# LUTHER AND THE BELOVED COMMUNITY

# Luther and the Beloved Community

*A Path for Christian Theology*
*after Christendom*

Paul R. Hinlicky

WILLIAM B. EERDMANS PUBLISHING COMPANY

GRAND RAPIDS, MICHIGAN / CAMBRIDGE, U.K.

Published 2010 by
Wm. B. Eerdmans Publishing Co.
2140 Oak Industrial Drive N.E., Grand Rapids, Michigan 49505 /
P.O. Box 163, Cambridge CB3 9PU U.K.

Printed in the United States of America

16  15  14  13  12  11  10       7  6  5  4  3  2  1


**Library of Congress Cataloging-in-Publication Data**

Hinlicky, Paul R.
     Luther and the beloved community: a path for Christian theology
     after Christendom / Paul R. Hinlicky.
          p.      cm.
     ISBN 978-0-8028-6492-5 (pbk.: alk. paper)
     1. Luther, Martin, 1483-1546.   I. Title.

BR333.3.H57    2010
230'.41092 — dc22

                                                    2010006439

www.eerdmans.com

*In Memoriam*
*William (†2000) and Marie (†1996),*
*who rest in the peace of the Israel of God, that Beloved Community,*
*which they served in life and trusted in death.*

# Contents

*Foreword,* by Mickey L. Mattox                                           xi

*Preface*                                                                 xv

*Abbreviations*                                                          xxv

**Part One: Luther's Creedal Theology**

1. The Problem of Christian Belief in Euro-America Today                   3
   *A Question Posed by Josiah Royce*                                      3
   *Critical Dogmatics as the Task of Interpretation*                      7
   *An Alternative: James's Experiential Theology*                        17
   *Saints amid Boas and Crocodiles*                                      21
   *Luther Fails to Map*                                                  25

2. "One of the Trinity Suffered": Luther's Neo-Chalcedonian
   Christology                                                            31
   *Epistemology at the Turn of the Ages*                                 32
   *"This Man Created the World"*                                         46
   *"One of the Trinity Suffered"*                                        51
   *The Erasure of the Communion of Attributes
     in Modern Christology*                                               60

Contents

3. God Surpassing God by "Christ Made to Be Sin"          66

    *Beyond the Wrath of God?*                            66

    *Propitiation, Not Expiation*                         73

    *What Anselm Really Taught*                           83

    *Luther's Radicalism*                                 91

    *But Is It Real?*                                     96

4. Trinitarian Advent: Resituating the Dialectic
   of Law and Gospel                                     105

    *The Faith of Jesus*                                  106

    *The "Necessity" of the Cross*                        118

    *Trinitarian Advent*                                  122

    *Teaching the Trinity*                                130

**Part Two: Explorations in Theological Anthropology**

5. Somatic Self, Ecstatic Self: Luther on Theonomy       139

    *Somatic, Ecstatic, and Centered Selves*              141

    *Lutherans against Luther on the Power of the Will*   149

    *Reading* De servo arbitrio *as Apocalyptic Theology* 153

    *Zwingli's Alternative Case for the Decentered Self*  162

    *New Agency in Christ*                                169

    *Appendix to Chapter Five: A Roman Catholic Objection:
    Does Luther's Rapture Rob Humans of the Freedom of Faith?*  175

6. The Redemption of the Body: Luther on Marriage        179

    *The Renewed Image of God*                            179

    *Marriage as Holy Estate*                             191

    *Luther's Biblical Theology of Marriage*              198

    *Dirty Sex? The Problem of Concupiscence*             201

    *The Christological Reading of Genesis 1–3*           209

    *Community in Suffering as in Joy*                    210

    *Same-Sex Unions and Other Hard Questions*            214

**Part Three: Some Objections regarding Justification,
the Church, and Political Theology**

7. "New, Old, and Different Perspectives" on Paul
   (Augustine and Luther)                                      221

   *The Perils of Repristinationism*                          221

   *Dunn's Claim for a New Perspective on Paul*               225

   *Sanders's Misidentified Insight*                          230

   *Stendahl's Misplaced Conscience*                          233

   *Käsemann's Critique of Salvation History*                 236

   *Beyond the Old and New Perspectives*                      242

   *The Law Battling the Law in Order to Liberate Us All*     249

   *Church in Service of the New Creation*                    254

8. Communio: Luther's Forgotten Ecclesiology                  258

   *A Catholic Luther?*                                       259

   *Heresiarch as Teacher of the Church?*                     262

   *The Achievement of the Second Vatican Council*            268

   *Ratzinger's Objection*                                    275

   *The Papal Confutation's Evasion of* Luthers Lehre         281

   *The Catholic Luther and Communio Ecclesiology*            287

   *Communio Ecclesiology*                                    292

   *A Counter-Challenge*                                      298

9. Passion and Action in Christ: Political Theology
   between the Times                                          301

   *A Man in Contradiction?*                                  301

   *Marxism as a Theological Problem*                         308

   Homo faber                                                 314

   *Marxism as a Christian Heresy*                            323

   *Vocation in Battle-Stations of the New Creation*          331

   *Luther's Admonition to Peace*                             337

   *Niebuhr's Rediscovery of Economic Power*                  343

Contents

The Reverend Dr. Martin Luther King Jr.'s Public Ministry
of Redemptive Love                                              348

Who Believes?                                                   354

10. By Way of Conclusion: What Luther Meant
by *theologia crucis*                                           358

What Luther Meant                                               358

Some Feminist Concerns                                          363

What's Wrong with Glory?                                        367

Three Conclusions                                               373

Appendix: The Problem of Demonization
in Luther's Apocalyptic Theology                                379

Works Cited                                                     386

Index of Names and Selected Topics                              401

# Foreword

Why look to Luther for help in meeting the many pressing theological and ecclesial challenges of today? A generation or two ago, theologians on all sides seemed to have an answer to that question, for they could everywhere be found looking to Luther and putting him to work in service to their cause(s). An impressive number of industrious and often daring Catholic scholars, for example, were excitedly retrieving theological treasures from Luther's voluminous writings even as they reluctantly identified elements in his theology that seemed inconsistent with their own Catholic faith. Protestant scholars could frequently be found working patiently alongside their Catholic counterparts in this endeavor, constructively arguing out the shape of Luther's thought and assessing its applicability to the present. At the same time, they were also caught up in the succeeding waves of scholarly energy released by the ongoing process of their own internal re-reception of the great Reformer's thought, which was being made clearer, at last, by painstaking historical and comparative theological research. Biblical scholars, too, even those who were not particularly beholden to the theological and ecclesial traditions that claim Luther's name, often found in his work and in his heroic story inspiration for their basic imaginative grasp of the meaning of the biblical text, the hermeneutical key, as it were, to such Pauline distinctions as letter and spirit, sin and righteousness, law and gospel. Biblical translators (for both the Hebrew and the Greek), ethicists, historians of the German language, of family life, of literacy, social and political theorists — nearly everyone, it seems, found something useful, and oftentimes much to like, in Luther's work.

Consistent with the decentering so common in intellectual currents in recent times, however, Luther was also — though hardly for the first time! — being examined critically through the lenses of various versions of the so-called "hermeneutic of suspicion." In fact, from the earliest studies of Luther's life, some found in him something quite different from the traditional hero of Protestant legend, or even the sadly erring "catholic" Luther dear to the ecumenists. Here he appears variously as the ideological toady of the rising Protestant princes, a traitor to the common man in the debacle of the Peasants' War, the inventor of the faulty "two kingdoms" theory that predictably resulted in Christian "quietism," or as the fearsome, and sometimes loathsome, opponent of the Jews, a man whose writings would be put to shameful use long after his death. In spite of the important advances made in recent times, some traditionalists, particularly among Roman Catholics, continue to see Luther in terms like these, or, even worse, in the all-too-easy demonic framework pioneered centuries ago by Catholic polemicists. Many theologians on the Anglo-American scene today adopt a less antagonistic stance toward Luther, but consider him too individualistic and thus insufficiently ecclesial, a naïve biblicist who sadly underestimated the crucial role of tradition in interpreting Scripture. Some theologically knowledgeable social historians see him as a man who not only sadly destroyed the sacramental unity of the Western church but also badly impaired its capacity for creating community across the various ethnic and national divides of modern Europe. Similarly, many of the New Testament scholars at work on the so-called "new perspective" on Paul fault Luther for having fundamentally misread the distinction between law and gospel. Nevertheless, confident Protestant voices, particularly within the relatively narrow circles of strict confessional Lutheranism, continue to lift up the image of the heroic Luther, a man for the ages who "rediscovered" a gospel that had somehow been lost, who stood for Christ and the truth when nearly everyone else failed. For his most ardent admirers, Luther remains the *doctor authenticus,* while for his detractors, Protestant and Catholic alike, he is hardly a teacher of the faith at all. There seems to be little hope, in the present ecumenical climate anyhow, that Luther can be recognized and received as a "common doctor" for the separated churches.

Readers who have taken up this book expecting another "business as usual" approach from any one of the angles sketched out above should be forewarned. The great strength of this book is not that it resolves all the questions about Luther's theology, but that it repositions Luther within the narratives that we theologians tell ourselves about the history of theology. Following in some ways the lead of the late Heiko Oberman, Hinlicky cuts Luther down to size. Making the most out of his own impressively broad reading in the scholarly literature on Luther's theology, Hinlicky eschews the hagiographic approach that looks for that certain something that made Luther different from all who came before — the Lutheran "*Sonderweg.*" As a theologian, however, he also rejects the historians' insistence that one must, as Bernhard Lohse once reportedly put it, *find* Luther in the sixteenth century and then *leave him there.*

Instead, Hinlicky seeks to retrieve Luther as a fallible but endlessly interesting and surprisingly resourceful conversation partner for contemporary theology. His Luther is one who, freed from the confessional/ hagiographical requirement that he speak *differently* from the antecedent catholic tradition, or the historians' insistence that he speak only *to* the sixteenth century, is able to speak *helpfully* on an impressively wide range of broadly catholic theological issues: Christology, Trinitarian theology, theological anthropology, Christian ethics, and much more. Hinlicky's Luther, in short, is much more than a one-trick pony who can run the syllogisms of forensic justification forward and back. To the contrary, he is a theologian grounded in the central teachings of the catholic faith and possessed of a remarkable capacity for applying that faith to perennial theological questions.

Both defensive and offensive theological analysis is essential to the task of bringing this Luther to light. In other words, Hinlicky has to try to carve out working space by, on the one hand, defending Luther against foes who dismiss him on account of his alleged theological faults, and, on the other hand, bursting the bubbles of uncritical admirers who need him to stand heroically as a quasi-infallible oracle for the *Grunddifferenzen* that make Protestants Protestant. Working both those ends against the salutary middle, Hinlicky seeks to engage Luther in the contemporary task of "critical dogmatics" without veering off into confessional apologetics. To the contrary, he clearly identifies aspects of Luther's theological outlook that must be repudiated in order to render him a theological resource fit for today. As he does so, he engages some of the very best, and most provocative, in contemporary Luther scholarship, reporting the findings of other scholars accurately and then deftly extending and correcting their arguments, advancing in a number of important ways our understanding of Luther's theology. Rejecting Luther's apocalypticism and the demonization that goes along with it, for example, Hinlicky nevertheless recognizes and demonstrates the importance of eschatological and proleptic elements in his thought, as well as their potential for contributing constructively to theology today. Elsewhere, he seizes forthrightly upon aspects of Luther's theology that have been considered problematic and unhelpful, particularly by Catholic scholars. In the case of Luther's well-known treatise against Erasmus, the *De servo arbitrio,* for instance, he endeavors to show how Luther could coherently insist on the sheer gratuity of divine grace and at the same time refuse to give in to the presumed rational requirement of a scheme of double predestination that would pit the "hidden" will of God against the will of God revealed in Christ.

This is a book, in short, that attempts, joyfully one might add, to rearrange the field on which the game of Luther studies is played. Hinlicky presses his case chapter by chapter, arguing insistently and consistently for Luther as a theologian fit to contribute to the contemporary Christian hope for the church and the kingdom of God, the "Beloved Community." But the book never devolves into mere scholarly inquiry into this or that in Luther's "thought." To the contrary, this is a deeply personal book in which the reader will discern over and again Hinlicky's own voice, the voice of a committed Lutheran minister and churchman whose ultimate concerns have to do with faith and faithfulness in the here and now, and one who never loses sight of the tragedy of the ecumenical division that came about in Luther's day. Wondrously, then, Hinlicky's book models the very thing it seeks to foster, i.e., engagement with Martin Luther as a living witness ready for continuing service to the church catholic. Let us attend!

MICKEY L. MATTOX

# Preface

In this book I build upon several previous books and contributions to books in preparation for writing in a discipline that I am inelegantly calling *critical dogmatics*.[1] In "Luther's Anti-Docetism in the *Disputatio de divinitate et humanitate*,"[2] I showed that Luther's Christology, as articulated in the patristic teaching about the communication of properties, provides the backing for the teaching of justification by faith alone, understood as the dramatic-narrative "joyful exchange" between Christ and the believing sinner. In *The Substance of Faith: Luther on Doctrinal Theology*[3] with Mickey Mattox and Dennis Bielfeldt, we demonstrated the salience of the old Luther's return to academic method and canonical hermeneutic to clarify logically classical Christian dogmatic assertions as something also needful in the life of churches reformed by the Word of God. We accordingly lifted up the evident seriousness with which the elder Luther applied himself to dogmatic questions in Trinitarian theology. In *Paths Not Taken: Theology from Luther Through Leibniz*,[4] I diagnosed the tragedy of theology in the tradition of Luther, which wanted simultaneously to deny to philosophy access to the theological region and at the same time to sponsor a new Christian philosophy to

---

1. See the discussion below, in Chapter One, of Royce's method of interpretation.

2. *Creator est creatura: Luthers Christologie als Lehre von der Idiomenkommunikation*, ed. O. Bayer and Benjamin Gleede (Berlin: Walter de Gruyter, 2007), pp. 139-85.

3. Dennis Bielfeldt, Mickey Mattox, and Paul R. Hinlicky, *The Substance of Faith: Luther on Doctrinal Theology* (Minneapolis: Fortress Press, 2008).

4. Paul R. Hinlicky, *Paths Not Taken: Theology from Luther through Leibniz* (Grand Rapids: Eerdmans, 2009).

guide culture where the Reformation had prevailed, in short, to sponsor a renewal of Christendom. These contradictory impulses, represented by Luther and Melanchthon respectively, canceled out each other in the brilliant but flawed endeavors of Gottfried Leibniz to harmonize the heritage of Augustinian faith with the ascendant Reason of the early Enlightenment. That "path not taken" of Leibniz's reconciliation left theology in a place of *homelessness* in Western culture that Karl Barth articulated nearly a century ago. Yet it also leaves theology free to reappropriate the thought of a theologian like Luther without the convoluted restraints and distortions manifest in the nineteenth century's anti-ecumenical confessionalism and/or the nationalist German *Kulturprotestantismus* of the so-called Luther renaissance (the dynamics of which formed Barth's hot and cold relation to Luther).[5]

How would Luther be appropriated for theology today without needing either to reinforce Protestant-Catholic or Protestant-Protestant schisms or to shore up an ever-shrinking cultural heritage? We can find out, if we strictly control our reappropriation by focusing on matters of ecumenical doctrine. In this book, therefore, I undertake a range of studies in *doctrinal* theology with the help of Martin Luther. By *doctrine,* I designate historically those teachings of the Christian faith which the ecumenical church has decided on as essential to its fidelity to the gospel and which are thus meant to function as *regula fidei,* essentially: the canonical narrative of Old and New Testaments; the Holy Trinity; the Personal Union of divine and human natures in Christ; and the doctrine of grace as salvation from sin and death. By doctrinal *theology,* I mean the contemporary endeavor to understand critically and articulate publicly such doctrinal decisions for the purpose of probing Christian belief today. Since Christian faith is monotheistic, these doctrines cannot consequently be taken as isolated nuggets of revealed truth but must be considered as cohering. Doctrinal theology teaches faith's knowledge of the *one* God: the almighty Father, creator from nothing of all that is not God; Christ, the only Son of the aforementioned Father, in His incarnate person and saving work; and the Spirit of this Father and Son, who spoke by the prophets and through the Scriptures still speaks today where those Scriptures are received as holy, that is, in the church. Theology thus works on the coherence of the Trinitarian articles of faith to glorify the redeeming God and to extend the knowledge of the sal-

---

5. "How could Barth's massive accord with Luther come to be so roundly overlooked?" George Hunsinger, *Disruptive Grace: Studies in the Theology of Karl Barth* (Grand Rapids: Eerdmans, 2000), p. 280.

vation of the sinner as inclusion in what the American philosopher Josiah Royce eloquently named the Beloved Community. I agree in this regard with Oswald Bayer that — alas, "rightly understood" — the doctrine of justification tells of God who, "in all the acts which He reserves to Himself alone" (Luther), is the One who creates *ex nihilo*.[6] But in some distinction from Bayer I take this insight of Luther's as key to the *coherence* of the faith.

Be that as it may, such considerations seem far from the consciousness of theology today. Today biblical scholars routinely dismantle the text's claim as canonical and then proceed as experts to opinionate on traditional dogmatic questions without method or rigor. Constructive theologians, so-called, build the kinds of metaphysical systems that Kant long ago demolished for philosophers with a conscience — or with great flourish and fanfare deconstruct systems long since fallen from power — in discourses that few outside their shrinking guilds read or understand. Historical theologians jealously guard the historical particularity of what once was, anointing themselves gatekeepers who effectively block the process of critical appropriation in traditional discourses like doctrinal theology. So the hard work of *critical dogmatics* in testing of the church's practice of faith in light of the aforementioned doctrinal norms freshly grasped and interpreted in every new generation has by and large given way to other models.

But theology is not philosophy, and the Holy Spirit is no skeptic.[7] As a critical retrieval and fresh assertion of definite meaning, the "new language of the Spirit"[8] is a hermeneutical process of appropriation that cannot proceed, to put it provocatively, without a certain measure of violence against the past.[9] Not only does it take up the past selectively and then put

---

6. Oswald Bayer, *Martin Luther's Theology: A Contemporary Interpretation,* trans. Thomas H. Trapp (Grand Rapids: Eerdmans, 2007), p. 38. Bayer rightly insists on the embattled experience in faith of God's claim to be the only Lord: "God's unity, along with the unity of reality and how reality is experienced, does not stand steadfast as an eternal and necessary principle that is never attacked; instead, questions are raised about these issues in actual and practical ways, as well as in an 'external' way. Whoever meditates upon the first commandment is entangled thereby in the battles between the one Lord and the many lords. One cannot extricate oneself from this entanglement by holding to a speculative idea about the unity of God" (p. 36). I acknowledge the issue Bayer raises here, and its basis in Luther's theology. But in this book I try to answer it in another way than by apparent dualism.

7. Martin Luther, *The Bondage of the Will,* trans. J. I. Packer and O. R. Johnston (Grand Rapids: Fleming Revell, 2000), pp. 66-70.

8. See *The Substance of Faith,* pp. 152-68.

9. I take the idea from Gary Percesepe, "Against Appropriation," in *Postmodern Philosophy and Christian Thought,* ed. Merold Westphal (Bloomington: Indiana University

these pieces to work in new ways, but it does so, as the critical historian sees things, from the uncontrolled perspective of the retriever. Of course, for critical dogmatics that uncontrolled perspective might be the fresh movement of the Holy Spirit. One cannot say in advance. It will be in any case some spirit! That must be discerned. The issue is less whether the appropriation repristinates any particular formation of the past than whether new formulations are faithful to the gospel of the crucified and risen Christ in His ongoing history in the world. Historians are rightly concerned to focus on the development of theological ideas and the precise exposition of their contextual meaning. Theologians depend on this work, since Christianity is a historical religion that can go forward only by coming to terms with its past. If at the end of the day, however, historians want to take their stand and object categorically — *Das ist aber nicht Jesus! Paulus! Luther!* — they may do so, but it begs the question — of Jesus, Paul, and Luther — whether *we* have found help moving forward on our pilgrim way.

So permit me to acknowledge from the outset that the Luther who appears in the pages to follow will be "my" Luther, Luther as I appropriate him, for which I, not Luther, am responsible. May I only offer back this re-

---

Press, 1999), chap. 4, pp. 69-87. "Back to the grammar of appropriation, which, I will argue (appropriating Deleuzoguattari for my purposes), is a grammar of possession and violence at odds with friendship — and necessarily so, according to one conception of philosophy. A resultant *recontextualization,* often called a 'reading of x . . .' Despite a generous spirit of inclusiveness on the part of some claimants, the logic of appropriation is a logic of exclusion: not everything concerning a proper name is to be appropriated, only that which is suitable, only those insights appropriate to the appropriator's own research program, which the appropriation of course, is meant to advance. Thus we might speak: of *a program of appropriation* into whose service a proper name is conscripted, often against his or her intent. Claimants lay claim to what they find serviceable in a proper name; invariably, someone will object to the claims, or in the case of living contestants (Derrida, Habermas) seek to be disowned. . . . My aim is not to show that programs or acts of appropriation are inappropriate [NB: the irony above of Percesepe's invocation of Deleuzoguattari] — in fact, I don't know what such a claim would mean, given the history of appropriation, which, in a certain sense, is the history of philosophy — nor, despite the title, is this a plea for philosophers to stop appropriating (they can't). I wish only to foreground the background assumptions and to highlight the limits of appropriation-as-a-means-of-inducing-discussion, conversation, or what is often called a 'dialogue' (which I have elsewhere called the most wistful term of the late twentieth century) as well as to suggest counterpossibilities for appropriation (I do not call these nonappropriations) . . ." (p. 72). The ambivalence here expressed is something only a contemporary postmodernist could love. I prefer to do my appropriations, violence and all, openly and honestly, sinning boldly but all the more boldly believing, etc.

flection to the gatekeepers?[10] Church historians deceive themselves if they think they are not guilty of the same transgression of illicitly crossing the boundary of the present and the past when they opinionate on contemporary issues on the mere authority of their historical-critical expertise — opinionate without the rigors of hermeneutical discipline, logical clarity, and systematic coherence, far too often nowadays (in inverse error of their apologist fathers) for the purpose of neutralizing the *prima facie* claim of the text as transmitted by the tradition.[11] My announced purpose to undertake *doctrinal* theology may be in such a climate unfashionable. But perhaps *critical dogmatics* has always been as unfashionable as it is necessary in the life of the church — for the same reason. The need to understand the faith and the need to criticize the church's practice of faith *are one and the same.*

This book begins in Chapter One by locating the question to be addressed in contemporary (Euro-)American culture. It considers two philosophies of religion that have vied with each in the last century in the representative figures of William James and Josiah Royce. Deciding in favor of Royce, the chapter asks with him whether we can be Christians today *in creed,* that is, in beliefs. Royce thinks yes, provided we have in mind a doctrine *for life,* that is, a doctrine that posits the goal of Beloved Community. Part One of this book looks to Luther's doctrinal theology as a resource for answering Royce's question positively, as in Ebeling's words: "Life is usually given precedence over doctrine, but instead Luther gives the pre-eminence to doctrine, precisely for the sake of the life created and desired by God. Doctrine is heaven, life is the earth. For doctrine, the word of God, is, to put it briefly, the bread of life."[12]

Chapter Two begins where Luther and his Apostle, Paul, began: with apocalyptic, that is, "revealed" Christology. The chapter accordingly argues against the naïveté of the first, second, and/or third Quest(s) for the Historical Jesus in the sense that these have sought a psychologically plausible Jesus who might be an inspirational figure for contemporary faith. Against

---

10. So G. R. Elton, "Commemorating Luther," *Journal of Ecclesiastical History* 35, no. 4 (October 1984): 614-19.

11. Every Luther scholar ought to suffer a sober reading of James M. Stayer, *Martin Luther: German Saviour. German Evangelical Theological Factions and the Interpretation of Luther, 1917-1933* (Kingston/Montreal: McGill-Queen's University Press, 2000), which shows in excruciating detail the abuse of history to fight covert theological battles.

12. Gerhard Ebeling, *Luther: An Introduction to His Thought* (Philadelphia: Fortress, 1972), p. 266.

this now dominant approach, it argues for Luther's rather different "anti-docetism": "This man created the world," i.e., the divine attributes are truly communicated to humanity in the person of the Incarnate Son of God. The result seems to be a monstrous paradox, but it is saved from logical meaninglessness by uncovering Luther's vigorous Trinitarian personalism, along the lines of the theopaschite Christology of the fifth ecumenical council: "This Son of God suffered and truly died." The logical point of Luther's paradoxical Christology then is not an abstract confusion or blending of divine and human natures, but rather that "one of the Trinity suffered," i.e., that the man Jesus, born of Mary, the friend of sinners and victor over the demons, who suffered under Pilate, is from all eternity the true self-interpretation of God to the creation fallen prey to anti-divine powers but now redeemed and on the way to fulfillment.

Chapter Three turns from this Christological affirmation to explore the neuralgic idea that the suffering Son of God bears sin in humanity's place under the wrath of God and just so satisfies divine righteousness. In fact, Luther is seen to integrate all three of the traditional atonement motifs: victory, substitution, and moral example/inspiration. While the penal substitution motif is for us today the most difficult, especially in light of certain feminist critiques, it is the key to Luther's integration of the motifs. To understand this, a very careful discrimination of Luther's view of satisfaction as propitiatory and passive over against Anselm's view of it as expiatory and active is required. In light of Girard's important work, this brings Luther's teaching into dialogue with the theology of gift in Radical Orthodoxy.

Chapter Four consolidates the results of the preceding two chapters. With Christine Helmer, it argues for re-situating the law-gospel dialectic in the larger canonical-narrative framework of "Trinitarian advent." It revisits Barth's famous attack on the law-gospel sequence in Lutheran theology. It finds Barth justified in echoing the exegetical-Pauline sequence of indicative-imperative, but not in failing to grasp sufficiently the dialectic in 2 Corinthians 3 of the letter which kills and the Spirit who makes alive. Taking up Barth's proposal to read Paul's *pistos Iesou* as the faith/faithfulness of the man Christ, Chapter Four then parses Luther's agreement with Anselm about the "necessity" of the cross over against Occamist-voluntarist annihilation of Luther's actual teaching, which dominates certain contemporary appropriations of Luther. The "necessity" of the cross proves to be the compassion of the Trinity in foreseeing and so willing creatures other than God, with wayward wills of their own, and so whose redemption and fulfillment would cost the Trinity the cross of the Son.

Thus the cross stands at the center of the coming of the Trinity into the depths of hell as the event by which the Risen One brings forth those redeemed for the Beloved Community. This concludes Part One of the book.

Part Two contains two studies in Luther's theological anthropology. Chapter Five explores the most difficult Luther text, *De servo arbitrio,* "On bound choice." It makes a Pauline exegetical argument about the somatic self, which in Adam is centered (egocentric) in illusory, yet inevitable ways until it becomes eccentric or ecstatic by Spirit-wrought conformation to Christ's cross and resurrection.[13] This reading is possible when *De servo arbitrio* is taken as apocalyptic theology, not philosophy. The reading of *De servo arbitrio* as philosophy by Melanchthon and later Lutherans, as also by Zwingli in his *De providentia Dei* (which was a critical response to Luther's *De servo arbitrio*), illuminates the chapter's claim that what Luther says about human nature and the human plight is said strictly in light of the revelation — concretely, the resurrection of the Crucified — not then as spontaneous self-understanding or even as a labored, rational account of experience. This apocalyptic reading yields a rich and suggestive idea of the new agency in Christ by the Holy Spirit active in the redemption of the body for the Beloved Community.

Chapter Six explores that new human agency in one of Luther's most historically significant applications: the new theology of marriage as a holy estate of God's creation and as the true "religious order," over against the antecedent Christian tradition's ambivalence about marriage and sometime veneration of the ideal of sexual renunciation. It tackles the controversial teaching of Luther that the believer is *simul iustus et peccator* by an exploration of sexual ambivalence. It also lifts up the notion of marriage as a community in suffering as in joy that corresponds to new agency in Christ in the time between the ages.

13. The critique of the centered self could also be made from a Melanchthonian position, e.g., Michael B. Aune, *To Move the Heart: Philip Melanchthon's Rhetorical View of Rite and Its Implications for Contemporary Ritual Theory* (San Francisco: Christian Universities Press, 1994). Aune cites Clifford Geertz's criticism of the Cartesian ego as "a bounded, unique, more or less integrated motivational and cognitive universe, a dynamic center of awareness, emotion, judgment, and action organized into a distinctive whole and set contrastively both against other such wholes and against its social and natural background" (p. 109). Aune comments, "'The autonomous, transcendent self,' writes theologian Timothy Sedgwick, 'is an illusion.' Such 'de-centering' of the human subject is 'old news' from both Classical and Christian perspectives. . . . The selfhood or 'moved heart' formed in the interaction between the Spirit and human being is an activity, not an autonomous, unique entity. It is a loving response experienced as *fiducia* and *notitia*" (p. 75).

Part Three entertains some likely objections to the present proposal for a path for Christian theology after Christendom that has now been sketched in Parts One and Two. Chapter Seven discusses the so-called New Perspective on Paul by retracing the footsteps of its evolution from Stendahl and Sanders through Dunn to N. T. Wright. In the process it identifies the antecedent nineteenth-century perspective of *Heilsgeschichte* that undergirds this "new" approach. It counterposes to this perspective Käsemann's position that "apocalyptic is the mother of Christian theology." It concludes by focusing on the difficult text of Galatians 3:10-14 about the "curse of the law," contrasting the exegesis of Martyn and Wright and showing how Luther's theological interpretation of this passage "as the Law (i.e., ethical content of love) battling the Law (i.e., the juridical curse upon the loveless) in order to liberate" achieves all three of the atonement motifs of victory over contra-divine powers, reconciliation with the holy God, and new agency in imitation of Christ.

Chapter Eight takes up a very different kind of contemporary objection to receiving Luther today as teacher of the ecumenical church from then Professor Joseph Ratzinger. Ratzinger's objection is studied and traced back to the heresiarch image created by papal opponents from very early on, which then became the pretext for Rome's failure to deal with Luther's teaching. Pelikan's complaint that Rome has never really listened to the witness of the Reformation is thus validated, as also Jenson's hope that Rome's consideration of that witness might provoke contemporary Protestants to recall the rock from which they were hewn. Setting that image and pretext aside, Luther's ecclesiology of *communio,* rooted in his Christological teaching of the joyful exchange, is uncovered and correlated with the ferment surrounding contemporary *communio*-ecclesiology, including Catholic thinking. Ratzinger's objection is thus met with the counterproposal that Rome should revoke the Bull of Excommunication against Luther, not of course in the sense of approving the polemical theology of the later Luther, but rather of dealing with the prophetic teaching of the early Luther anew as a possibility internal to its own life today.

Chapter Nine takes up what may be the profoundest objection to receiving Luther as theologian today. This is the objection stemming from Marx and his theological followers in the past century and a half about Luther's passivity in anthropology. The usual move by Lutheran apologists to recur to a Two Kingdoms doctrine is bracketed here on the grounds that the intervening Cartesian-Kantian dualism makes that distinction, admittedly crucial for Luther, virtually unintelligible to us. Instead, a different strategy is adopted: a fundamental theological critique of Marx's original refusal of the First Commandment with its catastrophic ethical implications and actually evil consequences. In this light, it becomes possible to lift up Luther's theology of creation, i.e., the doctrine of the three estates or forms of social life as modes of analysis for the new agency in Christ at work in the redemption of the body for life in the Beloved Community. The chapter concludes with illustrative sketches of such new agency in relation to the state (Luther's admonition to peace), the economy (Niebuhr's discovery of the power of labor for non-violent coercion in pursuit of justice in society), and public religion (King's mission to redeem America's soul from its founding betrayal in the race-based slave system). The Conclusion seeks to integrate the results of the foregoing with the widely discussed theme of Luther's *theologia crucis.*

First versions of Chapters Two, Three, and Four were composed as a series of lectures, "*Luthers Lehre* Today: Engaging Luther in Contemporary Doctrinal Theology" for the annual Pastor's Conference of ELCA Region Seven in Vancouver, BC, April 19-23, 2007 (unfortunately, I fell ill at the last minute and was unable to deliver the lectures in person). An early version of Chapter Six was presented at the Center for Catholic and Evangelical Theology's Conference on Marriage and the Family at St. Olaf College, June 12-14, 2005. Likewise a much earlier version of Chapter Eight appeared as "Luther's Forgotten Ecclesiology and Its Ecumenical Implications," in *Recent Research on Martin Luther* (Bratislava: The Evangelical Theological Faculty, Comenius University, 1999), pp. 123-33. A synopsis of this article appeared in *Luther Digest* 10 (2002): 60-63. Portions of Chapter Nine were presented as a lecture at Roanoke College, Salem, Virginia, in April 1999 when I visited from Bratislava as the Copenhaver Scholar-in-Residence. Portions of the Conclusion include material prepared for the seminar conducted by Dr. Bo Holm on the Relation between Doctrine and Life in Luther and Melanchthon at the 11th International Congress for Luther Research, July 2007, in São Paulo, Brazil.

I am grateful to all the partners in conversation indicated above, and also to those who have read and commented on all or part of this work: Ned Wisnefske, Brent Adkins, Sammeli Juntunen, Sarah Hinlicky Wilson, Gerry McDermott, and Mickey Mattox, who also graciously agreed to contribute the Foreword. I also express gratitude to my institution Roanoke College for its support of my scholarship. I am indebted to Norman Hjelm, who helped me to organize and present my ideas for this book to Eerdmans, and to the staff at Eerdmans who handled the copyediting and related matters. This book is dedicated to the memory of my parents, Marie and William, first teachers of piety and theology respectively.

I follow the rationale, though not all the details, of the *Lutheran Forum Guidelines* on inclusive language, which I have adapted for *my* language in this book (with the exception of the relative pronoun, Who, and the second Person, You, with respect to God); I have given others' language as it was written, translated, and published. The *Guidelines* read as follows: "Pronouns create confusion and mistakes in English-language letters nowadays, so we have to set an editorial policy about their use. If we are referring to hypothetical individuals, we find the most felicitous solution to be alternation between 'he' and 'she,' since 's/he' is cumbersome and 'one' can be a bit too formal and 'they' usually is followed by grammatical errors. (And when we talk about multiple members of the human race, we use terms like 'humanity' and 'people' rather than 'men,' since 'men' sounds like 'many males' rather than 'many persons.') When we speak of God and find it necessary to employ a pronoun, we use 'He' (also 'Him' and 'His') with the capital H. This is for two reasons. First, because Scripture authorizes the use of the masculine pronoun while clarifying that God is neither male nor masculine. Second, because the lowercase 'he' used in the same casual fashion as for human males can in fact be misleading about the non-maleness and non-masculinity of God. The person of Jesus Christ may be referred to with a lowercase 'he,' however, since he was truly human at the same time He was truly God. For consistency's sake, relative and second-person pronouns used of God will be capitalized as well (e.g., 'You' and 'Who'). We generally do not like endless repetition of the word 'God,' as in 'God Godself saved God's people,' as it implies a kind of robotic impersonality alongside the syntactical awkwardness. If, however, as an author you cannot in good conscience see your way to using the 'He,' you may use the repeated 'God,' but we ask you to provide a footnote explaining your rationale. 'She' as a referent to God has no canonical basis, and to our minds only encourages the erroneous notion that God is sexual or perhaps hermaphroditic, which neither mitigates the problem of the 'He' nor finds scriptural warrant. As such we decline to use it in these pages."

PAUL R. HINLICKY
*Easter 2009*

# Abbreviations

| | |
|---|---|
| BC | *The Book of Concord: The Confessions of the Evangelical Lutheran Church* |
| CA | *Confessio Augustana* |
| CT | *The Christian Tradition* |
| HD | *History of Dogma* |
| LC | Large Catechism |
| LCDUSA | *Lutheran-Catholic Dialogue in the USA* |
| LW | *Luther's Works* |
| SA | *Smalcald Articles* |
| ST | Systematic Theology |
| WA | Martin Luther, *Kritische Gesamtausgabe* (= "Weimar" edition) |

# PART ONE

# Luther's Creedal Theology

# The Problem of Christian Belief in Euro-America Today

## A Question Posed by Josiah Royce

This book is written in order to put dogmatic[1] insights of Martin Luther to work as resources for contemporary Christian theology in Euro-American[2] civilization. Yet obviously this is a question that was not and could not have been posed by Luther himself. It was posed almost one hundred years ago by the nearly forgotten Harvard philosopher Josiah Royce:[3] "In what sense, if in any, can the modern man consistently be, in creed, a Christian?"[4] In a final book, *The Problem of Christianity*, pub-

---

1. I will be using the word groups of dogma, doctrine, and creed interchangeably, with only slight differences in nuance: dogma as doctrine that has been defined by ecumenical council, doctrine for biblical teaching that remains undefined in the formal sense but widely acknowledged, and creed as the primal form of dogma with its *Sitz im Leben* in the baptismal profession and thence the liturgical act of confession in worship. Theology as critical dogmatics I take to be *both* first-order preaching, recitation, or confession of the gospel *and* second-order interpretation on an often imperceptibly sliding scale.

2. I rejoice in the development of indigenous Christian theologies outside the Euro-American sphere today, and restrict myself accordingly to the tradition to which I belong and its particular issues. On the other hand, I hope that the critique of theological habits still shaped by and attuned to Christendom undertaken in this book may be of some value to other-than-Western readers.

3. Bruce Kuklick, *Josiah Royce: An Intellectual Biography* (Indianapolis: Hackett, 1985).

4. Josiah Royce, *The Problem of Christianity* (Washington, DC: Catholic University of America Press, 2001), p. 62.

lished on the cusp of the First World War, Royce lifted up three tenets of creedal Christianity as "central" problems begging contemporary interpretation: the "idea of the spiritual community in union with which man is to win salvation, the idea of the hopeless and guilty burden of the individual when unaided by divine grace, [and] the idea of the atonement. . . ." Calling attention to these creedal notions, Royce knew that he was on the soil of Pauline Christianity: "Historically speaking, Christianity has never appeared simply as the religion taught by the Master. It has always been an interpretation of the Master and of his religion in the light of some doctrine concerning his mission, and also concerning God, man and man's salvation . . . [for] only after he had suffered and died, and — as was early reported — had risen again, did there become manifest, according to tradition, what, during his earthly life, could not become plain even to those who were nearest to him."[5] With Luther,[6] Royce sees that the (Pauline) kerygma of the cross and resurrection of the Christ constituted the hermeneutic of the traditions about Jesus of Nazareth in the rise of "normative Christianity."[7] Sharing that fundamental theological decision about the normative nature of Christian doctrine makes it possible to retrieve insights of Luther by means of a contemporary question which Luther himself may not have especially posed in his own historical particularity.[8]

---

5. Royce, *The Problem of Christianity*, p. 67.

6. See below, Chapter Two.

7. Arland J. Hultgren, *The Rise of Normative Christianity* (Minneapolis: Fortress, 1994).

8. And yet, in the words of Herman Otto Pesch: "When, however, one asks about God today, and does this against the background of our experience of reality, when evil is no longer counted as an element of the *perfectio universi*, when one asks about God immediately as the God of salvation and the meaningful basis of existence, when faith in God is continuously exposed to anxiety and inner turmoil [*Anfechtung*], threatened and challenged by reality, when the first tenet of God is his hiddenness in the opposite, when faith in the Creator and Father can come about only as faith in God as my Savior — then Luther's God question is a contemporary one." Otto Hermann Pesch, O.P., *The God Question in Thomas Aquinas and Martin Luther*, trans. Gottfried G. Krodel (Philadelphia: Fortress, 1972), p. 31. Pesch continues: "Does Luther not maintain that same outdated supernatural concept of God when he does not acknowledge the independent working of the powers and laws of nature, but attributes the meaningful events in nature directly to the working of God? Is it not a challenge to every 'secular world' if God is envisioned [as he is by Luther] as a factor in the physical world?" (p. 31). St. Thomas too can "contribute something": narrow-minded existentialism is "*our* danger," and "In this situation it is, then, a matter of life and death to call attention to the fact that God does not need us in order to be glorious but that he rather wills to be glorious by saving us" (p. 32).

Another factor that makes Royce's question pertinent is that he did not take his Pauline point of departure from Galatians as did Luther but found in the Corinthian correspondence the "ideal of a universal community." Needless to say, that hardly meant that Royce discounted the moral burden of the individual or the need of atonement, or that Luther has nothing to say about the coming kingdom of God, only that Royce gave the formation of the Beloved Community premier place in his exposition of the contemporary possibility of creedal Christianity's other two fundamental ideas.[9] This shift toward the "social intention of all the basic Christian concepts" (Bonhoeffer),[10] like the so-called "new perspective" on Paul (see Chapter Six below), represents important advances during the last century in understanding the "nature of doctrine" (Lindbeck) as in the first instance the *church's* self-regulation by its own constituting discourse. In the study that follows, I take this contemporary social orientation as the frame of reference in which I enlist Luther's insights into the church's constituting discourse as resource for critical dogmatics today.

In contrast to the project of this book, if one desired a presentation of Luther's theology on its own terms from the sixteenth century as a contemporary possibility, one could do no better than carefully to study Oswald Bayer's masterful *Martin Luther's Theology: A Contemporary Interpretation.* My appreciation of this insightful work will be evident in the ample use of Bayer's interpretations in the pages to follow. Yet it will also be clear that I do not think that the method of *Vergegungwärtigung* which Bayer deploys to approach Luther is finally either possible or for that matter desirable.[11] I do not think it is possible because Bayer himself inevitably modernizes, that is to say, corrects Luther by interposing contemporary questions;[12] this tacit procedure cannot but cast doubt on the viability of what purports to be a re-presentation of Luther's theology on

---

9. Royce, *The Problem of Christianity,* pp. 75-98.

10. Dietrich Bonhoeffer, *Sanctorum Communio* (Minneapolis: Fortress, 1998), p. 21.

11. Oswald Bayer, *Martin Luther's Theology: A Contemporary Interpretation,* trans. Thomas H. Trapp (Grand Rapids: Eerdmans, 2007), p. 346.

12. To mention but one case, modernizing is evident in Bayer's treatment of one of the most controversial theological matters, Luther's teaching on theodicy. Bayer's virtually Pascalian perception of the awful sublimity of nature hiding God's fatherly care for his human children substitutes for Luther's own understanding of the scandal of the light of grace, namely that grace is withheld from some, implying divine reprobation. See Bayer, *Luther's Theology,* p. 213, n. 53. Honest hermeneutical violence is to be preferred (see my Preface, n. 9, on Percesepe) to this; even better, dealing with the difficult text, e.g., Luther on reprobation. See Chapter Five below.

its own terms.[13] Nor do I think such re-presentation is desirable, if it tacitly lifts Luther out of the stream of Pauline-Augustinian tradition to which he belonged to offer a reconstructed Luther-theology as a *Sonderweg,* when we today should rather find ourselves within that same, broader stream of theological tradition. Thus I do not think such a Luther helps church and theology in North America, more broadly Euro-American civilization, today. Bayer, on the other hand, would deny that Luther can contribute or be made to contribute to "systematic theology": "presenting one's thinking as a system was foreign to him. . . . Those who think within a systematic framework are obsessed with unity and consistency. . . . Luther's theology raises fundamental questions about that enterprise."[14] *Tertium non datur?* There are to be sure problems with "systematic" or as I should say more precisely today "constructive" theology — not only from Luther's perspective;[15] but critical dogmatics of the kind

13. Bayer rightly underscores Luther's apocalypticism in the train of Paul the Apostle, as I shall also. But Bayer fails to deal with the huge obstacle entailed by this very insight: Luther's demonology and his slide into demonization of theological enemies. "Luther risked interpreting his era within the framework of the apocalyptic texts of the Bible and thus erred at times as well. A particularly dark chapter involves his late writings and sermons against the Jews" (Bayer, *Luther's Theology,* p. 333). True enough, but we today need a much better account of this error, not to mention a consequent treatment of Luther's demonology, which Bayer fails to provide. This account disallows any unbroken re-presentation of Luther's theology as a contemporary possibility. See the Appendix and additionally Hinlicky, *The Substance of Faith: Luther on Doctrinal Theology* (Minneapolis: Fortress Press, 2008), pp. 174ff.

14. Bayer, *Luther's Theology,* p. xv. Bayer himself presents Luther's theology by means of the creedal scheme in this book. Luther had a rather different explanation for his failure to produce a theological "system." In the "Preface to the Complete Edition of Luther's Latin Writings" (1545), he spoke with some personal modesty of his "confused lucubrations" (i.e., nocturnal studies, indicating the haste and stress under which he wrote): "But my books, as it happened, yes, as the lack of order in which the events transpired made it necessary, are accordingly crude and disordered chaos, which is now not easy to arrange even for me." He takes the opportunity to give thanks to God's grace that "a great many systematic books now exist, among which the Loci communes of Philip excel" (LW 34:327). Critical dogmatics will not be "theological system" in the sense that Bayer proscribes, a philosophical worldview decked out with Christian symbols, but it will find in the doctrine of the Trinity sketched in the creedal scheme and deriving from early Christian baptism the key to the unity of the scriptural God which embattled faith believes. Luther's undeniable witness to the hiddenness of God is first of all to the Son's experience of abandonment by the One whom He knew and obeyed as Abba, Father. That means, however, that the hiddenness of God is an experience of faith, not an alternative to faith, as I will argue in the Conclusion of this book.

15. Lewis Ayres, *Nicea and Its Legacy: An Approach to Fourth-Century Trinitarian Theology* (Oxford and New York: Oxford University Press, 2006), pp. 292-403.

I am advocating does not find these problems to lie centrally in a concern for unity and consistency.

Returning to Royce's question, then, he justified "philosophical" exploration of these creedal themes on the grounds that, "familiar as these three ideas are, they are still almost wholly misunderstood, both by the apologists who view them in the light of traditional dogmas, and by the critics who assail the letter of the dogmas, but who fail to grasp the spirit."[16] What is needed, Royce argued, is an approach to Christianity as a "problem," that is, "at least provisionally, not as the one true faith to be taught, and not as an outworn tradition to be treated with an enlightened indifference, but as a central, as an intensely interesting, life problem of humanity, to be appreciated, to be interpreted, to be thoughtfully reviewed, with the seriousness and the striving for reasonableness and for thoroughness which we owe to every life-problem whereupon human destiny is inseparably interwoven."[17] Royce thus sought a "philosophical" method, i.e., in distinction from partisan apologetics and equally partisan polemics, which would investigate hermeneutically just what it was that creedal Christianity was trying to communicate.

## Critical Dogmatics as the Task of Interpretation

In the process Royce generated a new, post-epistemological conception of philosophy as interpretation.[18] Not acknowledging (or rather, actively disowning) the fundamental philosophical task of *interpretation*, he argued, modern culture had witnessed the erection of a dualism between rival methods of description and appreciation, partitioning reality into the discrete domains of fact and value cordoned off from each other — no trespassing allowed.[19] This dualism in turn sponsored the cultural bifurcation

---

16. Royce, *The Problem of Christianity*, p. 74.

17. Royce, *The Problem of Christianity*, p. 61.

18. Royce, *The Problem of Christianity*, p. 295.

19. So Richard Rorty characterized Kantian culture, *Philosophy and the Mirror of Nature* (Princeton: Princeton University Press, 1979), pp. 3-13. Rorty also wants to "assert the possibility of a post-Kantian culture, one in which there is no all-encompassing discipline which legitimizes or grounds the others . . ." (p. 6) and thus he comes at the end of this seminal analysis to advocate passage "from epistemology to hermeneutics" (pp. 315-56). Yet I nowhere find in Rorty any appreciation for the American, semi-pragmatist precedent to be found in Royce's work.

of science and religion, giving a platform in this way to the equally uncomprehending claims of both critics and apologists of Christianity. Against the Cartesian-Kantian dualism of perception and conception in the construction of knowledge, "the striking aspect" of *The Problem of Christianity* was Royce's "defense of a novel kind of knowledge — interpretation — and it is not paradoxical to say that his explication of interpretation solves the two worlds problem [of fact and value] by denying it."[20] More precisely though perhaps less provocatively, Royce embedded the two cognitive functions of perception and conception in the wider world of human language, which he took after the fashion of German idealism's notion of *Geist* as dynamic, temporally extended waves of interpretation upon interpretation. "But interpretation, while always stimulated to fresh efforts by the inexhaustible wealth of the novel facts of the social world, demands, by virtue of its own nature, and even in the simplest conceivable case, an endless wealth of new interpretations. For every interpretation, as an expression of mental activity, addresses itself to a possible interpreter, and demands that it shall be, in its turn, interpreted."[21] Given this take on the encompassing reality of language in the human-social world, philosophical interpretation tells a story of stories, that is, of human persons understood as essentially storied figures — to themselves as to others, individually and communally. Within such a framework of understanding, it is far from paradoxical to think of a Word from God forming a community of faith and the discipline of theology as its "grammar" and "rhetoric." Indeed, I appropriate Royce's interpretive method in this book and retool it on behalf of *critical dogmatics.*

In exploring the all-embracing domain of language as interpretation, Royce was in fact developing into a philosophical method a procedure that had antecedents in classical Protestant theology: biblical hermeneutics, the task of understanding that arises from scriptural texts characterized by the genre of narrative. The problem of hermeneutics arises, that is to say, because biblical narrative, especially as understood

---

20. Kuklick, *Biography*, p. 212. "Metaphysically considered, the world of interpretation is the world in which, if indeed we are able to interpret at all, we learn to acknowledge the being and the inner life of our fellow-men; and to understand the constitution of temporal experience, with its endlessly accumulating sequence of significant deeds . . . [here] selves and communities may exist, past and future can be defined, and the realms of the spirit may find a place which neither barren conception nor the chaotic flow of interpenetrating perceptions could ever render significant." Royce, *The Problem of Christianity*, p. 294.

21. Royce, *The Problem of Christianity*, p. 294.

by the Protestant Reformers, is thought in sovereign fashion to call out and form its own audience. Hans Frei described the way in which biblical narrative absorbs hearers/readers into its world: "through the coincidence or even identity between a world being depicted and its reality being rendered to the reader (always under the form of the depiction) the reader or hearer in turn becomes part of that depicted reality and thus has to take a personal or life stance toward it."[22] The coincidence is possible, that is, on the assumption that language is all-encompassing, i.e., that there is no "mystical" alternative to language. There is here no revolt against language as such as an alien web of deception, no suspicion of language as such as a heteronomous power. "In the beginning was the Word. . . ." Rather language itself first creates the negative possibility of deception, of verbal violence into which abusive practice language users have surely fallen. Into this now ambiguous reality of language, Scripture's narrative way of communicating the "Word made flesh" comes and offers auditors a specific subjecthood — will you be Peter? or Judas? or Saul-turned-to-Paul? — and just so (a new) understanding of the self in relation to the God who speaks in the offer. With this, genuine consent or refusal takes place as well — provided that subjecthood is understood to exist antecedently, but not autonomously, timelessly, immutably, or alinguistically. (An antecedent subject exists, of course, but temporally and mutably, that is, as one answering to some other subjecthood-proffering narrative that has now been challenged and superseded by the coming of the biblical narrative.) In Frei's telling, however, it was just this latter notion of an antecedent self which was also timeless and immutable in its transcendental identity and autonomous by its critical power to secure knowledge of its objects that was soon to eclipse biblical narrative, and with it, the corresponding cognitive task of theology as interpretation of minds to other minds.[23]

---

22. So Hans W. Frei, *The Eclipse of Biblical Narrative: A Study in Eighteenth and Nineteenth Century Hermeneutics* (New Haven and London: Yale University Press, 1974), p. 24, characterized the "pre-critical" hermeneutics of the Reformers.

23. Frei's exhaustive analysis concludes that with the Cartesian turn to the subject, making "consciousness" the basic "element characterizing human being, the bond between society and individual being loosened, the mutual fitness of character with the suffering or doing of significant action or incident likewise becoming increasingly tenuous, the significance of [biblical] narrative . . . is bound to be minimal." Frei, *The Eclipse of Biblical Narrative,* p. 313. Frei is right to see Spinoza as the turning point in this development (pp. 42ff.), as from another angle I have argued in Chapter Two of *Paths Not Taken.* The correspondence

The problematic of hermeneutics had been mediated to Royce by German idealism, but the distinctive solution for which Royce argued in *The Problem of Christianity* derived from an insight of Charles Sanders Peirce (also dependent on the same sources) about the social (not private) and triadic (not dyadic) nature of understanding through language.[24] For if, as the prevailing theories held (corresponding to the rival epistemologies of empiricists and rationalists), objects of knowledge must be either things or ideas, Royce asked, "in which of these classes will you place your neighbor's mind, or any of the conscious acts of that mind? Is your neighbor's mind a *datum* that you could, were your perception 'unlimited,' simply find *present* to you, as *red* or as a 'change' can be present? Is your neighbor's mind, on the contrary, an abstraction, a mere sort of *being* which you merely conceive?"[25] Neither answer satisfies, because in the reality of language "interpretation is a triadic relationship."[26] In the realm of human language, that is to say, there is never only the isolated knower and the known object, but also always the audience to which the knower makes an object known (even when the audience is oneself): "Interpretation is a conversation, and not a lonely enterprise."[27] Such conversation takes time; it is an essentially temporal function by which any community of inquiry remembers the path traversed in order to chart its way forward. In reality, then, the human self, existing in and only in such communities of interpretation, is neither "a mere datum [n]or an abstract conception. A self is a life whose unity and connectedness depend upon some sort of interpretation of plans, of memories, of hopes, and of deeds. . . . Were there, then, no interpretations in the world, there would be neither selves nor communities."[28] Since in fact there are selves and communities, Royce presupposed, epistemology, whether empiricist or rationalist, is guilty of wanting to transcend language, to ground putative knowledge on timeless, wordless foundations, whether of pure experience by outstanding acts of perception or intellectual insight into innate conceptual processes,

---

with Royce's analysis is perfect: as the modern subject becomes a self-identity above the realm of temporal, changing, extending things, it has no need of self-interpretation in converse with other minds and indeed must resist the claims of narrative that would locate the self once again in the flux of becoming, where decisions that constitute the somatic, embodied, "extended" self threaten the "hell of the irrevocable" (see below, n. 44).

24. Royce, *The Problem of Christianity*, pp. 277ff.
25. Royce, *The Problem of Christianity*, p. 281.
26. Royce, *The Problem of Christianity*, p. 286.
27. Royce, *The Problem of Christianity*, p. 289.
28. Royce, *The Problem of Christianity*, p. 274.

and in this way to exempt itself from the fundamental temporal and linguistic process of human history: interpreting and being interpreted as minds relating to other minds about the passage to ideal community. For any account of the passage through time requires, as we have heard, narrative that posits (if only implicitly and unconsciously) an ideal, a goal of perfect communication, the Beloved Community of charitable interpretation. "Life may be a colloquy, or a prayer; but the life of a reasonable being is never a mere perception; nor a conception; nor a mere sequence of thoughtless deeds; nor yet an active process, however synthetic, wherein interpretation plays no part. Life is essentially, in its ideal, social. Hence interpretation is a necessary element of everything that, in life, has ideal value."[29]

It is a hotly debated question today whether there are selves, not to mention communities or final ends, as Royce assumed; Spinozist and Nietzschean ideas that agency is elusive, if not illusory,[30] that human selves might better be conceived as passing modes of being on the plane of immanence are in the ascendency. This is a topic that we will engage below in Chapter Five, where I argue that a decentered, theonomous self belonging to Christ as the one true Agent is nonetheless also an idiosyncratic self, with a definite albeit subordinate agency in the world. In the realm of human language, in any event, provided we find it trustworthy as Royce did (and so not the oppressive matrix of contemporary Gnosticism), the letter may be read in the light of the Spirit and the Spirit may be known on the basis of the letter. This is possible, provided that we are satisfied to know what is given for us to know in our own limited sequence. Such contentment with the finitude and fallibility of our formations of knowledge in the infinite process of interpretation depends on faith in the Giver of our sequence and His final reconciliation of all our provisional beliefs in the school of Heaven.[31] The dialectic of Word and Spirit can proceed in the interim, that is to say,

---

29. Royce, *The Problem of Christianity,* p. 293.

30. So Spinoza: "human power is very limited and is infinitely surpassed by the power of external causes, and so we do not have absolute power to adapt to our purposes things external to us. However, we shall patiently bear whatever happens to us that is contrary to what is required by consideration of our own advantage, if we are conscious that we have done our duty and that our power was not extensive enough for us to have avoided the said things, and that we are a part of the whole of Nature whose order we follow." Baruch Spinoza, *Ethics, Treatise on the Emendation of the Intellect and Selected Letters,* trans. S. Shirley (Indianapolis: Hackett, 1992), p. 158.

31. Philip Melanchthon, *Orations on Philosophy and Education,* ed. Sachiko Kusukawa (Cambridge: Cambridge University Press, 1999), p. 153.

insofar as the triadic relationships of interpreter, interpreted, and audience are *fully* taken into account — meaning then that the interpretive knowledge that we each so painfully and preciously acquire in our own time inevitably becomes in turn a new artifact, subject to new interpretations and so on to infinity. We will be superseded, but not forgotten. "Metaphysically considered, the world of interpretation is the world in which, if indeed we are able to interpret at all, we learn to acknowledge the being and the inner life of our fellow-men; and to understand the constitution of temporal experience, with its endlessly accumulating sequence of significant deeds. . . ."[32] To us, this process is infinite. Even in all eternity, we shall never comprehend the God who comprehends us all (Gregory of Nyssa).[33]

If we find *this* process nevertheless trustworthy, it is because, with Royce, we *believe* the dialectic of Word and Spirit to intend the Father's goal of the Beloved Community, that is to say in classical creedal language, it is because we believe that in the Spirit with the Son we will be presented — fragments of meaning that we are — purified and reconciled to all others, and so remembered eternally by the Father of the Son and Breather of the Spirit. This objective remembrance is a subjective participation in their eternal life. Over against this creedal faith in finality of the Beloved Community, premature desire for closure signifies the lethal Gnostic flight from history (even when dressed in Christian costume). For this world of infinite interpretation is still this world on which the cross of Jesus stood, indeed the one and only world where "selves and communities may exist, past and future can be defined, and the realms of the spirit may find a place which neither barren conception nor the chaotic flow of interpenetrating perceptions could ever render significant."[34] As interpretation, the infinite process deals with definite facts capable of interpretation, and as such these facts of past history may bear more significance than we bargain for. Royce knew this and indeed insisted on it. The cost of real though finite knowledge of minds in history is what Royce provocatively titled the "*hell* of the irrevocable."[35]

---

32. Royce, *The Problem of Christianity,* p. 294.

33. "There is nothing that can be supposed to embrace the infinite nature. And all the desire for the beautiful which is drawn towards the upward ascent never ceases in its incessant pursuit of the lovely. And the true vision of God consists in this, in never reaching the satiety of desire." "On the Life of Moses," in *Gregory of Nyssa,* trans. Anthony Meredith, S.J. (London and New York: Routledge, 1999), p. 107.

34. Royce, *The Problem of Christianity,* p. 294.

35. The irrevocable past becomes a living "hell" when the deed I have done and can-

Royce, in other words, has the right to say that real biographies (narrative interpretations of individuals and communities) can exist in definite, indeed, painfully significant ways because interpretation, as he explains, is not creative, as though it were the act of a Fichtean Ego, a sovereign self making its world *ex nihilo*. Interpretation is rather constructive, the act of a finite, social, and somatic self struggling to understand other selves, not to mention its own self, where the one thing that is shared is what has been, the transpired, the once-now-decided and henceforth-not-otherwise. In the flux of becoming, the past is one thing that is absolutely, dauntingly, and henceforth eternally true: "past time as irrevocable." That is to say, "the perception of an [sic] universe where all is fluent can be interpreted only through recognizing that the past returns not; that the deed once done is never to be recalled; that what has been done is at once the world's safest treasure, and its heaviest burden."[36] Because of this potential "*hell* of the irrevocable," Roycean interpretation arguably takes Heraclitus's world of flux more seriously than pop-Darwinian *Lebensphilosophie* (Royce is discussing Bergson): according to interpretation, human consciousness itself is nothing but the immanent and continuing process of interpreting the facticity of the self's own irrevocable past as held in memory to the prospective self, the imagined self, the future self. Consciousness *is* the passing present's continuing mediation of the past to the future, as embedded in the essentially temporal cosmos. This selfhood then is perilous. There is "no royal road to self knowledge" beyond or behind the flux, "no direct intuition or perception of the self . . ." that would lift us out of the womb of becoming, but rather only the "interior conversation, in which one discovers one's own mind through a process of inference analogous to the very modes of inference which guide us in a social effort to interpret our neighbors' minds."[37]

No wonder the Gnostic attraction! Royce's is a *somatic* self located in space-time, bounded by birth day and death day and sharing in the destiny of its particular society. This self is and can only be the biographical, historical act of constructing a future by the interpretation of a factual past: a perilous task liable to shipwreck in the world of Heraclitus's flux where what is

---

not undo is a veritable act of moral suicide, an act of treason committed against my own highest good, for which "I cannot forgive myself for having done." Royce, *The Problem of Christianity*, p. 162, emphasis added. Because of *this* threat of hell, the Gnostic alternative is and remains the abiding temptation.

36. Royce, *The Problem of Christianity*, p. 293.
37. Royce, *The Problem of Christianity*, p. 285.

done cannot ever be undone, where also what will be cannot be secured in advance. In such a world, the shipwreck of the self can occur in the several ways of despair, pride, and sloth. One can be so traumatized by brutality and abuse, that just to survive from moment to moment one abandons integration with a future in order to hold lethal memory at bay. Here the broken self needs a saving Word of its release from the anti-divine powers and of its healing, a theology of liberation. Or, out of anxiety to the secure future, one forgets that one has first received, transgresses the boundaries of one's particular time and place, rupturing the ecology of things to build bigger barns, yet then forgets what one has done to others, disowning one's own guilty past. Here the sinning self needs a saving Word of judgment and pardon, a theology of reconciliation. Or, out of resignation before a past that cannot be changed and a future that cannot be secured, an apathetic self abandons agency to float apathetically on the shifting tides. This slothful self needs a saving Word of command that speaks with authority, a theology of discipleship. Liberation, reconciliation, and new obedience are the three dimensions of salvation by which the morally burdened individual is atoned and brought anew into the Beloved Community.

Can we today, as the Creed speaks on the basis of 1 Peter 3:19, believe in the One who descended into hell to proclaim victory for "the spirits who are in prison"?[38] *Luther's* Christ wants us to so believe, to anticipate here what we shall study in Chapter Three: "Christ wants to say: 'Out of love for you I humble Myself and come to earth: I become an infant, assume body, soul, and human nature, am conceived by the Holy Spirit without sin, become a heavenly man and yet a true natural man endowed with flesh and blood, body and soul — all this to comfort you and that I may die and descend to hell for you. If you believe all this, even hell and the grave will be able to hold on to you no more than they were able to hold on to Me. Now you are a heavenly, not an earthly man; you no longer think, speak, and act in an earthly way but in a heavenly way.'"[39] The exodus of the enslaved from the land of bondage, the vacating of the grave of an executed criminal, the harrowing of hell — the biblical pattern is always the same. Salvation is the inclusion of the excluded into the Beloved Community, which itself comes into being by this new history of inclusion made by Jesus Christ, true man, true God, redeemer of the world.

---

38. Royce, *The Problem of Christianity,* p. 184.

39. "Sermons on the Gospel of St. John," 4:32 (1539?) LW 22:462. I will discuss the "spiritual sufferings of Christ" in the Conclusion.

Royce takes the creedal statement to ask whether we today can believe in an act of creative love that restores a true traitor, irrevocable past and all, to the Beloved Community. The "postulate" of creedal faith, now interpreted as a "doctrine of life," reads: "No baseness or cruelty of treason so deep and so tragic shall enter our human world, but that loyal love shall be able in due to time to oppose to just that deed of treason its fitting deed of atonement."[40] Notice: no magic, no fiat, no *deus ex machina*, but only a new creative act by a new actor making a new history on behalf of the failure: "triumph over treason can only be accomplished by the community, through some steadfastly loyal servant who acts, so to speak, as the incarnation of the very spirit of the community itself" in a creative deed that makes "the new world better than it was before the blow of treason fell."[41] New history is required, because there is and can be no world other than this temporally constituted one, with all its irrevocable past, hence the world that is "not godliness but the process of becoming godly, not health but getting well, not being but becoming, not rest but exercise."[42]

So again *Luther* famously re-described our reality as history in defense of his teaching that forgiveness of sins, life, and salvation come on the scene not as magic, fiat, sheer miracle, but as fitting miracle, creative fiat: not the magic of expiation but the heavy burden of propitiation. Or, in Royce's terms, we have the new and costly interpretation of the irrevocable past of failure by the Christ whose righteousness was to make that hellish history His own. Because of this new interpretation of our human past coming to us from Another's creative deed, Luther went on, "we are not now what we shall be, but we are on the way. The process is not yet finished, but it is actively going on. This is not the goal but it is the right road. At present, everything does not gleam and sparkle, but everything is being cleansed."[43] In Royce's words to the same point: "the suffering servant can thus transfigure this meaning [of the treason]; can bring out of the realm of death a new life that only this very death rendered possible."[44]

We have here, as is now visible, an intriguing set of interlocking ideas from Royce which I am connecting to Luther in a preliminary way. Whether from the perspective of Darwinian biology or of Christian eschatology, we have a take on reality as becoming, not being; a philosophical

40. Royce, *The Problem of Christianity,* p. 186.
41. Royce, *The Problem of Christianity,* p. 180.
42. Martin Luther, "Defense and Explanation of All the Articles" (1520) LW 32:24.
43. Luther, "Defense and Explanation of All the Articles" (1520) LW 32:24.
44. Royce, *The Problem of Christianity,* p. 181.

notion of knowledge as interpretation befitting the flux, which at the same time seems amenable to creedal theology, when what is at stake in the Christian creedal tradition is understood as a new history of inclusion of Luther's "sinner" or Royce's "traitor" into the Beloved Community.

It is not my purpose here to argue for or against the interpretations of sin and atonement that Royce went on to develop in *The Problem of Christianity,* but rather to take up the way by which he framed the question about the possibility of creedal Christianity for modern Euro-Americans — my purpose, of course, is to take up *Luther's* interpretations of sin and atonement and related matters. In fact, Royce died before his work was finished, leaving behind a work in progress with many perplexities unresolved, since *The Problem of Christianity* seems to mark Royce's own, late-in-life break from his earlier idealistic monism.[45] Even so, the questions he raised in it were not without effect. The fundamental notions here are that there is no private salvation in creedal Christianity but salvation is always salvation by inclusion of the person in the Beloved Community; that standing in the way of this inclusion are irrevocable histories of real betrayal, requiring creative love to make a new "atoning" history that may reconcile this "real, not fictitious sinner" (Luther). These arguably bore fruit in Martin Luther King Jr.'s life and work, as we shall have opportunity to study in Chapter Nine. Looking backward as well, Royce's *Fragestellung* aptly captured the great theme in Augustine's thought of a "universal society," along the lines urged by Etienne Gilson in the face of twentieth-century fascism: "the whole world, from its beginning until its final term, has as its unique end the constitution of a holy Society, in view of which everything has been made, even the universe itself. . . . Everything that is, except God Himself whose work the City is, is for the City and has no meaning apart from the City. . . ."[46] Gilson asserted this bad science but good theology in the face of Nazi racial theory: "all men, regardless of race, color or appearance, have their origin in

45. Kuklick, *Biography*, p. 21. ". . . Royce moved to pluralism" from monism, in the sense of granting a real, but subordinate agency to creatures. *The Problem of Christianity* "was a volume that brought Royce into the camp of Christian theism [that is, Trinitarianism] . . . human beings were [now] members of progressively larger groups that came to fruition in the widest community of religion. Rather than being parts of a larger whole, they were members of a more inclusive body, their separateness more strongly preserved, their oneness with the body more complexly defined." Bruce Kuklick, *A History of Philosophy in America, 1720-2000* (Oxford: Clarendon Press, 2001), p. 175.

46. St. Augustine, *City of God,* introduced by Etienne Gilson, ed. Vernon J. Bourke (Garden City, NY: Doubleday, 1958), p. 21.

the first man created by God . . . men are naturally brothers in Adam, even before being supernaturally brothers in Christ. . . ." He referred specifically to Augustine's "anti-racism."[47]

Broadly speaking, Augustinianism stretching back to Paul and then forward through Luther to modern figures like Royce and King stamps the tradition of creedal Christianity in the West, mostly for the good. For here, the pointed question is put to the City of Man: *Without justice, what is the state but organized crime?*[48] Here in turn salvation is understood socially as inclusion in the City of God, Jesus' *basileia tou theou,* Luther's "little flock," Royce's and King's Beloved Community — something greater than the visible church in history, although the visible church in history is both the bearer of this hope to the world and its true but ambiguous realization. In this Augustinian framework of *social* understanding, Martin Luther, taken then as the "modern Augustinian"[49] (*not* as the founder of a sect of individualistic anxieties of the introspective conscience), is an important resource for answering in the affirmative Royce's question: Can we be creedal Christians today?

## An Alternative: James's Experiential Theology

There is yet another factor at play in retrieving teachings of Luther relevant in Euro-American theology today by means of Royce's *Fragestellung.* Royce's book *The Problem of Christianity* was his critical response to the alternative philosophy of religion laid out by his lifelong friend and partner in philosophical dialogue, William James. In James's great and massively more influential study, *The Varieties of Religious Experience,*[50] he embraced from the outset the fact/value disjunction[51] and made it axiomatic

47. Augustine, *City of God,* p. 25. See Colin Kidd, *The Forging of Races: Race and Scripture in the Protestant Atlantic World, 1600-2000* (Cambridge: Cambridge University Press, 2006) and the author's review in *Sixteenth Century Journal* 39, no. 2 (Summer 2008): 513-14. Royce too, in his own time, battled against American racism.

48. Augustine, *City of God,* p. 88.

49. That is, Augustine appropriated by means of the newly developed logic tools of Nominalism. See Graham White, *Luther as Nominalist: A Study of the Logical Methods Used in Martin Luther's Disputations in the Light of Their Medieval Background,* Schriften der Luther-Agricola-Gesellschaft 30 (Helsinki: Luther-Agricola Society, 1994).

50. William James, *The Varieties of Religious Experience: A Study in Human Nature* (Mineola, NY: Dover, 2002).

51. James, *The Varieties,* p. 4. James called his method an "empirical" one, italicizing

for his approach to the study of religion: whereas the Bible's worth "would probably fare ill in our hands" if its credibility were to be judged by matters of fact, "the book may well be a revelation in spite of errors and passions and deliberate human compositions, if only it be a true record of the inner experiences of great-souled persons wrestling with the crises of their fate."[52] As this opening antithesis indicates, it was characteristic of James's approach to appeal to a prime level of pre-linguistic psychic experience, i.e., feelings that become articulate in symbolic language as judgments of value, not of fact.[53] Following the lead of the French liberal Protestant Sabatier, James accordingly relegated "worship and sacrifice, procedures for working on the dispositions of the deity, theology and ceremony and ecclesiastical organization" to "the essentials of religion in the institutional branch." James does not shy here from a value judgment. "Were we to limit our view to it, we should have to define religion as an external art, the art of winning the favor of the gods." In contrast to *that*, James directed attention to "the more personal branch of religion" where "the inner dispositions of man . . . form the entire centre of interest, his conscience, his deserts, his helplessness, his incompleteness." Here "the individual transacts the business by himself alone, and the ecclesiastical organization, with its priests and sacraments and other go-betweens, sinks to an altogether secondary place." So he concluded his methodological prolegomena: this study will "ignore the institutional branch entirely . . . and confine [it]self as far as [it] can to personal religion, pure and simple."[54] James has thus as-

---

the pronoun *we* in the following passage to underscore the Kantian limits of reason: "We cannot divide man sharply into an animal and a rational part. We cannot distinguish natural from supernatural effects; nor among the latter know which are favors of God, and which are counterfeit operations of the demon. We have merely to collect things together without any special a priori theological system, and out of the aggregate of piecemeal judgments as to the value of this or that experience — judgments in which our general philosophic prejudices, our instincts, and our common sense are the only guides — decide that *on the whole* one type of religion is approved by its fruits, and another type condemned." James, *The Varieties*, p. 327.

52. James, *The Varieties*, p. 5.

53. This stance on divine ineffability is presupposed throughout, but is discussed explicitly in James's lectures on mysticism. Here James holds that "personal religious experience has its root and centre in mystical states of consciousness; so for us, who in these lectures are treating personal experience as the exclusive subject of our study, such states of consciousness ought to form the vital chapter from which the other chapters get their light." James, *The Varieties*, p. 379.

54. James, *The Varieties*, p. 29.

sociated the prophetic critique of religion that uses God for human purposes with exteriority and social form and in contrast valorized interiority as the privileged realm of authentic and unmediated experience of the divine.

But it was just this fateful distinction at the root of James's approach, according to Royce, that constituted "a profound and momentous error in the whole religious philosophy of our greatest American master in the study of the psychology of religious experience."[55] The error stems from the artificial isolation of the individual and interiority from social experience. Royce thus urged that James's position is of a piece with the construction of the modern self stemming from Descartes; he argued this point in criticizing James's account of how one supposedly reasons by analogy to the existence of other minds: "I deem [your body] actuated, as is my own, by an inner life like mine."[56] In reality, Royce counters, the reason for postulating the existence of other minds is the primal experience in language: "the ideas which your words and movements have aroused within me are not my own ideas, cannot be interpreted in terms of my own ideas. . . ." In truth, the experience of others in language is the genesis of the individual's own self-awareness.[57] The experience of a real other through language, says Royce, induces us to "the fundamental hypothesis of my social consciousness, that all contrasts of ideas have a real interpretation and are interpreted."[58] Accordingly James's celebrated "pluralism," in Royce's critical reading, turns out to be a version of atomism according to which "unities are temporary, accidental and nonessential. . . . [This is a world where] each individual expression of the will to succeed, 'struts and frets its hour upon the stage, and then is heard no more.'"[59]

Royce finally rejected James's version of "pragmatism" as the Cartesian-Kantian "dualistic view of the cognitive process" tweaked in an empiricist direction with conceptions supplying "the banknotes, while only perception can supply the needed cash"[60] — thus leaving judgments of value in the lurch finally as but arbitrary expressions of irreducible psychological types. Such an epistemology indeed finds the "'cash' of experience in plenty," Royce grants, perhaps thinking of the vast repertoire on

55. Royce, *The Problem of Christianity*, p. 41.
56. Royce, *The Problem of Christianity*, p. 353.
57. Royce, *The Problem of Christianity*, pp. 107ff.
58. Royce, *The Problem of Christianity*, p. 361.
59. Royce, *The Problem of Christianity*, p. 354.
60. Royce, *The Problem of Christianity*, p. 291.

display in *Varieties*. "But [it] never find[s] what has created all the great religions, and all the deathless loyalties, and all the genuinely true insights of the human world, — namely, that interpretation of life which sends across the borders, both of our conceptual and of our perceptual life, to lay up treasures in other worlds, to interpret the meaning of the processes of time, to read the meaning of art and life."[61] Religions, taken as the creedal beliefs of communities, are interpretations of life as essentially social and historical. But James's approach yields only "wanton revels in mere perception"; it misses the target because it never rises to "the art of interpretation"[62] but rather sinks into the abyss of pre-linguistic intuition of the inexpressible.

This harsh judgment may be overstated, at least as pertains to *Varieties*, which as we shall see cannot avoid some measure of "interpretation." In any event, Royce's fundamental protest against James's approach largely went unheeded.[63] James's book seemed instead to demonstrate that the study of primal experience (understood in religion as the presence of the divine) could form the basis for a new kind of scholarship replacing the dogmatic theology of creedal Christianity. If philosophy, James wrote in conclusion, "will abandon metaphysics and deduction for criticism and induction, and frankly transform [it]self from theology into science of religion," it can then remove "historic incrustations . . . doctrines that are now known to be scientifically absurd or incongruous." It can further distill a residue of "conceptions that are at least possible," treating these as "hypotheses," distinguishing between "what is innocent over-belief and symbolism in the expression of it, and what is to be taken literally," in this way mediating "between different believers, and help[ing] to bring about consensus of opinion . . . discriminat[ing] the common and essential from the individual and local elements. . . ."[64]

61. Royce, *The Problem of Christianity*, p. 295.

62. Royce, *The Problem of Christianity*, p. 295. I have applied Royce's words to James's text, justly, I believe.

63. "James's student and famous biographer, Ralph Barton Perry, effectively portrayed Royce as outmoded and sentimental, ill-equipped to serve American thought in the new century. World War I also diminished Royce's reputation. . . . German thought was stigmatized. . . . [Perry] promoted a view of James as a utilitarian, humanist thinker who had rejected a romantic idealism. Perry's sleight of hand gained its wider credence later. . . . James was championed, in contrast to Royce, as more contemporary, forward-looking, and typically American. This was the first step in the construction of a scientific pragmatism, with James at its center, as the essential philosophy of the United States. . . . It was not a bad story." Kuklick, *History*, p. 176.

64. James, *The Varieties*, p. 455.

Needless to say, this project seemed enormously liberating and progressive at the time; in contrast Royce's Victorian prose already had an antiquarian ring. James's revisionist conception of the intellectual task in religion held far greater sway in American theology in the ensuing century.

There are several matters of interest here: a more general, having to do with the challenge of Darwinism and another quite specific, having to do with the conundrum Luther represents to James's scheme. First, and generally, what puts James and Royce on the same field of play is that both thinkers are dealing with the Darwinian revolution,[65] which they understood philosophically as bringing about a new ascendancy of Heraclitean dynamism after centuries of Parmenidean stagnation. Royce tried to incorporate the evolutionary perspective into his understanding of the "problem" of Christianity. Clear recognition of reality as temporal process entailed equally clear recognition that "great truths bear long sorrows." The "purgatory of time" requires the "complications of dogma, the strifes of the sects, the horrors of the religious wars in former centuries, the confusions of controversy in our own day. . . ." None of this must "make us despair. Such is the warfare of ideals. Such is the present world. . . . We have to do, not so much with apostasy, as with evolution."[66] James's engagement with Darwinism is arguably more profound; indeed, it is critical to a good reading of *Varieties* to take it into account, for between the lines James does mighty battle with the optimistic reading of evolution popular in his day.

## Saints amid Boas and Crocodiles

James laid out his analysis of religious experience along the fault-line between the "healthy-minded" on the one side and the "sick soul" on the other. He regarded these as two irreducible psychological types: "the causes of human diversity lie chiefly in our *differing susceptibilities of emotional excitement,* and in the *different impulses and inhibitions* which these bring in their train. . . ."[67] The healthy-minded simply does not feel "disease and death . . . the slaughter-house and indecencies without end on

---

65. For a thorough and enlightening account, see Louis Menand, *The Metaphysical Club: A Story of Ideas in America* (New York: Farrar, Straus & Giroux, 2001).

66. James, *The Varieties,* p. 79. See also the reference to the evolution controversy during his student years, p. 59.

67. James, *The Varieties,* p. 261. Emphasis original.

which our life is founded" with the sensitivity of the sick soul. For the healthy soul, all of nature "red in tooth and claw" is "huddled out of sight and never mentioned. . . ." Its "official" world is a "poetic fiction far handsomer and cleaner and better than the world really is."[68] So, according to this psychological theory, healthy-minded individuals will naturally gravitate to an optimistic religion, life siding with life. These "once-born" feel "that Nature, if you will only trust her sufficiently, is absolutely good."[69] Of course, for those "who naturally feel life as a tragic mystery, such optimism is a shallow dodge or mean evasion. It accepts, in lieu of a real deliverance, what is a lucky personal accident merely, a cranny to escape by."[70]

Yet there are indications that whatever the psychological basis of James's two basic types of religion, he is aware that the religious consciousness of the healthy-minded is of recent historical vintage: "The advance of liberalism, so-called, in Christianity, during the past fifty years, may fairly be called a victory of healthy-mindedness within the church over the morbidness with which the old hellfire theology was more harmoniously related."[71] James connects this new state of consciousness with the recent advance of the "theory of evolution," which has laid the ground, James claims, "for a new sort of religion of Nature, which has entirely displaced Christianity from the thought of a large part of our generation. The idea of universal evolution lends itself to a doctrine of general meliorism and progress which fits the religious needs of the healthy-minded so well that it seems almost as if it might have been created for their use." But, James notes, this is evolution interpreted "optimistically."[72] In another passage, James similarly notes the "strange moral transformation [which] has within the past century swept over our Western world. We no longer think that we are called on to face physical pain with equanimity . . . the recital of [such] cases makes our flesh creep morally as well as physically. The way in which our ancestors looked upon pain as an eternal ingredient of the world's order, and both caused and suffered it as a matter-of-course portion of their day's work, fill us with astonishment."[73] The inclusive "us" here is of course the liberal

---

68. James, *The Varieties,* p. 90.

69. James, *The Varieties,* p. 80.

70. James, *The Varieties,* p. 363.

71. James, *The Varieties,* p. 91.

72. James, *The Varieties,* p. 91.

73. James, *The Varieties,* pp. 297-98. See in this connection the acute analysis of Talal Asad, *Formations of the Secular: Christianity, Islam, Modernity* (Stanford, CA: Stanford University Press, 2003), chap. 2, "Thinking about Agency and Pain," pp. 67-99.

Protestant audience of the healthy-minded in attendance at the Gifford Lectures. James knew how to bring his audience along. While the "general optimism and healthy-mindedness of liberal Protestant circles to-day makes mortification for mortification's sake repugnant to us" — as James now turned tables — the despised "twice-born philosophy" symbolizes (however clumsily) "the belief that there is an element of real wrongness in this world, which is neither to be ignored nor evaded, but which must be squarely met and overcome by an appeal to the soul's heroic resources, and neutralized and cleansed away by suffering."[74] This latter conviction turns out to be James's own. In the book's climactic peroration to "the moral equivalent of war,"[75] James summoned his auditors/readers to a "renovated and revised ascetic discipline"[76] in the modern-saintly struggle to make the world a better place.

What makes *Varieties* such an interesting book, then, is that James comes to regard the religion of the healthy-minded as a not-so-beneficent illusion in what truly is the dark jungle of crocodiles and boa constrictors. If the religion of the healthy-minded is "a way of deliberately minimizing evil," a "radically opposite view, a way of maximizing evil" stands opposite it in the religion of the sick soul.[77] In this religion we "turn towards those persons who cannot so swiftly throw off the burden of the consciousness of evil, but are congenitally fated to suffer from its presence."[78] As unpleasant as James expects the exploration of this phenomenon to be for his healthy-minded audience of liberal Protestants, he begged their indulgence: "Let us see whether pity, pain, and fear, and the sentiment of human helplessness may not open a profounder view and put into our hands a more complicated key to the meaning of the situation."[79] It is not long before we find James coaching the hearer/reader along: "To ascribe religious value to mere happy-go-lucky contentment with one's brief chance at natural good is but the very consecration of forgetfulness and superficiality. Our troubles lie indeed too deep for *that* cure. The fact that we *can* die, that we *can* be ill at all, is what perplexes us. . . ." The sick-soul's awareness of the transiency of life brings "the worm at the core of all our usual springs of delight into full view, and turns us into melancholy metaphysi-

---

74. James, *The Varieties*, p. 362,
75. James, *The Varieties*, p. 367.
76. James, *The Varieties*, p. 365.
77. James, *The Varieties*, pp. 130-31.
78. James, *The Varieties*, pp. 133-34.
79. James, *The Varieties*, p. 136.

cians." So it is that the sick soul, should it attain to the second birth, arises to a "good that will not perish, a good in fact that flies beyond the Goods of nature."[80] It is evident that James's sympathy lies with these "twice-born"; most of his book is a description at once luxuriant and painful of the arduous path traveled from the "divided self" through "conversion" and on to "saintliness."

It is not until James assesses the "value of saintliness" that the depth of his engagement with contemporary Darwinism becomes explicit. Here he takes up the argument of Herbert Spencer that on naturalistic grounds the value of perfection is entirely relative to a given environment, with the implication "that in the world that actually is, the [saintly] virtues of sympathy, charity, and non-resistance" prove to be "folly when we are dealing with human crocodiles and boa-constrictors. The saint may simply give the universe into the hands of the enemy by his trustfulness." There is the kindred argument of Social Darwinism: "Here saintliness has to face the charge of preserving the unfit, and breeding parasites and beggars."[81] James cannot but feel the force of these objections, although he is not convinced. He is willing to acknowledge "the complexity of the moral life,"[82] but at the same time is sure that "were the world confined to these hard-headed, hard-hearted, and hard-fisted methods exclusively . . . [it] would be an infinitely worse place than it is now to live in."[83] Still, he is hard-pressed to refute these Darwinist extrapolations on their own grounds, since he shares them. In the end, he has — without admitting it in so many words — to resort to theology, that is, to Roycean interpretation: "Our final judgment on the worth of such a life as [the saint] will depend largely on our conception of God, and of the sort of conduct he is best pleased with in his creatures."[84] Or again, this time fending off Nietzsche's genealogical revelation of the saint's covert will to power: "the whole feud revolves essentially upon two pivots: Shall the seen world or the unseen world be our chief sphere of adaptation? And must our means of adaptation in this seen world be aggressiveness or non-resistance?"[85] In other words, how shall we *interpret* the fact of evolution?

80. James, *The Varieties*, p. 140.
81. James, *The Varieties*, p. 355.
82. James, *The Varieties*, p. 355.
83. James, *The Varieties*, p. 356.
84. James, *The Varieties*, p. 354.
85. James, *The Varieties*, p. 373.

## Luther Fails to Map

The very interesting personal answers James provides to these questions at the end of *Varieties,* like Royce's interpretations of sin and atonement, are not themselves pertinent to this study. What is of interest is how to frame the question about Christian belief today. At the end of *Varieties* James explicitly acknowledged his allegiance to the camp that "our ancestors used to brand as enthusiasm"[86] — Luther's term for those who appeal to an immediate experience of the Spirit apart from the *external* word, the *news* of the gospel. This admission helps us to see with fresh eyes the fork in the theological road between Royce's commitment to the *verbum externum* and James's self-professed "enthusiasm." In addition, however, we have James's apparent, last-minute retreat from his otherwise unbending commitments to naturalism, empiricism, and pragmatism when he finally appealed to our "conception of God" and the "unseen world" — appeals to old-fashioned theology which, however, James had not warranted and had no way to adjudicate.

Another, more specific clue to the theological dead-end to which the method of "enthusiasm" comes is the schizophrenic treatment accorded to Luther in *Varieties.* Luther appears in these pages as an exemplar both of healthy-mindedness and of the sick soul. James could lift up Luther's signature doctrine of justification by faith as an example of healthy "mind cure."[87] But this supposed mile marker on modern culture's road to religious inwardness could also be classified with the sick soul's "crisis of self-surrender,"[88] as James describes the sick old man Luther who "looked back on life as if it were an absolute failure."[89] Luther's ideas about repentance are said to bear "some very healthy-minded ideas, due in the main to the largeness of his conception of God";[90] indeed, James waxed eloquent in praise of the Luther who "in his immense manly way, swept off by a stroke of his hand the very notion of a debit and credit account kept with individuals by the Almighty[,] stretched the soul's imagination and saved theology from puerility."[91] Yet the very same Luther's theological God "of the humble, the miserable, the oppressed" is said to underwrite the sickly soul's idea that "the more literally lost you are, the more literally you are the very being

86. James, *The Varieties,* p. 486.
87. James, *The Varieties,* pp. 107-8.
88. James, *The Varieties,* p. 211.
89. James, *The Varieties,* p. 137.
90. James, *The Varieties,* pp. 128-29.
91. James, *The Varieties,* p. 348.

whom Christ's sacrifice has already saved."[92] Luther on the one hand illustrates the "mystical experience," when for example he told of being swept away by a deeper apprehension of the Creed's affirmation, "I believe in the forgiveness of sins."[93] But the same theologian, in words cited by James from Emerson, "would have cut off his right hand rather than nail his theses to the door at Wittenberg, if he had supposed that they were destined to lead to the pale negations of Boston Unitarianism."[94] Clearly Luther does not map well on the chart of religious experience that James has drawn.

One reason for James's confusion about Luther might be traced to his dependence on the scholarship of the contemporary giant of German liberal Protestantism, Adolph von Harnack.[95] Harnack, the eminent German Lutheran scholar of his times, proclaimed doctrine defunct: "The history of dogma comes to a close with Luther."[96] In seven probing volumes, Harnack argued the influential thesis that creedal dogma (such as Royce lifted up) is the historically contingent product of what he famously characterized as "the hellenization of the gospel." Hellenization is understandable, Harnack explained; it was even inevitable. But this creedal theology formulated the gospel in the thought forms of Greek substance metaphysics; as such, these ideas are unintelligible to the modern mind and constitute an actual obstacle to faith. As indicated, Harnack argued that it was none other than Martin Luther who in principle if not yet to full effect overcame the intellectualizing and reifying theology of the old church. Luther recovered Jesus' simple gospel of trust in the fatherly love of God. Couple this insight with the rise since Luther's time of the modern scientific understanding of the world — which threatens to crush the human spirit with knowledge of its insignificance and impotence in the vast and ancient cosmos — and Jesus' message of the fatherly God, rediscovered in principle by Luther's idea of trust, *fiducia,* is surely the "essence of Christianity" and the gospel for our times. Theology as belief, *theory,* intellectual *grasping* of the divine with antiquated, reifying *concepts* like "nature" or "substance," gives way to historically-critically founded preaching of existential trust in the world of Heraclitus.

92. James, *The Varieties,* p. 245.

93. James, *The Varieties,* p. 382.

94. James, *The Varieties,* p. 330.

95. James was well versed in German letters, and he cited the German title of Harnack's *The Essence of Christianity* in *The Varieties* (p. 100), though not *The History of Dogma.*

96. Adolph von Harnack, *The History of Dogma,* trans. N. Buchanan, 7 vols. (New York: Dover, 1961) [hereafter *HD*], vol. 7, p. 268.

Little in Harnack's analysis has stood up to critical scrutiny. For example, Jaroslav Pelikan's five-volume history of doctrine tells the counter-tale to Harnack of the *evangelization of Hellenism:* it is, he writes, a "distortion when the dogma formulated by the catholic tradition is described as 'in its conception and development a work of the Greek spirit on the soil of the gospel' [Harnack]. Indeed, in some ways it is more accurate to speak of dogma as the 'dehellenization' of the theology that had preceded it and to argue that 'by its dogma the church threw up a wall against an alien metaphysic'" [*Elert*].[97] Step by painful step, Pelikan methodically dismantles Harnack's construction of dogma as hellenization by means of a simple but crucial move: he takes dogma hermeneutically not *theoretically,* that is to say, as "what we believe, teach and confess on the basis of the Word of God" — an expression of the Lutheran Formulators[98] which Pelikan borrowed to define the subject matter of his study. "Without setting rigid boundaries, we shall identify what is 'believed' as the form of Christian doctrine present in the modalities of devotion, spirituality, and worship; what is 'taught' as the content of the word of God extracted by exegesis from the witness of the Bible and communicated to the people of the church through proclamation, instruction and churchly theology; and what is 'confessed' as the testimony of the church, both against false teaching from within and against attacks from without, articulated in polemics and in apologetics, in creed and in dogma."[99] When dogma is taken this way, as the complex act of the church's interpretation of the gospel word of God in (continuing!) history, Harnack's influential claim about Luther overcoming dogma turns out to be real sleight of hand.

Christine Helmer has recently shown this in some detail, especially in regard to the doctrine of the Trinity. "Luther's anti-speculative bent against a specific determination of the hidden God cannot be confused with the thematization of the immanent Trinity as a theological task of

---

97. Jaroslav Pelikan, *The Christian Tradition: A History of the Development of Doctrine*, vol. 1, *The Emergence of the Catholic Tradition (100-600)* (Chicago and London: University of Chicago Press, 1975) [hereafter *CT*], p. 55. Pelikan devoted another work explicitly to this theme: *Christianity and Classical Culture: The Metamorphosis of Natural Theology in the Christian Encounter with Hellenism* (New Haven: Yale University Press, 1995).

98. The refrain "We believe, teach and confess . . ." is repeated in the "affirmative theses" at the head of each of the articles in the Epitome of the Formula of Concord. See *The Book of Concord,* ed. Robert Kolb and Timothy J. Wengert (Minneapolis: Fortress, 2000) [hereafter *BC*], 486:1, 488:2, etc.

99. Pelikan, *CT* I:4.

reason in obedience to faith. In fact, Luther preached regularly on the immanent Trinity, and his disputations document lively exchanges concerning this locus in great detail."[100] Likewise, "Luther's sermons exude a doctrinal air."[101] "Even the classic terminology of the relations of origin is unapologetically preached from the chancel. Luther neither rejects thematizing the inner-Trinity, nor does he use a language for its articulation other than the technical language adopted by the church."[102] Indeed, one must preach and teach about the Trinity, according to Luther, because in natural life God is experienced in the undifferentiated unity of His work as an indistinct *res;* it is only in Christ and Spirit, i.e., in the realm of the church evoked by the gospel that God is revealed in His Trinitarian reality.[103] Luther takes up the traditional doctrine of revelation: "It is God who speaks from himself," an assertion from Hilary's *De Trinitate* that Luther often cites. "*Sic Hilarius: quis potest, inquit, melius de se loqui quam deus ipse?*"[104] Helmer locates the affirmation of creedal doctrine at the heart of Luther's *reformation* theology, *finitum capax infiniti:* "For Luther, the church's words are the language in which God speaks from God. The marvelous convergence points to the heart of a divine mystery. The divine desire is to be known as the triune God in eternity, and as such, to be known in a particular way: through the Spirit speaking to the church in its language."[105] In Luther's own words, for vivid example: "A papal decree condemns the Anthropomorphites for speaking about God as if they were speaking about a human being. . . . However, the condemnation is unjust. Indeed, how could men speak otherwise of God among men? If it is heresy to think of God in this manner, then a verdict has been rendered concerning the salvation of all children, who think and speak of God in this childlike fashion. But even apart from the children: give me the most learned doctor — how else will he teach and speak about God?"[106]

100. Christine Helmer, *The Trinity and Martin Luther: A Study on the Relationship between Genre, Language and the Trinity in Luther's Works (1523-1546)* (Mainz: Verlag Philipp von Zabern, 1999), pp. 22-23.

101. Helmer, *The Trinity,* p. 208. Her critique of German theology stemming from von Harnack is scathing (pp. 9-20).

102. Helmer, *The Trinity,* p. 218.

103. Helmer, *The Trinity,* p. 211.

104. "So Hillary: who is able, he says, to speak better of Himself than God Himself?" Helmer, *The Trinity,* p. 221.

105. Helmer, *The Trinity,* p. 221.

106. "Lectures on Genesis" LW 1:14.

Despite such weighty scholarly corrections by a Pelikan or a Helmer, the notion of an invidious "hellenization of the gospel" has only continued to grow in influence through a variety of permutations, taken up first by the influential philosopher Heidegger[107] and then by sundry theological camp followers up to the present day, especially in the increasingly secularized field of biblical studies. These moves effect a massive reduction of doctrine to "existential decision," or more recently, to ideology and power politics, in either case coupled hand in glove with bitter polemics against so-called "early Catholicism."[108] But Harnack already brought together all the objections here in a single, sharp question against the Luther who looked with favor upon the old church dogma as the veritable new language of the Spirit: "Who really ventures to restore again the 'entire Luther,' with the coarseness of his medieval superstition, the flat contradictions of his theology, the remarkable logic of his arguments, the mistakes of his exegesis and the unfairness and barbarisms of his polemic? Shall we forget, then, all that has been learned by us, but was unknown to Luther?"[109] Well, *of course not.* Let me stipulate that any possible appropriation of *Luthers Lehre* has to be a critical one, filtered rigorously through the sieve of all the questions just listed and more. Nevertheless, it was Harnack himself who conceded the one point that entitles us to proceed.

Harnack wrote: "The German Reformer restored life to the formulae of Greek Christianity; he gave them back to faith. . . . *Luther was the restorer of the old dogma.* . . . Of this there can be no doubt — that the gospel was for him 'saving *doctrine, doctrine* of the gospel' *(doctrina salutaris, doctrina evangelii),* which certainly included the old dogmas; the attempt to represent the matter otherwise has in my opinion been a failure: the gospel is sacred doctrine, contained in the Word of God, the purpose of which is to be learned, and to which there must be subjection" — Harnack here cites Luther's end of life *Short Confession on the Holy Supper:* "Therefore there must be a believing of everything, pure and simple, whole and

---

107. Benjamin D. Crowe, *Heidegger's Religious Origins: Destruction and Authenticity* (Bloomington and Indianapolis: Indiana University Press, 2006), p. 131. See Paul R. Hinlicky, "Luther and Heidegger," *Lutheran Quarterly* 32, no. 1 (Spring 2008): 78-86.

108. Walter Bauer, *Orthodoxy and Heresy in Early Christianity,* ed. R. Kraft and G. Krodel (Mifflintown, PA: Sigler Press, 1996); Martin Werner, *The Formation of Christian Dogma: An Historical Study of Its Problem* (New York: Harper, 1957). The same period, however, can also witness as splendid and insightful an account as J. N. D. Kelly, *Early Christian Doctrines,* Revised Edition (New York: Harper, 1978).

109. Harnack, *HD* VII:177.

entire, or a believing of nothing."[110] Either/or, the true doctrine or apostasy. The old man Luther here to be sure seems not to allow sufficiently for the difference between dogma and its theological interpretation (I will discuss this text below in Chapter Eight); this inflexibility may be a reflex of his apocalyptic impatience with all opponents, who become increasingly for the late Luther an undifferentiated mass of the devil's minions (see the Appendix to this book). Nor does this Luther seem to allow for the ways in which his own indulgence in the rhetoric of paradox has compounded confusion and hardened misunderstanding into fixed polarizations. Polemic as a method displaces interpretation. Harnack was the first of many to follow in the twentieth century who have held that the old man Luther is thus a "man in contradiction" (surely, in some respects he was), and that foremost among the "contradictions" in Luther's theology was that between his reformatory discovery of faith as *fiducia*, trust, on the one hand, and the, well, *dogmatic* "attitude . . . assumed towards the old dogma,"[111] on the other.

My operating hypothesis is clearly the inverse: if we succeed in interpreting the old dogmas as Luther interpreted them, they do indeed come to life, and in coming to life they can effect for us today a Luther-like critique and reform of the contemporary church's practice of faith. But the price of this is that hermeneutical act of "violence" against the historical Martin Luther: we must disavow Luther's unreflective and self-serving resort to demonization of theological opponents, not least to be able to put the demons to flight in a better way (see the Appendix). In any event, James's confusion about where to place Luther on his map of religious experience indicates that Luther can better be appropriated in answering the question Royce posed: Can *we* today be creedal Christians? That is, Luther's thought constitutes — not an automatic authority, certainly not today, after Christendom — but a resource when we understand creedal belief holistically as the "life-doctrine" (Royce) professed by the baptized at the Pauline "juncture of the ages": through this faith they enter into the promised Beloved Community by the new creative act of the Suffering Servant of the Lord on behalf of "real, not fictitious sinners." This entails, to be sure, some other scholarly project than the program that James pioneered and has since prevailed in the liberal Protestant establishment in America. To that alternative project we now turn.

---

110. Harnack, *HD* VII:174-75.
111. Harnack, *HD* VII:180.

# CHAPTER TWO

# "One of the Trinity Suffered": Luther's Neo-Chalcedonian Christology

*But Christ is the subject of the Gospel. What the Gospel teaches and shows me is a divine work given to me by sheer grace; neither human reason nor wisdom nor even the Law of God teaches this. And I accept this gift by faith alone. This sort of doctrine, which reveals the Son of God, is not taught, learned, or judged by any human wisdom or by the Law itself; it is revealed by God, first by the external Word and then inwardly through the Spirit. Therefore the Gospel is a divine Word that came down from heaven and is revealed by the Holy Spirit, who was sent for this very purpose. Yet this happens in such a way that the external Word must come first.*

Luther[1]

1. Commenting on Galatians 1:16 in "Lectures on Galatians" (1535) in LW 26:73. For justification in rendering the Latin *obiectum* as "subject," the translator refers to footnote 95 in LW 1:58, which asserts that a change in meaning in the antithesis between subject and object transpired in the seventeenth and eighteenth centuries but provides no further documentation of this claim.

## Epistemology at the Turn of the Ages[2]

Unlike James or even Royce, we will begin following Paul where Luther began:[3] with the *apocalypse* of the good news by Jesus Christ (Gal. 1:12) or, equivalently, God's *apocalypse* of Jesus who was crucified as His Son (Gal. 1:16). "This Son of God, that is to say, was not the earthly Jesus, but rather the one who was now the Lord, alive, present, and enthroned by God's having raised him from the realm of those who have died (1:1, 3)." So J. Louis Martyn explains Paul's opening salvo in the Epistle to the Galatians. "Henceforth the presence of the crucified, resurrected, and powerful Son of God determined, for Paul, the nature of Christian worship, the life of the church, and specifically Paul's daily work as an evangelist." To be sure, "this Son mysteriously remains the crucified Christ who enacted his faithful love for us in collision with the Law's curse (2:20; 3:13). The resurrection of the Son does not eclipse the Son's cross[,]" but rather established it as the divine and human deed of saving righteousness in combat with the anti-divine powers of Sin and Death.[4] This divine announcement *von oben* sets the agenda of Pauline theology.

Apocalyptic theology is *revealed* theology; it makes known to human

---

2. The fault in Paul's opponents in 2 Corinthians, writes J. Louis Martyn, "lies in their failure to view the cross as the absolute epistemological watershed. On a real cross in this world hangs the long awaited Jewish Messiah. How can that be anything other than an epistemological crisis?" "Epistemology at the Turn of the Ages: 2 Cor. 5:16," in *Christian History and Interpretation: Studies Presented to John Knox*, ed. W. R. Father, C. F. D. Moule, and R. R. Niebuhr (Cambridge: Cambridge University Press, 1967), p. 286.

3. Citing John 1:13, Luther had early commented on Galatians 1:4, "There is another reason why Paul refers to the will of the Father here, a reason cited in many passages in the Gospel of John also, where Christ, in asserting His commission, calls us back to the will of the Father, so that in His words and works we are to look, not at Him but at the Father. For Christ came into the world so that he might take hold of us and so that we, by gazing upon Christ, might be drawn and carried directly to the Father." "Lectures on Galatians" (1535) in *LW* 26:42. Accordingly I will argue in the Conclusion that apocalypse is the true import of the early Luther's *theologia crucis,* and also the reason why Luther abandoned this terminology of the Heidelberg Disputation as misleading (since, rightly understood as in this citation, there is also here below a proper *Johannine* theology of glory, i.e., John 1:18). There is an important dispute in the scholarship consequently about how to interpret the motif of the "withdrawal of the Deity" in Luther's discussions of the spiritual suffering of Christ, the hiddenness of God. In the Conclusion I take the position that the hiddenness of God is a function of revelation, not an alternative to it, an experience within faith, not an alternative to faith.

4. J. Louis Martyn, *Galatians*, The Anchor Bible, vol. 33A (New York: Doubleday, 1997), p. 166.

beings Jesus Christ's own "good news" (as "subject of the gospel") that now all are put right with the coming God by faith in Him, or equivalently, it shares with human beings the Father's knowledge of the Crucified as His own Son in the event of raising Him from death's grip, thus inaugurating the reign of God. The two apocalypses of Galatians 1:12 and 1:16 are complementary, two dimensions of the same event, the coordinate works respectively of the Son and the Father. Now the preaching of the good news (for Luther, as above, by the third coordinate work of the Spirit according to the old rule, *opera ad extra sunt indivisa*) extends the news of the Father's resurrection of the Crucified in the form of the resurrection to faith of those dead in their sins in the time and space of the passing age, or, alternatively in the present Christ's speaking of the joyful exchange. This extension — Martyn uses the military image of an "invasion" — inaugurates God's coming reality, the "new creation," what I am calling the Beloved Community. It does not "reveal" then in the sense of lifting the veil of obscurity on something that has timelessly obtained, but it reveals in the act of executing God's mysterious decree hidden from the ages but which is now coming to pass. Apocalypse reveals, as Martyn emphasizes, because it is first of all this assertion of God's reign, the invasive new creation, the event in time and space of incorporation of those dead in their sins to new life in the Beloved Community.

We shall engage Martyn's interpretation of Paul extensively in Chapter Six, even as we have begun here with his notion of the "epistemological crisis" that is rendered by the apocalyptic preaching of the gospel. Also with Luther,[5] Paul's pupil, this crisis is triggered by the *real presence* of the crucified and risen Lord to bestow Himself with His gifts in evoking human faith in the corporate assembly of those called out to the new creation. This real presence of Christ the subject both *for us* and *in us* accordingly constitutes for Luther the exclusive point of departure for theological

---

5. So also Bayer: "Luther's apocalyptic understanding of creation and history bars the door to him" from thinking in terms of a "comprehensive historical-philosophical perspective" such as "the modern concept of progress. The rupture between the old and the new world, which occurs in what happened on the cross of Christ and which marks each one biographically in baptism, ruptures metaphysical concepts of an overall unity as well as historical-theological thinking that one can achieve perfection." Oswald Bayer, *Martin Luther's Theology: A Contemporary Interpretation,* trans. Thomas H. Trapp (Grand Rapids: Eerdmans, 2007), p. 9. In apocalyptic the accent falls on discontinuity. The question is whether Christology modifies apocalyptic to provide its own accounts of continuity, e.g., the Pauline interpretation of the faith of Abraham, or eventually, the Trinitarian interpretation of monotheism. This does not remove faith from its embattled state in the world, but makes that state intelligible as experience of faith.

knowledge.[6] Without a firm grasp of this "crisis" of the ages, Paul's — and Luther's — Christological teaching that Christ is subject in the proclamation of the gospel cannot but seem the extravagant mythologizing of a mortal man — comprehensible only as symbolic expressions of judgments of value, not fact (as post-Kantian theology has been forced to think). But already with Paul (whose writings are the earliest extant texts of primitive Christianity),[7] the Easter revelation sheds its light backward in time:[8] the Crucified Son was already the One sent from the Father and anointed with His Spirit to be the doer, the agent, the subject of the work of redemption. Indeed in Paul's teaching the Son was sent from the Father's own eternity, as N. T. Wright has shown in several powerful exegetical studies (whose work we also further engage below in Chapter Six).[9] Indeed, only so can we speak of the cross of *Christ* and say that *here* the ages turned.

6. This centrally important motif of the "real presence of Christ" is already formulated at the climax of the *Heidelberg Disputation* (1518), although Luther is still thinking here primarily of Christ present in faith to fulfill the righteousness of the Law, and not yet so clearly of Christ present to bestow His own alien righteousness. So Thesis 26: "For through faith Christ is in us, indeed, one with us. Christ is just and has fulfilled all the commands of God, wherefore we also fulfill everything through him since he was made ours through faith." Thus Thesis 27: "Since Christ lives in us through faith so he arouses us to do good works through that living faith in his work" (LW 31:56). I will engage the interpretation of Luther's *theologia crucis* and the apparent tension with apocalypse as the agenda-setting point of departure for theology in the Conclusion below.

7. Independently called by the apocalypse of Christ, Paul nonetheless recognized as his own the faith in Christ in early Christian communities that preceded him. "From the beginning, the 'remembrance' of the death of Jesus and its saving effect 'for us,' along with the contemplation of the exalted Christ and his coming, expected in the near future, were constitutive elements in the Christian celebration of the eucharist." Martin Hengel, *Between Jesus and Paul: Studies in the Earliest History of Christianity*, trans. John Bowden (Minneapolis: Fortress, 1983), p. 93.

8. The "idea that Jesus had received divinity only as a consequence of his resurrection is not tenable . . . the resurrection event [had] the character of the confirmation of Jesus' pre-Easter claim. . . . To this extent the resurrection event has retroactive power. Jesus did not simply become something else that he previously had not been, but his pre-Easter claim was confirmed by God. This confirmation, the manifestation of Jesus' divine Sonship by God, is the new light brought about by the Easter event. However, as confirmation, the resurrection has retroactive force for Jesus' pre-Easter activity, which taken by itself was not yet recognizable as being divinely authorized, and its authorization was also not yet definitely settled." Wolfhart Pannenberg, *Jesus: God and Man*, trans. Lewis L. Wilkins and Duane A. Priebe (Philadelphia: Westminster, 1975), p. 135.

9. N. T. Wright, *The Climax of the Covenant: Christ and the Law in Pauline Theology* (Minneapolis: Fortress, 1991), pp. 18-136.

But if we can and must say that, then it becomes clear how Jesus' Easter glory reflected forward as well into the Trinitarian and Christological definitions of the ecumenical church, for this new point of departure for theological thinking in the apocalypse of the gospel required a thorough rethinking of who and what "God" is (and was and will be) if Jesus, who was crucified, nevertheless could be the Son sent from God, the messianic Subject of the apocalyptic invasion.[10] This (ongoing!) rethinking of God as Trinity on account of Jesus Christ the Mediator bore and bears the profoundest *reformatory* implications, as Robert Jenson, following up on insights of Karl Barth, has argued: "Eternity would be apprehended as the dramatic mutuality of Father and Spirit, of God as God's origin and God as God's goal, and therefore not as immunity to change but as faithfulness in action. Being would accordingly be apprehended not as persistence in what is but as anticipation of what is not yet. The church would know herself as the temporal mission not of resistance to time but of faithful change in time and know her own continuity in that mission not as hanging on to what is already there but rather as receiving what must come."[11] All this may follow because, as we have already noted, Luther took the apocalypse of Christ (in the sense specified above, as event) to require that we come to know our present reality as "becoming not being, labor not rest."

Yet many, perhaps most, twentieth-century interpreters of Luther

10. Luther famously held that all binding Christian doctrine is already given in the Holy Scriptures, so that Councils can only recognize and apply them, not invent or impose new articles of faith. But this must be understood in the loose way that Luther actually argues it. According to him, "this ancient article of faith that Christ is true God" was already held by Christians "ever since the days of the apostles [who] had believed in and worshiped the name of Jesus in prayer as true God." "On the Councils and the Church" (1539) LW 41:58. That is hardly the same thing as the developed Nicene *homoousios.* Luther allows for the development of doctrine in this sense, provided that the developed doctrine is recognizable as the work of the same Spirit who first inspired the Scriptures. In the same treatise, Luther shows a real historian's grasp of the development of the doctrine through the controversies, although he tends under the influence of Western, Pseudo-Athanasian writings (see Carolyn Schneider, "Luther's Preface to Bugenhagen's Edition of Athanasius," *Lutheran Quarterly* 7, no. 5 [2003]: 226-30) to take the Arian controversy as concerning a Christological rather than more strictly as a Trinitarian question.

11. Robert W. Jenson, *Unbaptized God: The Basic Flaw in Ecumenical Theology* (Minneapolis: Fortress, 1992), p. 138. Calling attention to this fundamental theological task, and seeing to its continuation, has been the special concern of Jenson's theological work. See also his seminal study, *The Triune Identity: God according to the Gospel* (Philadelphia: Fortress, 1982).

have sought a different point of departure for theological knowledge, namely, in some previous awareness of the human predicament, be it the misery of sin, the anxiety of existential decision, the perplexing loss of meaning in the modern world, or even from the universal rejection of the God who is by nature merciful.[12] They have appealed to Luther's own counsel to do theology *von unten,* that is to say, from the humanity of Christ as something that connects with our humanity. It is true that Luther so counsels, but these interpreters are guilty here of a category mistake.[13] The *human* Christ to whom Luther so appeals (and the *Christ* this human being is known to be by Luther as he makes this appeal) is none other than God's Incarnate Son, really present also here and now in his ubiquitous humanity (in the fashion described above by Martyn in regard to Paul), the same one as He once was.[14] As Sammeli Juntunen has pointed out, Luther with this counsel is pointing troubled believers *to* the *gospel narrative* and *away* from independent *philosophical speculation*[15] — not only, one may extrapolate, about divine predestination (which was Luther's particular pastoral concern) but also speculation about the human predicament.[16]

---

12. See Gerhard Forde, "Caught in the Act: Reflections on the Work of Christ," *Word and World* 3, no. 1 (1984): 28-30.

13. E.g., Gerhard Ebeling, *Luther: An Introduction to His Thought* (Philadelphia: Fortress, 1972), p. 235.

14. "Persons arrive at this knowledge of themselves, that is of the situation coram Deo, only by considering Christ, and not by considering themselves in mere introspection, which despises the passion of Christ on the cross. . . ." It is everywhere evident ". . . how much Luther underlines the necessity for persons to be touched in their heart *(affectus).*" Marc Lienhard, *Martin Luther: Witness to Jesus Christ, Stages and Themes of the Reformer's Christology,* trans. Edwin H. Robertson (Minneapolis: Augsburg, 1982), p. 104. Yet just this "work is not in our hands" (Martin Luther, *Kritische Gesamtausgabe* [= "Weimar" Edition, hereafter WA] 2, 139, 12). That is, "the union of the believer with Christ, effected by the Holy Spirit. It is within the framework of this union, and not outside of it, that the Holy Spirit touches the human conscience. . . . It produces a kind of identification between Christ and the believer. . . . United to Christ, Christians acknowledge their sin. They agree to be before God what Christ has agreed to be for human beings, that is, despoiled and poor (WA 1, 336, 24; 339, 3)" (p. 106).

15. Sammeli Juntunen, "The Christological Background of Luther's Understanding of Justification," Lecture (Salem, VA: Roanoke College, 2002); later published under the same title in the *Seminary Ridge Review* 2 (2003): 6-36.

16. Ebeling makes this point historically against "scholasticism": i.e., "a theology which does not keep strictly to its theme, man who is guilty and lost and God who justifies and saves, and to the event between God and man which follows this pattern — builds up its theological statements about man on the basis of a definition of man assumed in advance

Recognizing Christ the man presented in the gospel narrative (as opposed, say, to a critical reconstruction of the so-called historical Jesus as the "kernel behind the husk")[17] returns us to the fundamental point of apocalyptic theology: as in the gospel narrative, it is the heavenly Voice who declares about *this* man, who is the Son, *Hunc audite!* (Mark 9:7).[18]

Such Christology (in this Transfiguration sense, *von oben!*) is the lodestar of Luther's teaching of justification. In his theological maturity he was always careful, especially when attempting precise, public doctrinal formulations, to situate the doctrine of justification by faith in this Christology. An outstanding example of this is "the first and chief article" according to the *Smalcald Articles,* namely, "that Jesus Christ, our God and Lord, 'was handed over to death for our trespasses and raised for our justification' (Rom. 4[:25]); and he alone is 'the Lamb of God who takes away the sin of the world' (John 1[:29]); and 'the Lord has laid on him the iniquity of us all' (Isa. 53[:6]); furthermore, 'All have sinned,' and 'they are not

---

and not derived from that event that takes place between man and God." Ebeling, *Luther,* p. 224. One only wishes the same point would be made consistently against contemporary "theological" anthropologies that in the name of *Lebensbezug* haul in speculations in exactly the same fashion!

17. Luther's objection to allegorical interpretation is poorly understood because its background in Augustine's criticism of Origen is routinely ignored (e.g., *City of God,* IX, 23). On Luther's defense of narrative interpretation against allegorical reading of biblical history, see Manfred Schulze, "Martin Luther and the Church Fathers," in *The Reception of the Church Fathers in the West* (Leiden and New York: E. J. Brill, 1997): The biblical "*historiae* are not futile and must not be allegorized out of existence — they are indispensable practical presentations of the way in which God meets human beings. To Luther's mind, 'a young teacher comes upon *historiae* [stories] and thinks . . . a secret mystery is concealed in them, just as a kernel is concealed in a nut. . . .' Thus the *historiae* are dismissed as empty shells. . . . [But] allegorizing deprives Christians of their actual existential history *(Geschichte)* with God and in fact of that (hi)story of faith, love and also temptations in which a living God, not one who is spiritually withdrawn, encounters human beings in their everyday lives: 'I beg you to hold on to the kernel, the real treasure and preeminent element in Scripture — that you should in fact learn Holy Scripture by way of its *historiae*'" (pp. 618-19). Anyone familiar with the role the "kernel-husk" metaphor played in nineteenth-century theology — take heed! Kenneth Hagen has found in the concept of *enarratio* the key to Luther's mature theological method. Kenneth Hagen, *Luther's Approach to Scripture as Seen in His "Commentaries" on Galatians 1519-1538* (Tübingen: J. C. B. Mohr [Paul Siebeck], 1993).

18. "God sent us his Son to be our teacher and savior. Not satisfied with that, he himself preaches from his high, heavenly throne to us all, saying, 'Hunc audite,' 'Listen to Him' [Matt. 17:5]. Thus we should drop to our knees with the apostles and believe that we hear nothing else in the whole world. But we let the Father and the Son preach in vain, do things on our own, and invent our own sermon." "On the Councils and the Church" (1539) LW 41:130.

justified without merit by his grace, through the redemption that is in Christ Jesus . . . by his blood' (Rom. 3[:23-25])."[19] Here it is manifest that Luther's signature doctrine is all about Jesus Christ, that is, about the One who gives Himself with all His gifts to those who are otherwise helpless and "without merit," beginning then with the gift by the Spirit of the very faith to welcome Him. This Christology is the constant; the faith that appropriates Christ is the variable.[20]

From the same period as the *Smalcald Articles*,[21] we have the fruits of Luther's mature research into the history of doctrine. His settled reflection on the theological past proves to be infinitely far removed from those who advocate a Lutheran *Sonderweg*. His fundamental report is that *"all* those who have correctly had and kept the chief article of Jesus Christ have remained safe and secure in the right Christian faith . . . [namely] the belief that Jesus Christ is true God and man, that he died and has risen again for us. . . ." For Christ, Luther writes, is the *Heupt gut,* a double entendre meaning both Head of creation, as in Ephesians 1:22, and our true treasure, the "capital wealth" that Christians can bank on. In this same study, Luther went on to develop a scheme for understanding deviation in Christological teaching that is as clear and simple as it is penetrating. Some, he wrote, have attacked Christ's deity, turning Christ into a mortal who would himself need a savior. Others attack His humanity, turning Christ into a phantom who cannot reach us who are true flesh. Now contemporaries attack His saving work, leaving to Christ only the honor of having begun the work, making us "the heroes who will complete it with merits." Behind such deviations stands not mere human theological sloth, but "the devil . . . [who] attacks Christ in three lines of battle. One will not let him be God,

---

19. *BC*, ed. Kolb and Wengert, 301:1-3.

20. The justifying faith that makes "my own" the Christ, who in the specified way of gospel narrative is "for me," is always also an idiosyncratic formation specific to the believer's time and place, *as it must and ought to be.* For example, in the words of Wilfried Härle, "Their shared insight that doing the works of the law is not the way to salvation, but that salvation is received through faith in Jesus Christ, comes to Paul [sic] the Pharisee and Luther the monk not only in vastly different historical and *religionsgeschichtliche* situations, but apparently also in vastly different biographical situations, and leads therefore to quite different reactions and consequences." "Rethinking Paul and Luther," *Lutheran Quarterly* 20, no. 3 (2006): 308. To think otherwise is fundamentally to misunderstand the relation between the gospel and its tradition. This insight will be crucial to sorting our way through the debate on the New Perspective on Paul in Chapter Six below.

21. The historical connection has been made by William R. Russell, *The Schmalkald Articles: Luther's Theological Testament* (Minneapolis: Fortress, 1995), p. 83.

another will not let him be man, and the third will not let him do what He has done. Each of the three wants to reduce Christ to nothing." But to be the *something* that Christians can bank on in the apocalyptic battle, "all three articles must be truly believed. . . . If one article is lacking, then all are lacking, for the faith is supposed to be and must be whole and complete"[:] "Jesus Christ is true God and man, he who died and has risen again for us. . . ." Luther then concludes this discussion of Christological heresy by prophesying that from the third group of his contemporaries there will arise in the future a new deviation. These will deny "that Christ has risen from the dead. . . ." Then the world "will think nothing of a future life . . . of the resurrection and eternal life" and Europe will be returned to the religion of Epicureans and Sadducees.[22]

Is not this prophesied loss of apocalyptic theology prescient? In a previous work on Luther's Christology, I suggested that quests for the so-called historical Jesus that have dominated Protestant biblical studies since Schleiermacher are in fact searches for a psychologically plausible Jesus that becomes interesting once the kerygma of the cross-and-resurrection has been set aside as the (apocalyptic) hermeneutic of the traditions about Jesus.[23] It is the very desire for such an inward Jesus that is dubious in that light. In any event, after two hundred or more years and at least three major quests for the so-called historical (really, the psychologically plausible) Jesus, we should have learned by now how quixotic this quest is, given the nature of the sources. The gospel narratives exhibit no interest whatsoever in the psychology of Jesus but instead focus exclusively on the public figure, the *persona* of Jesus as the Spirit-endowed man sent on a mission by His Abba God — the *persona* who cannot be who He is apart from these relations to the Father and the Spirit. As I will argue below, one can and should affirm a "historical" Jesus in this latter sense of Jesus' *public* appearance in human history, *including* his relations to the Father and the Spirit. But any "historical" Jesus produced under the privatizing, neo-Gnostic presupposition of exposing His secret soul in relation to an undifferentiated Absolute or Transcendence — as Albert Schweitzer demonstrated already one hundred years ago — will tell us more about the searcher than the sought. The psychologically plausible Jesus is the Jesus who is plausible to the researcher.

---

22. "The Three Symbols or Creeds of the Christian Faith" (1538) LW 41:13, my emphasis.

23. Paul R. Hinlicky, "Luther's Anti-Docetism," in *Creator est creatura: Luthers Christologie als Lehre von der Idiomenkommunikation,* ed. O. Bayer and Benjamin Gleede (Berlin: Walter de Gruyter, 2007), pp. 139-85.

Indeed, the study of Albert Schweitzer's epochal *The Quest of the Historical Jesus* should be required reading, if not penitential discipline,[24] for all contemporaries naïvely undertaking "Jesus Research." No matter what the personal motives, this research tradition bears deep within it a definite, *anti-dogmatic* agenda. "The historical investigation of the life of Jesus did not take its rise from a purely historical interest; it turned to the Jesus of history as an ally in the struggle against the tyranny of dogma. . . ." Only then did it also seek "to present the historical Jesus in a form intelligible to its own time" — results exhaustively documented by Schweitzer in surveying the literature from Reimarus to his own day. So Schweitzer exposed the abuse of history in this tradition as a covert, and so undisciplined, speculative (i.e., not *critical*) dogmatics: "each successive epoch of theology found its own thoughts in Jesus; that was, indeed, the only way it which it could make Him live."[25] Having exposed this charade,[26] Schweitzer tried to drive a stake through its very heart once and for all:[27] he traced the problem all the way back to its root in the strange, apocalyptic Jesus of first-century Judaism, the one who forced his own dogmatism ("eschatology is simply 'dogmatic history' — history as molded by theological beliefs")[28] against the rocks of reality. In haunting words, Schweitzer unveiled the true secret of the historical Jesus: "in the knowledge that He is the coming Son of Man, [Jesus] lays hold of the wheel of the world to set it moving on that last revolution which is to bring all ordinary history to a close. It refuses to turn, and he throws Himself upon it. Then it does turn; and crushes Him."

---

24. This requirement might be dismissed on the grounds that, having debunked the historical Jesus of others, Schweitzer went on to reconstruct his own in the apocalyptic Jesus — so also, presumably, can we. This is profoundly to miss the entire point of the book: "The self-consciousness of Jesus cannot in fact be illustrated or explained; all that can be explained is the eschatological view, in which the Man who possessed that self-consciousness saw reflected in advance the coming events. . . ." Albert Schweitzer, *The Quest of the Historical Jesus,* with a new Introduction by James M. Robinson (New York: Macmillan, 1978), p. 367.

25. Schweitzer, *The Quest,* p. 4.

26. "The whole history of 'Christianity' down to the present day, that is to say, the real inner history of it, is based on the delay of the Parousia, the non-occurrence of the Parousia, the abandonment of eschatology, the progress and completion of the 'de-eschatologizing' of religion which has been connected herewith." Schweitzer, *The Quest,* p. 360.

27. "The want of connexion, the impossibility of applying any natural explanation [in the gospel narrative], is just what is historical, because the course of history was determined, not by outward events, but by the decisions of Jesus, and these were determined by dogmatic, eschatological considerations." Schweitzer, *The Quest,* p. 358.

28. Schweitzer, *The Quest,* p. 351.

Schweitzer's point is: end of story, that is, not only of creedal Christianity, but also the story of the covert and speculative dogmatics of liberal Protestantism, had liberals now the courage in light of Schweitzer's genealogy to apply to themselves the same critique previously applied to dogmatism. This critique must fall not only on the Catholic kind, indeed not only on its own historians, but the axe must fall to the root: the apocalyptic fanaticism of Jesus himself. All that survives the requisite disillusionment, Schweitzer concluded, are traces of "one immeasurably great Man who was strong enough to think of Himself as the spiritual ruler of mankind and to bend history to His purpose."[29]

Can we be creedal Christians today? Certainly not by evading the problem that Schweitzer laid bare, least of all with old[30] or new[31] attempts to "(re-)imagine" Jesus. Creedal Christology has a serious interest in testing its confession of *Jesus* Christ, the Son of God, for faithfulness to that man of first-century Judaism who once was crucified under Pontius Pilate. And it can do this by means of sober, modest, critical-historical analysis of the sources. An outstanding case for that kind of self-testing within the framework of the church's creedal theology can be derived from Leander E. Keck's *A Future for the Historical Jesus:*[32] precisely because the name "Jesus" refers not only to the Christ of God as depicted in the gospel narrative, but therewith also "to a historical figure of the public past and not to a private myth or meaning-syndrome . . . the door is open to inquiry concerning him to whom Christians give allegiance."[33] Indeed, the door is more than open. It must be *opened* in the work of *critical* dogmatics: "it is a

---

29. Schweitzer, *The Quest,* p. 371. A harrowing sentiment, given the German to emerge thirty years later with his doctrine of the "triumph of the will"!

30. For example, Bart D. Ehrman, *Lost Christianities: The Battles for Scripture and the Faiths We Never Knew* (New York: Oxford University Press, 2003); more carefully and less sensationally, Gregory J. Riley, *One Jesus, Many Christs: How Jesus Inspired Not One True Christianity but Many* (Minneapolis: Fortress, 2000).

31. E.g., Timothy Freke and Peter Gandy, *The Laughing Jesus: Religious Lies and Gnostic Wisdom* (New York: Three Rivers Press, 2005).

32. The "centrality of Jesus is constitutive of historical Christianity. Continuity with this tradition is evidenced in concentrating on Jesus as the decisive event, [though] one must do this without denigrating figures outside this tradition. . . . The preacher expresses the church's foundational conviction when he speaks of Jesus in a way in which he does not speak about others, and there is no reason to be on the defensive about it." Leander E. Keck, *A Future for the Historical Jesus: The Place of Jesus in Preaching and Theology* (Philadelphia: Fortress, 1981), p. 130.

33. Keck, *A Future,* p. 39.

question of whether Jesus is an expendable commodity to be used at will by the preacher," that is, a question of the "character and content" of faith in *Jesus* as the Christ.[34] The difficulty exposed by Schweitzer then is not at all to be evaded or avoided, but rather embraced. Knowledge of the Jesus of (public) history is a bastion against the arbitrary use of His name by private speculation; whatever Christology says of Him and in His Name even on the basis of the canonical Scriptures must comport with who Jesus was in His own particular (public) human history.

Keck's book masterfully summarizes the modern debate about the "historical Jesus," beginning with the crucial new dogma articulated by Lessing on behalf of the Enlightenment: "the inadequacy of historical fact as the basis of absolute certitude of faith." This new standard of credibility ran "through the entire subsequent story of Protestant theology"[35] to render suspect the (just alluded to) scandal of particularity at the font of revealed theology. But on reflection it is Lessing's rationalist notion of the certainty of faith that is quite inadequate to Jesus. Keck instructively notes in this connection that "there is absolutely no difference between the historical contemporary of Jesus and the modern believer."[36] That is to say, the kind of absolute certitude demanded by the rationalist Lessing is the certitude of a self for whom *any* historical relations are and must be dubious, even also contemporaneous ones. For that reason alone the Jesus of history can only be incertitude, since the aspiration here is to the chimera of Cartesian indubitability. How different the certitude of faith which Jesus as *persona* in the gospel narrative seeks and elicits: the *trust*[37] of a mutable,

---

34. Keck, *A Future*, p. 37. "Given man's infinite capacity to rationalize as well as the fact that Jesus has been the warrant for every sort of theological or social program, it is utterly essential to press the historical question against the church and its kerygma" (p. 71).

35. This is an important advance in understanding over Schweitzer's account, in which Reimarus and then David Friedrich Strauss are the key players. As I have argued in *Paths Not Taken*, chapter 2, the real — rationalist, naturalist — turning point comes with Spinoza; as previously pointed out with Frei, it is the construction of the sovereign self stemming from Descartes for which historical revelation cannot supply the requisite indubitability.

36. Keck, *A Future*, p. 37.

37. "Faith must remain venture and risk. Only when the ambiguous historical Jesus (ambiguous in the sense that he is not self-validating, not simply in the sense that 'historical Jesus' contains probabilities) is central does faith retain its venture." Keck, *A Future*, p. 67. But Keck does play trust off against belief. He criticizes Hermann for whom the problem was that trust in God "could not be derived from assent to beliefs about God" because today "beliefs about God cannot be assumed, hence the act of trusting and the act of understanding occur together or not at all" (p. 166).

unsecured self, a historical self that is "becoming, not being." In turn, for Keck, this notion of faith as trust historically traceable to Jesus signals the kind of contribution that historical scholarship can provide, with the insight that theologically "the deepest obstacles to trusting Jesus and the gospel are not lack of adequate data or an outmoded Weltanschauung but the moral enigma of life, personal and cultural."[38] Who can and would trust the Jesus who ended up crucified? Will he not take us to the same place? In this way, and to profound effect, Schweitzer's difficulty of the apparently deluded Jesus of apocalyptic faith is embraced by Keck. With Schweitzer, but against the covert dogmatics of Questers seeking the wrong kind of certitude from Schleiermacher to Fuchs and Ebeling, Keck rightly insists that "it is far from self-evident that either in Jesus' own day or in ours meeting [Jesus'] confidence elicits the same from those whom he encounters. . . . What is minimized . . . is the offense of Jesus."[39] The friend of sinners and tax-collectors, who ends up hoisted on the stake among criminal bandits, is morally ambiguous.

This is precisely right, as Dietrich Bonhoeffer insisted in the name of Luther's principle that "the person interprets the work." How, Bonhoeffer asked in the voice of the Questers, "can the person of Christ be comprehended other than by his work, i.e., otherwise than through history?" Bonhoeffer replied: "This objection [of the Questers] contains a most profound error. For even Christ's work is not unequivocal. It remains open to

---

38. Keck, *A Future,* p. 71.

39. Keck, *A Future,* p. 65. "Not surprisingly, Fuchs repeatedly insists that the disciples' faith did not break down between Good Friday and Easter, so that Easter faith is the renewal, confirmation, and release of pre-Easter faith." Keck, *A Future,* p. 65. Against this, Keck at times wants to argue apologetically that in our post-Christendom situation "the historical Jesus functions not as a secure basis for faith but as a crisis-creating figure, who makes hearing the gospel and coming to faith possible, though not inevitable." Keck, *A Future,* p. 55. "When the hearer finds himself drawn into a situation that evokes a re-examination of the mystery of his own life because Jesus has been introduced into his orbit, he is in a new situation, one not generated by himself. The immediate aim of preaching is to create such a situation; to this end the historical Jesus functions as a catalyst." Keck, *A Future,* p. 123. Keck coupled this with another argument: "Centralizing precisely the historical Jesus is more conducive to producing a grace-laden occasion than is presenting the Christ of Christian dogma, since the Christology of the church is not the door to faith." Keck, *A Future,* p. 125. I find this line of argument implausible, not least because it begs the question of the audience for preaching and in the process puts the possibility of grace into the hands of the artful preacher. In any case, this apologetic argument in Keck's book is in definite tension with another, in my view more compelling approach, where historical criticism functions as an aspect of critical dogmatics (see, e.g., Keck, *A Future,* pp. 130, 157, 181-82).

various interpretations." Only "when I know who he is, who does this, I will know what it is that he does."[40] Yet decisively, Bonhoeffer continued expositing Luther's principle, since only God knows who one is, since only God knows and searches the heart, only God knows the person. Knowledge of the person too is blocked from us. It is God's knowledge of the person of Jesus that is decisive, not ours. For just that reason "Christology is not soteriology."[41] Epistemically, we can know Jesus Christ, present for us — truly, as Bonhoeffer will go on to say, *for* us, *the* Man-for-Others — only as a function of God's apocalypse, that is to say, of the Father's sharing with us His knowledge of His Crucified Son by the sending of His own Spirit who had raised him from the grave.[42]

Returning to Keck, then, what historical critical scholarship can do as a function of such Christian theology is to insist on the question of "the ambiguous historical Jesus": "he functions as a question before he is affirmed to be the answer," so that it will be and ever remain the venture of *trusting* in Him which "is salvific."[43] That is the kind of certitude one has in history, not above or beyond history, the certitude in Another's promise to be for us as promised in a future made common. Just so, historical study makes clear that the real enigma of the Jesus of history, who prom-

---

40. Dietrich Bonhoeffer, *Christ the Center,* trans. Edwin H. Robertson (New York: Harper & Row, 1978), pp. 37-39.

41. Bonhoeffer, *Christ the Center,* p. 39. Bonhoeffer hastens to clarify, "the Christological question by its very nature must be addressed to the one complete Christ. This complete Christ is the historical Jesus, who can never in any way be separated from his work." Bonhoeffer's argument for the priority of Christology to soteriology, more precisely to the idea of the person interpreting the work, is the basis for the division of this chapter on the Person of Christ from the next on the saving work of Christ.

42. Wolfhart Pannenberg made the same argument. "There is no reason for the assumption that Jesus' claim to authority taken by itself justified faith in him. On the contrary, the pre-Easter Jesus' claim to authority stands from the beginning in relationship to the question of the future verification of his message through the occurrence of the future judgment. . . . Thus has been shown the proleptic structure of Jesus' claim to authority. . . . This means, however, that Jesus' claim to authority cannot by itself be made the basis of a Christology, as though this involved only the 'decision' in relation to him. Such Christology — and the preaching based upon it — would remain an empty assertion. Rather, everything depends upon the connection between Jesus' claim and its confirmation by God." *Jesus: God and Man,* p. 66.

43. Keck, *A Future,* p. 208. "In affirming that incarnation is not the most appropriate place to begin because it too commonly vitiates the historical, we leave open the question whether it may be the proper place to end — as one way of stating the ontic basis for what has occurred in and through Jesus" (pp. 211-12).

ised the nearness of God's reign to those far from God, is *inseparable from His relation to God:* "one simply cannot subtract God from Jesus and have Jesus left."[44] A "historical" Jesus without God — *that* historically and critically is to cut the Gordian knot. On the contrary, Keck argued, the historical data "are quite sufficient to be decisive for our understanding of God" when focused on "what can be known of the public life of Jesus which was set into motion by the kingdom of God" — not then "requiring our understanding of God to be traceable to Jesus' inferred selfhood."[45] In the *same* way as Schweitzer then, by *not* evading the challenge of the first-century, apocalyptic Jew Jesus, Keck leads us critically and historically to the cross: "Jesus was rejected in the name of the God of the law and prophets. Hence for Jews, no less than for gentiles, Jesus' execution is a crisis for the understanding of God . . . it was either Jesus' perception of God [as his Father] which was put to death with him" — this will be Keck's position — "or our pre-understanding of God by which we judge Jesus to be guilty of misplacing his trust . . . of misunderstanding the kingdom, and of misconstruing God" (Schweitzer's position) that will have to perish.[46] Does this choice not describe exactly the real state of biblical studies today?[47]

44. Keck, *A Future,* p. 212. See here the precious albeit forgotten study of Sir Edwin Hoskyns and Francis Noel Davey, *The Riddle of the New Testament* (London: Faber & Faber, 1941).

45. Keck, *A Future,* p. 217.

46. Keck, *A Future,* p. 231.

47. Hagen, following Luther, pleads for an "approach [to the Bible] which is consistent with and appropriate to the item under consideration . . ." *Luther's Approach,* p. 38. "Actually, theology is at stake. The Bible is all about God; it talks about God, to God, and for God. . . . To interpret Scripture with methods and techniques that are not only extraneous to Scripture but also contrary to its message is not consistent methodology. It takes Scripture out of its own environment and forces it into a different 'think system,' thought structure, or a different grammar" (p. 39). "There are obvious inconsistencies in the modern approach. Scripture is linked and limited to its historical settings, or historicized. Historicists historicize everything but historicism, or, more commonly put, philosophical relativists relativise everything but relativism. . . . Scripture is not primarily a historical document; it is theology in service of God. Just as theology should not dictate the conditions and limits of other disciplines be they philosophy or history, neither should other disciplines dictate the conditions and limits of theology" (pp. 61-62). There are of course thousands who have not bowed the knee to Baal. Quite specifically and limiting myself to the American context and the tradition of Luther's theology, I would mention the exemplary research that Nils Dahl took in *Jesus in the Memory of the Early Church* (Minneapolis: Augsburg, 1976) and *Jesus the Christ: The Historical Origins of Christological Doctrine,* ed.

The divided mind afflicts not only biblical studies. Keck rightly notes that "part of the confusion in today's pulpits is anchored in the widespread flight from identification with the Christian community, as if one could speak for God-as-such to man-as-such as an interpreter of faith-as-such in order to be legitimated by modern man. But post-Christendom culture will never license the church to talk about Jesus in terms consistent with Christian insight[,]" anymore than did pre-Christendom culture — or perhaps even Christendom. "The church," Keck continues, "must be clear about its own reasons for trusting Jesus and for commending him, and bear witness to that."[48] It is not, then, just a passing thought when Keck noted by way of conclusion that "actually a systematic theology might well restate afresh everything we have argued thus far, and do so from the standpoint of God's initiative — at least if one is prepared to think in a Trinitarian way."[49] Precisely *that* possibility of creedal faith today (not in the form of systematic theology but of critical dogmatics) leads us to Luther as resource.

## "This Man Created the World"[50]

Luther's statement strikes us as outrageous, as Luther of course knew it would.[51] Even more strangely (to us), Luther's point in making it is anti-Docetist, anti-Eutychian, anti-monophysite: Nestorius "does not want to

---

Donald H. Juel (Minneapolis: Fortress, 1991), together with his student, Donald H. Juel, *Messianic Exegesis: Christological Interpretation of the Old Testament in Early Christianity* (Philadelphia: Fortress, 1988).

48. Keck, *A Future*, p. 130.

49. Keck, *A Future*, p. 241.

50. Thesis 4 in *Disputation on the Humanity and Deity of Christ* translated from the Latin text of WA 39/2, pp. 92-121 by Christopher B. Brown for Project Wittenberg. The translation may be found at: www.iclnet.org/pub/resources/text/wittenberg/wittenberg-home.html. For a fuller account of this Disputation and the claims made about it in what follows, see the author's contribution to *Creator est creatura*, pp. 139-85.

51. In the words of Ian Siggins: "Faith is finally bound to confess that all His words and actions — even those by which we know Him to be a man — are in the fullest sense words and actions of the person of the Word. The implications of this confession stupefy the imagination; but this is Luther's confession." Ian D. Kingston Siggins, *Martin Luther's Doctrine of Christ* (New Haven and London: Yale University Press, 1970), p. 237. Siggins's sympathies in this matter lie with Zwingli (p. 236); in general, the reader may be referred to Siggins for an account quite other than the present one.

give the idiomata of humanity to the divinity of Christ[,]: but "Eutyches, on the other hand, does not want to give the *idiomata* of divinity to the humanity . . . if I . . . preach that this same man Christ is creator of heaven and earth, then Eutyches takes offense and is outraged at the words, 'A man created heaven and earth,' and says, 'No! Such a divine *idioma* (as creating heaven) does not appertain to man.'" Eutyches, then, "must deny the human nature of Christ if he rejects the divine *idiomata* of the human nature; for that would divide the person, and Christ would not remain man."[52] If we allow ourselves to be startled into the fundamental rethinking of things that Luther's startling claim intends, we would have to see that rethinking what God is in Trinitarian fashion also includes rethinking what that precious creature made in God's image is. For in Christ, Luther is saying, humanity is no longer to be defined philosophically as not-God, but in a new way, theologically, as united with God. What is "truly human" is not to be gathered from our experience apart from Christ; speculation about humanity, no less than divinity, is proscribed. For Luther, the notion of Docetism has as little then to do with the meat that hangs in the butcher shop (as he expressed it, in criticizing the notion of the resurrection of the flesh, following Paul's distinction between *soma* and *sarx*)[53] as with psychological plausibility. His fundamental intention here is clear, however, as expressed in another Disputation: this life is the material for the future life.[54] To be truly human is to rise from the dead. Jesus Christ is this new, true Adam. In Him, we too, and we all, are becoming truly human.

In the course of the church's early centuries, under the Easter assumption that the morally ambiguous historical relationship between Jesus and God had been resolved by the resurrection of the Crucified, the Trinitarian understanding of God was worked out, and with it the Christology of the Personal Union, the assumption of the human nature by the person of the Eternal Son to accomplish the work of human salvation. In

---

52. "On the Councils and the Church" (1539) LW 41:109.

53. Though not consistently. In "On the Councils and the Church," for example, he tries to distinguish the "temporal and transient idiomata" of eating, drinking, sleeping, suffering, sorrowing, and dying, which he maintains are left behind in the resurrection, from the "natural" idiomata that "remain," such as body and soul, skin and hair, flesh and blood, marrow and bones and all the limbs of an ordinary human. "On the Councils and the Church" (1539) LW 41:110. Luther did not achieve clarity on this critical point, which gave his Reformed critics the right to question the continuity of such glorified humanity with what human beings are here and now.

54. Thesis 35 of "The Disputation concerning Man" (1536) LW 34:139.

this work, the subject is the divine Person who not only uses the capacities of the two natures, but actually (not only verbally) communicates the capacities of each to the other in order to act as the one single agent/patient/public *persona:* Luther's "Christ who (was,) is (and will be) the subject of the gospel." So it is that in this unique case it conforms to *reality* to say things, as does the gospel narrative, like: This Man created the world. This Son of God has no place to lay His head. Luther's Christology accordingly makes *both* points. Doctrinal faithfulness to the real humanity of Jesus has nothing whatsoever to do with (wildly imaginative) reconstructions of a first-century human psyche (let alone conservative attempts to photograph, figuratively speaking, the Galilean Master). It rather has to do with the divine cause — the reign of God and our inclusion in it — which Jesus embodied in his own unique space-time, for which he was murdered in the same body but then, as faith believes, vindicated in that same body by the Abba Father at the Spirit's bidding.

We can say today again, as we saw in the last section, that Luther's anti-Docetism would require today that the public cause of Jesus and the primitive Christian testimony to and belief in His triumph be historically and critically verified. Such anti-Docetist historiography forms a contemporary bulwark for critical dogmatics against not only ecclesiastical but also secular-ideological hijacking of Jesus. Again, in Keck's words, "Historiography is by no means invulnerable to distortion and subversion, but it remains our major defense against absorbing Jesus into modern secular piety. Not least among the roles of historical study for theological work is its capacity to keep us honest. The point is that no one can deal with Jesus of Nazareth without confronting the question of God, because his concentration on God and his kingdom is what is constitutive of Jesus."[55] It is important for such historical understanding to set aside the uncomprehending caricature of Luther's Christology going back to David Friedrich Strauss or Ludwig Feuerbach, e.g., "pure mythology," a "god striding on the earth," "physical theory of redemption," and so on. The problems obscured by this self-satisfied polemic are far more baffling than imagined.

Indeed, from the beginning the meaning of "incarnation" affirmed in John 1:18 was by no means self-evident. Does "the Word became flesh" mean that the Logos morphs into flesh? Or that an otherworldly Spirit takes possession of a mortal body? In any case the classical doctrine does not, in Luther's understanding, pretend to fathom something ineffable, nor

---

55. Keck, *A Future,* p. 213.

in this way license speculation on the modality of the Incarnation. Rather the purpose is only to describe with concepts, so that we can more faithfully and effectively speak the God of the gospel, who is more *like a life than a thing,* whose way of being eternally, that is to say, includes a *capacity for, and the reality of, time, the creation taken (nature too) as history.* Augustine admitted how baffled he was at this in a seminal discussion in *The Confessions,* Book XI: even when we ascribe the entire course of the creation to God's creative foreknowledge in God's eternal Now, Augustine realized, we creatures of time must still think of God freely choosing one such course rather than the infinity of other possibilities (XI:11-13); indeed, we might add, as Christians who profess that God creates *ex nihilo* and out of abundance (and so also redeems and fulfills the creation in just the same divine way), that we are obliged to think of creation as a true, free decision (Luther indeed thinks that such free choice properly speaking belongs only to God). But if in eternity, God so takes counsel and decides, somehow then even in eternity God is involved in (to be sure, self-) movement of which time is in principle the measure. So Augustine left things, as a baffling paradox (e.g., XIII:37). Luther's Christology, however, to the extent that it was taken up and stimulated new thinking about the theological problem of eternity and time in Karl Barth, has since led to the Trinitarian renewal in contemporary systematic theology. In Jüngel's apt summary: "God's independent being must thus be understood from the event of revelation as an event granting this event of revelation. God's being as subsistence is self-movement. As self-movement God's independent being makes revelation possible. Revelation as God's interpretation of himself is the expression of this self-movement of the being of God."[56] This is needless to say a monumental revision of the as yet not fully baptized classical metaphysics which so baffled Augustine; we could say: *infinitas capax finiti est.*[57]

The Christological point then will be that the particular public *persona* who died on the cross is *the same One* as the Eternal Word by whom the cosmos was called into being and in the same event destined to its eschatological end. Conversely, the Word eternally born in the movement of

---

56. Eberhard Jüngel, *The Doctrine of the Trinity: God's Being Is in Becoming* (Grand Rapids: Eerdmans, 1976), p. 93.

57. Notice that the old, merely paradoxical Lutheran assertion, *finitum capax infiniti est,* has here been revised into a genuine evangelical insight. So also Bayer, *Luther's Theology,* p. 334, though he would likely dissent from crediting Barth and Jüngel, not to mention Augustine, this way.

God's self-subsistent, independent being is *the same person* as the man who was hoisted on the stake. In general, of course, and especially on biblical ground the ontological divide is firmly established between Creator and creature as between the eternal self-subsistent Life of self-movement and the life which comes from and returns to earth and ashes caught up in the causal nexus; it is pure nonsense to say abstractly: Divinity hangs on a cross, or, Humanity created the world. The divine nature has as its characteristic property not to die but simply to live and to make alive, if indeed by "divine" we are speaking of the being which is the creator of everything other than itself.[58] The creaturely nature has as its characteristic property to be born, to live not simply but so long as it lives by consuming other life-forms, and then to die and decompose, if indeed we are speaking of this embodied life of becoming. To confuse or blend together these natures is sheer confusion both ontologically and semantically. Yet, if one "is prepared to think in a Trinitarian way," Christological discourse is never only or chiefly about the conjunction, least of all the confusion, of two ontologically and semantically distinct sets of attributes.

Indeed, if such modalist Christology were all that was at stake, there would be no particular reason to identify the person of Jesus of Nazareth Christologically, and there could be very good reasons to refuse to do so. Even if we held on to Him, say, as the one, only, best, even direct source of information about God, in principle he would be like all the prophets who manifest in varying degrees the same conjunction of divine and human natures, functionally and dynamically, as they give voice to the word of the Lord. Both Judaism and Islam understand this. In its way, Islam acknowledges Jesus as a prophet in the line of the great prophets; likewise some in contemporary Judaism are at least in part willing to see Him too as a son of Israel and a rabbi. But creedal Christianity has wanted to say something different about this particular Proclaimer, certainly one with all the other prophets, but also the One who is now *proclaimed* as the eternal "Word made flesh," whose "glory" is to be "seen, full of grace and truth." It has

---

58. Lewis Ayres in recent discussion is particularly to be thanked for lifting up the pro-Nicene principle of divine simplicity as analytic to the biblical distinction of the being of the Creator from that of all else (the creature), and for insisting that it "serves to enhance the explanatory power of a fully Nicene Trinitarianism in which the order of the Trinitarian generation is preserved, and in which Father, Son and Spirit are all equally bound of the terms of divinity without ceasing to be 'other' to each other." *Nicea and Its Legacy: An Approach to Fourth-Century Trinitarian Theology* (Oxford and New York: Oxford University Press, 2006), p. 382.

wanted to say about Him, in the battle slogan of the Fifth Ecumenical Council, "One of the Trinity suffered."[59] It has wanted to say this in order to proclaim this particular Proclaimer as the Savior of all who suffer.

## "One of the Trinity Suffered"

In line with *this* fundamental intention of creedal faith to tell in Christ of the exalted man and the suffering God, the *communicatio idiomatum* was "the axle and motor of Luther's theology," as Johan Anselm Steiger elaborates in an exuberant study.[60] Luther, Steiger explains with appropriate subtlety, "thus *held on to* Greek metaphysics and to the Christological dogma grounded in it, but at the same time, by working out the doctrine of the *communicatio idiomatum* in detail, he helped to historicize this metaphysics. . . . Luther *kept up* an important theological matter of the early church and understood it better than they themselves were able to do."[61] This is correct, albeit somewhat immodestly expressed. Let us then first grasp Luther's abiding debt to the classical dogma, recognizing as well just how unusual it is for a Western theologian to appeal, in effect, not only to the axial notion of divine simplicity which establishes certain boundaries for Christology in the Formula of Chalcedon, but also to the Trinitarian personalism of the *Fifth* Ecumenical Council. For materially this would amount to an appeal to the victory of Cyril of Alexandria's Christological doctrine over the ambiguity left behind by Chalcedon's last-minute balancing act, when that Fourth Council hastily condemned the monophysite teaching of Eutyches to go along with the condemnation of Nestorius' conjunction Christology. We have already noted Luther's critique of Eutyches. The point here is not to urge some covert version of monophysitism. Rather, as Steiger's survey shows, it is becoming increasingly clear that Luther's Christological achievement in taking the communication of attributes as the account of Incarnation was to historicize the doctrine of being by means of Trinitarian personalism. This is the point, and this point becomes more comprehensible against the particular background of an appropriation of Cyrillian Christology. Luther's Christology is not particu-

---

59. See below, n. 69.

60. Johan Anselm Steiger, "The *communicatio idiomatum* as the Axle and Motor of Luther's Theology," *Lutheran Quarterly* 14, no. 2 (2000): 125-58.

61. Steiger, "The *communicatio*," pp. 147-48, emphasis added.

larly intelligible, by the same token, as mere Chalcedonianism, in terms of which the communication of idioms appears — indeed, has to appear — as sheer paradox, as rhetorical indulgence, as only a way of speaking, not of being, since a real becoming flesh of the divine nature would fatally compromise divine simplicity.[62]

First, then, concerning Luther's debt to the classical dogma: "in his theological reflection, Luther was altogether of the Alexandrian persuasion," writes Bernard Lohse, "putting most stress on the unity of the person of the God-Man . . . ," adopting and sharpening "the doctrine of the *enhypostasis* [sic; *anhypostasis?*] to read that the human nature of Jesus Christ has no *hypostasis* (separate existence) of its own but possesses it in the divine *nature.*"[63] Lohse means "possesses it in the divine *hypostasis,*" but the slip is telling for how difficult it has been in the shadow of von Harnack even for contemporary German scholarship to come to terms with what Luther actually taught, including his deep, actual dependence on patristic categories. But there is no denying that Luther holds not only, as for instance he once preached from the Wittenberg pulpit, that "the human nature in Christ shares in the glory of all the properties which otherwise pertain to God,"[64] and additionally that this mystery of Jesus' human majesty is to be explicated by a real, not merely verbal communication of properties, but also, at the same time, to a vibrant Trinitarian personalism (i.e., for which the personal distinctions still do real theological work): "We are not such stupid asses," Luther assures the congregation just moments later, "as to fabricate two or three gods. No, we worship only one

62. I am indebted here to an unpublished paper by Sarah Hinlicky Wilson, "Luther and Cyril on Christology" (Princeton Theological Seminary, 2006). See also David Yeago, "The Bread of Life: Patristic Christology and Evangelical Soteriology in Martin Luther's Sermons on John 6," *St. Vladimir's Theological Quarterly* 39, no. 3 (2004). See also Bayer, though the concession is still a grudging one: "The Christological concept of the communication of attributes was indeed known in theological tradition from the time of the early church on, but it had only a marginal meaning. Luther was the first one to place it into the center of Christology, indeed, in that of theology as a whole." *Luther's Theology,* p. 236.

63. Bernard Lohse, *Martin Luther's Theology: Its Historical and Systematic Development,* trans. Roy A. Harrisville (Minneapolis: Fortress, 1999), p. 229. Emphasis added to underscore the misstatements. Lohse's treatment of Luther's Christology, however, almost entirely takes its bearings from within the Augustinian tradition. Rightly, nonetheless, he rejects kenotic Christology for Luther, writing in conclusion that "the doctrine of ubiquity corresponds far better to the thrust of Luther's Christology . . ." (p. 231). I will take up the theme of the deity's "withdrawal" in the Conclusion.

64. "Sermons on the Gospel of St. John" (1539) LW 22:494.

God, and He is very God. Yet in this one God there are three Persons, one of whom is Christ. . . ."[65] Of Him (alone) it is true to say: "Mary suckles God with her breasts, bathes God, rocks Him, and carries Him; furthermore, that Pilate and Herod crucified and killed God."[66] This extravagant rhetoric of Luther was a deliberate "affront [to] the cultivated minds of his day[,]" Schulze rightly comments, a "description of the fact that God became human so unreservedly — but without sin — that human beings are in danger of being ashamed of the humanity of God."[67] Homiletical oratory aside, however, what Luther here proclaims is substantively at one with the "theopaschite" teaching of the Fifth Ecumenical Council: Luther too holds that "one of the Trinity suffered."

As mentioned, the Fourth Ecumenical Council at Chalcedon in 452 had ended in something of a split decision, ruling out both the Nestorian teaching of two sons, one of Mary and one of God, and the Eutychian teaching of a singular divine nature in Christ wrapped in a human cloak. The council rejected both those "daring to corrupt the mystery of the Lord's incarnation for us and refusing to use the name Mother of God in reference to the Virgin, while others, bringing in a confusion and mixture, and idly conceiving that the nature of the flesh and of the Godhead is all one, maintaining that the divine Nature of the only Begotten is, by mixture, capable of suffering. . . ." The concern for divine simplicity overrides the concern for the unity of person. Chalcedon accordingly spoke of *two* natures, divine and human, which must *each* be acknowledged "unconfusedly, immutably" and yet somehow *together* "indivisibly, inseparably." How this union of opposites was to be understood, however, was not expressed; nor indeed was it explained whether anything more than a conjunction was really required. With the latter omission lay the seeds of future controversy. Jenson points the finger at the contemporaneous *Tome* of Pope Leo, written against the Eutychian assimilation of the humanity into the nature of deity (rather than its assumption by the second Person). In rejecting this error, the *Tome* betrays its own tacit, and very problematic, conception of the union: "For each nature is agent of what is proper to it, working in fellowship with the other; the Word doing what belongs to the Word and the flesh what belongs to the flesh." Jenson comments acerbically: "This is either the Antiochene doctrine [of two agents]

---

65. "Sermons on the Gospel of St. John" (1539) LW 22:495.
66. "Sermons on the Gospel of St. John" (1539) LW 22:493.
67. Schulze, "Church Fathers," p. 592.

or something cruder."[68] This tacit understanding of two natures collaborating side by side like two independent operators threatened again, as had Nestorius's teaching of the two sons, the integrity of Christ as the one, singular agent/patient of the gospel narrative and thus the all-important role played in the drama of salvation by this one and the same incarnate life, death, and heavenly session, which *is* the public *persona.* Consequently Chalcedon's affirmation of the "one hypostasis" seemed like mere "verbiage." Jenson acutely diagnoses: "*Hypostasis* could carry the burden of denoting the one Christ in the continuity of his saving action only if it had an ontological weight in Christology matching that which it had in Trinitarian teaching."[69] To make a long story short, that is exactly how the Second Council of Constantinople in 553 tried to resolve the problem: it "recognized the key issue in the Christological controversy when it anathematized anyone 'who says that God the Logos who performed the miracles is one, and that the Christ who suffered is another.'"[70] In this decision it heeded Cyril, who had urged that if Christ performed miracles "only by virtue of an 'indwelling' of the divine Logos, he would have been no different from the prophets . . . [but] one must say that the Source of life was hungry, that the All-Powerful grew tired."[71] Thus, "if anyone does not confess that our Lord Jesus Christ who was crucified in the flesh is true God and the Lord of Glory and one of the Holy Trinity, let him be anathema."[72]

Why is that unity of person — rather, *as* person — so all-important? Marc Lienhard brings out nicely why this notion of the *unity* of the person in Christ matters so *to Luther.* "In this connection we find again [Luther's] theme of joyous exchange. In fact, Christ is stripped, he makes

68. Robert W. Jenson, *Systematic Theology,* vol. 1, *The Triune God* (New York and Oxford: Oxford University Press, 1997), p. 131. [Hereafter *ST.*]

69. Jenson, *ST* 1:132-33. He continues, "By a strong version of the communication of attributes, [Cyril's followers] made the one hypostasis be the 'synthetic' agent of the whole gospel narrative, both what is divine in it and what is human in it, and they identified the eternal Logos as himself this hypostasis. This 'neo-Chalcedonian' Christology was dogmatized by a Second Council of Constantinople in 553, although with little immediate effect outside Constantinople's narrow communion" (p. 133).

70. Jaroslav Pelikan, *The Christian Tradition: A History of the Development of Doctrine,* vol. 1, *The Emergence of the Catholic Tradition (100-600)* (Chicago and London: University of Chicago Press, 1975) [hereafter *CT*], p. 244.

71. Pelikan, *CT* I:245.

72. *Nicene and Post Nicene Fathers,* ed. Philip Schaff and Henry Wace (Peabody, MA: Hendrickson, 2004), 14:314.

himself a servant in order to assume our sin. Thus we become free. He snatches us from our slavery and makes us children of God . . . he insists that the divinity was truly present in the man Jesus. That is a fundamental intention which recurs incessantly in his thought, to which the Kenotic theologians of the 19th century do not remain faithful . . . love drives Christ to the incarnation and animates him during the whole of his earthly life. The true miracle is not the incarnation, but the love of Christ (WA 10, 3, 432)."[73] The gist of this is right, but, as we shall see, it must be more precisely formulated to avoid mere Chalcedonianism and the tacit modalism in much of the Western tradition: the man Jesus is not just a (even *the*) bodily expression of undifferentiated divinity or even of an un- differentiated "love," but *is* the second *persona* in the narrative sequence of the Father who sends, the Son who willingly goes, and the Spirit who at length returns the Son, with all the treasures He has now won, to the Fa- ther who sent Him.[74] In that case, the true miracle is not and cannot be incarnation as such. Rather, the true miracle consists in the coming in the flesh of *this* Person; *this* incarnation is the "miraculous love" of God for the *enemy* which leads *Jesus* to the *cross,* that is to say, not the *wrath* of God's love at the ruin of creation, but God's own self-surpassing love at- taining to *mercy* for the lost, the weak, and the enemy. Even more sharply, then, it is not *any* incarnation *as such* that will be saving (the incarnation of God in, say, Josef Stalin would *not* be good news), but that personally particular union of divine and human whose sense and purpose is made known in the personal history of *Jesus,* which by the same token is under- stood (by the anti-Arian *homoousios* clause of the Nicene Creed) to enact in time the Eternal Son's loving obedience to his Father in the Spirit.[75] The agape love of God expressed eternally *von oben,* the man Jesus' way of sorrows told in time *von unten,* are then irreducibly two necessary and complementary *descriptions* of *one and the same personal journey* of the Son of God's merciful way to enemies and failures. This suffering of love

---

73. Lienhard, *Martin Luther: Witness,* p. 176.

74. As Lienhard himself sees: ". . . the Father sends the Son who obeys the Father and whose work is made effective, in the present, as salvation by the Holy Spirit. It is not simply 'God' who acts, but it is God — Father, Son, and Holy Spirit — in the framework of a drama within God himself, with which human beings find themselves associated." He speaks also of the immanent Trinity, unlike Melanchthon: "the saving act of God in history only trans- lates what God is from all eternity. . . ." Lienhard, *Martin Luther: Witness,* p. 319.

75. On this claim, see Bruce Marshall, *Christology in Conflict: The Identity of a Sav- iour in Rahner and Barth* (Oxford: Basil Blackwell, 1987), pp. 161ff.

which ultimately prevails is, in Cyril's paradoxical but not unintelligible expression, Christ's "impassible possibility."[76]

Is the question then how to make sense of this apparently contradictory conjunction of logical opposites? On the contrary, it is the communication of attributes understood as this Person's free communicating in obedience to His Father's will that *yields* the theological account of "incarnation," so that "incarnation" does *not* denote abstract coincidence or mingling of divine and human natures in paradoxical or nonsensical violation of divine simplicity, but rather the concrete coming of Jesus Christ from the Father's bosom into the fallen and groaning world to set the prisoners free, hence yielding in turn a revised notion of divine simplicity that is not mere Platonic apophaticism, but infinitely generative and thus capable in its own divine way of time, thus also of finitude. In this light, Manfred Schulze is spot on to exclaim: "it becomes transparently clear how a center piece of [Luther's] theology burst into life with the *communicatio idiomatum*."[77] For we are not being asked by it to think literally of a body operated by a divine spirit, let alone that divine spirit somehow emptied out of its own reality and transformed into a body, or even figuratively to think of the personality of Jesus as a simile of God, a pointer to something beyond, as *signum* to *res,* who "shows us what God is like." We are instead to think *that* (per creedal *belief*) the *man* Jesus Christ rendered in the gospel narrative, *qua* this particular mortal being of manger and cross, *is* the coming to us of the Father's Eternal Son; and we are to think (again a *be-*

76. Sarah Hinlicky Wilson (unpublished paper, Princeton, 2006) is right to complain that Western sympathy for the Antiochenes is not well grounded. At stake for Cyril's opponents "was defending the impassiblity of God at all costs. When impassibility collided with the witness of Scripture, Antiochians stuck to the philosophical point, but Cyril went the other way and sided with the biblical narrative, even though it opened him up to the charge of theopaschitism." She goes on to make a decisive point. "Yet [Cyril] did so without sacrificing the principle of divine impassibility altogether. He was able to make the distinction on the basis of the economy: it is the Word in the flesh, not God the Word in himself, that is the subject of suffering. And this is the whole soteriological point of the incarnation, for in Christ God comes into direct contact with the world, instead of using a mediator as a buffer zone." "It turns out, then, that divine impassibility is an essential part of the equation that makes salvation happen, even what makes it wondrous. Any naturally passible being could not be God. . . . As Gavrilyuk further explains: 'If God could suffer as humans do without assuming humanity, the incarnation would be unnecessary.'" Granted. But the Incarnation so understood still requires a revision of metaphysics to ensure that divine impassiblity is conceived as including a capacity of love for suffering, rather than by the very misleading, traditional idea of apathy.

77. Schulze, "Church Fathers," p. 591.

*lief*) *that* the Eternal Son, God from God and Light from Light, *comes* from the Father by the Spirit to seek and find *us* in this particular man's journey to Golgotha. If we understand the exchanges of attributes entailed by this belief in the "one Lord, Jesus Christ" as the personal decision and various acts and passions of the Son in the Trinity's love for us, we understand all that there is to be understood theologically about the Incarnation: we bend the knee, confess Jesus as the saving Lord, and give glory in the Spirit to the Father in anticipation of the redemption of our bodies by membership in His Body, harbinger of the Beloved Community.

To grasp the communication of idioms as the theological account of "incarnation," then, the distinction between theological knowledge as theory and as interpretation once again becomes critically important. The entire critique of creedal belief stemming from Harnack, with all the incoherent attempts following him to salvage a nameless, contentless *fiducia* from an impossible *notitia,* trades on the false construal of the ecumenical dogmas as putative *theory,* i.e., as arrogant and impossible ambition to grasp the ineffable conceptually.[78] But the proclamation of the Crucified Man as God's Son given for the salvation of the hostile, the weary, and the lost is God's interpretation of Jesus for the world, which the church believes, teaches, and confesses, just as it is also God's self-interpretation to the world. Likewise the understanding of the Personal Union, that is, the sense of the *perichoresis* or exchange of human and divine attributes in Jesus Christ, aims at hermeneutical understanding of the "mind that was in Christ Jesus" (Phil. 2), the divine Person in its own intentionality in Christ, *not* the "how" of the Incarnation, which is and remains eternally ineffable. Manifestly, this is *not* the monophysite caricature Harnack concocted of a "natural[!] union," i.e., "that the God-Logos had taken up the human nature into the unity of his unique substance and made it the perfect organ of His deity. . . ."[79] Harnack's rendering (deliberately?) removes from view the *personal* nature of the exchange of properties, the wondrous divine *intention* of

---

78. See Dennis Bielfeldt, Mickey Mattox, and Paul Hinlicky, *The Substance of Faith: Luther on Doctrinal Theology* (Minneapolis: Fortress Press, 2008), pp. 162-68.

79. "If humanity was not deified in Christ, but if in His case His humanity was merely united with the divinity by the *prosopon* or person, then what effect can a union such as that have for us? That formula can only be of advantage either to the detested 'moralism' of the Antiochenes, or to mysticism, which bases its hope of redemption on the idea that the God-Logos continually unites himself anew with each individual soul so as to form a union." Harnack, *HD* IV:222. In this cunning fashion, Harnack indicates the background of Luther's "mystical" doctrine of the "joyful exchange" as also his genuine debt to Chalcedon.

love for the enemy, the decision "to become obedient, even to death, death on a cross," requiring the one divine Son to act in the humanity and suffer in the divinity to fulfill the mystery of the ages. Thus the Neo-Chalcedonian Christology rather advances a hermeneutical understanding appropriate to revealed theology. It gives us not merely the split decision of Chalcedon ruling out the extremes of Eutychian confusion and Nestorian separation, but the doctrine of the hypostatic, personal union, where the agent/patient in Jesus Christ is the divine Son in His eternal obedience of love, *the same thing* as the man Jesus' resolve to set his face to go up to Jerusalem.[80]

So much then for Luther's debts. He evidently knew this Alexandrian Christology from the medieval handbooks,[81] especially those that transmitted the teaching on the communication of attributes by John of Damascus, *On the Orthodox Faith*. But Luther did not only follow tradition here, as Bayer and Steiger correctly note. He actively retrieved a tradition that was overshadowed in the West by its modalist tendencies and developed it further in order to overcome the inadequate soteriology Western modalism sponsored.[82] Bayer in particular has labored to jolt German Lutherans (as Jörg Baur once put it to me) "out of their Christological forgetfulness." Aside from his important study, "Das Wort Ward Fleisch" in *Creator est creatura* on Luther's 1539 Disputation on the Johannine text (John 1:14), Bayer's analysis of the Luther hymn, "Dear Christians, One and All, Rejoice," is a particularly impressive endeavor to exposit in fittingly doxological form Luther's communication-of-attributes Christology as descriptive of the Victor's "descent into hell."[83] Even more profoundly, "the

---

80. On Justinian's anti-Docetism and neo-Chalcedonianism, see Pelikan, *CT* I:271.

81. This is a central discovery of Marc Lienhard: "Thus two realities are important to obtain salvation. First, *Christ*, i.e., the presence of Christ, thanks to the proclamation of the Word; then *faith*. The union of these two realities, *fides Christi*, constitutes one of the dominant themes in Luther's thought. When Christ is thus present in the *fides Christi* to save human beings, he takes upon himself the sin of believers and gives to them his righteousness. A kind of exchange is effected between Christ and the believer — what the reformer calls the 'the [sic] joyous exchange.'" Lienhard, *Martin Luther: Witness*, p. 59.

82. Jenson makes an acute correlation here that will figure greatly in the deliberations of Chapter Three on the saving work of Christ: "According to Anselm, the atoning work of Christ was the work of the human nature since only humans owed the debt and only a human could pay it. Then Christ also had to be God in order that the merit of the human's work be infinite and so available to all the race. 'Each nature does its own thing, in cooperation with the other' is the very summary of this soteriology." *Unbaptized*, p. 123.

83. Bayer, *Luther's Theology*, p. 219. I will, however, join in Christine Helmer's criticism of another aspect of Bayer's interpretation of this hymn in Chapter Four.

deepest conflict with Greek metaphysics and ontology," Bayer writes, "must of necessity come at the point where the biblical texts are taken with utter seriousness." Bayer then states: "What is ontologically unthinkable is described in Hosea 11:7-11, which ancient metaphysics would reject as mythology: an 'overthrow', a change within God himself."[84] As I will put it: God surpassing God.

This Christologically generated reflection now points us to the next chapter. I take a "change within God himself" to refer to the ultimate resolution by the Spirit of the confrontation at the cross between the obedient Son and the Father who hid His face from that Son when He willed His abandonment into the hands of sinners.[85] I do not think this "change" can be exposited successfully with a modalist theology that thinks figuratively of the Father as representing the divine and the Son representing the human, no matter whether one tries to work this out with Anselm or with Abelard.[86] Feminist critiques of this soteriology — How could the Father God's abandonment of His [sic] faithful human son ever be good news? — have a point, even if they fail to grant the premise of Trinitarianism, that the confrontation of the Father and the Son is *internal* to the divine Life and itself an implication of the costly decision for mercy — real

---

84. Bayer, *Luther's Theology,* p. 215. I am at one with Bayer so far as the cited text goes. But the text from Hosea gives as its reason for God's heart recoiling from destructive wrath that *God is God* and not like a jealous husband in a fit of rage. God's faithfulness to God's own promises through time, including through the time of God's well-merited wrath at human faithlessness, requires a different understanding of the unity of God than may be found generally in "Greek metaphysics" (as though this were a monolith), which the doctrine of the Trinity provides when the eternal divine Life it describes includes as such a free capacity for time. This "revision of metaphysics" does not diminish the miraculous change within God, but makes it intelligible as God's own *self*-overcoming — whereas in Bayer's account, we can never be sure that the overcoming is God's *own*.

85. ". . . the face to face encounter between the Father and Jesus is important. But it is not a question of the person Jesus acquiring merit. It is rather a matter of Jesus Christ, God and a man, interposing himself between sinful humanity and the wrath of God, bearing the punishment and thus dissipating the wrath of God. Such a work is not the achievement of the man Jesus considered in isolation, but of the Son become human, so that he is 'the happening of divine love among human beings living under the wrath of God' (Prenter)" Lienhard, *Martin Luther: Witness,* p. 110.

86. Lienhard notes here precisely how Luther differs from Anselm: ". . . Jesus is not a human representative, acting outwardly upon God, in order to render to him the honor which is due him and acquire merit by which he could benefit other human beings. It is the Son, sign of the Father's love, who offers himself in the place of sinners. Thus love triumphs over the wrath of God." Lienhard, *Martin Luther: Witness,* p. 76.

mercy, say, even for abusers and pimps. Even the corrective attempt of Gustaf Aulén to understand the divine Son as Victor over the anti-divine powers fails on the other side to grasp the need for any real confrontation between the really distinct persons of the Father and the Son, and so the "overcoming" within the divine Life, as Bayer invokes, when the Trinity "unthinkably" incorporates into its own blessed Life what is repulsive, sinful, and dying. To this the corresponding "unthinkable" thought is that of the "impassible possibility" of the "One of the Trinity who suffered." The results of the previous discussion are thus here once again confirmed: the man Christ, in his own most historical particularity as the beloved Son abandoned by His Father for His solidarity with enemies and failures *cannot be known by the analogy of history.*[87] To history he remains the enigma of Mark 15:34.

## The Erasure of the Communion of Attributes in Modern Christology

We may now conclude this chapter and prepare the way for the next by elaborating on the present claim about the Person of Christ as the Second of the divine Three. We will use as a resource the first five theses of Luther's *Disputation on the Humanity and Deity of Christ.* The first five theses read as follows:

1. This is the catholic faith, that we confess one Lord Jesus Christ, true God and man.
2. From this truth of the double substance and the unity of the person follows the communication of attributes, as it is called.
3. So that those things, which pertain to man, are rightly said of God, and, on the other hand, those things, which pertain to God, are said of man.

---

87. Agreeing (in an admittedly perverse way) with Ernst Troeltsch: "The dogmatic method accordingly lacks the main features of the method of secular historical scholarship, namely, criticism, analogy and correlation. . . . The dogmatic method cannot admit analogies or make use of them because it would then have to surrender its own inmost nature, which consists in the denial of any analogical similarity between Christianity and other forms of religious development." "Historical and Dogmatic Method in Theology," in *Religion in History,* trans. James Luther Adams and Walter F. Bense (Minneapolis: Fortress, 1991), p. 21.

4. It is true to say: This man created the world, and this God suffered, died, was buried, etc.

5. But these are not correct in the abstract (as it is said) of human nature.

Luther appeals to *fides catholica.*[88] He wants us to receive orthodox formulations of speech, such as "two natures in one person," as guiding truths *given by the Spirit,* who has not fallen silent since the publication of the Scriptures, but rather accompanies the church in "leading to all truth" in order "that we may confess the one Lord Christ true God and man." This language of confession once again indicates the hermeneutical, not theoretical understanding of cognition at work in doctrinal theology. The *point* of Luther's "confessional" (in the original "apocalyptic" meaning of the word as *witness* in a controversy) theology is to confess Christ in person, in his own New Testament body and blood, as the covenant of mercy between the redeeming God and sinful humanity, particularly in the time of trial, i.e., wherever and whenever Satan attacks to undo what God had done, dividing again reconciled God and suffering sinner. Christological talk for Luther, as *fides catholica* with its dogmatic *formulas loquendi,* is neither ecclesiastical dogmatism nor philosophical curiosity, but knowing *witness* within an apocalyptic-forensic conception of history, informed and well-grounded *testimony* given in the eschatological trial.

For such testimony, as for all other important speech aimed at successful communication, there need to be rules. The communication of properties is rightly characterized as a rule for talking rightly about Christ, but, as I have stressed, this rule is said by Luther *to follow* from the twofold substance and unity of person articulated in Thesis 2. The *communicatio idiomatum* is *analytic* to the catholic confession of the one person, i.e., it is a rule that articulates, or makes explicit to understanding, what the proclamation of the Incarnation affirms implicitly, to the end that confessors can put confession of Jesus Christ to intelligent and proper use in the cosmic struggle of the powers. As I have stressed, the predications are then not merely verbal for Luther. They guide our talk because they derive from and reflect back in properly guided speech to the mystery of the Person of Christ presented in the gospel narrative. Already Melanchthon, however, restricted the *communicatio idiomatum* to verbal predication; i.e., it is a

---

88. The following paragraphs are abstracted from the analysis in *Creator est creatura,* pp. 151ff.

way of talking for preaching, not of being for understanding. Thus the Cry of Dereliction does "not refer to being, but to the then present performance in which he humbled himself."[89] This restriction of Luther's teaching by his own first lieutenant requires a short excursion, since the cry of dereliction is a *crux intellectum* in the entire matter of our understanding of the Person of Christ.

Centuries later, for Schleiermacher too, admitting the Cry of Dereliction as reality would fatally compromise his doctrine of Christ's perfect God-consciousness: "I cannot think of this saying as an expression of Christ's self-consciousness."[90] In his *Glaubenslehre,* having just appropriated the Antiochene Christology of the Indwelling Logos, Schleiermacher turned to "the theory of a mutual communication of the attributes of the two natures to one another" as something "also to be banished from the system of doctrine and handed over to the history of doctrine," since in such a communication "nothing human could have been left in Christ since everything human is essentially a negation of omniscient omnipotence."[91] That latter definition of what is "essentially human" is precisely the characteristic demand of the nineteenth century for psychological plausibility, based upon modern self-knowledge, the search of which Schleiermacher pioneered in his afore-cited *Life of Jesus.* Ironically, however, not only then does one of the Trinity *not* suffer for Schleiermacher; *neither* does the perfectly God-conscious man Jesus truly suffer — that is,

89. Philip Melanchthon, *On Christian Doctrine: Loci Communes,* 1555, trans. C. L. Manschreck (Grand Rapids: Baker Book House, 1982), pp. 34-35.

90. Friedrich Schleiermacher, *The Life of Jesus,* ed. J. C. Verheyden (Philadelphia: Fortress, 1975), p. 423.

91. Friedrich Schleiermacher, *The Christian Faith,* vol. 2, ed. H. R. Macintosh and J. S. Steward (New York: Harper & Row, 1963), §97, 5 (412). "The theology of the hypostatic union could do justice to the predominant tendency of the Bible, which was to speak quite indiscriminately of the divine or the human in Christ while retaining the same subject; it could not do justice to those passages in which this tendency was replaced by language about the growth of Jesus." Jaroslav Pelikan, *CT* 1:251. Pelikan titles the view of Theodore of Mopsuestia and his followers "the indwelling Logos christology," i.e., the "indwelling of the Logos in a man whom he had assumed" (p. 252). The "religious intent" was "to take seriously the fact of moral development in the man Christ Jesus and thus to guarantee his status as simultaneously Redeemer and example" (p. 253). He notes that the Antiochenes could also describe this "moral" union of wills between the Logos and Jesus of Nazareth as a "personal" union, "neither a union according to ousia, as was the union in the Trinity, nor a union according to nature, as was the union of soul and body. Either of these definitions would obliterate the distinction between the divine and the human, produce a monstrosity, and make salvation through Christ impossible" (p. 252).

suffer *spiritually,* as Luther insisted (see Chapter Ten below). Hereafter, liberal Protestantism follows Melanchthon and Schleiermacher by regarding the communication of idioms at best as a way of popular talking, e.g., as edifying value judgments of the believer expressing devotion to the Savior, as Ritschl influentially taught.

Ritschl rather boldly sidestepped Luther's intended meaning. "In Luther we come upon a definite attempt to establish *theoretically* the old Christology by proving the *communicatio idiomatum.* At the same time, Luther's religious estimate of Christ does not depend upon a rigorous realisation of the theological formula of the one Person in two natures. . . . If faith no longer consists in assent to revealed dogmas, but in confidence toward God, then it follows that faith, i.e. trust in Jesus Christ and in the Holy Spirit, is a recognition of the Godhead of Christ and of the Holy Spirit, since trust of this kind can be given to God alone. Through this explanation of Luther's the Godhead of Christ is introduced as a judgment of value."[92] In the name of refusing *theory,* which motive he confusedly imputes to Luther who never separates *fiducia* from *notitia,* Ritschl's revision puts the believer with her value judgments in the Christological driver's seat. Luther's agency of the Spirit in providing the formulations of speech given to the community of the church goes absent. An individual believer of modern consciousness now makes Christ God by its trust, understood as a Kantian value judgment, expressive of its feeling of what God has done for it. Henceforth soteriology precedes and indeed yields up Christology as needed.

For Luther, to say the obvious, it is the living, really present crucified and risen Christ who evokes trust by the gospel told about Him, and the Spirit who formulates statements of belief about that trust which is true to Christ, who is both subject and object of faith. As to Ritschl's complaint that Luther attempts "theoretically to establish the old Christology" by means of the communication of attributes, we need here only to recall that a *personal* communion of properties in Christ is *always* presupposed, not some kind of *natural* fusion of them into a hybrid third thing.[93] The spec-

---

92. Albrecht Ritschl, *The Christian Doctrine of Justification and Reconciliation: The Positive Development of the Doctrine,* trans. H. R. MacIntosh and A. B. Macaulay (Clifton, NJ: Reference Book Publishers, 1966), pp. 391-92. Emphasis added.

93. So Calvin understood it: "But some are carried away with such contentiousness as to say that because of the natures joined in Christ, wherever Christ's divinity is, there also is his flesh, which cannot be separated from it. As if that union had compounded from two natures some sort of intermediate being which was neither God nor man!" *Institutes of the*

ter of the latter is a caricature, a smear. The personal union is *constituted* in the personal obedience of the Eternal Son in coming to redeem humanity, not *composed* out of some kind of interaction between discrete substances imagined in a quasi-physical manner to produce some kind of compounded thing. As such a personal act of the Son of God, the union revealed in the history of Jesus is and must remain (to all eternity!) ineffable with respect to its manner or mode. Luther is entirely uninterested in exploring *theoretically* how this union is to be explained; indeed he regards the use of earthly analogies (body and soul, fire and iron) as dangerous and misleading just because they are taken *theoretically* as potential explanations of the Incarnation's manner or mode. The point of the doctrine is not theoretical but interpretive, not to grasp God with a concept, but to recognize and appreciate the *decision* of the triune God to redeem humanity and its *actualization* seen *von unten* in the obedience of the man Jesus and his history with us, seen *von oben* in the Son's journey into a far country. Luther throughout presupposes the neo-Chalcedonian idea of the personal union.[94] Not the How of the Incarnation but the What and Why are of interest in the *communicatio idiomatum*, since the communicating of the attributes is always a matter of Jesus' own freedom of self-manifestation. "The risen Jesus is not passive or inert, and therefore not at the disposal of human beings, or anything created — except, of course, in so far as he freely gives himself to them." So Bruce Marshall interprets the Cyrillian paradox of this Person's "impassible possibility." "Jesus' being at their disposal, one could say, is not itself at their disposal, but only at his own. Upon his own action, therefore, depends any relation to him which creatures may come to have."[95]

Luther can say redundantly for emphasis: "The natures are joined *personally* in the unity of *person*"[96] and, in a second breath, "but these [predications] are not correct in the abstract (as it is said) of human nature." If that is

---

*Christian Religion* IV.17.32, ed. J. T. McNeil, trans. F. W. Battles (Philadelphia: Westminster, 1975), p. 1402.

94. T. F. Torrance, *The Trinitarian Faith: The Evangelical Theology of the Ancient Catholic Church* (Edinburgh: T. & T. Clark, 1993), pp. 146-90.

95. Bruce D. Marshall, *Trinity and Truth* (Cambridge: Cambridge University Press, 2000), p. 246.

96. WA 39/2, 98, 6. Emphasis added. Note the author's difference with Jörg Baur on this point in *Creator est creatura*, p. 174, n. 61, affirming Chemnitz's teaching of the *ubivolipraesenz* (being present wherever He wills) — the *only* way to account for the *kenosis* in the state of humiliation or the *restriction* of the gift of the body and blood to the meal.

so, historical analogy must *fail* in principle as the decisive test by which *this* Person is to be known in history. That would be to seek the living among the dead. Or to put the logical point more clearly: application of the historian's rule of analogy cannot discover Jesus in his own personal particularity, if that personal particularity consists precisely in the personal interchanges of divine and human attributes concretely rendered in the figure of the gospel narrative. Jesus cannot be remembered this way as person. Whatever is remembered in this way under the name of Jesus is not Jesus, i.e., that one of the Trinity who suffered in the flesh. Steiger cites Luther: "For He has become a sinner, yes, sin itself, and has thus erased and taken away the world's sin through his sin." He then comments: "As such a sinner Christ stood proxy for the whole of humanity in the divine judgment, and in the Garden of Gethsemane felt for a moment the eternal condemnation in the place of human beings." Or again, as Luther made the point concretely in the *Disputation on the Deity and Humanity of Christ:* "We must follow the guidance of the Holy Spirit, and as he himself prescribes, so we must speak. That Christ was made a curse for us, there signifies something truly concrete, that is, Christ was made a sacrifice, a victim for us." This concrete *persona* is truly remembered in the Eucharistic community, where this death is proclaimed until He comes again; for here He is willing and able to present Himself by the signs of bread broken and cup shared. This — *only* — is how the concrete Person is rightly remembered, that is, in accord with His own personal intention. That is also clue to a more adequate soteriology, to which we now turn.

# CHAPTER THREE

# God Surpassing God by "Christ Made to Be Sin"

*Suddenly we stand before the paradoxical and horrifying expedient that afforded temporary relief for tormented humanity, that stroke of genius on the part of Christianity: God himself sacrifices himself for the guilt of mankind, God himself makes payment to himself, God as the only being who can redeem man from what has become unredeemable for man himself — the creditor sacrifices himself for his debtor, out of love (can one credit that?), out of love for his debtor!*

Nietzsche[1]

## Beyond the Wrath of God?[2]

In the previous chapter, we concluded with the dictum of Luther: "We must follow the guidance of the Holy Spirit, and as he himself prescribes,

---

1. Friedrich Nietzsche, *Ecce Homo and Genealogy of Morals*, ed. Walter Kaufmann (New York: Vintage, 1967), p. 92. My thanks to Brent Adkins for calling this passage to my attention.

2. With apologies to Friedrich Nietzsche, *Beyond Good and Evil: Prelude to a Philosophy of the Future*, trans. Walter Kaufmann (New York: Vintage, 1966). "Modern men, obtuse to all Christian nomenclature, no longer feel the gruesome superlative that struck a classical taste in the paradoxical formula 'god on the cross.' Never yet and nowhere has there been an equal boldness in inversion, anything as horrible, questioning, and questionable as this formula: it promised a revaluation of all the values of antiquity" (#46 p. 60). If the thesis of the present chapter about God surpassing God in the cross and resurrection of Jesus holds, it will entail even more than a revaluation of the values of antiquity.

so we must speak. That Christ was made a curse for us, there signifies something truly concrete, that is, Christ was made a sacrifice, a victim for us." The statement about the concrete communication of attributes belonging to this unique man — "similar to none other" since He is also "one of the Trinity" — leads directly into Luther's view of His saving work. The primacy of Christology over soteriology does not deny that Christology "as such" is "already soteriology[,]" that it "teaches about salvation by its very nature,"[3] as indeed it does. But this apocalyptic primacy requires that our theological analysis of what Christ saves from is derived from Christ's own cross and not imposed on Him by wayward speculations on the human predicament: "The crooked man thinks crookedly and speaks crookedly even about his own crookedness" (Barth). Much contemporary theology (even a kind that fancies itself as "radically" Lutheran)[4] winces at this[5]

3. Oswald Bayer, *Martin Luthers Theologie: Eine Vergegenwaertigung,* 2. Auflage (Tübingen: Mohr Siebeck, 2004), p. 232.

4. Gerhard Forde, "Caught in the Act: Reflections on the Work of Christ," *Word and World* 3, no. 1 (1984): 22-23. The villain here is "metaphysics," by which Forde means "to look away from the actual events, translate them into 'eternal truths,' and thus to ignore or obscure what actually happened and our part in it. We interpret Christ's death as though it were an idea[,]" rather than a down-to-earth judicial murder in which we are all implicated. "In sum, each of the major types of atonement theory tends to obscure the truth of the murder of Jesus in the very attempt to convey its 'meaning' and 'significance' to us" (p. 25).

5. "Why should a God who is by nature merciful demand satisfaction? Is a God who consigns his Son to an excruciating death just to provide an example of what everyone already knew really a 'loving Father'? If God is God, could not the defeat of the demonic powers have been accomplished without the painful death? In other words, was the trip really necessary?" (Forde, "Caught in the Act," p. 25). These objections trade on sleight of hand: How do we already know that God is by nature merciful, a loving Father, sovereign and omnipotent over opposing powers? The traditional "theories" are trying to establish these claims, not simply to presuppose them. The same objection applies to Forde's contemporizing of the cross. Jesus, he says, asserts the mercy of God, "but we could not buy that. And so we killed him" (p. 26). Who is this "we"? How does it become you or I? Isn't this contemporizing move open to the same objection against the so-called metaphysical move to "eternal ideas," namely, that it obscures what actually happened, once, long ago, outside the walls of Jerusalem? This is not a marginal notion in Forde's analysis: "The universal significance of the death of Jesus has its roots first of all in the fact that he is *universally rejected* and killed by us, not in a theory about how his death is of infinite worth or universally 'satisfying'" (p. 27). While the appearance of even-handedly criticizing all the theories of atonement is maintained, the special target of Forde's polemic is Anselm: "When we skip over the actual event to deal first with the problem of the divine justice or wrath, we miss the point that we are the obstacles to reconciliation, not God" (p. 27). This latter is *not* Luther's view, as we shall see below.

and indeed goes to great lengths to regard it, whether in Paul or in Luther, as the mere remnant of a previous belief-system that has now in principle been overcome. Therefore we today too are free to discard it. In fact we are always on shaky ground when we evade the difficult text and exegesis turns into the exercise in bad faith of explaining why an author did not mean what she wrote.

Gerhard Forde was undoubtedly right, in the end, to teach that the resurrection is "the vindication of Jesus' life and proclamation of forgiveness, God's insistence that unconditional forgiveness actually be given 'in Jesus' name.'" He was also right to explain that to "accept such forgiveness is to die to the old man," who is *old* precisely in refusing God's mercy.[6] But that is because through the cross and resurrection of Jesus, God's mercy for enemies comes as *news*. Accordingly, if Forde's tacit claim is thus to have represented *Luther's* (not to mention, *Paul's*) theology of atonement,[7] one can hardly agree that for them we are entitled to assume that God is by nature (timelessly, universally, eternally, metaphysically) merciful to sinners and that the only issue is making this actual, the effective delivery of this mercy.[8] As with the "it is necessary" of the Synoptic passion predictions, we have in Luther's use of the Pauline texts a case of the divine passive: in fact *God the Abba Father* (Mark 14:36!) so treated and regarded His beloved Son in the merciless way of abandonment to death on a cross.[9] It is brutal even to repeat the thought. Nevertheless, in Luther's dictum cited above and a multitude of others like them, he is taking up the difficult but crucially important motif of the Apostle about *God* making Christ accursed (Gal. 3:13), sin (2 Cor. 5:21), and as such a sacrifice of atonement (Rom. 3:35). Luther's Paulinism is once again on display. So also is the root

---

6. Forde, "Caught in the Act," pp. 30, 31.

7. Lienhard cites WA 56, 37, 26: "He does not give grace freely to the point of requiring no satisfaction, but for us he gave Christ who satisfied [his righteousness] in order to give freely, nonetheless, grace to those who satisfy [his righteousness] through another." Also WA 56, 37, 14: "It is Jesus Christ alone who has redeemed our sins by satisfying [his righteousness] and by paying for us." Marc Lienhard, *Martin Luther: Witness to Jesus Christ, Stages and Themes of the Reformer's Christology*, trans. Edwin H. Robertson (Minneapolis: Augsburg, 1982), p. 76.

8. I grant that Forde does not want us to "mistake" his proposal "for a 'subjective' view of the atonement" (Forde, "Caught in the Act," p. 30); I deny, however, that his proposal succeeds in this respect.

9. "In Luther's view Christ was not only 'humiliated' by God, but 'abandoned' by him. God failed him. God withdrew himself from him" (p. 64). "He is 'a patre derelictus' (WA 57, 2, 28, 12)." Lienhard, *Martin Luther: Witness*, p. 67.

of the motif of the redemptive exchange: Christ suffers what properly befalls others and by means of this participation in their suffering wins the right over them and sets them free. Yet this entails, as Luther saw, that also we must speak theologically with Paul of the *wrath of God*[10] *as also of sin* as lethal power and guilt, not a putatively universal aversion to the merciful Jesus. Historically Lienhard was right to insist upon the uncomfortable fact: ". . . Luther placed his main emphasis on the wrath of God which must be appeased. . . . 'Therefore God has given us in the first place a man who satisfied the divine righteousness for us all.' . . . Forgiveness and new life are given to us, without any merit on our part, but they cost Christ dearly. . . . Luther returns again and again to this matter of the price of this grace, which is Christ himself and his work. . . . How is the saving work of Christ accomplished? By the fact that 'he has represented us in the fear of death, taken all our sins upon himself and has exterminated *(ausgeleschet)* them.'"[11]

The three traditional accounts of salvation through Christ's work (satisfaction, moral influence, and victory over anti-divine powers) all reflect teachings of the New Testament; surely any adequate teaching on the Work of Christ will integrate the three, not set them off against each other. But at least since Ritschl Protestant theology and Luther research have tended to discount the wrath of God as a "scholastic remnant" on the grounds that "it is impossible to conceive of sinners, at the same time and in the same respect, as objects both of God's love and God's wrath."[12] Ritschl's articulation of the fundamental objection assumes a simple self-identity in God, not thinking, as Luther thought, of an encounter at the cross between God and God and so of an "overcoming" or "surpassing" of God by God that we can intelligibly follow after in thought (if not in all eternity ever comprehend). If that latter teaching of a definite *becoming* of God in the *coming* of God in mercy can be sustained as the *news* in the good news, "satisfaction" has to re-emerge from the medieval shadows to which it was cast by liberal Protestantism. In Luther it can be seen, indeed, as the key also to the atonement motifs of Christ as Victor and as Example. That does not mean, as we shall see, merely repackaging Anselm's theology in Lutheran dress (that accusation can actually be made against

---

10. Lienhard, *Martin Luther: Witness,* p. 70.

11. Lienhard, *Martin Luther: Witness,* p. 180. The Luther references are to WA 10, 1,1, 123 and WA 10, 1,2, 236, 28 respectively.

12. Cited in David Lotz, *Luther and Ritschl: A Fresh Perspective on Albrecht Ritschl's Theology in the Light of His Luther Study* (Nashville: Abingdon, 1974), p. 41.

Melanchthon's theology of the atonement).[13] But it does require rather a more nuanced critique of Anselm than the commonplace smear about a "scholastic remnant."

Let then an honest opponent[14] of Luther's and Paul's theology of the Crucified's encounter with the wrath of God[15] for human salvation tell without apology or revision what both said and meant, as in the citation forming the epigraph to this chapter. Nietzsche[16] sees here with the genuine insight of an outsider. He charges that creative agape love, "born of the cross, which turns in the direction where it does not find good which it may enjoy, but where it may confer good upon a bad and needy person," as

13. It is typical of Melanchthon to make statements interpreting the *propter Christum,* which he shares with Luther, such as: "The Son of God became a sacrifice and merited grace for us, that is, forgiveness of sins, gracious acceptance by God and eternal justification and blessedness." *Loci Communes 1555,* p. 153. Or again: "The Mediator's entire obedience, from his Incarnation until the Resurrection, is the true justification which is pleasing to God, and is the merit for us. God forgives us our sins, and accepts us, in that he imputes righteousness to us for the sake of the Son, although we are still weak and sinful. We must, however, accept this imputed righteousness with faith" (p. 161). This is very much parallel to Anselm's idea of an active righteousness of Christ meriting a surplus of grace that can be credited to believers on application. What does not appear here is Luther's picture of God handing Christ over to wrath, of Christ's passive obedience.

14. ". . . theology owes Nietzsche a debt: I intend nothing facetious in saying that Nietzsche has bequeathed Christian thought a most beautiful gift, a needed anamnesis of itself — of its strangeness." David Bentley Hart, *The Beauty of the Infinite: The Aesthetics of Christian Truth* (Grand Rapids: Eerdmans, 2003), p. 126.

15. E.g., *"The Dawn,"* #68 in *The Portable Nietzsche,* ed. Walter Kaufmann (New York: Viking, 1969), p. 77.

16. See the various studies of Heinz Bluhm, especially "Nietzsche's View of Luther and the Reformation in *Morgenroethe* and *Die Froehliche Wissenschaft,"* PMLA 63 (1953): 111-27 and "Nietzsche's Final View of Luther and the Reformation," PMLA 71, no. 1 (1956): 75-83 which tells "the story of Nietzsche's exciting if unbalanced relationship to one of the abiding figures of the Christian tradition." Luther, Bluhm concludes, "is selected by Nietzsche to bear the brunt of his vicious and thorough-going assault on the historical fact of the re-Christianization of Europe in the sixteenth century. So far as Nietzsche is concerned, there are but two preeminent figures in the entire history of Christianity: Paul and Luther. The former is for him the real initiator of historic Christianity, the man who succeeded in putting Christianity on the map. The latter is its chief restorer after it had practically run its course in Europe and paganism was re-triumphant in the Renaissance. Nietzsche hates them both for what they perpetuated. . . . Paul and Luther are held to be in [agreement in] fundamental religious issues . . . of grace and faith . . ." (p. 77). Incidentally, Nietzsche's perception of the Reformation as re-Christianization comports with the instructive thesis of Scott H. Hendrix, *Recultivating the Vineyard: The Reformation Agendas of Christianization* (Louisville and London: Westminster/John Knox, 2004).

Luther put it in the Heidelberg Disputation,[17] affords only "temporary relief." Why? The "forgiveness of sins" is an imaginary solution to an imaginary problem.[18] Interestingly enough, however, the Christian God's "temporary relief" of forgiveness proves fictitious just because, for Nietzsche, the wrath of the gods is real. In one of the final formulations of his influential critique of the "Christian conception of God," Nietzsche wrote about "the *anti-natural castration* of a god, to make him a god of the good alone. . . ."[19] Nietzsche in other places traced this denaturing back to Plato and with wicked thrust and parry attributes it to the liberal Protestantism (e.g., the aforementioned Ritschl) of his day (Christianity as "Platonism for the people"). The secret of the contemporary "death of God" is thus exposed: we Christians have killed Him — with our *"pity."* "What would be the point of a god who knew nothing of wrath, revenge, envy, scorn, cunning, and violence?" Nietzsche asks in *The Antichrist.* The answer is that, "when a people is perishing . . . then its god has to change too. Now he becomes a sneak, timid, and modest; he counsels 'peace of soul,' hate-no-more, forbearance, even 'love' of friend and enemy. He moralizes constantly, he crawls into the cave of every private virtue, he becomes god for everyman, he becomes a private person, a cosmopolitan."[20]

Using Nietzsche's punishing analyses of the mind of modern Christianity for purposes of reconstruction in Christian theology, to be sure, is tricky business. Nietzsche is an opponent and cannot be turned into an ally; if one allies with him, one becomes an opponent. One has to disentangle the valuable insights provided in his hostile perspective from that perspective itself. Stimulating as are his penetrating sketches of shallow thinking and false living in contemporary Christianity, the practical *a priori* of Nietzsche's analysis of Christianity (along with his "precursor" Spinoza)[21] is radical denial of "the freedom of the will, teleology, the moral world order, the unegoistic, and evil."[22] Elements in this list might be reconciled with Pauline Christianity, but

---

17. LW 31:57.

18. *The Antichrist,* #15 in Kaufmann, *The Portable Nietzsche,* pp. 581-82.

19. *The Antichrist,* #16 in Kaufmann, *The Portable Nietzsche,* pp. 582-83.

20. *The Antichrist,* #16 in Kaufmann, *The Portable Nietzsche,* p. 583.

21. See Paul Hinlicky, *Paths Not Taken: Theology from Luther through Leibniz* (Grand Rapids: Eerdmans, 2009), chap. 2, pp. 43-86.

22. Letter to Overbeck, July 30, 1881, in Kaufmann, *The Portable Nietzsche,* p. 92. In fact, as we shall see in Chapter Five, Luther shares with Spinoza and Nietzsche certain "hedonistic" positions in psychology and thus a highly qualified notion of human freedom; Luther also denies that philosophy attains to any certainty on teleology and the moral world

not the package. What he has seen, however, is useful to us in this connection. A god who can only be good to us, and especially "good" *according* to us, is an idol, a convenient projection — neither Luther's nor Augustine's nor Paul's. Half-idolators, contemporary Christians *have* lost sense, if not stomach, for the "stern mercy" of the gospel (Augustine);[23] they have "cheapened grace" (Luther)[24] to the point that they can't give it away. That is why they cannot see and state plainly what Paul is saying in those painful texts, as Nietzsche sees and says. "Could it be," Leander Keck asked, "that one reason Christian theology often appears so bumblingly helpless today [after Verdun, Auschwitz, Dresden, and Vietnam] is that it has no real place for the wrath of God — precisely when we live in the midst of God's wrath and judgment?"[25]

Reinhold Niebuhr once wrote in elaboration of the gospel's stern mercy and costly grace: "The self-disclosure of God in Christ is significantly regarded by Christian faith as the final 'word' which God has spoken to man. The revelation of the Atonement is precisely a 'final' word because it discloses a transcendent divine mercy that represents the 'freedom' of God in quintessential terms: namely, God's freedom over His own law. Yet this freedom is not capricious. It is paradoxically related to God's law, to the structures of the world. This is the paradox of the Atonement, of the revelation of the mercy of God in its relation to the justice of God."[26] The task before us is to see movement internal to the life of God transpiring in the atonement clearly: far from presenting an alternative to the medieval Western doctrine of the *atonement as satisfaction,* Luther represents a profound retrieval (as well as a *corrective* development) of it. Burnell F. Eckhardt Jr., in an important and unjustly neglected study, so put the matter of Luther's teaching on the atonement (in full accord with Nietzsche!): "The fact that the vicarious victim is God is precisely what makes the sacrifice an act of God's mercy."[27] But that means that what God saves from — in at least one of the three di-

---

order, though he does think the phenomenon of religion attests to a sense of these things as well as an awareness of good and evil.

23. Augustine, *Confessions,* VIII:11.

24. Martin Luther, *The Bondage of the Will,* trans. J. I. Packer and O. R. Johnston (Grand Rapids: Fleming Revell, 2000), pp. 292-95.

25. Leander E. Keck, *A Future for the Historical Jesus: The Place of Jesus in Preaching and Theology* (Philadelphia: Fortress, 1981), p. 231.

26. Reinhold Niebuhr, *The Nature and Destiny of Man,* 2 vols. (New York: Scribner's, 1964), vol. 2, p. 67.

27. Burnell F. Eckhardt Jr., *Anselm and Luther on the Atonement: Was It "Necessary"?* (San Francisco: Mellen Research University Press, 1992), p. 42.

mensions of salvation mentioned above — is God. Centrally so, in that before salvation can be liberation from the ungodly powers or power for new life in God's reign, salvation is and must be reconciliation of the holy God and the sinful creature. Understanding this contention, in turn, radically challenges the usual practice of belief in American churches, as H. R. Niebuhr classically described their denatured deity, that pseudo-"God without wrath who brings men without sin into a kingdom without judgment through the ministrations of a Christ without a cross."[28]

## Propitiation, Not Expiation

Against modern theology of that denatured deity, Bayer rightly contends in Luther's name, "the criterion for truth is provided in this event in which Jesus Christ takes another person's place by a *propitiatory* death...."[29] Understanding Luther's teaching on this matter, "so difficult and yet so decisive," as Bayer notes, demands explicating it both in relation to and in distinction from the *expiatory* teaching of Anselm of Canterbury's *Cur Deus Homo.* Bayer declines to do this, however, opting instead to urge upon us in Luther's name a highly problematic distinction. On the one hand there is, he claims, God's "understandable" wrath, i.e., a voice from God that "can be understood, even though it is not the voice of his grace" in the "sphere of actions that bring about consequences." But on the other hand there is, as attested in the psalms of lament, an experience of God's wrath as something "incalculable, fearsome, and incomprehensible," something that cannot be "comprehended as a measured response to a specific mistaken action."[30] One wants immediately to ask: How then can this voiceless, incomprehensible experience be recognized as *God's* wrath? Why not rather Jesus' rain and sunshine which *the heavenly Father* sends upon the just and unjust alike?[31] Or the ac-

---

28. H. R. Niebuhr, *The Kingdom of God in America* (New York: Harper Torchbooks, 1959), p. 193.

29. Bayer, *Luther's Theology,* p. 235, emphasis added.

30. Bayer, *Luther's Theology,* p. 197. As the conclusion of *De servo arbitrio* makes plain, understanding of the wisdom and justice of God's judgments in history is, for Luther, something to be believed, something that will become evident in the light of glory. Faith in God's wisdom and justice even in judgments that appear inscrutable to us is what Luther calls for. Bayer's distinction between two kinds of experience of wrath is not true to Luther, since the scandal under discussion is the particularity of grace.

31. If I may again invoke Nietzsche as antidote to anthropocentric, narcissistic, piet-

tual, moral evil of Luther's *devil,* raging furiously to destroy what God creates? That God *permits* such natural or moral evils, to be sure, raises the question of *theodicy* as a serious theological problem. But Bayer declines to enter that debate,[32] preferring instead to represent a Luther who is attempting a "high-wire balancing act": denying that God is the author of evil even though God "uses evil as a tool that cannot escape his power."[33] The result is a Luther who prefers "logical inconsistencies" to denying the power, the goodness, or the unity of God. Predictably, the figure of the *deus absconditus* is hauled in here as a theological *deus ex machina,* i.e., to put a good face on a conceptual muddle. It may well be that the muddle goes back to Luther (we shall investigate the problem in Chapter Five below), but it *is* a muddle.

The biblical wrath that is *holy,* the wrath that is recognizable to faith in Jesus Christ as *God's* wrath, is no outburst of pagan Zeus in a fit of blind rage. It is the righteous wrath of the God of love against all that is against love. It is the wrath of the public God, not a massive private ego. It is the wrath of the Creator God over the ruin of His creation, revealed from heaven against all ungodliness and wickedness of those who suppress the truth. It is, moreover, this threatened wrath from which Jesus delivers us, not least in making it understandable to believing sinners, since this is the eternal wrath which He met in our place and overcame in the heart of God at Golgotha, provided then that we understand that event of atonement as something *internal* to the life of the God of love. Whether, in face of Nietzsche's challenge, this holy wrath can be understood to be real and not imaginary, is another question. We will take it up again at the end of this chapter.

But for the moment we need to see with unmistakable clarity that Luther in fact thinks of Christ's atoning death as providing a necessary *propitiation* (divine judgment against sin), which is redemptive for others (Mark 10:45, a "ransom"). While I will be leaning heavily on Eckhardt's

---

istic demands on God: as though "we should find a god who cures a cold at the right time or who bids us enter a coach at the very moment when a violent rainstorm begins, such an absurd god that we should have to abolish him if he existed. A god as servant, as mailman, as calendar man — at bottom, a word for the most stupid of all accidents!" *The Antichrist,* #52 in Kaufmann, *The Portable Nietzsche,* p. 636.

32. Theodicy, Bayer argues, is not a dispute about God as Leibniz held, but a dispute *with* God, as in Job. *Luther's Theology,* p. 213. Theodicy as theological dispute about God has to do with the urgent matter of discerning the evil against which God wills and works. The tragedy of German theology in the 1930s was exactly that it did not *know* how to distinguish God from the *devil.*

33. Bayer, *Luther's Theology,* p. 200.

study,[34] I present a thesis here that can be developed out of an analysis by Sarah Hinlicky Wilson. She writes: "Luther has three very important things in common with Anselm: a) the conviction that the incarnation is intrinsically related to the atonement; b) the belief that our merit cannot procure our own salvation; and c) an emphasis on God's providing Christ for us out of love and a desire to eliminate His own wrath. Luther's chief difference from Anselm in terms of content (not theological style) is that satisfaction for Luther means punishment, whereas for Anselm it means payment." Thus, as just argued: "the battle is not only on the outside, or on earth, or in us; it is also in God Himself."[35] As Luther himself says, "Thus the curse, which is divine wrath against the whole world, has the same conflict with the blessing, that is, with the eternal grace and mercy of God in Christ."[36] The divine curse *must* yield to the divine blessing, Luther urged dramatically in the 1535 Galatians commentary, or "God Himself would be conquered."[37] In some mysterious way, then, God strives with God in Christ, just as Christ battles sin "in His own body and in Himself."

So we may put forward a thesis: at the cross there is a confrontation between the Father and the Son that is to be reconciled, if it is reconciled, by the Spirit. I do not mean this thesis in any patripassionist sense, e.g., that the Father is helplessly stricken at the pain of His Son or any other such sentimentality parading as theology. In that the Son in the power of the Spirit bears human sin in obedience to the Father, and in this uncanny way truly perishes in solidarity with sinners under the aspect of the same Father's holy wrath, when, and if, the Father recognizes the Son's love for sinners to the cross as His own love for them as well, by the same the Spirit, they too are also raised by faith in Christ with Christ to the Father's newly opened arms. When Luther speaks of the "Law battling the Law to become liberty for me,"[38] the sense is Jesus' fulfillment of the double love

---

34. Eckhardt, *Anselm,* p. xi. "The Christological agreement between Anselm and Luther is to be expected in view of the appreciation both had for their Western tradition, and particularly for Augustine. That Anselm's Christology was as Chalcedonian as Luther's is beyond any legitimate dispute" (p. 53).

35. Sarah Hinlicky Wilson, "Luther on the 'Atonement'" (unpublished paper, Princeton Theological Seminary). Again, "there *is* a lot of continuity with Anselm here, more than Aulén recognized, though . . . Luther's satisfaction motif is associated with punishment (or propitiation) rather than payment (or expiation)."

36. "Commentary on Galatians" (1535) LW 26:281.

37. "Commentary on Galatians" (1535) LW 26:282.

38. "Commentary on Galatians" (1535) LW 26:164.

commandment colliding with the juridical power of the Law to condemn the lovelessness of the world in which Jesus is wrapped on account of His merciful solidarity with us; thus the Law is ethically fulfilled and given its juridical right and now superseded by the triumphant mercy of God. "For by the very fact that He permitted the Law to accuse Him, sin to damn Him, and death to devour Him He abrogated the Law, damned sin, destroyed death, and justified and saved me."[39] In this event, God surpasses God.

What is perhaps different about this thesis than previous attempts to articulate Luther's complex teaching is the "heaving lifting" this account requires of the doctrine of the Trinity.[40] Indeed, Gustaf Aulén, famous for a book criticizing the "Latin" theory of expiation represented by Anselm and contending for Luther's retrieval of patristic thought in the motif of Christ the Victor,[41] actually sought a certain, similar integration of the various motifs in his own dogmatics: "It is significant that Luther not only regards the ancient triad, sin, death and the devil, as destructive powers, but includes also the law (as Paul did) and wrath, the divine wrath. Through this insight of Luther, Christian faith is able to view the work of Christ in the most profound perspective."[42] But Aulén lacked the vigorous Trinitarian personalism that is needed to clarify the problem. In any case, we may accordingly take it for granted in arguing for this thesis in what follows that "satisfaction" (properly clarified) is not *all* that Luther will say about atonement, only a necessary component of it that demands particular attention today because of confused efforts in modern theology to banish it from the realm of theological possibility.

In fact Luther himself was not thrilled with the terminology: ". . . even if we should just keep the word satisfaction and interpret it to mean that Christ has made satisfaction for our sin, still it is too weak, and

---

39. "Commentary on Galatians" (1535) LW 26:163.

40. As Robert Jenson has seen with his typical acumen: *ST* I:189-93.

41. Gustav Aulén, *Christus Victor* (London: Society for Promoting Christian Knowledge; New York and Toronto: Macmillan, 1931).

42. Gustaf Aulén, *The Faith of the Christian Church,* trans. Eric H. Wahlstrom (Philadelphia: Muhlenberg, 1962), p. 200. Aulén argues the devil plays a double role, as the very "incarnation of that which is hostile to God" and as the prison-keeper of sinners, i.e., that "in accordance with God's will . . . because of sin, men have been placed under the dominion of the devil. . . . It then becomes clear that the victory over the destructive powers is at the same time a reconciliation" (p. 202). Unfortunately, Aulén did not explore this difficult complex of ideas with the depth demanded.

too little is said of the grace of Christ, and not enough honor paid the suffering of Christ, to whom we must give higher honor, that he not only made satisfaction for sin but also redeemed us from the power of death, the devil and hell, and establishes an eternal kingdom of grace and a daily forgiveness even of the remainder of sin that is in us."[43] Granted. The notion of "penal substitution" is not to stand on its own, unintegrated with the motifs of redemptive victory and example of love; in that case all-too-easy notions of an expiatory bribe by means of a scapegoat will displace the difficult notion of propitiation, i.e., real reckoning with divine wrath that must be faced and rightfully endured in order to be surpassed, releasing the prisoners from oppressive powers, freeing and empowering them for new lives. "Penal substitution" must then earn its way in the theology of the atonement by making intelligible redemptive victory over the anti-divine powers as something down-to-earth. In the same way it must illuminate the very act of Christ's love in such a way that, "if we look at [it], we are moved to imitate [it]"[44] in new obedience to God which is a mighty agency in the world. In any event, it is the revised, propitiatory (not expiatory) *concept,* not *term,* "satisfaction," that matters: Christ's love in making His own the sinner's moral place under holy wrath *fulfills the just requirement of the divine law of love*[45] and so *by right* trumps the same law's right to hold under indictment loveless failures, even hostile enemies for whom this Man for Others dies. The *concept* of satisfaction as penal substitution is that Christ by his death meets and endures, thus overcomes or surpasses (the word "satisfies" *is* too weak!) the real and righteous wrath *of God* in such a way that those who had been justly indicted are now justified by this *rightful* act of mercy; consequently, the demonic usurpation over them is *rightfully* as well as powerfully defeated as they arise to faith in the same heavenly Father, and so by the coming of the same Spirit who raised Jesus from the dead believers are born anew in new hope for the world that God has so loved, enflamed with new desire to love as Christ has loved them and given Himself for them.

43. Quoted in Lohse, *Luther's Theology,* p. 227, from *Crucigers Sommerpostille,* WA 21, 264, 27-33. Thanks to Sarah Hinlicky Wilson for the reference.

44. "The Heidelberg Disputation" (1518) LW 31:57. Like satisfaction and imputation, imitation is also too weak a word, when the new life in Christ is a matter of "delight" in what God commands, "being Good Samaritan as Christ has been our Samaritan." Risto Saarinen, "The Pauline Luther and the Law," *Pro Ecclesia* 15, no. 1 (Winter 2006): 76.

45. Antti Raunio, *Summe des Christlichen Lebens: Die 'Goldene Regel' als Gesetz der Liebe in der Theologie Martin Luthers von 1510 bis 1527* (Helsinki, 1993), pp. 311-18.

"Penal substitution" and "vicarious satisfaction" were common-places of the older literature. To take but one example, Robert S. Franks's book of one hundred years ago took its orientation from the well-known passages in the Large Catechism's explanation of the Creed's Second Article and the corresponding passage in the *Smalcald Articles* mentioned in the last chapter.[46] On this basis, Franks argued a critical clarification: that for Luther "Christ's satisfaction [was] not like the schoolmen after the analogy of private law as directed to appease God's injured honour, but rather after the analogy of public law as intended to placate His offended righteousness and His violated decree."[47] It is not, in other words, God's bruised ego that is offended and in need of soothing, but it is God's reign, the public administration of justice in His own creation which has been disordered by sin as a kind of contagion of moral ruin or corruption that is wreaking havoc.[48] This cosmic disorder is what needs rectifying, that somehow both sin be condemned and yet sinners redeemed. Franks went on to correlate this crucial shift in perspective from private to public justice with the "change from the medieval doctrine of Christ's satisfaction as essentially an active self-oblation to the Protestant view of it as fundamentally a passive endurance. . . ."[49] The former active, expiatory righteousness is, strictly speaking, an *unnecessary* work of supererogation by the sinless Christ, which just so earns a treasure of surplus merit (earned as human, but infinite in value as divine), freely available now for dispensation through the sacramental system. The latter passive, propitiatory righteousness refers to Christ's necessary substitution for the guilty suffering under the Law's curse, if indeed they are rightfully to be pardoned and set free. At this juncture, Franks provided a full plate of

46. Robert S. Franks, *A History of the Doctrine of the Work of Christ in Its Ecclesiastical Development* (London: Hodder & Stoughton, 1918), pp. 357ff.

47. Franks, *A History*, p. 376. The criticism is aimed at statements like this from Anselm's *Cur deus homo:* "Judge for yourself if it is not contrary to the honor of God for man to be reconciled to Him while man still bore the shame of this outrage inflicted on God, without first honoring God by overcoming the devil, just as he had dishonored Him by being overcome by the devil." Anselm of Canterbury, *Why God Became Man* and *The Virgin Conception and Original Sin,* translation, introduction, and notes by Joseph M. Colleran (Albany, NY: Magi Books, 1969), p. 111.

48. It may be noted here that the question so posed, "What was God in His goodness to do?" i.e., when sin is destroying the creation but mere forgiveness enables the destroyers, harkens back to Athanasius's seminal discussion of atonement theology in *On the Incarnation of the Word,* #8 in the *Nicene and Post-Nicene Fathers (N&PNF),* IV:40.

49. Franks, *A History*, p. 376.

citations[50] from Luther to show that the redemptive suffering of Christ is in some way *necessary,* lest following Paul in Galatians 2:21, Christ would be thought to have died "to no purpose." Forgiveness cannot transpire merely by fiat. Though free to us, grace is not free to God, if we are thinking, as mentioned, of God publicly as Creator and Judge, whose justification we need (not sentimentally and privately as our special friend in the sky, whose patronage we seek for our private needs), but as future citizens of the reign and members of the Beloved Community He is now bringing about in the new creation of all things.

Franks concluded by turning attention to a central contention of Luther's Galatians commentary of 1535:

> Christ is innocent so far as His own Person is concerned; therefore He should not have been hanged from the tree. But because, according to the Law, every thief should have been hanged, therefore, according to the Law of Moses, Christ Himself should have been hanged; for He bore the person of a sinner and a thief — and not of one but of all sinners and thieves. For we are sinners and thieves, and therefore we are worthy of death and eternal damnation. But Christ took all our sins upon Himself, and for them He died on the cross. . . . In short, He has and bears all the sins of all men in His body — not in the sense that He has committed them but in the sense that He took these sins, committed by us, upon His own body, in order to make satisfaction for them with His own blood.[51]

To this contention of Luther for Christ as sin-bearer, we add a few other notes from the second Galatians commentary: "Our sins are not removed by any other means than by the Son of God given into death. . . . He *was* given for them. . . ."[52] Or again: "But because there was no price in heaven or on earth except Christ, the Son of God, therefore it was extremely necessary that He be given for me."[53] Luther takes umbrage at an idea some-

---

50. E.g., God's "gracious imputation must first be bought and obtained for us from His righteousness"; or again that "Christ [is He] . . . who in thy place and for thee has made satisfaction superabundantly to every Divine command and to God's righteousness"; or again, "it could not come about that God's wrath, judgment, and all evil things should be removed and all good be won without satisfaction having to be made to the Divine righteousness, sin having to be paid for, and death having to be overcome in accordance with justice." Franks, *A History,* p. 376.

51. "Commentary on Galatians" (1535) LW 26:277.

52. "Commentary on Galatians" (1535) LW 26:32ff.

53. "Commentary on Galatians" (1535) LW 26:177.

times imputed to him, but which he imputes to the "enthusiasts": "You might as well tell me also that because faith alone justifies, Christ is not necessary."[54] *Note well in all this Luther's refusal of a theology of atonement based* solely *on divine omnipotence or freedom.*[55]

Surveying all such evidence from Luther's 1535 Galatians commentary and beyond, Eckhardt holds that Luther "mocks and rejects the idea that God in view of his omnipotence could perform salvation without Christ"[56] and concludes: "The abundance of references in Luther to the concepts of sacrifice and exchange lead one to wonder how Hofmann, Aulén, Forde and company could have convinced so many that their position is even worthy of consideration."[57] Theirs *is* in plain sight a *massive evasion* of these difficult *texts.*

How to proceed? Eckhardt helpfully reminds us in this connection that "Luther's discourse on justification most frequently speaks in terms of an exchange — the celebrated *fröhliche Wechsel* — between Christ and the sinner."[58] With equal right he notes that the "*fröhliche Wechsel* has been occasionally misunderstood and criticized as immature Luther, based on the mistaken premise that it occurs through the mystical presence of Christ, i.e., *propter Christum in nobis,* which would create a tension with forensic justification." The reference here is to the position of Osiander, i.e., "if the exchange is mystical, then it becomes in effect akin to the scholastic *gratia infusa.* . . ." The fear then would be that this teaching makes a religious experience of regeneration based upon the mystical presence of Christ in the soul the basis for the non-imputation of sin and reckoning of righteousness. The fear in Luther's case is ungrounded. For Luther, "the exchange is actually quite forensic. . . ." Here "[sin] is imputed forensically to [Christ]; and thus the reverse exchange must also be seen as one of imputation. For Luther, then, the *fröhliche Wechsel* occurs only by imputation; it may in fact be termed Luther's version of the vicarious satisfaction. . . ."[59]

---

54. "The Sacrament of the Body and Blood of Christ — Against the Fanatics" (1526) LW 36:344.

55. Lienhard, *Martin Luther: Witness,* p. 58.

56. Eckhardt, *Anselm,* p. 34.

57. Eckhardt, *Anselm,* p. 48. "Perhaps Forde's treatment is the most annoying because it is most clearly an effort to put words into Luther's mouth, words which are in fact far more convincing of Forde's antagonism towards the Anselmian view than of his accuracy in representing Luther here" (p. 6).

58. Eckhardt, *Anselm,* p. 44.

59. Eckhardt, *Anselm,* p. 46. Citing the 1535 Galatians commentary, LW 26:233, 278, 279, 283f., 290, 325, 373 and also from Luther's sermons.

Alas, like the word "satisfaction," so also the word "imputation" is too weak, in that it seems to leave the one spoken to untouched, unmoved, unchanged.[60] The joyful exchange is an event in language; it is an exchange of predications, "I am yours and you are mine," as in a nuptial vow, which in Luther's culture had legal force even if spoken secretly. Bearing in mind the legal status of betrothal in Luther's time, when such an exchange of promises constituted a legal engagement, Eckhardt is not wrong to characterize the language as "forensic" (provided we do not sneak in the law-court model here, where instead the image of nuptials belong). In the celebrated passage of the early Reformation treatise, *On the Freedom of the Christian*,[61] we see this engagement model. The Christ who comes to dwell in faith comes by the word of promise, like a bridegroom to his betrothed — "I am yours, you are mine" — although in this case the exchange is hardly symmetrical: "Your sins are mine; my righteousness is yours." The bearing away of the believer's sin and the bestowing in its place of Christ's own righteousness comes about — and this is the truth contained in the weak word, imputation — by the *external* word of a true Other coming as news. As such it is communicated by an act of promise, predication, imputation, attribution. Thus the action of the joyful exchange is not a magical, mystical infusion of invisible qualities, but down-to-earth speech, occurring in the ordinary way, to state and perform something quite extraordinary. Of course, this speaking entails the real presence of Christ to speak His own promise, not merely a report about what Christ once did. Just so, however, "to contend that the *fröhliche Wechsel* requires an infusion of righteousness is to misunderstand Luther's preference for this language."[62] Eckhardt is manifestly right, but understanding how Christ can be simultaneously *for us* as the Man who believed on our behalf and as the New Man who believes *in us,* requires a doctrine of the Holy Spirit — a topic reserved for the next chapter.[63]

Part of the confusion surrounding this difficult topic[64] is that the old Lutheran dogmaticians combined Luther and Anselm (via Melanchthon) in their teaching on the priestly office of Christ, in which Christ "is both priest and sacrifice in one person . . . that he may reconcile man with God."

---

60. So also Bayer, *Luther's Theology,* pp. 50-57.

61. "The Freedom of a Christian" (1520) LW 31:351.

62. Eckhardt, *Anselm,* pp. 97f. "The *Christus in nobis* is the *Christus pro nobis,* and is clearly not meant by Luther to be understood as an enabler of virtuous habits which justify" (p. 98).

63. Eckhardt, *Anselm,* p. 191.

64. On this, see *Paths Not Taken,* pp. 145-49.

This office consists in the satisfaction He rendered and the intercession He makes on behalf of the sinner. The satisfaction consists both in the active obedience of His life in fulfillment of the law and His passive obedience by which He suffered the penalty; both together are accomplished "to the praise of divine justice and mercy and for the procurement of our justification and salvation." The intercession at God's right hand is perpetual: "Christ is not content merely in silence to await the effect of His satisfaction, but . . . He actively, effectively, really avails Himself of His merit with the Father in such manner as becomes Him in His divine dignity." So Hollaz summarized: the "redemption of the human race is the spiritual, judicial, and most costly deliverance of all men, bound in the chains of sin, from guilt, from the wrath of God, and temporal and eternal punishment, accomplished by Christ, the God-man, through His active and passive obedience, which God, the most righteous judge, kindly accepted as the most perfect ransom (Gk.: *lytron*), so that the human race, introduced into spiritual liberty, may live forever with God."[65] This is Christ's *priestly* work. Note well, it is neither His prophetic preaching of the Kingdom summoning to discipleship (the moral influence motif of Christ as example for us in His martyrdom) nor His kingly work subduing those enemies under His feet (the *Christus Victor* motif of Christ's harrowing of hell). As mentioned above, any adequate teaching of the atonement will *integrate* these motifs, not play them off against each other. All the same, the integrative key among them belongs to the Priestly office. For the Christ who called to discipleship is the Christ who was condemned for offering forgiveness to disciples as God's free gift (Mark 2:1–3:6); and the Christ who empties hell is the Christ who suffered hell (Mark 15:33) on account of His solidarity with those disciples who could not follow Him in their own power (Mark 14:27-28; 16:7).

It is evident then that in some way Anselm (via Melanchthon) stands behind this old Lutheran synthesis, even though Anselm lacks Luther's central focus on Christ the Lamb, Christ the sin-bearer, which difference demarcates the new doctrinal development ensuing from Luther's reformation theology, that is, from the concrete and historical exchange of idioms.[66] Under the impact of the reformatory theology, in other words,

65. *The Doctrinal Theology of the Evangelical Lutheran Church*, ed. H. Schmid, trans. C. Hay and H. Jacobs (Philadelphia, 1899), pp. 342-46.

66. Harnack, *HD* VI:68. Forde made this Lutheran point against Anselm succinctly: "Jesus' death is not a substitution for our death; it is our death. It is the death of the one who

Anselm's question, *Cur deus homo?*, was both taken up and yet answered in a new way. As I urged in *Paths Not Taken*, Luther provides a Cyrillian Christ for Augustinian humanity in sharp distinction from the West's vulnerability, especially manifest in liberal Protestantism, to thinking of a Nestorian Christ for a Pelagian humanity.[67] This must be clearly understood.

## What Anselm Really Taught

Blanket criticism of Anselm's teaching on satisfaction, in Harnack's words as "untenable" as well as "unevangelical," goes unchallenged to the present day in the confused line of thought that passes from Ritschl and Hofmann through Aulén and Forde. Not overly to weary readers from outside the strange world of post-Kantian Luther theology in Germany and its lesser American imitators, for our purposes that criticism can be simplified to two points. Anselm's theory is judged by Harnack as "unevangelical" in that it "rests satisfied" in showing theoretically *"the possibility of the redemption of the individual from sin;* but as this possibility can afford no comfort whatsoever to any distressed conscience, as it only satisfies the understanding, it is a worthless substitute for a real doctrine of redemption — Luther would say it is of the *devil"* since as mere theory it does not deliver "the *certitudo salutis."*[68] If this critique is not to be taken as an ob-

---

stands against God. . . . Atonement occurs when God succeeds, at the cost of the death of his Son, in getting through to us who live under wrath." *Christian Dogmatics,* ed. Carl E. Braaten and Robert W. Jenson, 2 vols. (Philadelphia: Fortress, 1984), II:58. Granted. But at the same time, Forde resolutely repudiates any notion of representation and in the process confuses the old Lutheran revision of Anselm with Anselm himself. He calls the idea of "substitution" the "Achilles' heel" of the theory and seemingly agrees with the Socinian criticism that "the transfer of someone else's sin to the innocent is absurd and improper, just as in reverse the transfer of someone else's righteousness to the unrighteous." *Christian Dogmatics,* II:24-25, cf. also 16. Again, without recognizing his actual concurrence *with* Anselm and *against* the old Lutheran revision of him, Forde calls Christ's "active doing of the law for us in his life . . . a step in the right direction . . ." *Christian Dogmatics,* II:25. Adding honesty to confusion upon confusion, Forde confesses in the end that Luther's "happy exchange" retains "vestiges of something quasi-physical" and is "too abstract and mythological for contemporary eyes. If anything, Luther's formulations still have too much of the traditional metaphysical and mythological freight." *Christian Dogmatics,* II:61. One may be at least be grateful for this candid admission.

67. *Paths Not Taken,* pp. 18, 120.

68. *Christian Dogmatics,* II: 69. Thus Gerhard Forde: "We cannot be saved by a better

83

jection to understanding as such in the second-order discourse of theology, then this complaint simply reduces to the charge, as we shall see, that because Anselm lacks a sufficient understanding of Christ's participation in the human plight he will also lack a sufficient appreciation for the problem of Christ's availability to those in bondage. Additionally, Harnack holds Anselm's teaching to be "untenable" on account of "the mythological conception of God as the mighty private man, who is incensed at the injury done to His honour and does not forgo His wrath till He has received an at least adequately great equivalent . . . the frightful idea . . . that *mankind are delivered from the wrathful God*."[69] We have already noted how the Reformation theology construed God's wrath in the aspect of the public, divine office of the Creator, not in terms of the easily bruised since massively inflated ego of a medieval warlord. Nevertheless, the very "worst thing" that Harnack finds in Anselm is exactly what Luther finds *underdeveloped* in Anselm.[70] For Luther, as we have seen, what we are centrally delivered from is the *wrath* of God; for Luther, salvation is Christ harrowing *hell*. This makes Luther *even more guilty* of the mythological horror that Harnack imputes to the medieval Catholic Anselm. But what is actually the case with Anselm?

In fact it was both the evangelical impulse in Anselm's account *and his nomianism*[71] that made his account of atonement as satisfaction attrac-

theology, a better *idea* of God. God must *come* to save us" (p. 67). Granted. Then we need in theology to think of God who comes to save instead of otherwise: ". . . there is a very real sense in which God is not what he aims to be for us, until God actually succeeds in accomplishing that aim. God is not, in actuality, merciful for us until the reality of wrathful absence has been overcome." *Christian Dogmatics*, II:73. In this act of atonement "God changes objectively only by dying to himself as a God of wrath, saying no to that forever for us. . . . The cross is what it costs God to remain true to himself, to remain a God of mercy. . . . Admittedly there is discontinuity for thought: God changes; God remains the same; God does; God comes alive in Jesus. God gets a new name in this event. The gap cannot be closed in thought." *Christian Dogmatics*, II:75. But certainly it can and must be described conceptually!

69. Harnack, *HD* VI:76.

70. Harnack, *HD* VI:76. Forde echoes this criticism as well: "The more serious problems with Anselm's doctrine are theo-logical rather than logical. The most persistent one is the question of justice versus mercy and its consequences for the doctrine of God. The attempt to prove the necessity of satisfaction leads to the idea that mercy can be exercised only when the demands of justice have been fulfilled. But if God has to be paid and has been paid, how is God merciful?" Forde, *Christian Dogmatics*, II:23.

71. Luther: "When Isaiah 53[:8] declares that God has 'stricken him for the transgression of my people,' tell me, dear fellow, does this proclamation of Christ's suffering and of his

tive and useful to Melanchthon, to the old Lutheran dogmaticians (and at least necessary to Luther): "What greater mercy could be imagined," Anselm asked at the conclusion of *Cur deus homo,* "than for God the Father to say to the sinner condemned to eternal torments and having no way to redeem himself: 'Receive my only begotten Son and present Him instead of yourself'; and for the Son Himself to say, 'Take me and redeem yourself'? This is what they say, in effect, when they call us and draw us to the Christian faith. What could be more just, furthermore, than for Him to whom is given a price that surpasses all that is owed Him, provided the offering is made with proper dispositions, to remit the whole debt?"[72] In this text Anselm's intention in his treatise is manifest. Here we see what he regards — forgive the metaphor — as the "cash value" of his deliberations. Anselm has in fact been trying to understand the biblical text about "ransom" (Mark 10:45) by means of an *economic* metaphor: Christ paid our *debt.* His death was, or more precisely provides, expiation. Carefully read, his meaning is that the gratuitous and active obedience of Christ's life, culminating in his unobligated self-sacrifice, thus an act of love above and beyond the letter of the law, procured a treasury of infinite merit that may now be freely dispensed to the needy sinner by the sacraments of the church in order to satisfy the sinner's debt. While resort to the economic metaphor of debt has seemed to many calculating and legalistic, Anselm deployed it in search of a conceptual alternative to the predominant, popular theory that the "ransom" of Jesus' life was paid to the devil[73] and that, to

---

being stricken for our sin imply that the law is cast away? What does this expression, 'for the transgression of my people,' mean? Does it not mean 'because my people sinned against my law and did not keep my law'? . . . according to Romans 5[:13], where there is no law there is no sin. And if there is no sin, then Christ is nothing. Why should he die if there were no sin or law for which he must die? It is apparent from this that the devil's purpose in this fanaticism is not to remove the law *but to remove Christ, the fulfiller of the law.*" "Against the Antinomians" (1539) LW 40:274ff., emphasis added. How does this Luther differ from Anselm, who argues against the cheap grace of mere pardon, even if on account of Christ and mercy: "then God is relaxing the penalty and making a man happy on account of his Son. . . . But divine 'mercy' of this sort is quite opposed to God's justice which allows nothing but punishment to be the return for sin. Therefore, just as it is impossible for God to contradict Himself, so it is impossible for Him to be merciful in this way" (p. 115).

72. Anselm, *Why,* p. 162.

73. This explanation can already be found in Irenaeus, *Against Heresies,* V:1 (ANF I:527). Although Irenaeus insists that God committed no fraud in deceiving the devil, he does not explain how the ransom was in fact a righteous and fitting deed of redemption, as he insists that it was.

boot, by a kind of divine deception (i.e., the humanity impaled like a worm on the hook of the divinity only to snare the greedy, unsuspecting devil when he tried to devour Jesus).[74]

Anselm is rightly appalled at this ransom to the devil theory, often naïvely assumed in the *Christus Victor* tradition: "Whatever was exacted of man," he curtly writes, "was due to God, not to the devil."[75] And this debt was *honestly* to be satisfied; God does not cheat even that cheater, the devil. These contextual considerations are important for the proper estimation of Anselm's atonement theology. Just as Anselm's theological method — *sola ratione*[76] — aimed to liberate the work of critical dogmatics from superstitious biblicism and ecclesiastical authoritarianism by means of rational probing to uncover the good reasons for the truths of faith,[77] the relation with God is in turn understood by Anselm as a moral, not a magical one (in a fashion that even Karl Holl[78] would have had to approve): "A person who does not render God this honor due Him, takes from God what is His and dishonors God, and this is to commit sin . . . on account of the insult committed, he must give back more than he took away . . . some compensation for the injury of the pain he has inflicted."[79] We have already

---

74. Rufinus of Aquilea provides a particularly egregious version of this theory with the example of a "mousetrap" cited in *The Christian Theology Reader,* ed. Alister E. McGrath (Oxford: Blackwell, 1999), p. 180.

75. Anselm, *Why,* p. 161.

76. "Anselm's ". . . *sola ratione* principle lay at the root of his well-known *fides quaerens intellectum* — faith seeking understanding . . . methodology, according to which, simply put, all arguments in support of a point are made from reasoned or logical premises, entirely without recourse to any authoritative statements, whether from Scripture or from ecclesiastical tradition." Eckhardt, *Anselm,* p. 8.

77. According to Eckhardt, what really separates Luther and Anselm is the implications for theological method of sin. "Anselm's *fides quaerens intellectum* is faith seeking elsewhere than Scripture to obtain knowledge of what it believes, as though Scripture were unable to provide this, or at least unable to provide the higher levels of *intellectum* sought by faith . . . a rational reason for the Trinity's being what it is, an attempt to make discursive sense, *extra Scripturam,* of what Scripture teaches." Anselm, *Why,* p. 172. This otherwise acute analysis lacks the important distinction between reason as theory and reason as interpretation argued in the first chapter of this book.

78. Karl Holl, *The Reconstruction of Morality,* trans. F. W. Meuser and W. R. Wietzke (Minneapolis: Augsburg, 1979).

79. Anselm, *Why,* p. 84. "The will of every rational creature must be subject to the will of God." This is the "rectitude of the will . . . the only and total honor which we owe to God" so "that no one sins who pays it and anyone who does not pay it sins" (p. 84). Original justice was grounded in the gift of rationality: "created for the purpose of loving and choosing the

noted the danger in conceiving of this failure to give God His due in privatized fashion rather than as the public act of the creature giving glory to the Creator and thanksgiving for the gift of the creation.[80] The point here is that Anselm demands just what Holl found in the early Luther's passionate Augustinian contentions against *securitas*,[81] that the relationship to God cannot be less than an *ethical* one. But if the human relation to God is a moral one, it is one that *must* be repaired when violated, as in any other moral relation. That is why atonement is "necessary" — not absolutely necessary (in view of God's *potentia absoluta*), of course, but given God's moral relation to the human creature (in view then of God's *potentia ordinata*), necessary to sustaining that relation if and when it has been violated. This necessary repair of the creation damaged by moral disrespect of its Creator is ". . . the satisfaction, which every sinner must make to God."[82] God is not there either to be disregarded or to be used, let alone to be bribed. Neither can the public God administrating the universe forgive by mere fiat, by dint of superior divine power which would really be just caprice, without violating the justice by which God has bound Himself to the

---

supreme good above all things, not as a means toward something else but as a goal in itself . . . it was created simultaneously rational and just for this purpose" (p. 119).

80. But it is not clear to me that Anselm is actually guilty as charged. He can write "there is nothing more just than for the supreme justice, which is the same as God Himself, to preserve His honor in the order of the universe." Anselm, *Why*, p. 88. "Did [man] not take from God whatever He had intended to make out of human nature?" (p. 112). "When [the rational will] wills what it should, it honors God — not that it confers anything on Him, but that it freely subjects itself to His will and plans and keeps its place in the order of the universe, and to the best of its power, it preserves the beauty of the universe" (p. 90). Even "though a man or a fallen angel is unwilling to submit to the divine will and plan, still he cannot escape it; for if he wants to escape the dominion of the will that commands, he rushes under the dominion of the will that punishes. . . . If divine wisdom did not impose these sanctions where wickedness tries to disturb right order, there would arise in the very universe which God has to keep in order, a certain deformity from the violation of the beauty of order, and God would seem to be deficient in His providence . . . it is necessary that satisfaction or punishment follow every sin" (p. 91).

81. See here Wilhelm Pauck's "Introduction" to the early Luther's *Lectures on Romans*: Luther "regarded the piety which underlay this [Scholastic] theology as an irreligious affectation of religion (to use Calvin's phrase), because it was marked, he felt, by a concern for eternal happiness reflecting man's love of God for his own sake, not for God's sake. Luther calls this way of loving God through which men seek eternal bliss *amor concupiscentiae*, i.e. a covetous or selfish love." *Luther: Lecture on Romans*, trans. Wilhelm Pauck (Philadelphia: Westminster, 1961), p. lv.

82. Anselm, *Why*, pp. 85, 105.

creation. "Let the SS man die unshriven. Let him go to hell. Sooner the fly [buzzing the corpse] to God than he" (Cynthia Ozick).[83] Any such forgiveness by fiat simply rends further the moral fabric of things, aping the sin which it supposedly forgives. In this connection Anselm's theology of atonement, economic metaphor and all, is the original protest against *cheap* grace; grace is free to us, he argues, only because of its *dear* cost to God.[84]

At this juncture in Anselm's deliberations, Anselm's partner in conversation, Boso, is led to despair at the thought of the sinner repairing the violated relation to the Creator: "Nothing is more just, yet nothing is more impossible. But out of all this, the mercy of God and the hope of man seem to vanish, so far as the happiness for which man was created is concerned."[85] This very despair of Boso is not different in kind from what the early prophet Luther with his Augustinian railings against *securitas* sought to induce. They share a common root in Augustine's exposure of the spiritual root of idolatry in using God for human purposes rather than surrendering to God for service in God's purposes. Just like Luther, Anselm aims to necessitate Christ: "man can be saved through Christ, or else let them despair of being saved at all."[86] Seeing their true need, people are turned to Jesus' voluntary suffering to find again the mercy of God and the hope of guilty and indebted humanity. Anselm is already aware of the objection current nowadays that his theory makes God guilty of "divine child abuse,"[87] as "if God so derives delight from, or has need of, the blood of the

83. Cited in Meir Y. Soloveichik, "The Virtue of Hate," *First Things* (February 2003).

84. Anselm, *Why*, p. 70. It is "not fitting for God to remit sin without punishing it" (p. 85), because then both the innocent and the guilty "will be in the same position before God" and so "make injustice resemble God" (p. 86). If "it is not fitting for God to do anything unjustly or inordinately, it does not pertain to His freedom or kindness or will to pardon without punishment a sinner who does not make recompense to God for what he took away" (p. 87). "It is impossible for God to be deprived of His honor. For either the sinner freely pays what he owes, or God takes it from him against his will . . . man, by sinning, plunders what belongs to God, so God, by punishing, takes away what belongs to man" (p. 89). "God cannot admit into happiness anyone who is bound in any way by the debt of sin, because it would not be right for Him" (p. 110). "We are speaking of that ultimate mercy by which He makes man happy after this life. That this happiness must not be granted to anyone except to one whose sins are totally forgiven, and that this forgiveness must not be granted except after payment of the debt which is due for sin in proportion to the magnitude of the sin . . ." (p. 115).

85. Anselm, *Why*, p. 112, cf. 115.

86. Anselm, *Why*, p. 116.

87. Ted Peters has a useful discussion of Anselm's teaching on "Jesus as Our Satisfac-

innocent, that He neither wishes nor is able to spare the guilty without the death of the innocent."[88] But for Anselm Christ is no child; He is the divine equal of the Father who sends Him: "from the instant this man begins to exist, He will always be replete with Divinity, as constituting His very self."[89] In sending the Son, the Father is motivated by his own faithfulness to his creation, and in obeying, the Son is motivated by the Father's own love for the helplessly indebted creature.[90]

All the same, Anselm has argued for the necessity of Christ's satisfaction from the side of human need, the debtor. It is impossible for debtors to render the compensation due:[91] "No one but God can make this satisfaction . . . but no one ought to make it but man . . . then it is necessary for a God-Man to make it."[92] Christ's *suffering* for Anselm is essentially *act,* self-oblation, supremely voluntary, an "unforced willingness": "God draws or moves him, when He confers this willingness . . . implying not any compulsion of violence, but a spontaneous and loving tenacity of the good will that has been received . . . [that] simple and genuine obedience when a rational nature maintains, not by necessity but freely, the willingness it has received from God."[93] Christ's suffering is the act of a moral agent "to preserve justice, in which He persevered so unwaveringly that He incurred

---

tion" in light of Luther's "Happy Exchange" in critical response to Feminist theological objections; see Ted Peters, *God — the World's Future: Systematic Theology for a New Era,* 2nd ed. (Minneapolis: Fortress, 2000), pp. 221-28.

88. Anselm, *Why,* p. 83.

89. Anselm, *Why,* p. 139.

90. "But when he voluntarily subjects himself to the necessity of doing good and does not merely endure it unwillingly, then surely, he deserves greater gratitude for his favor . . . he does it spontaneously . . . we must ascribe the whole work to His graciousness, because He began this for our sakes, not for His own, since He is not in need of anything. He was not unaware, surely, of what the future conduct of man was to be. . . . He freely obligated Himself. . . . He does this by the necessity of preserving His honor. . . ." Anselm, *Why,* p. 123. But "it is only in a less proper sense that we say God cannot do anything, or that He does it necessarily. In fact, all necessity and all impossibility are subject to His will, but His will is not subject to any necessity or impossibility . . ." (p. 150). So "he performs it by the free decision by which he committed himself to it" (p. 152). Thus Anselm employs the important distinction between antecedent and consequent necessity (p. 153): "all these things occurred by necessity because He willed them. But there was no necessity antecedent to His choice . . . no one took his life from Him, but He laid it down . . ." (p. 154).

91. Anselm, *Why,* p. 107. "What a great burden sin is" (p. 108); "a very dangerous condition" (p. 209); "when I give attention to what 'against the will of God' means . . ." (p. 140).

92. Anselm, *Why,* p. 124.

93. Anselm, *Why,* p. 81.

death as a result."[94] The result of these considerations then is Anselm's theological account of Christ's sacrifice as an active, not passive obedience: "This 'giving' then, must be understood in the sense that in some way this man will offer Himself or something belonging to Himself, to the honor of God, without being in debt to God";[95] thus the death on the cross is Christ's *sinless* self-offering. "He will not be obliged to die, because there will be no sin in Him." But "he commits himself to death for God's honor."[96] As such this unobligated self-offering is infinitely meritorious: "this man represents a good incomparably greater than the evil of all sins which His murder immeasurably surpasses . . . this life is more worthy of love than sins are deserving of hate . . . such a great good, so worthy of love, can suffice to make recompense for what is owed for the sins of the whole world . . . it can do infinitely more than suffice . . . this life overcomes all sins, if it is given for their remission. . . ."[97]

As noted, Lutheran Orthodoxy retained Anselm's active obedience: it is out of love for God and for sinners that Christ lives and finally goes sinlessly — so actively — to that Godforsaken death where, passive in death and grave, God laid on Him the sin of the world. In this way, thanks originally to Anselm, the whole life of Christ's obedience, not only the suffering on the cross, is taken into consideration and integrated, with the result that Christ's prophetic summons to discipleship also finds place as a true aspect or dimension of the morally repaired relation to God.[98] Lutheran Orthodoxy added to this, however, a notion from Luther that is missing in Anselm: that in and on account of this active love of obedience the innocent Christ became the representative of sinful humanity who suffered as such the wrath and rejection of God. It gets this idea from Luther, who got it from Paul, who got it from the second Isaiah. "For our sake he made him to be sin who knew no sin, so that in him we might become the righteousness of God" (2 Cor. 5:21; cf. Isa. 53). Admittedly, it comes as something of a surprise today to learn from this analysis that penal substitution never crossed Anselm's mind, and that it is *this lack* which Luther criticizes. Without the penal element, in other words, Anselm's notion of expiation,

94. Anselm, *Why*, p. 77, cf. 82.
95. Anselm, *Why*, p. 136.
96. Anselm, *Why*, p. 136.
97. Anselm, *Why*, p. 141.
98. Saarinen calls attention here to the "extensive collection" of Luther's 1530/32 sermons on the Sermon on the Mount, which Luther interprets as a "cleansing of the Decalogue" and "an ethic for Christians." "Pauline Luther," p. 75.

purchasing a treasury of merit of which sinners may avail themselves to still God's anger, could be used to underwrite the vulgar sale of indulgences or even the "sacrifice of the mass." Fundamentally, for Luther, God cannot be bribed, not even if God graciously provides the cash. It would, however, be no more just to blame Anselm for the use of his half-understood theology hundreds of years later in the time of Luther than to blame Luther for the understandings of his theology by later generations who have claimed his name. The solution is to understand clearly. On the other hand, it is perhaps just as surprising to learn that all contemporary summons to discipleship, like that in Dietrich Bonhoeffer's reading of the Sermon on the Mount, along with the corresponding protest against cheapened grace as the "Lutheran heresy," are *indebted,* as it were, to Anselm of Canterbury. This too must be clearly understood and acknowledged.

## Luther's Radicalism

It is the Roman Catholic theologian Hans Urs von Balthasar — virtually alone among modern interpreters so far as I can see — who grasps then the true "radicalism of Luther": "the Christology of 'substitution' strikes like a thunderbolt. It is as if Luther's thought, right from its very beginnings, was bent upon filling precisely the gap that patristic theology had left open in the *admirabile commercium.* His Christology follows the doctrine of the *pro nobis* to its ultimate, exclusive conclusion and here it is understood as exchange *(mirabilis mutatio, opus conversum, transmutatio, suavissimum commercium). . . .* No one could take 2 Cor. 5:21 more literally. . . ."[99] Von Balthasar succinctly captures Luther's fundamental intuition: "Sins 'lie' on Christ: this is something that must be taken seriously. In bearing the sin of the entire world, he, 'the sole just and holy man,' becomes simultaneously 'the sole, the greatest sinner on earth.' 'Christ is more damned and forsaken than all the saints . . . in all reality and truth, he submitted to God the Father's eternal damnation for us.' . . . 'Indeed he felt hell's punishment.'" Von Balthasar went on from this appreciative description of Luther's radicalism to make typical Roman Catholic criticisms of Luther's Christology: "this picture represents Christ's sin-

---

99. Hans Urs von Balthasar, *Theo-Drama: Theological Dramatic Theory, IV: The Action,* trans. G. Harrison (San Francisco: Ignatius, 1994), p. 284.

bearing, crucified humanity as purely passive in the dramatic process: it is the bait that is 'swallowed'; victory lies with the deity that, hidden from the devil, holds the 'fishing line.'"[100] Von Balthasar here attributes to Luther the *Christus Victor* motif, without asking how it is integrated in a new way with the admittedly central motif of the penal sufferer. Like many other (not only Roman Catholic) Western thinkers, he finds the "obscurities and illogicality of the Lutheran doctrine of the 'exchange'" betrayed when, "as a result of a fortunate 'non sequitur,' [Luther] cannot restrain himself from urging the believer actively to 'seize' and 'lay hold of' faith and the benefits it contains — which doubtless looks very much like something achieved by man."[101] Likewise, here, von Balthasar does not notice how the *imitatio Christi* of Abelard's moral influence doctrine is being integrated into a new whole. In any case, he concludes that "we can no longer tell whether man, who is both sinner and righteous, is one or two; we can no longer tell whether he is a subject enjoying continuity."[102] So the criticism of Luther's Cyrillian Christology is mirrored in criticism of Luther's theological anthropology, where grace seems to destroy nature rather than fulfill it. We will try to prune this thicket in Chapter Nine below.

From here von Balthasar went on to track the theological conception of penal suffering and vicarious substitution in the contemporary Protestant theologies of Barth, Moltmann, and Pannenberg and to consider the important criticisms of sacrifice in the work of the René Girard (on Girard, see further below). The early Pannenberg is singled out by von Balthasar as one in the tradition of Luther's theology who impressively understood and indeed advanced Luther's radicalism. Pannenberg asked whether satisfaction means that "no else has to die in the complete rejection in which Jesus died." The question is an interesting one. If expiation is rejected in principle in favor of propitiation, that is, if the idea of salvation as release from punishment by virtue of a substitute's payment of the debt is rejected, and if in contrast Christian salvation is understood to entail not escape from punishment but the gift of new life beyond it, then is Jesus as savior really little more than a pioneer? That is, is Jesus only the One who clears a path for us through the cross to the crown, as

---

100. Balthasar, *Theo-Drama*, p. 288.

101. Balthasar, *Theo-Drama*, rightly pointing to Luther's notion of the two kinds of righteousness.

102. Balthasar, *Theo-Drama*, p. 290.

the Letter to the Hebrews can seem to teach (Hebrews 12:1-3)? Pannenberg writes: "Jesus' death meant his exclusion from the community with the God whose coming Kingship he had proclaimed. He died as one expelled by the entire weight of the legitimate authority of the divine law, excluded from the nearness of the God in whose nearness he had known himself to be in a unique way the messenger of the imminent Kingdom of God." There is then uniqueness to Jesus' death as the One and only (as holy, the "righteous for the unrighteous") so abandoned by God. Consequently, Pannenberg contends, "no one else must die this death of eternal damnation, to the extent that he has community with Jesus. Whoever is bound up with Jesus no longer dies alone. . . ."[103] Jesus has thus conquered the eternal death; His believers are delivered from that wrath to come (1 Thess. 1:10). There was a terror of Godforsakenness unique to Jesus, not merely in that He knew eternal death in that moment, but chiefly in that He endured that death innocently as the representative of others, out of holy love then for those justly condemned. This love vindicated on the third day, no one else ever has to die alone. Dying together with Christ spiritually by baptism, they must die only in order to be made new and be made whole.

Such reflections as Pannenberg's led von Balthasar at length to Isaiah 53 and to the key question: "Why the Cross, if God forgives in any case?" It will not do to demythologize the "Old Testament picture of God so that he changes from a violent, wrathful God and becomes a powerless God who does not engage in retribution. . . . What is the relationship between God's love and his justice, particularly in the case of the Cross?" Von Balthasar takes up the "discovery" (here attributed to Girard and Schwager, but in reality going back to Luther) that "it is sins (not only the punishment due to sin) that are transferred, on the Cross. . . ." In spite then of rather hackneyed criticisms, it is just this difficult innovation of Luther on Christ as sin-bearer that leads von Balthasar forward to the "final elements of the drama of reconciliation."[104] The Orthodox theologian Sergei Bulgakov is summoned to testify: "'in a kind of *oboedientia passiva*'" (which, recall, von Balthasar now proves himself *inconsequently* to have criticized in Luther), Christ "allows himself to be placed under God's anger against sin. Thus he 'drinks the chalice' and is 'forsaken by God.'

---

103. Wolfhart Pannenberg, *Jesus: God and Man,* trans. Lewis L. Wilkins and Duane A. Priebe (Philadelphia: Westminster, 1975), p. 263.

104. Balthasar, *Theo-Drama,* p. 313.

Through this experience of sin[-bearing] he 'destroys' the 'reality' of sin that men have created. His suffering is hypostatic and, as such, its intensity is supra-temporal and, in that sense, eternal." Thus also "the Cross is an event involving the whole Trinity. . . ."[105] "Jesus by his obedient death takes over the guilty death that is our fate. This, and this alone, can undermine death from within and draw its sting. . . . The forsakenness that prevails between the Father and his crucified Son is deeper and more deadly than any forsakenness, temporal or eternal, actual or possible, that separates a creature from God. Every sin committed in the world is borne and atoned for on the Cross . . . it follows that the Cross must be erected at the end of hell, without being equated with the latter."[106] That is to affirm not only that "the Son dies 'because of sin' but at a deeper level he dies 'because of God,' because God has definitively rejected what cannot be reconciled with the divine nature."[107]

Von Balthasar's interpreter Edward T. Oakes comments that the thought just expressed is "absolutely crucial" to understanding von Balthasar and "perhaps constitutes his greatest single innovation to the tradition" — well, an innovation borrowed from Luther — namely, that Christ "was punished because it was the essential moment of his mission to take on the sins of the world, to be our representative, assume in our stead what was rightly our destiny: meaning not just death as a natural termination to organic life but death as a banishment from the presence of God (which is the real meaning of hell)."[108] "This unique death of Jesus is final, unsurpassable," von Balthasar concluded, citing Revelation 1:18: "Behold, I have the keys of death and Hades." Satan is defeated; the gates are opened, the prisoners may come forth.

For Luther, the descent into hell is at once the apex of Christ's passive obedience as the Lamb of God bearing away the sin of the world and at the

105. Balthasar, *Theo-Drama*, p. 314.
106. Balthasar, *Theo-Drama*, p. 495.
107. Balthasar, *Theo-Drama*, p. 496.
108. Edward T. Oakes, *Pattern of Redemption: The Theology of Hans Urs von Balthasar* (New York: Continuum, 2002), p. 237. But of course the thought originates in Luther from whom von Balthasar retrieves it, as he laconically notes: "Luther's radicalism found no direct disciples among the other reformers. Melanchthon's interpretation of the *commercium*, that is, grace as *imputatio*, by no means expresses Luther's original intuition. However, another side of his theology of the 'exchange' does continue to exert an influence, although it was not his discovery but was known before his time. This is his teaching on Christ's penal suffering on our behalf (or his experience of hell)." *Theo-Drama*, p. 291.

same time the beginning of His royal rule as the coming judge and king of all creation. In the sense of Romans 8:31-39, then, there is no hell, no Godforsakenness, nothing in all creation that can separate us from the love of God in Jesus Christ. For in Christ, God has surpassed God in order to gain us all, consigned all to sin to have mercy on all. Just as Christ the King now entrusts this preaching of His victory for all perishing creatures to the church, He does not abandon or limit it to the church, which is the servant of the gospel, not its master.

This *potential* universalism, on the other hand, does not imply, as it may in von Balthasar's or Barth's theology, coercive salvation. For Barth, it is in the office of king and judge of creation that the love of Christ appears as something inevitably triumphant.[109] Among other paradoxes that result, this seems to make conversion to divine mercy finally unavoidable.[110] Against this I would argue that there remains the final possibility of remaining reprobate, since the universality of Christ's atoning love both in its breadth and in its depth consists in his priestly act of *offering,* not in the royal act of *commanding* (and the Spirit's work of *motivating,* not forcing). Christ enters hell to defeat Satan, to rob him of his right by wresting the law of God from his grip, by both the right and the power of His fulfillment of the commandment of love on behalf of the unlovable, which love the Father has now owned. Just so, Christ the Victor opens hell and victoriously leads its denizens forth. He commands the traumatized to stand up and walk. Yet even on this Exodus some may still hanker after the fleshpots of Egypt. Pharaoh himself is not reconciled but eternally condemned, "horse and rider thrown into the sea." History matters. The gospel of Jesus Christ is not a supernatural comedy. The Spirit is not impersonal force. Those may be forever lost, that is to say, who in full awareness and provided every motivation to the contrary prefer to hold on to their willful existence as to their own greatest love, as the personal substance activated in a once-and-for-all historical biography. It would be for them too much to let go of this identity of their own making in order to be redeemed by Another, whose history for them must prevail over them.[111] Not the trauma-

---

109. G. C. Berkouwer, *The Triumph of Grace in the Theology of Karl Barth,* trans. Harry R. Boer (Grand Rapids: Eerdmans, 1956).

110. For this critique of Barth, see *Paths Not Taken,* pp. 112-26.

111. So Luther: "The damned are tortured because they are not willing to be damned, nor resign themselves to this will of God." WA 56, 391, cited in Dietmar Lage, *Martin Luther's Christology and Ethics: Texts and Studies in Religion,* vol. 45 (Lewiston, Queenston, Lampeter: Edwin Mellen Press, 1990), p. 60.

tized, but the mighty He has cast down from their thrones; not the starving poor, but the rich He has sent empty away.

History is in any event far larger than we can visibly see. The same early Pannenberg wrote that the "concept of Jesus' descent into hell, of his preaching in the realm of the dead affirms . . . that men outside the visible church are not automatically excluded from salvation."[112] The church is not the fullness of the Beloved Community, but the bearer of its promise in the travail of human history and its partial, often deeply obscured, and always contested realization. Many beyond its visible walls may also be liberated in surrendering to the victorious Lamb of God — or not. That is what is at stake in history, even history expanded by the revelation of its depth in the descent of Christ into hell — how much more "reality" can we accord "this world" of *becoming*, the *history* that we *are?* Would not even Nietzsche have to agree?

## But Is It Real?

Nietzsche would not, of course, grant a certain premise of the foregoing Christian-theological interpretation of the reality of the wrath of the gods, and so the possibility of resolution of wrath by the self-sacrifice of the divine-and-human Christ. As we have seen, he would not deny the reality of the wrath of the gods. Indeed, he would celebrate it as a sign of life. But he would deny that gift is really possible, that a self-sacrifice can be real, in his own words from the epigraph to this chapter, that a "creditor sacrifices himself for his debtor, out of love . . . for his debtor." He asked, as if the answer were self-evident: "Can one credit that?" Jacques Derrida has contributed a probing reflection on Nietzsche's final question here, as if it were genuine, not rhetorical, in *The Gift of Death.* This study traces the notion of total sacrifice to God ("the gift of death") from the classic biblical tale of the "binding of Isaac," as parsed by Kierkegaard's *Fear and Trembling,* on to Derrida's own searching meditation on the Sermon on the Mount's Father in heaven who "sees in secret" and "rewards in secret." Briefly put, the outcome is that the true sacrifice of the entire self to God is the absolute sacrifice that renounces all remuneration, and in just this way, breaks free of the economy of calculation, reciprocity, and revenge, as in the early Luther's *odium sui* and *resignatio ad infernum.* Yet does one pay just this monstrous

---

112. Pannenberg, *Jesus: God and Man,* p. 272.

sacrifice, Derrida finally asks, if calculating on one's little secret, that is, the God who sees and knows in secret and just so guarantees repayment in a new key, on a higher order? Isn't this Pascalian wager the same old cruelty in a new key? "The moment the gift, however generous it be, is infected with the slightest hint of calculation, the moment it takes account of knowledge or recognition, it falls within the ambit of an economy: it exchanges, in short it gives counterfeit money, since it gives in exchange for payment. . . . This knowledge at the same time founds and destroys the Christian concept of responsibility and justice. . . ."[113] Perhaps, if all we have to go on is the theology of Matthew. But even as we move on to Paul or John, Nietzsche expressed astonishment at that "stroke of genius" of God surpassing God, as I have termed it in this chapter, the *Selbstaufhebung der Gerechtigkeit,* in Nietzsche's words, into grace as new creative possibility *Jenseits des Rechts, deus supra legem.* Derrida is not quite fooled, however, by Nietzsche's indignant rhetoric. In conclusion, he asks instead about "the reversal and infinitization that confers on God . . . the responsibility for that which remains more secret than ever, the irreducible experience of belief. . . ."[114] Derrida leaves the question dangling, but I take these final words to indicate the possibility that the "stroke of genius" may not be Christianity's but rather of the One designated in the ecstasy of faith by the word, God, as narrated.[115]

It is the question of this book: Can we be creedal Christians, i.e., those thinking that "for us and for our salvation, He came down from heaven . . . ," and still take responsibility for our little faith? Thinking that economy is both satisfied and surpassed in the economic metaphor of Luther's "joyful exchange"? Thinking otherwise, of course, Nietzsche demanded a genealogy of sacrifice, that is to say, a non-religious explanation of the ubiquitous phenomenon of religion. In this very attempt to grab Christianity by the throat, however, Nietzsche advances our thinking to a profounder conception of the phenomenon of religion. The notion of sacrifice is at the heart of things, naturally enough as Nietzsche thinks, to fend off the wrath of the gods, or, what is the same, to assert ourselves as gods by taking charge of the gods with our bribes. Interestingly, this take on the essence of religion as sacrifice could be confirmed theologically by the po-

---

113. Jacques Derrida, *The Gift of Death,* trans. David Wills (Chicago and London: University of Chicago Press, 1995), pp. 111-12.

114. Derrida, *The Gift,* p. 115.

115. Thus, turning against Derrida's apophatic turning against Christian kataphaticism, as in Derrida, *The Gift,* p. 108.

lemic of early Christian fathers against pagan sacrifice, as also of Martin Luther against what he regarded as relapse into that pagan sacrifice, the so-called "sacrifice of the mass." Because both the fathers and Luther held to the *ephapax* nature of Christ's divine self-sacrifice for us, in the sense of pure gift, and so exclusively, they held against our sacrifice to the gods, even if only by means of the symbol, the scapegoat: they knew this covert titanism at the heart of the phenomenon of religion. Both argued then in complex ways (befitting a complex reality!) that the once-for-all sacrifice of Christ canceled, corrected, and/or fulfilled the sacrifices of the nations. Sacrifice demarcated the field of battle. The *Christus Victor* mythology of Christ at war with the contra-divine powers now comes down to earth as the historical reality of the gospel's contention against sacrifice. Neo-orthodoxy sustained this polemic of the gospel against "religion" as the "idolatrous" attempt to grasp God in human symbols; but it is too shallow an understanding of the problem, more Platonic and Kantian, really, than prophetic. As Luther urged against Karlstadt, it is not the outward image or the external word that is an idol, but the inward images that serve the worship of human works as levers with which to move heaven and earth.[116] The heart of idolatry is not the image as such but the sacrifice it demands and enables.

Richard J. Mouw has drawn the right moral from this for Christian theology: "We do not have to — we *ought* not to — imitate Jesus' approach to dying. His suffering is in significant ways inimitable, because he bore the wrath of our cursed existence precisely in order that we do not have to suffer under that wrath."[117] Yet René Girard has argued that there "is a unity that underlies not only all mythologies and rituals but the whole of human culture, and this unity of unities depends on a single mechanism, continually functioning because perpetually misunderstood — the mechanism that assures the community's spontaneous and unanimous outburst of opposition to the surrogate victim"[118] — the scapegoat. Girard's analysis exposes a deep and broad mystification of violence that seemingly perpetuates a vicious syndrome of unconscious revenge-taking. When we think of attacks on Jews as "Christ-killers," for notorious historical example, it

116. "Against the Heavenly Prophets."

117. Richard J. Mouw, "Violence and the Atonement," chap. 10 in *Must Christianity Be Violent? Reflections on History, Practice and Theology*, ed. Kenneth R. Chase and Alan Jacobs (Grand Rapids: Brazos, 2003), p. 170.

118. René Girard, *Violence and the Sacred*, trans. Patrick Gregory (Baltimore: Johns Hopkins University Press, 1979), p. 301.

seems obvious that Mouw's "ought" is in no little tension with Girard's "is": perhaps Christianity's sacrifice of the Son of God for the life of the world is the quintessential mystification of the scapegoat mechanism. Nietzsche's genealogy of religion can be read this way. He famously reduced (at least in his positivist period) everything to the Hobbsean natural law of self-preservation, Spinoza's *conatus,* or, in his own famous retitling of classical entelechy, the will-to-power. What appears religiously then as gift in Christianity, as divine self-sacrifice, is only appearance, no matter how mesmerizing appearance can be, especially in the symbols and rites of the Mass. But if we reduce these appearances to the underlying power relations — aspirations and frustrations, cunning stratagems and desperate follies — we see what is really going on in the world where the Christian God has died (culturally) and does not (never did) exist (in reality). Given that non-existence, we see that "the wrath of God" is invented by the same will-to-power — albeit of those less powerful in the world, the slaves — to snare the consciences of the strong, the nobles. We see likewise the self-sacrifice of the Son of God exposed as an "expedient," a "stroke of genius" to console the snared consciences. And we see further, that in the process of enjoying such "temporary relief," the snared conscience is obligated anew, of all things, from *within,* by *gratitude.* What we see is that the apparent divine gift always turns out to have strings attached. An imaginary solution to an imaginary problem, to be sure, but real in its own cunning way of irrepressible will-to-power.

In a classic exercise of Durkheimian sociology Girard took up Nietzsche's challenge to understand what really transpires under the cloak of religion by means of a penetrating study of Greek tragedy. The Nietzschean nature of this genealogical project in *Violence and the Sacred* may not be immediately evident on account of Girard's manifest humanist concerns (and later, liberal Protestant Christian sympathies): he tells us explicitly that he is not interested in theological debates about the death of God and/or the death of man because they "draw a veil over the subject of vengeance, which threatens to become quite real once again, in the form not of a philosophical debate but of unlimited violence, in a world with no absolute values." We today have desperately, in other words, to catch up with the loss of the "essential quality of transcendence" by which functional religion with its mystified, ritualized sacrifice at the religious heart of cultural life once was able to "define the legitimate form of violence and to recognize it among the multitude of illegitimate forms." But lacking today that essential quality of transcendence, traditional religion is no longer functional, even though the social needs it filled remain — and will *demand* their *satisfaction*. Consequently things are unraveling. Contemporary culture can no longer parse the difference on which civilized life depends, "the fundamental difference between sacrifice and revenge, between a judicial system and vengeance." Discrimination between legitimate and illegitimate forms of violence becomes "a matter of mere opinion, with each man free to reach his own decision." This explains the agonizing paradox of contemporary life, that "demystification leads to constantly increasing violence, a violence perhaps less 'hypocritical' than the violence it seeks to expose, but more energetic, more virulent, and the harbinger of something far worse — a violence that knows no bounds."[119] *Such* is the problem that *Violence and the Sacred* sets out to solve — if the moral concern is not very Nietzschean, the diagnosis is.

The details of Girard's exceedingly interesting and rich account need not detain us here. What I wish to underscore is the warning about the reality, psycho-sociologically considered, of the wrath of the gods. For Girard, the illusion of enlightened thought is that religion is or was simply illusion, when in reality religion has always been dealing with the imminent threat of catastrophic outbreaks of fury, rage, and blind vengeance. This ever-imminent threat is what has necessitated ubiquitous rites of sacrifice. "Any phenomenon associated with the acts of remembering, commemorating, and perpetuating a unanimity that springs from the murder of a surrogate victim can be termed 'religious.'"[120] Sacrifice is a mechanism for objectifying, externalizing, and expelling the threat of the *bellum omnes contra omnem* by fixing it on a victim. If we regard sacrifice in the self-congratulatory manner of "modern thinkers" who "continue to see religion as an isolated, wholly fictitious phenomenon cherished only by a few backwards peoples or milieus[,]" we blindly "project upon religion alone the responsibility for a violent projection of violence that truly pertains to all societies *including our own*."[121] Girard is speaking of course of Hitler, Hiroshima, and Stalin — signifying those technologically sublime descents of the *novus ordo seclorum* into the fury of "reciprocal violence," making the crimes of Crusade and Inquisition child's play in comparison. But "we, the spoiled children of privilege, consider the god's anger as something illusory. It is in fact a terrible reality. Its justice is implacable, its

---

119. Girard, *Violence*, p. 24.
120. Girard, *Violence*, p. 315.
121. Girard, *Violence*, p. 317.

impartiality truly divine."[122] The wrath is real. The description matches Luther's to the tee: "God hidden in majesty neither deplores nor takes away death, but works life, death and all in all. . . ."[123]

To be sure, it a legitimate question here whether in this way pagan notions of the wrath of the gods sneak into Christian theology by the back door, or whether Christian theology correctly interprets in this Girardian way the professed tragedy of pagan existence. "Oh Theseus, dear friend, only the gods can never age, the gods can never die. All else in the world almighty Time obliterates, crushes all to nothing. The earth's strength wastes away, the strength of a man's body wastes and dies, faith dies and bad faith comes to life, and the same wind of friendship cannot blow forever, holding steady and strong between two friends, much less between two cities. For some of us soon, for others later, joy turns to hate and back again to love . . . infinite Time, sweeping through its rounds gives birth to infinite nights and days. . . ."[124] The nemesis of almighty Time — what *do* we make of it theologically? It is in any case a sign of how alienated contemporary theologians are from any deep understanding of their own traditions that so many rushed into simplistic, non-tragic, morally optimistic readings of Girard, as if it backed up liberal Protestant critiques of the crude, bloody atonement theology of medieval Catholics or contemporary fundamentalists. The exception to this shallow trendiness was the penetrating Augustinian, indeed *Anselmian* account that John Milbank made of Girard in *Theology and Social Theory.*

Milbank exposed the Hobbsean script in the background of Girard's tragic view of origins[125] as well as the "positivism" of *any* analysis of religion by "rigorous social science" pretending at last "to decipher religion and so unlock the secrets of human culture as a whole."[126] This is in accord with the tenor of Milbank's entire book: theologians cannot defer to methodologically atheistic accounts of reality without giving away the store. But chiefly, and what is of special interest here, Milbank takes on a certain re-

---

122. Girard, *Violence,* p. 259.

123. Luther, *Bondage,* p. 170.

124. "Oedipus at Colonus" (lines 685-700), in *Sophocles: The Three Theban Plays,* trans. Robert Fagles (London: Penguin, 1984), p. 322.

125. On Hobbes, see further Paul R. Hinlicky, "Luther and Liberalism," in *A Report from the Front Lines: Conversations on Public Theology. A Festschrift in Honor of Robert Benne,* ed. Michael Shahan (Grand Rapids: Eerdmans, 2009), pp. 89-104.

126. John Milbank, *Theology and Social Theory: Beyond Secular Reason* (Oxford: Blackwell, 1997), p. 393.

reading of Christianity in the light of *Violence and the Sacred* (beginning with the later Girard himself). In this (liberal Protestant) reading, we discover a non-sacrificial Jesus who refuses mimetic rivalry (i.e., infinite, insatiable envy), and thus also violence. But such a Jesus, says Milbank, is no more than a "unique individual," not a "positive, alternative practice, but only a negative refusal."[127] With this critique of too shallow a take on the theological implications of Girard's discovery of the uncanny reality of the wrath of the gods, and therewith the urgent need of sacrifice to stave off outbreaks of blind, catastrophic violence, Milbank argues a rehabilitation of Anselmian theology along the lines of the preceding account of Christ's active obedience, Christ's self-oblation. "Anselm argued (in essence) that only God himself, free from the blindness of sin, could fully 'suffer sin,' and so make an offering to God, or a return of love fully commensurate with the ontological gulf caused by sin, and therefore able to cancel it out." Understood in this way, the "'shape' of Jesus' life and death [is] of the type of an exemplary practice which we can imitate and which can form the context for our lives together, so that we can call ourselves the 'body of Christ.'"[128] That is to say, the Anselmian Christ enables us to refuse the usually mystified sacrifice of others to save ourselves by providing participation in His own self-sacrifice of love for others. In this way, we do not fend off a threatened outbreak of rage and revenge, misunderstood as supernatural wrath; rather we protest such rage and revenge, identify it as the self-punishment sin brings on itself, and manifest socially the alternative society of Christ with His church, "bearing one another's burdens" as our own form of self-sacrifice in union with His. This alternative praxis would represent, of course, the ethics of Luther's "joyful exchange."

In light of what I have argued above, Milbank's claim for Anselm here must be judged imprecise, i.e., the strong theological idea of "suffering sin," "bearing the burdens of others, even of our accusers," is not found in Anselm. The notion of Christ as the sin-bearer is *Luther's* retrieval and revision of this theology of atonement.[129] In any event, what ought to fol-

---

127. Milbank, *Theology and Social Theory,* p. 395.

128. Milbank, *Theology and Social Theory,* p. 396.

129. The point would be trivial, if Milbank did not begin to lose grip on his Augustinianism at just this juncture in the argument of this grand book. Invoking John Scotus Eriugena, Milbank finally argues that God does not punish sin because "God is not in time, and he only knows sin as it happens, in terms of its negative effects. He does not will to punish sin, because punishment is not the act of a real nature upon another nature, and God always remains within his nature. Punishment is ontologically 'self-inflicted,' the only punishment is the delete-

low from Girard's discoveries about the nature of sacrifice, according to Milbank, is a vigorous retrieval of the dramatic distinction between the two Cities, between the self-giver who is Christ with His church, and the other-sacrificers, those scapegoaters "who know not what they do." This provisional division of the two Cities follows from the reality of the "wrath of the gods," and its overcoming by the alternative praxis of the God-man with all who follow Him. If we add Luther to this, those who follow Him are always first of all those whom He has found, in the hell they share with all the other sacrificers of others.

If this is right, one will be first the sinner for whom Christ lived, died, and reigns forever or not. This real alternative between the two societies is dramatized for us in Luke's account of the two thieves crucified with Christ in Luke 23:39-42. "One of the criminals who were hanged there kept deriding him and saying, 'Are you not the Messiah? Save yourself and us!' But the other rebuked him, saying, 'Do you not fear God, since you are under the same sentence of condemnation? And we indeed have been condemned justly, for we are getting what we deserve for our deeds, but this man has done nothing wrong.' Then he said, 'Jesus, remember me when you come into your kingdom. He replied, 'Truly I tell you, today you will be with me in Paradise.'" In this climactic Lucan episode, Jesus already reigns from the cross, already able to assure inclusion of those who surrender by faith to His merciful reign. In this division, then, we have an answer to Nietzsche's complaint against the notion of the triumphant love of God for the enemy — impressive even to him — as an "imaginary solution to an imaginary problem." If the wrath of God is as real as dikes collapsing before the threatening surge of mutual recrimination and vengeance, the overcoming of wrath is as real on this earth as this foretaste of Beloved Community, that is, when the society of the church is experienced as the bearer of the story of Christ's saving deed of righteousness, which was His passion, that singular act of creative agape making good out of evil by enduring that evil as His own, there to seize fast the evildoer and reconcile just this one, if only she will come into this truth by telling the truth of what now has transpired.

rious effect of sin itself upon nature, and the torment of knowing reality only in terms of one's estrangement from it." Milbank, *Theology and Social Theory,* p. 420. In *Paths Not Taken,* I have argued for the theological insufficiency of a purely privative view of evil and in favor of actual evil, hence evil that is also finally actually punished. Milbank claims here that "Eriugena's improvement of Augustine's ontology of evil [may also be read as] a critical modification of 'political Augustinianism'" (p. 420). I am not convinced of improvement on either score.

Despite the ". . . fundamental identity between Christ's lordship and the Church with regard to their temporal nature," however, "the area covered by Christ's lordship" — that is to say, the reach of the Beloved Community — exceeds the visible boundaries of the church's witness to include all of creation. "Christ rules also over the invisible powers which stand behind empirical institutions"[130] — even those that "do not necessarily know the role assigned to them within his lordship."[131] Christians consequently may in good conscience (Rom. 13:5!) live also in the world as citizens, not of Augustine's two cities (for no one can serve both God and the devil), but of Luther's two kingdoms (for one can serve God in both church and state), therefore even obey the state (except when it "abandons its proper role and deifies itself[,]")[132] knowing with Luther that law apart from mercy is tyranny and with Augustine that apart from justice the state is organized crime. In this tension mortals can live really on the earth, until Christ at last comes as king of creation to resolve forever the conflict of good and evil. Just so, the interim "solution" of the "forgiveness of sins" is no more *imaginary* than the wrath revealed from heaven, provided we look for it where it is to be found, in broken bread and wine poured out: the Sacrifice that ends all sacrifice but the sacrifice of praise.

130. Oscar Cullmann, *The Christology of the New Testament,* trans. Shirley C. Guthrie and Charles A. M. Hall (London: SCM Press, 1963), p. 227.

131. Cullmann, *The Christology,* p. 230.

132. Cullmann, *The Christology.* This notation, of course, indicates disagreement with Milbank on political theology; see below, Chapter Nine.

# CHAPTER FOUR

# Trinitarian Advent: Resituating the Dialectic of Law and Gospel

*God's grace runs into our hatred of grace. But this is the proper work of grace, that his eternal Word — by his becoming flesh, by his remaining obedient in the flesh, by his suffering punishment and therefore dying, because of this obedience — undertook to give the saving answer in our place, to expose our human autocracy and godlessness, to confess man's lostness, to acknowledge the justice of God's judgment against us, and thus to accept the grace of God. This is what Jesus Christ did for us during his whole lifetime on earth, but especially at its end. . . . He quite simply believed* (pistos Iesou *in Romans 3:22; Galatians 2:16, etc. should certainly be translated as a subjective genitive!). And in this faith he bore our punishment — not first of all, for instance, to give us an example (he certainly also did that!), but first of all and above all representatively. This is God's grace: that our humanity is, insofar as it is ours, not only condemned and lost because of our sins (our perpetually new sins!), but at the same time, insofar as it is the humanity of Jesus Christ, it is justified by God and accepted in the judgment and in the lostness because Jesus Christ — only the eternal Word of God could do this — believed, i.e., he said not "no" but "yes" to grace and thus to man's state of being judged and lost. But this justification and acceptance of our humanity is really accomplished in the resurrection of Jesus Christ from the dead.*

Barth[1]

1. Karl Barth, "Gospel and Law," in *Community, State and Church* (Garden City, NY: Doubleday, 1960), pp. 74-75.

## The Faith of Jesus

The unsuspecting reader might imagine the epigraph to come from the pen of a theologian in Luther's tradition, perhaps even from the Reformer himself. For the argument is to be found everywhere in Luther that faith which glories in God's favor in spite of unworthiness treats God as the Giver of all good gifts and so fulfills the First Commandment.[2] As Luther put it in summing up a central argument in the Reformation treatise, *On the Freedom of the Christian:* "This is what the promises of God provide: what the commandments demand; they fulfill what the commandments demand, so that everything is from God himself, both commandment and fulfillment. He alone commands; he alone also fulfills."[3] What could be more Luther-like, then, than to trace this fulfilling of the law on our behalf to Jesus, to His own "obedience of faith," and so to underline that our believing, such as it is, does not justify as a religious work that we perform,[4] but rather as the Spirit-wrought participation in Jesus' own faith as first and ever the beneficiaries of His faithfulness? At least one Luther scholar (other than and before the Mannermaa school) detected just that reasoning in Luther's description of justifying faith as *fides Christo formata,* "faith is nothing other than Christ living and acting in the believer."[5] It is striking that my teacher, David Lotz, came to this interpretation in the process of disentangling a Melanchthonized Luther from his ambiguous reception by

2. Admittedly Luther does not agree grammatically-exegetically with Barth's rendering of *pistos Iesou*, but the passage in which he urges taking the expression as an objective genitive, i.e., faith directed to Jesus as its object, Luther nevertheless substantively exposits faith as the same daring confidence in God's grace, the faith that Barth grounds in Jesus himself. Luther, *The Bondage of the Will*, trans. J. I. Packer and O. R. Johnston (Westwood, NJ: Fleming Revell, 2000), p. 291. Luther would have understood this faith as the obedience of Jesus in his true, spiritual sufferings.

3. Cited from Oswald Bayer, *Martin Luther's Theology: A Contemporary Interpretation,* trans. Thomas H. Trapp (Grand Rapids: Eerdmans, 2007), p. 60. To be sure, Bayer hastens to fend off Barth, as he understands Barth, lest Luther's words be taken to mean merging law and gospel into "a third Word — to describe something like a self-revelation of God" (p. 61).

4. Barth mocks faith as a good work, which turns Jesus Christ into the "indispensable companion, the useful lever arm . . . the personification of the wonderful ideas . . . the great creditor who again and again is just good enough to cover the cost of our ventures in righteousness." Barth, "Gospel and Law," p. 90. Here "the offense, the saving offense of the cross, has been removed." Barth, "Gospel and Law," p. 91.

5. David Lotz, *Luther and Ritschl: A Fresh Perspective on Albrecht Ritschl's Theology in the Light of His Luther Study* (Nashville: Abingdon, 1974), p. 130.

the Ritschl school. "Thus Ritschl also posed those sterile choices which ever since have led to repeated controversies and a polarization of viewpoints in Luther research: in the matter of justification one must supposedly opt for either imputed righteousness or infused righteousness; either God's forensic sentence outside us *(extra nos)* or his sanative process within us *(in nobis):* either the 'for Christ's sake' or the 'in view of the new obedience.' Luther himself would not have recognized these options as mutually exclusive. His theology of the real presence of Christ, effected in the believer by the Spirit through faith in the living Word, held together what his interpreters have not infrequently put asunder."[6] I think that it is safe to say that in 1974 Lotz had not been "corrupted" either by the ecumenical dialogues or by reading Mannermaa!

In fact, the words cited in the epigraph above come from the pen of the Swiss Reformed theologian, Karl Barth, in a polemical tract, *Gospel and Law,* that was aimed, fired, and almost hit a traditional shibboleth of Lutheran theology, *Law and Gospel* — in *that* order! The questions are subtle, but in spirit Barth arguably stands in the tradition of theology stemming from Luther, as George Hunsinger has argued,[7] while much that has passed as "Lutheran" through the centuries stems equally from Melanchthon (although "according to the letter," as I have argued elsewhere, Barth's theological positions resemble neither Luther's nor Calvin's so much as Melanchthon's).[8] It is not my purpose here to sort out shifting school- and party-allegiances, but to tackle a matter of deep and debilitating confusion in Protestant theology, intimated in the feisty quote from Barth: the right relationship of law and gospel. Since the Holocaust of European Jewry at the hands of the Nazis, and with increased sensitivity of the contribution to this horror made by Christian anti-Judaism,[9] the theological problem of the status of the law in Christian theology has become a question of no lit-

---

6. Lotz, *Luther and Ritschl,* p. 136.

7. George Hunsinger, *Disruptive Grace: Studies in the Theology of Karl Barth* (Grand Rapids: Eerdmans, 2000), pp. 279-304.

8. Paul Hinlicky, *Paths Not Taken: Theology from Luther through Leibniz* (Grand Rapids: Eerdmans, 2009), pp. 170-76.

9. I have found most instructive: Richard Steigmann-Gall, *The Holy Reich: Nazi Conceptions of Christianity* (Cambridge: Cambridge University Press, 2003); Doris L. Bergen, *Twisted Cross: The German Christian Movement in the Third Reich* (Chapel Hill: University of North Carolina Press, 1996); Susannah Heschel, *The Aryan Jesus: Christian Theologians and the Bible in Nazi Germany* (Princeton: Princeton University Press, 2008); and *German Churches and the Holocaust,* ed. Robert P. Ericksen and Susannah Heschel (Minneapolis: Fortress, 1999).

tle urgency.[10] We will deal with this question directly in Chapter Six. Within the life of the church as prolepsis of the Beloved Community (so we concluded the preceding chapter), the theological question about the law and its relation to the Christian message of gracious justification for Christ's sake is perennially urgent (as the original dispute in Galatia over table-fellowship indicated). It is perhaps too easy to ask whether the church is to be either a hospital for sinners or a sanctuary of the saints, since rightly understood it is to be both. But right understanding of a paradox like *simul iustus et peccator* does not come easy.[11]

With his striking translation of the Greek *pistos Iesou* as Jesus' own faith, representing us who do not believe, to tell of the one righteous man who in our godless place nevertheless believed in God's merciful acceptance, Barth sought to retrieve that crucial argument of Martin Luther which had been forgotten, if not actually suppressed within Lutheranism: justifying faith is the electing Spirit's rapture by which the newborn believer gives to God the glory which is God's, and so begins to give to the neighbor the love which befits the creature of this God.[12] So faith comes to fulfill the ethical intention of the holy law of God; simultaneously faith liberates from the same law's curse upon the faithless, loveless, hopeless human being sold under the power of sin. Barth applied this idea of faith concretely and originally to Christ who believed for us.[13] As *His* faith in God and faithfulness to sinners is the true fulfillment of the law, the faith of Jesus is the gracious reason why faith in Him puts the sinner right with God and why such faith now alive to God springs into action in the form of new obedience.

10. See Hinlicky, "A Lutheran Contribution to the Theology of Judaism," *Journal of Ecumenical Studies* 31, nos. 1-2 (Winter-Spring 1994): 123-52.

11. Nor is it clear that this paradox ever went much further than its early formulations by Luther, who by the time of the Antinomian controversy is learning to say that progress in good works is necessary. See the discussion of *fides abstracta* and *fides incarnata* below in Chapter Nine.

12. As in the *Preface to the Epistle to the Romans* (1546, revised from 1522) LW 35:365-80. See also the "Disputation concerning Faith and Law" (1535) LW 34:105-32.

13. Maybe *exclusively* to Christ. Bruce McCormack is probably right to read Barth's own version of the doctrine of justification as extreme and consistent extrinsicism. That is McCormack's own position. Bruce McCormack, "What's at Stake in Current Debates over Justification: The Crisis of Protestantism in the West," in *Justification: What's at Stake in the Current Debates*, ed. Mark Husbands and Daniel Treier (Downers Grove: InterVarsity; Leicester, UK: Apollos, 2004), p. 95. In Luther, it is no stretch to say with Lotz that it is the Crucified and Risen Jesus who believes in us.

But is this Luther? None other than Oswald Bayer has impressively shown in this connection that what matters is the "enduring systematic meaning of Luther's distinction" between the form of God's Word which demands and exposes, and the form of God's Word which promises and clothes.[14] If I read Bayer rightly here, one must then be cautious about a blind defense of the traditional Lutheran (really, psychologizing, Melanchthonian) sequence law and gospel (i.e., first terrorizing law, then consoling gospel), lest manipulative preaching imply that the gospel is but an "accessory of the law," and in this way in fact take "priority over the gospel."[15] That could happen if the precedence of the law meant that it defined the problem on its own terms. Then the gospel becomes nothing but an answer to a question posed by the law. This occurs not infrequently in evangelical churches. The law demands perfect works, so it is said. The gospel mercifully provides one work that compensates for all the missing others, the decision to accept Christ. Not only does the legalistic scheme stay in force in this understanding, but the gospel reduces to a good deal, and faith in Christ, in effect, becomes a tawdry bribe. But this was not the intent of the traditional sequence of law and gospel, according to Bayer; it was rather meant to indicate a *universal, juridical fact,* i.e., that before the coming of the gospel as news, "the law, as it functions, is there already determining human existence."[16] This is as much as to say with Girard, as we have interpreted him in the last chapter, that a *lex talionis,* a nemesis, a karma, a *deus absconditus,* the Pauline *stoicheia tou kosmou* operates juridically, universally, fatefully, fatally before the news of Christ comes on the scene and is revealed (so Gal. 3:23). In that sequence, then, the gospel brings in and brings about God's promise in Christ: "I am yours and you are mine." Ethics, or rather, the new obedience follows from this divine initiative of grace and does not precede it. A concession to Barth here is not explicit; Bayer does not name names. Yet substantively he lifts up Luther's conviction that "the preamble of the Decalogue — God's self-introduction and self-communication — is pure gospel. In the same way, the threat of death (Gen. 2:17) can really be understood only in relation to the preceding promise of life and free provision of gifts (Gen. 2:16)."[17] Rightly understood, then, the sequence gospel-law is possible.

14. Bayer, *Luther's Theology,* p. 62.

15. Bayer, *Luther's Theology,* p. 62.

16. Bayer, *Luther's Theology,* p. 62. In Chapter Seven I will connect this idea with the Pauline *stoicheia tou kosmou* in Galatians 4.

17. Bayer, *Luther's Theology,* p. 63.

Charitably read, just this was the meaning of Barth's revisionist sequence in the essay "Gospel and Law." Barth's reference to the law here is not to the juridical nemesis, the pedagogue of Galatians 3:23, but to the newness of life before God and for the neighbor that arises from faith in the divine and unilateral promise. So Barth repeated in the essay *verbatim* (though unnamed) Luther's own teaching that "all commandments are included in the first commandment and must be understood and explained as especially emphasizing the first commandment."[18] In this vein Barth pointed to the evangelical *parenesis* of the New Testament, the Pauline "obedience of faith," with its imperative to realize the indicative of grace. This line of thought led him, however, to a "general and comprehensive statement" that scandalized the stiff-necked Lutherans of his day: "the Law is nothing else than the necessary *form of the Gospel,* whose content is grace."[19] Here too, Barth was trying (without naming names!) to retrieve from the tangled web of Lutheranism a teaching of Luther that had become for various reasons embarrassing to contemporary Lutherans: "Given the validity of this indicative, 'that I am not my own but his, my faithful savior Jesus Christ' [an allusion to, among others, *Luther's* Catechism!], then precisely this . . . establishes the *Ten Commandments,* together with its exposition in the *Sermon on the Mount,* and its application in the *apostolic instructions.*"[20]

Taking this as a confessional provocation, however, a frustrating and inconclusive debate ensued in the volatile climate of the Germany of the 1930s. Werner Elert took a narrowly focused polemical position to the contrary, fixated on a claim that Barth had made in passing, i.e., "The very fact that God speaks to us, that, under all circumstances, is, in itself, grace."[21] This statement, Elert contended, cannot be reconciled with the *lex semper accusat.*[22] Althaus attempted a mediating position. He showed that in Luther's exegesis of the Genesis story of Paradise, the original form of the life-giving divine Command was neither demand nor promise; the law that demands and the gospel that promises consequently must be understood as forms that the creative command of God for life takes on in response to the outbreak of Sin.[23] The divine command to live then can be understood to

---

18. Barth, "Gospel and Law," p. 82.
19. Barth, "Gospel and Law," p. 80.
20. Barth, "Gospel and Law," p. 78.
21. Barth, "Gospel and Law," p. 72.
22. Werner Elert, *Law and Gospel* (Philadelphia: Fortress, 1967).
23. Paul Althaus, *The Divine Command: A New Perspective on Law and Gospel* (Philadelphia: Fortress, 1966).

stand behind both law and gospel, and in this way provide some theological understanding of the unity of the One God, or put otherwise, the basis for recognition of both law and gospel as the Word of the one God. Nuances aside, however, these two self-proclaimed "voices of genuine Lutheranism" (as they said of themselves in defense of the Führer at the Ansbach Council in 1934)[24] refused to understand Barth's essay as he intended it to be understood, i.e., that by the sequence of gospel and law Barth meant the Pauline-exegetical distinction between indicative and imperative (not the equally Pauline distinction of 2 Corinthians 3 between the letter that kills and the Spirit who makes alive, as the sequence law and gospel was understood by traditional Lutheranism).[25] Elert and Althaus now required all true-blue Lutherans to impose on Barth's essay their own (not fully successful) reconstructions of Luther's famous distinction, deploying the dubious tactic of polemical theology of drawing implications far from Barth's mind from a concoction of their own making. The cognitive task of interpretation was eschewed. Coupled with the urgent and volatile politics, the ensuing polarizations compounded confusions that then hardened into fixed positions.

The foregoing analysis admittedly opens up the proverbial can of worms. What is clear upon reflection is that Barth and his opponents hold in mind different background narratives by which they cast the roles of law and gospel. It is important to Barth's narrative that God from eternity is the God who has freely chosen to be the God of grace, the God for humanity in Jesus Christ. It is important (let us call to the stand a better representative of Luther's tradition than Althaus or Elert) in Bayer's narrative that God's election of sinful humanity be understood as a costly decision, entailing an incalculable struggle and "overcoming" in God, a true miracle of God entering into time to become what He had not been. Thus for Barth

---

24. William H. Lazareth, *Christians in Society: Luther, the Bible and Social Ethics* (Minneapolis: Fortress, 2001), p. 8. Lazareth makes this sharp judgment on Althaus, yet follows his interpretation of the divine Command, pp. 58-84.

25. Barth explicitly acknowledges the Lutheran reading of 2 Corinthians 3: "This is the law of which it was said and must be said: either entirely the Law and then death, or entirely the Gospel and then life, there is not third possibility." The hitch is that, according to Barth's reasoning, this is "the Law, dishonored and emptied by sin's deception, which, with the power of the *wrath* of God, nevertheless is and remains *His* Law." "Gospel and Law," p. 94. This is the Law not as God ethically intends it, but functioning juridically as "our autocracy takes possession of it," to use it for self-justification (p. 91). If this gets to the bottom of the dispute, it indicates that the issue is the proper place of the law in the economy of salvation.

there cannot finally be any true opposition between law and gospel, since as God's Word both alike are expressions of the same eternal election of grace, differing only as form and content, each in its own way "repeating" in time what God eternally has determined Himself to be. For Bayer, the opposition between the law of God which rejects the sinner and the gospel of God which mercifully receives her, represents more than human-ocentric states of religious consciousness. It indicates a real movement in the life of God, a becoming of God of something God had not been, a God then capable of time who acts on that capacity in sending Jesus Christ and the Holy Spirit — a passage internal to the life of God. I am not the first to suggest that this impasse comes as a result of an insufficiently vigorous Trinitarian *personalism* on both sides. I think, following the lead of Christine Helmer's criticism of Bayer's interpretation of the Luther hymn, "Good Christian Friends, Rejoice," we can begin to chart a way forward.[26] Before we get to that task, however, let me acknowledge how a full discussion of the thorny issues raised thus far in this chapter would require extended explorations. I can think of at least the following four theses for further reflection that arise from it.

*First,* Karl Barth was right in proposing the sequence of gospel and law to see in the gospel imperatives (i.e., the "law of Christ" from the same Letter to the Galatians 6:2) a second form of the gospel, the summons to new obedience (Augsburg Confession VI!). Note well: a second use of the gospel is still the *gospel* — of the God who *gives* what He commands, namely the Holy Spirit both to will and do the will of God. In Trinitarian terms, one needs here a Holy Spirit who is more than the Fifth Wheel of mainline Protestantism, whether Lutheran or Reformed. Taken in this Pneumatological sense, however, a second use of the gospel[27] to empower new life in the hope of righteousness is greatly to be preferred to the bogus,

---

26. According to that singular *obsession* of German Luther research, Bernhard Lohse follows Ebeling in distinguishing Luther's teaching on law and gospel *from Augustine's* in that Luther's "is no longer structured in salvation-historical but in dialectical fashion" and that as such the "distinction between law and gospel cannot be made once for all, but must be drawn ever anew." Lohse, *Martin Luther's Theology: Its Historical and Systematic Development,* trans. Roy A. Harrisville (Minneapolis: Fortress, 1999), p. 269. This is true for Luther, so far as it goes, but it certainly does not go far enough. "Trinitarian advent" is *not* to be taken as a surrogate for a triumphalist salvation-history scheme in which law and Judaism are superseded by grace and Christianity.

27. "Sanctification here [i.e., Romans 6] is justification maintained in the field of action and suffering." Ernst Käsemann, *Commentary on Romans,* trans. Geoffrey W. Bromiley (Grand Rapids: Eerdmans, 1980), p. 174.

incoherent "Third Use of the Law" found in Formula of Concord VI (the first two uses are law enough). On the other hand, Barth was wrong to treat grace, or rather love, as a master category that elides the real tension between demand and promise, wrath and mercy. Elert, who misread everything else, was onto something here. That God is loving, in other words, does not entail that God is merciful to the sinner, for the sinner is the one who *is* against love. That is what being sold under the power of Sin means. There is a true contradiction here that cannot be dialectically mitigated. It is eminently evident that love entails wrath, hating the evil that is against love, or at least abandoning it to self-inflicted non-being. The real opposite of love is not wrath, but apathy (Rom. 12:9), which would yield, as the church father Lactantius saw, a Stoic deity. That the loving God comes nevertheless in *mercy* to the unloving and hard-hearted opponent of God indicates a self-surpassing of the God of love, a true passage, a becoming that is fitting to the God who is eternally a divine life of love in motion, the Holy Trinity. This divine self-surpassing in a true passage from wrath to mercy is the cost of the *assumptio carnis.*

*Second,* if Jesus Christ is not God's second thought, an improvisation, as it were, then the wrath of God which God overcomes in the life, death, and resurrection of Christ is *anticipated* in God's eternal self-determination to create, redeem, and fulfill the world through the missions of Christ and His Spirit. This thesis agrees with Karl Barth's Christocentric revision of the doctrine of election on the basis of the Lutheran teaching of the universality of the atonement, as I argued in *Paths Not Taken.*[28] Here I would add that this grounding of God's becoming in time in the eternal Trinity's self-determination issues in the kind of meditation on "God's Love for the World" that Bethge placed at the beginning of Bonhoeffer's posthumous *Ethics,* taking the word "love" with the connotation of mercy, as laid out above. "Love is the reconciliation of man with God in Jesus Christ. The disunion of men with God, with other men, with the world and with themselves, is at an end. Man's origin is given back to him. . . . And so love is something which happens to man, something passive, something over which he does not himself dispose. . . . Love means the understanding of the transformation of one's entire existence by God; it means being drawn into the world as it lives and must live before God and in God. Love, therefore, is not man's choice, but it is the

28. I have made my case for this reading of Barth in *Paths Not Taken,* chap. 2, pp. 87-126.

election of man by God." As election is election to membership in, and service (Eph. 2:10) on behalf of, the Beloved Community (Eph. 1:3-10), the eternal divine counsel is the starting point for a new kind of Christian "ethics" (*before* "good and evil")[29] which Bonhoeffer envisaged, i.e., concrete exploration of a qualitatively *new* form of life, "being drawn into the world as it lives and must live before God and in God." We will explore this idea of passivity before (this) God as powerful new agency in the world in Chapter Eight.

*Third,* such attention to the doctrine of the eternal, divine counsel requires us to resituate (not abandon) the vital distinction between law and gospel within the Genesis-to-Revelation narrative of "Trinitarian advent" (Helmer). If that is right, it is wrong to set up the law-gospel dialectic, so to say, as an independent operator that picks, chooses, and (ab)uses biblical texts to kill or to make alive, as preacher or would-be prophet deems fit. Crucial as the law-gospel distinction is, not only for preaching and pastoral care but indeed and above all for faith's knowledge of the merciful God (which is the *point* of preaching and pastoral care!),[30] the law-gospel distinction is not self-validating, nor is it self-interpreting. It arises out of reflection on the apocalyptic gospel. Its meaning, in other words, is not detachable from the particular story it arose to interpret, the gospel narrative of the sending of the Son in the fullness of time, born under the law to redeem those under the law (Gal. 4:4-5). The law-gospel dialectic is meant for the interpretation and application of biblical narrative, that is,

29. Did Bonhoeffer have a response to Nietzsche in mind when he denied that Christian ethics shares in the aim of all ethical reflection to know good and evil, but rather sees in such ambition already a falling away from the origin, which must be reconciled, before the question of living can be asked at all?

30. With this, I agree with exactly half of the premise in Mark C. Mattes's interesting, erudite, but ultimately confused critique of contemporary systematic theology, *The Role of Justification in Contemporary Theology,* Lutheran Quarterly Books (Grand Rapids: Eerdmans, 2004): "The doctrine of justification itself sets appropriate boundaries in the quest for coherent, consistent, and comprehensive theological, metaphysical, and ethical systems, insofar as reflection can establish them in the light of the law-gospel distinction" (p. 4). But the doctrine of justification or equivalently the proper distinction of law and gospel is never "itself," i.e., self-interpreting and self-validating, but always proving itself in the interpretation of Scripture and validating itself in delivering to faith true knowledge of God, to wit, Trinitarian advent. The real motive here, one fears, is Kantian, and the real target is faith's knowledge of the God of the gospel: "Sight entails a transparency that would be able to defend or explain human suffering, guilt, and finitude from God's point of view. This is simply not humanly possible" (p. 5). Whoever claimed it was humanly possible? Not an apocalyptic theology of revelation. *Hunc audite!* Does Mattes take faith to be a human possibility?

the canonical narrative organized by the kerygma of the resurrection of the Crucified. Thus its apt usage is subject to the test question whether it in fact illumines the difficult text and brings *it* to life as *viva vox Dei*, thus to kill and to make alive, as pleases the Spirit of Jesus and His Father — that means, so far as we can see or control, *ubi et quando Deo visum est!* What that latter qualification critically implies is that in preaching and pastoral care, the *minister is not in control*, not even the theologically educated minister, the one whose theology is ever so carefully, even exclusively honed for preaching. The preaching of God's mercy can in fact anger the hearts of those who want to refuse it. The preaching of God's wrath can in fact liberate a confused conscience that wants to be free of sin but does not know how or what or to whom to let go. The psychological effects of the proclamation of Jesus Christ are as variable as the human audience to which it speaks; they cannot be controlled without falling into artifice and manipulation, which in the present case, is sinful unbelief.

To put the point theologically: the economic distinction between the Word of God as letter that kills and as Spirit who gives life, or rhetorically, between the Word of God as a demand that exposes human incapacity and the Word of God as promise that gives what God commands, is a function of the procession/missions from the Father of the divine Word and the Spirit into the world. In the gospel narrative, the Word Incarnate comes as the Letter that killed and was killed (recall the previous chapter's discussion of the ambiguity of Jesus). And the Spirit who makes alive first of all is the Spirit who raised that Incarnate Word from death and exalted Him as Lord and who in parallel raises to faith those dead to God by the preaching of the Incarnate Word crucified for our sins but raised for our justification. The law-gospel dialectic as interpretation of Scripture then subsists within the Trinitarian dialectic of the external Word which points to the Spirit in order to be understood and of the Spirit which points to the Word in order to be received. To argue this resituating of the sequence law and gospel in the mission/processions of the Word and the Spirit is the narrower task of what remains in this chapter.

*Fourth,* this latter notion that God *is* the missions of the Word and Spirit sent from the Father and that God's election in time is accordingly election to membership in and service on behalf of the Beloved Community continues to *entail* the evangelical mission to the nations. At the same time, it entails Christian participation today in a dialogue with (at least) Judaism and Islam intending friendship with these others before God. This aspiration is both possible and necessary, since the gospel has a history in the world that is itself relevant to the understanding of the gospel. A renewed theological discipline of church history, as was previously argued in regard to biblical studies, would be one that understood itself as a function of critical dogmatics. It would inquire into the history of the proclamation of Jesus Christ to learn what can be learned from this history to further the mission to the nations. Surely one thing we have learned (if indeed we are true children of the Reformation) is that while Christianity is the historical bearer of the gospel to the nations, it has this treasure in the earthen vessel of a religion alongside other religions. If Paul had not been mistaken in his near expectation of the Parousia, we would not be troubled by this perplexing paradox of a religion like all the others, yet whose first rule of faith is to be "new creation" (Gal. 6:15-16). On the other hand, if Paul had been right, we would not be here to be perplexed by this problem or any other problem. So perhaps it is a good problem that the Parousia has been delayed indefinitely. Luke-Acts in fact constitutes one-quarter of the New Testament, and the Johannine writings quite a large fraction of the remainder. The moral to be drawn from the delay of the Parousia is that Christianity is not the gospel, and the Beloved Community that the gospel promises exceeds Christianity. Yet Christianity bears the gospel, and the Beloved Community subsists in the Christian church. Not observing in Christianity just such vital and self-critical distinctions, first Judaism and then Islam executed fundamental critiques on Christianity that God in His providence has deemed needful for Christians to hear and to appreciate with fear and trembling (Rom. 11:17-24). Theology today that would be able to conduct such dialogue while also sustaining the mission to the nations faces an enormous task. Such a missiology (inclusive of ecumenical and interfaith theological dialogue) vastly exceeds the scope of the present book, but mention of it serves to illustrate the work before us, if this book succeeds in commending Luther, not as a *Sonderweg*, but as an ecumenical resource for theological reconstruction today at the end of the American empire.[31]

The present question, then, is whether we can resituate the dialectic of law and gospel in the canonical narrative of Trinitarian advent. To answer this question, we have once again to come first to a qualified defense

---

31. Concurring here with the profounder point of Samuel P. Huntington's poorly understood and even more badly criticized *The Clash of Civilizations and the Remaking of World Order* (London: Simon & Schuster, 2002): "In the emerging world of ethnic conflict and civilizational clash, Western belief in the universality of Western culture suffers three problems: it is false; it is immoral; and it is dangerous" (p. 310).

of Anselm of Canterbury and his theological method — apparently so far removed from Luther! — the *sola ratione*. Luther's warnings against (speculative) reason in theology are fundamentally misunderstood, however, when we take "reason" to mean logic, rather than the metaphysical tradition of natural theology which he knows in classical form from Aristotle and Cicero.[32] Likewise, Anselm's battle-cry, "by reason alone," is fundamentally misunderstood when we take this to mean "outside of faith" rather than "faith seeking clarity in its own ground and object." Even so, there will still be a difference between the two. Luther cannot do theology without constantly re-preaching the gospel, lest the necessary work of second-order reflection take on a life of its own. Anselm's theology by contrast is staged; it is a piece of theater that pretends to argue "by reason alone" in order dramatically to present its results as the same as those given in the deposit of faith. We have to see past these apparent and real contradictions in order to see why Luther sides with Anselm, against Ockham, on the "necessity" of atonement. It is a "necessity," as we shall see, befitting the triune God of love. It is a narrative necessity of Trinitarian advent. In the process we discover that Luther does not at all decline to apply logical tools in reasoning about the truths of Scripture,[33] indeed in reasoning from Scripture to the mind of God. Interpretation of the mind and will of God is for Luther the particular kind of cognition that revealed theology

32. B. A. Gerrish, *Grace and Reason: A Study in the Theology of Luther* (Oxford: Clarendon Press, 1962). Luther's natural reason may not know much about God, but it can and often does know that it did not create itself, so that if there is a Creator, it is someone or something not-I. This intellectual distinction of Creator and creature (*not* thankful acknowledgment of the Creator!) can be understood by natural reason, but Creator and creature are only united by grace, as faith understands Christ. Thus, both nature and faith are ways of knowing; both are forms of cognition. Luther takes up the Pauline distinction between *sarx* and *pneuma* to execute a thorough critique of the faculty psychology with its root dualism between matter and mind. Natural reason is then subsumed under self-reliant flesh, which abuses the natural knowledge of God by the *opinio legis;* this is the false inference that sacrificial religious works gain divine approbation. The root problem is not idolatry; idolatry is the by-product of works-righteousness, which is self-reliance, self-worship, self obsession. The importation of the mind-matter scheme from Aristotle, displacing the *sarx-pneuma* scheme of Paul, according to Luther, is what corrupted theology as a form of cognition into philosophy as an alternative form of cognition.

33. Graham White, *Luther as Nominalist: A Study of the Logical Methods Used in Martin Luther's Disputations in the Light of Their Medieval Background,* Schriften der Luther-Agricola-Gesellschaft 30 (Helsinki: Luther-Agricola Society, 1994). See also Dennis Bielfeldt's contribution in *The Substance of Faith: Luther on Doctrinal Theology* (Minneapolis: Fortress, 2008), pp. 59-130.

exercises. For him theology never rests content with an authoritarian, "It is written." Luther says this, to be sure, to insist upon the difficult text, to require that in listening to the witness of Scripture we hear something more than the echo of our own thoughts, but rather hear what we did not already know and could not have imagined.[34] Yet once the text is established, Luther's theologian wants to know what the Holy Spirit meant by it, why indeed God has said what God has said. "Theology is understanding Scripture in spiritu (in the Spirit). It describes the grace, the salvation, the liberation of God in the form of Psalm and praise. In the text of Luther reflecting the text being narrated, a flow and unity in the praise of God exists. . . . The use of Scripture in such a manner *is* the 'interpretation,' the setting forth in detail the praise to the glory, the grace, and justice of God."[35] Delivering that interpretation of the mind of God is the art of theology as interpretation, to bring the believing mind to the awesome cognition of the "fiery furnace — aflame with love for us." The first and ancient question, then, is why the cross? Why *this* story of redemption?

## The "Necessity" of the Cross

The problem of "sin," we have seen, is not the problem that poor Nietzsche imagined in his heroic struggle to free himself from Pietism's legacy of guilt-ridden inwardness (his schoolmates taunted this grave child as "the little pastor").[36] Nor in turn is Luther's doctrine of justification by faith in Christ a product of the West's supposedly introspective conscience, as a Swedish Lutheran influentially claimed a generation ago (further discussed in Chapter Six below).[37] The young prophet Luther, imitating his models Augustine and Paul, assails *securitas*. In divine response to the destruction of human *securitas*, Luther's justification by faith does not mean justification by introspection but by "extra-spection," as it were. There is such a host of misunderstanding bound up in Nietzsche's accusations and Stendahl's attempted apology and the Pietism to which both go back that a

---

34. So Kenneth Hagen, *Luther's Approach to Scripture as Seen in His "Commentaries" on Galatians 1519-1538* (Tübingen: J. C. B. Mohr [Paul Siebeck] 1993), pp. 17, 83.

35. Hagen, *Approach to Scripture*, p. 58.

36. Rüdiger Safranski, *Nietzsche: A Philosophical Biography*, trans. Shelley Frisch (New York: Norton, 2002), p. 30. Perhaps it was this same legacy that helped make him such a master psychologist!

37. Krister Stendahl, *Paul among Jews and Gentiles* (Philadelphia: Fortress, 1976).

veritable Hercules is needed to clean out the stables. Something less heroic will by necessity be attempted here, beginning with a painfully obvious piece of pastoral wisdom. Anything so private and pitiable stemming from the weakness of nature God our Maker can and really will in His fatherly mercy overlook, as the Psalms assure us, so long as we are merely truthful before Him. This is what Augustine taught us all, including Luther. Confession is *therapy*[38] a *liberating* recognition and farewell to that old and pitiable self (*Confessions* XI:1), a daily putting on of the new self under the bold petition of the children of grace, "Command what you will, O God, but *give* what you command!" (*Confessions* X:29). The merciful heavenly Father can and will simply overlook all failings that cling to the old nature; that is to say, *venial* sins are forgiven and not imputed just because they are not *mortal* sin, which by distinction is to succumb to that dominating power in lethal guilt that deadens the heart and blinds the mind to God our true Life. Sin, properly speaking, is that anti-divine force which none less than the Christ *crucified and risen* defeats. Sin, we should think with the Apostle, is the dominating *power* that makes us in our *public* lives *enemies* of God's *reign,* personally guilty in that we have willingly yielded our bodies to its cause. Anselm was in one decisive respect aware of this.

What "provide[s] the final link in Anselm's chain of arguments for the necessity for the vicarious satisfaction, is that God, having undertaken the cause of creation, cannot allow *the world* to go unsaved. God must 'complete what he began' *with human nature.* So not to have created in vain, 'it is therefore necessary that God complete what he began with human nature.' If God does not accomplish this, His *creation* is foiled rather than vindicated, and such an outcome is inadmissible, being unfitting."[39] What kind of "necessity" is indicated here? Is it some kind of philosophical logic, some metaphysical system presumptuously imposed on the freedom of God forbidding God to do whatever God pleases?[40] Or, has Anselm learned from the Bible to look for true beauty in God's faithfulness to His good purpose and in His wisdom to use the right means in attaining those ends? "We may say that 'necessity' for Anselm means stylistic consistency, that it is in God's style as an artist to use this medium of salvation, and not

---

38. Peter Brown, *Augustine of Hippo: A Biography* (Berkeley and Los Angeles: University of California Press, 1969), p. 165.

39. Burnell F. Eckhardt Jr., *Anselm and Luther on the Atonement: Was It "Necessary"?* (San Francisco: Mellen Research University Press, 1992), p. 35. Emphases added.

40. "The concept of fittingness [or beauty] is critical to Anselm . . ." Eckhardt, *Anselm,* p. 23.

another. God cannot be inconsistent with his own *pulchritudo* and still be God."[41] God cannot be the God that God actually is, according to the Scriptures, if God were not faithful to the wayward creation, if God did not bring to completion in a fitting way the work He had begun but which has now gone awry due to sin.

To make Eckhardt's point about Anselm another way: God is not to be conceived as mere naked omnipotence, the unbounded freedom of all possibles. As a Trinitarian, Anselm thinks of God not only as power, but also always as wisdom and love, the almighty Father who by His own Word and Spirit works all in all. The "all things" that God is concretely able to do are not all things absolutely or abstractly, since not all things are wise or good. But they are those things, beyond human imagination let alone power, that conform to divine wisdom and goodness to accomplish God's purpose. "So there are for Anselm some things not even God can do . . ." not for lack of ability or strength, but because they are inconceivable for God as the perfect harmony of power, wisdom, and love. It is not because God is impotent, or because we have limited God by imposing on Him our ideas of what is fitting, but because God really would contradict His own divine nature as the perfect harmony of the perfections and so fail to correspond to Himself, that is, would cease fitting together who God will be with who He was and is. It is in this sense that Anselm contends that God cannot bring the wayward creation to rectification without atonement, that it befits God both to require and to provide atonement, if indeed, as is fitting, He desires to save His own lost creature from the debtor's prison.[42] The "necessity" of the cross is a necessity of divine wisdom in matching means (power) to end (goodness), which doctrinal theology can reason after and so come to *ponder, worship, and rejoice in, in the way any beautiful thing gives birth to wonder, praise, and delight.*

But is this in any way amenable to Luther? Eckhardt rightly contends in this light that Luther "would agree with Anselm that God cannot dispense with his rules of forensic justice in dealing with sinners."[43] Pointing to Luther's 1518 *Disputation against Scholastic Theology,* Eckhardt highlights Luther's criticism of the view of the nominalist theologian William of Ockham, who held that God in absolute power and freedom could ac-

---

41. Eckhardt, *Anselm,* p. 177. ". . . there must be beauty and symmetry in all things pertaining to God. For Anselm fittingness, which turns out always to be requisite in conceiving of God, has to do with symmetry and order" (p. 40).

42. Eckhardt, *Anselm,* p. 25.

43. Eckhardt, *Anselm,* p. 26.

cept the sinner without justifying grace.[44] Luther's rejection of Ockham's argument here is tantamount to a rejection of the nominalist distinction between God's *potentia absoluta* and *potentia ordinata*.[45] "Considerations of the *potentia absoluta* lead inevitably to the question whether divine *acceptatio* of sinners without atonement is conceivable in another order. . . . Luther's answer is to reject the question; he sticks adamantly to the order which is in existence, refusing to consider another, and *insisting that God is bound*. . . . For Luther God cannot accept man without the fulfillment of a certain precondition, viz., God's 'justifying grace.'"[46] This contention against the Master of the *via moderna* is significant. Here Luther "recognizes that there are certain things which not even God can do, if he is to be true to himself,"[47] i.e., when God's being true to God from the beginning is not anything available to a *potentia absoluta,* but from all eternity the Trinitarian coinherence of power, wisdom, and love. Faith seeking to understand the wisdom of the cross (*folly* to the perishing) *disbelieves* any putative God who is simply such unbridled "freedom," sheer, absolute *potential*.[48] No, for Trinitarian theology, God is, always has been, and always will be the perfect (albeit ineffable) harmony of power, wisdom, and love — *never* power alone. *That* would be Arianism, the "Father" without His own Son-Word, the Father and Son without the Spirit-Bond of love. To argue that Luther is a voluntarist in theology, if Eckhardt is right, is not "radically Lutheran," but radically to misunderstand Luther, who is no Unitarian but a thoroughgoing Trinitarian.[49]

So Luther "begins to look very Anselmian."[50] There is, says Eckhardt, "a tacit agreement in principle with Anselm's refusal to skirt the justice of God. . . ."[51] Righteousness is required, which is exactly why the righteousness of Christ is for Luther so central. "The reason faith justifies is precisely

---

44. Eckhardt, *Anselm,* p. 13 cited from WA 1, 227:4-5; LW 31, 13.

45. Eckhardt, *Anselm,* p. 162.

46. Eckhardt, *Anselm,* p. 158, cf. 182.

47. Eckhardt, *Anselm,* p. 29.

48. Christopher Morse, *Not Every Spirit: A Dogmatics of Christian Disbelief* (Harrisburg, PA: Trinity Press International, 1994).

49. "Accordingly we may conclude that Luther was no nominalist bent on demonstrating the dubious credibility of any theological use of reason, his admission of 1520 notwithstanding, that philosophically he was still a nominalist." Eckhardt, *Anselm,* p. 159. The famous remark refers to Luther's training in nominalist logic, not subscription to Ockhamist metaphysics.

50. Eckhardt, *Anselm,* p. 30.

51. Eckhardt, *Anselm,* p. 31.

because it embraces Christ"[52] who embraces believers. Just so, justification is not introspection at all. To think so would mean drawing Luther's distinction between law and gospel as an anthropological-psychological distinction between states of consciousness, between, say, misery and blessedness (Schleiermacher), or terror and consolation (Melanchthon), or boasting and obedience (Bultmann). Just so, that approach fails to understand the distinction theologically, as the Trinitarian dialectic of the Word and the Spirit, i.e., as the execution in our midst of the cross by the Word and resurrection to faith by the Spirit. Justification as introspection cannot in principle grasp the distinction between law and gospel as *public* harbinger of the destiny of the world, calling out into the *ek-klesia* of the coming Kingdom. Not only is faith individualized, it is thus privatized by introspection. Salvation as inclusion of the burdened individual in the Beloved Community by an act of atonement cannot here even be conceived. When justification is by "extra-spection," i.e., faith in Christ, the distinction between the Word of God as law and gospel is therefore not in the first place a grammatical-rhetorical distinction in how language performs (though it is, in the second place, also that), nor is it a psychological distinction in human affect (it is *not* that *at all*). On these levels, the law-gospel distinction is regulative for preaching (i.e., how Christians use language to curse or bless, to bind or loose) but it is not prescriptive for experience, since people are brought to faith in all sorts of ways, psychologically speaking. The proper distinction between law and gospel is the sequence given within the broader story of "Trinitarian advent," when it is clear that the theological distinction actually reflects the theological event of God surpassing God.

## Trinitarian Advent

We turn for the remainder of this chapter to Christine Helmer's dispute with Oswald Bayer about the interpretation of the 1523 Luther hymn, *Nun freut euch, lieben Christen gmein,* "Dear Christians, One and All Rejoice," given with amendments from the German *Evangelisches Kirchengesangbuch* in the *Lutheran Book of Worship* translation (#299):[53]

52. Eckhardt, *Anselm,* p. 32.

53. I have adapted the latter translation as follows with bracketed emendations to render the text more literally from the *Evangelisches Kirchengesangbuch* (Evangelisch-Lutherische Kirche in Bayern), #239, which modernizes the form of Luther's sixteenth-century German, but closely follows Luther's wording (cf. WA 35:422-25).

1. Dear Christians, one and all rejoice, With exultation springing,
   And, with united heart and voice and holy rapture singing,
   Proclaim the wonders God has done, [his sweet and wondrous deed]
   [How dearly he had bought it!]

2. Fast bound in Satan's chains I lay, Death brooded darkly o'er me,
   Sin was my torment night and day; In sin my mother bore me.
   But daily deeper still I fell; my life became a living hell,
   So firmly sin possessed me.

3. My own good works all came to naught, No grace or merit gaining;
   Free will [hated] God's judgment, dead to all good remaining.
   [Angst drove me to doubt], left only death to be my share;
   [I had to sink to hell.]

4. But God has seen my wretched state before the world's foundation,
   And, mindful of his mercies great, He planned for my salvation.
   He turned to me a father's heart; He did not choose the easy part,
   [It cost] his dearest treasure.

5. God said to his beloved Son: 'Tis time to have compassion.
   Then go, bright jewel of my crown, [be salvation to the poor];
   From sin and sorrow set them free; slay bitter death that they
   May live with you forever.

6. The Son obeyed his Father's will, was born of virgin mother;
   And, God's good pleasure to fulfill, He came to be my brother.
   His royal pow'r disguised he bore, a servant's form, like mine, he wore,
   To lead the devil captive.

7. To me he said: "Stay close to me, I am your rock and castle.
   [I wholly give myself for you]; for you I strive and wrestle;
   For I am yours and you are mine, and where I am you may remain;
   The foe shall not divide us.

8. Though he will shed my precious blood, of life me thus bereaving,
   All this I suffer for your good; be steadfast and believing.
   [My life will devour death]; my innocence shall bear your sin;
   And you are blest forever.

9. Now to my Father I depart, from earth to heaven ascending,
   [There I want to be your Lord], the Holy Spirit sending;
   In trouble he will comfort you [and teach you to acknowledge me]
   And into truth shall guide you.

10. What I on earth have done and taught, guide all your life and teaching;
    So shall the kingdom's work be wrought and honored in your preaching.
    But watch lest foes with base alloy the heav'nly treasure should destroy;
    This final word I leave you.

The *crux intellectum* is how to situate verses 2 and 3 with their poignant description of the human person lost and alone and helpless.

Bayer deserves great credit for bringing this Luther-hymn to the forefront of the discussion, since in fact, as we might *prima facie* suppose, it tells the story of the eternal Trinity's compassionate self-determination to create that He might redeem, and redeem just that which He has created: "But God has seen my wretched state before the world's foundation, and, mindful of his mercies great, *He planned for my salvation.*" In just this way, the hymn seems to expose the human plight as a living hell, not to be sure in a simplistic and triumphalistic theology of salvation history, as though it were some former epoch now safely left behind, but rather in the manner of apocalyptic theology, revealing the mystery hidden from the ages. This is the mystery of the God "who kills *in order* to make alive,"[54] that is, of the God who foresees and wills both Adam's defection and the costly, redeeming obedience of the New Adam at the cross. It is this *linkage* of a "plan of salvation" given in the purpose clause, "*in order to,*" that is disputed in general by Bayer and so also in the interpretation of this particular passage. In spite of the manifest setting of verses 4 and 5 in the eternal counsel and purpose of God, Bayer claims to have found something quite different in the hymn: "a rupture between the first and second parts of the hymn . . . so deep" that it cannot be conceptualized, a rupture that "renders impotent" the usual theological account "that God became man because it was necessary to bring to reality an eternal decision about predestination and that this is God's reaction to human sin."[55] I cannot read these words

---

54. For what is at stake in this little purpose clause, and why it is not compatible with the existential reading of Luther, see Hinlicky, "Luther and Heidegger," *Lutheran Quarterly* 22, no. 1 (Spring 2008): 78-86. See also for Luther's resort to the Pauline text of Romans 11:32 in time of trial, David C. Steinmetz, *Luther in Context* (Grand Rapids: Baker Academic, 2002), pp. 1-11.

55. Bayer, *Luther's Theology*, p. 221.

except as a manifest attempt to force the hymn to say exactly what it does not say.

What motivates this? Once again we have to raise here an objection against Bayer's apparent dualism in the name of genuine Luther theology. Or to put my point another way, for Bayer the "overthrow" in Luther's God — that I wish also to acknowledge — is theologically incomprehensible because *any* conception of divine unity connecting "before" and "after" is renounced in telling the story of the "overthrow"; consequently we have no way of recognizing the God "after" as the same God "before." It could be, after all, another (say, true) God replacing the former (say, imposter) God — not at all a preposterous thought, but rather the perennially seductive idea of Gnosticism. Against this, I want to argue that because of the implied purpose clause there is a narrative here, which we can follow *(nachdenken)* and interpret (with the help of vigorous Trinitarian personalism) as God surpassing God, where the wrath of the God of love who is against what is against love finds the way also to love the enemy and reconcile the offender. But most of this work has been done for us by Helmer in her analysis of this Luther-hymn.

In this hymn, "Luther suspends the I's captivity in the narrative of trinitarian advent."[56] In this path-breaking theological, not only historical, study, Helmer carefully analyzed the text to demonstrate that thesis. The first verse requires us to regard the hymn as a *retrospect,* a memory *shaped or constructed* by the promised Spirit[57] about the coming of the Incarnate Son from the wellspring of the Father's mercy to rescue.[58] "The lament" that next follows "is articulated as a confession of sin. Confession recalls the 'before' as captivity . . . and as the incapacity for the good. From the perspective of the 'after,' the preceding enmity with the law is acknowl-

---

56. Christine Helmer, *The Trinity and Martin Luther: A Study on the Relationship between Genre, Language and the Trinity in Luther's Works (1523-1546)* (Mainz: Verlag Philipp von Zabern, 1999), p. 146. Helmer's purpose is to subvert an anthropological narrative from law to gospel and replace it with a narrative of Trinitarian advent (p. 135). Following Yeago, against Elert, she writes: "When the law/gospel paradigm is privileged, the doctrine of the Trinity is moved to the margin" (p. 147).

57. It is the Spirit who convicts of sin as well as summons to praise: "Luther does not metaphysically divide the aspect of the divine nature as judgment from the advent as the summons to joy." Helmer, *The Trinity,* p. 154.

58. A "narrative of trinitarian advent, however, plots the I's lament as an interruption." Helmer, *The Trinity,* p. 151; locating the lament within the praise "converts present tense agony to past tense of remembrance" (p. 152), i.e., not "erased from memory, but rendered in a distinct type of speech" (p. 153).

edged and confessed."[59] So the law is implicitly situated in the second and third verses. Helmer in this light "challenge[s] the usual [i.e., Bayer's] way of viewing the hymn from an alleged anthropological starting-point by focusing on its literal beginning, the advent of the Spirit [in verse 1], as well as the genre in which the subsequent narrative is cast."[60] Her point is that verses 2 and 3 are hardly some spontaneous self-interpretation, giving us what people naturally think about their plight. This *retrospective* self-interpretation in verses 2 and 3 is rather a function of *revealed* theology, the self-interpretation of the past self from the present perspective of the faith announced in verse 1.[61]

On the other hand, if we try to launch gospel discourse on the basis of self-understood human misery or terror, we would have to think of the Trinity's compassion and resolve to help in verse 5, not as something foreseen from eternity as the Luther text expressly states in verse 4, but as a contingent temporal reaction to suffering that thankfully the deity happens to notice and with which it spontaneously sympathizes, "insisting on [an] unprecedented act of mercy eluding final explanation. . . ."[62] God, in this non-interpretation, spontaneously gushes, as it were, on a whim. How could anyone *rely* on that? Luther's German is rather clear, however: *Da jammert' Gott in Ewigkeit, mein Elend übermassen*. Far from some temporally contingent eruption of spontaneous feeling, God in eternity, according to the text, foresees, feels, and resolves to create the world in which verses 2 and 3 will take place because the remaining verses will also come to pass. So Helmer writes, "when the law/gospel principle is projected into the nature of God," requiring that the word of compassion spontaneously erupt in an unmediated flood, "a wedge symmetrically splits it apart into the two sides of wrath and mercy. The divine conversion to the gospel is experienced as an unprecedented revolution in the divine nature, a turnaround unmediated by conceptual explanation . . . the 'general' view of God is split off from the 'specific' trinitarian story of divine mercy."[63] In

59. Helmer, *The Trinity,* p. 155.

60. Helmer, *The Trinity,* p. 121, cf. 136, 139, 156, 162.

61. In accord with what Luther wrote in the *Smalcald Articles* (hereafter SA): "inherited sin has caused such a deep, evil corruption of nature that reason does not comprehend it; rather, it must be believed on the basis of the revelation in the Scriptures. . . ." SA III:1, 3 in *The Book of Concord,* ed. Robert Kolb and Timothy J. Wengert (Minneapolis: Fortress, 2000), p. 311.

62. Helmer, *The Trinity,* p. 148. This is Oswald Bayer's interpretation, ruling out any *felix culpa.*

63. Helmer, *The Trinity,* p. 149. Bayer expressly owns the position that Helmer here

place of this dualism between an apparent God of wrath and a secret God of love,[64] Helmer wants to show that Luther's God is *motivated* by the "divine essence of mercy and in terms of the trinitarian persons as subjects of speech."[65] Verses 4 and 5 tell of God in eternity, the *Ratschluss zur Erlösung*, the Trinitarian decision for salvation.[66] In this narrative framework, the memory of misery and death by the redeemed is bracketed "on one side by its conversion into the confession of sin, and on the other side, in the Father's speech as the *promissio* of life." The miracle of inner-Trinitarian mercy is Christologically mediated: it is Christ who "has endured the full impact of death, hell and devil in such a way as to suspend it as the lament of a totality in a hymn of praise."[67]

---

criticizes in *Luther's Theology*, pp. 337-40. Lotz traces this loss of "Luther's profound doctrine of God in which the divine love and wrath were held together in dialectical tension" to "the wooden fashion Harnack fitted Luther's distinctions between wrath and love, law and gospel, sin and grace, etc. into this overarching distinction between God as he is known outside Christ and God as he is known in Christ. This procedure means, in effect, that the one type of knowledge must finally be less true than the other, and so God's wrath is only relatively true while his love is absolutely true." Lotz, *Luther and Ritschl*, p. 185, n. 86.

64. Concerning "the distinction between 'right speculation' on the inner-Trinity, and a type of speculation that incites the divine anger. . . ." Helmer, *The Trinity*, p. 250, those to whom Christ has been shown are nevertheless "tempted to climb above revelation, and search out the divine ways that have not been revealed. . . . Luther gives the original example of Satan who, using his own wisdom, inquired into the depths of the divine Majesty, and fell into the abyss" (p. 251). "What Luther insists to be the demonic threat is the forcing of the separation of God from his revealed way . . . the demonic attack against revelation . . . the devil who attempted to speculate on the way in which God is 'tecum' apart from the trinitarian revelation" (p. 252). Thus "when Luther preaches that there is an aspect of God that God desires to remain hidden, he is not referring to a 'rest' that is held back in the revelation of the christological center of salvation" (p. 253).

65. Helmer, *The Trinity*, p. 122.

66. Helmer, *The Trinity*, p. 161.

67. Helmer, *The Trinity*, p. 157. "The most central mystery of the Christian faith is concentrated on the one who endures the silence of God to its extreme, and then mediates this experience in speech: the cross and resurrection of Jesus Christ. The lament articulating the totality of an experience terminating in death and in the descent to hell is placed in the mouth of the individual who alone experiences the totality of death, and mediates its silence into the lament" (p. 160). Helmer goes on to argue then that the lament in verses 2 through 4 actually belongs to the Incarnate and Ascended Christ: it is the Crucified's "silence that takes upon itself death [which] points to the mystery rupturing the heart of the Trinity" (p. 162). In verse 9 we learn of the Ascended Christ (p. 182), of "Christ, speaking from the inner-trinitarian mercy seat that has been sprinkled with his blood. Imported into the relation between the Father and the Son is Christ's blood that has become the promissio

Helmer, it seems to me, is clearly right in regarding this sweeping narrative as "a summary of Luther's richly concentrated theology that reveals Luther's own understanding of the scope of Scripture"[68] as the narrative of Trinitarian advent. "This is the mystery of the divine mercy that is turned from the inner- to the outer-Trinity, binding the ties of love so tightly that no unholy power can prevent or separate Christ from those to whom he declares his love."[69] Curiously, however, yet no doubt as a result of her polemical objection to Bayer's unmediated "overthrow" within God, Helmer rejects any "interpretation that locates the turn from wrath to mercy in the inner-Trinity," on the grounds that in this hymn "the movement unfolds from the lament, heard by God in eternity, to the heartfelt compassion compelling God to remember God's mercy and desire to help . . . an inner-trinitarian turn precedes Christ's advent."[70] In fact, however, in this hymn the wrath of God is no more an express theme than the law of God, though it is of course implied by the tyranny of Satan and the lamented experience of a living hell. In other words, this most difficult thought in Luther's atonement theology does not appear expressly in the hymn. Helmer here needs to deny that it nevertheless lies in the background, only because Bayer has imposed his dualism on the text. She is in any case right that the infinite ground beyond all comprehension is the divine *Barmherzigkeit.* "Dislocated from its usual anthropological context, the lament is now identified with the inner-Trinity in eternity. The divine essence is characterized by the deepest identification of God with human exile and misery. . . . Already in the inner-Trinity, the claim of reciprocity, *'Denn ich bin dein und du bist mein,'* communicates the lament into the divine essence . . . 'mercy' signals the center of Luther's understanding of the divine nature."[71] That center is *Barmherzigkeit,* "by which God remembers and acts. It is this attribute that ultimately grounds the communication of the lament into the divine nature. Mercy is designated as the ground of the inner-trinitarian passion."[72] In conclusion, she reiterates: "The anthropo-

---

of mercy . . . the lament in its totality can only be spoken by Christ before the Father" (pp. 180-81). These latter reflections may amount to something of an overinterpretation of the text, but arguably a legitimate development of the hymn's implicit theology.

68. Helmer, *The Trinity,* p. 126.

69. Helmer, *The Trinity,* p. 178.

70. Helmer, *The Trinity,* p. 164. "Not a turn from wrath to love, the inner-trinitarian turn is told as the narrative of the attribute of mercy" (p. 169).

71. Helmer, *The Trinity,* p. 165.

72. Helmer, *The Trinity,* p. 166. "No ultimate explanation is offered, neither for the di-

logical view resulting from the rigid application of the law/gospel relation is displaced by the trinitarian/theological privileging of the divine mercy."[73]

A question that could arise here is whether Helmer's argument over-reaches and effectively annuls the law-gospel dialectic (in the sense of minimizing the obstacle to mercy formed by actual evil and its condemnation by the law) rather than resituating it in the Trinitarian dialectic of the procession/missions of the Word and the Spirit. Annulling the law-gospel dialectic of course could no longer pass muster as Luther-interpretation. The potential for such misunderstanding becomes particularly acute when she polemicizes against the picture of a temporal and unmediated "turn from wrath to love" in God, when in reality her polemic is directed against the reduction of Trinitarian theology to the articulation of human states of consciousness[74] or, what is the same, the projection of these states of consciousness in the name of the law-gospel dialectic onto God. What she wants to affirm, as we have seen, is the eternal turn of the triune God out of mercy to come in time in mercy to and for the sinner as integral to the very divine counsel to create, redeem, and fulfill the world. This turn may be described as an eternal turn "from wrath to mercy," as we heard in the previous chapter, if wrath itself is rightly understood as the alien form of divine love, entailing then a real history of God with His creature, including in it a true divine self-surpassing, motivated all the same by the well-spring of *Barmherzigkeit,* which the Trinity is.[75] Helmer then would have made her point more clearly, in my view, if she had articulated Luther's Augustinian notions of "severe mercy" or of "the wrath of love." The opposite of Pauline agape is not, in any case, hate but apathy, that widespread Stoic indifference that in our day has become the pale, politically correct virtue of hopeless, loveless "toleration." "Let love be genuine; hate what is evil, hold fast to what is good" (Rom. 12:9). The sin that is real and powerful and lethal, the sin that God hates, is whatever God hates out of love, and the wrath that God surpasses in reconciling the real, not fictitious, sinner is a self-surpassing that moves God and so also the sinner forward onto a

---

vine capacity to suffer, nor for the turn towards the Son, other than the inexplicable ground of the divine nature itself. . . . Mercy is the groundless ground of the divine turn towards creation" (p. 168).

73. Helmer, *The Trinity,* p. 272.

74. Helmer, *The Trinity,* p. 67.

75. Thus Helmer's tacit criticism of Anselm is quite precisely formulated: "God is not determined by a structure of payment." Helmer, *The Trinity,* p. 239.

new relationship in a new creation. A formulation like this, it seems to me, captures the eternal ground of *Barmherzigkeit* which is the life of the Trinity, accounts for the recognizability and fittingness of the Suffering Servant's way to the cross, and makes intelligible the self-surpassing temporal event of the Incarnation as divine becoming, which turns the lament of verses 2-3 to doxology.

## Teaching the Trinity

Since the Trinity *is* the story of its advent, not only must Christians know the Trinity in order to sustain their telling of the gospel story, the Trinity itself must be eminently teachable. Luther "preaches in detail on the revelation and the knowledge of the inner-trinitarian side of God . . . trinitarian doctrine is to be understood and preached, not only adored in silence."[76] *God speaks, God is spoken, God is heard;* in Jesus Christ we are incorporated into this linguistic *event* which God *is.*[77] The Father speaks, the Son is spoken, and in the Holy Spirit God is heard, as human beings come by faith to repentance in Jesus Christ. This Trinitarian structure of Luther's theology of the Word is a veritable prescription for the new evangelization of Euro-American culture, among other missions to the nations, in that it radically eschews the manipulative theatrics of revival, and rather summons Jesus and discipleship, leaving to the Spirit both to will and to do. For there is no other way in which the Word of the Father is Heard but in all rigor *ubi et quando Deo visum est.*

*God speaks.* As we have heard, Luther takes his theological point of departure *von oben,* as in the heavenly command in the Transfiguration story, the Father's *Hunc audite.* "Then a cloud overshadowed them, and from the cloud there came a voice, 'This is my Son, the Beloved; listen to him!'" (Mark 9:7 and parallels). Helmer draws out two implications from this about the time and place of Christian theology. First, the Father's command to listen to the Son requires first-order theology *always* to *begin* its work in acknowledging the "intimate relation . . . of their natural unity. . . ." The church's creedal belief in "God from God, Light from Light, true God from true God, begotten not made" is placed by Luther "under the author-

---

76. Helmer, *The Trinity,* p. 203.

77. Luther's 1537 Trinity sermon begins in eternity with the Father's voice speaking of the cross of his Son for the salvation of his creatures. Helmer, *The Trinity,* pp. 235-43.

ity of the Father's speech, a position already implying a trinitarian theological claim of a natural unity between Father and Son. . . ."[78] Second, in this same way the boundaries of first-order theology are drawn. "Luther succeeds in demarcating the theological region inside which no disputations are necessary" — indeed, allowed. Christian theology — not Cicero or Aristotle — does not begin from nowhere or anywhere, least of all with pretentions to some universal discourse, in which case it would have to dispute about what it is and is supposed to do.[79] The starting point and boundaries are *given* in the gospel, and apart from this *Deus dixit,* there is no Christian theology. Christian theology begins with the Father's *Hunc audite,* and so it proceeds in that region in the world where the Father's command is heard and obeyed in the Spirit. "If, on the contrary, the Father's voice is disobeyed, a cloud of suspicion is moved over the Father's natural unity with the Son, and the issue becomes the subject for dispute"[80] — in the sense of disputing deviations from this specific time and place which are destructive of the very possibility in the world of such discourse. In this region of church and faith, then, any attempt to separate the Father and the Son will have to be regarded as a *demonic* assault on the very possibility of theological teaching; consequently second-order theology (e.g., in the form of the academic disputation) is undertaken as not mere academic exercise, but "to demonstrate obedience to the Father in a defense against those who, like the devil, attempt to separate the Father from his word."[81]

Second, *God is spoken.* Studying Luther's Trinity Sunday sermons from 1537, Helmer argues against the sufficiency of the "word-event" model of a so-called relational ontology that justifies the hearer in a performative act. This can be little more than fiat, even if it is the case that language works in such and such a way. In this word-event model, "justification takes place when the word effects an anthropological displacement from law to gospel. It is a kerygmatic moment, an existential transfer that occurs."[82]

---

78. Helmer, *The Trinity,* p. 59.

79. "Different grammars require different disciplines. Theology as the rigorous study of the sacred page has a unique discipline. . . . To state the argument succinctly: Paul is not Aristotle; Scripture is not philosophy; Augustine is not philosophy. Luther sought to follow Isaiah, Paul, and Augustine. For Luther, theology is focused on God. Its text is the sacred page. The sacred page is a gift from the Creator, Redeemer, and Sanctifier. It is the sacred page against the pagans and their pagan gods." Hagen, *Approach to Scripture,* pp. 84-85.

80. Helmer, *The Trinity,* p. 60.

81. Helmer, *The Trinity,* p. 61.

82. Helmer, *The Trinity,* p. 200.

Here "the relationship between the active word and its passive appropriation is discussed as a word-faith correlation, or as the word's invitation to faith, or as the word's intention to awaken faith in God and love towards the neighbor."[83] The problem with this model, as interpretation of Luther, is that, in Helmer's own words, "when the sermon is reduced to kerygmatic intention, the location of reception in the hearer tends to be privileged over the objective extreme of the word's content. The subjective moment is upheld as the location at which the word-faith correlation is constituted."[84]

I take this critique of the word-event model to center on two points that I would lay out as follows. First, the hearer's decision of faith in this model becomes the event that effectively replaces the free and incalculable work of the electing Holy Spirit in Luther's teaching. For Luther it is by the Spirit that *God spoken* becomes also *God heard;* true hearing comes by impartation of divine faith, by the unprogrammable coming of the Spirit and not by mechanics of linguistic performance as such. Divine faith is not and cannot be construed as any kind of natural human response to an inviting word, like faith in my promise to buy you lunch tomorrow, for it is the *invisible* God who so invites in the gospel and promises in the offensive form of the *sub contrario.* Even if we were in a position to assess this Speaker's competence and good character to do as is promised, we are repelled by the form of the invitation and the content of the promise. To think that performative language can *ex opera operato* do its magic in theology as proclamation is to remove the offense of Jesus, the offense of the cross, to abstract from the invisible Father's promise of life in His Name a contentless promise of benevolent divine presence that one would be a fool not to include among one's life-options.

Second, then, while certainly the Word spoken may *function* as an invitation to faith, that is not what it *is.* The event of the Word spoken is not its inviting to some benefit or promising of some good, but is the Word of that appalling crucified flesh, the stone of stumbling, who is Jesus in agony. The Word spoken as event is the oxymoron "Christ crucified." God is spoken in the unfollowable story of Jesus' way to Golgotha, until the Spirit of the resurrection makes new people who can now follow Him through the cross to His glory. This is the true preaching of the law, as the law accuses Jesus who believed for us and puts Him to death for His solidarity

---

83. Helmer, *The Trinity,* p. 198.

84. Helmer, *The Trinity,* p. 200, on Elert's collapse of "any substantial content Luther might give to the justifying word into a 'mathematical point . . . without extension . . .'" (pp. 201-2).

with us. *He* is the event "set for the rising and falling of many in Israel." This event is *not* and cannot lie in the preacher's persuasiveness nor the winsomeness of the presentation, but only in the uncanny assertion of the Messiah hoisted on the imperial stake. *That* can be *heard* as God *spoken* only by the personal Pentecost of the Spirit's coming.

Third, *God is heard.* Apocalyptic revelation effects incorporation into the Trinitarian life of God; faith is *divine* faith, *hearing* God *spoken* as God *intends.* The Word of the cross exhibits the power of God to save as the Spirit raises the hearer to faith. That is the true preaching of the gospel, as the Father vindicates accursed Jesus with all those for whom He believed, also for us if we have, or rather are given, ears to hear. Trinitarian advent so situates the preaching of law and gospel then that effective preaching is never in the power of the preacher. On the contrary, whether or not God's spoken Word, who is Jesus Christ the Crucified, is heard by us as God hears it (that means, raising, vindicating, exalting, enthroning the Crucified with all those for whom He believed) — such hearing turns on the free movement of that Spirit, who blows as He will, who cannot be manipulated, bribed, or otherwise conjured. If this is right, the Spirit's mission to the nations in Jesus' name has nothing whatsoever to do with psychologically terrorizing auditors, nor with the refined ambulance-chasing of the modern Protestant middle-class chaplaincy, running after the weaknesses, the failures, the crises, and anomie of modern life, not to mention any kind of blessing spoken upon its fantasies for power, health, wealth, and personal liberation. All this business of religion is but a contemporary trade in indulgences, which turns the house of the Lord from a house of prayer for all peoples into a den of thieves. But God is spoken when Jesus says: "Whoever would come after me, let them deny themselves and take up their cross and follow me." Try selling that! We can't even *hear* it! But where *God is heard,* "as the hearers are gathered into the Spirit's view, they learn to speak about what they have been shown."[85] The infallible sign of the Spirit's hearing among us is the new hunger for theology that teaches: *catechesis.*[86] Here we

---

85. Helmer, *The Trinity,* p. 230. "When humans are determined as subjects according to experiential, cognitive and religious capacities, then the words they speak cannot be narrowed to a passive instrument directed at a transcendental I . . ." (pp. 232-33).

86. "There is a knowledge of the Trinity that, although not separated from soteriology, adds another dimension to it," Helmer writes. "I have used the terminology of incorporation to show that the sermon is not crystallized into a kerygma, to be appropriated existentially by faith, but that it invites a full immersion into learning, speaking and glorifying the Trinity. . . ." Helmer, *The Trinity,* p. 266.

learn to speak in a new and theological language, according to which God kills *in order to* make alive.

How does the human world come to look in view of Trinitarian advent and how then can we live at this turn of the ages — members if not citizens of two societies? In the next two chapters, I want to offer several studies on topics in theological anthropology. The topics are timely. Today the human body is a battleground to such an extent that many even in the churches entertain considerable doubts that Christian theology can teach anything touching on personal behavior beyond a thin ethic of responsibility. That would be quite a fall from New Testament *paranesis.* New Testament *paranesis* in any case touches on "personal" matters, but always in the quite specific form of address to those made members of Christ, citizens of the coming Beloved Community.[87] So our fall from grace today would have to be diagnosed as a double fall, not only from the individual Christian's discipleship but also from membership in the holy community. Of course, it is also no small challenge today even to assert an ethic of responsibility, since we are not sure whether we control our bodies — who and what on earth, we ask, is this "we" in control? — or whether as members of vastly overpowering physical, linguistic, and cultural systems it is rather our controlled bodies that control us. That is how the issue is usually posed: an increasingly desperate belief in personal autonomy obligating an increasingly implausible personal responsibility or sober recognition of the heteronomous powers demanding in turn a humane and enlightened libertarianism so far as "private" matters go. Some choice: sad or happy Stoicism, as the case may be. A frank Epicureanism sounds better. Christian theology is expected as a rule to pipe up on behalf of the ghost of its former self that appears in the sad Stoicism of the Ethic of Responsibility. But the latter *is* a ghostly, if not ghastly business. Responsible for what? Responsible to whom?[88] As Hannah Arendt so painfully showed us, Adolph Eichmann acted "responsi-

---

87. "The leveling down of Pauline exhortation to a general ethics and the underlying concentration on anthropology separate the two foci of Pauline theology, play off the subjective and the objective perspectives against one another, change the thesis of freedom from the power of sin into morality, and thus make individual acts of sin the real subject of debate. The resultant contradictions are then blamed without inhibition on the apostle." Käsemann, *Romans,* p. 173. In detail, J. Lewis Martyn, *Galatians,* The Anchor Bible, vol. 33A (New York: Doubleday, 1997), pp. 416-558.

88. Jacques Derrida, *The Gift of Death,* trans. David Wills (Chicago and London: University of Chicago Press, 1995).

bly."[89] That conundrum of the banality of evil in our kind of post-Christendom world ironically indicates that the contemporary decentering of the self allows a return of the repressed, the Enlightenment's dark and shadowy "other" — that is to say, Luther's daunting teaching on *the bondage of the will.*

89. Hannah Arendt, *Eichmann in Jerusalem: A Report on the Banality of Evil,* rev. and enlarged edition (London: Penguin, 1994), pp. 278-79.

# PART TWO

# Explorations in Theological Anthropology

# CHAPTER FIVE

# Somatic Self, Ecstatic Self: Luther on Theonomy

*Corporeality is standing in a world for which different forces contend and in whose conflict each individual is caught up, belonging to one lord or the other and representing this lord both actively and passively. If in such a context Paul speaks of our members, or even our bodies themselves are called members, it is clear that we are never autonomous, but always participate in a definite world and stand under lordship. . . . There thus arises a dialectical understanding of Christian existence. It belongs to the sphere of power of the risen Lord, but it does so on earth and therefore it is still exposed to the attack of the powers which rule this aeon, is always under assault . . . and is constantly summoned to preserve and verify eschatological freedom in the service of its true and only Lord . . . the Creator who is bringing back his world in his justice. . . . Bodily obedience is necessary as an anticipation of the reality of bodily resurrection.*

Käsemann[1]

I have already indicated in preceding chapters a position I worked out in *Paths Not Taken:* I concur with Karl Barth's monumental revision of the supralapsarian Reformed doctrine of election on the basis of the Lutheran

---

1. Ernst Käsemann, *Commentary on Romans,* trans. Geoffrey W. Bromiley (Grand Rapids: Eerdmans, 1980), pp. 176-77.

contention for universal atonement.[2] In this chapter, I seek to give grounds for sustaining a doctrine of election and corresponding theological anthropology, which might recognizably claim the Luther of *De servo arbitrio* [hereafter *DSA*] as resource. This would be a doctrine of election focused on the mystery of humanity's election in Christ, revealed in the gospel, to the end of Beloved Community, *not* consisting of predetermined lists of the saved and the damned. Much contemporary theology, be it admitted, has simply ditched the problem altogether, whether under the mantle of Kant's practical postulate of "free-will" to contend against wicked naturalists and metaphysical determinists, or thinking like good Platonists to spare the God who spared not His own Son from the authorship of moral evil. So effectively, many have decided for the skepticism and Pelagianism of Erasmus, which found its modern restatement in Kant's philosophy of religion.[3] How one imagines continuing in the tradition of Luther's theology on this basis escapes me. In any event, I eschew both of these motives. I hold that nothing is more important today than to bring to bear Christian theology's Pauline-Augustinian-Lutheran critique of Pelagianism, that is, "works-righteousness," or "expiation" (not "idolatry" per se but "sacrifice" as noted in the previous chapter's discussion of Girard) as the mask of *false* agents whose works are *not good* and in its place to offer the one true image of God, Jesus Christ. In Him faith apprehends the one true *Agent* of human good, the New Adam who did the righteous deed, in whom we too can be refashioned as members of His Body, and just so, doers as also hearers of a salutary Word of life against death.

To accomplish this task, I need to exposit Luther's admittedly over-the-top rhetoric in *DSA* in the light of a strict and precise definition of Luther's theological intention, *not* then as an inept and indeed unintelligible treatise in philosophical anthropology. In fact, this latter was how Luther's

2. See Paul Hinlicky, *Paths Not Taken: Theology from Luther through Leibniz* (Grand Rapids: Eerdmans, 2009), chap. 2, pp. 87-126.

3. A basic line of argument running through *DSA* is about God's intention in giving the law. Erasmus argues that God would not command obedience if addressees were not free to obey; Luther argues that God commands obedience to show that addressees are incapable of obedience. Hence the reign of law up to Christ is for Luther juridical, not ethical: "God is trying us, that by His law he may bring us to a knowledge of our impotence . . . as Paul teaches, [this] is the intent of divine legislation." Luther, *The Bondage of the Will*, trans. J. I. Packer and O. R. Johnston (Westwood, NJ: Fleming Revell, 2000), p. 153. In contrast, the fundamental move Kant makes in postulating practical freedom is precisely the Erasmian-Pelagian position, that Ought implies Can. See Charles R. Pigden, "Ought-Implies-Can: Erasmus, Luther and R. M. Hare," *Sophia* 29, no. 1 (1990): 2-30.

rival in Zurich, Huldrich Zwingli, read *DSA,* setting an influential precedent for its reception. In turn, however, it will be Zwingli's rebuttal of Luther, *De providentia Dei, On the Providence of God* [hereafter *DPD*], which allows us to read *DSA* in true, historical context, that is, against the immanent horizon of possibilities of its age, neither setting Luther against some earlier medieval position like those of Ockham, Scotus, Thomas, or Augustine, or, as mentioned, against some modern thinker, especially Kant, reading Erasmus as his surrogate.[4] When we read Luther and Zwingli side by side, the features of what precisely Luther intended to say to his own day and age becomes much crisper.[5] Yet first we need to clarify some basic concepts that we will be using.

## Somatic, Ecstatic, and Centered Selves

In the epigraph to this chapter, we witness Ernst Käsemann's vigorous attempt to make intelligible the Pauline understanding of creaturely existence and corresponding creaturely freedom on the stage of the apocalyptic battle of the aeons. Martin Luther also contended for this theological anthropology in his Latin treatise against Erasmus, *DSA* (*On Bound Choice,* usually rendered in English as *The Bondage of the Will*):[6] We "acquiesce in [Satan's] rule," wrote Luther, explaining his Pauline understanding of the will's creaturely freedom, "willingly and readily, according to the nature of willingness, which, if constrained, is not 'willingness'; for constraint means rather, as one would say, 'unwillingness.' But if a stronger one appears, and overcomes Satan, we are once more servants and captives, but now desiring and willingly doing what *He* wills — which is royal free-

4. For a helpful recapitulation of Erasmus's treatise on free-will, see B. A. Gerrish, "Piety, Theology, and the Lutheran Dogma: Erasmus' Book on Free Will," chap. 1 in B. A. Gerrish, *The Reformation Heritage* (Chicago: University of Chicago Press, 1982), pp. 11-26.

5. I can also note here, though I cannot pursue it at this time, that Zwingli's thought on providence proved to have significant philosophical influence, overshadowing Luther's treatise in at least one important line of development. It appears that Zwingli's recasting of Luther's teaching on the immutability of divine foreknowledge *as philosophy* somehow shaped those decisive early-modern thinkers Spinoza and perhaps also Leibniz, setting a trap for the would-be theological Lutheran Leibniz from which he could not finally free himself.

6. As Kolb thankfully translates correctly Luther's title: Robert Kolb, *Bound Choice, Election, and Wittenberg Theological Method: From Martin Luther to the Formula of Concord,* Lutheran Quarterly Books (Grand Rapids: Eerdmans, 2005).

dom."[7] What matters with creatures, one might say, is not *that* one loves, but *what* one loves; what matters is not *whether* life has meaning, but *what* meaning is found. For the existence of a creature is, so to say, outside itself. So the self here is a de-centered or ecstatic one. In one of Luther's more attractive depictions: "Christ is displayed by the enlightening of the Spirit, and by it man is rapt to Christ with the sweetest rapture, he being passive while God speaks, teaches and draws, rather than seeking or running himself."[8] Indeed the very vocabulary of "creature" already contains such a construction of the self, as that mutable nature with a desire for the supernatural, as Augustine thought.[9] Luther indeed leaves no doubt that in composing *DSA*, he had books of the Bishop of Hippo open before him. The very title of the book, he claims, is drawn from Augustine's second book against Julian, where he learned that if we attribute to the human will the power to will, that is, to move itself, we "completely exclude the Holy Spirit and His power as if superfluous and unnecessary."[10]

It is as if Luther is saying that human nature, as God intended it to be in creation, would naturally have been ecstatic, captivated and led by the Spirit, with the Son, to the Father — though now fallen we see it captivated by other powers leading to other destinations. If so, it is as a good student of Augustine's theological anthropology, as also of his Pneumatology, that Luther has drawn that fundamental argument for justification by faith (as

---

7. Luther, *Bondage*, p. 103.

8. Luther, *Bondage*, p. 311. Ebeling explicated faith as such ecstatic existence: Gerhard Ebeling, *Luther: An Introduction to His Thought* (Philadelphia: Fortress, 1972), pp. 254-56, and of God as "event" (p. 258).

9. Henri de Lubac, S.J., *Augustinianism and Modern Theology,* trans. Lancelot Sheppard (New York: Crossroad, 2000), p. 121. De Lubac's fundamental point is that Christian thought must interpret the desire for God as natural to that creature made in God's image, not a supernatural add on. "To ensure that over one region of human activity grace should prevail, [modern theology] exposed another whole region to the danger of secularization. In opposition to the pessimistic exaggerations [this is de Lubac's recurring caricature of Luther, e.g., p. 232, as though he were of one mind with the Jansenists] concerning the present corruption of nature, there was claimed [by the Molinists] for fallen man the power of performing certain morally good actions at least, for the reason that since free will was not destroyed by original sin there was no need for a special help to take its place or to restore it" (p. 240). So both modern friend and foe of Augustine conspired to extirpate from nature the "desire to see God," in this way "yielding to the prevalent naturalism and making the most dangerous concessions to a world entirely unconcerned about its higher destiny" (p. 262). De Lubac is evidently ignorant of Luther's true teaching on this question in the Genesis commentary.

10. Luther, *Bondage*, p. 142.

we discussed in the previous chapter in connection with Barth), that the law which commands love of God above all and for all creatures in and under God is only fulfilled by Spirit-wrought faith: "The love of God is required no less than our conversion and the keeping of all the commandments; for the love of God is our true conversion."[11] This is the ecstatic love of Spirit-wrought faith, not the self-seeking centeredness of free-will which uses God and all creatures only for its own purposes. The true good of genuine love consists in turning from the centered existence (*incurvatus in se,* in Luther's well-known expression) freely willing its own in all things to the new world which God is and brings, still invisible but promised in Christ, which *is* the ecstatic self bound now to God's will and purpose for the Beloved Community, which primordially the Holy Trinity *is.*

The background in Augustine is thus unmistakable. Jan Lindhardt has pointed to the tension created in the Augustinian theological tradition in which Luther was educated by the appropriation of Aristotle's anthropology. "Just as a good mirror reproduces objects correctly, so the reason represents the world and nature as they actually are. This is why the highest type of reason was termed during the Middle Ages *speculatio,* that is, reflection. By way of contrast, the feelings or passions are unreliable, a judgment that applies to both the affective states of the soul *(pathe)* and the bodily drives . . . the function of the reason is to guide the will, which in turn is to govern the passions and drives. . . ."[12] Quite in contrast to this picture of reason as pilot bridling the passions, Augustine held "in extension of the Platonic tradition, that a man was identical with his love. He defined love itself as *concupiscentia* (desire)."[13] Here a view emerged of "man more as a unity than as a creature subdivided into various departments. . . . It was not the distinction between body/soul/reason, which occupied his attention, but the direction adopted by the soul or will, or drive." This unitary person "was interpreted during the Renaissance as representing a completely different view of man . . . ,"[14] "not conceived of as an active subject, but as a receptive object."[15]

11. Luther, *Bondage,* p. 164. I am grateful to Robert Wilken for pressing upon me this question about love for God in Luther.

12. Jan Lindhardt, *Martin Luther: Knowledge and Mediation in the Renaissance,* Texts and Studies in Religion, vol. 29 (Lewiston, NY: Edwin Mellen Press, 1986), p. 23.

13. Lindhardt, *Martin Luther,* p. 25.

14. Lindhardt, *Martin Luther,* p. 27.

15. Lindhardt, *Martin Luther,* p. 30. According to Lindhardt, Luther appropriated the revival of Augustinian anthropology in humanist rhetoric. Yet Augustine's "theology was

This may be overstated. The Augustinian notion of desire is more complex than a simple reversal from active subject to passive object. Desire too is "active," which is why it can be either self-seeking or seeking God's glory; in principle it is *seeking* fulfillment of the needs of a *creature*, that is, of one who does *not* have life in itself. In its very action, however, desire is restless, exposed, vulnerable, dependent, something to be shaped and formed, in that the self's notions of its "need" are concretely formed by socially mediated experience in language and culture. In this sense, *affectus* is a receptive object, informed or misinformed, shaped or misshaped, guided or led astray by demands and promises communicated in language. All by nature seek the good; what good we seek depends on what is presented and so seems good to us as situated by our bodies in particular human cultures at particular times and places. Our perception of the good is formed by the forces that speak to us, telling stories of weal and woe; our agency arises as a function of this patiency, as we yield or resist the contending voices appealing for our allegiance. This reception then is an actual effect in the world, this yielding or resistance of patiency, which the old word *obedience* once captured. Obedience actively gives the ear to one voice or another. Obedience thus becomes an actual effect in the world, which matters immensely in the world of creatures. And obedience is an effect that belongs to no one else but the biographical self who so yields or refuses to yield its body in service. If this behavior were coerced, of course, it would take place, as we say, under duress and we would not count it as the patient-agent's own (at least before a human court). But if one freely yields, if one concurs with the demand, or promise, or command, it is justifiably called one's own and no one else's action. *Bodily obedience is necessary* (we might say, reasoning from the particular to the universal) *not only as an anticipation of the reality of bodily resurrection, as Käsemann rightly states of Paul, but in anticipation of any demand, threat, promise, hope.*

Thus on analysis the underlying picture of the "creature" here may

---

only a modification of the tripartite view of man . . . [which] created some odd misunderstandings" (p. 72). This latter judgment is doubtful. One might say the same of Luther and Melanchthon, who also retain the terms "reason," "will," and "affections" just as Augustine does. They are put to work in a new scheme. Lindhardt in another passage tries to explain the difference between Luther and Augustine with the claim Luther and Augustine agree that "a man is his love, with the difference that for Luther *affectus* is a receiver-concept, which is to say that *affectus* is not characterized as a drive or desire (contra Augustine) but as an experience that comes to one from Augustine [sic; outside?]" (p. 108). But this is surely wrong.

not be such a flattering one: the ecstatic self's "will is like a beast standing between two riders,"[16] Luther continued (knowingly or not, reversing Plato's dualistic and rationalistic image in the *Phaedrus*),[17] in that such humans have no power to move themselves, that is, to cause, command, or demand their own desire into existence or to change its direction. "Ask experience how impervious to dissuasion are those whose hearts are set on anything! If they abandon their quest of it, they do so only under pressure, or because of some counter-attraction, never freely. . . ."[18] In Luther's Pauline imagination, it is not the pilot of free-will or charioteer of the soul that masters its internally contending desires, but God and Satan who contend over the creature's unitary love.

One may wonder whether Käsemann has been any more successful than Luther was in his generation. Both theologians battled against the precious illusion of the centered, sovereign self, in Luther's time emergent, in Käsemann's dominant. Talal Asad has trenchantly described its appearance in recent guise as a "historical project": "Given the essential freedom, or the natural sovereignty, of the human subject, and given, too, its own desires and interests, what should human beings do to realize their free-

---

16. Luther, *Bondage*, p. 103. Gustaf Wingren nicely captured Luther's picture: "Man is set between God and the devil. When he is bound by God, he is free against the devil. When he is bound by the devil, he is free against God. . . . Before God man can be free only as evil. He cannot be separated from God and independent of God without being a captive to God's adversary and foe, a slave of the devil." Gustaf Wingren, *Luther on Vocation*, trans. Carl C. Rasmussen (Philadelphia: Muhlenberg Press, 1957), p. 105. "Man would be free from the bondage of the will only if the will were free and unengaged, with the ability to choose its rider or to pursue existence with no rider at all" (p. 106). "In God's power man's entire status is called freedom; in the devil's power it is called thralldom" (p. 106). Man "has to take God as he is and suffer him" (p. 107).

17. In the *Phaedrus* Plato argues both for desire as fundamental and for its dualistic split: "We must go on to observe that within each one of us there are two sorts of ruling or guiding principle that we follow. One is an innate desire for pleasure, the other an acquired judgment that aims at what is best. Sometimes these internal guides are in accord, sometimes at variance; now one gains the mastery, now the other. And when judgment guides us rationally towards what is best, and has the mastery, that mastery is called temperance, but when desire drags us irrationally towards pleasure and has come to rule within us, the name given to that rule is wantonness." *Phaedrus* 237d-e, in *The Collected Dialogues of Plato*, ed. Edith Hamilton and Huntington Cairns (Princeton: Princeton University Press, 1971), p. 485. The immortal soul is here likened to a charioteer, driving two steeds, representing irrational and rational desires, 246b (p. 493). I am indebted to Brent Adkins for calling this reference to my attention.

18. Luther, *Bondage*, p. 104.

dom, empower themselves, and choose pleasure? The assumption here is that power — and so too pain — is external to and repressive of the agent, that it 'subjects' him or her, and that nevertheless the agent as 'active subject' has both the desire to oppose power and the responsibility to become more powerful so that disempowerment — suffering — can be overcome." Asad adds immediately, "I shall argue against this assumption";[19] i.e., Asad argues that power and pain can only appear as "external" to a self "insanely" centered on its self as essentially free and naturally sovereign. The "insanity" of this project is evident not only in the fact that for "the self to be liberated from external control [it] must be subjected to the control of a liberated self already and always free, aware, and in control of its desires"[20] — the project presupposes the very freedom it lacks and so in fact ends up exchanging one form of bondage for another. But the aspiration itself for centeredness and sovereignty is not a sane "'desire to be connected to the world in a certain way . . . [even] controlled by the world in certain ways and not others.'"[21] That connectedness, indeed, dependency is sane, if indeed our selves are somatic and eccentric.

Yet this centered self has claimed to be the more "natural" self-interpretation, like William James's once-born healthy-mindedness, under the conditions of modernity, which Asad, following Milbank, calls "secularism." This centered self is clearly *not* what we described as an ecstatic self, for the latter is its own self only as a (precarious) integration of experience *in respect to the unique body which it* is *with its own space and time* amid contending claims to allegiance. Luther thinks that somatic receptivity is the clue to a proper way of speaking of the self as ecstatic (rather than centered): "Are not things which we did not produce ourselves, but received from others, spoken of as 'ours' in the most proper sense . . . ? If we create the things that are called ours, it follows that we created our eyes . . . hands . . . feet. . . . [But], says Paul, what have we that we did not receive?"[22] The ecstatic self *is* inextricably based in its own *somatic* receptor,[23] understood from out of its fundamental *corporeality*. Here, recalling Royce, the present of consciousness is located by the *body's* place, and consists in the self's ongoing interpretation of its past recollected *by virtue of the organic*

19. Talal Asad, *Formations of the Secular: Christianity, Islam, Modernity* (Stanford, CA: Stanford University Press, 2003), p. 71.

20. Asad, *Formations,* p. 73.

21. Asad, *Formations,* p. 73, citing Susan Wolf.

22. Luther, *Bondage,* pp. 185-86.

23. Lindhardt, *Martin Luther,* p. 23.

continuity of the body to its current aspirations for its *body's* future. Such corporeality, as Käsemann tried to capture Paul's usage of *soma,* designates one definite position in space-time that is one's own, and no one else's, where possibilities are given with the voices that contend for our hearing and bodily allegiance, where freedom or agency consists in bodily obedience to one or another such claims in that same space-time. This is the *soma* that Paul believes God has created for Himself, but has fallen prey to usurpers and yet which God will redeem for Himself at the resurrection (Rom. 8:23). The somatic self is not free then by the merit of making its own choices, as it were, decreeing in this way what will be its own good or evil; rather it is effectively free in choosing the good which is God, its maker and redeemer, as its own bodily future in the Beloved Community to come, if in fact it so freely, willingly chooses. In point of fact, however, for Paul, it must first *be freed* before it can effectively choose that good, a view that Luther, quoting Augustine, endorses: God, who "creates and preserves us without ourselves . . . , does not work in us without us; for He created and preserves us for this very purpose, that he might work in us and we might co-operate with Him, whether that occurs outside His kingdom by His general omnipotence, or within His kingdom, by the special power of His Spirit."[24] In terms of theological anthropology, divine faith which justifies, for Luther, is the bodily cooperation of the new, ecstatic self with God.

There is another interpretation of the self, however, which would be illusory and indeed exist as an evasion, in Paul's, Augustine's, Luther's, Käsemann's, or Asad's mind, of this precarious, embattled place of the somatic self. This other, *centered* self can imaginatively distance itself from its body (e.g., *Phaedrus* 250b-c). This self imagines to create its own future since it can willfully forget its past; more precisely, for this self, memory of past bodily states is optional, since this self centers as its own self in the present moment's awareness. Consequently this self can also disregard the claims of external forces contending for its ears; it can do this because it in turn regards the one position occupied by its body through space-time as itself illusory, a deceptive, heteronomous interpretation of its true existence, namely, the one centered in the ever-passing parade of present awareness. This self is decidedly not the "extended thing" with which it is, as it were, associated. This self regards its present state of consciousness floating along on the stream of time as all that it is from one moment to the

---

24. Luther, *Bondage,* p. 268.

next; just so it disowns what it has been given, forgets the accident of its seeming identity with any past bodily state (and associated memory), and consequently creates (not too weak a word!) its own (well, virtual) reality, that is, adopts a creative attitude toward the next moment of consciousness and so on to infinity.[25] This self is as protean as it is promethean. Whether we call it the Platonic soul, the Gnostic spirit, the Pelagian agent, the Cartesian thinking thing, the secular Sovereign Self, or the promethean *Homo faber* makes little theological difference. Whatever it is called, whatever form it has assumed historically with whatever new shade of meaning, it *is* the belief in "free-will."

In the last chapter, we saw how Luther put the verse on the lips of the faithful: "My own good works all came to naught, No grace or merit gaining; Free will [hated] God's judgment, Dead to all good remaining. [Angst drove me to doubt] Left only death to be my share; [I had to sink to hell]." We argued that this depiction does not represent a spontaneous self-interpretation but rather the retrospective analysis of the (old) self's plight from the new perspective of redemption by the Son's coming in the body to redeem the lost body from Satan's usurpation for life and service in the coming reign of God. Here "free-will" is not cast as a neutral human capacity for self-determination, but as an enemy at war with the God who comes to reign in the form of the Beloved Community. Free-will then is a peculiar (yet inevitable) illusion about the self and its powers absent news of the coming of God, an almost necessary evasion of the precarious reality of the embodied self with its moral burden of the irrevocable past. When Luther "denies" free-will to expose to the depths this human predicament, this apocalyptic theological framework of his thinking must ever be kept in mind. "You imagine," he addresses Erasmus, "that the human will is something placed in an intermediate position of 'freedom' and left to itself . . . you imagine that God and the devil are far away, mere spectators, as it were, of this mutable free will; you do not believe that they are prompters and drivers of an enslaved will, and each waging relentless war against the other."[26] What Erasmus imagines, of course, is what the philosophical tradition attests going back to Plato's construction of the tripartite soul: it is the picture of the will as a charioteer mediating between rational and irra-

---

25. E.g., the discussion of Paul de Man in Alasdair MacIntyre, *Three Rival Versions of Moral Enquiry: Encyclopaedia, Genealogy and Tradition* (Notre Dame: University of Notre Dame Press, 1990), pp. 210-13.

26. Luther, *Bondage*, p. 262.

tional desires. Luther's denial of "free-will" cannot be taken then as a "philosophical" thesis alongside others, even though, as we shall see, neither he nor we can avoid reckoning with the tension that the introduction of his theological anthropology of somatic-ecstatic creatures creates with philosophical accounts of centered experience and the accompanying analyses of its capacities. Luther's own self-identified followers in fact tried to disown that tension, as we shall next explore.

## Lutherans against Luther on the Power of the Will

To the end of his life, Luther regarded the treatise against Erasmus, *On Bound Choice,* as one of two from his voluminous writings that might be preserved for posterity. The other was his Catechisms. He paid Erasmus the backhanded compliment at the end of the treatise, that he alone had seen through to the "hinge" on which the whole matter turns.[27] This is interesting to note for several reasons. First, both of the writings that Luther would have seen preserved are works in dogmatic theology,[28] not the exegetical works or occasional essays and polemical tracts that otherwise dominate his oeuvre. Luther was proud of them as works in which he put his reformatory teachings together in an ordered and coherent way, the Catechisms to instruct preachers and the faithful, the treatise against Erasmus to do battle for them against damaging misinterpretations of the faith. We need to know God in this way. "For if I am ignorant of the nature, extent and limits of what I can and must do with reference to God, I shall be equally ignorant and uncertain of the nature, extent and limits of what God can and will do in me — though God, in fact works all in all (cf. 1 Cor. 12:6). Now, if I am ignorant of God's works and power, I am ignorant of God himself; and if I do not know God, I cannot worship, praise, give

---

27. Luther, *Bondage,* p. 319.

28. So Ebeling: "It is foolish to deny, as is often done, that [Luther] possesses the power of systematic thought. But he displays it not in the summarizing and harmonizing architectural structure of a system of doctrine, nor in the speculative derivation of numerous lines of thought from a single principle, but rather by a critical and liberating demonstration that God is God indeed, in the language of biblical tradition" (*Luther,* p. 247). The critical aspect of Luther's dogmatics is that "one must exclude everything which prevents God from being God, and which gives an opportunity of speaking of theological matters in an untheological or pseudo-theological way" (p. 246). Indeed, "Christian doctrine is a guide to the right way to speak of God" (p. 248).

thanks or serve Him, for I do not know how much I should attribute to myself and how much to Him. We need, therefore, to have in mind a clear-cut distinction between God's power and ours, and God's work and ours, if we would live a godly life."[29] Luther's writings to the end of knowledge of God and of self do not of course add up to a "system," but neither does most of the material produced in systematic theology, which discipline of Christian teaching (better called, though scandalously nowadays, dogmatics) is "systematic" in thinking consequently and coherently in teaching the gospel to those who believe or would believe and "live godly lives." "Systematic" theology is this art of consequent interpretation, and in *DSA* we see Luther at the top of his game.

There is a second reason for interest. While the portion of posterity that claimed Luther's name for itself did treasure the Catechisms, the treatise *On Bound Choice* quickly became something of an embarrassment to them.[30] It had not been controversial among the sixteenth-century theological parties that later came to be known as the Lutherans, the Calvinists, and the Thomists that God foresaw Adam's fall, yet in the same foreknowledge elected some of those fallen to be saved and so predestined them to eternal life in Christ who would in time become the source and means of their salvation. That much seemed to all parties the manifest witness of the Scriptures, even though the "modern" theology of the Ockhamists had recently put forward a rival to it. The *via moderna* put forward a "natural" theology, argued philosophically on grounds of a tacit divine compact *(potentia ordinata)* with creatures entered into by the *potentia absoluta,* that the Deity could and would accept creatures on this contracted basis, if in principle creatures were *facere quod in se,* that is, "to do what is in them,"

---

29. Luther, *Bondage*, p. 78.

30. See Robert Kolb, *Bound Choice,* for a thorough documentation of this claim. Jill Raitt vividly dramatizes this embarrassment in her account of a public debate between Calvin's heir and a pupil of Melanchthon: "Beza denied that the doctrine he expounded perturbed consciences or robbed people of their consolation since the Holy Spirit is given to the elect and testifies to their spirits that they are indeed children of God. Indeed, claimed Beza[,] . . . the Genevan doctrine was in accord with Luther's treatise against Erasmus. In fact, Beza wrote nothing more in his Responsio and allowed Luther to speak for him." Jill Raitt, *The Colloquy of Montbéliard: Religion and Politics in the Sixteenth Century* (New York and Oxford: Oxford University Press, 1993), p. 154. She concludes: "Beza's use of Luther's Bondage of the Will should have been a master stroke. It turned against the Lutherans a fundamental work of Luther himself in which the arguments strongly underpin the very points that Andreae found so horrible, namely, that, by his secret will God could will the damnation of anyone" (p. 210).

i.e., act on their natural powers.[31] After Luther's protest erupted against this new Pelagianism, all parties, the Thomists too, rejected human salvation by natural power according to the modernist scheme and apart from the assisting grace of God.[32] The issue between the earliest protesters against and defenders of the papacy was *not* grace, but *faith,* that is, between Luther's faith alone in Christ alone, and the papal party's faith formed by charity, as the condition of divine acceptance. What rapidly did become church-dividing controversy between the protesting parties, however, was second-generation Calvinism's embrace under the press and duress of sixteenth-century polemics of what seemed a clear and unavoidable inference from the non-controversial affirmation of divine election to salvation in Christ, namely, that the number and identity of the elect had been settled by an eternal, secret, and absolute decree of the Deity, which also included reprobation, that is, the deliberate withholding from some of the Spirit, lest they turn again and believe.

A problem arose here for the would-be heirs of Luther. In *DSA* Luther not infrequently argues against the goddess Fortuna in the process of arguing for divine election: "But if God is thus robbed of His power and wisdom in election, what will He be but just that idol, Chance, under whose sway all things happen at random?"[33] Fundamentally, Luther thinks of Christ the Savior together with His people in the Beloved Community as the content of God's election, and not a predetermined list of the saved and the damned.[34] But it also seems evident here in time that God both gives and withholds the Spirit needed to come to Christ, and thus to meet the condition of His gracious acceptance. Hence the inference is hard to avoid of "a dreadful hidden will of God, Who, according to His own counsel, ordains such persons as He wills to receive and partake of the mercy preached and offered. . . ." Luther's reticence in such a formulation is evi-

---

31. See the classic studies of Heiko A. Oberman, *The Harvest of Medieval Theology: Gabriel Biel and Late Medieval Nominalism* (Grand Rapids: Baker Academic, 2000) and *The Dawn of the Reformation: Essays in Late Medieval and Early Reformation Thought* (Edinburgh: T. & T. Clark, 1986).

32. See the first three canons concerning justification by the Council of Trent which anathematize the *facere quod in se* of merely natural powers, against which Luther had fundamentally protested. *Canons and Decrees of the Council of Trent,* trans. Rev. H. J. Schroeder, O.P. (St. Louis and London: Herder, 1960), p. 42.

33. Luther, *Bondage,* p. 199.

34. The Pauline "wisdom hidden in a mystery . . . revealed in the gospel" which philosophical reason never imagined, Luther, *Bondage,* p. 306.

dent. He will not plainly articulate a decree of reprobation, but the sense is implied. He immediately warns against inquiry into this "most awesome secret of the Divine Majesty."[35]

"Lutherans" eventually united to reject the teachings that eternal reprobation is an effect of God's justice, since God in Christ justifies the ungodly; that mercy is restricted to the chosen, since Christ has died for all; that God ordained Adam's sin (which was nevertheless spontaneous, even though Adam had no alternative) since the origin of sin is a mystery; that God's love and hate have no cause in their objects but only in God's arbitrary choice, since God's choices are wise and knowing as well as powerful; that the cause of Adam's fall, indeed of all things, was God's foreknowledge and foreordination, since the particular object of God's foreordination was redemption in Christ.[36] Of course, these rejections, pastorally sensible as they were, left all the burning questions to go begging with little more than what seemed to be a pious appeal to "faith." The "Lutherans" had no idea how to put their denials together in an affirmation. The embarrassing problem to boot, as we have seen, for this unified front of "Lutherans" against the "Calvinists'" doctrine of the double decree was that their own church father, Martin Luther, arguably held the same or very similar monergistic views. In contrast to Luther's teaching, their own slowly evolving synergistic view of free will as also a "cause" of justification alongside divine grace derived instead from Philip Melanchthon. Indeed, Melanchthon[37] had grown away from his earliest views on human bondage under the influence of Luther. He was increasingly displeased with the fatalism, as it seemed to him, to which Luther's arguments against Chance inclined, especially the leading argument in *DSA* about the "immutability of divine foreknowledge" — Luther's own words for what was centrally at issue between himself and Erasmus.[38] So confessionalized Lutheranism came to birth, containing a

35. Luther, *Bondage*, p. 169.
36. Raitt, *The Colloquy*, pp. 147-48.
37. On Melanchthon's alienation from Luther's teaching here, see Hinlicky, *Paths Not Taken*, pp. 150-69. See also Oswald Bayer's brief but precise analysis, "Freedom? The Anthropological Concepts in Luther and Melanchthon Compared," *Harvard Theological Review* 91, no. 4 (1998): 373-78.
38. Interestingly enough, according to Steinmetz, also the Anabaptist Hubmaier, who had been Zwingli's follower, "understood Luther's doctrine of predestination as his denial of the freedom of the human will as another form of the Stoic assault on freedom and responsibility." David Steinmetz, *Luther in Context* (Grand Rapids: Baker Academic, 2002), p. 67.

difficult and profound contradiction within itself. But what had Luther actually meant to say?

## Reading *De servo arbitrio* as Apocalyptic Theology

Luther's theological intention[39] in the treatise was to re-preach[40] the Pauline gospel to Erasmus (and of course all the readership) as an act of apocalyptic battle, falling back as need be on second-order theological reflection in order to meet and overcome objections, and then to advance the line of battle into the enemy's camp by exposing fallacies and tacit but false assumptions Erasmus held about the human situation. The task, Luther writes, "is to assert with precision, and consistency, and warmth, and give solid, skillful, substantial proof of my teaching."[41] This act of *assertion* conveys the clear teaching of God on which embattled faith depends in the conflict that "breaks in upon the world." "The Spirit asserts to such purpose that He breaks in upon the whole world and convinces it of sin, as if challenging it to battle."[42] Without doubt, Christian teaching "breaking in upon the whole world" cannot be pigeon-holed, safely compartmentalized into a region of privacy called religion. It thus overlaps with claims in the region of philosophy, which reads the human situation in another way. It is not for Luther a question of "double truth,"[43] as Bayer rightly maintains,[44] but it certainly requires the frank admission of twofold or two-tiered perspectives on reality, perspectives that in their own ways shape perception of the very reality in dispute.[45] Recalling the major theme of his *theologia crucis* from the Heidelberg Disputation, Luther at one point exclaims:

39. For an alternative account based on Luther's pastoral intention, see Kolb, *Bound Choice*, pp. 31-66; also Oswald Bayer, *Martin Luther's Theology: A Contemporary Interpretation*, trans. Thomas H. Trapp (Grand Rapids: Eerdmans, 2007), pp. 185-92, which similarly argues that the purpose of the book is to "forget" the question of the self.

40. Kenneth Hagen, *Luther's Approach to Scripture as Seen in His "Commentaries" on Galatians 1519-1538* (Tübingen: J. C. B. Mohr [Paul Siebeck] 1993), p. 152.

41. Luther, *Bondage*, p. 219.

42. Luther, *Bondage*, p. 67.

43. "Disputation concerning the Passage, 'The Word Made Flesh'" (1536) LW 38:239-77.

44. Oswald Bayer, *Theology the Lutheran Way*, ed. and trans. Jeffery G. Silcock and Mark C. Mattes, Lutheran Quarterly Books (Grand Rapids: Eerdmans, 2007), pp. 78-80.

45. On Luther's distinction between the old and new languages of philosophy and theology, see *Creator est creatura*, pp. 178-80.

"Many things seem, and are, very good to God which seem, and are, very bad to us. Thus, afflictions, sorrows, errors, hell, and all God's best works are in the world's eyes very bad and damnable. What is better than Christ and the gospel? But what is there that the world abominates more?" Since, however, the theologian, who is to "see with God's eyes, that is, [as one] who [has] the Spirit,"[46] is also a philosopher (that is, a human creature with her own incorrigible experience and interpretation of self), sorting out these shifting perspectives of reason and revelation, of nature thinking and of faith thinking, of the lights of nature, grace, and glory, is itself a fundamental theological act.

Thus early on in the treatise, Luther lays his theological cards on the table: "If, then, we are taught and believe that we ought to be ignorant of the necessary foreknowledge of God and the necessity of events, Christian faith is utterly destroyed, and the promises of God and the whole gospel fall to the ground completely; for the Christian's chief and only comfort in every adversity lies in knowing that God does not lie, but brings to pass all things immutably, and that His will cannot be resisted, altered or impeded."[47] With this "comfort in adversity" of the Christian at stake, Luther goes on expressly to reject the usual compatibilism: the problem, he writes, is "insoluble" if you try "to establish both the foreknowledge of God and the freedom of man together; for what is harder, yes, more impossible, than maintaining that contraries and contradictories do not clash?"[48] Thus the Thomistic and later Lutheran view that God elects by foreseeing the free (but just so meritorious) act of faith is ruled out. Objections to injustice on God's part that consequently arise are also summarily indicted, tried, and executed. They are based on the fallacy of treating Creator and creature alike, as if equals; we should rather "revere the majesty of God's power and will, against which we have no rights, but which has full rights against us to do what it pleases. No injustice is done to us, for God owes us nothing."[49] We can hardly be surprised then, as mentioned, when Luther does not shy from implying, if not expressly inferring, the dreaded corollary. Yet it is interesting how and why he avoids a frank, non-dialectical statement of a doctrine of reprobation.

In tackling this, he tries to show that it is *fallen* reason that once

---

46. Luther, *Bondage,* p. 203.
47. Luther, *Bondage,* p. 84.
48. Luther, *Bondage,* p. 215.
49. Luther, *Bondage,* p. 216.

again *asserts* its hostility to God and so *confirms* its guilt in protesting God's injustice at the very thought of reprobation. It is "faith and the Spirit [which] judge otherwise, believing that God is good even though he should destroy all men"[50] — the logical point under the harsh rhetoric being that it is question-begging to set up another authority (such as self-serving human ideas of justice) over God. "God is He for Whose will no cause or ground may be laid down as its rule or standard. . . . Causes and grounds are laid down for the will of the creature, but not for the will of the Creator — unless you set another Creator over him!"[51] With this move, Luther goes on the offensive: reason exposes its sinful fallenness when it does not protest the "good luck" of grace and mercy, betraying that it secretly considers such "good fortune" as merited reward. Reason only protests the "bad luck" of reprobation: "because this is against its interest, it finds the action iniquitous and intolerable . . . [it does] not judge in this matter according to equity, but according to passionate regard for its own interest."[52] Having shown that reason is not neutral in disputing God's justice, but rather a covert combatant in the apocalyptic battle, Luther is on the other hand eager to concede that it is incomprehensible also to believing reason how it is just on God's part to crown the unworthy, but then to punish those no more unworthy from whom grace has been withheld. But believing reason, he says, trusts on the basis of the mercy revealed in Christ what it cannot yet comprehend; incomprehension will give way to understanding God's justice when faith gives way to sight.[53] That's the gist of the case.

Little wonder that Philip and his followers ran in another direction!

Yet, what if, in accord with the theological subversion of classical metaphysics that we have been implicitly and explicitly urging throughout this book, human beings really are their history on the earth? What if it is this history that matters — eternally? What if we cannot count on a *comical resolution* in an afterlife, let alone such a happy ending for us and for all *as our due*? What if we cannot count either on peaceful stillness at death? Nor on the good memory the polis will have of us? What if we rather exist on this good earth for God's purposes, to be workers in God's kingdom, and what then if we have missed our calling and now live by resisting it?

50. Luther, *Bondage,* p. 202.
51. Luther, *Bondage,* p. 209.
52. Luther, *Bondage,* p. 234.
53. Luther, *Bondage,* p. 234.

Would it not be the case then that *the* religious *illusion* would be the easy gospel that "God hardens none and damns none, but has mercy on all and saves all, so that hell is destroyed, and the fear of death may be put away, and no future punishment need be dreaded"?[54] By contrast, the faith of the martyr is in a hard gospel — Luther's Christian, whose "chief and only comfort in every adversity lies in knowing that God does not lie, but brings to pass all things immutably." This then would be a defiant faith *in the teeth* of heteronomous and seductive powers, holding against them that the very things one suffers and does *in the body, as time,* are *the* matters of eternal consequence. Perhaps that is far more meaning than we bargain for, and we should well prefer Erasmus's skepticism to it. What's a little existentialist angst about modern meaninglessness, after all, in comparison to the God *who owes us nothing* but *demands our all?*

To interpret this treatise on theonomous existence, with its ruthless, relentless assault on the centered self's illusion of autonomy, and its Christian faith in redemption from the heteronomous and seductive powers that enslave above all those who will not see as guilt their very protest against the sovereign justice of the kingdom *of God* — to understand *Luther's* meaning, we must read this most "systematic" and "philosophical" of his writings as theology, revealed theology, apocalyptic theology. That will be clear for several reasons.

The first reason is our need to clean up the shoddy imprecision of Luther's terminology in this treatise, which has baffled generations of interpreters who cannot finally decide for or against him because they are simply unsure of what he means to say. This is Luther's personal weakness; it is the reason why he preferred Melanchthon's clear, ordered, patient writing to his own volcanic eruptions. Luther in fact does not take the time to explain in this treatise, for example, how differently he (generally!) uses the words *voluntas* and *arbitrium,* nor then the differing senses in which these capacities are said to be servile. "The co-existence of two ways of asserting the bondage of the will, which are apparently fundamentally different, makes the task of understanding Luther very difficult."[55] At the risk of imposing my own order on chaos, I would in brief organize terminology as follows.

*Voluntas,* desire, is spontaneously bound to seek the good and avert from evil; a freedom to seek what is ugly or foul or to flee from what is

54. Luther, *Bondage,* p. 202.
55. Ebeling, *Luther,* p. 217.

beautiful or delightful would be pathological. This is the non-controversial truism borrowed from Plato with which Aristotle launched the *Nichomachean Ethics:* "All by nature seek the good."[56] On reflection it is evident then that there is no freedom of desire; the will, taken as desire, spontaneously and necessarily seeks what appears good to it and flees what appears evil. This capacity is what Luther has in mind when he denies that the will can move itself, that is, cause itself to desire something. "Free-will," Luther says, would mean to ascribe to desire such power of "freely turning itself in any direction, yielding to none and subject to none."[57] This is what, he says, Erasmus commits himself to by insisting on "free-will." How odd then when Erasmus adds the little postscript, as he does, that such "free-will" is "ineffective without God's grace." This, Luther retorts, amounts to a contradiction: "What is ineffective power but (in plain language) no power?"[58] Likewise *voluntas* is the capacity Luther has in mind when he goes on to write that free-will, properly speaking, belongs only to God, meaning that a capacity for self-determination in the radical sense belongs only to the divine nature. God can move God's own will and so become God in a new way by virtue of a divine attribute, namely, the omnipotent "power of freely turning in any direction, yielding to none and subject to none." So Luther affirms radically divine omnipotence: God can be who God will be.

But what divine nature? The affirmation that God is such power, be it noted, does not entail that God is without other essential attributes, such as wisdom and love, which then mutually qualify each another in the act of God's being and the actions of God *ad extra.* God can be whatever God wills, but not all such possibilities are wise or good, which attributes are also essential to God. Otherwise, indeed, any self-movement of God would not be followable as *God's* and would be instead unrecognizable as *God's* self-movement. If omnipotence alone defines deity, if God simply and primordially is *potentia absoluta* (not Holy Trinity), then God's life (if we may even call it that) is a sheer, incalculable, unfollowable, ever-spontaneous reinvention, so to say, *deus exlex.* (Consider here the picture that the perhaps already half-mad Nietzsche eventually came to draw: a ". . . *Dionysian* world of the eternally self-creating, the eternally self-

---

56. Cf. Steinmetz's discussion of *synderis,* "the natural human longing for the good" in the Ockhamist background of his thought in *Luther in Context,* pp. 64-65.

57. Luther, *Bondage,* p. 105.

58. Luther, *Bondage,* p. 104.

destroying, this mystery world of the twofold voluptuous delight, my 'beyond good and evil,' without goal, unless the joy of the circle is itself a goal. . . . *This world is the will to power — and nothing besides!* And you yourselves are also this will to power — and nothing besides!")[59]

*Arbitrium*, choice, is in principle freedom to choose between logically non-contradictory paths to a desired goal; e.g., I can take either I-81 or the Blue Ridge Parkway from Roanoke to Lexington. I have before me in this actual space-time a real choice. In relation to God, free-choice would have originally indicated many, non-contradictory paths of obedience, as the human race would have multiplied and flourished to maximal diversity in harmony with God's will to create the Beloved Community by means of human cooperation. But Luther holds that such free choice since Adam's fall exists in name only, that humanity has since inherited only bad choices in relation to God. Exiled from paradise, as the story goes, all Adam's posterity have now lost his original free choice to obey God in purity of heart. In relation to God, now, they have nothing but bad choices, *including all their religious choices.* This latter especially is the illusion of religion that like a prophet of old Luther wishes to shatter. Our religious choices are no better before God than our irreligious choices: "should they do good works in order to obtain the kingdom, they never would obtain it, but would belong rather to the number of the ungodly, who with an evil, mercenary eye seek the things of self even in God."[60] If we think of a reform, not only of abuses, but of church and theology, this latter critique of the religious *amor concupiscentiae* is what Luther here bequeaths us.

We could also add here *freedom of action,* for which I find in Luther no special terminology, though the idea is there. Even if hypothetically we desired to love God above all (as Scotus taught), for example, Luther denies that we would succeed in acting so, because we have inherited from Adam such deep mistrust in and uncertainty about God. Even if wistfully we could imagine love of God for God's sake, we do not act on that fantasy, let alone sustain a life of such love, because uncertainty and suspicion cannot overcome our inherited inertia. Yet Luther never denies that we have freedom of action with respect to the things that are, as he puts it, "below us."[61] That is, we do not *have to* act on our immediate desires with respect

---

59. Friedrich Nietzsche, *The Will to Power,* trans. W. Kaufmann and R. J. Hollingdale (New York: Vintage, 1967), #1067, p. 550.

60. Luther, *Bondage,* p. 182.

61. Luther, *Bondage,* p. 107.

to fellow creatures. We can critically reflect on the goods and evils that appear to us, and we can query whether they are really such. Consequently, we can withhold action or commit to action as the case may be. Granting this, Luther allows enough of the relevant freedom in civil society to reward good citizens and punish evildoers, at least with a rough kind of justice. Luther roots this freedom over things "below us" in the *imago Dei* passage of Genesis 1:26-28: "that man was made a lord of all things so that he might freely rule over them. . . . For there man certainly could act according to his own will, all these things being put under his control."[62] On this basis, he finds a theological foundation for speaking of a certain, delimited freedom of action in the realm of nature. In the dispute with Erasmus, however, he insists "we are discussing, not nature, but grace; we ask, not what we are on earth, but what we are in heaven, before God. We know that man was made lord over things below him, and that he has a right and a free will with respect to them, that they should obey him and do as he wills and thinks. But our question is this: whether he has 'free-will' Godward. . . ."[63]

With the foregoing Luther thinks he has cordoned off his topic. Luther wants to talk about the human, created will in relation to God, not in relation to creatures. But Zwingli, as we shall see, asks a penetrating counter-question here, whether the theological region of things "above us" can be so neatly separated from the natural realm of philosophy, the things "below us." Had not Luther himself equated the necessary foreknowledge of God *with the necessity of events,* the knowledge that God does not lie but brings to pass *all things* immutably? How indeed can we separate the circumstances in which the martyr is put on the witness stand from the web of decisions creatures make concerning things below? Zwingli will represent a clear and forceful alternative here: "For before the creation of the world Divine Providence had just as much determined about their acts and life as about their creation and birth. For if the hairs of our head are numbered, if nothing can escape Divine Wisdom, if Providence is nowhere at rest, if Goodness neither neglects nor postpones anything, it is clear that what follows life and existence is just as much regulated as the bestowal of these."[64] He puts this objection directly to Luther: "the things lower than man do not

---

62. Luther, *Bondage,* p. 150.
63. Luther, *Bondage,* p. 310.
64. "The Providence of God," in *The Latin Works of Huldreich Zwingli,* 2 vols., trans. Samuel Macauley Jackson (Philadelphia: Heidelberg Press, 1922), 2:205 [hereafter Zwingli, "Providence"].

happen by chance but are regulated by Providence. . . ."[65] We will return to this powerful objection, not least to probe further how Luther understands the distinction between nature and grace. In any case, Luther's intention is clear: it is "with regard to God, and in all that bears on salvation or damnation, [that man] has no 'free-will,' but is captive, prisoner and bondslave, either to the will of God, or to the will of Satan."[66] Theologically, in this relation, Luther wants to defend an exclusive thesis: God has taken salvation out of the (incompetent, unworthy) hands of (self-deluded) creatures and put it into His own. *This* action — we might say *this* distinguishing of nature and grace, *this* sorting out the shifting perspectives of reason and revelation — *is* the enlightening work of God the Holy Spirit.

That yields a second reason why we must read *DSA* as apocalyptic theology. "What need is there of the Spirit, or Christ, or God, if 'free-will' can overcome the motions of the mind to evil?"[67] When I assign this text for students to read, I often instruct them at any given point to go through several pages and circle in red ink every occurrence of the name, the Holy Spirit. They are astonished to learn as a result that *DSA* might as readily have been titled *De Spiritu sancti*.[68] "I call a man ungodly if he is without the Spirit of God; for the Scripture says that the Spirit is given to justify the ungodly . . . it obviously follows that whatever is flesh is ungodly, under God's wrath, and a stranger to his kingdom. And if it is a stranger to God's kingdom and Spirit, it follows of necessity that it is under the kingdom and spirit of Satan. For there is no middle kingdom between the kingdom of God and the kingdom of Satan, which are ever at war with each other."[69] Luther needs to assert in full Trinitarian personalism the Holy Spirit as Lord and Giver of life in battle with that unholy spirit, Satan. It is the Holy Spirit who takes salvation out of the uncertain hands of mortals in order to steel these very mortals now as the Spirit's defenseless witnesses against the heteronomous usurpers, even as within they still battle within themselves against old, still seductive desires. The martyrs need to know with full conviction that when they have fallen into the hands of the persecutors, they have not fallen out of the hands of God. Where apocalyptic war between

---

65. Zwingli, "Providence," p. 208, though Luther is not named. The point against Luther is reiterated in the Epilogue (p. 225).

66. Zwingli, "Providence," p. 208.

67. Luther, *Bondage*, p. 157.

68. Robert W. Jenson, "An Ontology of Freedom in the DSA of Luther," *Modern Theology* 10, no. 3 (July 1994): 247-52.

69. Luther, *Bondage*, p. 253.

the two Cities rages, theology is Spirit-given instruction for battle (Mark 13:11). This warfare in which there is and can be no neutrality determines theology as the (new) form of human reason, a cognitive process of interpretation needed in the fog and friction of "God's apocalyptic invasion" (Martyn), quite in distinction then from any philosophical inquiry into human will-power as such.

Nevertheless, Luther's contentions about human bondage could not have failed to have philosophical fallout, not least in making human bondage and liberation future themes for philosophical reflection. Nor could the uncomfortable implications about reprobation be ignored, as much as Luther tried to push them to the side. Above all, Luther's tortured attempts in *DSA*'s dialectic of *deus absconditus et revelatus* to describe the God who surpasses God in coming mercifully to that mortal being "fast bound in Satan's chains . . . so firmly sin possessed" in order rightfully and powerfully to overthrow that usurper, had to generate as much confusion as insight, given the metaphysical tradition's operating assumption that to be god is to be perfectly self-identical and so perfectly unrelated. As we shall see, this notion of divine perfection marks the precise point at which Zwingli's counterattack begins and to which it ever returns. Interpreting Luther's meaning in the rhetoric of God hidden and revealed, moreover, against Zwingli's theology of perfect, transparent divine lucidity, helps us past the false but convenient interpretation of Luther here as ultimately an Ockhamist, holding to divine voluntarism, positing a *deus exlex.*[70] Certainly Luther employs the idiom in which he was educated, indeed to chilling effect: "But God hidden in Majesty neither deplores nor takes away death, but works life, and death, and all in all; nor has He set bounds to Himself by His Word, but has kept Himself free over all things."[71] Luther

70. So the insightful analysis of Paul Vignaux, "On Luther and Ockham," in *The Reformation in Medieval Perspective,* ed. Steven E. Ozment (Chicago: Quadrangle Books, 1971), pp. 107-18.

71. Luther, *Bondage,* p. 170. Jakob Wolf has disputed this translation of Luther's Latin, "neque enim tum verbo suo definivit sese," on the grounds that it neglects the little word "tum," which would render a translation "for neither has God *as such* defined himself by His word." The idea is not that there is another God, a hidden One not defined by His Word, over and beyond Jesus Christ, but rather that the revealed God who has defined Himself in this way for us, remains veiled *then, when, in the case that* we look away from that Word at His omnipotence at work in and over all things. "Luther's Concept of Deus Absconditus" (unpublished lecture, University of Aarhus, 2003). If Wolf is right, that would mitigate the antithesis between Bayer and Barth, both of whom presuppose a more dualistic rendering of Luther's meaning, in the perspectivalist direction I am urging throughout this study.

knows that a God unbounded by His Word is Trinitarian heresy. Yet Luther even presses this apparently heretical dualism: "It belongs to the same God Incarnate [= *deus revelatus*] to weep, lament, and groan over the perdition of the ungodly, though that will of Majesty purposely leaves and reprobates some to perish. Nor is it for us to ask why he does so, but to stand in awe of God, Who can do, and wills to do, such things."[72] The objection to this provocation is immediately evident. How could we ever know that we are talking about one and the same entity? Luther attains to the decisive question in the rhetoric of the hidden and revealed God in *DSA*, but not yet clearly to an answer — in one sense, his theological answer is that the real answer awaits the light of glory, so that faith in the revealed God remains in the interim faith against a background of true inscrutability. A better theological answer, as we have been arguing throughout this book, comes when we take this appearance of God as hidden to (fallen, not physical) nature in contradistinction to the God revealed to faith as something followable, as a narrative, as a passage, as a real becoming of God. At the conclusion of this chapter, we will see that Luther did express regret at the dualistic implications of his provocative formulations in *DSA* and that he also hinted at just the kind of narrative resolution that I am proposing. The need for this will become apparent in light of Zwingli's *DPD*.

## Zwingli's Alternative Case for the Decentered Self

Zwingli did not share the conviction of Luther's that the Spirit works through the Word concerning Christ to conform to His death and resurrection. One looks in vain throughout *DPD* for anything like it. That is because in Zwingli's perspective Luther's focus on the Spirit's new work of the new self as conformation to the death and resurrection of Christ actually distracts from the true resolution of the "strife about free will and merit which arising long ago still continues, one side seeing that Providence and the free gratuitous election of God are the essential thing, the other side declaring that it is freedom of will and the reward of good works."[73] Certainly Zwingli puts Luther on the right side of "this evil strife" for defending the free, gratuitous election of God against human merit; but notice

72. Luther, *Bondage*, p. 176.
73. Zwingli, "Providence," p. 189.

what has subtly shifted here. The strife about this for Zwingli is no longer the Spirit's strife with Satan and against human illusions for the sake of the redemption of our bodies, but a theological-philosophical brouhaha about externals that ought then to be resolved, not prosecuted, by penetrating conceptually to the root of the confusion. So he continued: "This evil strife could be concluded immediately, if men would once turn to the contemplation of the Deity as the safest bulwark of religion. The supreme good is the Deity."[74] This text coming in the middle of *De providentia Dei* is the key to its interpretation, harkening back as it does to the opening thesis, "Providence must exist, because the supreme good necessarily cares for and regulates all things,"[75] and pointing forward to the summation: "It is clear, therefore, that by ascending in this way from our intelligence we arrive at the Deity, and when we have reached Him we have searched out providence also."[76] It is with this precise nuance of intellectual radicalness, cutting off Luther's still "half-papist" dependence on the *verbum externum*, that Zwingli here teaches that "recognition of the one true God is [faith's] salvation and horn of plenty. . . ."[77] Such recognition is not bound to that *news* concerning Christ, that *external* Word speaking His death and resurrection, and binding newborn believers to it by the Spirit's free election, since "externals can do nothing more than proclaim and represent . . . and since faith is a gift of the Holy Spirit, it is clear that the Spirit operated before the external symbols were introduced."[78]

In Gaebler's acute parsing of the import of these key statements: "Zwingli opposed the statements, essential for Luther, about the 'hidden' God with the 'simplicity' of God whose will can be totally recognized in his revelation."[79] One could also say: for Zwingli there is no difference in kind between philosophy and theology, since the "simplicity" of perfect being is in principle transparent to the mind made lucid, whether by ratiocination or by revelation. For Luther, there is a difference in kind between theology and philosophy, because the perfection of God does not reside in a timeless simplicity of self-identity, but in a real becoming of the Word made flesh and the body made divine, thus in a perfect capacity for time. Surely

74. Luther, *Bondage*, p. 189.

75. Luther, *Bondage*, p. 130.

76. Luther, *Bondage*, p. 233.

77. Luther, *Bondage*, p. 197.

78. Luther, *Bondage*, p. 188.

79. Ulrich Gaebler, *Huldrych Zwingli: His Life and Work*, trans. Ruth C. L. Gritsch (Philadelphia: Fortress, 1986), p. 147.

what is most striking about *DPD* when reading it on the heels of *DSA* is that we are now on the soil of the philosophical quest for the Deity, the *Arche,* the cause of causes in which the mind can rest and in turn direct the body to its proper work. As McSorley acknowledges, Luther teaches a perfectly "Catholic and biblical" *Alleswirksamseit Gottes;* that means that God the Creator and Sustainer of all that is impels secondary causes forward, even when the secondary causes commit evil. In this Luther follows the Augustinian maxim that God is the cause of all causes, though not the maker of all choices. God's responsibility for any evil act does not lie in immediately causing the evil choice, but in enabling a world in which evil choices can occur (that is, to be sure, a huge responsibility). By contrast, Zwingli teaches an *Alleinwirksamseit Gottes;*[80] that means that he denies secondary causes altogether.[81] Nor does Zwingli flinch from the consequence: God who is *deus exlex,* above the law, immediately instigates[82] the evil choice in the reprobate, though this is no sin on God's part, since God is above and beyond the law.[83] Interestingly, a corollary argument in support of God's sinlessness in immediately instigating the evil choices of the reprobate is based on divine simplicity, in that God is "uninfluenced by any evil emotion"[84] in so causing Pharaoh to hold on to his slaves or Judas to betray his Master with a kiss. Reprobation, then, is forthrightly taught: "And if a good part of mankind are bound over to everlasting imprisonment and chains, and though they deserve that for their rebelliousness, yet they were born by Divine Providence to the end that, being made examples of, they might proclaim his justice."[85]

Zwingli's treatise originated in a series of sermons delivered before Philip of Hesse in advance of the abortive Marburg Colloquy in October 1529, when Zwingli and Luther were brought face to face to resolve the controversy that had broken out about the Lord's Supper among the antipapist protesters. In January 1530, Philip wrote to Zwingli asking for a copy of those sermons from the year before; on this request Zwingli developed the sermon material into the "comprehensive Latin discourse on providence," which he then published.[86] The circumstances of its conception

---

80. Zwingli, "Providence," pp. 137, 203-4.
81. Zwingli, "Providence," pp. 138, 154.
82. Zwingli, "Providence," p. 176.
83. Zwingli, "Providence," p. 169.
84. Zwingli, "Providence," p. 182.
85. Zwingli, "Providence," p. 170.
86. Gaebler, *Huldrych Zwingli,* p. 146.

and composition thus betray Zwingli's rivalry with Luther for theological leadership of a united Protestant front against Rome. True enough, but more profoundly, they point to Zwingli's "most detailed, most thorough, and most comprehensive alternative" to Luther's case for apocalyptic Christianity in *DSA*. It would not be misleading to capture the alternatives in exactly that way: (Pauline) apocalyptic versus (Seneca's Stoic) providentialism. In Gaebler's summary: "agreement with Luther is confined to this point" of denying freedom of the will. "The treatise is otherwise permeated with a refutation of chief statements of Lutheran [sic, i.e., Luther's] theology, especially of those developed against Erasmus in Luther's *On the Bondage of the Will.*"[87] We can briefly survey that series of refutations.

Fundamentally, Zwingli attacks Luther's distinction between the two forms of the Word of God, as law and as gospel, maintaining instead: "The law is the divine order, expressing His nature and will . . . the law is the constant will of God." Lest there be any doubt about who is under attack here, Zwingli continues: "Hence it is clear that at our time some persons of the first importance, as they think, have spoken without sufficient circumspection about the law saying that the law is only to terrify, damn, and deliver over to torments. In reality, the law does not do that at all, but, on the contrary, sets forth the will and nature of the Deity."[88] Thus the gospel is interpreted as (renewed, refined, clarified) law: "What more welcome message than that God announces Himself as that which is to be cherished and loved above all things?" What matters immensely to Luther's sinner who is uncertain of God's mercy, or Luther's martyr who is standing defenseless in the face of heteronomous powers, is for Zwingli a logical inference drawn from the gospel interpreted as law: "For unless He loved us, why, pray, should He disclose Himself to us?" God's self-revelation as such is the gospel, which is the disclosure of the law, which is God Himself.[89] One can ask, however, whether this affirmation of the law as the revelation of "the will and nature of God" contradicts Zwingli's teaching that the law applies to the creature, not the Creator who is above the law. There is a real tension here.[90]

---

87. Gaebler, *Huldrych Zwingli,* p. 147.
88. Zwingli, "Providence," p. 166. In the next paragraph, Zwingli accuses Luther of "sheer ignorance of rhetoric" in so interpreting Paul, since "the law can no more be abolished or cease to be . . . than can God Himself . . ." (p. 167).
89. Zwingli, "Providence," p. 174.
90. Spinoza's famous formula, *deus sive natura,* is anticipated by Zwingli, "Provi-

Several corollaries to the foregoing can be noted. Zwingli takes his definition of faith from Hebrews 11:1 and interprets the "things hoped for" as a "paraphrase for the Supreme Deity." Faith is thus defined as "a real and substantial thing, that is, the clear light and certainty of the soul,"[91] in that it apprehends God as Being itself (a residual Thomism). Here too Zwingli is disputing Luther's definitions, for whom faith sees in the dark, as through a mirror dimly, pressing through the hidden to the revealed God. Zwingli thus goes on to discuss aspects of faith that Luther had previously lifted up, such as *plerophoria*, full conviction, and faith as "gift of God," giving these his own interpretation. It is a matter of some subtlety, but Zwingli comes to the anti-Luther point in this discussion about the nature of faith when he concludes: "Faith is given to those who have been elected and ordained to eternal life, but so that election precedes, and faith follows election as a sign of it."[92] In just this way Zwingli severs once again Luther's strict correlation of external Word and internal witness of the Spirit, which locate election in history because these inseparable processions/missions of the Son and the Spirit involve eternity in time.[93] Still, the external Word is not wholly without significance for Zwingli: following Anselm's expiatory (not propitiatory) teaching on atonement, Zwingli regards Christ's sacrifice as a past event that "atoned" (that is, paid the debt) for "original sin."[94] Remembrance of Christ's satisfaction of our debt has moral influence: when "the mind of man has been so taught by God as to know that His Son was made an offering for our sins, it is so charmed by the taste of Divine Goodness as to trust in that only and alone. . . ."[95] Notwithstanding, in principle "election is free" and "nothing prevents God from choosing among the heathen men to revere Him, to honor Him, and after death to be united to Him."[96] The remembrance of Christ is not, strictly speaking, necessary.

This latter is seemingly, to this very day, the great attraction of

---

dence," pp. 210, 226. I can only note here the hunch that Zwingli thinks of this along lines that parallel the famous distinction later made by Spinoza between *natura naturans* and *natura naturata*.

91. Zwingli, "Providence," p. 193.

92. Zwingli, "Providence," p. 197.

93. Zwingli, "Providence," p. 198. "For the apostle's work also is from the hand of God, but indirectly, the internal drawing is the work of the Spirit acting directly" (p. 203).

94. Zwingli, "Providence," p. 207.

95. Zwingli, "Providence," p. 198.

96. Zwingli, "Providence," p. 201.

Zwingli's liberal vision. Since, arguably, the theology of *DPD* is drawn more from Seneca than from Paul, it is only seemly for Zwingli to acknowledge that, were he given a vote in the matter of who should be in heaven, he would cast his lot for "Socrates or Seneca" over the Pope and his minions![97] But, as we have seen in Pannenberg and von Balthasar, there is nothing to prevent theology in the tradition of Luther from likewise expanding the scope of redemption. The real question is whether the redemption remains Christ's.

How can we make sense of Zwingli's sharp and consequent dissent from Luther, particularly this dramatic insistence on a virtually pantheistic[98] determinism? In turn, how can we make sense of Luther's theological anthropology in a way that clearly avoids theopanism? Much like later arguments that Leibniz is in truth a crypto-Spinozist, we face here a conundrum. Has Zwingli caught Luther in a fatal contradiction, such that either Luther must, as did his followers, return to semi-Pelagianism (or rather, the incoherence of claiming faith in the "paradox" when a conceptual muddle stares us straight in the face), or, must Luther overcome his human-all-too-human scruples and follow Zwingli into the brave new world that Seneca once blazed and Spinoza will finally open? Zwingli in any event sought to impale Luther on the horns of this dilemma. Luther refused to reply (although, as mentioned, he did offer a few reconsiderations to his students years later in the Genesis lectures, which we will take up in conclusion).[99]

As for Zwingli himself, he was undoubtedly convinced that the fearless journey into theopanism he was charting was the only way to avoid atheism. The anxiety about atheism is manifest in almost every discussion of the matter: "When the mind begins to contemplate God, to talk and commune with Him about the things it has in common with Him, suddenly the flesh, fashioned from clay, draws it back. 'Fool,' it cries, 'Where are you going? There is no Deity; much less one that cares for our affairs.'"[100] The "flesh" says this because sense experience sees only unorganized, chance events in the material order, not the harmony intuited by mind. But if the flesh is right, "if anything takes place by chance and at random, if anything exists of its own right and independently of the direction

---

97. Zwingli, "Providence," p. 201.

98. See above, n. 535.

99. Kolb, *Bound Choice*, p. 37, cf. also 53.

100. Zwingli, "Providence," p. 162.

of the Deity, then everything is at random and drifts along by chance. . . ."[101] The deeper reason why Zwingli must correct Luther's error in permitting contingency to "things below us" now becomes evident. If "everything comes by chance, Providence is done away with, and if Providence is done away with, the Deity also is done away with."[102] "Providence cares for all things and is nowhere idle or listless, or there is no Providence at all . . . there is no Deity."[103] Pantheism is the alternative to atheism, Seneca to Lucretius, Epictetus to Epicurus.

What is intriguing here is Zwingli's anthropological rooting of the conflict between the flesh which perceives only random physical events and the mind which sees into the harmony of things. This is quite deliberate and quite central in the argument of *DPD*.[104] Whatever the value of that observation about an innate conflict between fleshly perception and mental conception for philosophical accounts of human experience, here we see from yet another angle a real fork in the road between the pupil of Paul and the pupil of Seneca. For nothing so animates Luther in *DSA* — the argument recurs continually in its pages — as his discovery that the Pauline antinomy of *pneuma* and *sarx* is not the equivalent of the Stoic or Platonic anthropological dualism of mind and matter, of *nous* and *soma (sema)*.

For Luther, the human being is and can be an enemy of God only in its higher powers. He follows Augustine's anti-Manichaean reading of Paul: it is not the evil body that causes the good soul to sin, but the evil soul that leads astray the good body. The Spirit, properly speaking, is not a creature at all, but God who mediates the love of the Father and the Son, that is to say, the Spirit persuading believers that they are with Jesus beloved children and so empowering these beloved to rise up to live anew to the Father. Flesh likewise is not meat, but the "spirit" of human self-seeking and self-reliance. This is the sense in which the Spirit wars against the flesh and the flesh against the Spirit (Gal. 5:17). From this Pauline insight, Luther holds against Erasmus's Hellenizing that "it is not one part of man, even the most excellent or principal part, that is flesh, but that the whole of man is flesh; and not only so, but the whole people is flesh; and even this is not all, but the whole human race is flesh!"[105] Therefore, Erasmus, "you cannot find a way out by saying: though they are under sin, yet

---

101. Zwingli, "Providence," p. 158.
102. Zwingli, "Providence," p. 210.
103. Zwingli, "Providence," p. 233.
104. Zwingli, "Providence," pp. 163ff.
105. Zwingli, "Providence," p. 250.

the best part in them, that is, reason and will, makes endeavors toward good."[106] Ignorance and contempt of God "are not seated in the flesh, in the sense of the lower and grosser affections, but in the highest and most excellent powers of man, in which righteousness, godliness, and knowledge and reverence of God should reign — that is, in reason and will, and so in the very power of 'free-will,' in the very seat of uprightness, the most excellent thing in man!"[107] The traditional anthropological dualism, on the other hand, leaves the body to the devil, so long as the "spirit" can be saved.[108] Yet this "spirit" is no neutral actor, but rather "is wholly turned to self and to his own. He does not seek God, nor care for the things of God; he seeks his own riches and glory, and works, and wisdom, and power, and sovereignty in everything, and wants to enjoy it in peace . . . he can no more stop his self-seeking than he can stop existing. . . ."[109] This ungodly flesh, this "spirit" looking down on its own grosser parts, overlooking or disowning its own past sins, seeking itself in all future things, even in God, wearing the mask of religion to crown its self-centeredness, is "without the Spirit, Who alone fulfills the law. Men may try to keep it in their own strength, but they can accomplish nothing."[110] That latter is flesh. As Luther had put it almost a decade before in the *Disputation against Scholastic Theology:* the solution to self-seeking desire is not to satisfy it (it is unsatisfiable), but to extinguish it (which the Spirit does by the cross and resurrection of Jesus).

## New Agency in Christ

"For through faith, Christ is in us, indeed one with us. Christ is just and has fulfilled all the commands of God, wherefore we also fulfill everything through him since he was made ours by faith."[111] Jesus Christ is the true human being, the image of God, the Agent of a new humanity, and it is by participation in Him through the ecstatic selfhood of faith, that we acquire agency in the world. The issue that emerges out of the comparison of Luther and Zwingli is whether we can account for both of Luther's affirma-

---

106. Zwingli, "Providence," p. 279.
107. Zwingli, "Providence," p. 280.
108. Zwingli, "Providence," p. 309.
109. Zwingli, "Providence," p. 205, cf. 234.
110. Zwingli, "Providence," p. 285.
111. Thesis 26 "Heidelberg Disputation" in LW 31:56.

tions without contradiction, avoiding both Stoicism and Pelagianism, that (1) in the region of theology God's foreknowledge is the immutable necessity by which His purposes come to pass, and that (2) in the region of philosophy, the human race is free lord of the earth and its well-being. Such an account is possible, if and when the interface between the region of theology and the region of philosophy is occupied by Christ, or the equivalent, the ecstatic self in Christ. Luther seeks in ever-fresh verbal portraits to convey this image of a new and liberated humanity in Christ, most famously perhaps in the paradoxical Reformation manifesto on freedom: "A Christian is a perfectly free lord of all, subject to none. A Christian is a perfectly dutiful servant of all, subject to all."[112] In faith, the ecstatic self lives in the confidence of God's call into in His Beloved Community, knowing that "all things work for good to them that love God, who are called according to His purpose." In love, this ecstatic self lives on the earth in the needs of the neighbor. In hope, it lives on the earth amid the groaning of the creation for the apocalypse of the "the glorious liberty of the children of God." So true freedom on the earth consists in such decentering: freedom from self for others and all in love and hope; freedom in faith from all other claims of allegiance, and just so the Spirit's martyrs refusing to bend the knee to the bullies or to sell the soul to their sycophants. Decentering is to dwell in Christ by faith that works in love (and hope).

In the background here is Luther's exegesis of the "theodicy of faith" in Romans 8, especially verse 28, on which verse, he had commented, "depends the entire passage." The exegetical musings of Luther on Romans 8 from a decade prior to the composition of *DSA* show us that Luther's perspectivalism has deep roots,[113] as also does the language of necessity

---

112. "Heidelberg Disputation" in LW 31:344.

113. Gerhard Ebeling's well-known juxtaposition of relations *coram Deo* and *coram hominibus* as Luther's device for excluding "non-theological talk about God," i.e., talk about God apart from sin and redemption, might rather be understood and explicated in terms of what I am calling perspectivalism, i.e., as epistemology at the turn of the ages, rather than as a "relational ontology" (whatever that may mean). Ebeling cites Luther: "For to us who look down into the depths, things appear arbitrary and fortuitous, but to those who look up, everything is necessary, for we live, act and suffer not as we will, but as [God] wills, and so does everything that exists. Free will, which is only apparent with regard to us and temporal things, disappears in the sight of God." Ebeling, *Luther*, pp. 215-16. He comments, "For that which we do, and everything that happens at all, appears to us to be something which could have been different, and is therefore fortuitous and freely chosen in any given case, is only the aspect of events which we see as long as we do not take God into account. It is mere illusion which only persists as long as things are not considered in the light of God" (p. 219). To

and immutability, in his grappling with Paul's message with the help of Augustine. "For if it were not the purpose of God, and if our salvation depended upon our will and works, it would depend upon chance. . . ." Who can trust luck in this world of crocodiles and boa-constrictors, bullies, and sycophants? That is not faith, but superstition. But in Romans 8 the Apostle is showing that "the elect are not saved by chance but by necessity . . . purely by His own election and immutable will, in the very face of so many rapacious and terrifying adversaries who try in vain to harm us. . . . But now He shows us that we are saved by His immutable love."[114] Luther entertains the objection that arises from the experience of those "terrifying adversaries": "Does the contingency of an event impede the sure predestination of God? And the answer is that with God there simply is no contingency, but it is only in our eyes. For not even the leaf of a tree falls to the ground without the will of the Father."[115] If we believe with Jesus by His Spirit in His Father, Luther is laying bare, then there are — really — two perspectives, the alienated creature's and the Creator's (and also then the reconciled creature's) on this one and the same creation. These two see the same thing differently.

It is the "prudence of the flesh" that treats its perspective as if it were final; so it proceeds, divinizing itself, until "it is strangled to death" and comes to understand that "salvation comes in no way from something working in itself but only from the outside, namely, from God."[116] But then it is no longer the "prudence of the flesh"; it has died and been raised again and become the "prudence of the Spirit." This leads to one final reversal: it is those who fear God in His election that manifest their own election. Why? What does this fear represent? Of what is it the sure sign? It signifies acknowledgment of the God who *has a choice,* which is what an *election* is and actualizes. But this choice in God is the very thing that "the reprobate despise . . ."; they "pay it no attention, or in desperation they become pre-

---

be sure, Ebeling denies the actual import of these words when he denies as a "complete misunderstanding of Luther" the imputation to him of "metaphysical determinism . . . interpreted in a causal scheme foreign to Luther and not expounded in terms of the coram-relationship which determines his thought" (p. 223). Thus Luther's affirmation that all things happen immutably by the will of God is not a "theoretical statement" but a "confession of faith" (p. 223). I find this latter distinction unintelligible for reasons made clear in Chapter One above.

114. "Commentary on Romans" (1516) LW 25:371.
115. "Commentary on Romans" (1516) LW 25:373.
116. "Commentary on Romans" (1516) LW 25:377.

sumptuous, saying, 'If I am damned, then I will be damned.'"[117] In other words, the elect fearfully acknowledge the gracious *choice* of God; the reprobate recklessly impute a *fatalism* to God, thinking that God is unable to surpass His own wrath and their damnation, that is, to justify the ungodly, to harrow hell, "consigning all to sin in order to have mercy on all." As you believe, so you have. Whether it is the leaf falling to the ground or the Gestapo knocking at the door (Rom. 8:35-36), "all things work for good to them that love God, who are called according to His purpose," since *this* God is the One who raised Jesus from the dead. But that means that God is active and innovative in time, causing incalculable contingencies to serve His purpose, that God turns actual evils to good, though seeing this transparently awaits the final event and so the "light of glory."[118]

The notion of God's temporal activity here, in both the Spirit's electing to faith and weaving the web of events to good, threatens to burst the bonds of what I have called elsewhere the "protological" bias[119] of the theological tradition stemming from Augustine. This bias reflects Hellenism's search for an *arche,* a principle of origin that would explain all subsequent becoming. This protological bias is evident in Augustine's idea of God's "eternal now," in which the temporal past, present, and future of the world are all equally present to the divine Mind, who willed the entire sequence into existence in one eternal act. We cannot but then think of God's eternity as a paradoxical "time before time," from which everything unfolds fixed and determined. The Bible too takes interest in the origin, yet primarily to give God the Creator a choice in creating this world rather than some other, and hence in the ongoing supervision of the creation, to give God choices in creative response to human choices, which are real on the earth, even if "Godward" they avail nothing. By referring us in the end to a justice of God yet to be accomplished and so disclosed in the "light of glory," Luther pressed this protological bias to the limit by intimating not just a future insight from the comprehensive perspective, but new light radiating from a real passage in God's history with humanity. As argued in previous chapters, God's eternity should consequently be thought to include a capacity for time. That is to say, that God's eternity is as much, indeed even more in the Bible, God's "time after time," the *eschaton.* In that

---

117. "Commentary on Romans" (1516) LW 25:378.

118. Luther concludes *DSA* with a discussion of these three lights, *Bondage,* pp. 317-18, which I will take up in the Conclusion.

119. Hinlicky, *Paths Not Taken,* chap. 6.

case, the Spirit's election on the earth, in time, marks real passage of the eternal God from hiddenness to revealedness, from wrath to mercy. Luther has thought through the problem to this point.

This would mean, as Barth saw, that God's immutable foreknowledge of events is God's *self*-determination to create, redeem, and fulfill the world in Christ. To this progression in thought, theology today must think of God's Spirit as infinitely adaptive in time in relating to created wills really other than God's own and of human freedom over creation, bringing with it maximal biographical diversity, as the *fulfillment* of this divine self-determination bringing to pass the Beloved Community. Yet, by the same token, it is also the failure of this passage in hells of the irrevocable; it is *civitas terrena,* mad raging Pharaoh, who will not let the people go. These affirmations of faith go together in Christ, who reveals by enacting the mystery of God's plan and just so restores human nature to its exalted divine destiny. In the interim, however, creaturely freedom in things below actualizes real evils, making choices of what God does not will, making havoc in the web of life. In turn, the Spirit freely improvises new stratagems, elicits new initiatives, actualizing real righteousness, healing and renewing the torn web of life. So the apocalyptic battle rages. So ecstatic selfhood, which in faith reconciles divine sovereignty and human freedom, is and remains an embattled body on the earth, *not* believing what one sees with the evidence of one's own eyes in natural light, enduring ghastly episodes of God's hiddenness. There is evidence that some years after the publication of *DSA* Luther came to interpret his own treatise *DSA* along these lines.

Robert Kolb calls attention to the so-called Jena paragraph, which Luther's editor Georg Rörer inserted into the 1546 Wittenberg and Jena editions of *DSA* in Luther's Works. Speaking in Luther's first person, the text adds, "I could wish indeed that another and better word had been introduced into our discussion than this usual one, 'necessity,' which is not rightly applied either to the divine or human will." It goes on to complain that "necessity" "suggests a kind of compulsion" which would be the very "opposite of willingness. . . . For neither the divine nor the human will does what it does, whether good or evil, under any compulsion, but from sheer pleasure and desire, as with true freedom; and yet, the will of God is immutable and infallible, and it governs our mutable will. . . ."[120] It is impossible to say whether Luther, who was still alive, authorized this insertion but,

---

120. Kolb, *Bound Choice*, p. 27; cf. Luther, *Bondage*, p. 81.

Kolb writes, what "must be acknowledged is that Luther was constructing a new theological paradigm" at this time and experimenting with "new vocabulary." For that experimentation, Kolb points us to the Lectures on Genesis 26,[121] where Luther "took the opportunity" to look back critically on his work in *DSA* and forcefully reject a fatalist interpretation (such as we saw Zwingli demand). Luther now wants to align God's immutability, not with the hidden predestination of individuals, but with His promises in Christ.[122] Curiosity about the former is the sin of origin, for it wants to uncover God's secret[123] rather than await its revealing. This is a new thought, as if to say, "God hides in order to reveal." Luther puts these words in God's mouth: "I will reveal My foreknowledge and predestination to you in an extraordinary manner, but not by this way of reason and carnal wisdom. This is how I will do so: From an unrevealed God I will become a revealed God. Nevertheless I will remain the same God."[124] Or again, a little later: "If you believe in the revealed God and accept His Word, He will gradually also reveal the hidden God."[125]

From here Luther goes on, as customary, to speak of the manger and the cross. *Hunc audite!* This *listening* is what you can *do* as new agents in faith; how different from the fatalist conclusion of "the Epicureans. . . . 'If this is how it must happen, let it happen.'"[126] But if someone protests, "I cannot believe," Luther refers to the creedal faith of the church: "If you think all these things are true, there is no reason why you should complain about your unbelief." For the creed tells of the Son who died for you — what else can you lack, since "to believe is nothing else than to regard these facts as the sure and unquestionable truth."[127] This statement of Luther's might be misunderstood today, as if he meant that believing supposed facts of history were the point; rather, his point is that the Creed tells of the Son's existence "for you," and that the narrated existence of the Son for you *is* your immutable, infallible election, "learning to cling to the Child and Son Jesus, who is your God and was made flesh for you."[128] Thus the im-

---

121. Kolb, *Bound Choice*, p. 27.

122. "Commentary on Genesis" in LW 26:43.

123. Adam "wanted to search out why God had forbidden him to enjoy the fruits of that one tree." "Commentary on Genesis" in LW 26:49.

124. "Commentary on Genesis" in LW 26:44-45.

125. "Commentary on Genesis" in LW 26:46.

126. "Commentary on Genesis" in LW 26:45.

127. "Commentary on Genesis" in LW 26:46.

128. "Commentary on Genesis" in LW 26:48.

mutable necessity of God's foreknowledge is now interpreted to mean that this God in Christ for you "cannot deny Himself but keeps His promises." Yes, he admits, "I have written that everything is absolute and unavoidable; but at the same time I have added that one must look at the revealed God, as we sing in the hymn [Luther's own composition]: *Er heist Jesu Christ, der HERR Zabaoth,* **und ist kein ander Gott.**"

Can Luther mean anything other than that all authority in heaven and on earth has been given to the man for others, our brother, Jesus Christ? That it is this man "who created the world" and for whom the world was created? Luther's reticence remains. He does not openly state what remains in a real sense yet to be seen. But he does state this belief, correcting a false reading of what he had written in *DSA*. The dialectic in Christian experience of the hidden and revealed God — which could have told of a *deus exlex* above and beyond the triune God bound to His Word — is an experience *within* faith (think of Jesus in the Garden of Gethsemane) not any *alternative* to faith, even as faith from baptism day to resurrection day is tested, tried, embattled faith. We will pick up this matter afresh in the conclusion of this book.

---

## Appendix to Chapter Five

### A Roman Catholic Objection:
### Does Luther's Rapture Rob Humans of the Freedom of Faith?

The account from a generation ago by the Catholic scholar, Harry J. McSorley (who went on to play a major role in Lutheran-Catholic doctrinal dialogue), surveyed the range of modern interpretation of Luther's *DSA*. From his work, two things can be gained. The first is to confirm how the *crux intellectum* still turns on the very point where Zwingli attacked, the univocity of God. The second will be to parry McSorley's classical Catholic objection, namely, the complaint that Luther's theological anthropology robs faith of its own freedom.

To the first question, McSorley finds three "broad categories of interpretation." In the first are those "who consider only that part . . . which treats the biblical doctrine of bondage to sin and who emphasize that Luther allows for free will in the things that are 'beneath' us, the natural things[. But these] do not take seriously Luther's teaching that, as a result of God's infallible foreknowledge, all things happen by absolute necessity." This first group we could call the "dualists," since they simply disregard the contradiction outlined above to which Zwingli called attention. A second group tries to read into Luther "certain modern philosophical-theological categories," which McSorley does not find useful on principle (e.g., existentialism). Neither do I. A third group includes "authors who see that the affirmation of universal necessity . . . has deterministic overtones which exclude any activity of free will and deprives faith of its decision-character." This last group, which does not cut the Gordian knot like the dualists, subdivides. There are those "who reject this aspect of Luther's teaching"; there are those "who seem to accept this teaching in all its radicality"; and there are those "who try to distinguish what they consider to be Luther's sometimes misleading statements and expressions from his sound, biblical intention." It is evident that the present effort belongs in this last subgroup.

Interpreting Luther according to his biblical and Catholic intentions, McSorley himself concluded that "Luther teaches a doctrine not of absolute, but of conditional necessity, a *necessitas consequentiae,* which the Scholastics regarded as being compatible with free will. . . . It is not a rejection of *liberum arbitrium* in the Catholic sense, but of a pagan concept of autonomous *liberum arbitrium* which would somehow be independent of God's sovereign and universal rule of his creatures."[129] What McSorley means is that given the bad choices which the natural human will has inherited from Adam, it is in consequence necessarily so that the sinner is unable to choose for God; but when God restores to the sinner through Christ the good choice to obey, then the obedience of faith becomes its own renewed and free possibility. So far as it goes, McSorley is arguably right, even though in *DSA* Luther impatiently repudiated the distinction between antecedent and consequent necessity. Since Luther does not hold to philosophical determinism, he does not imagine (as for example in Scotus's encounter with Averroes or Leibniz's encounter with Spinoza) what is the relevance of the distinction between antecedent and conse-

---

129. Luther, *Bondage*, p. 328.

quent necessity: "This is to say that God's action is necessary, if He wills it, but the thing done is not in itself necessary." So Luther correctly grasps the distinction, but then protests, "what do they establish by this play on words?"[130] Luther finds the introduction of this distinction off-topic. "But what need was there to tell us that? — as though there were any fear of our claiming that things which happen are God, or possess a divine and necessary existent nature!"[131] As we shall shortly see, that fear is right around the corner. Notwithstanding Luther's exasperation then, McSorley points to the apparent contradiction, which evidently escapes Luther. Luther "explicitly and repeatedly affirms that man has *liberum arbitrium* 'in the realm of things below him,' or 'in respect of what is below him' or 'in his own kingdom' where man 'is led by his own will and not by the precepts of another' and where God 'has granted him a free use of things at his own will' . . . eat, drink, beget, rule, etc."[132] Does this concession not involve Luther in a "flat contradiction"? "For surely God 'foresees and decrees' what man shall do 'in the realms of things below him' such as eating and ruling. Surely God foresees that men and angels will sin. But if God's infallible foreknowledge causes all things to happen by *absolute* necessity *to the exclusion of free will,* then it would be impossible for Luther to say that these events 'in the kingdom of man' happen freely. But Luther says precisely this! . . . Luther is guilty of a contradiction when he makes an 'exception' to the rule of universal necessity."[133] With this, McSorley nicely captures the crux for understanding sketched above. It is exactly the same objection that Zwingli raises, though with an opposite intent, for Zwingli wants to deny contingency altogether.

As to the second point about the freedom of faith, after an exhaustive analysis, McSorley came to his own, seemingly differentiated interpretation of *DSA*, which is worth our attention in that for all ecumenical progress it continues to raise the classic Catholic objection against Luther's ecstatic self, who is as such justified by faith, when faith is faith in Christ. In the words of the Council of Trent: "If anyone says that the sinner is justi-

---

130. Luther, *Bondage,* p. 83. But very shortly Zwingli will come within a cat's whisker of saying just that, picking up a line of argument stretching back to Averroes and forward to Spinoza.

131. Luther, *Bondage.*

132. Harry J. McSorley, C.S.P., *Luther: Right or Wrong? An Ecumenical-Theological Study of Luther's Major Work,* The Bondage of the Will (New York: Newman Press; Minneapolis: Augsburg, 1969), p. 327.

133. McSorley, *Right or Wrong?* p. 328.

fied by faith alone, meaning that nothing else is required to cooperate in order to obtain the grace of justification, and that it is not in any way necessary that he be prepared and disposed by the action of his own will, let him be anathema."[134] For Luther, as we have seen, this analysis of the creaturely self and its corresponding unfreedom of desire does not dig deep enough; it considers only the bound choice inherited from Adam, not the servile desire of any conceivable creature, which does not have life in itself, but must live by wanting what it does not have, and so lives in history as a formed, concrete, irrevocable biography. "Cooperation and preparation by the action of one's own will" abstracts from this latter somatic self; it posits a neutral desire, one that can simply make good choices, once a good choice is restored to it. It is telling in the perspective of the present apocalyptic interpretation that McSorley singles out for special criticism this aspect of Luther's soteriological vision: "But when Luther says that the change of our wills from sin to justice depends solely on the overcoming and the defeat of Satan by someone stronger — Christ — and neglects entirely to mention that the personal, free decision of the sinner — made possible, to be sure, only by the healing and liberating grace of God — is essential to justification, then he is no longer on biblical or Catholic ground. . . . For the call to justification and salvation is addressed to the sinner from whom the response of free obedience to Christ and to justice is required."[135]

But Luther's sinner under Satan's thrall can only *resist* that very call (Luther lifts up the biblical precedent of Paul who was Saul before the encounter on the Damascus Road),[136] all the more so in thinking that a response of free obedience is its own right, power, and responsibility. There must be a new work of the Holy Spirit, in parallel to the turn of the ages that occurred once for all in the resurrection of the Crucified and conforming to it: the death of the centered self and the raising from those ruins of the newborn child of God, the ecstatic self, which by definition is this Spirit-led, free, and happy cooperator with God.

---

134. In *Trent*, p. 43.

135. McSorley, *Right or Wrong?* pp. 334-35.

136. For the importance of this motif to Luther, see Mickey L. Mattox, "Martin Luther's Reception of Paul," in *The Reception of Paul in the Sixteenth Century*, ed. Ward Holder (Leiden/Boston: E. J. Brill, forthcoming), "Sermons on Acts 9" (pp. 116-27). I am indebted to the author for sharing the page proofs with me.

# CHAPTER SIX

# The Redemption of the Body: Luther on Marriage

*[Christ] is not a foe of nature. No, He shows that He wishes to help na-
ture and subdue its enemy, death and devil. He has compassion with
our misery, for He sees that we are now drowned by the devil's poison
and by death and are so submerged in it that we cannot extricate ourselves. He wants to wreak vengeance on him as on His own foe, who
poisoned and spoiled His work.*

Luther[1]

## The Renewed Image of God

In this chapter I want to turn our inquiry in theological anthropology in
the tradition of Luther in a rather different direction from the ground covered in the previous chapter: to the "nature" that grace claims and redeems, as in the epigraph above, where Luther interprets Pauline theology
of the resurrection of the body. In line with the cumulative argument of
this book, that means a turn to the new interpretation of the human social
prospect in the light of the Beloved Community, to the earthly potency of
the hope for the "redemption of our bodies," concretely to one illustrative
sampling of that new agency of somatic-ecstatic selves in Christ here, now,
on this good but groaning earth (Rom. 8:22). This move is possible because the Pauline teaching of salvation as the redemption of the body

---

1. "Commentary on 1 Corinthians" (1534) LW 28:205.

stands witness against an ever-tempting Marcionite-Gnostic reading of the Apostle; it requires, when all is said and done, the interpretation of his apocalyptic gospel as the fulfillment, not supersession, of the "Israel of God" (Gal. 6:16). Even more than the Apostle could have realized against the horizon of near-expectation of the Parousia which stamped his mission and ministry (1 Cor. 7:29-31), that means that what we mean by "nature" is not whatever we find "natural," but rather is something to be learned, as Luther learned, from the Scriptures of Israel.[2] Luther, lifelong professor of Old Testament Scripture, was not wrong to look in this direction to understand the body's redemption, if N. T. Wright is correct in claiming about the same Pauline passage of 1 Corinthians 15: "As the last Adam, the representative of the people of God in their eschatological task and role, the Messiah completes his work of obedience on the cross . . . and being raised up after death, enters upon a new mode of human existence, becoming in one sense the pattern and in another sense the life-giving source for the future resurrection life of those who belong to him."[3] The question before us, larger than Paul but finding here its Pauline basis, is how that last Adam may, and may not, be said to redeem the first.

We concluded the previous chapter by looking at the real though qualified agency Luther sees in the ecstatic self belonging to Christ, the redeeming Lord. Defending the authenticity of Luther's Paulinism — but also in turn Luther's humane interpretation of Paul for the sake of the creation which Paul himself was convinced was about to be dissolved and replaced — Wilfried Härle takes up that notion of agency in Christ and places it within the cosmic sweep of the Genesis-to-Revelation narrative of Scripture: ". . . *the destiny originally given by God to human beings of bearing God's image,* which can only be expected in its full and complete form in the eschaton, but which is already now fulfilled under the conditions of the present in *Jesus Christ[:] He* is the image of God — yet not in the sense of excluding the rest of us human beings, but rather appointing us to become participants now by faith in him, and in the righteousness actualized in him. This participation in the image of the Son of God, who is the image of God and thus also the fulfillment of human destiny is what Luther is aiming at when he says that Christ's

---

2. It is true, of course, that Luther denies that Mosaic legislation is addressed to us, and invokes the "law written on our hearts," the so-called "natural law" as the basis for ethics. But he denies this because he finds this distinction itself in Scripture. "How Christians Should Regard Moses" (1525) LW 35:164-66.

3. N. T. Wright, *The Climax of the Covenant: Christ and the Law in Pauline Theology* (Minneapolis: Fortress, 1991), p. 35.

righteousness is imputed to the believer. Thus we can say: God's mercy *(sedaqah)* consists in God reckoning and confirming Christ's righteousness to sinners and thereby *awakening faith* in them, which is justification before God."[4] The details of Härle's language here — righteousness as mercy, faith as participation, justification as faith-awakening imputation — will be explored in the next chapter on the so-called "New Perspective on Paul." What matters here is the rather different connection he has made between the first and the second Adam as bearers of the image. This connection indicates that the redemption of that body, inherited from the first Adam, comes about by participation in the body of Christ, the last Adam, in whom the image of God already now approaches from the eschaton.

We have already encountered the importance of Genesis 1:26-28 for Luther. The *imago Dei* passage is his biblical basis for teaching the freedom of humanity over the things "below," in the realm of fellow creatures, that is, for human agency understood as the Creator God's regents on the earth. It is a notable feature, however, of the somatic self which we are according to Genesis 1:26-28 that it is expressly designated "male and female" and that the image and corresponding task is assigned to them as partners. Is it then Adam *with Eve* (i.e., assuming for the present the canonical text inclusive of the second creation story in Gen. 2–3) from which Christ redeems? Correctly translated, the celebrated text of Galatians 3:28 tells us that in Christ: "there is *neither* Jew *nor* Greek; there is *neither* slave *nor* free; there is *no* 'male and female.'" This latter variation in the form of the negation occurring in the last clause, Martyn writes, "suggests that the author of the [early Christian baptismal] formula drew on Genesis 1:27, thereby saying that in baptism the structure of the original creation had been set aside" by the "newly created unity" in Christ.[5] Noting the grammatically masculine form of "one" which the baptized have become, Martyn like Wright above takes this to indicate incorporation: the new "members of the church are not one *thing*; they are one *person*, having been taken into the corpus of the One New Man."[6]

---

4. Wilfried Härle, "Rethinking Paul and Luther," *Lutheran Quarterly* 20, no. 3 (Autumn 2006): 311.

5. J. Louis Martyn, *Galatians,* The Anchor Bible, vol. 33A (New York: Doubleday, 1997), pp. 376-77.

6. Martyn, *Galatians,* p. 377; Martyn notes that Paul became aware of the "fact that even in the church, the beachhead of God's new creation, there were as yet some marks of sexual and social differentiation (e.g., 1 Corinthians 7; Philemon). He had later, therefore, to think very seriously about the tension between the affirmation of the real unity in Christ

More broadly, Martyn goes on to point to the "remarkable tension" in the traditions about Jesus in "matters of sexual differentiation and the family." Side by side in the same gospel traditions we find *both* some texts construing redemption as the restoration of God's original intention in creation (Mark 10:6-7) *and* others construing redemption as the new formation of an eschatological family not based on kinship (Mark 3:33-35). Is it redemption *of* the image indicated in Genesis 1:26 or redemption *from* that image? Martyn is surely right to see that "the traditions about Jesus find him arguing both on the basis of creation and on the basis of the gospel's power to bring about a new creation. . . ."[7] Were then the seeds for the ethical schism over "matters of sexual differentiation and the family" which have run just under the surface through *all* (not just today regarding same-sex unions) of Christian history sown already at the very beginning? As pertains to the first and second clauses of Galatians 3:27, Martyn is right to say that "incorporation into the Christ" as new creation makes the church "a family made up of former Jews and former Gentiles" with the important consequence that the "baptismal liturgy" is not a "rallying cry in favor of a new religion, Christianity, against an older one, Judaism."[8] The final peroration of Galatians makes that clear to all who have eyes to see: "Neither circumcision nor uncircumcision means anything; what counts is a new creation" (Gal. 6:15). That much is clear. Paul found grounds for urging but not requiring some recognition of the import of the second clause, as may be seen in the Letter to Philemon. But Martyn does not, and perhaps cannot, make the third clause "no male-and-female" fit with this reasoning about the supersession of ethnic, religious, and class distinctions in Christ. First Corinthians 7:29-31 would be as close as Paul comes to anticipating already now that future life of the resurrection, and if 1 Corinthians 11:2-16 is authentic, Paul — in the same epistle — can revert to a nearly reactionary appeal to the old creation.

Early Christians tried very hard to anticipate the life of the resurrection in regard to the perceived burden of sexuality. Many considered "sexual renunciation" a manifestation already now of that future life of the resurrection, as Peter Brown has so insightfully and thoroughly described for us across the early centuries of the church.[9] If the curse of Genesis 3 on the

---

and the disconcerting continuation of the distinguishing marks of the old creation. In writing to the Galatians, he does not pause over that matter" (p. 377).

7. Martyn, *Galatians*, pp. 380-81.

8. Martyn, *Galatians*, p. 382.

9. Peter Brown, *The Body and Society: Men, Women and Sexual Renunciation in Early Christianity* (New York: Columbia University Press, 1988).

disobedient couple had subordinated Eve to Adam from whom she had come, and Adam to the soil from which he had been made, then escape from these curses of the law (the woman's yoke of childbearing and the man's yoke of tilling the soil by the sweat of the brow to provide for woman and child) was within reach by means of sexual renunciation, now empowered by the Spirit of the resurrection at work in God's new creation. It is hard for us today even to imagine the world in which such aspirations for sexual renunciation seemed the gospel itself: a world before aspirin, before antibiotics, before the germ theory of disease and sanitation, before contraception, when a moment's sexual pleasure could bring in exchange death of mother or infant at birth as regularly as the burden of hungry mouths to feed for those men who would not abandon their women and offspring. In such a world it was very easy to imagine that sexual love was the dirty trick of the devil; Gnostic literature is replete with this bitter accusation against Yahweh,[10] the false god of the Hebrew Scriptures, author of the deception encoded in Genesis 1:26-28.

With its inheritance from Judaism preserved after the second-century struggle with Gnosticism, early catholic Christianity could not move wholly in this direction; and bitter experience taught quickly how illusory sexual renunciation would prove in the mass. Brown's hero in the long, amazing story of sexual renunciation in early Christianity is Augustine, whose eschatological vision of new innocence and reconciliation in the Beloved Community also put the human predicament here "below" in better light:

> [T]he catastrophe that needed to be explained was not the fact of a human society, where men and women married, made love and begot children. That would have happened had Adam and Eve not fallen. What remained a dark enigma to [Augustine] was the distortion of the will of those who now made up society. The twisted human will, not marriage, not even the sexual drive, was what was new in the human condition after Adam's fall. The fallen will, subject to the original, God-given bonds of human society — friendship, marriage, and paternal command — [was now subject] to sickening shocks of willfulness, that caused these to sway, to fissure, and to change their nature. It was the present twisted will that had led to the development of slavery and

10. See Paul R. Hinlicky with Ellen I. Hinlicky, "Gnosticism: Old and New," *Dialog* 28, no. 1 (Winter 1989): 12-17.

to the sinister emergence of the state as a necessary agent of coercion. . . . Men and women had not fallen "into" society from an angelic state of Paradise; they had swept even society into their fall.[11]

The point Brown is making here is of broad relevance to Christian political theology: quite in contrast to modern social contract theory, which tells the Hobbsean narrative of a transition from a violent state of nature to civil society, and yields a one-city theology, Augustine's reading of the Bible's opening chapters tells of a transition from primal community to a world plagued by violence, and yields accordingly a two-city theology. The community of marriage suffers this latter fate in the transition from Genesis 1:26-28 to Genesis 3. Yet in spite of the differentiated curse there laid upon it, Augustine found marriage to remain blessed by God with the blessings of children, loyalty, and love as surely as the creative command, "Let there be . . ." remained in force. Needless to say, this is a complex teaching and ambivalent. To it Luther added, as we shall see, his characteristic Christological orientation by lifting up the text of Genesis 3:15 as the Protoevangelium, making this divine consolation and promise central to the sense of the story as whole. Thus it would be through the great Nevertheless in face of death and sin, through the Yes to life in bearing and raising of children, that the bodies of the exiled would one day discover redemption.

If the more fanatical attempts at "sexual renunciation" in any case seemed in Augustine's hindsight to have represented a false attempt to storm heaven, perhaps it was also based on a false reading of Galatians 3:27. Perhaps the break in the parallelism with the two previous clauses to say in the third instance, no "male-and-female" with an allusion to Genesis 1:26-28, indicates a different contrast from the ethnic, religious, and class structures rising out of the fallenness of the old creation. In that case the sense would not be that the partnership of heterosexual marriage no longer exists or even ought not to exist in the church, but that the image of God renewed in Christ by incorporation into His Person is expanded beyond the confines of heterosexual marriage where Genesis 1:26-28 had seemed to locate and as such confine it. As Christopher Morse has rightly noted in this connection, such an interpretation "would be in effect to claim that only married men and women who cling to each other as one flesh are human beings made in the image of God and that all unmarried

11. Brown, *The Body and Society,* pp. 404-5.

people are not human beings. Such a teaching clearly violates the love that comes to embodied expression in the way that Jesus Christ is confessed in Christian faith to relate to the church."[12] What *had been* the apparent meaning of Genesis 1:26-28 is not a meaning that has been annulled for Paul, but rather relativized and subordinated to God's eschatological family, where in Jesus Christ there is place for the child, the single, the widower, the eunuch, the celibate as well.[13] Such a reading has the advantage of overcoming the tension Martyn finds in the traditions about Jesus: the new eschatological family of God does not cancel and annul married life, but (since Christ is not a foe of nature!) it lifts the curse of Genesis 3, restores the Creator's original intention of blessing upon the equal partnership of man and woman,[14] and at the same time relativizes and subordinates married life to the greater righteousness of the new creation. As it happens, such a reading would correspond to the twofold theological move Luther made in demoting marriage as sacrament yet elevating marriage as a definite form of Beloved Community, indeed the true "religious order" (as opposed to the monastery or the convent), as Scott Hendrix has described with appropriate nuance.[15]

We have in that event an illustrative case of the nature that grace

12. Christopher Morse, *Not Every Spirit: A Dogmatics of Christian Disbelief* (Harrisburg, PA: Trinity Press International, 1994), p. 275. Dr. Morse is the author's esteemed doctor-father. My disagreement with him here is as theologically subtle as it is personally painful.

13. As Morse goes on beautifully to describe "what is done at a celebration of Christian marriage blesses us all, married or unmarried, widowed, single, or divorced. Freed from the anxiety of both exclusion and compulsion, we are in this hearing brought to see signified in the couple's special love as gift that mystery of the special union between Christ and every one of us." Morse, *Not Every Spirit*, p. 278. But there is another dimension to this shared blessing: we have all, male and female, gay and straight, married or unmarried, been *children*. That is *the* factor that precludes any annulment of Genesis 1:26-28 on the basis of Christological heroism, and makes the blessing, though not recognition, of homophile unions problematic. See below.

14. Mickey L. Mattox makes a strong argument for this tendency in Luther's later exegesis, *"Defender of the Most Holy Matriarchs": Martin Luther's Interpretation of the Women of Genesis in the* Enarrationes in Genesin, *1535-45* (Leiden and Boston: E. J. Brill, 2003), pp. 74-75.

15. Scott Hendrix, "Luther on Marriage," *Lutheran Quarterly* 14, no. 3 (2000): 335-50. Certain feminist critics of Luther who then accuse him of bringing "the monastery into the bedroom" have a real insight, even if their construal of it is hostile. Cf. *Luther on Women: A Sourcebook,* ed. and trans. Susan C. Karant-Nunn and Merry E. Wiesner-Hanks (Cambridge: Cambridge University Press, 2003).

comes to redeem in Luther's teaching on marriage. Hendrix cites a letter of Luther to Amsdorf about his decision to marry: "I also wanted to confirm what I have taught by practicing it; for I find so many timid people in spite of such great light from the gospel." Hendrix comments: the "recovery of the gospel has revealed that marriage was better than celibacy and that it was also intended by God for most people; Luther wanted not only to teach that insight but also to demonstrate it in his own life."[16] The observation dovetails with an overriding argument of this book for Luther's apocalyptic theology: the "nature" that the believer has in common with others nevertheless is now constructed differently, that is, when perceived in the light of grace (although this new construction in turn creates problems of its own that will not resolve until all is seen new in the light of glory). So the task before us in this chapter is to probe in these shifting perspectives issues involved in Luther's teaching on marriage as a test case in his evangelical theological anthropology.[17] After taking note of the scholarly recovery of the public and social nature of "the holy estate of marriage" in the understanding of Luther and his tradition, I will with help from Dietrich Bonhoeffer lay bare the biblical basis of Luther's theology of marriage in the Christological interpretation of the first three chapters of the Book of Genesis. In the process, I will be trying to put my finger on a difficulty that subverts retrieval, i.e., Luther's Augustinian linkage of sexual love to procreation.[18] Luther does not find this link in the sheer fact of heterosexual

---

16. Hendrix, "Luther on Marriage," p. 343.

17. Jane Strohl's plenary address to the 2007 International Congress for Luther Research in São Paulo, Brazil, "Luther's New View of Marriage, Sexuality and the Family" is a splendid contribution. Among historical accounts of Luther's teaching on marriage, I have been informed principally by William Lazareth's *Luther on the Christian Home* (Philadelphia: Muhlenberg Press, 1960), with the republication of its final chapter and new preface in the *Lutheran Quarterly* (1993): 235-68; relevant chapters in Paul Althaus, *Ethics of Martin Luther*, trans. and with a foreword by Robert C. Schultz (Philadelphia: Fortress Press 1972); H. G. Haile, *Luther: An Experiment in Biography* (Garden City, NY: Doubleday, 1980); Heiko A. Oberman, *Luther: Man between God and the Devil*, trans. E. Walliser-Schwarzbart (New Haven: Yale University Press, 1989); and the unpublished study of my friend, the Finnish Luther scholar Sammeli Juntunen, "Sex in Luther." I am particularly indebted to Juntunen, not only for his excellent research, but for deliberating with me on these matters when he came to Roanoke College to lecture in October 2004. Roland H. Bainton's chapter "The School for Character" in his famous biography, *Here I Stand: A Life of Martin Luther* (New York: Mentor, 1955), is still useful for congregational study, as is Thomas P. Azar, "The Estate of Marriage, 1522," *Lutheran Forum* 30, no. 2 (May 1996): 41-43.

18. Hendrix, "On Marriage," rightly stresses Luther's abiding Augustinianism on this topic, p. 336.

fertility, but rather, as I will show, in the true, albeit counterintuitive good of marital community. Marriage as a form of Beloved Community is not only community in life's joys but also in its sorrows; in language familiar to English-speaking peoples from the *Book of Common Prayer:* "to have and to hold from this day forward, for better or for worse, for richer or for poorer, in sickness and in health, to love and to cherish, until parted by death." I will probe Luther's own reformed liturgy for weddings, among other sources, to bring out this community in suffering as in joy as the test of married life's anticipation of the Beloved Community.

This thesis, however, opens up in the process a problematic ambivalence at the heart of things. Oberman, to be sure, has rightly laid the weight upon Luther's defiant affirmation: "'whoever is ashamed of marriage is also ashamed of being and being called human,' . . . 'it is the God of this world, the Devil, who so slanders the marital state and makes it shameful.'"[19] Luther's exegesis of Genesis 2:18 "is truly epoch-making. 'This is the Word of God, by virtue of which . . . the passionate, natural inclination toward woman is created and maintained. It may not be prevented by vow and law. For it is God's Word and work.'"[20] *That* is Luther's greater "breakthrough" in the sense of the epigraph to this chapter: *Christ is not a foe of nature, but has come to wreak vengeance on [the Usurper of nature] as on His own foe, who poisoned and spoiled His work.* Yet what are we to make, then, of Luther's occasional but unmistakably negative construals of sexual love as sinful concupiscence — even within marriage? This is often dismissed by scholars under the rubrics of "post-monastic tinges" (Lazareth), a leftover from "Augustine's negative view of sexual passion" (Althaus), "the legacy of Augustine's Stoic psychology" (Juntunen). Undoubtedly there is basis in the corpus of Luther's writings for these pronouncements, but Luther is responsible for the sources he takes up and uses (not those sources). I hope in what follows to put these very (problematic) sentiments in a different light by taking, as I do in general, Luther's relation to Augustine more positively than is the habit in Protestant church-history, where the tacit assumption of a Lutheran *Sonderweg* still informs certain habits of scholarship.[21]

19. Oberman, *Luther: Man Between,* pp. 272-73, cited from WA *Briefe* 1.471, 352f.; Aug. 1519. "What made Luther's theology so vivid and intelligible was not the outer rhetoric, but the connection of the Word of God with corporeality . . . he understood God's Word as truly creative, 'God spoke and it was so.'"

20. Oberman, *Luther: Man Between,* pp. 273-74, cited from WA 18.275, 19-28, 1525.

21. For a recent example, witness the rather tortured reasoning of Timothy J.

Sexual love that can be affirmed and enjoyed in spite of ineluctable emotional complexity in a world at once fallen, claimed for redemption, but not yet fulfilled, is politically superior to the alternately sanitized, mechanized, or spiritualized sexualities of today's puritan and libertine alike.[22] The point is very much *political.* In Robert W. Jenson's acerbic judgment: "we should deprecate the recent 'sexual revolution' not so much for the behavior released, pitiful though most of it is, as for its consequences as a political choice. A sexually anarchic society cannot be a free society. For no society can endure mere shapelessness; when the objective foundation of community is systematically violated the society must and will hold itself together by arbitrary force," i.e., fascism.[23] The atomized individuals created by our recent sexual license, Jenson is saying, will eventually be organized in uniformitarian ways by authoritarian politics as the resulting *Lumpenproletariat* becomes dependent on the monopolistic state as surrogate parent. The task of a Christian theology of marriage under such post-Christendom conditions is to lay claim to a public space *in pro-*

Wengert, "Philip Melanchthon and Augustine of Hippo," *Lutheran Quarterly* 22, no. 3 (Autumn 2008): 249-67. Contrast this with the nuanced appraisal of David Steinmetz, in *Luther in Context,* pp. 12-22.

22. Herbert Marcuse's manifesto of the New Left, *Eros and Civilization: A Philosophical Inquiry into Freud* (Boston: Beacon Press, 1955), proclaimed revolt against the repressive order of procreative sexuality and a glorious return to the primary narcissism of unfettered "polymorphous perversity." In years since, second thoughts are expressed in the writings, e.g., of tough-minded feminist Ann Douglas, who makes clear the economic differences between the pre-modern and modern family which have so profoundly distressed the partnership of male and female in industrial and post-industrial societies: Ann Douglas, *The Feminization of American Culture* (New York: Anchor Press/Doubleday, 1977); or, e.g., of Christopher Lasch, whose study of modern political economy's penetration of the home showed how the contemporary family has been transformed into an expression of, not a "haven" from, this "heartless world." Christopher Lasch, *Haven in a Heartless World: The Family Besieged* (New York: Basic Books, 1977). Lasch's jeremiad against the contemporary culture of narcissism hit the nail on the head: "The most prevalent form of escape from emotional complexity is promiscuity: the attempt to achieve a strict separation between sex and feeling. Here again, escape masquerades as liberation, regression as progress. The progressive ideology of 'nonbinding commitments' and 'cool sex' makes a virtue of emotional disengagement, while purporting to criticize the depersonalization of sex. . . . This program seeks to allay emotional tension, in effect, by reducing the demands men and women make on each other, instead of making men and women better able to meet them." Christopher Lasch, *The Culture of Narcissism: American Life in an Age of Diminishing Expectations* (New York: W. W. Norton, 1978), p. 200.

23. Robert W. Jenson, *Systematic Theology,* [hereafter *ST*] vol. 2: *The Triune God* (New York and Oxford: Oxford University Press, 1997), p. 91.

tection of children, there to help men and women better to enjoy the "blessing" as well as better to meet the high moral demands of God's creative "mandate"[24] in Genesis 1:26-28.[25] This is accomplished by understanding this partnership as singular, foundational, and social, constituting the image of God in things "below," that is, in dominion of the earth — a nest of resistance against the totalizing prospect. Yet this very understanding comes about by relativizing and subordinating married life to the Christological fulfillment found in the love of Christ and the church (which community includes all sorts of *unmarried* people).

The notion assumed in this chapter's undertaking, that evangelical teaching on marriage (or any other "ethical" topic) is intended to help us occupy public space, meet moral demands, and attain to creation's promised blessing,[26] offends a certain school of Lutheran thought, though in my view wrongly.[27] Antinomians hold that Christ is "the end of the law"

---

24. Bonhoeffer proposed the dynamic term "mandate" in place of the traditional terminology of "estate" or "order" because the traditional language "would involve the danger of directing attention towards the actual state of the institution than towards its foundation, which lies solely in the divine warrant, legitimation and authorization. The consequence of this can all too easily be the assumption of a divine sanction for all existing orders and institutions in general and a romantic conservatism which is entirely at variance with the Christian doctrine. . . . The concept of the 'estate' . . . did good service at the time of Reformation onwards but in the course of history it has acquired so many new connotations that it is now quite impossible to employ it in its pure original sense." *Ethics*, ed. E. Bethge (New York: Macmillan, 1978), p. 288.

25. So Mattox, *Defender*, pp. 70-71.

26. I am following William H. Lazareth's distinction between creative command and accusing and constraining law in *Christians in Society: Luther, the Bible and Social Ethics* (Minneapolis: Fortress, 2001), pp. 71-85, and Reinhard Hütter's incisive analysis in "The Twofold Center of Lutheran Ethics," in *The Promise of Lutheran Ethics*, ed. K. Bloomquist and J. Stumme (Minneapolis: Fortress, 1998), pp. 31-54.

27. See Timothy J. Wengert's detailed analysis in *Law and Gospel: Philip Melanchthon's Debate with John Agricola of Eisleben over Poenitentia* (Grand Rapids: Baker Books, 1997). The massive fact that stands against every antinomian interpretation of Luther is his catechisms with their exposition of the Decalogue. Recognizing that "Wittenberg's gospel had led to a kind of gross antinomianism" (p. 149), Luther explicated the commandments: "More than just a threat, the commands are the font of all good works; outside of obeying them no work or being can please God" (p. 150). For Melanchthon (see his own socially oriented exposition of the commandments in *Loci communes 1555*, pp. 83ff.), "The Decalogue has not been abrogated . . . although the *accusatio* has been dropped, the *notitia* remains. . . . The law shows us works, not so that we may be justified through them, but so that, since we cannot get through this life without works, God may reveal to us the particular works to be done" (p. 165). Wengert's criticism of the antinomian Agricola is telling: "by avoiding the law in one

(Rom. 10:4) not chiefly (or today at all) in Luther's sense that His holy obedience to God's law fulfills God's ethical purpose and so counts for the helpless sinner who trusts in Him. Rather, they hold that Christ is the end of the law in the sense that Christ saves by a new revelation of true and higher morality, which overthrows the false morality of this world, exposing it as oppressive ideology — the anti-Judaism of this new Marcionism is scarcely concealed. The grain of truth in this (at least as a claim to interpret Luther) is that the fallen creature no longer understands itself as creature of God; that the "law written in her heart" has consequently become obscured by a legalistic mentality *(opinio legis)*, namely, that the gods can be bribed by sacrifice and their wrath in this way averted (recall the discussion of Girard in Chapter Three). The entire Reformation critique of self-chosen meritorious works of religious sacrifice/devotion in place of the truly good works commanded by God for the good of others in society loses its ground, however, if this "antinomian" reading of Luther prevails. Then Christ is the not the end of the law's *jurisdiction* as the pedagogue to Christ (Gal. 3:23) but rather the end of the law's (old, oppressive) ethical content (but see Rom. 7:12; 13:8-10). Luther insightfully wrote against such antinomianism that it takes the grounds out from under Christ's propitiatory death, which is the basis in reality for the sinner's free justification.[28] Aside from its affinity with Gnosticism,[29] the real problem with antinomianism is that according to Luther the law *as God's* is both the source of prophetic criticism of oppressive morality and that authentic prophetic criticism always recoils back upon the critic, whose own need is thus revealed as the same reconciliation with God (Rom. 2).[30]

Consider, for example, how Luther has the evangelical pastor conclude the reformed liturgy for weddings with a prayer that addresses God as the One "who has created man and woman and hast ordained them for

---

place, he let it in the back door without realizing what he was doing. He regards the promise of baptism as the motivating factor in asking for forgiveness ('remember the Trinity'), but prescribed a series of actions, concluding with a prayer that beseeched God not to remove the gift of the Holy Spirit" (pp. 127-28). This latter gospel-reductionism amounts to a contemporary description of ethics in mainline denominations.

28. "Against the Antinomians" (1539) LW 47:99-119.

29. Philip J. Lee, *Against the Protestant Gnostics* (New York: Oxford University Press, 1987).

30. To say therefore against Lutheran libertarians that "the gospel is ordered to the law" is rightly intended, but the nuance is wrong. Pastor Greg Fryer puts the matter this way in his remarkable correspondence with Bishop Stephen Boumann in a Web publication under the title, "Theology in the Metropolitan New York Synod, ELCA, 2005."

the married estate, hast blessed them also with the fruits of the womb, and hast typified therein the sacramental union of thy dear Son, the Lord Jesus Christ, and the church, his bride. . . ."[31] Along these lines we should teach today in accord with the anti-Gnosticism of the catholic tradition: God has created us in order to redeem us; God redeems precisely what He has created.[32] Jesus Christ in His love for the church and the church in its love for Him by the Spirit form the renewed image of God (as Härle rightly sees) in which the married partnership of male and female in social and personal commitment is affirmed, corrected, and fulfilled (alongside other social forms, see below Chapter Nine).[33] If the gospel is "ordered to the law," it is the law as corrected by Jesus (Matt. 5 & 19), fulfilled in his obedience (Rom. 5), and realized in us by the Spirit (Gal. 5). Recent scholarship has underscored the *socially* reformatory intention and effect of this "Lutheran" correction of the law in the light of the gospel,[34] to which we now turn.

## Marriage as Holy Estate

No one in recent memory expressed as elegantly the old Lutheran notion of marriage as public estate — and that under the duress of the conditions of modernity *in extremis* — as did Dietrich Bonhoeffer in a wedding sermon he composed in his prison cell for friends Eberhard and Renate in May 1943. The sermon speaks common Christian themes: of God who

---

31. "The Order of Marriage for Common Pastors" (1529) LW 53:110ff. See also Mattox, *Defender,* p. 71.

32. "Conclusion of the Ten Commandments, Large Catechism" [hereafter LC], *The Book of Concord,* ed. Robert Kolb and Timothy J. Wengert (Minneapolis: Fortress, 2000) [hereafter *BC*], pp. 428ff.

33. Lutheran orthodoxy considered the orders as "estates in the church." The "domestic estate" included marital, parental, and servile (i.e., labor) relations. *The Doctrinal Theology of the Evangelical Lutheran Church,* ed. H. Schmid, trans. C. Hay and H. Jacobs (Philadelphia, 1899), p. 619. It is this tradition to which Bonhoeffer is giving sharper Christological focus (to guard against a proclivity to mere conservatism in the alliance of Throne and Altar of German Lutheranism) and which I take up in Chapter Nine. Oswald Bayer makes an interesting attempt at retrieval in *Martin Luther's Theology: A Contemporary Interpretation,* trans. Thomas H. Trapp (Grand Rapids: Eerdmans, 2007), pp. 120-53.

34. John Witte Jr., *Law and Protestantism: The Legal Teachings of the Lutheran Reformation,* with a foreword by Martin E. Marty (Cambridge: Cambridge University Press, 2002); also the author's review in *Sixteenth Century Journal* 35, no. 2 (2004): 534-36.

joins together and thus of the indissolubility of the partnership; the rule for married life that makes it a type of the love of Christ and the church; the blessing that orders married life to children in tandem with the burden of suffering and mortality entailed; and finally the common order of charity in Christ which provides the real basis of happiness in the new home. The decisive passage on marriage as public estate comes early on and reads as follows:

> Marriage is more than your love for each other. It has a higher dignity and power, for it is God's holy ordinance, through which he wills to perpetuate the human race till the end of time. In your love you see only your two selves in the world, but in marriage you are a link in the chain of the generations, which God causes to come and to pass away to his glory, and calls into his kingdom. In your love you see only the heaven of your own happiness, but in marriage you are placed at a post of responsibility towards the world and mankind. Your love is your own private possession, but marriage is more than something personal — it is a status and office . . . love comes from you, but marriage from above, from God. As high as God is above man, so high are the sanctity, the rights, and the promise of love. It is not your love that sustains the marriage, but from now on, the marriage that sustains your love.[35]

Bonhoeffer's emphasis here on the social nature of marriage is of a piece with his larger, lifelong quest to retrieve the "social intention of all the basic Christian concepts"[36] over against the dominant individualism of modern theology stemming from the Cartesian revolution that had made *Mitsein* categorically suspect and at length unintelligible to the atomistic individualism of the modern mind.

What is striking in the newer scholarship is such recovery of this *so-*

---

35. Dietrich Bonhoeffer, *Letters and Papers from Prison*, new greatly enlarged ed., ed. E. Bethge (New York: Macmillan Collier, 1972), pp. 42-43. I am grateful to Charles Ford for reminding me of this passage. Oberman remarks in the same vein upon Luther's own happy marriage: "But the decisive factor was that both of them regarded marriage as a profession and divine vocation without the romantic expectations of love that were later to increase so enormously the number of disappointments and marital breakups." *Luther: Man Between*, p. 280.

36. Dietrich Bonhoeffer, *Sanctorum Communio: A Theological Study of the Sociology of the Church*, ed. C. J. Green, trans. R. Kraus and N. Lukens, Dietrich Bonhoeffer Works, vol. 1 (Minneapolis: Fortress, 1998), p. 21.

*cial* nature of Luther's teaching on marriage as the actual "nest" for love in the world. In his instructive study of the history of marriage in Western law, John Witte rightly accents the tradition's teaching stemming from Luther of marriage-and-household (the pre-modern "domestic economy") as the fundamental social order or "estate" instituted by the Creator. For early Lutherans, Witte writes, "all persons should heed the duty of marriage for the sake of society. In the reformers' view, marriage was an important, independent institution of creation — in Luther's words, 'a divine and holy estate of life,' a 'blessed holy calling' with its own created sphere of authority and responsibility. Indeed, marriage was the foundation of society and of churches, states, schools and other institutions that comprised it."[37] Similarly Steven Ozment concluded his careful study of family life in Reformation Europe with this pointed challenge to tacit assumptions of today's "atomistic and expressive" individualism (Bellah): "To the people of Reformation Europe no specter was more fearsome than a society in which the desires of individuals eclipsed their sense of social duty."[38] In an intriguing article, Scott Hendrix underscores the gravamen of reformatory reconstructions of masculinity: "in the conflict between their needs as men and society's expectations of them as patriarchs . . . to be a man was to sacrifice one's own desire for the good of a woman, a child to be born, and the community."[39] Martin Brecht puts the new perspective summarily: "One should not underestimate the effect of Luther's writings on marriage, for they initiated a change in society. First of all, marriage and women were valued more highly. . . ."[40]

In the light of these scholarly reassessments, it is indeed striking when we turn to Luther himself to see how this social purpose — at the expense of almost any celebration of romantic love as such — leaps out at us. Whatever the justice with which Luther treated canon law in often scathing remarks, the substantial 1530 legal treatise *On Marriage Matters* is nothing but an extended and detailed plea for public recognition and legal protection of marriage: "because marriage is a public estate which is to be

---

37. John Witte Jr., *From Sacrament to Contract: Marriage, Religion and Law in the Western Tradition* (Louisville: Westminster/John Knox, 1997), p. 49.

38. Steven Ozment, *When Fathers Ruled: Family Life in Reformation Europe* (Cambridge, MA: Harvard University Press, 1983), p. 177.

39. Scott Hendrix, "Masculinity and Patriarchy in Reformation Germany," *Journal of the History of Ideas* 56, no. 2 (April 1995): 193.

40. Martin Brecht, *Martin Luther: Shaping and Defining the Reformation, 1521-1532,* trans. J. L. Schaaf (Minneapolis: Fortress, 1990), p. 95.

entered into and recognized publicly before the church, it is fitting that it should also be established and begun publicly with witnesses," not without "the knowledge and consent of those who are in authority and have the right and power to establish a marriage, such as father, mother, and whoever may act in their stead."[41] This plea for social recognition and legal protection of marriage does not constitute in the modern sense of the word a "secularization" of marriage, as Althaus rightly underscored, as if (in Luther's own words) marriage were "'nothing more than a purely human and secular state, with which God has nothing to do.'" Likewise, Hendrix warns against a one-sided reading of the new social perspective: Luther "is not trying to secularize marriage in the sense of separating it from God or religion."[42] On the contrary, in accord with his teaching on the two regiments of *divine* rule, it is more a matter of demanding that the state take responsibility *before God* for marriage than it is chiefly or simply a rejection "of the claim of Roman clericalism that the church is responsible for the legal aspects of marriage."[43]

At least several contemporary theologians coming from the tradition of Luther have followed Bonhoeffer's lead here, retrieving Luther's interpretation of marriage as the primal form of co-humanity and so of public life of which Genesis 1–3 actually speaks.[44] Robert Jenson, building upon Karl Barth's critique of the Cartesian-dualistic disjunction of person and body, has argued that sexuality is "the way in which our directedness to each other, the intrinsic commonality of human being, is built into the very objects as which we are there for one another. It is sexuality that rescues the communal character of human being from being a mere ideal or

---

41. Martin Luther, "On Marriage Matters" (1530) LW 46:259-319.

42. Hendrix, "Luther on Marriage," p. 340. The concern is expressed against Witte's claim that the Lutherans "regarded marriage as a social estate of the earthly kingdom alone" (p. 349, n. 22). The confusion, as Hendrix acknowledges later in this article, derives from that labyrinth for understanding which is the Two Kingdoms doctrine.

43. Althaus, *Ethics*, p. 89. Mattox also corrects the secularizing tendency of the modern Two Kingdoms theology here, when he calls "attention to the very different shape Luther's thought on marriage assumes when interpreted in the context of his theology of orders." *Defender*, p. 71.

44. "Whatever the husband has, this the wife has and possesses in its entirety. Their partnership involves not only their means but children, food, bed, and dwelling; their purposes, too, are the same. The result is that the husband differs from the wife in no other respect than sex; otherwise the woman is altogether a [*Mensch*] . . . she differs only in sex . . . she is the mistress of the house just as you are its master, except that the wife was made subject to the man by the Law which was given after sin." "Commentary on Genesis" LW 1:137-38.

demand laid upon and makes it a *fact* about us."[45] Jenson's formulation here virtually echoes Luther's words from the Large Catechism: "God has established [marriage] before all others as the first of all institutions, and he created man and woman differently (as is evident) not for indecency but to be true to each other, to be fruitful, to beget children, and to nurture and bring them up to the glory of God. . . ."[46] Likewise Jenson's correlation of sexual and political order in this instructive chapter of his *Systematic Theology* echoes the public-social intention of Luther's teaching on marriage: "For it is of utmost importance to [God] that persons be brought up to serve the world, to promote knowledge of God, godly living, and all virtues, and to fight against wickedness and the devil. . . ."[47]

Oswald Bayer also "re-presents" Luther's social theology[48] of marriage "in einer Zeit des Individualismus und des Generationenbruches," advising that "whoever wants to grasp Luther's understanding of marriage must first look at the family."[49] Although it "sounds banal," we must "newly learn that the world and our life, indeed our own biography, did not begin with ourselves. Rather we much more owe thanks to a word, a will, an affirmation which our own life presupposes, which came before it." Penultimately that will be the word, will, and affirmation of our parents, but ultimately it is God's creative, commanding Word as seen in Genesis 1:26-28.[50] The Decalogue's commandment protecting marriage from adultery *theologically,* not only chronologically, *follows and presupposes* the commandment protecting elders in Luther's understanding. Accordingly it is in recognition of this debt to the generations, going back to the will of the

---

45. Jenson, *ST* II:89.

46. *BC,* p. 414.

47. *BC,* p. 414.

48. Luther's theology of the Word "lässet sich von 'Person' nie individualistisch, sondern nur im Zusammenhang eines Wortwechsels sprechen: Wer bin ich, ergibt sich daraus, dass ich angeredet bin und mich deshalb auch verantworten kann und muss . . . das wahrhaft Personale gerade in seiner Institutionalität, in seiner institutionellen Verfassheit besteht und ohne sie leere Pesonalität wäre." Oswald Bayer, *Martin Luthers Theologie: Eine Vergegenwaertigung,* 2. Auflage (Tübingen: Mohr Siebeck, 2004), pp. 133-34. The author acknowledges that research here was undertaken before Bayer's book was translated into English, and, with the reader's indulgence, he retains his own translations here. The reader may consult Bayer, *Luther's Theology,* pp. 140-51.

49. Bayer, *Martin Luthers Theologie,* pp. 129-34. All translations are my own.

50. In Bonhoeffer's words from the marriage sermon: "Today God adds his 'Yes' to your 'Yes,' as he confirms your will with his will . . . and creates out of your love something quite new — the holy estate of matrimony." Bonhoeffer, *Letters,* p. 42.

Creator "in the beginning" according to Jesus' word in Mark 10:9, that Luther, according to Bayer, finds firm ground on which to build marriage. This recognition of the course of the generations through time in which a married couple take their place comes from the Word of God, as "it creates an unreserved and unlimited sharing of a definite man and a definite woman . . . ," that is, as God's Word "confers definite form upon the chaotic naturalness of human drives and brings forth a definite distinction" and relation of man for the woman and woman for the man. Although Bayer does not draw it out explicitly, this argument can only mean that marriage is ordered by God to procreation. Does that imply, however, that apart from God's directive command in Genesis, and even in spite of the human body's heterosexual form, sexuality as a matter of human consciousness and historical experience is polymorphous, indeed, narcissistic and anarchistic in tendency? Bayer does not say, but the implication of his argument that sexual drives are otherwise something formless is that in any case they will somehow be formed (or misformed) socially, no doubt chiefly by that debt of thanks (or pain) of each human child to its parents. In this situation, the *Kraft zur Gemeinschaft,* according to Bayer's reading of Luther, is the Word of God which commands marriage.

We might detect in the background of Bayer's reticence here Dietrich Bonhoeffer's unappreciated effort to restore the concept of the "natural" to theology in Luther's tradition, not nature as opposed to grace in the exaggerated way demanded by anti-Catholic polemics, but rather here, down on the earth, as opposed then to the "unnatural": "Natural life is formed life. . . . If life detaches itself from this form, if it is unwilling to allow itself to be served by the form of the natural, then it destroys itself to the very roots. Life which posits itself as an absolute, as an end in itself, is its own destroyer. Vitalism cannot but end in nihilism. . . ."[51] Form is social, public, ordered; the furious, vitalist revolt of *Lebensphilosophie* against all form as heteronomous raged around Bonhoeffer as he penned these thoughts under the shadow of Nazi nihilism. Formlessness led not to human liberation but finally to arbitrary unification of formless peoples singing, *Ein Volk! Ein Reich! Ein Führer!* So Bonhoeffer counterproposed: we should understand "the natural [as] that which, after the Fall, is directed toward the coming of Christ. The unnatural is that which, after the Fall, closes its doors to Christ."[52] The theological task for social ethics is not to abandon

---

51. Bonhoeffer, *Ethics,* p. 149.
52. Bonhoeffer, *Ethics,* p. 144.

form, nor to defend at all costs existing formations, but to re-form the natural toward the image of God made known in Christ.

In this light we may say something that both Bayer and Jenson imply, but do not further explicate, which is actually central to Luther's theology of marriage. Bonhoeffer expressed it in the wedding sermon for Eberhard and Renate thusly: "In your love you see only your two selves in the world, but in marriage you are a link in the chain of the generations, which God causes to come and to pass away to his glory, and calls into his kingdom."

Jenson is concerned to show that homosexual unions cannot substitute for heterosexual unions, if the "body" is not merely instrumental in relation to free-floating nonsomatic "persons," but the inalienable biological form of created personhood. Bayer is concerned to show over against the apparent infinity of sexual desire (Marcuse's polymorphous perverse) that commitment and fidelity are possible by faith in the Word which commands marriage and gives what it commands. These are both worthy concerns which I share. But in what follows I am interested in bringing out what Edmund Burke once called the "covenant between the generations" as the integral and integrating link in retrieval of Luther's teaching on marriage.[53]

---

53. Edmund Burke, *Reflections on the Revolution in France* (New York: Knopf), p. 38. Admirers of the French Revolution do well to consider Bonhoeffer's trenchant commentary (penned upon Hitler's fawning visit to the tomb of Napoleon in fallen Paris?): "The emancipation of the masses leads to the reign of terror and guillotine. Nationalism leads inevitably to war. The liberation of man as an absolute ideal leads only to man's self-destruction. At the end of the path which was first trodden in the French Revolution there is nihilism. The new unity which the French Revolution brought to Europe — and what we are experiencing today in the crisis of this unity [i.e., under Hitlerism] — is therefore western godlessness . . . not the theoretical denial of the existence of God. It is itself a religion, a religion of hostility to God. . . . The American democracy is not founded upon the emancipated man but, quite the contrary, upon the kingdom of God and the limitation of all earthly powers by the sovereignty of God. It is indeed significant when, in contrast to the [French Revolution's] *Declaration of the Rights of Man,* American historians can say that the federal constitution was written by men who were conscious of original sin and the wickedness of the human heart. Earthly wielders of authority, and also the people, are directed into their proper bounds, in due consideration of man's innate longing for power and of the fact that power pertains only to God." Bonhoeffer, *Ethics,* pp. 102, 104. Herbert Marcuse is one such admirer. Commenting on Marcuse's attack on Luther for "limiting the concern of freedom to the inward man, and thus with diverting the Germans from their true needs for freedom. . . ," Martin Brecht writes, "this begs the fundamental question of how freedom is to be achieved. Luther's answer was: by liberation as a gift, not through activistic self-realization." Gift presupposes Giver: real freedom consists in humanity's "election to communion with God. This understanding was just as contrary to the conventional view of man at the time as it is to the mod-

## Luther's Biblical Theology of Marriage

The theological grounding of marriage in the divine mandate spoken in Genesis 1:26-28 is universal in Christian tradition. Within this wide tradition, as Oberman remarked, Luther's particular iteration of it had wide, indeed world-historical influence. For complex historical reasons that need not detain us,[54] it entailed culturally a new conception of the human and its good which overthrew the antecedent cultural-religious idealization of virginity. Opponents among the monks "argue that chastity is a thing of incomparable worth and its equal is nowhere to be found."[55] But Luther, himself still living as a monk, replies, "if anyone is unable to keep his vow of chastity and takes a wife, confident of God's mercy, as he grows in this faith he will discover a merciful and understanding Father . . . that is what God's mercy is like. In no sense does God attribute sin to the conjugal rights of married people. . . ."[56] Whatever other problems the Wittenberg professor of Old Testament notoriously had with rabbinic Judaism and its exegesis of the same Scriptures on which he too labored, Luther recovered and reasserted the Hebrew Bible's celebration of the monogamous heterosexual union which, in the words of the conservative Jewish cultural commentator Dennis Prager, had worked through the centuries to force "the sexual genie into the marital bottle. [The Torah's original sexual revolution] ensured that sex no longer dominated society, heightened male-female love (and thereby almost alone created the possibility of love and eroticism within marriage), and began the arduous task of elevating the

---

ern views of human possibilities." *Martin Luther: His Road to Reformation 1483-1521*, trans. J. L. Schaf (Minneapolis: Fortress, 1993), p. 409. The "progressive" possibilities of Burke's notion in this age of ecological anxiety might be seen in Jonathan Schell, *The Fate of the Earth* (New York: Knopf, 1982).

54. In his conclusion to *The Body and Society*, p. 425, Brown identifies a deep ambivalence in the doctrine of desire, *concupiscentia nuptiarum* and *concupiscentia carnis*, behind the Christian tradition of sexual renunciation: "The fatal flaw of concupiscence would not have seemed so tragic to Augustine, if he had not become ever more deeply convinced [from the Bible] that human beings had been created to embrace the material world. The body was a problem to him precisely because it was to be loved and cherished."

55. "The Judgment of Martin Luther on Monastic Vows" (1521) LW 44:346.

56. "Monastic Vows" (1521) LW 44:376. The sentence continues: ". . . which is due solely to his mercy, although Psalm 51 refers to it as sin and iniquity in no way differing from adultery and whoredom, because it springs from passion and impure lust." I will take up this ambivalence in Luther's evaluation of sexual love — in itself apparently sinful, yet mercifully forgiven — below.

status of women."[57] *Prima facie,* Luther's affinity with the Torah's reformatory program in world history is obvious,[58] as should also be his sourcing of it in the same Bible shared with Judaism.

Significantly, he concluded the Scripture readings in his reformed liturgy for the wedding with this blessing pronounced by the pastor, based upon the *imago Dei* text of the first creation story: "[T]his is your comfort that you may know and believe that your estate is pleasing to God and blessed by him, For it is written: 'God created man in his own image; in the image of God created he them; male and female created he them. And God blessed them, and God said unto them, Be fruitful, and multiply and replenish the earth, and subdue it: and have dominion. . . . And God saw everything that he had made, and, behold, it was very good' [Gen. 1:27-28]."[59] Luther's purpose in reiterating this text in the marriage liturgy is not merely polemical, i.e., to attack the reign of the antecedent ideal of celibacy in the conscience of people. It is also performative: the pastoral repetition of the blessing from Genesis evokes and informs faith in the newlyweds that their marriage is a work of God under His blessing and command. So the liturgically climactic pronouncement of God's blessing upon the new couple reveals-and-puts-into-effect the true good of their sexual union by promising God's approbation and care; thus they may believe with Christian faith in their marriage in this specific way and conduct themselves accordingly.

But what is that true good for Luther? It is always, in part, a negative good, a "remedy against sin," a wall against polymorphous perverse. But as early as 1519, Luther's preaching about marriage identified its "real fruit as children, whose rearing was the special responsibility of the married estate. . . . In the raising of children one obtains the greatest indulgence. Children brought up correctly are the good works . . . which one leaves behind, and which shine in one's death and thereafter."[60] This good of marriage *in children* is a leading motif in Luther, from which he never departs. Sammeli Juntunen advances the following definition of marriage from his study of the Luther texts: "Marriage is a divine and legitimate union *(coniunctio)* of a husband and wife in the hope of children, and in order to

---

57. Dennis Prager, "Judaism's Sexual Revolution: Why Judaism (and Then Christianity) Rejected Homosexuality," *Crisis* 11, no. 8 (September 1993).

58. Paul R. Hinlicky, "Luther Against the Contempt of Women," *Lutheran Quarterly* 2, no. 4 (Winter 1989): 515-30.

59. "The Order of Marriage" (1529) LW 53:110ff.

60. Brecht, *Road,* pp. 355-56.

avoid fornication and sin, to the glory of God. The ultimate goal is to obey God, to avoid sin, to call on God for help, to ask for children, to love and raise them to God's glory, to live with the wife in fear of God and to carry the cross."[61] This fuller and more complex definition of marriage and its true goods reflects the larger story of Genesis 1–3, i.e., taking into account the dissonance introduced by the disobedience of the first couple: the sinful concupiscence that fills the vacated place of love of God in forming the chaotic desires of the human heart. The new situation of life in exile from paradise makes marriage necessary, not only as divine mandate or as command (Gen. 1:26-28) spontaneously assented to (Gen. 2:23), but now also as social institution and legal demand, as duty imposed with its legal constraints and threats (Gen. 3:16-19). Now married life is also the *duty* to procreate and the wall against sin. Luther therefore also included readings from Genesis 3 in his reformed wedding liturgy to tell about "the cross laid upon this estate" and realistically to indicate this post-paradisiacal marital community *in suffering* as well as in joy.

As duty to procreate and remedy against sin, marriage after Eden does double duty. It defends *externally* by erecting a legal wall of separation against wayward desire as well as *internally* through cross-bearing: "it is a precious and noble work . . . to endure much misfortune and many difficulties in the person of wife, children, servants and others . . . he who believes it and rightly understands it, sees how good it is for the soul, although it is an evil for the flesh and its lusts."[62] Luther's meaning here, so offensive to William James's healthy-minded religion, is that community in suffering as also in joy morally purifies and so sanctifies desire. It does this by giving each partner to care for the other in the inevitable troubles that their united form of life entails. Marriage takes such a form in the frustrated creation, fallen and groaning under the power of sin.[63] But this

61. Juntunen, "Sex in Luther."

62. Cited by Lazareth, *Christians in Society,* p. 265.

63. At the beginning of his discussion of the "curses" pronounced in Genesis 3, Luther writes thematically: "But he heals sin, like a wound, with a health-giving plaster, that is, with the promise concerning Christ, while He also applies the harsh cautery which the devil had brought on. Just as health-giving plasters also damage the flesh while they effect their cure, so the curative promise is put to Adam in such a way that at the same time it includes a threat, to serve as a cure for the lust of the flesh. But by 'lust' I mean not only the hideous prurience of the flesh, but also that filthiness of spirit. . . . There was need of this harsh cautery to keep this depravity of our nature in check." "Commentary on Genesis" LW 1:183.

is its true good for human beings who learn in this "real religious order"[64] compassion, patience, and trust in God.

## Dirty Sex? The Problem of Concupiscence

Where is the positive human good of marriage in all this? One can readily imagine today a host of objections to Luther's rather sobering account of marriage after Eden as duty to procreate and remedy against sin, for example: that it proffers a reform and renewal of patriarchy, not its overcoming;[65] that we today can have no such confidence as Luther did in the procreative ideology of the post-exilic priestly writer of Genesis 1 who wants Jews to make babies to ensure ethnic-cultural survival (while we today face problems of global overpopulation); that the antithesis between *amor concupiscentiae* and *amor crucis* disparages the intrinsic good of sexual pleasure; that such earthly pleasures are certain goods to be enjoyed now, not sacrificed for uncertain heavenly rewards; that reason and nature, not theology and Bible, must be our guide on things "below."

The root of all such objections, however, appears to be the self-evident legitimacy of "concupiscence" in modern minds, i.e., we today regard self-seeking love, especially when marketed as erotic pleasure, as an "imperative" of evolutionary biology, simply a natural "given," therefore a non-negotiable "need" that we have a "natural" right to satisfy as best we can in just the way that individually suits us. Luther does not share this assumption about the chaotic infinity of unformed desire or the misshapen ways in which it inevitably expresses itself in the common life of humanity. In general, he does not think that any such thing as pre-linguistic, asocial "needs" exist, since "needs" are always somehow constructed by language and culture in service of definite forms of social life, be they words of man or words of God. For Luther, whose word we believe about our "needs" and "nature" is precisely what is at issue. "Just compare God and man! God says, 'It is my will that you have a helper and not be alone; this seems good to me.' Man replies, 'Not so; you are mistaken. I vow to you to do without a helper; to be alone seems good to me.' What is that but to correct God?"[66]

To be sure, Luther *does* agree with us moderns in disagreeing with

---

64. Hendrix, "On Marriage," p. 338.
65. See Ozment's nuanced characterization in *When Fathers Ruled,* p. 49.
66. "Exhortation to the Knights of the Teutonic Order" (1523) LW 45:145.

the venerable ideal of celibacy, which he counts as something "unnatural": "Must I keep my vow if I have vowed to cling to the sky or to ride on sunbeams or float on the clouds?" No, for sexual desire is something ". . . implanted in us, as is proved by our bodily members, our daily emotions, and the example of all mankind. Now unless God himself performs a miracle, if you vow celibacy and remain unmarried you do exactly the same as he who vows adultery or something else which God has forbidden."[67] But even in this apparent agreement between us, so far as it goes, Luther all the more significantly disagrees with us. For he construes the sexual desire "implanted in us" and "experienced in our members and emotions" in the light of Word of God as intended by God for procreation: "We were all created to do as our parents have done, to beget and rear children. This is a duty which God has laid on us, commanded and implanted in us. . . ."[68] The divine purpose of procreation revealed in the biblical text covers, so to say, with blessing and forgiveness the considerably mixed motives at work even in marital union: "Marriage is an inseparable uniting of one husband and one wife, not on the basis of natural law alone, but also on the basis of divine will and (if I may say so) divine lust. This approbation and good pleasure of God covers the miserable shamefulness of the libido, and removes the wrath of God, which is immanent in its concupiscence and sin."[69] It is God's holy and merciful "lust" to continue creating the human race in spite of sin, which lustily uses concupiscent human desire, mercifully overlooking its ignorance and disregard of His purpose.

Consequently, we can hardly draw any straight line from Luther the liberator of marital love from ascetic prejudice and the ideal of sexual renunciation to today's sexual liberation. He regarded sexual desire unformed by the procreative purpose of God within the marriage covenant as disordered. Luther, to be sure, does not mean this psychologically — as if the lovers have to be thinking about babies during love-making for the loving to please the lusty God, who rather more gladly overlooks their ulterior motives. He really thinks socially not individualistically, theologically not anthropologically, politically not psychologically. He is teaching on the basis of the Word of God that lovemaking pleases God in spite of ambiguous motives, when it is set in the social structure with the corresponding personal commitment that makes time and space for children — that makes

67. "Teutonic Order" (1523) LW 45:155.
68. "Teutonic Order" (1523) LW 45:155.
69. Cited by Juntunen, "Sex in Luther," from WA 43, 294:40–295:3.

for them a "nest." It is all about the children, giving little ones safe place and haven in the fallen world, so that they are loved with God's love by parents who act in God's stead, fulfilling in this nurture their calling to image God in this most concrete form of dominion over the earth.[70] Thus Luther can at the same time brutally observe that "if you judge according to reason and outward appearance, marital coitus is in no way different from adultery."[71] The human consciousness (divided, complex, ambivalent) is not decisive, but rather service to the public God's purpose of Beloved Community.

Thus Brecht remarks that the early Luther who approved of marriage "as the highest state of human relationships" and "superior to clerical celibacy," "still considered sexuality to be burdened by sin."[72] But there is no evidence that an older Luther moved beyond this view.[73] According to Juntunen, Luther speaks regularly of love-making even in marriage as *"böser lust, misera libido"* and expresses Augustinian embarrassment at non-rational sexual arousal comparable to the animals with neither knowledge of God nor faith in the act. The impression is that sexual union remains for Luther "something dirty in itself, even within marriage." As mentioned at the outset, Juntunen thinks that this negative commentary on love-making can be blamed on Augustine's legacy, specifically the dependence on the tripartite soul of Stoic anthropology. Althaus too leaves us with an unresolved statement of the tension and the same shopworn reference to Augustine: "At this point Luther is still caught up in the traditional Augustinian negative attitude toward sexual passion. However, this also expresses a basic truth: the demonic character of selfish desire is most clearly apparent in sexual love."[74] Lazareth simultaneously approves of Luther's "biblical realism" about sex and chastises the "ex-monk" for "hedg[ing] away from too positive an evaluation of the husband-wife" sexual relation in marriage.[75] All these authors maintain that there are resources in Luther for a more positive theological evaluation of sexual plea-

---

70. *BC,* pp. 400-401.

71. Cited by Juntunen, "Sex in Luther," from WA 43, 302:24-28.

72. Brecht, *Road,* pp. 355-56.

73. Brecht tacitly acknowledges this in *Luther: Shaping and Defining,* pp. 91-92, commenting on the "exquisite writing" of 1522 on *The Estate of Marriage:* "Luther had not lost sight of the fact that there was sin in marriage, too; in fact, here we find more of the biblical view of the sinfulness of marital relationships."

74. Althaus, *Ethics,* pp. 84-85. One might comment: a forgotten truth today.

75. Lazareth, *Family,* p. 255.

sure. But this is simply to state the problem of Luther's ambivalence, and in a typically tendentious fashion that makes a villain of the Catholic Augustine and a victim of the not quite yet fully Protestant pioneer Luther. Whatever else Luther has done, however, he has broken in principle with the medieval faculty psychology and this with the help of Augustine.[76] When Luther writes in the Genesis commentary that Adam and Eve's original "righteousness was not a gift which came from without, separate from man's nature, but that it was truly part of his nature, so that it was Adam's nature to love God, to believe God, to know God, etc.,"[77] he is reiterating Augustine's unitary conception of human nature as a temporally and socially constituted desire that is formed by the actual object of its love in its own unique somatic sequence in space-time. Reinhard Hütter is on the right track, in my view, to bring out the Augustinian relation of nature and grace that Luther always presupposes. "Without desire we would cease to be human; without God as desire's ultimate end, we become inhumane. Therefore Christian freedom has to be understood as true *askesis* or chastity: to let all our desires be ordered by and fulfilled in the communion with God that begins in grasping Christ in faith. Instead of being governed by the insatiability of our desires seeking fulfillment in finite goods, we become free to desire our ultimate good. In communion with God we receive the finite goods of creation that we also desire."[78] True *askesis* or chastity does not consist for Luther in renunciation of sex as something dirty, but integration of sex, including "dirty" sex, in God's purposes.

If we disregard Luther's fundamental Augustinianism, it is possible to think that Luther was simply of a divided mind and never attained clarity. But we should not presume so. The still young and as yet unmarried Reformer praised conjugal love as greatest and purest, since "all other kinds of love seek something other than the loved one: this kind wants only to have the beloved's own self completely." Luther dramatized this in the voice of the bride, whose love "glows like a fire and desires nothing but the husband. She says, 'It is you I want, not what is yours: I want neither your silver nor your gold; I want neither. I want only you. I want you in your entirety, or not at all.'"[79] Luther brusquely then acknowledged that in actual experience this bridal love is mixed with and corrupted by sinful de-

---

76. Jan Lindhardt, *Martin Luther: Knowledge and Mediation in the Renaissance,* Texts and Studies in Religion, vol. 29 (Lewiston, NY: Edwin Mellen Press, 1986), pp. 23-30.

77. LW 1:165. De Lubac ought to have entertained this not-incidental teaching of Luther!

78. Hütter in "Lutheran Ethics," p. 47.

79. "A Sermon on the Estate of Marriage" (1519) LW 44:9.

sire to use the beloved for self, a desire that can subvert marital love and finally destroy it, since self-seeking love is *never* satisfied, not even with the spouse whom God has given.[80] Years later, we find the same ambivalence. Juntunen calls to attention a letter to Spalatin, in which Luther writes, "Sweet greetings to your wife. . . . When you take her, your Catharina, with sweet kisses and embrace her, you should think: 'This human being, this wonderful work of God, has my Christ given to me. Glory and honor to him!' In the evening of the same day, when you receive this letter, I will love my wife in the same way and remember you." Yet around the same time, he acknowledged in his male voice to the male students in the classroom (as recorded in the Genesis commentary): "we can hardly speak of her without a feeling of shame, and surely we cannot make use of her without shame. The reason is sin."[81] What are we to make of this?

Ambivalence is not revulsion. Ambivalence is "emotionally complex." Ambivalence is witness of a contest of competing loves in the self. Ambivalence is the cry of the believer's torn being from Romans 7:14-20. So what exactly are these competing values of pure "bridal love" and *"misera libido"*? For Luther the sin of concupiscence is clearly not the creature's created and divinely blessed erotic desire for its beloved, the love that wants "only you, not your goods, you in your entirety or not at all." This he calls "an overwhelmingly passionate love," a "desire to live with her and to accede to God's will by procreating descendants."[82] God declares categorically: "it is not good for the man to be alone." The good of "bridal love" is still lacking at this point in the second creation story in that Adam, accord-

---

80. Already in "The Disputation against Scholastic Theology" (1517) Luther had maintained that "every act of concupiscence against God is evil and a fornication of the spirit," i.e., concupiscence is not to be identified with sexual love but is a spiritual phenomenon (that can and does, of course, also corrupt sexual love): "man is by [fallen] nature unable to want God to be God. Indeed, he himself wants to be God, and does not want God to be God" (LW 31:10). A year later in "The Heidelberg Disputation" (1518), Luther spelled out the implication of this notion of concupiscence as spiritual, not erotic: "The remedy for curing desire does not lie in satisfying it, but in extinguishing it" (LW 31:54). Luther finds his distinction "abundantly" in the Bible and it forms the basis for his entire dispute with Erasmus: "that it is not one part of man, even the most excellent or principal part, that is flesh, but that the whole of man is flesh. . . ." Luther, *Bondage*, p. 250, so that "ignorance and contempt [of God] are not seated in the flesh, in the sense of the lower and grosser affections, but in the highest and most excellent powers of man, in which righteousness, godliness, and knowledge and reverence of God, should reign — that is, in reason and will . . ." (p. 280).

81. Luther, "Commentary on Genesis" LW 1:118-19.

82. Luther, "Commentary on Genesis" LW 1:136.

ing to Luther, "still has no partner for that magnificent work of begetting and preserving his kind."[83] Neither companionship nor the Pauline antidote to fornication has yet come into view in Luther's reading of the second creation story, but rather God's purpose of procreation provides the motive for that "overwhelmingly passionate love, the desire to live with her and to accede to God's will. . . ." This is primary, as primal as the earth and the rib, as "dirty" as the dirt from which Adam is formed and from whose side Eve is taken. It is the thrall of "bridal love." In this light, what then is the concupiscence that spoils holy eros, if concupiscence is *not* this overwhelmingly passionate desire to make love to the bride/bridegroom and see its fruit someday in children?

Will it not be an unnatural desire for something else, something more, something better than this "earthly," i.e., "dirty" good, the definite creature presented by God as complement, one to the other, with all that this entails? Sinful desire in general for Luther, not eros but concupiscence, signifies the whole person turned away from reliance on God's power, wisdom, and love and turned instead to self-seeking self-reliance in doubt of God's power, wisdom, and good favor. Commenting on Genesis 3:1, he writes: "the serpent directs its attack at God's good will and makes it its business to prove from the prohibition of the tree that God's good will toward man is not good. Therefore it launches its attack *against the very image of God* and the most excellent powers in the uncorrupted nature."[84] If that attack succeeds, it will on Luther's suppositions distort everything, sexual desire included. Self-seeking rather than the other-seeking of bridal love under the supreme love of God the Giver despoils this image of God, so that it seeks itself in all things. Luther's ambivalence on sexual love echoes the difficult relation of eros and agape, of nature and grace, in the Augustinian tradition, while the perception of an antinomy here, inflamed by Protestant-Catholic polemics, cuts the Gordian knot of understanding. This latter view, given classic expression in Anders Nygren's *Agape and Eros*,[85] has often misled Lutheran theology into a very un-Lutherlike "as-

83. Luther, "Commentary on Genesis" LW 1:116.

84. Luther, "Commentary on Genesis" LW 1:146. Emphasis added.

85. Anders Nygren famously wrote in conclusion that what Luther "seeks to destroy is that interpretation of Christian love which fundamentally contains more Hellenistic Eros-love than primitive Christian Agape-love . . . in Catholicism — the idea of acquisitive love is the bond which ultimately holds the whole together . . . in Luther — it is the religion of eros and Agape that we meet." *Agape and Eros,* trans. Philip S. Watson (New York and Evanston: Harper & Row, 1969), pp. 739-40.

ceticism" — the Kantian suspicion of "inclination," a disregard (often tinged with misogyny)[86] of human desire, feeling, and passion which are disparaged as possessive and prejudicial, as carnal, subrational, and womanish. A modern combination of rationalism and prudishness set the stage in turn for the revolt of the irrational and return of the repressed that erupted in twentieth-century Europe. It would take us too far afield to explore this sketch of an alternative account to Nygren's, but let me at least indicate *in nuce* that the very notion of "selfless love" is simply incoherent (unless one is surreptitiously hypostasizing a concept), if love is the will and deed of a real agent.[87] What is meant by agape is self-giving love, primordially the love which the Father has toward the Son and the Son toward the Father in the unity of the Spirit. Self-giving love is divine, in its capacity to generate community, when by "God" we mean the Father, the Son, and the Holy Spirit. This divine love is not opposed to nature, but redeems and fulfills it. Natural love, eros, seeks its own happiness in another as befits a creature who "does not have life in itself."[88] It becomes concupiscence when it finds happiness by means of another but apart from the happiness of that other given to it by the Trinity, creator, redeemer, and fulfiller of the two, together, as together. Here, as everywhere, there is no "separate peace," no salvation of the individual other than incorporation into the Beloved Community. Married life, with its holy eros, is a form of this.

One modern possibility of an account of agape and eros other than Nygren's might be found in the insightful discussion of concupiscence provided by Paul Tillich in his *Systematic Theology*. He writes: "Love does not exclude desire; it receives libido into itself. But the libido that is united with love is not infinite. It is directed, as all love is, toward a definite subject with whom it wants to unite the bearer of love. Love wants the other being, whether in the form of *libido, eros, philia,* or *agape*. Concupiscence, or distorted libido, wants one's own pleasure through the other being, but it does not want the other being. This is the contrast between libido as love and libido as concupiscence. Freud did not make this distinction because of his puritanical attitude toward sex. Only through repression and sublimation of libido can man become creative. In Freud's thought there is no creative eros which includes sex. In comparison with a man like Luther,

---

86. Luther, "Commentary on Genesis" LW 1:118.
87. John Milbank, "The Ethics of Self-Sacrifice," *First Things* 1 (March 1999): 33-38.
88. LC in *BC*, p. 433.

Freud is ascetic . . . in man's essential nature the desire to be united with the object of one's love for its own sake . . . is not infinite but definite. It is not concupiscence but love."[89] This interpretation of sinful concupiscence as infinite erotic desire amounts to a reading of Luther in continuity with Augustine.[90] The idea here is that the Augustinian hierarchy of love integrates and orders eros, and just so identifies and excludes the disordered eros of concupiscence. Divine creative self-giving love makes creaturely eros specific and definite, as befits creatures; it divests eros of its self-divinizing fantasies of infinity and puts it back to work and to enjoy on the earth, in honoring the past and preparing the future, by the embrace of the definite spouse, in the "covenant of the generations." If we allow such an Augustinian background to Luther's complex and ambivalent evaluations of lovemaking, his view that concupiscence still attends marital love takes on a different aspect than prudish disgust or prurient fascination with "dirty sex." The persistence of sin in the life of the redeemed does not manifest in some degrading (or titillating) resort to forbidden ecstasy, but rather consists in the failure wholly to love that definite beloved "as oneself" in this specific form of life (the sexual) with all that it entails (the prospect of children).

That Luther thought along these lines, as Tillich maintained, is suggested by the ideal of "chaste" sexual love which he developed by the time of writing the Large Catechism.[91] Chaste love, over against sinful concupiscence, is that desire which is directed to the definite "spouse whom God has given." In Christian faith each one's marriage is something concretely to be believed. The commandment, he therefore writes, requires each "to love and cherish the spouse *whom God has given them.* Therefore, wherever marital chastity is to be maintained, above all it is essential that hus-

89. Paul Tillich, *Systematic Theology* (Chicago: University of Chicago Press, 1967), II:54.

90. If it sets at rest hearts nervous about *that continuity,* we can parenthetically note that — coming from a theologian like Tillich — such continuity naturally does not include taking over Augustine's or for that matter Luther's pre-scientific, "venereal" theory of sin's transmission, based on Psalm 51!

91. Lazareth holds that *"Luther had already arrived at an evangelical marriage ethic by 1523, almost two years before his own marriage,"* that is, "derived from his biblical understanding of the Christian faith relatively independent of his own personal experience" (*Family,* p. 246, emphasis original). That is correct in the sense that "faith transforms the lives of people and enables them to view historical reality from the perspective of eternity." Faith transforms marriage from a human institution into a divine calling "since I am now certain that it is well pleasing to God" (p. 254).

band and wife live together in love and harmony, cherishing each other wholeheartedly and with perfect fidelity. This is one of the chief ways to make chastity attractive and desirable. Under such conditions chastity always follows spontaneously without any command."[92] Why would spouses in faith regard each other this way, as the one whom God has given? Which union, therefore, no one ought to tear apart, beginning with they themselves? Why can they not just walk away from each other, when they no longer desire to share themselves in this united form of life?

### The Christological Reading of Genesis 1–3

Obviously, in one sense they can just walk away, tear asunder, disregard, or repudiate what God has given in the life's partner. The story of the fall already indicates this possibility in principle: "The woman whom you gave to be with me, she gave me fruit from the tree and I ate." Luther comments: Adam "does not say, 'Lord, I have sinned; forgive me my debt; be merciful'; but he passes on the guilt to the woman."[93] In spirit, Adam walks away from her. His desperate act of self-justification before God is at the same time refusal of the community he assuredly has with Eve in guilt and in suffering the threatened punishment. Their community of love has in fact become a community of guilt and a community in suffering. But Adam does not want that for himself. So he breaks faith with Eve. Before God he divorces himself from her. So according to Luther, it is not until after the conclusion of the "trial" before God in Paradise with the promise of the coming Redeemer from Eve's seed, that the couple is spiritually reconciled and reunited. This happens when Adam names Eve "mother of all living," indicating the restoration of communion with her. This reconciliation can only happen now, for "unless grace comes, it is impossible for a man to act otherwise than to excuse his sin and to want it considered as righteousness."[94] What has intervened between Adam's recrimination of Eve (and of God who gave Eve to him) and his new embrace of Eve as "mother of all living" is the promise of the "forgiveness of sins by the Seed of Eve." Luther writes: "He calls her Eve to remind himself of the promise through which he himself also received new life, and to pass on the hope of eternal life to

---

92. In *BC,* p. 415, emphasis added.
93. Luther, "Commentary on Genesis" LW 1:177.
94. Luther, "Commentary on Genesis" LW 1:181.

his descendants. This hope and faith he writes on his wife's forehead by means of this name, as with colors. . . ."[95] The renewed marriage is thus, in Luther's reading, an act of Christological hope. To answer the question posed above then: (1) they do not walk away from each other because of the divine promise of forgiveness; (2) they cannot divorce before God because in fact they share inseparably in a common guilt; (3) they receive one another anew as the spouse whom God has given — even in face of moral betrayal — in an act of messianic hope for their descendants. Their renewed community in suffering as in joy is a form that the Beloved Community assumes under the post-paradisiacal conditions of exile and hope.

What is the alternative? Sexual desire that wants to be infinite, that will not yield time and place to the new generation, becomes demonic desire that devours finally also the devourer. Indeed, I write these words in a "sexually liberated" nation which is not accidentally casting upon future generations a crushing, catastrophic load of debt because it will not make the sacrifices needed today for justice in society and peace in the world, beginning with the sacrifice of infantile polymorphous perverse in order to grow up to that adult and creative love for the definite spouse and the definite children whom God gives. The difficult argument I am making in this chapter with Luther as resource is written in anticipation of the painful encounter with the white-hot wrath of God in store for this wicked and adulterous generation, when those who will pick up the pieces from its sins will have to learn this community in suffering as in joy, if only to survive.

## Community in Suffering as in Joy

The linkage between sex and children is not for Luther the typical bow nowadays to the sheer biological fact of heterosexual fertility, since that relation between sex and babies can be rationally managed by abstinence, contraception and other technologies, other formations of family (polygamy, serial monogamy), or the treatment of children as chattel (our property, clay in our hands, a project). In these ways and others, the linkage is managed quite *apart* from *marriage* as Luther has defined this *holy union* of human partnership in God's creative work, i.e., not only to make babies but above all to raise them to the glory of God and for public service to hu-

95. Luther, "Commentary on Genesis" LW 1:220.

manity in its dire situation of exile and hope after Adam's fall. The reflection is surely true so far as it goes that biologically "the presupposition of the history in which human nature is enacted is the provision of new humans in succession," and that by dint of "sheer plumbing . . . the vagina and the penis are made for each other."[96] But neither of these undeniable facts as such entails the community of marriage. There are other ways to manage fertility, including unholy ways such as the abortion industry with its cohort of shameless theological apologists.

But what kind of linkage is this community in suffering as in joy to be? Suffering isolates and destroys, we might object; there is nothing creative or redemptive about it. Pain cannot link anything, least of all sexual love and children; it merely isolates. Yes, pain can do that. That is exactly why for Luther, unbelief perceives and experiences the cross as the incomprehensible end of the story of Jesus, something at all costs to be avoided and never to be undertaken. Yet such flight from physical and historical reality is not, for Luther, how the God who spared not his own Son faces suffering. Luther's unbribable, non-manipulable God afflicts, yes, but as faith in the risen Christ perceives, *in order to* heal, casts down *in order to* exalt, kills *in order to* make alive, destroys the *concupiscentia carnis in order to* redeem and fulfill the *concupiscentia nuptiarum*. Take away this purpose clause, and you have taken away the risen Christ and the faith which after [Him and in the power of His Spirit takes up the cross to follow him.]

So Luther's own words of pastoral counsel in this connection attest: "that even married people have mostly unhappiness and misery is no wonder, because they have no knowledge from God's word about their estate of marriage. That is why they are just as unhappy as monks and nuns. On both sides people live without trust and consolation about God's being pleased with them. Therefore it is impossible that they could bear external unhappiness and trouble. . . . If they don't know their estate internally, that it is pleasing to God, then there is already unhappiness. . . . God's order and way of working has to be taken from his Word. Trust must be put in God's Word, or the estates will be harmed and become unbearable."[97] It is faith's knowledge of God's good pleasure that makes the marital community in suffering as in joy into a hospice of compassion. But apart from this, marriage is — as we see all around us today — "unbearable."

But why? Why *suffering* as an integral *key* to the marital link of sex-

---

96. Jenson, *ST* II:89.
97. Cited by Juntunen, "Sex in Luther," from WA 10/II, 298:9-21.

ual love and children? It could be maudlin, though not untrue, to invoke here the grateful sense of self-giving sacrifice that children honor in good parents (and painfully suffer the absence of in bad parents). We can take a more scientific clue from evolutionary biology. *Human* reproduction is remarkable for the extraordinarily long dependency of children on parents, which in evolutionary terms provided time and space for development of their equally extraordinary brain capacity.[98] Already in the pre-historical state of nature, it is the infant-nursing, child-nurturing family — in its community in suffering as in joy, its covenant between the generations and its school of compassion — for which and out of which marriage as the human form of sexual order emerged and evolves until it fulfills the promise of the image of God in human dominion here "below" on this earth. The natural presupposition of the history of salvation and the role in it of marriage is therefore not "sheer plumbing," but the pre-historical form of human family, as socio-biologists have rightly pointed out. The state of nature is not to be imagined as alpha males fighting for gain and glory, from which violence and anarchy we emerge by social contract, beasts arising from the jungle to civilized life.[99] This Hobbsean narrative reverses the canonical story of the sinful Fall from Paradise into anti-social forms of society, the Augustinian *civitas terrena*. Locke was surely right to attack this Hobbesian inversion of the biblical narrative of creation and fall and in his political philosophy to insist that the state of nature involves community from the beginning, especially the primal form of the family.[100]

98. Matt Ridley, *The Origins of Virtue* (London: Penguin, 1997); Antonia R. Damasio, *Descartes' Error: Emotion, Reason and the Human Brain* (London: Papermac, 1996).

99. Thomas Hobbes, *Leviathan*, with selected variants from the Latin edition of 1668, ed. E. Curley (Indianapolis: Hackett, 1994): "in the state of mere nature . . . there are supposed no laws of matrimony, no laws for the education of children, but the law of nature, and the natural inclination of the sexes, one to another, and to their children . . ." (p. 129). *Leviathan* is a work of (anti-)theology, specifically, a radically anti-Augustinian brief for the city of man against the city of God. This entails inverting the biblical narrative of creation and fall, so that we regard humanity no longer as fallen and redeemed beings, but as rising beasts. Of course, that makes human community something unnatural, artificial, conventional, contractual, and it makes the *Leviathan* of the total secular state necessary to fend off the war of all against all.

100. John Locke, *Second Treatise of Government*, ed. C. B. Macpherson (Indianapolis: Hackett, 1980). "Paternal or parental power is nothing but that which parents have over their children, to govern them for the children's good, till they come to the use of reason . . . [and] live as freemen. . . . The affection and tenderness which God hath planted in the breast of parents toward their children, makes it evident, that this is not intended to be a severe arbi-

Theologically, the command to be fruitful and multiply is scripted biologically in all living creatures. But the command to marry, i.e., to form the partnership of male and female as the human image of God in dominion over the earth comes from above, as it must, if it is to join sexual love and care of children together in human consciousness as faith's embrace of community in suffering as in joy. That marriage does so emerge in history, therefore, is no foregone conclusion, any more than in any other respect that we attain to the Beloved Community, "shar[ing] one another's burdens and so fulfill[ing] the law of Christ" (Gal. 6:2). The matter is controverted. The battle for the gospel is not only over the proper proclamation in and of the church, but also on behalf of the groaning creation and its liberation from the anti-divine powers of sin and death. Disobedience and unbelief are possible here in the realm of nature as also there in the realm of grace. Fallen nature is wracked with uncertainty about God's will and so it can rationalize anything. Unfaithfulness may destroy what was well begun.[101] The community in suffering as in joy which married love with its care of children entails has from the dawn of time waxed and waned, as the cultural history of sexuality amply demonstrates. It is through the Word concerning the crucified and risen Jesus that this aversion to marriage is met and overcome, even as his death and resurrection is the secret vindication and guarantee of all fragmentary and ambiguous experience of human community in the world, which remains in hope God's creation on the way to fulfillment in the Beloved Community, in spite of, rather, in de-

---

trary government, but only for the help, instruction and preservation of their offspring . . . the paternal is a natural government . . ." which terminates when the child becomes an adult (pp. 88-89). See Paul R. Hinlicky, "Luther and Liberalism," in *A Report from the Front Lines: Conversations on Public Theology. A Festschrift in Honor of Robert Benne,* ed. Michael Shahan (Grand Rapids: Eerdmans, 2009), pp. 89-104.

101. Witte in *Sacrament to Contract* emphasizes that among other reforms of law, the early Lutherans permitted divorce, beginning with Luther who wrote: "Since people are as evil as they are, any other way of governing is impossible. Frequently something must be tolerated even though it is not a good thing to do, to prevent something even worse from happening" (cited from LW 21:94). Likewise Bugenhagen: "The reality is that some households become broken beyond repair" (cited from *Vom ehebruch und weglauffen,* folios miii-oiii; p. 67). Witte summarizes: "By conjoining these arguments from scripture, utility, and history, the reformers concluded that (1) divorce in the modern sense had been instituted by Moses and Christ; (2) the expansion of divorce was a result of sin and a remedy against greater sin; and (3) God had revealed the expanded grounds for divorce from history" (p. 68). I apply this reasoning to the possibility of church recognition — not celebration or blessing — of same-sex unions in Paul R. Hinlicky, "Recognition not Blessing," August 2005 *Journal of Lutheran Ethics* (online), vol. 5, issue 8.

fiance of sin and death. This is what Bonhoeffer meant when he spoke of Christ the center, albeit hidden, of all of life, also, indeed preeminently of married life.[102] Unveiled by the gospel and appropriated in faith, the suffering love of Jesus who makes the unworthy His own heals and sanctifies every spouse who lives for the sake of its other, however ambivalently.

## Same-Sex Unions and Other Hard Questions[103]

All who are unworthy? Does this ambivalence include also partners in same-sex unions? Christopher Morse has posed the matter this way: "In sum, doctrinally, the issue boils down to whether a homosexual orientation is ever God's good creation, or always an evidence of the 'fall' as a rejection of one's good creation, and whether it is ever the fit of God's Holy Spirit for human wholeness templed in the human body, or always an idolatrous defiance of God's embodied gift."[104] There is clarity to putting the doctrinal question this way, even if the actual life of those who live between the times as *simul iustus et peccator* is more ambiguous. Nor is the question necessarily antinomian.[105] It is evident that such unions are not the marriages blessed and also burdened by God according to Genesis 1–3 in Luther's Christological interpretation. Yet, spiritually, as God's forgiving love covers the abiding concupiscence at work even in married love, might it also be understood to cover the disordered love of gay or lesbian partners when this very desire is understood in repentance and faith as a cross to be born, not a work of God to be celebrated? Likewise politically, since "it is better to marry than to burn," cannot exclusive same-sex unions as community in suffering as in joy be aligned socially with the "covenant of

---

102. Bonhoeffer, *Ethics:* "The world, like all created things, is created through Christ and with Christ as its end, and consists in Christ alone (John 1.10, Col. 1.16). To speak of the world without speaking of Christ is empty and abstract. The world is relative to Christ, no matter whether it knows it or not. The relativeness of the world to Christ assumes concrete form in certain mandates of God in the world . . ." (p. 207). "This means that marriage is not only a matter of producing children, but also of educating them to be obedient to Jesus Christ" (p. 210).

103. See Hinlicky, "Recognition not Blessing," and, Paul R. Hinlicky, "Appreciation and Critique of the ELCA Draft Social Statement on Sexuality," August 2008 *Journal of Lutheran Ethics* (online), vol. 8, issue 8.

104. Morse, *Not Every Spirit,* p. 282.

105. ELCA Metro New York Synod Bishop Stephen Boumann in his correspondence with Pastor Fryer, referenced above in n. 15, has made that compellingly clear.

the generations"? Politically, that would be better than the destructive illusions of Marcusian sexual liberation, and spiritually, a concrete gesture of redemptive love to gays and lesbians now adrift in the fierce tides of polymorphous perverse. It is imaginable that such unions would be recognized as analogous to marriage in Christian community life under the following, carefully specified theological conditions.

First, God's inclusive love in Christ entails repentance as well as faith. It is not simply sinners but penitent sinners who are embraced in the holy communion of the church. Same-sex partners seeking the recognition of the Christian community (just like the divorced) must clearly acknowledge normative Christian teaching that their union falls short of the marriage God intends for his creature, concretely, in that homophile desire reflects the brokenness of the fallen creation (Rom. 1), not the original intention of the Creator (Mark 10).

Second, in that case the church can and should recognize and support such civil unions because repentance in this life does not achieve the perfection of sin eliminated, but only of sin controlled.[106] Arguably, this latter is something the church has done intuitively and pastorally, if quietly and discretely, for a very long time. Public recognition of this pastoral practice is more mature and less hypocritical as also more beneficial in holding gay or lesbian unions publicly accountable.

This possibility of recognition, argued by using Luther as resource, admittedly falls painfully short for those seeking the public blessing of same-sex unions, that is to say, approval of these unions as the creative will and work of God, as we saw Morse frame the question. Why is it necessary theologically to maintain that homophile desire is disordered, that is to say, not the will of God articulated in the Genesis passage, as Christologically interpreted? As it is necessary theologically to maintain that even marital love is afflicted by concupiscent desire for an infinity of objects, it is by analogy necessary also to maintain that polymorphous sexual desire is disordered; attraction to the same sex intrinsically refuses the procreative purpose of God, from which the blessing of Genesis 1:26-28 obviously cannot be separated. Nor is there any other "blessing" from the Word of God for the church to pronounce over a marriage.

Note well, however, that "disorder" is not the same as "sinful." Disor-

---

106. "Luther insists that the crucial distinction for a Christian is not 'sin' or 'no sin,' but rather 'controlling sin' *(peccatum regnans)* or 'controlled sin' *(peccatum regnatum)*." Lazareth, *Family,* p. 247.

der is more like disease than sin, just as — closely read — Romans 1:18ff. regards homophile relations as one particular consequence of a universal sinful idolatry. It is not precisely right then to put the question as Morse does, as if the traditional teaching on homosexuality as disordered as such accused any given homosexual individual of personally rejecting her own good creation, of idolatrously defying God's embodied gift, any more than heterosexuals could on that basis boast of personally accepting their creation and worshipfully embodying it by the mere fact of their spontaneous desire for the other sex. Nor then is this to deny the cruelty of homophobic bullying, but rather to expose its very groundlessness. We can accept theologically the testimony of both straight and gay that sexual attraction is not something most people choose but rather is something to which one awakens and which can by then hardly be cast off like an acquired habit. Here, more than ever, it is critical to grasp the social intention of Christian teaching, to avoid biological determinism, and to engage social-constructivist interpretations of the formation of sexual identity.

But does this present appeal to Luther's Christological interpretation of Genesis 1:26-28 bind us to pre-scientific thinking, in a particularly regressive fashion?[107] One can argue on Augustinian lines and without recourse to biblical literalism, as I noted above, that sexual greed in breaking the covenant of the generations portends ecological and economic catastrophe and that this enormous sinfulness of our times falls upon heterosexuals, not on a vulnerable sexual minority. What is most striking of all in these considerations, in Luther's perspective, is the power of destructive illusions to which reason (even in the name of science!) succumbs apart from the Word of God. That is why Luther is adamant that apart from faith in the Word of God commanding marriage, reason is deaf and blind to the true linkage of sex and children, namely, that to continue in God's work of creation *we must replace ourselves.* We must give birth, and care for the children of our love, indeed order our sexuality in marriage to that end, and in that way prepare to die. Just as each has received, so each is bound also to pass on to the new generation the gift of life, truly the *gift* of our time and space which cannot be hoarded but only spent. Because *we must die,*[108] we ought to care for our children, if we wish in the little time-space

---

107. "The traditional interpretation of the third chapter of Genesis that there was a 'historical Fall,' an action by our human progenitors that is the explanation of biological death, has to be rejected." Arthur Peacocke, *Theology for a Scientific Age,* enlarged ed. (London: SCM Press, 1993), p. 222.

108. Thus I can concur with Peacocke that "evolution can operate only through the

of our life, including preeminently our sexual life, to cooperate with God's creative purpose for the human race. Gays and lesbians can, in the resource of such Christian faith and in recognized unions, practically and politically align themselves with this divine purpose, bearing their own crosses just as heterosexual couples must. The problem for both is that we flee the holy cross. For Luther this unwillingness is lethal sin and the devil's victory. In Augustine's perspective, it is to refuse one's niche in the ecology of creation, and so to send a ripple of contagious destruction through the whole system of things. If this line of reflection may be dismissed as "prescientific," then I dare say we have dismissed theology altogether.

But we need better science. Must we not raise the politically suppressed question today about the psychogenesis of homosexuality? If one maintains theologically that homophile desire is disordered, I do not see how one can avoid difficult explorations into the sexual abuse or emotional neglect of children by parents and other adult figures that positively correlates with adult homosexual identity.[109] As Catholic thinkers have similarly suggested, social thinking that comes from Luther should turn us away from the atomistic and utilitarian individualism presupposed by so many social scientists and urge us instead to think "ecologically" about family life. The hard question about same-sex unions is the "hot-button" issue of today, but as just indicated, Luther's theology of marriage ought to focus our attention on children as the test case. What about economic conditions that take away time and space for children? How is that connected with the painful difficulty today for so many singles to find suitable partners? What about children born without benefit of married and faithful parents? What about the pain of infertility? How might these latter two questions be better linked? What about the least wanted orphans and the loving homes that gay and lesbian couples might provide them? What about the legally sanctioned massacre of the unborn and poignant desire of the infertile to adopt?[110]

I have argued that the deeper theme in Luther's theology of marriage is — not surprisingly on reflection — the cross and resurrection of Jesus. My point in this has not been to make marriage attractive in this present

---

death of individuals — new forms of matter arise only through the dissolution of the old; new life only through the death of the old." Peacocke, *Theology for a Scientific Age,* p. 221.

109. Merton P. Strommen, *The Church and Homosexuality: Searching for a Middle Ground,* 2nd ed. (Minneapolis: Kirk, 2001), pp. 25ff.

110. Sarah Hinlicky Wilson, "Blessed Are the Barren," *Christianity Today* 51, no. 12 (December 2007): 22-28.

culture of narcissism, but to make it appear impossible. That is to say, theology that would really follow in Luther's train will have no choice but to criticize social arrangements and cultural dispositions that fail to support marriage politically as well as church practice that no longer consoles and strengthens those who suffer to do the will of God in their sexual lives, but rather is blind and deaf to those who so suffer.

# PART THREE

# Some Objections regarding Justification, the Church, and Political Theology

# "New, Old, and Different Perspectives" on Paul (Augustine and Luther)

*Paul's view of salvation history does not differ from Augustine's. Salvation history is the battlefield of the civitas dei and the civitas terrena. No conception which disregards this reality and does not, from this starting point, assume a constitutively dialectical form can invoke the authority of the apostle. . . . No one can take on the likeness of Christ in the birth-pangs of the Messiah without having become a disciple of the one who was crucified. Although the enthusiasts raise their cry of victory, according to Rom. 8:36 believers are regarded as sheep to be slaughtered. Measured by human criteria, salvation is fundamentally rooted in disaster. That means that the Pauline proclamation of the reality of salvation history is deeply paradoxical.*

Käsemann[1]

## The Perils of Repristinationism

With this chapter and the next several, I wish to consider some objections to the project of this book, which is to appropriate Luther as resource for a contemporary theology of the Beloved Community in the form of critical

---

1. Ernst Käsemann, *Perspectives on Paul,* trans. Margaret Kohl (Philadelphia: Fortress, 1978), pp. 67-68.

The title of this chapter is taken from a phrase of N. T. Wright, *Paul in Fresh Perspective* (Minneapolis: Fortress, 2005), p. 13.

dogmatics — without, that is, any need to *repristinate*.[2] In that regard, it has, I hope, been striking that thus far we have not deliberately or systematically entertained Luther's *articulus stantis et cadentis ecclesiae* — the doctrine of justification. That "oversight" has been deliberate, not only because Luther's doctrine of justification today *is* regarded as grounds for a searching objection to the Reformer's claim to "the authority of the apostle" Paul, as we shall consider in this chapter. But I have also delayed this discussion because the doctrine of justification in some respects has become a "Lutheran" shibboleth: not the proper Pauline stone of stumbling that signals the Spirit's saving shift in human perspective to faith in the Crucified as the Risen One of God, but a barrier wall of incomprehension among foe and friend alike. This is particularly so, as we have had occasion to note in passing, when a sloppy and merely anti-Catholic notion of justification "by grace" (opposed then to "works") substitutes for Luther's teaching of *faith alone in Christ alone* (opposed then to "sacrifice" in Girard's sense). There is a morass of confusion here that must be dissolved before one can clearly consider any contemporary objection to the "Lutheran" doctrine of justification. Alas, it has always been so, going back to the rhetorical form of *paradox*[3] which Luther chose to express his ideas, but which also rendered his theological concern unintelligible to those outside the circle, without a key to unlock his riddles (cf. Mark 4:11).

How deliberate this rhetorical decision to employ paradox was on Luther's part is hard to say. If Käsemann is right, as in the epigraph above, Luther could have been seeking to follow Paul and Augustine in rhetorical form as well as in material content. There is material content at stake here that I wish to appropriate as resource. In addition, properly understood as a form of rhetoric aimed at subverting accustomed ways of thinking, and *not* as the assertion of logical contradictions, paradox in preaching may also be a resource for us today. But what is or ought to be plain today after the labors of Lutheran–Roman Catholic dialogue[4] (as we shall see in the next

---

2. In response to Stendahl's invocation of Cadbury's *The Peril of Modernizing Jesus*, I have treated Cadbury's question with the discussion of Albert Schweitzer, *The Quest of the Historical Jesus* (New York: Macmillan, 1978), above in Chapter One.

3. As per the introduction of his theological program in the "Heidelberg Disputation," LW 31:39.

4. Paul R. Hinlicky, "The Lutheran Dilemma," *Pro Ecclesia* 8, no. 4 (Fall 1999): 391-422; "A Response to the Vatican's Response: I. The Persistence of Sin in the Life of the Redeemed," *Lutheran Forum* 32, no. 3 (Fall, 1998): 5-7; "A Response to the Vatican's Response: II. Is There a Lutheran Communion?" *Lutheran Forum* 32, no. 4 (Winter 1998): 9-11; "Pro-

chapter) is that Luther's use of the rhetoric of paradox sowed endless seeds of confusion, undoubtedly among his opponents, yet also within his inner circle, perhaps also in Luther himself,[5] until finally and necessarily the Reformers returned to medieval methods of patient reasoning in the scholastic disputation.[6] By then, however, the ecumenical damage was done.

Paradox-mongering posing as radical theology is *not* something to be commended.[7] Theology is not just preaching the paradox of Christ crucified (let alone all sorts of speculative inversions of meaning) but also interpreting the paradox to those who don't get it. Thus the irenic method of ecumenical theology today strives for charitable readings as the basis for genuine criticism.[8] The hole of unintelligibility and indeed mistrust is only dug deeper when we are counseled to desist from consequent, clear reasoning in theology with an ecumenical intention and instead to assert the paradox all the more passionately, all the more exclusively, in this fashion claiming for ourselves the banner of *the* Lutheran way.[9] In a probing recent study, Olli-Pekka Vainio finds no less than five contending doctrines of justification among "Lutherans" in the course of the sixteenth century until the Formula of Concord cobbled several together and ruled out the others.[10] The import is that one cannot talk honestly about *the* Lutheran doctrine of justification, since not even "the Lutherans" agreed (or agree) on what they were (are) talking about. Luther as resource for us today therefore is not and cannot be the harmonized Luther of confessionalized Lutheranism, supposedly with a chief doctrine of a purely forensic declaration of divine acceptance offering consolation for troubled consciences (sort of Bultmann, made edifying, or Tillich, made simple). In reality, this

---

cess, Convergence, Declaration: Reflections on Doctrinal Dialogue," *The Cresset* 64, no. 6 (Pentecost 2001): 13-18; "A Lutheran Encyclical: Benedict's Deus Caritas Est," August 2006 *Journal of Lutheran Ethics* (online), vol. 6, issue 8.

5. Timothy J. Wengert, *Law and Gospel: Philip Melanchthon's Debate with John Agricola of Eisleben over Poenitentia* (Grand Rapids: Baker Books, 1997).

6. Paul Hinlicky (with Dennis Bielfeldt and Mickey Mattox), *The Substance of Faith: Luther on Doctrinal Theology* (Minneapolis: Fortress, 2008), pp. 1-3.

7. *Pace* Oswald Bayer, *Martin Luther's Theology: A Contemporary Interpretation,* trans. Thomas H. Trapp (Grand Rapids: Eerdmans, 2007), p. xv.

8. Hinlicky, "Process, Convergence, Declaration."

9. Mark Mattes, *The Role of Justification in Contemporary Theology,* Lutheran Quarterly Books (Grand Rapids: Eerdmans, 2004).

10. Olli-Pekka Vainio, *Justification and Participation in Christ: The Development of the Lutheran Doctrine of Justification from Luther to the Formula of Concord* (1580) (Leiden and Boston: E. J. Brill, 2008).

post-Kantian trajectory of an existentialist *Sonderweg* grows ever and ever thinner in dogmatic content, even as it fails to ask genuinely radical, that is, self-critical questions about the failure of the Reformation. One task in this book consequently has been to liberate our reading of Luther from the filters of those who later took his name upon themselves — not because such readings are in fact wholly defective or unworthy, but to free us from the inevitable need of confessionalism (whether in conservative or radical form) to read Luther selectively (if unconsciously so) and appropriate him (as a result) inconsequently as the Source (not a resource).

What I mean, concretely, is this. After Oberman, it is quite impossible to read Luther and fail to see that for good and for ill apocalypticism stamps everything, such that his theology is inextricable from it (and so I have taken Luther in this book). In the Appendix to this book, I explore the need in this regard for an act of hermeneutical "violence" that rigorously eschews Luther's habitual resort to demonization of theological opponents in place of reasoned disputation. Even those who self-identify as "radically" Lutheran, for all their alienation from conservative confessionalism or ecclesiastical Lutheranism, still want to appropriate Luther under the mantle of *the* Reformation, *the* Protestant principle, *the* Scripture principle, *the* doctrine of justification. It never occurs to them that this is more of the same self-privileging, which ineluctably contains within it the original demonization of the opponent. This is why repristination, whether conservative or radical, is not only hermeneutically impossible but morally suspect. It never occurs in such thinking, for example, that the sixteenth-century "Reformation" might with equal justice be labeled the schism of Western Christianity, that even prophetic protest presupposes something substantial in need of reform, that the Bible did not fall out of heaven for them to pick up and fall upon a decisive word to the contemporary hour, or that even among sixteenth-century Lutherans one has to ask, *Which* doctrine of justification? Failing to ask these self-critical questions, "Lutherans" will continue to monkey with Luther's bombast in the interest of denominational identity-politics at the expense of others rather than learn from Luther's teaching of "Jesus Christ, the same yesterday, today and forever." But this, rather *He,* is the One we need to learn. Jesus the Crucified Christ is the constant; doctrines of justification are the variable, as indeed they must be, since in every new generation the teaching of justification via the exegetical encounter with Paul the Apostle is, as Ernst Käsemann so often put it, applied Christology.

It should be no objection, on the other hand, that Augustine or Luther or Barth or Royce developed Paul's message of the righteousness of God revealed in Jesus Christ beyond Paul's own original thoughts by applying the Jesus Christ of the gospel to their own situation. This is what we all do, even covertly as historians who think that instead we are strictly seeking to get Jesus, or Paul, or Augustine, or Luther "right." As N. T. Wright has recently acknowledged, we are in fact "fighting" over Paul's "legacy."[11] It cannot be otherwise, since all bring to the topic of historical study the concerns and questions of their own day (notably today, as we shall see, the Nazi murder of the Jews and the complicity of Christian anti-Judaism in that singular crime of the twentieth century). Such considerations consciously and unconsciously shape the narrative we think to discover in the facts. If historians would understand this, they would not distance themselves from theologians who notice that these texts, unlike other texts, are about God and our salvation, and who want as a result to pass on what they have received from those same sources as the Word of God. They would understand that within the economy of theology as critical dogmatics, historians have that honorable theological task — not of repristination — but of self-critical testing our appropriations, for example, whether and how Luther's or Augustine's development of the doctrine of justification can be found fitting with Paul's own. Then a claim to the legacy of Paul can be justified (or denied!), without the impossible requirement that its contemporary application be a mirroring re-presentation of a so-called historical Paul. Only under this latter assumption in any case are the New Perspective's noteworthy objections to the "Lutheran" doctrine of justification as a false guide to the historical Paul cogent, indeed helpful to us in the interpretive project of this book.

## Dunn's Claim for a New Perspective on Paul

*Which* doctrine of justification? That is the question. Nowhere in contemporary theology is such contention about justification more evident than in the debate about the "New Perspective on Paul," as James D. G. Dunn in 1983 labeled a ferment in Pauline studies that continues to this day. Since then the New Perspective has evolved. In fact today the New Perspective is not any one set of ideas about Paul, though it does have some basic, common concerns: to correct anti-Judaism in Pauline studies, to overcome in-

---

11. Wright, *Paul in Fresh Perspective*, p. 13.

trospective piety, to use Paul as a resource for social justice engagement, and to rehabilitate the reputation of good works in the life of the believer — all this, by means of a polemical accent against the "Lutheran" doctrine of the law and of justification. Lutheran theologians to date have grappled piecemeal with these concerns, especially it seems with the New Perspective's denial that Romans 7 describes the life of the believer as *simul iustus et peccator*.[12] But I have been more concerned in this book to appropriate Luther by means of a contemporary question in Euro-America about the creedal themes of the Beloved Community, the moral burden of the individual, and the need for atonement. Thus I wish in this chapter to deal with the challenge of the New Perspective in a more systematic way. I can do so within the parameters of this book by narrowly focusing on a difficult text, Galatians 3:10-14, the passage about the "curse of the law." On this level of engagement, the New Perspective as we shall see helps liberate Luther as resource, but in the process also gets some help from Luther in turn. But first we retrace the constituting steps taken in the formation of the New Perspective.

In that 1983 lecture,[13] Dunn translated Galatians 2:16, probably the very first occurrence in Paul of the word-group *dikaio, dikaiosyne,* this way: "We who are Jews by nature and not Gentile sinners, know that a man is not justified by the works of the law *except* through faith in Christ Jesus. And we have believed in Christ Jesus, in order that we may be justified by faith in Christ *and not by works of the law, because by works of the law shall no flesh be justified.*" The italics indicate the focal points of Dunn's exposition. In this verse, according to Dunn, Paul is recalling the very words he had said to Peter in Antioch when he confronted him for withdrawing from table-fellowship with Gentile Christians. At first Paul reminded his fellow Jew Peter of their common Christian Jewish belief, namely, that the works of the law do not help *except* with the aid of faith in Christ Jesus. There is in this initial formulation of their common faith no antithesis. Works are good, but not good enough until aided by faith in Christ. Yet as Paul continues to argue with Peter, seeking to find a theological basis to protest the exclusion of the Gentile believers from table-fellowship on the grounds of ritual impurity, he is led to formulate a new antithesis in the

---

12. Wilfried Härle, "Rethinking Paul and Luther," *Lutheran Quarterly* 20, no. 3 (Autumn 2006): 303-17, and Risto Saarinen, "The Pauline Luther and the Law: Lutheran Theology Reengages the Study of Paul," *Pro Ecclesia* 15, no. 1 (Winter 2006): 64-86.

13. James D. G. Dunn, "The New Perspective on Paul," *Bulletin of the John Rylands Library* 65 (1983): 95-122. Accessed online at http://www.thepaulpage.com.

second half of the verse. The last part of the verse no longer speaks of justification by works of the law *helped* by faith in Christ, but rather justification by faith in Christ *and not* by works of the law. Thus Dunn held that in Galatians 2:16 we may see laid bare before our eyes the fateful turn from one religion, primitive *Jewish* belief in Jesus as the Christ with Torah observance, to another religion, the *Christian* belief in Christ alone without the ritual accoutrements of Jewish identity: "[I]n this verse faith in Jesus Messiah begins to emerge not simply as a narrower definition of the elect of God [within Judaism], but as an alternative definition of the elect of God [incipient Christianity]." Thus, the Pauline doctrine of justification by faith turns out not to be about the secret evil of pride in good works in the human psyche but rather about inclusiveness in the Christian community. We are dealing, as Dunn concluded, with "the salvation-history significance of Christ"; what Paul accordingly "is concerned to exclude is the *racial* not the *ritual* expression of faith; it is *nationalism* not *activism*" which he rejects. Thus the traditional "Lutheran" polemic against good works is fundamentally misleading; it misses completely the Jewish racism and ethnocentrism which were Paul's real targets and in the process makes suspect the good works of faith operating through love in favor of passivity and quietism.

Thus the import of Dunn's history of religions exegesis cum observation was that the doctrine of justification by faith constructed by Paul at this moment in the heat of that church-political battle was but, as Krister Stendahl had contended some years earlier, a stratagem, certainly not the eternal gospel that it later became at the hands of Augustine and Luther, and certainly not along the anti-Pelagian line as they understood it. The exegetical case Dunn made in that lecture has not stood up to critical scrutiny — in brief, his translation of the Greek as *except* rather than as *but* in the clause "man is not justified by the works of the law *except* through faith in Christ Jesus" has hardly convinced scholarship.[14] Yet this new vision of Paul's ministry in terms of a progressive theology of salvation history caught on quickly. It was seen in continuity with the progressive and inclusive impulses of Hebrew prophetism, now in Paul breaking through the restrictive barriers of Jewish nationalist-racist exclusivism. Dunn's announcement of the New Perspective caught fire therefore as a reading of the Apostle more usable for social justice engagements today. Now justifi-

---

14. E.g., J. Louis Martyn, *Galatians*, The Anchor Bible, vol. 33A (New York: Doubleday, 1997), p. 251.

cation by faith no longer meant: "*Absolvo te!* Christ's righteousness avails for you the troubled sinner as you entrust yourself to Him." For this version of Pauline proclamation falsely focused the message of the Apostle on the introspective individual, taken as a burdened conscience in need of relief from the weight of guilt. Now justification by faith meant: "Christ has torn down the walls of taboo separating the ungodly from the godly. All are welcome!" The message now focuses on society, taken as laden with prejudices, exclusions, and inferiorizations. Nor is the church any longer to be like a hospital for sick souls, a zone of passivity allergic to social activism, but rather a mustering of robust consciences eager to do the good work of human redemption in society, undertaking William James's "moral equivalent of war."

The stage had been set for Dunn's announcement of the New Perspective by two previous scholars, on whom he lavished praise as the "mold-breakers": E. P. Sanders and Krister Stendahl. We will first examine Sanders's important study, *Paul and Palestinian Judaism,* to extract the notion of the "Lutheran" doctrines of the law and of justification that this author was working with. We will then consider the same complex of ideas in Krister Stendahl's famous essay about the introspective consciousness of the West. In both scholars we will discover important critiques that are useful to the project of this book, though also in each case in need themselves of significant correction. The theological issue we will thereby get to is what Käsemann sniffed out but rather clumsily attacked as the re-emergence in the New Perspective of the old scheme (really, as old as Luke-Acts) of an undialectical, immanent salvation-history scheme of progressive revelation. One advantage of this scheme is supposedly its positive view of the Old Testament/Hebrew Scriptures in correction of Christian anti-Judaism rooted in the negative "Lutheran" view of "the works of the law." But Dunn's reconstructed Pauline view of the "works of the law" as Jewish "identity-badges," as we have just seen, is hardly less negative. Early normative Judaism[15] does not fare very well in the salvation-history

---

15. If "Jesus had [to be] de-Christologized, as it were [by nineteenth-century liberal Protestant biblical scholarship] then the Torah had to be delegalized." David Novak, *Jewish-Christian Dialogue: A Jewish Justification* (New York and Oxford: Oxford University Press, 1989), p. 76. Ironically, the "new, more secular emphasis on Jesus' ethical teaching often led to a new denigration of Judaism as 'legalism,' as opposed to the Christian ethics of love" (p. 75). In truth, the scheme of progressive historical revelation "distorts both traditional Judaism and traditional Christianity in the service of a secular state that, in truth, require[s] neither faith" (p. 123).

scheme: it is stigmatized as the ethnocentric, if not racist obstacle to the advance of the reign of God, inclusive of all peoples. It is therefore eminently questionable whether this represents genuine progress in getting to the root of, and so eradicating, Christian anti-Judaism.[16] The critique of the tacit scheme of salvation history in the New Perspective will bring into consideration the work of a contemporary scholar in Käsemann's school of "apocalyptic as the mother of Christian theology," J. Louis Martyn, whose reading of Galatians expressly invokes the tradition of Luther[17] in tacit response to the claims of the New Perspective.[18] We will then be prepared to entertain some more recent advances in the New Perspective represented by N. T. Wright, before concluding with several salient features of Luther's own interpretation of Galatians on "the curse of the law." In this fashion the New Perspective's objections to Luther's view of the law and justification might be profitably met, moving the argument forward. For I will show that Martyn and Wright come to an exegetically well-grounded impasse in the interpretation of the "curse of the law," which calls out for the

---

16. E. P. Sanders acutely noted, as we shall explore below, the "degree to which scholars need an inferior religion to serve as the foil to the 'higher' and 'worthier' view." E. P. Sanders, *Paul and Palestinian Judaism: A Comparison of Patterns of Religions* (London and Philadelphia: SCM and Fortress, 1977), p. 97. What Sanders did not sufficiently recognize is the specific, post-Kantian location of this scholarly "need" in the new departure for theology represented by Schleiermacher. His neo-Protestant typology of "religious communions" inferiorized Judaism on account of its "limitation of the love of Jehovah to the race of Abraham" in invidious comparison with Christianity, "the most perfect of the most highly developed forms of religion." Schleiermacher, *The Christian Faith*, ed. H. R. Macintosh and J. S. Steward (New York: Harper & Row, 1963), vol. 1, pp. 37-38. Sanders the historian's manifest contempt for "systematic theology" (e.g., p. 141) blinds him to this kind of insight. The casual smear of "Lutherans" then proceeds apace through the pages of this very long book (e.g., inter alia p. 228). The inadequacies of Sanders's own account of the difference between Paul and Palestinian Judaism (pp. 431ff.) have been pointed out from opposing perspectives by Dunn, i.e., that Sanders did not carry through on his insight by locating Paul *within* Palestinian Judaism ("The New Perspective on Paul") and Stuhlmacher, i.e., for Sanders's overreliance on Schweitzer's improbable thesis of competing juristic-Jewish and participationist-Hellenist soteriologies in Paul. See Peter Stuhlmacher, *Revisting Paul's Doctrine of Justification: A Challenge to the New Perspective*, with an essay by Donald A. Hagner, trans. Daniel P. Bailey (Downers Grove, IL: InterVarsity Press Academic, 2001), pp. 28ff.

17. Martyn, *Galatians*, p. 35.

18. Martyn's response is explicit (to Dunn) in "Events in Galatia: Modified Covenantal Nomism versus God's Invasion of the Cosmos in the Singular Gospel: A Response to J. D. G. Dunn and B. R. Gaventa," *Pauline Theology*, vol. 1: *Thessalonians, Philippians, Galatians, Philemon*, ed. Jouette M. Bassler (Minneapolis: Fortress, 1991), chap. 12, pp. 160-80.

kind of theologically imaginative solution Luther brought to the same text, when he spoke of the "Law battling the Law in order to liberate" us all.

## Sanders's Misidentified Insight

"One must note in particular," wrote Sanders, "the projection on to Judaism of the view which Protestants find most objectionable in Roman Catholicism: the existence of a treasury of merits established by works of supererogation. We have here the retrojection of the Protestant-Catholic debate into ancient history, with Judaism taking the role of Catholicism and Christianity the role of Lutheranism."[19] Or again, "the principal element is the theory that works *earn* salvation; that one's fate is determined by *weighing* fulfillments against transgressions. Maintaining this view necessarily involves *denying* or getting around in some way *the grace of God in the election*."[20] In reality, however, the results of Sanders's study of first-century Palestinian Judaism demonstrate that early Judaism was a religion of "covenantal nomism," that is, "the view that one's place in God's plan is established on the basis of the covenant and that the covenant requires as the proper response of man his obedience to its commandments, while providing means of atonement for transgression."[21] These observations have constituted a point of departure for the New Perspective.

Several things may be noted. We have already had occasion to register emphatically the fact that the issue between sixteenth-century Catholics, Lutherans, and Calvinists was not grace. All these children of Augustine, Catholics too, taught salvation by grace. The issue that divided Luther and his papal opponents, as Luther saw it in his Galatians commentary of 1535, was the doctrinal definition of justifying faith: faith formed by Christ or faith formed by love.[22] The issue concerned *which* doctrine of justification was to be received in the church and with *what* critical force. Also, we have noted Oswald Bayer's grounding of Luther's doctrine of faith in the preface to the Decalogue with those words of gracious divine election, "I am the Lord your God." These two not theologically insignificant observations should already cause us to wonder about whom Sanders is speaking

19. Sanders, *Paul and Palestinian Judaism*, p. 57.
20. Sanders, *Paul and Palestinian Judaism*, p. 54.
21. Sanders, *Paul and Palestinian Judaism*, p. 75.
22. E.g., inter alia, "Commentary on Galatians" (1535) LW 26:161.

when throughout this important book he recurs to the "Lutheran" doctrine of the law or justification. The veil lifts when we note *precisely* to whom Sanders ascribed this retrojection of a (badly described) Protestant-Catholic conflict onto early, normative Judaism. Sanders made this important discovery about the history of *modern* critical research into ancient Judaism by nineteenth-century Christians, especially in *Germany* (not the Anglo-Saxon world!).[23] "A fundamental change," he wrote, "had taken place in the nineteenth century in works by Christian authors about Judaism. Through the eighteenth century Christian literature had primarily tried to show the agreement of Jewish views with Christian theology. . . . With F. Weber, however, everything changed. For him, Judaism was the antithesis of Christianity."[24]

One may add here a further note about Protestant theological arguments with Catholicism up to the turn of the nineteenth century. Luther's argument had never been with Catholicism, but with the papacy: this latter was the "Antichrist" who had arisen to oppress Christendom, that is, Catholicism. Thus Luther and his followers sought ever and again to establish the *catholic* credentials of their teaching; they accused the papists of being the innovators, the modernists. (We shall both document and consider further the implications of this original ecclesiology in the next chapter.) In addition, we have also to note that the same argumentative relationship to Judaism that prevailed prior to Weber, as Sanders notes, also stamps Luther's relationship to the Hebrew Scriptures. As with the antecedent tradition, it was not that Judaism was the antithesis of Christianity for Luther but rather that Judaism had failed to recognize its own Messiah, from its own Scriptures. Mickey Mattox, a scholar devoted especially to Luther's Old Testament exegesis, rightly notes that "Luther clearly saw the religion of Israel up to the time of Jesus

---

23. Sanders, *Paul and Palestinian Judaism*, p. 55.

24. Sanders, *Paul and Palestinian Judaism*, p. 33. Similarly Blenkinsopp on Julius Wellhausen: "In keeping with nineteenth century moral idealism and certain dominant emphases in German Evangelical Christianity, the prophets were read as exponents of ethical individualism, an unmediated approach to God without benefit of priesthood and sacrificial ritual and, in brief, a religion in which personal experience counts for more than institutions and the traditions which they mediate." Joseph Blenkinsopp, "Tanakh and the New Testament," in *Biblical Studies: Meeting Ground of Jews and Christians*, ed. Lawrence Boadt, Helga Croner, and Leon Klenicki (New York: Paulist Press, 1980), p. 104. It was, in brief, liberal Protestantism that executed the anti-Catholic polemic by means of an anti-Jewish smear: "The Church is not [Christ's] work, but an inheritance from Judaism to Christianity" (p. 105).

as a religion of grace and faith that was founded on God's word of promise given to Adam and Eve even before their expulsion from the garden." So Luther knew how to talk about the "faithful synagogue," evincing "his love for the people and religion of the Old Testament . . . embody[ing] a love for the law of God that is almost rabbinic."[25] Even the "Jews" who appear as opponents in Luther's exegetical work on the Hebrew Scriptures are "abstract" or "theological Jews" — motifs, types, not "actual persons," since Luther "had little firsthand knowledge of Jewish people" and what he knew of rabbinic Judaism he knew from citations in Christian biblical commentators. To be sure, this ignorance allowed for the rise of prejudice ripening into bigotry unchecked by reality, and in the end Luther reflects the ghettoized Christendom in which he lived and thought and did not transcend, as gratefully we do and we must.[26] Yet even this relation of abstract opposition in his exegetical work remains largely a "family quarrel." It does not rise to the level of demonization, as we witness in Luther's apocalyptic-polemical writings (see the Appendix to this book).

The comment of the contemporary Catholic biblical scholar Joseph Blenkinsopp about this relation of hermeneutical opposition (which I have elsewhere characterized as a "sibling rivalry," like "Jacob and Esau")[27] is apropos: "Given its origin and nature, Christianity must of necessity address a critique to Judaism as Judaism must to Christianity, and such a critique will necessarily inform any attempt, Christian or Jewish, to give a theological account of the classic texts to which both bodies appeal."[28] If any such critique is what is meant by "anti-Judaism," it would bear the absurd implication that the writings of the Hebrew prophets, which are echoed in those New Testament writings that continue the critique of the Temple cult, would be the source in history of anti-Semitism. Neither Jesus nor Paul, but rather Marcion and his followers up to Adolph von Harnack designate historically the source of Christian anti-Judaism as a theological position. In that case, nothing could be more valuable to the contemporary theological task of interpretation than actually to hear the critique of the other,[29]

25. Mattox, *The Substance of Faith*, pp. 32-33. These words are addressed to the "so-called new perspective on Paul."

26. Mattox, *The Substance of Faith*, p. 29.

27. Hinlicky, "A Lutheran Contribution," pp. 123-52.

28. Blenkinsopp, "Tanakh and the New Testament," p. 113.

29. A brief but vigorous sample of this is Meir Soloveichik's essay, "The Virtue of Hate," *First Things* (February 2003).

which is the conversation among friends in living Judaism, as also in Islam, to which a critical dogmatics in Christian faith today oriented toward the Beloved Community aspires.

Sanders, we can safely say, shoots with a scattergun, where a laser beam is needed. The cost of this imprecision is great. His real insight is that the salvation-history approach in the background of emerging comparative religions scholarship in the nineteenth century, with its need to compare and contrast and in this way to evaluate religions on the assumption of a progressive historical development, inevitably requires inferiorization. But this insight gets mixed up with the shallow tact of painting with a broad brush German Lutheranism (on the ethnocentric Anglo-American assumption of a direct line, Luther-Bismarck-Hitler?), taken in turn as a theological position exalting grace and despising works. So the thesis lives on in the antithesis. Sanders, no doubt, is vulnerable to this invidious confusion because he too works with a religious studies approach dominated by the post-Holocaust need to shift the evaluation of Judaism in a happier direction and to lay bare Christian attitudes of anti-Judaism which may have contributed to the Nazi genocide. These valid concerns are far too serious, however, for such amateurish theology in the guise of historical scholarship. While the rich and fascinating scholarship on early Judaism in his book, with its vivid portrait of covenantal nomism, is a lasting contribution to understanding, the method adopted self-destructs in the process. The ensuing conversation in the New Perspective demonstrates as a result that theology as interpretation becomes inescapable.

## Stendahl's Misplaced Conscience

The term "salvation history" *(Heilsgeschichte)* originated in the nineteenth century as a technical term. It did not refer to the pre-critical notion that the Genesis-to-Revelation canon of normative Christianity tells the story of the One God who is determined to create, redeem, and fulfill this world. While the widespread use of the term by many parties since the nineteenth century has made its technical sense vague, the notion originally meant to point to an immanent, non-supernaturalist unfolding of salvation in history, a progressive revelation through human religious development up to the building of the kingdom of God on earth (as Kant concluded and mandated for the nineteenth century in Part Three of *Religion within the Limits of Mere Reason).*[30] From this perspective, then, the portrait of a historical process developing under the guidance of the Spirit from Jerusalem to Rome as we find it depicted in the Book of Acts is fundamentally justified. Within history there is a progressive unfolding of the divine plan of salvation moving out from the Jews onto the Gentiles. Paul the Apostle can be fitted into this movement from Judaism to Christianity. Yet this history of salvation, with its progressive social implications for us today, has been fundamentally misunderstood insofar as it has been read through the filter of the West's "introspective conscience." It has taken Paul's doctrine of faith, as if it were an answer to the supposedly perennial questions of human existence rather than God's mandate for social structures progressively more inclusive. Such was the stunning (at the time) thesis of Krister Stendahl: "it is exactly at this point [of introspective conscience] that Western interpreters have found the common denominator between Paul and the experience of man, since Paul's statements about "justification by faith" have been hailed as the answer to the problem which faces the ruthlessly honest man. . . ."[31] So Stendahl argued some years before Dunn in his influential essay, "The Apostle Paul and the Introspective Conscience of the West." But in fact, he maintained, "justification by faith" was no such thing. It was the fruit of Paul's "grappling with the question about the place of the Gentiles in the Church and in the plan of God . . . which had driven him to that interpretation of the Law. . . ."[32] It is evident then that Dunn was more than justified in giving credit to Stendahl as a "mold-breaker": not only for breaking the grip of the introspective, individualistic "Lutheran" doctrine of the tyranny of the law, but also for restoring to honor the salvation-history framework of Pauline theology.

There is much that is of lasting value in Stendahl's *tour de force.* He was surely right to note that Bultmann's existentialist interpretation of Paul "is an even more drastic translation and an even more far-reaching generalization of the original Pauline material than that found in the Reformers"[33] — an insight about the (mis-)location of the "introspective conscience" which we should immediately correlate with the previous discussion of Sanders's misplaced insight into the source of anti-Judaism.

30. Immanuel Kant, *Religion and Rational Theology,* trans. Allen W. Wood and George di Giovanni (Cambridge: Cambridge University Press, 2001), pp. 129ff.

31. Krister Stendahl, *Paul among Jews and Gentiles* (Philadelphia: Fortress, 1976), p. 79.

32. Stendahl, *Paul among Jews and Gentiles,* p. 84.

33. Stendahl, *Paul among Jews and Gentiles,* p. 88.

Extremely valuable is Stendahl's further criticism of Bultmann's assumption that "continuity in human self-consciousness" can provide a hermeneutical bridge between ourselves and the New Testament, when in fact "sayings which originally meant something later on were interpreted to mean something else, something which was felt to be more relevant. . . ."[34] In this way Stendahl could be understood to have put his finger on the real problem of theological interpretation in the New Testament and of the New Testament, which according to the argument of this book should lead us to critical dogmatics as the tradition-discourse of interpretation along the lines that Royce sketched. But instead he takes this insight only to indicate the danger of "modernizing,"[35] along the lines of Albert Schweitzer's concern, as discussed above in Chapter One. There is no awareness in Stendahl's essay of the corresponding danger (especially for the rigorous historian concerned with historical particularity) of repristinating, as argued at the outset of this chapter. Stendahl is certainly right to connect Luther with Augustine in terms of "conscience," but wrong to overlook the role for each of these monks that daily recitation of the Psalms played in forming that conscience and also connecting it to the cosmic struggle between the *civitas dei* and *civitas terrena.* The crucial association Stendahl makes between introspection and individualism stretching back through Luther to Augustine, in other words, is *misplaced.*[36] For *that* separation of conscience from *society* one has to look at the modern dualism of thinking things and extended things, and so between inward religion and external institutions, as characterized James's philosophy of religion which we studied in Chapter One. Stendhal is right to point to the apparently "robust conscience" of Saul the blameless Pharisee, though also here the significance of a good insight is *misplaced.* What else would Saul's robust conscience mean than that at his blameless best in zeal for the law and the traditions of his elders he proved an enemy of Christ, that the apocalypse of Jesus Christ required of him a new interpretation of his former blameless self as exactly that to which his robust conscience and healthy-minded activism had led him? In Saul-now-Paul's case, introspection is not the presupposition of Christian grace, but it certainly is its fruit.[37]

34. Stendahl, *Paul among Jews and Gentiles,* p. 94.
35. Stendahl, *Paul among Jews and Gentiles,* p. 95.
36. For a nuanced discussion of the relation of Luther to Augustine, see David C. Steinmetz, *Luther in Context* (Grand Rapids: Baker Academic, 2002), pp. 12-22.
37. One has the sense in reading Stendahl's essay that a certain brand of pietistic

Stendahl would have acknowledged in reply to this objection, I imagine, that the radical discontinuity of Paul's supposed Damascus apocalypse as an event in time and space cannot be explained on the basis of salvation history, i.e., that the apocalypse is a mythic production expressing the immanent evolution of religion; thus it is rather to be explained by salvation history. In any event the "framework of 'Sacred History' that we have found to be that of Pauline theology" frees us, Stendahl concluded, from the old scheme that the soul must first be terrorized by the preaching of the law before it is ripe for the consolation of the gospel, the pretension "that the only door into the church was that of evermore introspective awareness of sin and guilt."[38] In its own way, this too is a valuable insight, yet it is, once again, *misplaced*. There is some basis in Melanchthon's theology for such a psychologically prescriptive (rather than theologically regulative) *ordo salutis*,[39] but given the scope of Stendahl's massive claims in this little essay, he stands far more guilty of retrojecting Pietism and Cartesianism onto Luther and Augustine. The price for this misplacement is very steep, if we must assimilate Paul to Luke.

## Käsemann's Critique of Salvation History

*Which* doctrine of justification? Paul's or Luke's? That is the kind of question that, I submit, we can in retrospect today see that Martin Luther *actually* raised; in the form of a question it is and indeed remains the question every new generation must answer in its own wrestling with the message of Paul the Apostle. It is not in other words Luther's sixteenth-century exegesis of the righteousness of God as *die Gerechtigkeit, die vor Gott gilt* that is as such bequeathed to theologians who stand in his tradition. It is rather his fundamental insight that the critical Pauline expression is not to be understood from Aristotle but from the Hebrew Scriptures.[40] Paul is not

---

Lutheranism hovers in the background like a demon needing to be exorcized: "Nobody can attain a true faith in Christ unless his self-righteousness has been crushed by the Law. The function of the Second Use of the Law is to make man see his desperate need for a Savior." Stendahl, *Paul among Jews and Gentiles*, p. 87.

38. Stendahl, *Paul among Jews and Gentiles*, p. 96.

39. See Hinlicky, *Paths Not Taken: Theology from Luther through Leibniz* (Grand Rapids: Eerdmans, 2009), pp. 148-61.

40. "Preface to the Latin Writings" (1545) LW 34:337, where Luther also invokes Augustine's "On the Spirit and the Letter." See the helpful survey by Mickey L. Mattox, "Martin

speaking then of righteousness as an essential attribute of God by which mortals are evaluated but rather, taking the phrase as a genitive of the author, Paul speaks with the Scriptures of Israel of the righteousness of the saving God keeping covenant faithfulness in Jesus Christ to rescue His people and reclaim them for His Kingdom.[41] Such was the impassioned conviction of Ernst Käsemann, even though his Lutheran-all-too-Lutheran penchant for bombast, polemic, and hasty judgment damaged him as a theologian in the same way it damaged Luther before him. Like Luther, however, Käsemann lived in "a world gone mad";[42] this requires of interpretation a certain extra measure of charity.

Käsemann took on Stendahl's "Introspective Conscience" in an essay, "Justification and Salvation History in the Epistle to the Romans," where like a dog on a bone he fastened onto Stendahl's remark about the "framework of Sacred History" in Paul to locate Stendahl in "the context of an established theological tradition" (of the nineteenth century, as noted above).[43] Käsemann made three comments about this theological tradition of *Heilsgeschichte* to set off the exegetical counter-arguments that followed: (1) The authority of Scripture in the Reformation sense is eclipsed here, because a scholarly scheme of religious development in history not only replaces the form of theological argument by means of concrete exegesis of authoritative Scripture, but this scheme always — covertly in Protestantism, overtly in Catholicism — leads to the present moment of (the scholar's or the church's) enlightened understanding as to the very goal of God and standard of all judgment. Adoption of *Heilsgeschichte,* to borrow a term from Bonhoeffer, represents neo-"Protestantism without Reformation."[44] (2) Käsemann clarifies the nature of his critique. He "has nothing against the phrase salvation history" in spite of reservations about its misuse. In fact, he "would even say that it is impossible to understand the bible in general or Paul in particular without the perspective of salvation history" — meaning that God's faithfulness through time constitutes a history on the earth, to which the Scriptures bear witness. His worry, however, is

---

Luther's Reception of Paul," in *The Reception of Paul in the Sixteenth Century,* ed. Ward Holder (Leiden and Boston: E. J. Brill, forthcoming), pp. 93-128.

41. Ernst Käsemann, *Commentary on Romans,* trans. Geoffrey W. Bromiley (Grand Rapids: Eerdmans, 1980), pp. 24-32.

42. See the enlightening account of Roy A. Harrisville, "The Life and Work of Ernst Käsemann (1906-1998)," *Lutheran Quarterly* 21, no. 3 (2007): 294-319.

43. Käsemann, *Perspectives on Paul,* p. 61.

44. Käsemann, *Perspectives on Paul,* pp. 62-63.

that "the divine plan of salvation [can] be absorbed by an immanent evolutionary process whose meaning can be grasped on earth, or which we can control and calculate."[45] He then tells about the disillusionment of the liberal faith in progress after World War I and the nightmare of "a conception of salvation history which broke in on us in secularized and political form in the Third Reich and its ideology."[46] (3) Käsemann noted Stendahl's attack on Bultmann in his article. But he did not in turn focus on Bultmann's theory of universal human self-consciousness as the bridge for understanding, which had been the object of Stendahl's criticism. Rather Käsemann focused on the fact that Bultmann too held Paul's doctrine of justification to be theologically central, thus to be and mean more than "an early Christian defense against Judaism, conditioned by its time."[47] In the light of these remarks, Käsemann claimed, as he turned to the exegesis of Romans, that the history of salvation undoubtedly "forms the horizon of Paul's theology" but "the significance" of this fact "is anything but decided."[48]

Invoking the conflict in Romans 5:12ff. between the two humanities, Adam and Christ, Käsemann made here the statement that forms the epigraph to this chapter. The significant fact is that both Adam and Christ are corporate realities. That is why salvation must be something followable, narratable, written as history: salvation is "power which changes the old world into a new one and which becomes incarnate in the earthly sphere." To deny this "incarnation," to abandon this "corporeality" and narratability, would turn Paul into Marcion. That is the anti-Gnostic vindication of what is valid in the notion of *Heilsgeschichte*. But "when all this is conceded, so that the idea of incarnation receives its due, dialectic and paradox must not be overlooked."[49] The real, canonical salvation history is not a progressive, forward march from victory unto victory. "Sarah's laughter is faith's constant companion . . . [in] the story of Adam and the prodigal son, of the crucified Christ, the sheep without a shepherd, the warring confessions; a story in which both faith and superstition cross and recross each other without pause."[50] The continuity of this story of salvation is not immanent in history, to be read off the pages uncritically or critically de-

---

45. Käsemann, *Perspectives on Paul*, p. 63.
46. Käsemann, *Perspectives on Paul*, p. 64.
47. Käsemann, *Perspectives on Paul*, p. 63.
48. Käsemann, *Perspectives on Paul*, p. 66.
49. Käsemann, *Perspectives on Paul*, p. 68.
50. Käsemann, *Perspectives on Paul*, p. 69.

tected behind the pages of Scripture, because the story of salvation in Scripture continues only "when God's Word, contrary to the earthly realities, creates for itself children and communities of the pure in spirit."[51] Take away the uncontrollable living God with His free Word and Spirit and the history of salvation falls to pieces.

For the remainder of his response to Stendahl, Käsemann made observations on the fate of the Reformation doctrine of justification. Quite contrary to the picture Sanders would draw of German scholarship dominated by the "Lutheran" reading of Paul, contrary to Stendahl's retooling of the cliché about the troubled monk seeking a gracious God, Käsemann pointed out that the real Reformation doctrine of justification has long since been eclipsed, that "the portrait of the benevolent God has more or less pushed out the picture of the judge, and the function of the Holy Spirit is now only viewed as edification, although the New Testament ceaselessly shows him as a polemicist."[52] This predominant shift to neo-Protestant religious consciousness has long since made the very notion of justification nugatory. Then, in a fateful depiction of the Pauline sphere of *nomos* as dominating power, Käsemann sketched in his own (polemically slanted, alas, as usual) words the very picture of "covenantal nomism" (of course, without knowledge of Sanders, whose book had not yet been written): *Nomos* "creates the sphere within which man tries to sunder himself from immorality and godlessness, views the history of his father's redemption as the guarantee of his own election and claims God's grace as his personal privilege."[53] Note well: in this depiction the issue is *not* grace. The sphere of *nomos* knows very well about *grace*. It knows it so well it takes ownership of grace, as a possession. *That,* just *that,* and *only* that is what is at issue, according to Käsemann, in Paul's contention for the counter-righteousness of the sphere of faith as opposed to *nomos*. Grace is not what is in dispute theologically between works and faith, but *which* justification, that of the ungodly or that of the pious? *Nomos* "represents the community of 'good' people which turns God's promises into their own privileges and God's commandments into the instrument of self-sanctification."[54] That usurpation is what was at issue in the righteousness of God revealed in the gospel.

Is *this* "struggle," Käsemann asked in conclusion, "really superseded"

---

51. Käsemann, *Perspectives on Paul,* p. 70.
52. Käsemann, *Perspectives on Paul,* p. 71.
53. Käsemann, *Perspectives on Paul,* p. 72.
54. Käsemann, *Perspectives on Paul,* p. 72.

today, since, according to Stendahl, it had originally been "a merely anti-Jewish affair"?[55] Stendahl was not wrong to challenge interpretation of Paul's gospel "in exclusively individual terms," but he risks losing the dimension of anthropological depth and the personal discipleship that derives from the *absolvo te*. It is impossible and it is wrong, then, "to play off justification and salvation history against one another . . . [rather] everything depends on the right co-ordination of the two" so that what is incarnated in history is not the gathering of those good in their own eyes, but the justification of the ungodly.[56]

Käsemann's considerable strengths are on display in this rejoinder to Stendahl but so also are some of his weaknesses. Like Luther, his method entails re-preaching the gospel (Hagen's *ennaratio*) in the very act of interpreting it, sometimes at the expense of patient elaboration. It is a method, moreover, that is explicitly, even aggressively theological, to the chagrin of "serious" historians. A real deficiency lies in the fact that Käsemann lacked training in philosophy (although he incisively identified the idealist thought stemming from Kant as the basis for the German intelligentsia's incomprehension of the Reformation gospel).[57] He was also a student "victim," as it were, of German scholarship's hostility to patristic theology (i.e., Harnack's "hellenization of the gospel" thesis).[58] Accordingly, he lacked the tools needed to make the ambitious arguments he intended. Thus it is not surprising to hear Stendahl reply in response to Käsemann's essay, "I find it difficult to answer [him]." Stendahl protested that his own exegetical proposal simply became the occasion for Käsemann to go on a rant against the evils of *Heilsgeschichte*. If this is the game, he rejoined, "[s]imilarly, I could list how pogroms and the Holocaust found fuel and comfort in an understanding of Judaism as the eternally condemned and evil way to serve God . . . ," implying, of course, that just this stereotype of Judaism is condoned by Käsemann's description of the sphere of *nomos*.[59] Indeed, Stendahl explicitly registers "a profound warning against that kind of theological imperialism

---

55. Käsemann, *Perspectives on Paul*, pp. 72-73.

56. Käsemann, *Perspectives on Paul*, p. 76.

57. Harrisville, "The Life and Work of Ernst Käsemann," pp. 299-300.

58. In the present essay, Käsemann parrots the parody of Patristic theology, which according to the argument made in Chapter Two of this book must also make Luther's own Christology opaque to him: Gentile Christianity's "Christ became the God of the mystery plays, the conqueror through suffering, who makes his believers like himself. He becomes man so that we can become as gods." *Perspectives on Paul*, p. 73.

59. Stendahl, *Paul among Jews and Gentiles*, p. 131.

which triumphs in its doctrine of the justification of the ungodly by making Judaism a code word for all wrong attitudes toward God."[60]

Käsemann chose to make Nazism the illustration of the perils of *Heilsgeschichte;* Stendahl chose to make Christian anti-Judaism the theme of his rejoinder against Käsemann's "justification of the ungodly." In this exchange of insults, Stendahl did not defend his commitment to salvation-history, but rather reiterated that the question for debate he had posed concerned Paul's question about Gentiles in God's plan over against Augustine's and Luther's question about comfort for troubled souls. He thus accused Käsemann of begging the question.[61] Dunn's proclamation of the New Perspective, as we have seen, sided with Stendahl against Käsemann at just this point, and so escaped the force of Käsemann's theological critique and exegetical refutation which, admittedly, has to be dug out from underneath the impassioned preaching. If I have succeeded in extracting the gravamen of Käsemann's case out for consideration, however, what emerges from this exchange is something of *crux intellectum* for Pauline studies — and not one to be settled by the Nazi Holocaust blame game.

While Käsemann indeed sketches the sphere of *nomos* as the sphere of self-righteousness, he equally well grasps that behind the *nomos* is not merely the self-deception of human boasting but the specter of the judgment *of God.* The "curse of the law," in other words, cannot *finally* be something on the plane of anthropology; it cannot finally be either the boasting of the godly *coram deo* or their ritual exclusion of the Gentiles *coram hominibus.* In fact, penultimately the "curse of the law" manifests in *both* these ways for Paul and should be seen together, not pitted off against each other: spiritual pride excludes, and exclusion is the manifestation of spiritual pride. But both interpretations fall short so far as they leave the impression that the "curse of the law" is a mere consequence of its *human* misuse. Moreover, it is worth stressing that if things are left on the plane of anthropology, it is the hapless Jew who appears in *either* case as the stereotypical abuser of the law: boasting of their separated superiority (so Käsemann), insisting upon ritual purity against dirty Gentiles (so the New Perspective). As to anti-Judaism, then, it is a wash between the two perspectives, old and new. But there is possibility of moving the discussion beyond the impasse just narrated, if we follow Käsemann's hint about the judgment of God. For in that case, behind the Pauline tyranny of the law

60. Stendahl, *Paul among Jews and Gentiles,* p. 132.
61. Stendahl, *Paul among Jews and Gentiles,* p. 131.

stands the wrath of God, God's holy judgment on the creation fallen short of its intended glory. The "curse of the law" is not in that case anything especially Jewish at all, but something that is and can be revealed from heaven against *all* wickedness and ungodliness, both Jewish and Gentile, something that as *stoixeia tou kosmou* already afflicts Gentiles who have not known the Torah of Moses.

## Beyond the Old and the New Perspectives

In the light of the foregoing impasse, I wish now to stage an *Auseinandersetzung* between two outstanding representatives of the salvation-history and apocalyptic approaches to Paul: N. T. Wright and J. Louis Martyn, respectively. The issue is how to understand the "curse of the law" in Galatians 3:10 — and whether, in the end, Luther as a resource liberated from certain misleading features of the "old" perspective can be a help, rather than an obstacle, in achieving a better perspective on Paul's views of law and justification. We begin with Martyn's provocative analysis of the passage in question.

The Galatian interlopers, to whom Martyn assigned the title "the Teachers," have come to frighten the Gentile Christians. They are criticizing Paul because he has failed to teach them the Torah's two ways — of blessing on those who observe it, and curse upon those who do not (Deut. 27). Now to be blessed, the Gentile Galatians must commit to observing the prescribed works of the law by submitting to circumcision as the divinely ordained sign of assuming the yoke of the covenant. In Galatians 3:10-14, Paul is concerned to turn back that threatened "curse of the law" upon the interlopers. It is the Teachers, who want to live under the Torah's curse and blessing, who are in fact cursed by it, since the *Nomos* (Torah) does not have the power to bless, only to curse. This is universally true, Paul argues. The observant have no real advantage. Paul's sense becomes clear as he passes from speaking about observance and non-observance (the Teachers' focus) "and begins to speak of the Law itself. . . . By the power of its universal curse, the Law has established its own realm, and in that cursed realm no one is being set right. Why not? Doubtless because the Law has as its business to pronounce a curse (v 10); but also because the source of rectification [= justification] lies elsewhere"[62] — namely with

---

62. Martyn, *Galatians*, p. 312.

the gospel which is the power of God already promised to father Abraham's seed to bless those who have faith. In accord with Martyn's apocalyptic approach, the coming of the gospel onto the scene has initiated a new antinomy, a new opposition. The gospel effectively takes blessing from out of the law's scope and leaves the law with only the power to curse. It can do this because the faith which is blessed has now appeared in Abraham's seed, the faithful man Jesus Christ. The preaching of Him who is the "reflection of God's faithfulness . . ." has brought faith and the Spirit to the Galatians, a faith "elicited, kindled, incited by the faith of Christ, enacted in his atoning death."[63]

Verse 12 now becomes extraordinarily significant, especially when we look ahead to 3:19-20: "Paul here disqualifies the Law on the basis of its origin . . ." since it does not come from faith. The impotence of the law to bless is due to the fact that it is based on a "false promise,"[64] that is, a promise now known to be false by the coming of faith apart from the law and its works and instead by the preaching of Christ's faithfulness to God and to us at the cross. Thus it is that "Christ redeemed us from the Law's curse," the key word being *redemption,* i.e., the "universal curse would have had no terminus except for the appearance of a greater power . . . the person of Christ, who embodied the faith."[65] In Christ the Crucified, Paul saw "the only juncture at which that embodied faith met that embodied curse in all of its power."[66] This is the impressive fundamental insight of Martyn's apocalyptic exegesis. Yet at this juncture, it comes perilously near to Marcion, or, as Martyn no doubt would say, Paul's argumentation could seem (falsely) here to anticipate Marcion.[67] Omitting the words "by God" from the citation of Deuteronomy 21:23, "cursed by God," in Galatians 3:14, Paul dissociates "the curse from God, linking it solely to the Law. . . . The voice of God and the voice of the Law are by no means the same. It was the

---

63. Martyn, *Galatians,* p. 314.

64. Martyn, *Galatians,* p. 316.

65. Martyn, *Galatians,* p. 317.

66. Martyn, *Galatians,* p. 318. Thus Martyn's interpretation falls emphatically within the *Christus Victor* tradition: "the human dilemma consists at its base, not of guilt, but of enslavement to powers lying beyond the human being's control" (p. 308). "Central to the action in this apocalyptic struggle is, therefore, not forgiveness, but rather victory, God's victory in Christ and the resultant emancipation of human beings" (p. 18, n. 110).

67. But for Paul "these polar opposites were not wooden, ontological antitheses, but rather dynamic, apocalyptic antinomies. The difference is monumental. . . . Marcion's antithesis between a creator God and a redeemer God[,] . . . altogether unlike Paul's apocalyptic antinomies, became anti-Judaic." Martyn, *Galatians,* p. 34.

Law, not God, that pronounced a curse on the crucified one."[68] How is that to be understood, if not with Marcion?

Summarizing this apocalyptic exegesis on the "curse of the law," Martyn lists the following the results: (1) The law curses, God blesses. (2) Blessing and curse are not of equal age, but the curse has intervened between God's promise to Abraham and its fulfillment in Christ. (3) The voice of the curse was "robbed of its power when, approved by God in his law-cursed death, Christ vanquished that curse, freeing the whole of humanity from its power." Martyn acknowledges that the resulting picture is "highly paradoxical" in that Paul never takes his eyes off the cross as if the victory of blessing over curse took place "in the apparent defeat of the crucifixion itself." This suggests that "in that event God fundamentally redefined both strength and weakness."[69] Perhaps the paradox of victory in apparent defeat opens up to understanding, Martyn finally suggests, when we see that the false promise of Torah observance in fact had blocked the coming of the promise to the Gentiles by separating observant Jews from them. But in effecting just this separation, the law enacts its curse on both the observant and the non-observant, who are cursed by being separated, the pious from the ungodly. The curse consists "precisely in its act of differentiating and separating observant from non-observant, the pious from the godless, the Jew from the Gentile."[70] Just so, the "issue is not whether a human being observes the Law or fails to do so," but whether "blessing prevails over curse."[71]

The strange view of the law that seems to result from this reading may be off-putting. Martyn immediately acknowledges that even in Galatians Paul's view of the law is richer and more complex than the nearly Marcionite position indicated in his exegesis of Galatians 3:10-14. He also readily acknowledges a significantly different theology of the law in Romans.[72] Nevertheless, there are real strengths to his exposition. First, it takes seriously the evident distancing of God from the law (which is explicit in Gal. 3:19-20). Second, it depicts curse and blessing as powers contending for humanity. Third, it explains how Christ for Paul can defeat the curse by embodying faith in face of its full fury. Fourth, it does the foregoing by arguing tightly the development of Paul's course of thought in his

---

68. Martyn, *Galatians*, pp. 320-21.
69. Martyn, *Galatians*, p. 326.
70. Martyn, *Galatians*, p. 327.
71. Martyn, *Galatians*, p. 328.
72. Martyn, *Galatians*, pp. 30ff.

actual, historical contest with the Teachers "by listening with Galatian ears"[73] (rather than superimposing on Paul complexes of thought discovered in background sources). Finally, the apocalyptic approach turns the understanding of the history of salvation in the minds of the Teachers on its head: *Lex semper accusat.*

N. T. Wright published a potent analysis of exactly the same text, from the perspective of "covenant theology,"[74] i.e., his more sophisticated version of *Heilsgeschichte.*[75] The text is important to the New Perspective. It was Stendahl's case that the law as pedagogue in Galatians 3:23 *until,* not *unto* Christ, disclosed the supposed pattern of salvation-history theology in the letter to the Galatians.[76] But language of the "curse of the law" preceding this correlates with the language of enslavement and imprisonment under the pedagogy of the law (not a benevolent schoolmaster for the immature but rather a cruel custodian). This speaks against any effortless, organic unfolding of salvation immanent in history. Wright is far more attuned to this objection from the side of apocalyptic theology. The position he takes on Galatians 3:10-14, however, in one respect squarely (or rather, almost squarely) contradicts Martyn's. Paul does not say, Wright urges, "the law cursed Jesus, but the resurrection showed the law to be wrong." Rather, Paul's argument "actually *depends on the validity of the law's curse,* and on the propriety of Jesus, as Messiah, bearing it on Israel's behalf."[77] Presumably Wright means the *divine* validity of the curse. The "Torah was

---

73. Martyn, *Galatians,* pp. 41-42.

74. Wright, *Climax,* p. 156.

75. Not least in regard to what Wright has learned from Käsemann: "If I had to choose the works of one Pauline exegete to take with me to a desert island, it would be Käsemann." N. T. Wright, *What Saint Paul Really Said: Was Paul of Tarsus the Real Founder of Christianity?* (Grand Rapids: Eerdmans, 1997), p. 18. In the conclusion of this book, Wright sums up Paul's doctrine of justification as follows: (1) it is a covenant declaration, (2) modeled after the law court, (3) anticipating the eschatological day of judgment, (4) demarcating those who have faith in Christ Jesus by the gospel message of His Lordship as already vindicated (p. 131). "'Faith, for Paul, is therefore not a substitute 'work' in a moralistic sense . . . [nor] a general religious awareness. . . . It is very precise and specific. It is faith in the gospel message, the announcement of the true God as defined in and through Jesus Christ . . . the proclamation of the lordship of Jesus Christ. . . . 'Justification' is the doctrine which insists that all those who have this faith belong as full members of this family, on this basis and no other" (pp. 132-33). I will be forgiven for failing to detect the dramatic break here with the "Lutheran" doctrine of justification!

76. Stendahl, *Paul among Jews and Gentiles,* p. 87.

77. N. T. Wright, *The Climax of the Covenant: Christ and the Law in Pauline Theology* (Minneapolis: Fortress, 1991), p. 152.

correct to pronounce the curse. It merely did not have the last word."[78] That, as we shall see, is an interesting take on *divine* validity as something somehow surpassable. In any case, behind the (near) head-on collision with Martyn's fundamental claim stands one significant strength of Wright's "covenant theology" approach to the interpretation of Paul. That is the consistent and thorough resolve to understand the New Testament writings on the basis of their spiritual homeland, which is the Scriptures of Israel and early Judaism's attempt to understand her destiny theologically on that basis. Wright worked out a rich and persuasive notion of the corporate Messiah on this basis, as mentioned above in Chapter One. Thus the "curse of the law" here designates no subordinate attack on faithful Jesus by wayward *stoixeia* of the rebellious cosmos, the Torah among them. It is rather the "covenantal curse, Israel's curse, being taken on by Israel's anointed representative in an act which itself symbolized very precisely all that the curse of exile stood for. The death of the king, hanged on a tree in the midst of his own land . . ." is no abstract curse falling on abstract sin, but the God of Israel's own curse upon Israel's failure, the Messiah absorbing in one concentrated blow the people's punishment.[79] What transpires is not the punishment of individual transgressors, Wright stresses, but of the corporate failure of Israel to be blessing and light to the nations. Thus this verdict can be resolved in the cross of the Messiah, in the process setting free the promised blessing of all nations, which may now pass through the Jews to the Gentiles by the same faith. "The dual problem caused by the clash of Torah and Abrahamic promise is given a dual solution: blessing for the Gentiles, which they had looked like being denied, and new covenant for Israel, which she had looked like failing to attain."[80] This is the *theological* fulfillment for Paul, not of a few proof texts, but "of the whole paradoxical history of Israel."[81]

The plight designated by the "curse of the law" then was Israel's exile (Wright argues that the Babylonian exile had never truly ended in the minds of first-century Judaism, but Israel still languished in diaspora, even on the soil of Palestine still under foreign occupation). Agreeing with one of the chief claims of the New Perspective, Wright explains that "Paul, like all first-century Jews, had a 'plight,' though it is not to be identified with that of

---

78. Wright, *Climax*, p. 152.
79. Wright, *Climax*, p. 153.
80. Wright, *Climax*, p. 154.
81. Wright, *Climax*, p. 155.

the puzzled existentialist, or for that matter of the conscience-stricken Protestant." Rather the plight was "the sorry state of Israel," which provoked a painful question of theodicy regarding "the covenant faithfulness and justice of the creator God who had called her to be his chosen people." Interestingly, Wright acknowledges here in a way what Stendahl would not, that so far as Israel's sorry state includes also "the present sinfulness of Jews as individuals, the normal 'Lutheran' reading can be contained within this analysis." Likewise so far as Israel's plight included "crippling uncertainty" about the future, Wright adds, the "existentialist" reading finds a home. But decisively "only the framework of covenant theology" does justice to Paul, for whom, as for most Jews of that time, "as long as Herod or Pilate ruled over her, Israel was still under the curse."[82] All this, however, is but background to what is foregrounded in the Letter to the Galatians. Here, more like Käsemann and Martyn, Wright acknowledges the discontinuity: the Damascus apocalypse not only turned the Pharisee into the Apostle but also turned this framework of covenant theology on its head, challenging "the normal Jewish analysis and understanding of its plight at its root."[83] Now Paul sees that it is the way of the obedient and suffering Messiah that is "the necessary if paradoxical outworking of God's plan, to save the world by focusing its problems, through the Torah, first on to Israel and then on to her Messiah." At the same time, this reversal was no absolute "*novum*, a Christian invention. It was based on Torah, Prophets, and Psalms, read (he would have said) with eyes now at last unveiled."[84]

Wright's analysis of the "curse of the law" represents a real advance beyond the *Heilsgeschichte* approach inherited by the New Perspective through Stendahl and programmatically laid out by Dunn. This is in part because Wright takes the paradox and discontinuity in the history of salvation demanded by the apocalyptic approach without succumbing to virtual dualism, i.e., Marcionism, in the interpretation of the "curse." Moreover, this approach has the virtue of taking Paul's theology seriously as "worldview" (to use an unfortunately encumbered word), meaning here that "the belief-structure which informed and directed [Paul's] life and work, and through which he perceived the world was itself thoroughly theological."[85] This attention to Paul's theological beliefs has the merit of

82. Wright, *Climax*, p. 261.
83. Wright, *Climax*, p. 261.
84. Wright, *Climax*, p. 262.
85. Wright, *Climax*, p. 262.

lifting up and underscoring the saving goal of Beloved Community. Paul "writes in order to call into being, and sustain in being, communities composed of men, women and children of every race and every class of society, believing that in so doing he is acting as midwife (or even mother, as in Galatians 4:19) to the renewed covenant people of God, which can know no boundaries because it is precisely the renewed human race."[86] Finally, the cost of birthing the Beloved Community is not theologically cheap to God; it costs the Messiah that death accursed by God for the failure of His chosen humanity to become such light to the nations.

There is nonetheless one significant weakness in Wright's approach: unlike Martyn's method of "listening with Galatian ears," there is a tendency to allow the reconstruction of the background worldview to overdetermine the reading of the text, with the result that the subtle tensions and theological difficulties discerned by Martyn do not sufficiently surface in Wright's reading. Wright's theological solution to the problem of God's covenant faithfulness by the paradox of a crucified Messiah does not note, or deal with, the scandalous distancing of the God of blessing ·from the curse of the law which the difficult text attests, as Martyn has so acutely laid out. From this follows a further difficulty: How is it according to Wright's account that the accursed death of the Messiah avails also for Gentile sinners under the wrath of God, as surely they — the Gentile audience at Galatia — also are in Paul's theology?

Thus both theologians each in their own way have theological difficulty with the antagonism between the curse of the law and the blessing of God. Martyn's powerful invasion of God in the person of Christ faithful on the cross virtually makes of the law a power independent of and opposed to God. Wright so assimilates the cross of the Messiah into the covenant plan and purpose of God that the drama of that antagonism diminishes, unfolding instead like the surprise ending of a mystery novel, engaging, but all the same moving along according to a predetermined script, as one now sees once eyes have been opened and the veil removed. This has the consequence of making ignorance rather than resistance the opponent of the gospel. Wright is correct to say that the curse of the law is valid and validly falls on the Messiah as representative of the failed people of God; Martyn is correct to see that cursing is not blessing, and that the question of how these two contraries can be ascribed to one and the same God is daunting. Can Luther help?

---

86. Wright, *Climax*, p. 263.

## The Law Battling the Law in Order to Liberate Us All

It depends of course on what kind of help he might offer. Certainly exegesis from the sixteenth century cannot settle critical-historical disputes of the twenty-first. Nor is it a matter of superimposing a "Lutheran" dogmatic formulation about the righteousness that prevails before God. In the present case, however, we have two exemplary exegetes who are powerfully engaged with the theology of the Apostle. The kind of contradiction we have uncovered between them regarding the "curse of the law" is built on the respective strengths of the two approaches of apocalyptic and covenant theology. The exegetical observations are strong. Paul *both* distances the God of blessing from the "curse of the law" *and yet* the "curse of the law" is somehow valid, and that is why the Messiah's accursed death justifies and redeems those under the law that they may enjoy the blessing of Abraham promised to faith. The law is only a temporary pedagogue and yet in the fullness of time this pedagogue must be both satisfied and overpowered. How then must we learn to think about a God *in motion*, the Sender and the Sent and the Sending of Galatians 4:4-7, the God who becomes in that He comes in time, not to destroy but to create anew out of the ashes of a dying world? Such theological questions seem to arise from the exegesis and the difficulties it raises. We today, however, are not the first to notice or deal with the tensions that arise from close reading of the biblical texts, or to generate creative theological interpretation by facing, rather than effacing difficulties. Luther as resource can help on this level of theological imagination.

An entire monograph could be devoted to Luther's second commentary on Galatians of 1535, which contains Luther's mature statement of his (not Lutheranism's!) doctrine of justification by faith. Indeed, Luther here is engaged in subtle debate with the recent development in the thought of his closest ally: Philip Melanchthon's exclusively forensic restatement of the doctrine. Of necessity, our focus here is very narrow and precise. Can Luther's own account of the "curse of the law" reconcile the contradiction previously described?

First, we must clearly see that for Luther it is not the law taken over by sin and causing boasting or exclusion that identifies our true plight. True, law seized from God's hands and put to work for our purposes rather than God's promotes just that boasting, with all the inferiorization of others — for good reasons and not-so-good reasons — that goes along with it, as Paul teaches in Romans 2. But that is not our true plight, any more than its opposite: the godless flight from the law of God into wasted lives of lawlessness, as in Jesus' parable of the prodigal son or Paul's first chapter to the Romans. That really is a waste, a sinful waste. But neither is that our true plight. Both the godly and the ungodly have their respective issues with the law. Luther in any case would never be so perverse as to despise the relative rectitude in this world of the "good" people, whom Käsemann so recklessly and often clumsily attacked. *Coram hominibus,* good people make better neighbors than bad people. (Ask anyone who has ever lived in a bad neighborhood, especially the poor who are stuck in them.) Thus "Aristotle or a Sadducee or a man who is good in a civic sense calls it right reason and good will if he seeks the common welfare of the state and tranquility and honesty."[87] And so far as this goes, that's right. The issue here is subtler than a crude inversion of civic righteousness, deeper than exposing its inevitable bourgeois hypocrisies, hypocrisy being the tribute that vice pays to virtue. Luther insists on the distinction between earthly and heavenly righteousness to get at this subtler level of analysis, though it is not clear that this way of making the distinction illuminates much for us today. Ebeling helpfully re-described the distinction between earthly and heavenly righteousness as a relational one: righteousness *coram deo,* in relation to God, and *coram hominibus,* in relation to human beings. Yet even the foggy notion of a "relational ontology" tends to separate where Luther means only to distinguish aspects of or perspectives on one and the same thing. At issue in Luther's distinction is rather the goodness of those good people, which would also truly be goodness for those bad people. What makes a good work truly good, that is, a divine work, a work of the good God who creates *ex nihilo?* What makes an earthly doer of a good work truly a good person, that is, a person united with the person of God the Giver of good without reserve? This *is* a *subtle* issue, demanding an insight that does not come easily or naturally to the *opinio legis,* the naturally legalistic mentality of good people (Luther is thinking of Aristotle's *Nichomachean Ethics,* not the rabbis) who know and act upon the difference between right and wrong in civic society, but also the bad people (if they are not sociopaths) who know that they are bad in the eyes of others. For in either case, "the human heart neither understands nor believes that such a great prize as the Holy Spirit [the real doer of good works] can be granted solely through hearing with faith. . . ."[88]

---

87. "Commentary on Galatians" (1535) LW 26:262.
88. "Commentary on Galatians" (1535) LW 26:213.

Hearing *what?* A supposedly radical, counterintuitive polemic to the effect that our goodness is really just badness? How is that not just perverse? Or a theological case for the fittingness of a crucified Messiah as the paradoxical agent realizing God's plan?[89] As reflections, I do not deny, nor do I think that Luther denies, that either of these reflections can help faith to understand. But we have not yet, according to Luther, come to that point of faith where understanding might be sought, for we have not yet even raised the question about truly good works, works that do good to those who are not so good by those who are not so good. That is to say, we do not yet understand our true plight, namely, that even in our civic goodness at its best we are not the active agents of *His* kingdom for which God created us. So again, *what* hearing penetrates our natural defenses and reveals *that* to us? One way that Luther talks about that is to tell of the law taken out of our hands to serve our purposes, so that instead, perhaps for the first time, we hear the law as God's own voice. When we hear the law as God's own voice demanding of us God's own purposes, that is the "proper task of the Law[,]" wresting us "from our peace and self-confidence, to set us into the sight of God, and to reveal the wrath of God to us."[90]

Martyn was right to see in this *event* that the law only curses, just as it is made bereft of its false promise by which observers would bless themselves. Yet for Luther, this action of cursing occurs as *God* seizes the law from out of our hands, as Käsemann would say, to act as our Judge. So now we understand our true plight! Or do we? What we have just heard is another theological explanation — the true one in Luther's view — but still it does not tell us what we hear when the Spirit is granted as a free gift. The Spirit as gift — that *was* the original question in Galatians. Indeed, recalling that, if receiving the Spirit as a gift is what is to happen by hearing with faith, it is impossible to regard this hearing about wrath by the revelation of the law as the true measure of our plight. For all it does and can do now is to curse us. Who can listen to that? It would be like lying down to die. It would not actually reach us but rather send us running. Moreover, who

---

89. Gerhard Ebeling's warning here is surely apropos: "The concealment of revelation under its opposite is a theme that dominates everything which Luther has to say. . . . At the same time, one must be on one's guard not to succumb to the emotional force of such utterances, or to resist it, without understanding the true reason for such a way of speaking, a reason which leads to much more than such paradoxical language, and which is not satisfied by the ecstasy of paradox." *Luther: An Introduction to His Thought* (Philadelphia: Fortress, 1972), p. 238.

90. "Commentary on Galatians" (1535) LW 26:150.

wants or needs the Spirit? Who wants or needs the Spirit as a free gift? The curse cannot reach and convince us, only attack us. We do not yet understand why we need the Spirit as a gift. No, we have not gotten to the bottom of our plight, even when we hear that voice of the holy law as God's, not ours, not even when attacking false security and revealing holy wrath.

So the question must be posed afresh: *What* do we hear, when the explanation is apropos that "the Law is torn from our self-serving uses and works instead to reveal the wrath of God"? What we grasp here by hearing with faith, Luther will answer, is faithful Jesus with us, right here in this our place, rather more in our own person, assuming our identity, making it His own. In looking at faithful Jesus "who loved me and gave Himself for me" just here, under the curse of the law, we come to apprehend our true plight by the light of the innocent One who shares it with us, the righteous for the unrighteous: "not by the law or by works, but by a reason or an intellect that has been illumined by faith . . . a theological, faithful, and divine consideration of the serpent hanging from the pole, that is, of Christ hanging on the cross for my sins, for your sins, for the sins of the entire world."[91] When we hear with faith about Christ crucified for us all, so that we receive the Spirit as a free gift in this hearing, we are hearing on the primary level, reaching to our hearts, saying "for you as for all." This is the story, according to Luther, behind Paul's words of the *pistos Iesou*. If I may condense several pages of Luther's commentary on Galatians 3:13, "He was made a curse for us," that story runs something like this:

> Thus the whole emphasis is on the phrase "for us." For Christ is innocent so far as His own Person is concerned . . . [but] He bore the person of a sinner and a thief — and not of one but of all sinners and thieves. . . . Therefore it was appropriate for Him to become a thief and, as Isaiah says (53:12) to be "numbered among the thieves." . . . He has and bears all the sins of all men in His body — not in the sense that He has committed them but in the sense that He took these sins, committed by us, upon His own body, in order to make satisfaction for them with His own blood. Therefore this general Law of Moses included Him, although He was innocent so far as His own person was concerned; for it found Him among sinners and thieves. . . .
>
> Christ was not only found among sinners; but of His own free will and by the will of the Father He wanted to be an associate of sin-

---

91. "Commentary on Galatians" (1535) LW 26:287.

ners. . . . But it is highly absurd and insulting to call the Son of God a sinner and a curse! If you want to deny that He is a sinner and a curse, then deny also that He suffered, was crucified, and died. . . . Now the Law comes and says: "I find Him a sinner, who takes upon Himself the sins of all men. I do not see any other sins than those in Him. Therefore let Him die on the cross!" . . .

Now let us see how two such extremely contrary things come together in this Person . . . the sins of the entire world, past, present, and future, attack Him, try to damn Him, and do in fact damn Him. But because in the same Person, who is the highest, the greatest, and the only sinner, there is also eternal and invincible righteousness, therefore these two converge: the highest, the greatest, and the only sin, and the highest, the greatest, the only righteousness. Here one of them must yield and be conquered, since they come together and collide with such a powerful impact. . . .

[In sum,] He attached Himself to those who were accursed, assuming their flesh and blood; and thus He interposed Himself as the Mediator between God and men. . . . And being joined with us who were accursed, he became a curse for us; and He concealed His blessing in our sin, death, and curse, which condemned and killed Him. But because He was the Son of God, He could not be held by them. He conquered them and triumphed over them. He took along with Him whatever clung to the flesh that He had assumed for our sake. Therefore all who cling to this flesh are blessed and are delivered from the curse.[92]

In Luther's narrative of the *pistos Iesou*, we witness a battle, as Martyn rightly maintains, between powers of blessing and curse. At the same time, as Wright insists, we see a propitiation which gives the Victor the right to ransom His redeemed from the curse and bestow on them the promised blessing. How does Luther think these two together rather than as alternatives? Luther sees the law fulfilled in its ethical demand by the loving faithfulness of Christ meeting the rightful curse of the law upon the lovelessness of both pious and impious. Thus Christ defeats the law's power by "satisfying" (too weak a word, rather fulfilling) its right: Christ Crucified is the "Law battling the Law in order to become liberty" for all. When proclamation of this deed of righteousness for the unrighteous is heard *pro me*, the Spirit has fallen from heaven onto the earth, with this *news*, this

---

92. "Commentary on Galatians" (1535) LW 26:277-90.

*Verbum externum* killing to make alive, raising a somatic self to an ecstatic posture. "I have been crucified with Christ; I no longer live, but Christ lives in me. And the life I live in the body, I live by *the faith of* the Son of God, who loved me and gave Himself for me" (Gal. 2:20). An idea of Martyn's in translating *pistos Iesou* as the faith/faithfulness of Christ lends part of the solution, then, as also Wright's idea of the Messiah's representative death. Luther unites these two motifs in the idea that Christ, in His own Person innocent, freely assumed out of love the person of all sinners under the wrath of God. Taking their place, He has the power to overthrow the curse of the law for them, since in attacking Him the curse of the law *has overreached and transgressed its boundary,* resulting in the loss of both its power and its right. For hidden under the sin of the world which He bears, He is the Son of God and Lord of the law who has jurisdiction over all creatures. When He rises, the power of the law to curse guilty creatures is therewith pushed back and banished from those who cling to His crucified and risen body. Hidden under the Godforsaken death, He was also innocent, not only by divine nature, but by this perfect human obedience of love on behalf of others. By this loving faithfulness to sinners, the Son has actually fulfilled the law's true intent in the double love commandment, to love the neighbor as oneself, to fear, love, and trust God above all, in one and the same action. This obedience is what faithful, innocent Jesus has actually done in dying, making *his passion the supreme action: as* the accursed before God, He has loved those accursed. Therefore He has both the power and the right to make the curse of the law guilty and send it away in chains.[93]

## Church in Service of the New Creation

One may conclude then that in the light of Christ the Crucified, the Torah ceases to be the unitary phenomenon that it is for normative Judaism and, as Jacob Neusner has rightly insisted, a new hermeneutical whole with the Scriptures of Israel is formed for Paul and ensuing Christianity.[94]

93. In this analysis I am indebted to my seminary professor, Robert W. Bertram, "The Human Subject as the Object of Theology: Luther by Way of Barth" (University of Chicago Ph.D. dissertation, 1964).

94. Jacob Neusner, with William Scott Green, *Writing with Scripture: The Authority and the Uses of the Hebrew Bible in the Torah of Formative Judaism* (Minneapolis: Augsburg/Fortress, 1989), p. 4.

Covenantal nomism reflects the irrevocable calling of Israel (so Rom. 12:29), but for Luther's Paul, Christ embodies the true, just, and holy intention of the Torah. Dramatically, this embodiment acts to surpass its holy curse on all that is untrue, unjust, and unholy, both to condemn sin in the flesh and to make new those who now by faith pass through the spiritual crucifixion to newness of life for the Beloved Community, the Israel of God. From the beginning of this book, we have taken the hope of the Beloved Community as our theological point of departure: as social and somatic selves, there is no salvation for the individual except by reconciliation to the community. When Luther is taken as a representative of the Augustinian tradition (and not as the pioneer of an existentialist *Sonderweg*), the tacit understanding of the social nature of eschatological salvation in the City of God is not only visible in Luther, but actually may be seen to undergird his doctrine of justification by faith in the Christ who was made a curse *for us all.* Such is Luther's Paulinism: "For God has consigned all to sin, in order that he may have mercy on all."[95]

Thus I have been more than happy to agree with the New Perspective's elevation of the broad historical, social, even cosmic dimensions of Pauline salvation and accordingly to make common cause with the New Perspective's justified attacks on pietist and existentialist reductions of the Reformer's theology to pious consolation or existential authenticity. On the other hand, liberated from such restrictive Lutheran traditions, Luther has some challenges for the New Perspective in turn. As Käsemann noted, it does little good to neglect theologically the moral burden of the individual, even to try to banish this topic from Pauline purview, since Paul's gospel makes those who hear it with faith responsible to God, yet amid a humanity that is not yet redeemed, in which the powers are still at war, in which the believer surely will be found as described in Romans 7 *simul iustus et peccator.* The advance of God's reign is not a straightforward story, beginning with Paul's own disappointed hope in the imminent Parousia and the *irony* — what other word can we use? — that following Paul's death (estranged from the Jerusalem church, perhaps not reconciled with Peter, isolated, his literary legacy vulnerable to early Gnostic appropriation), it was the author we call Luke who saved him for the future. We have access to the real, radical Paul only through Luke, that is, only through the church catholic which saved his letters and embedded them in her rule of faith, the emergent canon. The Spirit always has the last laugh. Paul's message of

95. On the importance of this text for Luther, see Steinmetz, *Luther in Context,* p. 1.

the Victory for us of Him who was accursed breaks out *ubi et quando Deo visum est* to remind the church that she is not yet the Beloved Community but only its groaning anticipation, not the good news but only its bearer to the ungodly (herself included!), not the Lord who saved by an accursed death but only His unworthy servant (just as Luke too teaches, Luke 17:10). So if ironically Luke saved Paul for the early catholic church, in the same way, the church catholic bears in its own Scriptures the Pauline canon of faith: "Neither circumcision nor uncircumcision means anything; what counts is a new creation. Peace and mercy to all who follow this rule, even to the Israel of God" (Gal. 6:15-16). We may, with rough justice, take Paul's canon here as the theological equivalent of Luther's chief article of justification by faith, i.e., as a hermeneutical principle or criterion for ascertaining fidelity to the gospel in the life of the church. There are at least three imperatives for ecclesiology arising from these critical insights.

First, what matters in ecclesiology is the Beloved Community, which as Augustine taught is greater than the visible church in history. This is so in a twofold sense: it is in its reality and fullness the heavenly Jerusalem coming down from above, thus here below it manifests in the visible church as a *corpus permixtum*. Here some who appear visibly within her gates will prove to be imposters, and others who appear visibly as enemies on the outside will prove sisters and brothers. Just so, the visible church on earth remains a wandering people of God on its pilgrim way, which always exists for the sake of that Beloved Community to come, not the other way around. Second, Paul's gospel tied up as it was with his expectation of the Lord's imminent return, has no resources for its own perpetuation into history other than the bare missionary imperative to the nations. The deutero-Pauline epistles, the Pastorals, and Luke-Acts all bear witness to the theological fact that the delay of the Parousia mandates the organization of the visible church to sustain the mission to the nations, which to be sure now means that Christianity appears in history as one religion alongside others. The primal disbelief of Judaism and the rise of Islam as a critique of Christianity are reminders from the Lord of History that Christianity is not yet the Beloved Community but the bearer in history of its promise and its realization in time only by anticipation in faith, hope, and love, thus in fragmentary, often paradoxical ways. Third, to respect the foregoing imperatives, the church militant does not merely hold, but rather essentially structures itself by a set of binding beliefs. This is *not* to say that the individual believer is justified by submitting to the beliefs of the church as an organized religion. The individual believer is justified in the surrender of trust to the Lord Jesus Christ, arising in the Spirit to new obedience in the Father's kingdom, the "hope of righteousness" (Gal. 5:5). It is to say, however, that in the visibility of earthly history we have no access to the living Lord Jesus Christ apart from the binding beliefs about him borne by the church catholic, beginning with and ever normed by the Pauline canon of Galatians 6:15-16.[96] It is also to say that, for this very reason, those binding beliefs are not, as it were, decorative. The imperative is that they actually structure the life of the church. Discerning this is one task undertaken in critical dogmatics, which tests the life of the church against those binding beliefs that must structure it.

---

96. Bruce Marshall, *Trinity and Truth* (Cambridge: Cambridge University Press, 2000), p. 244.

# CHAPTER EIGHT

# Communio: Luther's Forgotten Ecclesiology

*O dear man! If someone does not want to believe the article of faith concerning the Lord's Supper, how will he ever believe the article of faith concerning the humanity and divinity of Christ in one person? If you have doubts about whether you are receiving the body of Christ orally when you eat the bread from the altar, likewise, that you are receiving the blood of Christ orally when you drink the wine in the Lord's Supper, then you surely have serious doubts (especially when the end of your life draws near) about how the infinite and incomprehensible Godhead, which is and must essentially be everywhere, can be bodily enclosed and included in the Virgin's Body, as St. Paul says in Colossians 1 [2:9]: "In him the whole fullness of deity dwells bodily." And how is it possible for you to believe that the Son alone became man, not the Father or the Holy Spirit, since the three persons are nothing but the one God in a most completely single essence and nature of the one Godhead? How can this be explained? How is it possible that the single, completely perfect Godhead of the Son should divide or separate itself so that at one and the same time it is united with the humanity, and the same single Godhead of the Father and the Holy Spirit is not united with the humanity? Yet it is at the same time one and the same Godhead; one person is in Christ with the humanity, and it is not the Father or the Holy Spirit.*

Luther[1]

---

1. "Brief Confession concerning the Holy Sacrament" (1544) LW 38:307.

## A Catholic Luther?

*Sanctorum communio* — I believe in the Holy Spirit's creatures, those called out from the *civitas terrena* and assembled around holy things, as the new and holy people, the body of Christ, the temple of the Spirit, the foretaste of the Messianic banquet, the anticipation in faith, hope, and love of the Beloved Community that comes down from heaven, the end of all things. So the creedal faith instructs. Luther shared this creedal faith[2] and theologically developed it in his own distinctive way, although scholarship for the most part has neglected this discourse about the church in preference for the polemical idioms forced upon him when he spoke of an oppressed and hidden church in the ruins of apocalyptic warfare with the Antichrist. *Abscondita est ecclesia, latent sancti* — Bayer lifts up this lament over the ruin of the church in the sixteenth century as if it were a permanent and central principle of ecclesiology in the tradition of Luther.[3] But placing the accent here surely obscures the tragedy of the Reformation's failure, and Luther's real but limited responsibility for the catastrophe.

One depressing theme that runs like the proverbial red thread through Brecht's three-volume biography of Luther is that of his reform's utter dependence on the good favor of the princes. "Luther once stated the relationship generally: 'If the government tolerates me as a teacher of the Word, I will honor it and recognize it as my ruler with all respect.'"[4] But "with all respect" quickly became "in all respects." The program for an evangelical episcopacy laid out in *Confessio Augustana* (hereafter CA) XXVIII was never realized, neither in Rome of course but also not, fatefully not, in the emerging "Lutheran" churches. In its place the fateful alliance of "Throne and Altar" evolved. Now the "hiddenness" of the church in the ambiguities that attend apocalyptic warfare easily slide into an ideological rationalization for the church's loss of autonomy and subservience to the powers that be. The *corpus permixtum* in Augustine's sense of the

---

2. So Bernard Lohse: We "need to be aware that throughout his life, even in the midst of controversies, he held fast to fundamental aspects of the traditional ecclesiology." *Martin Luther's Theology: Its Historical and Systematic Development,* trans. Roy A. Harrisville (Minneapolis: Fortress, 1999), p. 277.

3. Oswald Bayer, *Martin Luther's Theology: A Contemporary Interpretation,* trans. Thomas H. Trapp (Grand Rapids: Eerdmans, 2007), pp. 278-79, though in a footnote, #105, Bayer rejects a dualism between visible and invisible churches.

4. Martin Brecht, *Martin Luther: The Preservation of the Church, 1532-1546,* trans. J. L. Schaaf (Minneapolis: Fortress, 1993), p. 267.

Parable of the Wheat and Tares sown together becomes standard operating procedure for a church whose mission is no longer to the nations but instead that of a chaplaincy of the *Volk* on behalf of the state. This is among the cruelest of ironies that befell Luther's theology.

Consider by contrast the Luther text above which forms the epigraph to this chapter on ecclesiology. It is interesting from any number of angles, not least for its acknowledgment of the visibility and hence testability of creedal faith as mark of the church. It comes, as we may recall from Chapter One, from the late treatise that von Harnack cited when he announced the impossibility of creedal belief for us today. Von Harnack's objection to this text is one to which this entire book has been addressed. In this chapter the objection will be more narrowly focused, namely, the objection against the possibility of the community of faith, not merely holding, but rather being essentially structured by such a set of binding beliefs in its life and mission as expressed in the epigraph. The text comes from the end of Luther's life as he prepares for death (thus the reference to "serious doubts" as death draws near), as Luther wishes to leave behind a public testimony to his teaching. In it Luther is particularly interested in differentiating the catholic beliefs he holds from those of Zwingli, though here the topic is not divine providence and election as discussed previously in Chapter Five, but the Lord's Supper, Christ, and the Trinity. In that light, what is remarkable about the text is not only the systematic linkage Luther discerns between the various articles of belief, but also the fact that the teaching about the Lord's Supper drives his teaching on the community of faith, the church. For this Meal marks the place upon the earth where the exalted, ubiquitous[5] Lord who rules over all in His indivisible Person gives Himself anew and anew "for us" in just that New Testament[6] gathering of somatic

---

5. Scott Hendrix translates a passage from a 1525 sermon (thus prior to the Eucharistic controversy with Zwingli): "The sum of the matter is this: Depressed or exalted, circumscribed in whatsoever way, dragged hither or thither, I still find Christ. For he holds in his hands everything in heaven and on earth, and all are subject to him — angels, the devil, the world, sin, death and hell. Therefore, so long as he dwells in my heart, I have courage, wherever I go, I cannot get lost. I dwell wherever my Lord Christ dwells. . . . We are, through Christ, better fortified [than with reason]. We are assured that he dwells everywhere, be it in honor or dishonor, hunger, sorrow, illness, imprisonment, death or life, blessing or affliction. It is Paul's desire for the Ephesians [3:18] that God gives them grace and strength to embrace [the rule of Christ] with their heart." From *Eyn Sermon von Staerke und Zunehmen des Glaubens und der Liebe* (October 1, 1525?) WA 17, 1:437.32–438.4, presented to the International Congress for Luther Research, Copenhagen, 2002.

6. Kenneth Hagen, "From Testament to Covenant in the Early Sixteenth Century,"

selves, visible upon the earth, that forms His earthly body. The One who is the hidden Lord of the cosmos manifests here in the assembly as the Head of the Body, the Bridegroom of the Bride.

As boldly as these things are asserted, we once again observe Luther's refusal to inquire into the mechanism of these ineffable mysteries; the asserted beliefs or articulations of the faith describe and communicate, but do not (even try to) penetrate with comprehension.[7] We see as well the insistence that *fiducia* cannot be divorced from *notitia,* any more than Christ can be separated from His body, any more than the Incarnate Son can be severed from His Father and their Spirit. Such inseparability of the various articulations of the one faith provides the sense of Luther's affirmation that "everything is to be believed completely and without exception, or nothing is to be believed. The Holy Spirit does not let himself be divided or cut up . . ."[8] — the thought that von Harnack impugned as a kind of fundamentalist demand for blind faith in a laundry-list of supernatural facts. When taken in context, as we now see, it means rather a demand within the Eucharistic community for knowing faith in the Christ who is for us, together with His Father and their Spirit. Thus it is hard to imagine a more "catholic" Luther. An interesting question arises out of renewed knowledge of this Luther, here writing in this final will and testament on the creedal belief of the church catholic. In light of the imperatives for ecclesiology that we have drawn from our discussion of the New Perspective on Paul, it runs like this: Can Luther's (not Luther-

---

*Sixteenth Century Journal* 3, no. 1 (April 1972): 1-24, also describes the theological difference between Luther and Zwingli with respect to differing accounts of covenant between them: Luther's *promissio* and Zwingli's *compactum.*

7. "Here . . . one rarely if ever succeeds in making affirmations with ontological import [i.e., truth claims], but rather engages in explaining, defending, analyzing, and regulating the liturgical, kerygmatic, and ethical modes of speech and action within which such [ontological] affirmations from time to time occur. Just as a grammar by itself affirms nothing either true or false regarding the world in which the language is used, but only about language, so theology and doctrine, to the extent that they are second-order activities, assert nothing either true or false about God and his relation to creatures, but only speak about such assertions. These assertions, in turn, cannot be made except when speaking religiously, i.e., when seeking to align oneself and others performatively with what one takes to be most important in the universe by worshiping, promising, obeying, exhorting, preaching." George Lindbeck, *The Nature of Doctrine: Religion and Theology in a Postliberal Age* (Louisville: Westminster/John Knox, 1984), p. 69.

8. "If the ring is broken at one point, it is no longer a perfect ring; it no longer holds together and constantly comes apart." "Brief Confession concerning the Holy Sacrament" (1544) LW 38:307.

anism's) doctrine of justification by faith be a resource also for the Church of Rome today? It seemed at least possible after the Second Vatican Council.[9]

## Heresiarch as Teacher of the Church?

In the wake of the changes in the Roman Catholic Church caused by that Council's Decree on Ecumenism, *Unitatis Redintegratio,* and on the basis of decades of Catholic Luther research that had preceded, Cardinal Willebrand, the Vatican's ecumenical officer, made a historic statement before the Lutheran World Federation assembly at Évian in 1970. There he spoke of Martin Luther as a "Teacher of the Church."[10] This statement could only have meant that the Roman Catholic Church would now be involved in a long-term, necessarily difficult process of fundamentally reevaluating its previous judgment on the Reformer. In listening to Luther's voice as it was being recovered in Luther research, especially of Roman Catholic scholarship during the course of the twentieth century,[11] Roman Catholics were in fact discovering in Luther nothing less than an authentic doctor of the church, including today's Roman Catholic Church. How did this reassessment come about?

It did not come about in a vacuum. It was in fact built upon a new, far truer image of the historical Martin Luther overthrowing nearly 500 years of accumulated misrepresentations. It is no exaggeration to state that beginning in Luther's own life, already in the time following the publication of the Ninety-Five Theses in late 1517, polemicists like Johannes Eck created a monstrous image of Martin Luther as a morally derelict and diabolically inspired opponent of all Christian authority and tradition (a script the irascible Luther was pleased to perform on occasion to taunt opponents in anti-papist polemic). Such malicious caricatures of Luther's person as well as of his teaching falsely determined the Roman Catholic perception of the Reformer for the future. The Jesuit theologian and

9. Portions of the following pages are abstracted from Paul R. Hinlicky, "Process, Convergence, Declaration: Reflections on Doctrinal Dialogue," *The Cresset* 64, no. 6 (Pentecost 2001): 13-18.

10. *The Documents of Vatican II,* ed. Walter M. Abbott, S.J. (New York: American Press, 1966).

11. For an overview and evaluation, see *Lutherforschung im 20. Jarhundert: Rückblick-Bilanz-Ausblick,* ed. Rainer Vinke (Mainz: Philipp von Zabern, 2004), pp. 191-260.

contemporary ecumenist, Jared Wicks, writes at the beginning of his significant study, *Luther and His Spiritual Legacy:*

> In 1549, three years after Luther's death, a German Catholic writer, Johann Cochlaeus, published his *Commentary on Luther's Actions and Writings,* a book that deeply influenced the image of Luther held by Catholics for more than two centuries. Sad to say, Cochlaeus wrote in the white heat of excited anger against Luther. By his own admission, Cochlaeus set out to make his readers feel revulsion toward Luther. . . . Cochlaeus had an eye especially for passages in which Luther attacked Catholic doctrines and institutions. The excerpts [from Luther's writings which Cochlaeus reprinted in his *Commentary*] were to show the readers a Luther quite reckless in polemics, clearly destructive of Church, clergy, and Sacraments. Cochlaeus depicts Luther as the cause of the violence in Germany in 1525, when the peasants revolted. . . . Luther, according to Cochlaeus, was not even consistent, but kept changing his views as occasion suggested. . . . In spite of the disorganization and carelessness [of his *Commentary*], Cochlaeus's image of the devilishly destructive Luther dominated Catholic popular understanding of Luther for centuries.[12]

In the *Joint Commentary on the Augsburg Confession,* theologians Müller and Pfnür make the same point:

> One cannot overestimate the importance for the traditional Catholic view of the Reformation and of the Lutheran position of the catalogs of heresies drawn chiefly from the statements by the Reformers of the first half of the 1520s, principally by Johannes Cochlaeus, Johannes Eck, Johannes Faber, and Alphonsus de Castro. According to this view, the focal point of the Lutheran doctrine and the "source and origin of almost all other heresies" is Luther's doctrine "that faith alone is suffi-

---

12. Jared Wicks, S.J., *Luther and His Spiritual Legacy* (Collegeville, MN: Michael Glazer, 1984), pp. 15-16. Wicks goes on to identify "three serious, central points of doctrine" where he finds even the "substance of Luther's positions erroneous." These are enumerated as Luther's doctrine of complete human passivity in conversion (the "bondage of the will"); Luther's rejection of the Eucharist as "a prayer of praise and dedication addressed to the Father in the Holy Spirit" (the "Mass as sacrifice"); and finally, Luther's claim that Scripture has "a power of self-interpretation" (the "perspicuity of Scripture"). Wicks, *Spiritual Legacy,* pp. 29-30.

cient for the salvation of everyone." The Reformation way of speaking about faith alone justifying was interpreted as teaching that the Sacraments accomplish nothing, that good works are superfluous, and that nothing can endanger faith. This view was supported by quotations of exaggerated Reformation statements taken out of context, and often obtained second or third-hand.[13]

Wicks points out that not until the 1930s did a Roman Catholic scholar in Germany, Adolph Herte, publish historical studies which demonstrated that "Cochlaeus had intentionally sketched Luther in the worst possible light so as to arouse suspicion and hatred toward his person."[14] Roman Catholic Luther research since then represents a sustained effort to overcome the traditional image of Luther and engage his message and theology fairly and accurately. Can one say the same for Lutheran theological attention to Roman Catholic thought?

The prospect of a new Rome motivated Jaroslav Pelikan's seminal *The Riddle of Roman Catholicism,* which broke just this ground when it was published in 1959 in anticipation of the Second Vatican Council. The real enigma that Roman Catholicism has been to Protestants was opened up to understanding as Pelikan sympathetically exposed the genuinely evangelical, biblical, and ecumenical value of Roman Catholicism's commitment to the visible unity of the church. The exclusive claim by the Church of Rome to possess catholicity should no longer, Pelikan argued, blind Protestants to the Lord's will for visible unity. Why? The reform of Roman Catholicism can be anticipated at the approaching council. "Rome has never really listened to the witness of the Reformation,"[15] but that very deafness is now about to be overcome. At the same time, it needs to be acknowledged that the state of Protestantism is equally unhealthy on account of four hundred some years in reaction against the value of catholicity manifest in the visible unity of Eucharistic fellowship. Protestantism has consequently disintegrated into hundreds of competing sects, deeply

---

13. *Confessing the One Faith: A Joint Commentary on the Augsburg Confession by Lutheran and Catholic Theologians,* ed. George W. Forell and James F. McCue (Minneapolis: Augsburg, 1982), p. 134.

14. Wicks, *Spiritual Legacy,* p. 16.

15. Jaroslav Pelikan, *The Riddle of Roman Catholicism* (New York: Abingdon, 1959), p. 212. Pelikan wrote a complementary study of Lutheranism's ecumenical potential *Obedient Rebels: Catholic Substance and Protestant Principle in Luther's Reformation* (New York and Evanston: Harper & Row, 1964).

polarized into modernist and fundamentalist wings with respect to Christianity's relation to the modern world. Pelikan's book taught many Protestants to think positively for the first time of the authentic Christian values uniquely preserved in Roman Catholicism, values which Protestants needed to recover.

Pelikan taught Lutherans especially to think of the "tragic necessity of the Reformation": "Partisans on both sides have difficulty acknowledging that the Reformation was indeed a tragic necessity. Roman Catholics agree that it was tragic, because it separated many millions from the true church; but they cannot see that it was really necessary. Protestants agree that it was necessary, because the Roman church was so corrupt; but they cannot see that it was such a great tragedy after all."[16] Such partisanship belongs to a past that today needs to be overcome, Pelikan urged. Lutherans in particular should think of themselves as "evangelical catholics," as the Swedish Bishop Söderblom had proposed.[17] Years later, the same Pelikan would write in correction of Adolph von Harnack's influential interpretation of the "end of dogma" in the Reformer, "Luther had always valued such continuity with ancient doctrine, above all with the creeds of the ancient church. . . . In opposition to the Anabaptist rejection of infant baptism, Luther argued for the correctness of this practice from its continuity throughout Christian history, going so far as to declare: 'We confess that under the papacy there is the correct Holy Scripture, correct baptism, the correct Sacrament of the Altar, the correct keys for the forgiveness of sins, the correct office of the ministry, the correct catechism. . . .' He was able to take over a medieval Eucharistic hymn celebrating the identity of the body in Sacrament with the body born of Mary, adding stanzas of his own."[18]

It is not an exaggeration then to see this new historical scholarship on both sides opening up to theological dialogue and disputation the theological claims and reformatory proposals of the historic Martin Luther. These claims and proposals of course had been violently foreclosed in his own time by the efforts of the local pro-papist party, together with the Curia in Rome, who lobbied for and eventually obtained, to Luther's shock and dismay, the Bull of Excommunication in 1519. Yet during the decade

16. Pelikan, *The Riddle*, p. 46.

17. Pelikan, *The Riddle*, p. 75.

18. Jaroslav Pelikan, *The Christian Tradition: A History of the Development of Doctrine* (Chicago and London: University of Chicago Press, 1975), IV:176-77.

between this violent and premature cessation of debate and the Diet at Augsburg in 1530 before the Emperor, the territories under the influence of Luther's theology nevertheless proceeded with the "reform of certain abuses," as the CA would later put it. These reforms included offering the Sacrament in both kinds for the laity, permitting the marriage of priests, liturgical reform that eliminated the use of the Mass as a private, expiatory sacrifice that could be sold, suspension of many regulations regarding mandatory confession of sins, distinction of foods, and permission for the renunciation of monastic vows that had been taken before the age of maturity. To opponents these "reforms" rather appeared as renegade destruction of all authority and tradition. With the issue of the papal bull of Luther's excommunication at the end of 1519, there was in their eyes no further need of discussion, debate, or deliberation. Luther was condemned and the matter was in principle settled; the only issue was enforcement and conformity, or at worst, containment of the influence of Luther's heretical theology. The polemics of the opponents therefore aimed at discrediting Luther in the public eye through whatever propagandistic distortions of his meaning or slanders of his reputation could be mustered.

Pelikan summed up the beginning of Counter-Reformation thinking among Roman Catholics this way: The prime mover was the "heresiarch" Luther. Although he had said some sensible things at the beginning, he "steadily deteriorated" and became "the first to break the bond of peace and unity. . . . The whole business depends on the one man, namely, the author of the schism": Luther himself had become the chief issue, "Martin the heretic, Martin the schismatic, Martin the prince of utter pride and temerity"; and he remained so also after his death.[19] Luther qua person, not qua *doctor ecclesiae,* became the issue. As much as contemporary Roman Catholic scholarship deplores such malicious, willfully ignorant characterization of Luther, it will be necessary to rehearse in even further detail this polemic in order to appreciate the true nature of the contemporary, now precarious ecumenical hope of a new Rome. As we shall see, Joseph Cardinal Ratzinger, who is now Pope Benedict XVI, in an important respect *sustained* the traditional Catholic objection to the *person* of Luther against this possibility of receiving Luther instead as *teacher.* Indeed, this acute objection to *Luther* as teacher also for the Church of Rome forms the specific objection that this chapter must take up and meet. But we still have some spadework ahead us before we can state Ratzinger's objection precisely.

19. Pelikan, *The Christian Tradition,* IV:246.

Presumably in a doctrinal dialogue between churches, ecclesial communities, or confessions aimed at reconciliation and restoration of Eucharistic fellowship, an individual person, even of Martin Luther's stature, is not or should not be the issue, positively or negatively. This was the principled position of someone like Arthur Carl Piepkorn on the Lutheran side.[20] Overcoming the traditional Roman Catholic perspective which focused on Luther personally as the "heresiarch" is likewise a matter of ecumenical principle, not just rectification of the historic injustice of a biased, hostile, manipulated image of Luther with all the centuries of damage it dragged along behind it. Throughout this book, we have argued that the corresponding Protestant idea that the Reformation was a "breakthrough" or a "breakout" that can chiefly be blamed or credited to Luther's personal religious experience is equally false. Modern Protestants especially have seen the issue in this same way, thinking of Luther as their hero of faith, or hero of conscience, a solitary religious and/or cultural genius who broke the regressive shackles of the authoritarian past and opened the way to a progressive future of freedom.[21] Although positively evaluated, this neo-Protestant interpretation of the Reformation as Luther's liberating act of personal heroism is the obverse image of the traditional Roman Catholic view of the schism as due to the personal villainy of Luther. In either such approach, however, *the essentially Christian and ecclesial nature of this great and terrible event of Western Church history is obscured.* But when that ecclesial context is obscured, the unfinished business of the Reformation's theological proposals for the renewal and reform of the one church and so their reception by Roman Catholicism, that is to say, the ecumenical intention of Reformation theology, is not sufficiently grasped. It is Luther as creedal Christian, Luther as teacher and *doctor ecclesiae* that matters here.

This is a serious failing with great contemporary import. What is at stake in the vision of a new Rome is atonement in Royce's sense, the overcoming of a bad history with a new one that redeems that past. This new history takes place in part by the new event of Roman Catholics hearing the authentic voice of Martin Luther as a "teacher of the Church," as Willebrand said, i.e., as a dogmatic resource for the healing and reintegra-

---

20. Harry McSorley, "Use and Underuse of Luther in the Lutheran–Roman Catholic Dialogues in the United States," *Lutheran Theological Seminary Bulletin* 71 (Winter 1991): 3.

21. See Paul Hinlicky, "Luther and Liberalism," in *A Report from the Front Lines: Conversations on Public Theology. A Festschrift in Honor of Robert Benne,* ed. Michael Shahan (Grand Rapids: Eerdmans, 2009), pp. 91-97.

tion of the one church. Luther's theology might provide an aid to unity — provided we can free our minds enough to discover and take up the originally ecumenical intention of renewal and reform. The scholarly investigation of Luther's theology by Roman Catholics in the past 75 years is a major catalyst of this event and possibility. But another chapter in the writing of that new history would be along the lines of the project of this book, demoting Luther on the Protestant side as Hero of Faith in order also to regain him as teacher of the common, that is, the Catholic faith. Thus we next review the opening to this possibility created by the Second Vatican Council and the summons to doctrinal dialogue that ensued in order to set the context in which Ratzinger posed his objection.

## The Achievement of the Second Vatican Council

Christian "discord," the Second Vatican Council's *Decree on Ecumenism* maintained, "openly contradicts the will of Christ, provides a stumbling block to the world and inflicts damage on the most holy cause of proclaiming the good news to every creature."[22] The *Decree on Ecumenism* therefore mandated work aimed at new resolutions of the historic impasses in doctrine through the method of dialogue. The method of dialogue seeks to "eliminate words, judgments, and actions which do not respond to the condition of separated brethren with truth and fairness"; instead, it seeks "a truer knowledge and more just appreciation of the teaching and religious life of both Communions." Finally, it leads each to self-examination in face of Christ's will, so that "wherever necessary, [each will] undertake with vigor the task of renewal and reform."[23] The particular goal of ecumenical dialogue is to overcome the *doctrinal* division between the churches, i.e., the divide in *official* teaching concerning the gospel. The dialogue envisioned is between churches, not individuals, concerning official teaching, not popular ideas. Roman Catholicism by this commitment to doctrinal dialogue began to recognize and acknowledge the existence of other, separated Christians as *"eccesial communities,"* whose teaching pertains to the common Christian gospel. Rome thus ceased to regard Protestants solely as misled individuals who ought to return to the bosom of Mother Church.

22. *The Documents of Vatican II*, p. 341.
23. *The Documents of Vatican II*, p. 341.

In the Lutheran–Roman Catholic dialogue in North America, Catholic theologian Harry McSorley, whose study of *De servo arbitrio* we took note of in the Appendix to Chapter Five, commented in the dialogue on "Eucharist and Ministry" that in the *Decree on Ecumenism*, ". . . for the first time the Catholic Church speaks officially on the Lord's Supper celebrated by the separated Christian communities in the West. . . . This Decree did not say that these liturgies are simply invalid or non-sacraments because they are not led by 'legitimate' ministers. On the contrary, the drafter of the decree for the Secretariat for Promoting Christian unity explicitly turned back the proposal of 152 council fathers who wished to have the decree say: 'especially because of a defect of the sacrament of orders [these separated Christian communities of the West] do not have the reality of the Eucharist.' Thirteen of these bishops gave as their reason that, in the absence of orders, there is neither the full nor partial reality of the Eucharist but only a non-efficacious sign. This view, widely held by Catholics prior to Vatican II, but lacking foundation in the official doctrinal statements of the church, was repudiated by the drafter of the decree."[24] Ecumenical dialogue thus presupposed in some real but not-yet-defined form the common dignity of the "ecclesial communities" involved. By the same token, it implied that the Roman Catholic Church is not the whole church. In the same North American dialogue on "Eucharist and Ministry," Catholic theologian Kilian McDonnell interpreted a famous statement from Vatican II's *Constitution on the Church,* which says that the mystical Body of Christ "*subsists* in the Catholic Church": "In setting aside the word *est* [of a previous draft] and substituting the word *subsistit,* the council was able to express the identification between the church which Christ founded and the Roman Catholic church, without making the absolute claim of being the only manifestation of that church. The move from *est* to *subsistit* is clearly a move to loosen up the exclusive claim of the Roman church to be the one and only manifestation of Christ's church."[25] Yet this "loosening" inevitably im-

---

24. *Lutherans and Catholics in Dialogue IV,* p. 135; hereafter cited as *LCDUSA* by volume and page number. *Lutherans and Catholics in Dialogue I-III,* ed. Paul C. Empie and T. Austin Murphy (Minneapolis: Augsburg, n.d.); *Lutherans and Catholics in Dialogue IV: Eucharist and Ministry* (USA National Committee of the Lutheran World Federation and the Bishops' Committee for Ecumenical and Interreligious Affairs, 1970); *Lutherans and Catholics in Dialogue V: Papal Primacy and the Universal Church,* ed. Paul C. Empie and T. Austin Murphy (Minneapolis: Augsburg, 1974); *Lutherans and Catholics in Dialogue VIII: The One Mediator, the Saints, and Mary,* ed. H. George Anderson, J. Francis Stafford, and Joseph A. Burgess (Minneapolis: Augsburg, 1992).

25. *LCDUSA IV:*313.

plies that the Church of Rome also shares in the defectiveness of the divided church, having lost fellowship with the churches of the Reformation, not to mention those of the East.

The new ecumenical attitude aimed at doctrinal reconciliation through the process of dialogue between Christian communions also derives from the transformed state of the church in modern, secular society. The renunciation of resort to the secular sword at the First Vatican Council and the positive theological and moral evaluation of religious liberty at Vatican II came to expression in the *Decree on Religious Liberty,* which excluded on the grounds of revelation itself the possibility of resorting to coercion when dialogue and persuasion fail: "Man's response to God in faith must be free. Therefore no one is to be forced to embrace the Christian faith against his own will. . . . God calls men to serve Him in spirit and in truth. Hence they are bound in conscience but they stand under no compulsion. God has regard for the dignity of the human person whom He Himself created; man is to be guided by his own judgment and he is to enjoy freedom."[26] This affirmation of religious liberty in civil society does not directly touch upon intra-Christian theological dialogue between churches. But, given the resort to persecution and religious war in the aftermath of the Reformation, it points to a dramatically changed context in which ecumenical dialogue becomes thinkable.

More theologically, mention must also be made of Vatican II's *Constitution on the Sacred Liturgy,* which supported the movement for liturgical renewal, along with the corresponding return to Scripture and the Fathers. In one of the first Lutheran–Roman Catholic dialogues in the United States, Roman Catholic theologian Godfrey Diekman emphasized the Council's new theology of worship as an ecumenical resource that roots all the Sacraments in "the Paschal [Easter] mysteries," in "Christ the High Priest." Hence, he stressed, "sacraments are our personal faith-encounter with Christ in the priestly assembly."[27] Some years later, Roman Catholic theologian Avery Dulles envisioned Lutheran–Roman Catholic reconciliation proceeding on the basis of liturgical renewal. He wrote about a "new Catholicism" less captivated by the "objectifying categories of the Scholastic tradition," and "more strongly oriented toward mystery and symbol." This new Catholicism, he predicted, would succeed "in transcending the impasses of the sixteenth century and inaugurating a fruitful dialogue with

26. *The Documents of Vatican II,* pp. 689-90.
27. *LCDUSA I-III:*69.

Lutheranism." Dulles could even imagine a renewal of the preaching of Christ within Roman Catholicism inspired by distinctively Lutheran themes. "Both Roman Catholicism and Lutheranism have sought to steer a middle course between antinomianism and legalism. According to each tradition, the law of God imposes a genuine obligation, but it must not be allowed to preclude the word of pardon and grace that comes to us in Christ without our deserving it and hence, in a certain sense, in spite of the law which condemns us. A theology of law and Gospel, therefore, can be, by Catholic standards, fully orthodox."[28] When we bear in mind that the Reformation was essentially a movement of liturgical renewal and reform, chiefly concerned with what actually happened in the church service, this movement from the side of the "new Catholicism" seemed promising indeed.

Finally, the Second Vatican Council's work of rethinking the nature of the church as a communion, *communio ecclesiology,* is noteworthy. In the fifth round of the North American dialogue, Catholic theologian Patrick Burns explained the new thinking about the Catholic Church as a "communion of communions." He began by affirming that the principle of unity in any church fellowship is "the saving presence of Christ in Word and Sacrament." Such communion with the really present Christ requires awareness in each congregation of its own "essential relationship to the other local Christian communities through the world," where Christ is also present. This relation in and through Christ is expressed in the community of their bishops/pastors as a communion of communions. In turn, there exists one pastor among the community of bishops devoted to the whole, i.e., the pope.[29] This ecclesiology of *communio* lends itself to ecumenical flexibility and conciliation because the concept of *communio* is far more relational than the legal-juridical categories of traditional Roman Catholic thought. It allows for various sorts of relationships. For example, Roman Catholics in the U.S. dialogue on Mary and the Saints could recall that (just as traditional Lutherans held), "*full* ecclesial communion would involve agreement with regard to all truths that either church holds to be binding in faith or inseparable from the gospel." At the same time, however, they recalled that "it is Catholic teaching that a measure of communion already exists between Catholic and Lutheran churches"[30] because of

28. *LCDUSA IV*:276-77.
29. *LCDUSA V*:152.
30. *LCDUSA VIII*:123.

the common baptism into Christ and the common confession of the Incarnation and the Trinity made in the Nicene Creed. This flexibility opens up possibilities for degrees of fellowship in spite of the lack of Lutheran assent, for instance, to the modern Marian and Papal dogmas. This thinking about the church as communion around Word and Sacrament thus builds a bridge across what previously were regarded as impassible chasms.

These positions of the Second Vatican Council on ecumenism, religious liberty, the sacred liturgy, and *communio* ecclesiology were the presuppositions of the forty plus years of Lutheran–Roman Catholic dialogue that followed. Harding Meyer of the Lutheran World Federation's Ecumenical Institute in Strasbourg recounted the enthusiasm with which this concept of dialogue was welcomed after Vatican II: "One spoke no longer 'about' them but rather 'with them' as partners. *Par cum pari,* equal to equal, this was the great new motto. It meant that before talking to the other one had to listen to them: to their convictions, their concerns, their fears, their experiences. And the goal of dialogue was to affirm together — rather than over against each other — what each wanted to affirm. What finally could be affirmed together could not be known in advance. The dialogue process itself had to answer that question. Thus the dialogue was an eminently open manner of talking and dealing with one another."[31] Of course, such dialogue had before it the enormous challenge of overcoming 450 years of separation, mutual hostility, and new historical developments. Careful, historical scholarship, good will, and the perception of somehow sharing in the common apostolic faith worked to clarify the historic disputes and to effect what is called in ecumenical parlance "convergence."

Convergence in doctrine does not mean a fully harmonious agreement in all aspects. Rather, convergence denotes the discovery of new formulations of teaching that cease to be mutually contradictory and so cease to form independent causes of the division of the church. In other words, the goal of dialogue is to reformulate teaching in such ways that both sides affirm what each holds to be essential but avoids offending against what the other affirms to be essential. Such reformulations presuppose that a sufficient basis of unity already exists in the apostolic faith in the Incarnation and the Trinity, as defined by the Nicene Creed; they also presuppose that in the course of history the church has witnessed a legitimate variety of theological interpretations of the common faith. So a distinction is

---

31. Harding Meyer, "The Ecumenical Dialogues: Situations, Problems, Perspectives," *Pro Ecclesia* 3, no. 1 (Winter 1994): 25.

made between doctrine or dogma, which is ecumenically binding interpretation of revelation, and various theologies, which are contextual attempts to interpret the dogmatic content of the Christian faith in a systematic way to a specific audience. As McSorley put it in the third round of the
U.S. Lutheran–Roman Catholic dialogue: "Christians are not in full communion when they disagree on binding dogmas of faith. It is one of the
tasks of ecumenical theological dialogue to overcome such dogmatic disunity between churches. But this is not to say that theological unity must
be sought. A variety of theologies can legitimately be developed within the
one confession of faith."[32] The burden of proof is thereby shifted. "To have
the right to live in separate churches, one would have to be sure . . . that
one is clearly in disagreement about the truth" (Karl Rahner). The American dialogue on *Mary and the Saints* reiterated this understanding: "The
goal of ecumenical dialogue is not to eliminate all differences, but to make
certain that the remaining differences are consonant with a fundamental
consensus in the apostolic faith and therefore legitimate or at least tolera-
ble. Reconciliation is a process admitting of many degrees, leading up to
full fellowship in faith. . . ."[33] In a doctrinally reconciling church, there assuredly would still be vigorous theological contention about the truth of
the one gospel, one Lord, one faith, one baptism.[34]

These examples show that *ecumenical dialogue is not a way of ignor-
ing or suppressing doctrinal differences but rather of making them constructive by taking them up anew in a mutual way, in the strength of the shared
Christian meta-doctrines, so to say, concerning the person of Christ and the
Trinity — and now, we may add, the convergence on justification* represented by the Joint Declaration on Justification in 1999. Two notes are per-

---

32. *LCDUSA I-III*:24-25.

33. *LCDUSA VIII*:55.

34. We can further illustrate this with an example from the aforementioned dialogue
on *Mary and the Saints*. It asks the two churches to engage questions such as: "Does the
Catholic Church *require* its members to invoke saints? Could Lutherans live in union with a
church in which this practice was encouraged but not imposed? Could the Catholic Church
live in union with Lutherans who preach Christ as sole Mediator with the conviction that the
invocation of saints will thereby recede?" *LCDUSA VIII*:56. In another place, the dialogue
states, ". . . in spite of our real differences [on invocation of Mary and the Saints], we are not
as far apart as it seemed at first glance. From a common basis of belief Catholics challenge
Lutherans to give clearer expression in ecclesial practice to the *koinonia* of saints which includes the living and the dead in Christ. At the same time, Lutherans challenge Catholics to
give clearer expression to the sole mediatorship of Christ in the devotional practices involving the saints and Mary . . ." *LCDUSA VIII*:122.

tinent here. First, the *Joint Declaration* does not simply regard the condemnations of the sixteenth century as wrong. Rather it says that in principle these condemnations said something true, i.e., pointed out a danger that had to be identified and rejected. What is being said today is that these, in principle, correct condemnations do not apply to today's ecumenical partners, who do not sanction these errors. Second, one may wonder if the *Joint Declaration* does not point to a better solution to the teaching on justification than either side had traditionally imagined, namely, that the previously contending ideas that "faith alone justifies" and that "faith justifies by its active love" can be brought together because *Christ himself is present for us and active in us by faith.* This has been the central contention of Tuomo Mannermaa, whose seminal study of Luther's second Galatians commentary in fact lies behind the Joint Declaration's reformulations of the classic Lutheran position. He had written: "It has become a commonplace to assert that the thought of justifying faith is alone the center of Luther's thought. This conception is in need of revision. Justifying faith is as such according to the Reformer a *fides abstracta*, an abstract faith. It is not the content of the common Christian life and faith, which first finds its own expression as *fides concreta* or *fides incarnata*. Faith always together with love forms incarnate, concrete faith."[35] The sixteenth-century doctrinal formulations were in spite of their best intentions *anthropocentric*, focused on what transpires in the justified person rather than on the agency of the crucified and risen Lord in his people. In its *Christ-centered* reformulation of the teaching on justification, the *Joint Declaration* points us to a better solution than previously known.

---

35. Tuomo Mannermaa, *Der im Glauben Gegenwärtige Christus: Rechtfertigung und Vergottung. Zum ökumenischen Dialog,* Arbeiten zur Geschichte und Theologie des Luthertums, Neue Folge Band 8 (Hannover: Lutherisches Verlagshaus, 1989), p. 104, my translation. So also Dietmar Lage on *fides incarnata:* "Works of love are a necessary component of the very meaning of faith. Love of the neighbor is understood as the inherent natural consequence of the structure of faith itself. The *necessitas* aspect, the theological impetus to act, is preserved within Luther's conception of *sola fide* as a *fides incarnata*. Faith is thereby denied the status of a universal Protestant virtue in its own right and it becomes illegitimate to conceive of faith as, itself, a good work. This understanding of *sola fide* as *fides incarnata* clearly invalidates the critique of Luther's doctrine of faith and works made by Karlstadt and the Anabaptists." Dietmar Lage, *Martin Luther's Christology and Ethics: Texts and Studies in Religion,* vol. 45 (Lewiston, NY: Edwin Mellen Press, 1990), p. 153. *Fides abstracta* is "forensic justification, 'cheap' grace, a 'sweet' Christ and a privation or spiritualization of faith. Such a person reduces works to an option within the Christian ethos which ultimately turns faith into a form of quietism" (p. 154).

## Ratzinger's Objection[36]

In the ferment of the discussions stemming from the Second Vatican Council just described (although long before the Joint Declaration on Justification), there arose during the 1970s an "impassioned debate," as then Regensburg theologian Josef Ratzinger wrote, of a "Catholic recognition of the *Confessio Augustana*," which would lead to "a reciprocal recognition of ministries and, in consequence, the formation of a eucharistic community, thus, after 450 years of separation, healing the rift that began with the misunderstanding of this text [the CA], the real purpose of which was in fact unification."[37] Ratzinger then proceeded to delineate an incisive series of

36. Critical as I shall be of Ratzinger in this discussion, I should like to note for the record that I regard him as "my pope" too. See Paul R. Hinlicky, "A Lutheran Encyclical: Benedict's Deus Caritas Est," August 2006 *Journal of Lutheran Ethics* (online) vol. 6, issue 8. In *First Things* (October 2006), the late Richard John Neuhaus commented on my review as follows: "In my commentary on Pope Benedict's first encyclical, *Deus Caritas Est* (*First Things,* May 2006), I noted some striking parallels with Martin Luther's treatment of the 'right hand' and 'left hand' rule of God and the distinction between love and justice. I opined that other theologians might want to explore that aspect of the encyclical more fully. Which is just what Paul Hinlicky, professor of Luther studies at Roanoke College, Virginia, has done. Writing in the *Journal of Lutheran Ethics,* he says: 'Assured faith, certainly faith in the love of God in spite of contrary experience. The theology of the cross in the face of incomprehensible suffering. The freedom of the Christian — also from political correctness. The simple, direct ministry of charity to the neighbor in need. The two-kingdoms theology requiring the patient, political, non-utopian work for justice in society. The redemption and sanctification of eros rather than its suppression or renunciation. The primacy of grace over human choice. The real presence of Christ in the Eucharist as the source of Christian discipleship. The firm rejection of terrorism and fanaticism in religion. Faith forming love in the image of the Crucified. All this 'taught with authority, unlike the scribes and the Pharisees.' Shall I go on? Is it any wonder that Lutherans who have any substantial memory of their own tradition slip away to the bosom of the erstwhile foe where that theological tradition, though not (yet) honored by name, is nevertheless honored in fact? It is no wonder. What is a wonder is the Lord of the Church, who works stunning reversals. Prof. Hinlicky sums up with this: 'Benedict is our pope, too, even though we remain "separated" sisters and brothers belonging to an "ecclesiastical community." I hope many of us "separated" will read this encyclical and ones to come. There are perhaps sticking points that others will find more important than the deep commonalities with our forgotten tradition that I have uncovered in this review. No doubt they exist. But it ought deeply to perplex us that our tradition is better preserved today in the Roman Catholic Church than in our own nominally Lutheran Church in America.'"

37. Joseph Cardinal Ratzinger, *Principles of Catholic Theology: Building Stones for a Fundamental Theology,* trans. Sister Mary Frances McCarthy, S.N.D. (San Francisco: Ignatius, 1987), p. 218.

fundamental objections to this possibility. He was undoubtedly right to maintain that once the genuine possibility of reunion materialized in the 1970s, it actually "caused both sides to be uneasy about the threatened dissolution of what was peculiarly their own and led, consequently, to a cooling of the ecumenical climate."[38] He was also right as a result to maintain that "unification requires of the whole faith community a thorough state of inner readiness,"[39] which cannot be coerced by mandates either of bishops or of theologians. Instead, we have before us "a very demanding process" of working through real difficulties to find the "starting point of a new way."[40] This is the task that Ratzinger commended "as a goal for ecumenism and hence as an indication of the right course for it to follow."[41] These affirmations form bookends to the series of difficulties that Ratzinger then enumerated. What, then, given the new atmosphere described in the preceding section, are the serious objections to Luther as resource according to the theologian who now sits on the chair of St. Peter?

First, Ratzinger raised the objection of the so-called ecclesial "density" of the "ecclesiological communities that trace their origin to Luther": To what extent, he asked, is the CA to be "regarded as a valid and adequate expression"[42] of their faith and life? The question is necessary because the Lutheran "movement continued to develop with the result that the CA became just one confessional text among many others. . . ."[43] The particular stone of stumbling is Luther's own composition, the *Smalcald Articles,* "in which the Pope is designated as Antichrist and an understanding with Rome is declared impossible in itself and unthinkable."[44] The underlying issue that comes to the surface with this query about the relative weight of the CA is the extent to which "Luther's writings are to be regarded as the real foundation of the Reformation, the normative basis for interpretation. . . ."[45] Ratzinger alludes here to the Catholic Luther scholar Peter Manns's interesting, contemporary objection to recognition of the CA as an attempt "to bypass Luther," hence as ecumenism on the cheap.[46]

38. Ratzinger, *Principles,* p. 218.
39. Ratzinger, *Principles,* pp. 218-19.
40. Ratzinger, *Principles,* p. 228.
41. Ratzinger, *Principles,* p. 218.
42. Ratzinger, *Principles,* p. 219.
43. Ratzinger, *Principles,* p. 220.
44. Ratzinger, *Principles,* p. 220.
45. Ratzinger, *Principles,* p. 220.
46. Peter Manns protested that talk in the 1970s about recognizing the Augsburg

Ratzinger regards Manns's objection as beside the point, since the CA is the "official ecclesiological text." But, he continues, Manns's objection does call attention to two important problems: (1) the distinction between theological opinion and church doctrine is not drawn so clearly in Lutheranism as in Catholicism, thus rendering a real meeting of partners on the same level difficult; (2) the historical fact that Luther "regarded himself not merely as a theologian but as possessed of an *auctoritas* comparable to that of the Apostle Paul," just as Lutherans have in fact looked upon him "as a kind of prophetic founder." In this way, in spite of Ratzinger's official focus on the CA, the issue of Luther's person reintrudes in his objection to Catholic recognition of the CA. A thorny problem becomes visible: "According to what norm is Luther himself to be read and interpreted — solely according to the ecclesiological norm [i.e., the CA] or, in a more revolutionary fashion, as fundamentally critical of the Church and her institutions?"

Ratzinger sees here "contradictory possibilities of development, with the options of deciding in one direction or the other."[47] Yet, since history does not have the last word, "new steps" are conceivable that "leave the past behind" or "assimilat[e] from the legacy whatever is of permanent value." Clearly, what is not of value but rather constitutes an enduring objection to Luther as common resource is his personal claim to *auctoritas* on the level of Paul the Apostle, and his corresponding status in the eyes of Lutherans as prophetic founder of a new church. Were that not difficulty enough, Ratzinger continued with an incisive critique of the CA itself, questioning both its actual authority in Lutheran churches as "binding and definitive teaching of the Church as Church"[48] and the compatibility of its content with Catholic doctrine.

In connection with the former, Ratzinger raised an acute objection to the "one-sided *sola Scriptura*" principle, which he argued could hold only so long as Luther and Melanchthon ascribed infallible certainty to their interpretation of the Bible. Yet, as exegesis continues in every new age and situation, and so "the ambiguity of history makes its appearance," the prob-

---

Confession "was clearly directed against Luther as developed by its Catholic promoters." *Luther's Ecumenical Significance: An Interconfessional Consultation,* ed. Peter Manns and Harding Meyer in collaboration with Carter Lindberg and Harry McSorley (Philadelphia: Fortress, 1984), p. 4. Manns's conviction that the rediscovered Luther is neither "Roman" nor "Lutheran" but an "ecumenical authority as against both churches" (p. 18) is searching.

47. Ratzinger, *Principles,* p. 221.
48. Ratzinger, *Principles,* p. 222.

lem of normative tradition reappears; over against the shifting tides of scholarly opinion, the "church teaches and can teach precisely as church." Ratzinger accordingly summoned the Protestant churches to their own "recognition" of the principle of tradition which would in turn "restore the official realm of 'ecclesia' in which official unity" with Rome could be conceivable.[49] All the same, materially, the CA itself is not and cannot be recognized as a Catholic confession of faith and thus as the vehicle for reconciliation between the divided churches.[50] This, Ratzinger argues, becomes unmistakably clear when it is read side by side with the *Confutatio Pontificia,* the response of the papal party to the CA at the Diet of Augsburg. We need to examine the papal Confutation, for in Ratzinger's view, it is in its light that it becomes evident how Luther's *Smalcald Articles* prevail over the ambiguous language of Melanchthon in the CA.

What is Ratzinger pointing at? Melanchthon's distinction in the CA between use and abuse, he argues, obscured the true nature of the conflict (attested at Smalcald), since "for the Catholic Church, what he called *abusus* is, in fact, a part of her faith. But Luther was well aware of what the real issue was." It was "a quarrel in principle and about principles,"[51] not customs or usages. Moreover, the use Melanchthon makes of the subjective principle of faith to discern abuses reduces Catholic ontological affirmation to the level of immediate human consciousness or experience, "the experienced certainty of salvation...."[52] Such psychological reduction in the name of faith is indeed *not* compatible with Catholic doctrine and that explains in turn why all the abiding disputes about the nature of ministry and worship life turn on this Lutheran reductionism, whether formally in the name of the Scripture principle or materially in the name of the subjective principle of faith.[53] In the end, Ratzinger makes but one concession to a genuine abuse registered in the CA: "the combination of spiritual and secular power" in the bishops-princes of that time together with the practice of excommunication. But the fundamental question that emerges from this critique of the CA is that of "binding doctrine in and through the Church," as the "immediate counterpoint of 'gospel'"; this would not de-

---

49. Ratzinger, *Principles,* p. 223. The author's quixotic "The Lutheran Dilemma" (*Pro Ecclesia* 8, no. 4 [Fall 1999]) was an attempt to argue Ratzinger's summons here to the Lutheran World Federation.

50. Ratzinger, *Principles,* p. 227.

51. Ratzinger, *Principles,* p. 224.

52. Ratzinger, *Principles,* p. 225.

53. Ratzinger, *Principles,* p. 226.

prive experience of its meaning, but relativize it in importance by linking it "to the objective teaching of the Church."[54]

Where do we go from here? If we can transcend the matter of Luther's personal defiance of papal authority, or his later self-image as prophet of the end-time, or for that matter the injustice of the papal treatment of Luther (which Ratzinger fails to acknowledge in this discussion, but only alludes to in the final concession to CA XXVIII on the genuine abuse of excommunication by the warlord bishops of the sixteenth century), we can agree with Ratzinger that the fundamental *question of authority in the church is a particular question about the authority of the gospel itself and that binding doctrine in and through the church is and must be warranted by this superior norm of the saving Word of God which doctrine in turn serves.* In other words, if binding doctrine is the immediate counterpoint of the gospel, binding doctrine answers questions like: Why should sinners believe that their sins are forgiven? Why should the dying believe the promise of life? Why should the world believe in the coming of the reign of God, the promised Beloved Community? Is the answer to such questions to be some version of the claim that Christ handed on jurisdiction over the church to Peter and his successors? That is, the *petitio principii* of a mere assertion of authority to which one submits, then to discover the possibility of assured faith? How would that be any better than *sola scriptura,* i.e., that one is to believe because the Bible says so? What is at stake in this dispute is rather the Beloved Community, for the sake of which the church exists in history. The church above all, for its own sake as also for the sake of the world, must ask and answer the "why" question put to the message it bears, the gospel of inclusion in God's coming reign. Probing this question belongs at the heart of critical dogmatics, in the future church life in Euro-America after Christendom, "without emperor, without pope" (Bonhoeffer, i.e., at least as we have known emperor or pope).[55] Even when it is granted that Scripture, creed, and ministry all direct us to believe the gospel, the question remains all the same: Why should Scripture, creed, and ministry do just that? Why is the gospel good and how does it remain news?[56]

Today Roman Catholics and Lutherans are alike confronted with this

54. Ratzinger, *Principles,* p. 226.

55. Cited in Reinhard Hütter, *Suffering Divine Things: Theology as Church Practice,* trans. D. Scott (Grand Rapids: Eerdmans, 2000), pp. 10-11.

56. I learned from my seminary professor, Robert W. Bertram, to put the question of binding doctrine in this way.

larger theological problem of the authority of the Word of God, if neither *sola scriptura* nor an infallible papacy may credibly claim to answer questions that are in immediate counterpoint to the gospel and bind us together in common confession. What is not involved then is an assertion that Scripture should be authoritative over against tradition or human arrangements any more than an assertion that an infallible teaching office should be authoritative over the gospel. Luther, as we have seen, thinks of Scripture, and its normative interpretation by the creeds, as a hermeneutical whole, to which he is unashamed to appeal, the *fides catholica*. But the question is why the particular Word rendered in Scripture, the Gospel of God, ought to be authoritative in the church's life, also over its traditions (including the Bible!) and institutional arrangements. Given that we have already in this book argued the necessity and the possibility of retrieving Luther as *doctor ecclesiae* and leaving behind Luther as prophetic founder of a new religion, hero, and apocalyptic demonizer of the Pope among others, the issue really is and really is to be seen as *Luthers Lehre* (which in fact stands behind the CA as the "real issue," just as Ratzinger sees).

Robert Jenson tried to pose the question in just this way at the time. Recognition of the Augsburg Confession "is not fundamentally," he maintained, "a question of Roman Catholic recognition of the Lutheran denomination."[57] On the contrary, Roman Catholic recognition of the Augsburg Confession could only mean that the polemic which the Augsburg Confession contains in its agitation for church reform in light of the doctrine of the gospel, i.e., justification by faith, has a "legitimate object" also on the Roman Catholic "side of the denominational line." Recognition would mean Roman Catholic acceptance and internalization of the Reformation critique. That would also imply the critique of today's Lutheranism by Reformation theology. Jenson surmised that "Roman Catholic recognition of the Augsburg Confession might even recall official Lutherans to the Augsburg Confession's actual meaning."[58] In Jenson's words: ". . . the object of Roman Catholic consideration and of Lutheran advocacy must be the Augsburg Confession and not the theology of Luther as such. If both sides of ecumenical discussions could keep this rigorously in mind, much would be gained. But just so, it is vital to remember with equal rigor how radical a document

---

57. *The Role of the Augsburg Confession: Catholic and Lutheran Views,* ed. Joseph A. Burgess (Philadelphia: Fortress, 1980).

58. *Catholic and Lutheran Views,* ed. Joseph A. Burgess, p. 163.

the Augsburg Confession is. It was an ecumenical statement and claim, but that does not mean that it was or is a list of existing agreements. It is a proposal to subject all churchly teaching and practice to the critique formulated by the proposition that we are justified by faith alone. Recognition of the Augsburg Confession — by whomever — is recognition of the need and biblical-traditional legitimacy of this critical enterprise."[59] Here Jenson lifts up the so-called hermeneutical function of the doctrine of justification by faith to test the church's practice, as in the Pauline canon of Galatians 6:15-16. This latter is the actual content of *Luthers Lehre,* i.e., not justification as some peculiar theory of the salvation of the individual, but justification as *regula fidei:* in Word and Sacrament and in everything else set forth the good news of Christ clearly, in a manner that does nothing to obscure the all-sufficiency of Christ's saving person and work, but rather lucidly and compellingly sets it forth for faith to appropriate.

To meet Ratzinger's objections, then, to Luther's doctrine so understood as criteriological resource also for the new Rome, it is necessary in what follows to establish the following: (1) that the image of Luther as heretic still lingers in Ratzinger's re-focusing on the person of Luther in his objection to the recognition of the CA, which can be shown by rendering the *Confutatio* itself suspect as a credible statement of Catholic doctrine; (2) that the teaching of the "catholic" Luther on the church as communion accords with the best of recent Catholic ecclesiology while deriving from the center of the Reformer's teaching, the Christological basis of the doctrine of justification by faith in the "joyful exchange." This rejoinder, be it noted, hardly suggests that the institutional objections that Ratzinger has raised against real, existing Lutheranism (Jenson's "the Lutheran denomination") will be refuted by it. On the contrary, it rather will indicate how estranged from Luther are those today who bear false witness by retaining his name for themselves. But that is another matter.

## The Papal Confutation's Evasion of *Luthers Lehre*

The tendency of traditional Roman Catholic polemic has been to blame the schism on the person of Martin Luther, without accepting blame for its own resort to verbal, then physical violence. Luther pointed to this in the conclusion of the problematic *Smalcald Articles:* "they are not now and do

---

59. *Catholic and Lutheran Views,* ed. Joseph A. Burgess, p. 156.

not want to be true bishops. Rather, they are political lords and princes who do not want to preach, teach, baptize, commune, or perform any proper work or office of the church. In addition, they persecute and condemn those who do take up a call to such an office."[60] The connection here between the original demonization of Luther and the corresponding resort to violence has never been adequately grasped on the Catholic side, up to and including Ratzinger's meager concession to the CA on this point. But this tendency already manifests in the first draft of the *Confutatio* of the Augsburg Confession, to which I would especially call attention here.

The stage had been prepared for the *Confutatio* by the 404 Articles of Eck, Luther's decade-long antagonist, who wrote to the Emperor in the months preceding the meeting in Augsburg: "Martin Luther, the Church's enemy within the Church, has refused to heed the admonitions addressed to him by your Majesty and hurled himself into a veritable whirlpool of godlessness: he calls the Pope of Rome the 'Antichrist,' the Church a 'harlot,' the bishops 'worms and idols,' the schools of theology *(studia generalia)* 'synagogues of Satan'; monasteries he calls 'brothels,' theologians 'bats,' secular princes 'louse's eggs, fools, insane drunkards worse than the Turks'. . . . He has fallen into a deep pit of despair; he blasphemes God; he has no reverence for saints or sacraments and no respect for ecclesiastical or secular magistrates. . . ."[61] With Luther's inventiveness in language thus on display,[62] Eck created the shocking collage from snippets of Luther's violent language. Eck knew that Luther had repudiated the left wing of the Reformation movement, and he anticipated that in the Augsburg Confession Melanchthon would also repudiate those "who put forward all kinds of harmful and dangerous doctrines attacking the Christian Sacrament, that was instituted by God" — as Philip actually expressed it in one early draft of the conclusion of the CA. But Eck nevertheless laid the blame for all the turbulence of the preceding decade, and

---

60. "The SA" in *The Book of Concord* [hereafter *BC*], ed. Robert Kolb and Timothy J. Wengert (Minneapolis: Fortress, 2000), 324:2.

61. *The Augsburg Confession: A Collection of Sources*, ed. J. M. Reu (reprinted by Concordia Seminary Press, Winter 1966), pp. 97-98.

62. On Luther's scatology, see the instructive study, Heiko Oberman, "Teufelsdreck: Eschatology and Scatology in the 'Old' Luther," *Sixteenth Century Journal* 19, no. 3 (1998): 435-50. The insight does not apply only to the "old" Luther: "at ego indied magis provoco Satanam et suas squamas, ut acceleretur dies ille Christi destructurus Antichristum istum." Words from 1522, in Luther's "last appeal to Staupitz," cited from WA *Briefe* 2. 567, 35f.

particularly for the radical rejection of the Lord's Supper, on Luther personally: "We must acknowledge as Luther's sons the iconoclasts, the sacramentarians, the Capernaites, the Neo-Hussites and their descendants, the Anabaptists, the Neo-Epicureans who declare the soul to be mortal, the enthusiasts, also the Neo-Cerinthians who deny the deity of Christ . . . destroy the churches, demolish the altars, trample upon the most holy Eucharist. . . ."[63] After listing 404 such quotations from Luther and his "sons," taken out of context and patched together to form a single whole, Eck concluded, "all the articles above noted, both those of Luther himself, as clearly a man familiar with the devil, and those of his followers who, being infatuated with his errors, have so degenerated as to become deaf to the truth, we reject and anathematize. . . ."[64]

The *Confutatio,* tragically, would take up the line initiated by Eck. Admittedly this first draft to which I am calling attention, prepared as a refutation of the Augsburg Confession by the papal party, was such an embarrassment that the Emperor sent it back for a rewrite. Even the rewrite (which was adopted by the Emperor as the official papal refutation of the Augsburg Confession and to which he demanded subscription by the Lutheran princes) is regarded today by Roman Catholic ecumenists as an embarrassment.[65] Nevertheless, the first version of the *Confutatio* remains important for several reasons. First, an analysis of the rejected first draft shows how the tendency to place personal blame on Martin Luther allowed Roman Catholic theologians to evade the force of the arguments set forth in the Augsburg Confession, an evasion that continues in the final draft, even if its basis in *ad hominem* has been muffled. Second, while it is true that the Council of Trent, not the text of the *Confutatio,* became authoritative for confessionalized Roman Catholicism, nevertheless, it was in terms of the second official draft of the *Confutatio* that the Lutheran Confessors at Augsburg experienced their repudiation and condemnation. Modern interpreters dare not minimize, as Ratzinger did in his discussion, the threat which the Imperial demand for subscription to the *Confutatio* as proof of orthodoxy had to represent to the first Lutherans. The *Confutatio* would, therefore, have decisive import at least for the future of Lutheranism in defining the terms of debate for Melanchthon's *Apology of the Augsburg Con-*

63. *Sources,* ed. J. M. Reu, p. 97.
64. *Sources,* ed. J. M. Reu, p. 120.
65. See the characterization it receives in *LCDUSA VIII*:27-28.

fession, the longest, most sustained work among the confessional documents and theologically perhaps the most enduring of them. We restrict ourselves here to a brief analysis of the rejected first draft of the *Confutatio* to show how the focus on the person of the heresiarch permitted the massive and systematic sidestepping of the issues posed by the Reformer's theology. The original draft of the *Confutatio* opened with the following five points. First, it acknowledged that some articles of the Augsburg Confession are orthodox. Second, it asserted that other articles of the Augsburg Confession appeared to disown sectarian error and agitation of the previous decade (the so-called Radical Reformation with its repudiation of the sacraments). Third, it declared that "a good many articles emerge . . . which neither agree with the Holy Scripture nor with the doctrines of those doctors whom the Church has sanctioned."[66] At this point, the draft impatiently but in revealing fashion erupted. The Lutheran princes ought at once "to renounce their heresies and errors, and consent with the Catholic Church which truly is the pillar and ground of the truth, and also the Bride of Christ, and governed forever by the Holy Spirit."[67] An interpretive remark is demanded by this telling outburst. One can make an appeal to authority like this only in disputes in which authority is not in dispute. The appeal to authority is intelligible only where a community of discourse has already decided upon principles of authority that are essential to its identity. In the present case, however, "consent with the Catholic Church" was precisely what was in dispute. Which catholic church? The new church of militant papalism, emerging from the bull *Unam Sanctam* in 1302, which claimed for the papacy authority over the secular sword? Or the previous catholic church, defined by the witness of the martyrs, the canon of Scripture at whose center is a crucified Christ, the consensus of the Fathers, and the creeds of the Ecumenical Councils (the fourth of which declines imperialistic Roman claims to primacy of jurisdiction)? Appeal to authority begged the question, since this was a radical dispute "in principle and about principles" (Ratzinger), i.e., about what properly constitutes authority in the "catholic Church." Fourth, the *Confutatio* maintained that the Augsburg Confession silently ignored ten years of error and confusion created by the defiant publications of the condemned heretic, Martin Luther. Behind the irenic words of the Augsburg Confession, the confutators complained, "many other heresies and doctrines in-

66. *Sources,* ed. J. M. Reu, p. 327.
67. *Sources,* ed. J. M. Reu, p. 327.

vented to raise tumults are left in the writings, books and pamphlets published within several years, Luther being the primary author and source of them all; for he has thought out some new and unheard of heresies and resuscitated and restored [old heresies]."[68] Fifth, the "unheard-of, foreign, wicked, criminal and absolutely intolerable heresies and sects" that now plague Germany are said to have "suddenly sprung up ... by the recent discord"[69] among the Lutherans themselves. This remark is also revealing, since it indicates once again how the confutators insisted against all evidence that all the dissidents without differentiation belonged to one and the same party stemming from Luther. The *Confutatio* thus concluded about the foregoing five points: "It is apparent that the fountainhead and origin of [all these heresies and hostile sects] is Luther and his wicked, frivolous and self-contradictory doctrine."[70] Luther, the draft will go on to say, is "the principal preacher and the instigator of these dissensions,"[71] even questioning the true divinity of the Son of God; again: "Luther has taught wickedly that the Sacraments had been only recently invented,"[72] and so on.

From this brief survey, it is very clear that the first draft of the *Confutatio* had never tried to understand the text of the CA on its own terms. The confutators came to the Diet at Augsburg with a predetermined agenda *not* to re-engage the theological argument but only to reiterate the decade-old papal condemnation of Luther, i.e., to deflect any new debate that would shift the question away from the controversial person, the condemned heretic. Nevertheless, the reference above to Luther's "self-contradictory" doctrine is once again telling. For we find "self-contradictory" those statements that come from a conceptual frame of reference that we do not understand or appreciate. This is a virtual truism; it is the reason why we have to struggle to understand texts, positions, and arguments sympathetically on their own terms, before we pass judgment on them. This is especially true in theology, in which words and conceptual frameworks are the basic material of the discipline. The alternative is sheer confusion and arbitrariness. For example: "although they everywhere make much ado about the Word of God, yet their doctrine, so far, is very unstable and self-contradictory."[73] The confutators ex-

68. *Sources,* ed. J. M. Reu, p. 327.
69. *Sources,* ed. J. M. Reu, p. 327.
70. *Sources,* ed. J. M. Reu, p. 328.
71. *Sources,* ed. J. M. Reu, p. 329.
72. *Sources,* ed. J. M. Reu, p. 336.
73. *Sources,* ed. J. M. Reu, p. 341.

plain themselves this way: "... in accordance with Luther's doctrine that faith alone justifies, [the CA] leaves no repayment or reward of good works which, although they may have been done in the best manner, Luther holds to be sin. . . . [Therefore] people are very torpid to do good works since they have ever so often heard . . . that we merit nothing by good works."[74] To the confutators, it was exactly Luther's chief teaching that "faith alone justifies," which appeared self-contradictory. It seemed to them to destroy any motive for good works. This made no sense to them, especially because they also correctly read Luther otherwise to lift up and celebrate the good works of Christian love. This combination of faith alone that justifies with works of true love (*fides incarnata*, as formed and normed by Christ's love for the sinner, thus not expiatory religious works) that flow from justifying faith, seemed to them self-contradictory. In reality, we may well suspect here a clash of conceptual frameworks, in which the very terms "faith," "works," "rewards" have different significations, relations, and hence meanings.

Such confusion is inevitable when the coherence and sincerity of an opposing argument are not assumed and the hard work of understanding is not undertaken, which is the basic cognitive task of theology as critical dogmatics, according to the argument of this book. One should observe the rule in theology[75] that no argument of refutation is permitted until an opponent's position is restated with such clarity and sympathy that the opponent herself will acknowledge it as her own. By this rule, all false representation and consequent obfuscation are excluded. Lacking that discipline, however, it is but a small step from dealing in caricatures of opponents' arguments and *ad hominem* attacks on personal motives to the conclusion that the opponent is irrational and obstinate, incorrigible and insincere, a hardened minion of the devil. The draft of the *Confutatio* took this small but disastrous step, concluding that what reason had failed to achieve, political power must now resolve: "these heresies must, therefore, not be referred to a future council, but now they must be successfully stamped out, covered up and abolished forever by your Imperial Majesty. . . ."[76] Clearly in the mind of contemporary papal proponents, Martin Luther personally was the chief issue, not a dissenting or erring brother to be corrected but an obstinate false prophet leading many souls to destruc-

---

74. *Sources*, ed. J. M. Reu, p. 341.

75. A rule that has its source in Thomas Aquinas, but which I learned from my doctor-father, Christopher Morse.

76. *Sources*, ed. J. M. Reu, p. 343.

tion, to be vilified and if possible crushed. He had caused, as the first draft of the *Confutatio* declared, "the wretched common people to vacillate in doubt and to be involved in inextricable errors."[77] The first draft of the *Confutatio* did not regard the dispute as an ecclesial crisis, something implicating all the parties. Rather it treated the "Lutherans" as a misled group of individuals who were defecting from the church under the influence of a singular heretic, Martin Luther.

To the point that I am making here it is not necessary to examine the content of the final draft any more than it is necessary to study here the content of the CA. The point is that the vitriol directed against Luther as malevolent person served to evade the force of his reformatory arguments, also for the final draft, even though much of the *ad hominem* was edited out. This evasion is something very different from saying that a dispute about Christian truth and its implications for the life of the one church has occurred, that opponents are to be understood and argued with in the best light under the direction of the divine Word, that a decision about the controversies must be awaited by the work of the Spirit through the consensus of the faithful as expressed in a council: this, roughly summarized, was Melanchthon's irenic stance and proposal in composing the CA, which self-consciously spoke in the name of the regional churches that had adopted Luther's reforms, appealing therefore from the Church to the Church for the sake of the Church.

## The Catholic Luther and *Communio* Ecclesiology

The notion that Luther might be recognized as a teacher of the whole church implies the notion that Luther is not the founder of a sect, but rather taught as a member of the whole church for the sake of the whole church. Many modern Roman Catholics have been astonished actually to discover such a Luther, the one whom the pioneering Roman Catholic scholar Joseph Lortz called the "catholic Luther." Roman Catholic theologian George Tavard, for example, quotes this statement of the early Luther, "I make a long, wide, deep distinction between the Roman Church and the Roman Curia. The former I know to be the most pure dwelling-place of Christ, the mother of churches, the mistress of the world, though in the Spirit . . . the bride of Christ, the daughter of God. . . . The latter is known

77. *Sources,* ed. J. M. Reu, p. 343.

by its fruits. . . .ˮ[78] Tavard points out that "such a distinction is not unknown among Catholics." In any case, the "important fact" is that Luther's
"doctrine of justification was not developed against Roman teaching. It antedates the violent opposition to everything Roman that will merge from
his condemnation by Leo X."[79] It follows that Roman Catholics today have
no *a priori* reason to be suspicious of this teaching on faith and works by
the "catholic Luther." This term, "catholic Luther," points to a Luther driven
by a classical Christological passion that is deeply informed by the theme
of the believer's communion with Christ.

As we have seen again and again throughout this book, it is possible
to understand Luther's doctrine of justification from the angle of the "joyful exchange" in which the believer by faith gives to Christ his sin, and
Christ in turn gives the believer His righteousness. Luther indeed consistently exposited justification in the dramatic, participatory, and communal
language of the joyful interchange between faith and Christ, the bride and
the bridegroom. The Roman Catholic scholar Jared Wicks sees this with
real clarity; commenting on "the exchange with Christ outside myself,"
Wicks writes: "At the exact center of spiritual existence, according to Luther, the believer is realizing his situation as one of participation and exchange with Christ, of Christ's inhesion and cementing him to himself,
and of a transforming exchange between his sin and Christ's righteousness. In 'apprehending faith' I lay hold of his victory as the death of my sin
and of his consummate righteousness as mine by grace. In passivity under
the rapture of grace, I am taken out of my lost state into the sphere of
Christ's invincible righteousness."[80] Already in 1519, Luther is drawing the
ecclesiological implications of this renewed understanding of the union of
Christ and faith. He wrote, "Christ with all his saints, by his love, takes
upon himself our form [Phil. 2:7], fights with us against sin, death and all

---

78. George Tavard, *Justification: An Ecumenical Study* (New York: Paulist Press, 1983),
p. 51, cited from WA II:446-47.

79. Tavard, *Justification*, p. 51. Tavard concluded: "In his central doctrine of justification by faith, Luther was right, and the conditions of his times made him a strenuous defender of the truth. This strikes me as the inescapable conclusion from an unbiased reading
of his less polemical writings. . . . But the irony of Luther's situation is that he was right on
the chief point of the Christian understanding of human life in its relationship to God at a
time when the Church's hierarchy, caught in the exciting turmoil of the Renaissance and the
power politics of the emerging European nations, was blind to the point he was making"
(p. 107).

80. Wicks, *Spiritual Legacy*, p. 137.

evil. This enkindles in us such love that we take on his form, rely upon his righteousness, life and blessedness. And through this interchange of his blessings and our misfortunes we become one loaf, one bread, one body, one drink, and have all things in common. O this is a great sacrament!"[81]

In this light are we not entitled to ask whether the real patrimony of the early Luther's reformation theology — before the tumult of apocalyptic catastrophe polemically colored everything — is such a Christocentric ecclesiology of communion anchored in the Eucharist, when the sacrifice of the Eucharist is the sacrifice of praise in the Spirit, by virtue of union with Christ who anew and anew condescends to meet and feed His people, to the glory of the Father? Not then an expiatory sacrifice of Christ the scapegoat by the clergy on behalf of unworthy observers to placate an angry God, but rather on the basis of the once-for-all propitiation on Golgotha, a Spirit-wrought participation in Jesus' own self-giving to the Father for all?

The case for a "catholic Luther," not only at home with but deeply dependent upon the legacy of patristic theology, is not only a contemporary Roman Catholic discovery. In a seminal article,[82] Lutheran theologian David Yeago challenged the interpretation according to which "Luther stands in no significant relationship to the preceding Christian tradition. . . . [As if] the catholic tradition figures in the story only as that which Luther had to overcome, to 'break through,' on his way to 'rediscovering the gospel.'" In Yeago's considered view, "the western schism, far from being the appropriate historical outcome of principled theological disagreement, was instead a tragic chapter of accidents." His case, in part, goes like this. The "celebrated question" of so much modern Protestant interpretation of the origin of the Reformation, "'*How can I get a gracious God?*', is rather conspicuous by its absence" in the writings of the early Luther. Yeago finds instead an angry young prophet driven by the question, "Where can I find the *real* God?" i.e., the God who cannot be bribed or manipulated, not with our best endeavors, let alone anything so gauche as indulgences. It was the "threat of idolatry, not a craving for assurance of forgiveness, that troubled Luther's conscience if anything did." The real God commands

81. "The Blessed Sacrament of the Holy and True Body and Blood of Christ, and the Brotherhoods" (1519) LW 35:58.

82. David Yeago, "The Catholic Luther," *First Things* 61 (March 1996): 37-41; originally a paper delivered at "The Catholicity of the Reformation" conference in Northfield, MN, on 27 February 1995; revised 24 October 1995. All citations in the following three paragraphs are from the original paper.

that we love God wholly and purely, for God's sake, and not for the sake of whatever benefits we can derive from God. Luther inherits this searching demand from Augustine, and it is the axis on which his early prophetic critique of the idolatry of the *amor concupiscentiae* turns, as that came to outstanding expression in the Heidelberg Disputation's theology of the cross. Here the question under discussion is, "How can I be sure that I truly love God *for his own sake* and am not merely using him as a source of elevated pleasures and a more satisfying self-image?" In fact, such a deity that we could put to use for our purposes has no real existence. It is an empty idol. The real God cannot be so manipulated. Only now and on this basis does the question of the certainty of salvation and the gracious God become actual.[83]

We will return in the conclusion to this book to Yeago's insightful critique of the inadequacy of Luther's early *theologia crucis* as a solution to *this* question of spiritual certainty, that is, after one has been divested of *securitas* by the prophetic Word. It is in any case evident that this radical young *Augustinian* of the *theologia crucis* is also a *catholic* Christian. By the end of 1518, after the onset of the controversy over indulgences, Luther's mature doctrine of the certainty of faith supplanted the theology of the cross, which Luther never again explicitly invoked. What accounts for this evolution? Yeago persuasively argues[84] that it is at this juncture of his thinking that Luther finally discovered the theological significance of the Sacraments as the personal communication of Jesus Christ. "The concrete, external, public sacramental act in the church is *the concrete, external, public act of Jesus Christ in the church*." Here the direct, first-person speech of the risen Lord transpires, "I baptize you. . . . Be of good cheer, your sins are forgiven. . . . This is my body, given for you." Is Jesus Christ telling the truth in this declaration of forgiveness in the place and time of gathering of those called out by the gospel? Assured faith is faith that takes Him at His word, here and now, according to His command and institution. The sacraments of the church are the "locus of assurance, of certitude," because they are the locus of Jesus Christ himself, here and now, on the earth. "For

---

83. For a somewhat more nuanced historical account of the early Luther's struggle in the context of contemporary penitential traditions, see David C. Steinmetz, *Luther in Context* (Grand Rapids: Baker Academic, 2002), pp. 1-11. Steinmetz argues that the "Reformation discovery of the gospel did not put an end to [Luther's] *Anfectungen*" (p. 1), "since only the already justified can experience sorrow for their sins" (p. 11). Certain faith is the faith which, continually tested, continually finds consolation anew.

84. This account accords with Bayer, *Luther's Theology*, pp. 49-56.

Luther after 1518, Christ is central not as pattern but as person; we are saved by the faith which acknowledges his authority, competence, and willingness to rescue those who call on him." Consequently, Luther can "quite straightforwardly identify the doctrine of justification with the Christological dogma of the ancient Church." Yeago concluded that we are quite mistaken if we take the Reformation as a turn "away from the catholic tradition, [as] the founding of a new Christianity." It was, on the contrary, a "turn towards the very heart of the catholic tradition," i.e., a rediscovery of the evangelical significance of the sacraments.

All this new knowledge of the "catholic" Luther puts even Luther's anti-papalism in new light. Consider Luther's argument in the tract of 1527 (!) against the Radical Reformation, *Concerning Rebaptism*. It is just because "Antichrist" is to "take his seat in the temple of God . . . , [so] the Christendom that is now under the papacy is truly the body of Christ and a member of it. If it is his body, then it has the true spirit, gospel, faith, baptism, sacrament, keys, the office of the ministry, prayer, holy Scripture, and everything that pertains to Christendom. So we are all still under the papacy and therefrom have received our Christian treasures."[85] Even this anti-papal indictment of the Antichrist is a dialectical affirmation of the catholic church, not its renunciation as some Egypt to be left behind. Scott H. Hendrix in *Luther and the Papacy: Stages in a Reformation Conflict* studied the evolution of Luther's thinking about the papacy. He found in Luther both a changing empirical assessment in response to the treatment he received from the papacy and an underlying standard of judgment that remained remarkably uniform. Luther's judgment about the papacy as an institution changed from youthful veneration to early skepticism to open defiance and finally to the condemnation of the papacy as Antichrist. Given the unjust treatment Luther received from the papacy, these judgments are historically understandable, even if we must regard them today as hyperbolic at best and ecumenically injurious. It should be enough to say that the papacy sinned, indeed, sinned against its own divine office and calling, and that as well, the papacy is capable of repentance and renewal. Luther, however, became convinced that the papacy was irreformable in this spiritual sense.[86] This conviction, reinforced by the principled deafness and blindness of Rome to what the "heretics" were ac-

---

85. "Concerning Rebaptism" LW 40:232.

86. Scott H. Hendrix, *Luther and the Papacy: Stages in a Reformation Conflict* (Philadelphia: Fortress, 1981), p. 148.

tually saying, had massive influence on "the Protestant cause" and its self-understanding.[87]

What Hendrix brings out, which is not so well known, is Luther's underlying and consistent criterion of judgment in all stages of his life: *the papacy is by divine right a pastoral office "of nourishing people in the church with the Word of God."*[88] This pastoral function is for Luther "the criterion for claiming legitimate authority in the church."[89] True pastors are "servants of the present Christ and not vicars of an absent Christ."[90] Even his disobedience to the Pope is based on this criterion.[91] Luther's outrage is directed "at the perversion of the pastoral office."[92] In fact Luther "was protesting against the usurpation of the church by an unfaithful hierarchy on behalf of the faithful people, not against the church on behalf of the individual"[93] as he was so often falsely understood, especially in Pietism and the Enlightenment. Luther's own historical judgment about the incorrigibility of the papacy in the *Smalcald Articles* notwithstanding, in light of the "pastoral principle" Hendrix has uncovered, do we not have to ask whether Luther would have welcomed, indeed celebrated, a renewed and faithful papacy that would properly exercise its pastoral office? Wouldn't his own principle compel him to rejoice to be proven *wrong*? And would not a new reception of Luther as teacher of the church catholic be just that renewal of the papacy in faithfulness to the gospel?

## *Communio* Ecclesiology

It is no stretch to say that Luther defines the church as essentially communion, as in his celebrated explanation of the Third Article of the Creed in the Large Catechism: "I believe that there is on earth a little holy flock or community of pure saints under one head, Christ. It is called together by the Holy Spirit in one faith, mind, and understanding. It possesses a variety of gifts, yet is united in love without sect or schism. Of this community I also am a part and member, a participant and co-partner in all the bless-

---

87. Hendrix, *Papacy,* p. 159.
88. Hendrix, *Papacy,* p. xi, emphasis added.
89. *LCDUSA* V:21.
90. "Letter to Cardinal Albrecht" LW 48:342.
91. Hendrix, *Papacy,* p. 70.
92. Hendrix, *Papacy,* p. 136.
93. Hendrix, *Papacy,* p. 134.

ings it possesses."[94] Linkage of this idea of Beloved Community to the new *communio* ecclesiology of the ecumenical movement is organic and natural. There is considerable ferment around this idea, which is being worked out both by Protestant and Orthodox theologians associated with the World Council of Churches' Faith and Order movement, as well as by Roman Catholic theologians, but the basic intuition is that the church is the *event of sharing* that is set into motion and sustained by the gospel. The saving message of Christ creates community, reconciled fellowship with God, and on this basis new human fellowship. The most basic image and actualization of the church as *communio* is the assembly gathered for the Eucharist, in which the life of God and the life of the world are concretely communicated to one another — a social "joyful exchange." Local Eucharistic assemblies are likewise linked to each other through time and space in the fellowship of their pastors. The universal church is thought of as a "communion of communions" spread across the earth. Perhaps a renewed papacy faithful to the gospel could minister communion with the church of the past (Ratzinger's principle of tradition) as well as steward the unity of churches across the globe.

The Ecumenical Institute at Strasbourg published a study of *communio/koinonia* in 1990 that described the concept in terms of the following elements: (1) "The Church as a human fellowship is by nature a fellowship in solidarity"; (2) This "fellowship . . . impels a common participation in material and spiritual needs, in material and spiritual resources"; (3) "This fellowship presupposes fellowship in the confession of the faith and includes fellowship in the office of Word and Sacraments, in common actions and decisions . . . [which] take on an authoritative character. . . . *[It] is by nature a committed fellowship. Commitment is not optional; it impels the community toward common life and action*"; (4) This fellowship is "simultaneously universal and particular. Repeatedly, historical challenges arise in the face of which the relation to the universal Church is decisive for the particular church and its decisions. Conversely, the needs of a particular church demand action and decision from the universal fellowship . . ."; (5) This fellowship is "not a coerced and prescribed uniformity. It realizes itself in a variety of forms." And finally, (6) this fellowship "looks beyond itself. It lives from its communion with the Lord, who is Lord and Savior of all creation and serves him as sign and instrument for the salvation of the world." The Strasbourg study in addition accented the fact that

---

94. *BC*, p. 419, #49-53.

"fellowship in the Eucharist is unthinkable . . . without fellowship in the faith . . . which takes on a normative form through councils and synods. *Those who do not accept the faith in this normative, doctrinal form exclude themselves from the* communio."[95] Several things are to be noted from this description, which now allow us to begin meeting the objections of Ratzinger to Luther as resource in ecclesiology. First, there is a clear affirmation of "binding doctrine" as *sine qua non* of the sharing that is and claims to be ecclesial. Second, there is a clear affirmation of commitment to common life and action. These two affirmations would meet Ratzinger's objection on several points. For they link "binding doctrine in and through the Church" to a commitment to common life and action, hence constitute "teaching authority." Certainly in a *communio* ecclesiology teaching authority will not be conceived in the juridical fashion traditional in Roman Catholicism since it became a confessionalized denomination like others after the sixteenth century. Rather, teaching authority in *communio* would be structured by the process of mutual admonition that Luther envisioned in those same, problematic *Smalcald Articles:* "the church could not be better ruled and preserved than if we all live under one head, Christ, and all the bishops — equal according to the office (although they may be unequal in their gifts) — keep diligently together in unity of teaching, faith, sacraments, prayers and works of love, etc."[96] Mutual admonition, let it be repeated for emphasis, is no free-for-all, but that admonition which is based upon and indeed made possible by the ecumenical doctrinal consensus, minimally: "since justifying faith is awakened and the Church is gathered only by the pure preaching of the Gospel and the evangelical celebration of the sacraments, communion and its preservation require agreement in the right understanding of the Gospel (Augsburg Confession VII). The Reformation sought such agreement primarily by means of explicit confessional consensus documents adopted by congregations and churches. In such a confessional communion the communion of churches also finds visible expression."[97] This new ecclesiological thinking also finds expression from the Catholic and Orthodox sides. J. M. R. Tillard has written a sweeping rein-

95. *A Commentary on "Ecumenism: The Vision of the ELCA,"* ed. William G. Rusch (Minneapolis: Augsburg, 1990).

96. *BC*, 308:9.

97. *A Commentary on "Ecumenism,"* ed. Rusch, p. 127.

terpretation of Roman Catholic ecclesiology from this perspective. Everything is directly grounded in the redemptive mission of Jesus. "The event in which [Jesus'] Lordship and his messianic role burst forth in full light, his Cross culminating in his Resurrection, is the event in which he takes upon himself the human condition in its deepest level of poverty. . . . He is made the Lord of the Kingdom in the supreme moment of his communion with the rejected, the despondent, the hated, the excluded, the scorned, the ridiculed, the martyrs. . . . The Kingdom is a Kingdom of the 'poor,' not only because they are heirs of it but also because it is by identifying himself with their fate that Jesus has overcome it."[98] Salvation is grounded in the Son of God's sharing of human nature, partaking of human woe, taking on Himself the sin of the world, even perishing with humanity in the death of the Godforsaken. Through this very solidarity established as the Crucified, the Risen Christ is bringing about the reunion of humanity with God. From this Christological center — note well, not a conveyance of jurisdiction from the departing and soon-to-be-absent Christ to Peter and his successors — new thinking about the church radiates, including about the Petrine ministry to the church's visible unity. The church is to be in every way an expression of this saving communion between God and humanity as established in the cross and resurrection of Jesus. So one comes to think that the true unity of the church is the visible communion with Christ, and through Christ with His Father, and by their Spirit with all who believe. In this way the pastoral ministry of Peter to and on behalf of the church's unity through time and space might be understood as the Spirit's gift and intention in the development and reform of the institution.

Likewise the Orthodox theologian Kallistos Ware writes from out of the patristic tradition: "This notion of salvation as sharing implies — although many have been reluctant to say this openly — that Christ assumed not just unfallen but *fallen* human nature. . . . Christ lives out his life on earth under the conditions of the fall. He is not himself a sinful person, but in his solidarity with fallen man he accepts to the full the consequences of Adam's sin. He accepts to the full not only the physical consequences, such as weariness, bodily pain, and eventually the separation of body and soul in death. He accepts also the moral consequences, the loneliness, the alienation, the inward conflict. It may seem a bold thing to ascribe all this to the living God, but a consistent doctrine of the Incarnation requires nothing

---

98. J.-M. R. Tillard, O.P., *Church of Churches: The Ecclesiology of Communion,* trans. R. C. DePeaux, O.P. (Collegeville, MN: Liturgical Press, 1992), p. 70.

less."[99] "A consistent doctrine of the Incarnation," i.e., a soteriology that articulated the ancient church's definition of Christ's divine person in terms of His earthly life's work, as we have seen in Chapter Three, stands behind and grounds Luther's doctrine of justification — no reduction then of the ontological affirmations of the church's faith to human experience or faith subjectively understood. On the contrary, this indicates how Luther's ecclesiological thinking about the church as a communion is not floral decoration, but flows out from the very center of his theology. In all such thinking, the fundamental intuition is that the end of all things (Mark 13:27) is the Beloved Community, which already now impinges upon the present in the gathering of the people of God around that holy meal, which proclaims the death of Christ till He comes again.

The Beloved Community, it is clear, exists here and now by faith not sight, in hope, not yet in palpable reality, and that is why what we often see in the church is still the same old sin, betrayal, vanity, cruelty, and confusion, covering up and obscuring from view the fellowship of disciples who love one another. This ugly fact reflects the truth in the later Luther's teaching of the church's hiddenness, not in the sense of invisibility, but in the sense of moral ambiguity. The church is at best always becoming the Beloved Community. But it does not and will not arrive there, until that heavenly Jerusalem descends from above, as a bride prepared to meet her groom. That is why, moreover, the doctrinal-creedal commitment to the truth of the gospel in this life takes precedence over any empirical demand or claim to realize here and now the love which will only prevail eternally in eternity. The justification for the church's existence is not ever that it has realized the Beloved Community, but rather that it bears the divine promise and surety of it, and so realizes it in its own life as foretaste, not yet as feast. This realization of Beloved Community under the conditions of fallen existence is real. But it is often hidden. We will try in the next chapter to describe that renewed human agency "between the times."

In this light, however, we can see that Ratzinger mischaracterized the CA's principle of faith as psychological subjectivity by failing to understand what the dialoguers call the hermeneutical use of the doctrine of justification by faith, i.e., as a principle of interpretation of the church's life by the criterion of gospel faithfulness, as in the Pauline canon of Galatians 6:15-16. "Justification by faith" is not an answer to the doctrinal question:

---

99. Kallistos Ware, *The Orthodox Way* (Crestwood, NY: St. Vladimir's Seminary Press, 1979), p. 107.

*quid sit?* It is not saying what ontologically or otherwise the object of faith is, as do the Scriptures and the Creeds. "Justification by faith" takes over as an answer to such questions exactly what the ancient and ecumenical church defined in its creedal theology (CA I-III!). It rather asks and answers the question about how the deposit of faith is to be *used,* so that the gospel, as doctrinally identified by those ecumenical standards, actually gets communicated by the ministry and in the worship of the Eucharistic assembly. It stipulates a rule: so communicate Christ (both orally and visibly) that He with all His blessings becomes ours by the mere surrender of faith to His promise of communion, "I am yours and you are mine."

As Jenson puts it, this rule for communication befits the thing communicated: "Jesus' sacrificial act on the Cross is his giving of himself to the Father for us and inseparably his giving of himself to us in obedience to the Father. What he gives is therefore communion: our communion with him, and just so our communion with the Father and with one another."[100] The dogmatic content is not betrayed then by an alien, even inimical means of communication. Nor is this dogmatic content betrayed by an alien notion of its gravamen in history, something less than Beloved Community, but rather points to the true inclusiveness of the church mercifully to include "the rejected, the despondent, the hated, the excluded, the scorned, the ridiculed, the martyrs." Such fellowship is to be the aim of every sermon, baptism, and Supper of the Lord. It therefore has ongoing force for the life of the church, which can never truthfully be anything other than this table-fellowship of divinely claimed, forgiven, and renewed sinners on their way to "the hope of righteousness." As Jenson continued, "the content of this encompassing communion is our sharing of Jesus' own life and fate, which is to say in his self-giving, his sacrifice."[101] That allows for a stronger sense of the church as a genuine agent under the reign of Christ, a true servant of Christ's own saving presence. Susan K. Wood describes the same thinking in contemporary Roman Catholic idiom: "'Communion' integrates the two dominant images of the church at the time of the Second Vatican Council: the church as the body of Christ . . . and the church as the people of God. . . . Within this integration the image of communion retrieves a biblical and patristic idea of the whole Christ, the *totus Christus,* by which all of humanity through grace in a covenant relation with the

---

100. Robert W. Jenson, *Unbaptized God: The Basic Flaw in Ecumenical Theology* (Minneapolis: Fortress, 1992), p. 40.

101. Jenson, *Unbaptized God,* p. 40.

head, Christ, are not only joined to the body of Christ, but participate in Christ in such a way that we form a single being."[102]

It is now apparent that we have a gospel answer to the question why anyone should believe the church, an answer that obtains for both Protestant and Catholic and transcends the form of the question that historically divided them. When the church is understood as communion, it follows that "the slogan: 'Jesus, yes — the Church, no' . . . cannot be used by either Catholic or Protestant theology. Christology and ecclesiology cannot be separated."[103] *Totus Christus* is not a familiar way of speaking among modern Christians, yet this Augustinian concept of the church as a visible yet spiritual fellowship of faith in Christ should be in principle agreeable.[104] Vilmos Vajta has demonstrated that, as opposed to his early polemical use of dualistic language (also inherited from Augustine) about the inner and outer Christendom, Luther in fact makes such a purely analytical distinction only in order to emphasize the "spiritual, sacramental" meaning of the one outward, physical fellowship. In reality, these constitute one, whole, indivisible church, a visible but spiritual fellowship of faith in Christ, "the Church as spiritual-sacramental *Communio* with Christ."[105] But in that case, "are faith in Christ and identification with the church-community distinguishable spiritual acts? Or is the Christ who is both the ground and object of faith the *totus Christus,* the embodied person whose body is the church?"[106]

## A Counter-Challenge

Ratzinger was not wrong to radicalize the question about Roman Catholic recognition of the CA, even if the deep current that carried him to that

102. Susan K. Wood, "Communion Ecclesiology: Source of Hope, Source of Controversy," *Pro Ecclesia* 2, no. 4 (Fall 1993): 425.

103. Walter Kasper, *In Search of Christian Unity: Basic Consensus/Basic Differences,* ed. Joseph A. Burgess (Philadelphia: Fortress, 1991), p. 31.

104. The concept may be sharply distinguished from that of *Christus prolongatus,* ". . . which Protestant theologians often unjustly accuse Catholics of holding. Whereas the first stresses the distinction between Christ as head and the Church as the body of Christ and subordinates the body to the head, the second extends Christology into ecclesiology." Kasper, *In Search,* p. 43, #29.

105. Vilmos Vajta, "The Church as Spiritual-Sacramental Communion with Christ and His Saints in the Theology of Martin Luther," in *Luther's Ecumenical Significance,* ed. Peter Manns and Harding Meyer (Stuttgart: Franz Steiner, 1988), p. 129.

106. Jenson, *Unbaptized,* p. 97.

challenge was the traditional image of Luther as heresiarch, as we have shown in our study of the first draft of the *Confutatio*. This systematic evasion of Luther's teaching, we may safely assume, no one today would want to own as a credible statement of Catholic doctrine. The profounder point, however, is that Ratzinger's demand actually requires a reckoning with Luther as would-be teacher of the church catholic. We have seen that the ecclesiological teaching of the "catholic" Luther on the church as communion not only accords with the best of recent Catholic ecclesiology but that it derives from the center of his teaching, the Christological basis of the doctrine of justification by faith, the "joyful exchange." Thus Ratzinger's objections to Luther as resource for the new Rome are met. Now a counter-question may be posed. What would it mean for the hope of a new Rome if the papal office today would rescind Leo X's Bull of Excommunication, not in the sense of endorsing the theology of the 1519 Luther as catholic and approved, let alone the teachings that developed after that, but rather in the sense of re-opening the debate at the point where it had been violently foreclosed? This would be to admit honestly and openly what in fact all know, that churches and councils can err, though by the grace of the Holy Spirit without the fatal loss of faith and saving truth, just as even the apocalyptic Luther acknowledged regarding the oppressed church under the papal "Antichrist." In a stroke, the heavy burden of history which is borne by the papal claim to this day would be lifted and the real truth of the Petrine office, namely, that he who denied his Lord was nevertheless restored to feed the sheep and tend the lambs, would be vindicated. The old Rome was not better off for externalizing the challenge of Luther the theologian; the new Rome will be better off for internalizing it.

We need the new Rome, and some of us must continue to suffer the pain of separation as witness to this as our common need. George Lindbeck's reflection in this regard is prescient: "The primary need in our day is for doctrinally normed and community oriented catechesis, life, and worship analogous, though not identical, to the practices that enabled churches to survive and grow amidst the religiously pluralistic and wholly non-Christian cultures of the first centuries." To continue in the sixteenth-century polemics, in a vain attempt to hold onto an antiquated confessional identity by oppositional contrast under the tacit assumption of "Christendom," turns a blind eye to "the loneliness, anomie, depression and meaninglessness characteristic of purportedly autonomous and self-actualizing individuals inhabiting the globalizing consumerist society of twenty-first century capitalism," where churches in any case can "no longer chiefly rely on ordinary familial and communal processes of socialization to transmit and sustain [Christian] identity."[107] The matters of ecumenical convergence and a new evangelization of post-Christian societies in Euro-America, in other words, turn out to be one and the same question. This is not surprising, since the disunity of the churches has been a basic factor in the de-Christianization of the West, which, after one hundred years of religious wars, gave up on the religion of the Prince of Peace. The future of the ecumenical movement is not other than the future of Christianity itself (at least in Euro-America), if it is the justification of the ungodly that at once unites each person to God in Christ and through Christ to one other.

It is no accident that the ecumenical movement was born on the mission fields, and that the mission field now returns to Euro-America with the same demand for Christian unity. In the dialectic of Luke-Acts and Paul that this chapter has proposed, mission is the common denominator. Missiology, that is to say, the practical doctrine of the Holy Spirit, assigns to each its task: to Peter, the preservation of the gospel into the future; to Paul, its extension to the nations. Such missiological reflection would involve also the Johannine witness of the Eastern churches. Let that be firmly noted, even though it falls outside the scope of this book.[108]

107. In *Justification and the Future of the Ecumenical Movement,* ed. William G. Rusch (Collegeville, MN: Liturgical Press, 2003), p. 11.

108. David Yeago has begun the mining of Luther's Johannine theology as a resource for today. See above n. 82.

# CHAPTER NINE

# Passion and Action in Christ:
# Political Theology between the Times

*Religious misery is in one way the expression of real misery and in an-*
*other a protest against real misery. Religion is the sigh of the afflicted*
*creature, the soul of a heartless world, as it is also the spirit of spiritless*
*conditions. It is the opium of the people. The abolition of religion as the*
*illusory happiness of the people is the demand for their real happiness.*
*The demand to abandon illusions about their condition is the demand*
*to give up a condition that requires illusions. Hence criticism of religion*
*is in embryo a criticism of this vale of tears whose halo is religion. . . .*
*Luther, to be sure, vanquished the bondage of devotion when he re-*
*placed it with the bondage of conviction. He shattered faith in author-*
*ity while he restored the authority of faith. He transformed parsons*
*into laymen and laymen into parsons. He freed man from outward re-*
*ligiosity while he made religiosity the innerness of man. He emanci-*
*pated the body from its chain while he put the chains on the heart.*

Marx[1]

## A Man in Contradiction?

We use the word "political" in a bewildering variety of ways today. For example, if by "political" one means public, having to do with matters of

1. Karl Marx, *On Religion*, trans. Saul K. Padover (New York: McGraw-Hill, 1974), pp.
35-37.

common human destiny, the word seems more than apt as a descriptor of the gospel, which is about our human destination in the Beloved Community of God through Jesus Christ and the Holy Spirit. Yet if by "political" one means power, having to do with the defeat of some and victory of others, we grow uneasy. We might understand that God's victory for us all over the contra-divine powers is part and parcel of the establishment of the reign of God, but we worry about who gets to parse this victory and defeat. And if by "political" one means partisan, as in the victory of one interest group at whatever costs over another, specters of the Crusades, the Inquisition, the imperial Conquests cum subjugation of native peoples arise and we positively repudiate political in this sense as an apt modifier of the gospel (except when our political party loses an election). Sorting through these various senses of the political today as public, as power, and as partisan is one task of political theology, which in the tradition of Paul, Augustine, and Luther, is in affirmation of the first sense, qualified approval of the second, and a repudiation of the third.[2]

In this chapter I take up Marx's well-known objection to Luther as resource for political theology[3] today. In some ways, his is the profoundest of objections and goes to the heart of things: the problem of human agency in a world in which humans are not finally in control (well, for Marx, *not yet* in *final* control). Marx understands the phenomenon of religion as emblematic of false consciousness arising out of human powerlessness. Following Feuerbach,[4] he believed that in a state of self-alienation, humanity creates images of the gods in order to give expression to its own lost essence. If humans are powerless, they imagine the all-powerful God. If humans are unloved, they worship the God of love. With such illusory conceptions, alienated humanity compensates for its loss, worshiping its own lost essence. At this point Marx added something to Feuerbach's criticism of religion. He says that in this act of worship, the oppressed human being secretly protests against its earthly state. Religion, Marx says appreciatively

---

2. For a contemporary sorting, see Robert Benne, *The Paradoxical Vision: A Public Theology for the Twenty-first Century* (Minneapolis: Fortress, 1995).

3. The term "political theology" originated as a pejorative term in Germany for what I have just described as "partisan" theology; in American English, however, the phrase does not necessarily bear that connotation and makes the unmistakable point that the Christian proclamation in its very essence cannot be privatized without transforming it into Gnosticism.

4. Ludwig Feuerbach, *The Essence of Christianity,* trans. G. Eliot (New York: Harper Torchbooks, 1957).

in dialectical Hegelian fashion, is the sigh of the afflicted, the soul of a heartless world. While appreciating that, Marx went on to insist that religion compensates like a narcotic, which the powerful classes are happy to see supplied in order to maintain their domination over the drugged masses, since people who believe that they will have happiness in heaven will not fight for it on earth. Thus religion is the opium of the people in a double sense. Religion is both a comfort for the oppressed under inhumane conditions, but also a narcotic that disables the oppressed from rising up to become the revolutionary agents of their own history. As we see in the epigraph above, the German Marx concretely traced the problem of religion as opiate to Luther. Is it not so?

It can seem so. As Dietmar Lage writes, Luther's "attempt to provide a positive theological foundation for Christian discipleship is fraught with inconsistencies, ambiguities and confusion."[5] It seems unprincipled: ". . . Luther rejects the fides incarnata when advocated by the papists and fanatics yet affirms his own fides incarnata. . . ."[6] This inconsistency is due to the fact that the *two* sources of Luther's idea of faith remain in tension with each other: "his adoption of the notion of faith as passivity is precisely why Luther is forced into ambiguity and confusion. . . . [It goes back to] his inability to resolve properly from the outset of his career the irreconcilable differences between the *obedientia activa* and *obedientia passiva* traditions. . . ."[7] The result of this conceptual confusion and ambivalent foundation for Christian activism in society is Luther's social conservatism. "Luther's understanding of Beruf remained a basically conservative medieval political view of social stratification and mobility. In fact, it can be argued that Luther's doctrine of Beruf, in adding theological sanctification to the static nature of the stations, in itself helped to maintain the prevalent medieval economic and political order against the onslaught of other social forces that had been unleashed."[8] Luther himself was not passive; rather he acted, but as a social conservative: "fear of chaos and need

---

5. Dietmar Lage, *Martin Luther's Christology and Ethics: Texts and Studies in Religion,* vol. 45 (Lewiston, NY: Edwin Mellen Press, 1990), p. 155.

6. Thus, both Majorists and Gnesio-Lutherans "must be regarded as legitimate heirs of Luther's apparent inability to come to terms with the issue of faith and works." Lage, *Christology and Ethics,* p. 156.

7. Lage, *Christology and Ethics,* p. 160. These are ". . . two distinctive interpretations of faith which in many senses are mutually exclusive" (p. 161).

8. Lage, *Christology and Ethics,* pp. 121, nn. 8, 127 and 11, 128 trace the social conservatism to Tauler, p. 128.

to preserve the reformation drove him to side with the power and might of the princes."[9]

Historically, Luther's social conservatism, Lage explains, emerged in response to the challenge of the Radical Reformation with its call for the active imitation of Christ. "For the Anabaptists, as for Karlstadt, it was obvious that works do not necessarily 'issue spontaneously from faith' as Luther claimed. It was not enough to recommend that 'good works ought to be done.' The Christian faith not only advocated, but demanded a moral change of behavior as evidence of total transformation . . . much more comprehensive than what they regarded as the mere forensic or declaratory justification offered by Luther and the 'solafideists.' . . ." Luther's "solafideism is the mistaken attempt 'to bring more people to heaven than God wants there.'"[10] Ironically Luther had to accept this ethical criticism as in part legitimate; he too held that "we should keep the Law and be justified by keeping it. . . ." The problem, however, is that "sin gets in the way." Sin remains an oppressive power afflicting the believer and the church as well as society. In face of its persistent power in the life of the redeemed, Luther maintained that the good news of Christ as sacramental gift and so faith as passive reception must have precedence over Christ as example and thus faith as active imitation.

So it seems indeed that it was Luther's self-contradictory notion of faith which led him into a dilemma, as he himself acknowledged: "If works alone are taught — as happened under the papacy, faith is lost. If faith alone is taught, unspiritual men will immediately suppose that works are not necessary."[11] Luther's response to the criticism was to embrace the dilemma. He saw no other choice, since an unresolved question afflicted any endeavor to be justified by Christian discipleship, namely, "to what degree the example of Christ should provide normative guidance and direction for the Christian life."[12] Since we cannot know with requisite certainty "what Jesus would do" to be justified by the very best attempt to imitate Him, defense of the *sola fide* against works righteousness had to prevail in a world sold under the power of sin, including as a consequence a measure of ethical uncertainty about any concrete action. Luther consequently was led to harsh polemic against all who would "turn from the great important articles to minor ones" like Christian activism for social reform.[13]

---

9. Lage, *Christology and Ethics*, p. 122.
10. Lage, *Christology and Ethics*, p. 135.
11. "Commentary on Galatians" (1535) LW 27:63.
12. Lage, *Christology and Ethics*, p. 138.
13. Lage, *Christology and Ethics*, p. 125.

Lage draws back from a charge of radical incoherence. In Luther's defense, he maintains that both "forms of proclamation have their proper time; if this is not observed, the proclamation of salvation becomes a curse," comforting the comfortable and further afflicting the afflicted. In the 1535 Galatians commentary, Luther counseled such pastoral wisdom as a matter of discernment: "To those who are afraid and have already been terrified by the burden of their sins Christ the Savior and gift should be announced, not Christ the example and lawgiver. But to those who are smug and stubborn the example of Christ should be set forth, lest they use the Gospel as a pretext for the freedom of the flesh and thus become smug."[14] We see again that the proper distinction between law and gospel for Luther is regulative for preaching, not prescriptive for experience. What decides the variable of proclamation is "the demands of the historical context. . . ." Christology is the constant;[15] the doctrine of justification, whether by faith or by works, is the variable, since in either case it is "a proclamation which nevertheless has its source in the sacramentum et exemplum of the one reality of Jesus the Christ."[16] Because one must discern the times, Luther "makes little attempt to resolve the discrepancies, choosing instead to affirm both a fides abstracta and a fides incarnata. Both are valid depending upon the nature of the situation. . . ."[17] This dependence on the situation should not lead into the "straits of confessional dogmatics" but into the "ambiguity" of political theology between the times. This "demands that the theological enterprise be radically creative in each new historical circumstance and situation . . . a view of faith which corresponds to, and allows us to participate in, the essential paradox found at the very heart of Christianity itself — Jesus Christ, fully human, fully Divine, suspended on

14. "Commentary on Galatians" (1535) in LW 27:35.

15. Lage rightly sees that "Augustine, the *Doctor gratiae,* provided Luther with more than his anti-Pelagian thesis. He also provided him with a new Christological formulation which made it possible for Luther to come to terms with the emphasis upon the Christus exemplum which dominated the construction of late medieval Christologies. Augustine's Christology included not only the *Christus exemplum,* but also the *Christus sacramentum —* Christ as the sign that God had acted for our salvation through the sacrifice and death of Christ for the sins of humanity. Luther makes note of the sacramentum et exemplum Christology for the first time in his marginalia to Augustine's De trinitate (Book IV, Chap. III) upon which he lectured in 1509 and from which the concept was originally borrowed." Lage, *Christology and Ethics,* p. 94. Luther comes to maintain "that Christ's sacramental significance has priority over his exemplary significance" (p. 96).

16. Lage, *Christology and Ethics,* p. 163.

17. Lage, *Christology and Ethics,* p. 164.

a cross between heaven and earth."[18] According to the argument of this book, such political theology between the times is a function of critical (not confessionalized) dogmatics.

The objection to this reaching back to the Radical Reformation, and finding its modern formulation in Marx who aimed at overcoming passivity in liberating new human agency, is nevertheless a profound one. On the level of anthropology, it is the objection that faith in Christ the savior is false consolation that mystifies the reality of dehumanization and leads to passivity in society and paralysis in ethics. On the level of Christology, it is the objection that for the sake of preserving the *Volkskirche* of *Kulturprotestantismus,* Christ is torn in half. The Master who calls to discipleship is left behind and forgotten, and with that the possibility of the true church of radical witness to that Beloved Community (which at present is *neither* church nor society). These objections, moreover, seem to have no little empirical evidence on their side, as noted in the last chapter's criticism of the alliance of Throne and Altar in historic Lutheranism.[19] Finally and fundamentally, as Lage's study bears ambivalent witness, it may be that the target of these objections hits home in penetrating to a deep confusion in Luther's own mind. For Luther *does* speak of faith in a double way. It is *both* a living, mighty, active thing *and* pure receptivity, almost Buddhist *Gelassenheit.* Thus the problem of the ecstatic self discussed above in Chapters Five and Six re-emerges here, now in social and political form. How indeed can divine sovereignty and human freedom be reconciled in Luther as resource for political theology?

To meet this objection, I will not take the usual route of standard Lutheran apologetics and try once more to explain the inexplicable *Zweireichenlehre.* I have nothing against it, properly understood; the problem is properly understanding it. With justice it has been faulted as a "labyrinth" of misunderstanding, so thoroughly mixed up with Cartesian and Kantian dualisms as to make it unworkable for us. I will return to it briefly at the conclusion of this chapter. But I won't make it the means to meeting the present objection. Rather I have to show that the Marxist objection itself succumbs to a similar paradox as the one alleged against Luther — not surprising in a way, since Marx's program was intended as a polemical inversion of Luther's, as we saw in the epigraph at the head of this chapter. If that

18. Lage, *Christology and Ethics,* p. 165.

19. Ernst Troeltsch, *The Social Teachings of the Christian Churches,* vol. 2, trans. O. Wyon (New York: Harper Torchbooks, 1961).

is so, then the solution to Luther's apparently equivocal notion of faith is one that Marx cannot resort to on his own materialist assumptions, namely, that the true human agent is the total Christ, the collective New Adam, the Head with His earthly Body. The agent of the new humanity is not then the individual Christian believer, who, as an individual caught in the earthly strife between the powers, never integrates perfectly passive and active obedience until perfectly healed and made whole in the light of glory. The true new Agent, however, already now includes this struggling believer and that individual truly participates in His righteousness — but only together with all the others from baptism day to resurrection day. It is these together through time and space who form the public, political body of the new humanity in the world, whose Head is Christ. Here, taken as the whole which it actually and essentially is and is yet to be, there is a perfect integration of the passive and active obedience in the labor of Beloved Community.

Aiming at the solution just sketched, I will be able next, resorting to new formulations of the doctrine of *Beruf* or vocation in Benne, Wingren, and Bayer, to ask whether Lage has gotten it right in associating notions of earthly station and Christian vocation with a static, injurious social conservatism and the loss of Christian discipleship. Roughly speaking, as we shall see, Luther spoke of three areas of social existence — state, domestic economy,[20] and religion; these constitute the traditional "orders of creation," which, however, I take in the dynamic sense of "mandates," as Bonhoeffer argued in his retrieval and revision of the old Lutheran political theology.[21] Luther never spoke of *Volkstum,* that racist concoction that Paul Althaus dreamed up[22] which so discredited this important dimension

---

20. That is, the domestic economy, the pre-modern household. I have discussed marriage and family above in Chapter Six.

21. Dietrich Bonhoeffer, *Ethics,* ed. E. Bethge (New York: Macmillan, 1978), pp. 286-92; H. Schmid, ed., *The Doctrinal Theology of the Evangelical Lutheran Church,* trans. C. Hay and H. Jacobs (Philadelphia: Lutheran Publication Society, 1899), pp. 604-23.

22. "The belief that God has created me includes also my Volk. Whatever I am and have, God has given me out of the wellspring of my Volk. . . . God has determined my life from its outermost to its innermost elements through my Volk, through its blood, through its spiritual style, which above all endows and stamps me in the language, and through its history. My Volk is my outer and inner destiny. This womb of my being is God's means, his Ordnung, by which to create and to endow me. . . . As a creation of God, the Volk is a law of our life. . . . We are responsible for the inheritance, the blood inheritance and the spiritual inheritance, for Bios and Nomos, that it be preserved in its distinctive style and authenticity." Paul Althaus, 1937 lecture cited in Robert B. Ericksen, *Theologians Under Hitler: Gerhard Kittel, Paul Althaus and Emanuel Hirsch* (New Haven and London: Yale University Press, 1985), p. 103.

of Luther's theology of creation and social ethic. Here we will find instead a rich theology of creation begging to interpret social experience as well as to direct the creature's labor to the tasks of Beloved Community. Accordingly we can seek and find resources for political theology today not only in Luther but also in several of our near contemporaries in Christian faith, whose theological lives manifest this true new agency in Christ. This is so enormous a task (really, a call to reinvent the discipline that goes by the name Christian Ethics as a function of critical dogmatics) that I can only illustrate rather than rigorously argue for what I have in mind. I will do so in a twofold way.

So, first, I will present sketches tightly focused on the agency of three representative public theologians and second, I will do so by situating each of them in the domain of one of the three estates. First, then, in regard to the political state, I will discuss Luther's own — forgotten, obscured — witness against war. Second, in regard to political economy, I will discuss the early Niebuhr's witness against class oppression at home and the struggle, in the language of his day, for the emancipation of "the American Negro" by the non-violent means of economic coercion. Third, in regard to public religion, I will discuss Martin Luther King's ministry from the church to the society for the redemption of the American soul from the founding betrayal of the national covenant by the sin of the race-based slave system. Then, and only then, will I say in conclusion what is of crucial and enduring importance about the *Zweireichenlehre:* its *Augustinian* realism about the state as a monopoly on the means of violence such that it cannot, in principle, belong to the Beloved Community, even if in God's economy it can and should be made to serve its coming. For Marx was not wrong to think that upon the achievement of socialism the state would wither away. Rather, he erred in rejecting the Beloved Community as God's gift and the work of the *totus Christus* as the path to it.

## Marxism as a Theological Problem

Western intellectual circles have been reluctant to come to terms with the bad facts surrounding the catastrophic failure of Marxism in the century past. This is so for several reasons. Anticommunism in the West invokes the unhappy memories of McCarthyism and an almost equally fanatical self-understanding of a certain kind of "bear any burden, pay any price" cold war ideology that turned a deaf ear to the cries of the poor and a blind eye to the socio-economic causes of revolutionary discontent in the developing world and rather made sweetheart deals with dictators. Moreover, Marxism for a very long time provided Western intellectuals with the only viable secular alternative to the juggernaut expansion of the McDonalds and Disneyland cultural hegemony of globally expanding capitalism. More darkly, the spell of fascination that Marxism cast was that it provided a comprehensive explanation and critique of the cultural marginalization of intellectuals,[23] who were perhaps not fully conscious of their own frustrated aspirations to be the philosopher-kings of the new secular civilization to which the Enlightenment had given birth, a culture that instead is driven by vulgar tastes for "bread and circuses" in the unregulated market. I know these motives well, for I very much shared them in my student years.

If I may then be allowed a personal preface to the theological criticism of Marxism: in six years living in central Europe in the 1990s I had the frequently unsettling experience of visiting castle museums. I say "unsettling" because, lacking these romantic relics of medieval warfare in our land, Americans tend to have fairy-tale conceptions of them. One visit to the torture chamber, taking a close-hand look at the ingenious inventions of human cruelty preserved there, disabuses one of Disneyworld fantasies. In the country where I taught for six years, Slovakia, a folk legend grew up among the poor about a Robin Hood figure, Janošik. He organized a band of brigands and tormented the aristocracy with raids and robberies until he was captured. In the city where he was executed, Liptovský Míkulaš, there is a museum dedicated to him, which preserves a contemporary woodcut of his execution. It depicts the dying Janošik hung on an enormous iron hook stuck through the ribs, the tortured bandit so exhibited on the town square for all to see and be warned — not unlike an imperial Roman crucifixion. Slovakia is not a wealthy country. Its museums, many of which were established during the communist period, were not high-priority items in the national budget. As a result, explanatory texts in the exhibits had not been updated since the fall of communism in 1989. So I could still read indignant Marxist explanations at such exhibits when I lived there in the 1990s, for example, that the torture instruments are proof of the injustice and inhumanity of the feudal system,

---

23. Ann Douglas brilliantly diagnoses the marginalization of clergy, women, and traditional humanist intellectuals during the nineteenth-century rise of capitalism in America in *The Feminization of American Culture* (New York: Anchor Press/Doubleday, 1977).

which by terror crushed the revolutionary aspirations of the peasants as personified in the bandit Janošik. No doubt there is truth in that. But knowing what we know today about Lenin's mass murder of the aristocracy and the Russian Orthodox clergy, Stalin's intentional starvation of the Ukrainian kulaks, the purges, the show trials, the complicity with Hitler over Poland, the Gulag, 1968, Normalization and the brutal defense of Real Existing Socialism (one could go endlessly on), one thing seems certain. It is not so much that the instruments of torture were abolished by Marxism as that they were merely modernized — and changed hands.[24] Slovak Lutherans saw what was coming: Hitlerism and Bolshevism, both of them plagues.[25]

I am about to diagnose a uniquely Marxian cruelty, but by this I do not intend to disregard other manifestations of well-organized modern barbarism. Contemporary theology pays ample attention to these others, as well it should. But oddly, it ignores the Marxian cruelty. One could rightly point to the feudal cruelty, as I just did with the example of Janošik, and argue that it provoked the Marxist reaction. Very well, but that only proves the point that Marxism was just another spin on the cycle of human violence, another chapter in our long-running tragedy of institutionalized human cruelty. But this is silly. Marxism has been quintessentially modern. It is exemplary of modern tendencies that are also present in fascism and liberalism, though fascism's modernism is romantic, reactionary, and racist while liberalism's is agnostic and diffident. Marxism's exaggerated, consequent modernism is what I have in mind now in speaking of a uniquely Marxian cruelty. Let it then be very clear that I am *not* contending that *only* Marxism is cruel, or that *only* it has made persons vicious. Much of the same critique can also be directed at contemporaneous capitalist regimes, where traditional feudal oligarchies have merely been exchanged for new moneyed ones or where populist "democratic" but illiberal regimes have come to power. Moreover the type of theological critique

24. The instructive parallel between fascism and Marxism as modern totalitarianisms is worked out by Alan Bullock, *Hitler and Stalin: Parallel Lives* (London: Fontana Press, 1991), which also amply documents the catalogue of crimes that may be charged to real, historical Marxism.

25. Samuel Stefan Osusky, "The Philosophy of Bolshevism, Fascism and Hitlerism: A Lecture presented at the Academic Conference of the Ministerium of the Liptovsky, Oravsky, Turiec, and Zvolen Districts of the Evangelical Lutheran Church of the Augsburg Confession on November 22, 1937 in Ruzomberok, Czechoslovakia," translation forthcoming by Paul R. Hinlicky, from *Styri Prednasky* [Four Lectures] (Mikulas: Tranoscius, 1938).

of Marxism that I want to undertake here may prove surprisingly pertinent to its erstwhile antipode, liberal capitalism, insofar as both modern ideologies may be understood as the sibling rivals of the Enlightenment's attempt to refound morality on a non-religious, rational, and secular basis.

"The fundamental issue between Marxists and Christians concerns the question: Is there a place for Prometheus in the Christian calendar? Are the biblical-Christian and the promethean-Marxist perspectives of human nature and destiny mutually exclusive? Is Christ the antipode of Prometheus? If Christ and Prometheus were two mutually exclusive alternatives, then the only responsible encounter between Christians and Marxists would be in terms of confrontation and not dialogue."[26] So the Czech Reformed theologian Jan Milič Lochman rightly posed the question, which, however, I wish to answer somewhat differently than he. Marxism was *uniquely* vicious because of its consequent, systematic atheism vis-à-vis the Christian God upon whom faith *waits* (as per Marx's critique of Luther in the epigraph). This eschatological refusal as a result made the promethean agents of the new humanity *uncommonly* cruel in that they committed their enormous, monstrous crimes because of moral illusions *peculiar* to them. It was precisely as the promise of earthly agency of the new humanity[27] that Marxism worked its spell and also its unprecedented evils. The fanatical, messianic self-understanding of Marxism as the redemptive "key to the riddle of history" bestowed on Marxists a good conscience in behavior that from outside their all-absorbing world looks plainly sadistic. "The success of the revolution is our highest good" — this was the practical maxim and guiding ethical light.[28] Marxism was uniquely destructive of civic virtue because this peculiar illusion about ushering in a new order of the ages on the basis of scientific insight was the source of its actual use, or rather systematic abuse, of the coercive powers of the monopolistic modern state. Marxism could have no patience with human beings *simul iustus et peccator,* no tolerance for the moral ambiguity that human beings are and remain, until all things are made new.

---

26. Jan Milič Lochman, *Christ and Prometheus? A Quest for Theological Identity* (Geneva: WCC Publications, 1988), p. 25.

27. Glenn Tinder, *The Political Meaning of Christianity* (Baton Rouge and London: Louisiana State University Press, 1989), instructively contrasts "the God-man" with "the man-God."

28. This problem of "means and ends" in Marxist morality is lucidly and convincingly dissected in chap. 6 of Steven Lukes, *Marxism and Morality* (Oxford: Oxford University Press, 1987), pp. 100-138.

With this counter-claim, one points to an immense irony. The very ideology that wanted to overcome human alienation and liberate humanity for creative, social existence instead raped the environment in massive, grandiose acts of mindless industrialization; imposed cultural uniformity of the most deadening kind; debased the understanding of public life to that of animals fighting for survival in a Darwinian jungle; and drove citizens to wall themselves off psychologically from a Kafkaesque world which Arthur Koestler already in the 1930s unforgettably described in his knowingly titled book, *The God That Failed.*[29] Let one poignant testimony here suffice. The following declaration of the Congress of Russian Intellectuals appeared in the Bratislava newspapers on August 15, 1998, commenting on the 30th anniversary of the Warsaw Pact invasion of the former Czechoslovakia, which crushed Alexander Dubcek's liberalization policies for "socialism with a human face":

> Thirty years ago in the night of August 20 tanks of the countries of the Warsaw Pact crossed the Czechoslovak borders on orders from Moscow. In the morning they entered Prague, in order to crush the Prague Spring. Bolshevik socialism once again showed the world its real face. Now it is too simple to point at the criminal irresponsibility of our former leaders. Today we must also speak of our own responsibility as citizens for everything which this country does which acquired the humiliating nickname, "the evil empire." In the difficult battle with evil, which is still not definitively defeated, in sufferings, in chaos, a new democratic Russia is being born in the present time. We are filled with faith that our land will really become a prosperous, democratic country. A few brave persons also believed this, who in protest against the evil committed in Czechoslovakia came to Red Square thirty years ago and paid for that with their own freedom. Today we proclaim: The Russian democratic public does everything to the end that imperialistic autocracy and violence against one's own people as well as against the nations of other lands not return. We challenge our friends in other countries: Be in solidarity with the democratic, reforming part of Russia. We need your support.[30]

29. Arthur Koestler, *The God That Failed* (New York: Harper, 1949).

30. *Sme* (Bratislava, Slovakia: vol. 6 and 51, no. 189: August 15, 1998). My translation from the Slovak.

Ronald Reagan's denunciation of the "evil empire" still makes Western intellectuals shudder, especially German Protestants who remember all too well Hitler's playing of the Bolshevism card to marshal domestic support. To the extent that a self-serving indictment of a now defeated opponent blinds Westerners to their own sins, it should. But in order to respond to this plea for support today from "the democratic, reforming part of Russia," indeed, of many other places in the world, as Euro-American Christian intellectuals surely ought, we need to come to terms with what Marxism really was. We need to do this not only to be rid of an infantile fantasy, but to come to terms with our own destiny in the troubled ship of liberal democracy. This of course is not to say that liberal democracy is the Beloved Community, only that is the form of the modern political state which is in principle open to it and further, that it is the only power, monopoly of violence and all, capable of restraining the juggernaut of global capitalism and the nightmare of the commodification of all things.[31]

The word "Marxism" represents an enormous and diverse tradition of social thought, beginning with Marx's original warning against the "commodification of all things." It is true in a highly diffuse sense that "we are all Marxists today," that is, that we appreciate and utilize the sociology of knowledge that descends from Hegel through Marx as we struggle to think ourselves out of the atomistic individualism of consumer capitalism. I would prefer then to say in this respect that "we are all Hegelians now." Some will still wish to distinguish redeemable elements in this tradition from the "Bolshevik socialism" referred to above. Certainly any attempt to criticize Marxism without allowing for alternative readings would be an unjust and foolhardy oversimplification. That being acknowledged, a certain simplification is allowable here. Theological criticism of Marxism has a *prima facie* right to focus in on Marxist *atheism and its corresponding prometheanism,* other valuable insights notwithstanding. One undertakes that, not to gild the obituary of a foe already fallen (atheism vis-à-vis the Christian God on whom we have in faith to *wait* has hardly fallen!), but in order to contribute to an urgent need to reconceptualize human social and political progress. In this vein, I want to indicate how the evil ironies to which I have pointed are not some secondary corruption of an originally innocent social theory, attributable, say, to Stalin or Lenin. The evil ironies go back to Marx's own Marxism. This becomes apparent when we under-

31. Talal Asad, *Formations of the Secular: Christianity, Islam, Modernity* (Stanford, CA: Stanford University Press, 2003), pp. 157-58.

stand Marx's own Marxism as an anti-theology, indeed as a distinctively Christian apostasy, as I shall explain.[32] From this specific perspective, moreover, it is possible to focus narrowly on what is essential in the Marxism that inevitably grew into Bolshevik socialism, namely, the false image it presents of humanity as *Homo faber,* as maker, as creator. This is but the inverse side of its consistent atheism.

## Homo faber

The formal resemblances between Christianity and Marxism are well recognized. Where Christianity speaks of the calling of humanity as God's covenant partner and representative on earth, Marxism speaks of *Homo faber,* humanity as worker whose destiny is to conquer nature and create his own world. Where Christianity speaks of the fall into sin by which humanity is alienated from God, neighbor, and self, Marxism speaks of the alienation effected by the division of labor, which divides humanity into mutually hostile classes. Where Christianity speaks of a prophetic critique that reveals sin, Marxism sponsors the relentless criticism of all philosophies, religions, and ideologies which conceal unjust relationships in society. Where Christianity speaks of the messianic hope of the coming of the Prince of Peace, Marxism points to the proletarian class as the bearer of universal liberation. Where Christianity is summoned to the evangelization of the nations and the battle against sin, Marxism awakens international class-consciousness and summons to revolutionary praxis. Where Christianity has spiritual pastors who lead the people of God, Marxism gives the leading role in the workers' movement to the Communist party. Where Christianity holds to dogmas of faith, Marxism elaborates the sci-

---

32. Reinhold Niebuhr made this critique of Marxism as messianism gone awry with unforgettable force in various writings. John Milbank, "The Poverty of Niebuhrianism," in *The Word Made Strange: Theology, Language, Culture* (Cambridge, MA: Blackwell, 1997), pp. 219-32, is an important critique of the theological liberalism (Stoicism) that Niebuhr never fully overcame, but fails to take into sufficient account the historical situation in which Niebuhr had to develop a stance of "hopeful realism" against Marxist illusions. This critique might better have been directed at Paul Tillich's Christian realism, since Tillich openly advocated the Hegelian equation of finitude and the fall, against which Niebuhr argued. See Paul Tillich, "Reinhold Niebuhr's Doctrine of Knowledge," in *Reinhold Niebuhr: His Religious, Social, and Political Theology,* ed. Robert W. Bretall and Charles W. Kegley (New York: Macmillan, 1956), chap. 2, pp. 35-49, and Niebuhr's reply to Tillich in the same volume, pp. 431-33. I will discuss Niebuhr and Milbank's critique of Niebuhr further below.

entific principles of historical development. Where Christianity sees a need for repentance, Marxism speaks of the need to overcome false consciousness. Where Christianity promises eternal salvation in the kingdom of God, Marxism foresees the coming of the dictatorship of the proletariat, the building of socialism, and the withering away of the state. In general we see that Marxism follows Christianity step by step in a meta-narrative of creation, fall, redemption, and final salvation. Marxism offers Christianity's history of salvation, yet without God or the kingdom of God.

Marx understood this resemblance. Recall the words of the early Marx's *Critique of Hegel's 'Philosophy of Right'*: "To be radical is to grasp things by the root. But for man, the root is man himself. The clear proof of the radicalism of German theory [Marx is thinking of the young Hegelians], and hence of its political energy is that it proceeds from the decisive *positive* transcendence of religion. The criticism of religion ends with the doctrine that *man* is *the highest being for man,* hence with the *categorical imperative to overthrow all conditions* in which man is a degraded, enslaved, neglected, contemptible being. . . ."[33] We take note of three interlocking steps here. First, the radical program for human liberation directly follows upon a refusal of the First Commandment. What is refused here is the reign of God, the command and promise of the Lord God of Israel, Creator and Redeemer of the entire world, to be "the highest being for humanity." Second, this refusal issues in a moral claim that is at the ethical heart of revolutionary praxis: a new categorical imperative to relentlessly criticize all social orders in which humanity is abased. From this, third, the practical precept (as previously mentioned) will flow: "the success of the revolution is our highest good." To understand Marxist morality, one must always come back to this original refusal of the First Commandment, this repudiation of the reign of the biblical God, as the basis of a positive act of faith in the prospective divinity of man against which human abasement in the present is to be measured.

This forms as direct an antithesis to Luther's teaching as can be conceived: "They deny faith and try to bless themselves by their own works, that is, to justify themselves, to set themselves free from sin and death, to overcome the devil, and to capture heaven by force, which is to deny God and to set oneself up in the place of God. For all these are exclusively the

---

33. "Towards the Critique of Hegel's Philosophy of Law," in *Writings of the Young Marx on Philosophy and Society,* trans. Loyd D. Easton and Kurt H. Guddat (Garden City, NY: Anchor, 1967), p. 259.

works of the Divine Majesty, not of any creature. . . . For those who teach that some other worship is necessary for salvation than the worship set down in the First Commandment — which is fear, trust, and love toward God — are antichrists and are setting themselves up in the place of God. . . ."[34] The metaphysical posit "that man is the highest being for man" is the act of "initial faith"[35] out of which Marxist rationality proceeds. This intersects directly with Luther's conviction that, in Bayer's words, "atheism is the highpoint among religions, which is most clearly seen in the religion of self-actualization, in which the human being seeks to make himself reliant simply on himself."[36] Marxism understood this very well. "Coercive atheization" (a term Slovaks used to describe Marxist proselytism) is mandatory policy in building socialism. In order to build a kingdom of righteousness on earth, it is necessary to root out from the mind of humanity the illusory hope of a kingdom of bliss in heaven above.

We can rehearse basic features of Marxism[37] in this respect around the central image of humanity as maker, producer, worker, creator. Work, or praxis, is the basic activity of humanity, according to Marx. In work the human community intentionally and thoughtfully alters the given, natural environment in the interest of its own survival and betterment. Marx uses the Greek word *praxis* to indicate that thought, theory, intellectual activity is also a material act, an aspect of labor. Thought also belongs integrally to the intentional labor of transforming the natural world to satisfy human needs and realize human dreams. The concept of praxis locates human thought in purposive human labor and thus disallows any religious or philosophical dualism of brains and brawn, theory and practice, mind and matter. It specifically rejects the Kantian, liberal notion that Reason represents a universal, neutral capacity that can objectively survey competing values, interests, and ideologies to judge between them. There is no such disembodied transcendent Reason, Marx says, but only the concrete the-

---

34. "Commentary on Galatians" (1535) LW 26:257-58.

35. For the Augustinian concept of "initial faith," see Alan Richardson, *Christian Apologetics* (New York: Harper & Brothers, 1947), especially chap. 3, "Christianity and Ideology," pp. 65-88.

36. Oswald Bayer, *Martin Luther's Theology: A Contemporary Interpretation,* trans. Thomas H. Trapp (Grand Rapids: Eerdmans, 2007), p. 137.

37. Making no pretense to original Marxist scholarship, I follow David McLellan, *The Thought of Karl Marx: An Introduction* (New York: Harper Torchbooks, 1971) as the basis for my presentation and interpretation of Marx's voluminous work. Also Sir Isaiah Berlin, *Karl Marx: His Life and Environment* (New York: Time, 1963).

ory of some particular praxis. Marx's own theory is a theory of *revolutionary* praxis, i.e., it is the doctrine of those who are intentionally working to overcome human alienation and to achieve human liberation. So the theoretical question arises for revolutionaries: How did alienation come about and why is there a need for liberation? Revolutionary social theory needs to construct a compelling and illuminating narrative of the human conflict in which the agents of the new humanity find themselves in order to map the way forward through revolution to communism.

It goes something like this. In order to survive merciless natural forces, primitive humanity had to organize as a workforce. By means of this economic organization of society, humanity began to force nature to serve its needs. But in order for human beings to rule over nature, they had to institute rule among themselves. This took place by the division of labor in the distribution of various economic tasks. Thus slaves and kings, serfs and lords, workers and bosses came into being. In the course of history this division of labor became increasingly extended and complex, bringing with it great material progress. Indeed by the time of capitalism, the growth of wealth seemed both inevitable and infinite. Capitalism projected the total scientific and technical conquest of nature. Marx himself (in dialectical, Hegelian fashion) praised capitalism for its historical role in the creation of wealth and scientific culture, which are the material presuppositions of socialism. Marx attacked romantics and idealists on the far left who wanted to return to some sort of primitive state prior to the conquest of nature, who thus ignored or devalued humanity's actual need for the economic progress that capitalism effects in its conquest of nature. Note well that Marxism in principle *never promises to overcome the basic human alienation from nature, not even in the communist utopia.* On the contrary the *human conflict with nature is understood as the driving force in all of history.* "Economy" is the name for the mechanism of this human conflict with nature. In the communist utopia nature will have been *conquered,* forced into submission to do the will of humanity, *not* reconciled.

In human history, however, a second type of alienation transpires that can someday be overcome; it is a distinctively human alienation from one's own human essence as both a productive and a social being. In buying and selling her labor the worker both loses control over her product and becomes a competitor with others on the labor market. Consequently, in place of the natural collaboration among social beings, cutthroat competition comes about, which at once atomizes and dehumanizes the competitors, who lose control and ownership of themselves as *Homo faber* as well as the fruits of their labor. On this basis, Marx developed a rhetorically potent *moral* critique of capitalism. Human labor in social collaboration represents the true value of products, so morally (i.e., on the assumption of the equal value of all human workers) prices should be determined, not by what a given product might fetch in an unregulated market, but by the labor value that goes into making the product. Moreover, since labor is in essence a social undertaking, the return in any event belongs to all. The very existence of private property betrays the true human value of things. Property should rather be regarded as an expression of the creative social labor of the human community, which should serve everyone equally in return. But this true (moral) evaluation and use of labor and property is impossible under capitalism; true value and use is systematically subverted by the amoral juggernaut of the unregulated market to maximize profit by maximizing efficiency, leading to the commodification of all things (i.e., nothing is sacred; everything and everyone has its price).

Just here, however, an enormous perplexity emerges. How is this true moral evaluation of labor possible in the social theorizing of revolutionary praxis, which arises still under the dark shadow of capitalism? How could anyone, even the revolutionary, ever know that humans are equal in value or regard their labor as stolen in proportion to the value by which the finished product transcends the raw materials from which it was made? How can it be seen that the initiative of the entrepreneur is in fact beholden to social collaboration? Who deprograms the revolutionaries to see and judge truly in this way? On what basis then could a revolutionary thinker execute even roughly such a *moral* critique? Faced with this enigma, Marx himself, while deploying morally potent rhetoric tactically as occasion required, increasingly turned away from evaluative claims toward the task of grounding revolutionary praxis in a scientific social theory that appealed to reason alone, as Sir Isaiah Berlin particularly underscored.[38] Here light dawns to the extent that the contradictions of late capitalism force themselves upon consciousness. It is not a matter of moral evaluation at all, but of scientific insight.

So "scientific" social theory of the surplus value of labor now generated a grand theory of history. The ex-appropriation of the value of the workers' labor by capitalists produces profits. This creates surplus money, that is, new capital. Capital in turn finances technical progress, and the fruits of this progress in principle increasingly satisfy human needs, even if

38. Berlin, *Marx*, pp. 5-8.

in practice all this comes about at the expense of the workers, in that the benefits of material progress are far from equally distributed. As the imperative of the capitalist juggernaut is to maximize profit by maximizing efficiency, technical progress increasingly displaces human workers with automation. In the fullness of time this leads to massive accumulation of wealth among a diminishing number of monopoly capitalists and massive unemployment among the increasingly replaced workers. These woes, however, are the birth pangs of the new creation, a *kairos* pregnant with new possibilities. Class war finally explodes, as the contradiction between the surplus of capital in the hands of the few and the pauperization of the working-class masses becomes unsustainable. That in sketch was Marx's social-scientific prediction for communist revolution in industrialized Europe. It was the theory of revolutionary praxis, scientifically reasoned, rigorously replacing in the process moral judgments of value with cognitive insights having predictive power.

In developing this theory, Marx was guided by the Hegelian conviction (the "real is rational, and the rational is real") that history is driven by a hidden law, namely that basic conflict of spirit (human intelligence) with nature (matter in motion according to physical law indifferent to human purposes). In scientific Marxism, beginning with the mature Marx himself, the story of cataclysmic historical development through class conflict culminating in the dramatic collapse of capitalism acquired the status of a law of historical development. It told that the essential capacity of humanity intelligently and intentionally to forge its own destiny is what had been lost; liberation means somehow reacquiring and reasserting this capacity to act as agent of one's own destiny. Thus the revolutionary worker instructed by revolutionary theory *actively awaits* the *kairos, anticipating* the liberating denouement of the drama of historical conflict in the final crisis of capitalism. They are open to such instruction. As vast numbers of industrial workers became pauperized, they are in the process also stripped of the vestiges of antecedent consciousness — religious, nationalist, or other particularist forms of human identity — and thus come to acquire a new consciousness of belonging to an emergent universal class, the proletariat. The proletariat purged and purified by these fires and instructed by scientific theory thus becomes the bearer of the universal future of humanity. This is the class that has nothing to lose but its chains. Its humiliation has been its preparation.

In the final crisis of capitalism, there is a convergence of developments. Under capitalism, humanity has attained to a stage of sufficient scientific and material progress in the conquest of nature to provide for the building of socialism. In the proletariat, humanity has reached the necessary state of universal consciousness for the building of socialism. Now, according to the secret cunning of history, a new human agency is ripe for seizing that long lost agency by seizing the future. The workers rise up, seize power, and appropriate the material success of capitalism for the building of a consciously classless society. What seals this convergence of forces, and bridges the gap between essence and existence, is this new agent and act of revolutionary praxis in which the workers reappropriate their alienated human essence. Taking history into their own hands, liberating themselves, they reacquire not only stolen property. More profoundly, in acting as revolutionaries, they above all reacquire the lost status of creators of their own common future. They are no longer passive and atomized objects of nature and historical-economic forces.

In developing this analysis, it must be emphasized again, Marx was not at all an ethical idealist who preached morality to the capitalists, in the hope that they might change their ways and behave more justly. In reality Marx was contemptuous of idealistic or religious socialism. Later, Lenin called such people "useful idiots," that is, those whom scientific Marxists could politically manipulate while disdaining their convictions. The new science of revolution was not founded idealistically on a moral appeal to the Ought, but on the scientific truth about human history and its once hidden, but now revealed, rationality. In place of idealism, Marx (with the aid of Engels) put forward the new science of historical materialism, where all reality proceeds from the dynamic motion of matter in accord with law. The conflict of the human species with nature is the original social fact, which a materialist theory of history uncovers and employs as an explanation of the hidden rationality of historical-economic development. Morality and idealism, like religion, have no place here but as mystification.

Yet, and in spite of all that has been said, Marx often *does* speak in a moral if not moralistic way, as if based upon a genuine knowledge of value. For example, as previously mentioned, he speaks of the injustice of capitalists ex-appropriating the value of the workers' labors, or of the injustice that the benefits of material progress are not distributed equally to all, or above all as we saw, he voiced the "categorical imperative" to overthrow all conditions that degrade human beings as measured by a metaphysical posit of human essence and its value.[39] On the one hand, Marx makes

---

39. "In short, like Marx, Engels, Kautsky and Lenin, Trotsky was committed on the one

moral evaluations of capitalist theft of workers' labor. On the other hand, Marx denies that moral evaluation is possible under these conditions of systematic, thoroughgoing alienation. Some kind of epistemological privilege is thus being ascribed to revolutionary theory. *A key move, indeed leap is made here. True moral evaluation is impossible under the conditions of alienation; it waits the overcoming of alienation in the workers' paradise. But in that case, how do Marxists rationally evaluate exploitation, as they manifestly do, and more seriously, how could Marxists ever critically evaluate their own revolutionary activity until* after *the revolution and the actual achievement of communism?*

This ambiguity in Marx is fateful. It reflects the strange fusion of determinism and freedom at the heart of his philosophy of history, borrowed of course from Hegel. On a purely scientific level, according to Marx's own theory, the argument is and has to be that capitalism is a necessary stage of human development and that the transition to socialism comes inevitably — but only when the time is ripe for it, that is, when the capitalist epoch has created both the material and spiritual presuppositions for building socialism. But in that case the moral activity of criticizing capitalism seems to be nugatory: exhorting proletarians to class-consciousness, organizing workers, theorizing about the laws of historical development, indeed the existential decision for revolutionary praxis itself. All this active anticipating revolution as evaluative action seems not only superfluous but also ungrounded. Does someone undertake revolutionary praxis as if by this he or she could help along the historical process with a merely subjective decision? How is such a merely subjective decision possible anyway under the conditions of total alienation? Can history be exhorted? Paradoxically, it seems that Marx uses the language of morality whenever he wants to summon readers to a change in consciousness grounded in *moral* decision for revolutionary praxis. Yet he disowns the language of value when revolutionary praxis is itself critically evaluated. Such a privileged stance is morally absolute, in other words, self-justifying. How are we to understand this?

Marx and his chief followers disavowed any need to ground moral discourse before the court of universal reason, but the fateful price of that

---

hand to the moral condemnation of capitalist evils and the advocacy and pursuit of socialist ends, and indeed to the justification of these ends in terms of a 'liberating morality'; and on the other, to the dismissal of all moral talk as dangerous ideological illusion, rendered anachronistic by the discovery of scientific laws of economic development." Lukes, *Marxism and Morality,* p. 25. I am calling a conundrum what Lukes here identifies as a "paradox."

disavowal was the failure to develop middle axioms by means of which they would be able to apply their own implicit morality self-critically to their own practice. In the "siege mentality" of class war, they were content to affirm that the success of the revolution is the highest good of humanity itself. Nor would it be easy to revise Marxism at this point, because the meta-narrative turns on the depiction of a total class war in which one must be located in either camp. As in Luther, there is no neutrality. Siege mentality is ingredient to the narrative itself, and militates against any recognition of a common human rationality or morality (i.e., natural law) by means of which one could give *reasons* (short of total conversion to the Marxist meta-narrative) why the revolution is the highest good of *humanity* (since "humanity" is divided into classes at war with each other), reasons that could function in turn as *criteria* for assessing revolutionary praxis self-critically. Why, after all, should it be unjust for the strong to direct the weak, the wise to govern the foolish, the wealthy to rule the poor? Parental authority, the model for political authority in much pre-modern thought, thinks it both natural and right that strong and wise parents rule weak and inexperienced children, not to dominate them but to nurture, protect, and enable them.[40] But beyond standard rationalistic attacks on the ideological pretensions of feudal paternalism, Marxists refused such considerations in principle. Marxists declined rational justification of their tacit moral claims in favor of strategic, tactical, or utilitarian considerations about the way forward to the revolution. Undertaking rational moral argument with opponents, like undertaking reform politics in the framework of the existing capitalist system, inevitably entangles one in the dynamics of alienation, which should rather be relentlessly criticized.

---

40. "Out of the authority of parents all other authority is derived and developed" (*The Book of Concord*, ed. Robert Kolb and Timothy J. Wengert [Minneapolis: Fortress, 2000], 407:150ff.), a position that Kant's influential contrast of heteronomy in ethics takes dead aim at: "Enlightenment is humanity's leaving behind its self-caused immaturity. Immaturity is the incapacity to use one's intelligence without the guidance of another. Such immaturity is self-caused if it is not caused by lack of intelligence, but by lack of determination and courage to use one's intelligence without being guided by another. Have the courage to use your intelligence! — that is the motto of the Enlightenment." "What Is Enlightenment?" in *The Philosophy of Kant: Immanuel Kant's Moral and Political Writings*, ed. Carl J. Friedrich (New York: The Modern Library, 1949), pp. 132-39. Jean Bethke Elshtain, *Public Man, Private Woman* (Princeton: Princeton University Press, 1981), correctly contrasts Luther's stance with contractarian theories by pointing to the necessary absence of children, childbearing and nurturing women, the aged, and the infirm in liberal theories, and to the presence of caring, providing, and disciplining fathers in Luther's.

There is for Marx, one might say, no bargaining with the devil (nor is there, we may note, any alternative to demonizing class enemies). The amelioration of conditions by reform politics in the framework of liberal democracy simply strengthens the capitalist system and delays the day of revolutionary reckoning. The moral justification of revolutionary praxis before the law court of universal reason is the Trojan Horse of class warfare; playing that game only saps the movement of clarity of vision and purity of purpose.

Even more decisively, for Marx the final objection to reform politics and rational disputation about moral decisions with class enemies is a *religious* one, though it is hardly acknowledged as such, *against the passivity of waiting* and, if I may express it this way, the *patience* of life together, the basic morality of *Mitsein*. Reform politics will never be able to overcome *this* self-alienation of humanity, as Marx has diagnosed that, but the true human is *Homo faber*. Nor can conventional moral disputation attain to the radical diagnosis, since the assumption is that disputants interact as moral equals, when in fact they are oppressor and oppressed. Marx then objects, not to tactical, but to moral compromises with the old order, because such compromises betray the radical salvation that is both needed and actively sought. This stance is religiously absolute, self-validating like a conversion experience. The revolutionary worker now bears the authentic image of humanity; she is the highest being for humanity, who does not need to be justified, but before whom all others must justify themselves. No other moral justification of this creative praxis can be given or required, for it constitutes a virtually metaphysical revelation for Marx of the reappropriated human essence as creator. No matter how alluring reform politics that ameliorate the plight of workers might be, no matter how plausible the objections of bourgeois moralists, for Marx, *one should choose revolutionary practice as the right way to overcome the evil system in principle, for here, and only here, in this way, and only in this way, "man becomes the highest being for man."*

## Marxism as a Christian Heresy

With this, the theological objection against Marx is made. Has not Marx's deterministic system resolved itself astonishingly enough into a pure option, willful choice, a metaphysical or religious posit of a highest being, which is and appears self-validating? Marx is surely not an idealist who thinks that there is another, truer realm above. But he is a perfectly modern *Gnostic*, who appeals to the fellow elect on the basis of a revelatory insight that he, modern Revealer of the key to the riddle of history, discloses now to all who are able to receive it. Like the ancient Gnostics, Marx tells a tale of the fall of the children of light into the alien world of matter, until at last coming to consciousness of their true nature and power, they rise as conquerors in the conflict with matter. This modernized Gnostic myth lies in the immediate background of Marxian social theory. If that is so, there is good reason why Marx disregarded the tacitly moral dimension of his doctrine of humanity. Consideration of this incoherence would have led him back to the Christian theological doctrine about somatic selves created in the image of God for *Mitsein*, that is, to the morally culpable refusal of the God of the Bible with which his project was launched.

In 1968 the celebrated moral philosopher Alasdair MacIntyre (who at the time regarded himself a Trotskyite) published a penetrating analysis in which he claimed that "only one secular doctrine retains the scope of traditional religion in offering an interpretation of human existence by means of which men may situate themselves in the world and direct their actions to ends which transcend those offered by their immediate situation: Marxism."[41] Indeed, "Marxism shares in good measure both the content and the functions of Christianity as an interpretation of human existence, and it does so because it is the historical successor of Christianity."[42] MacIntyre went on to identify the Hegelian doctrine of human alienation as the humanistic core of an original, prophetic Marxian praxis, which had been overshadowed by dogmatic, positivistic readings of Marx, beginning with Engels and culminating in Stalin. This is a kind of interpretation that has been taken up by many humanistic Marxists and sympathizing theologians, which I now claim to revise fundamentally in several respects on the

---

41. Alasdair MacIntyre, *Marxism and Christianity* (Notre Dame: University of Notre Dame Press, 1984), p. 2. As John Milbank shows, Hegel "makes a profound attempt to identify the difference which Christianity has made to western history, and does not, like sociology or Marxism, try to reduce the unique aspects of Christian social experience to some supposedly more 'basic' dimension of society. . . . The most extraordinary aspect to this attempt is that he attributes a great causal efficacy to the incarnation and crucifixion of Christ, and the early Church's experience of resurrection." Milbank, *Theology and Social Theory: Beyond Secular Reason* (Oxford: Blackwell, 1997), p. 163. This accounts for the basic correctness of the thesis about the dependence of the Marxist narrative via Hegel on Christianity.

42. MacIntyre, *Marxism and Christianity*, p. 6. I am here following Milbank, *Social Theory*, p. 189.

basis of the foregoing analysis. First, we should speak of Marxism as the historical *usurper* of Christianity rather than its successor. And second, while it is correct to locate the religious roots of Marxism in Hegel's doctrine of alienation, we must also see that the Hegelian doctrine of alienation and liberation is already substantively a *Gnostic* deviation from Christian orthodoxy.[43] In short, Marxism is not simply a secularization of Christianity, but a secularization of a deviant, heretical Christianity. Gnosticism does not envision a fall into sin to be overcome by God's grace, but a fall into finitude that stigmatizes all future history with inevitable conflict and violence, until finitude itself is overcome by a titanic revolutionary act realizing human divinity. These revisions of MacIntyre's thesis account not only for Marxism's messianism, but also for the peculiar moral blindness of Marxism to its own unique cruelty.

How is that unique cruelty *thought?* In Marx's critique of religion as opiate, it is not only God who must be demystified. When Marx uses the word "humanity," he is not thinking of an individual or a person or even a society of persons, let alone the Beloved Community, but of a natural species, just like all the other species. Humanity is but a species, just as, according to consistent materialism, the phenomena of human consciousness should not be reified into the idea of substantial soul. Personality, consciousness, or personhood is nothing more than the passing ensemble of social relations in some particular individual's brain. Thus, just as there is no God, neither is there any substantial soul nor, in modern language, any person who bears inalienable rights and transcendent dignity. It corresponds to this that it is not humanity as an individual or as a person or as a community of persons who enters into the communist paradise, but rather humanity as species. All individuals who suffered and died in the past on

---

43. Precisely insofar as Marx remains a Hegelian. See Cyril O'Regan, *The Heterodox Hegel* (Albany: State University of New York Press, 1994). See also Milbank, "For and Against Hegel," in *Social Theory,* chap. 6, pp. 147-76. "Hegel attempts to reason to the infinite from a finite 'starting point', and to such 'gnosticism' appropriately adds a gnostic myth of a necessarily self-estranged and self-returning God who leaves behind him the scattered husks of the merely material and indifferent" (p. 160). Marx only demythologizes this myth, taking it over in a secular version which makes it all the more vulnerable to terrorist interpretations (p. 195). Lukes cites Engels: "A 'revolution is certainly the most authoritarian thing there is': it is the act whereby one part of the population imposes its will upon the other part by means of rifles, bayonets, and cannon — authoritarian means if ever there were any; and if the victorious party does not want to have fought in vain, it must maintain this rule by means of the terror which its arms inspire in the reactionaries" (Lukes, *Marxism and Morality,* p. 103, cited from Engels, *Selected Works,* 1874, "On Authority," p. 639).

the way to the revolution are lost forever in the tragedies of alienated history. What has been is tragedy, to be left behind and forgotten. On the other hand, according to Marx, human personality will flourish when alienation has been overcome. In the communist paradise, human beings will all become artists, inventing their own selves in perfect harmony with others in a world of technologically secured abundance. Meanwhile, under the conditions of alienation, any given "person," that is, consciousness, is but a passive mirror reflecting the passing parade of unjust social relations. It is only potentially an agent capable of initiating history and directing life in liberating social praxis. Thus for Marx the true human person does not yet exist but is being born in the proletariat, arising in revolutionary praxis. From this doctrine, the chilling deduction from cruelty in thought to practical cruelty lies close at hand. If the true human person does not yet exist, neither do existing individuals bearing inalienable rights or transcendent dignity corresponding to a presently acknowledged personhood. (We can note here in passing what is at stake in the theological grounding of human rights.)

We are now in position to understand a revealing discrepancy: Marxism appealed morally more to the poor and disenfranchised of the emergent world than to the Western working classes of industrialized society whom Marx originally had in mind, while in the West Marxism's enduring appeal has been to intellectuals marginalized by the capitalist system. This *actual* appeal that Marxism exercised is an important clue to why Marxism ultimately failed, for Marxism, recall, was supposed to be the theory of the revolutionary praxis of industrial workers, not the academic social science of alienated Western intellectuals or the prophetic rallying cry of rural peasants against colonialism and imperialism. The peasantry, tied to the land and trapped in what Marx contemptuously derided as "the idiocy of rural life," could not yet become the bearer of universal human values as the proletariat was supposed to be, nor could their backwards societies, which had not yet passed through the crucial stage of capitalist industrialization, provide the material infrastructure for building socialism. In Europe itself the revolutionary workers movements never fully became Marxist because liberal and/or nationalistic ideologies with their ideals of civil rights and national culture dissipated the resolve of workers, while economic growth, education, and social reforms defused discontent. Trade-unionism was the death of Marxist appeal among the real working class of Euro-America.

Frustrated with the petty bourgeois failure of workers' movements in the industrialized countries, it was Lenin who seized the opportunity to take power in collapsing Czarist Russia by fusing together these two poles of Marxism's *actual* appeal. Russia was a feudal peasant society, Lenin and his colleagues were Westernized intellectuals. Under the centralized guidance of the Party, revolutionary peasants and workers in Russia could avoid the fate of the compromised workers' movements in Western Europe. Being centrally directed, they would skip an entire historical stage of capitalist economic development and proceed at once to the construction of socialism. In this respect, not only is Lenin's innovation a concession that Marx's own script for historical development had somehow gone amiss (Lenin attempted to explain this with his theory of imperialism, i.e., that industrialized nations bought time by exporting their crisis to the colonies). But this very correction of Marx by Lenin in the notion of "democratic centralism" (i.e., the dictatorship of the Party in the workers' movement) snuffed out whatever democratic potential remained to Marx's key notion of social praxis[44] and entrenched the totalitarian reading of Marx, which would culminate in the massive murders of Stalin, the blundering brutality of Brezhnev, Mao's "cultural revolution," Pol Pot's killing fields.

Yet it was Marx himself, as we have seen, who equivocated on the question of the relation of intentional human agency to social change; indeed this unresolved question is at the heart of his stance. Is Lenin's idea sheer nonsense, that guided by Marx's analysis revolutionary intellectuals could dictate to the proletariat, and command them perchance to leap over the entire stage of capitalist development in history by a sheer exertion of revolutionary will? Here we encounter again the fundamental conundrum we found in Marx himself. On the one side Marx, with the encouragement of Engels, claims a scientific knowledge of the laws of historical development, which seem to make conscious, willed revolutionary aspiration and praxis no more than a predetermined manifestation of underlying materialist, economic processes. Here we could perhaps fault Marxists for misreading the signs of the times, but not for choosing evilly. On the other side, Marx thinks this scientific knowledge is itself a material act, a human relation to the natural world that effects change in the world that is known. Revolutionary knowledge is itself a key catalyst, if not cause of revolutionary change. This means that the human action of conceiving and under-

---

44. John Dewey's instrumentalism might be read as a consciously liberal-democratic attempt to retrieve and redeem the Hegelian-Marxian doctrine of praxis.

standing social change has a material role in effecting the revolution by the revolutionary praxis of active waiting. Consequently, we can speak of revolutionary morality and revolutionary virtues. In that case, however, there is also culpability. Here we would have to fault Leninists for choosing evilly in constructing a pseudo-revolution that turned Russia and its minions into nothing but the Gulag, an institutionalization of violence against all difference which rivaled Hitlerism.

The bitter moral and intellectual failures of this revolutionary program have enormous consequences for humanity's future. The discrediting of Marxism seems also to discredit the very aspiration to overcome human alienation and to liberate humanity as a social being; distrust of the Marxist meta-narrative brings in its wake refusal of all meta-narratives of human salvation, while the memory of its scathing exposure of the hypocrisies of bourgeois liberalism linger on. But this reaction, understandable among disillusioned secular postmodernists, is too crude by far. It fails to penetrate to the Hegelian-Gnostic paradigm of the human predicament as *alienation* and its understanding of human salvation as *liberation*, which Marx took over from Hegel. That Hegelian-Gnostic conception of our fall and of our deliverance is, however, fundamentally flawed; it posits what John Milbank calls "ontological violence," and so inevitably reaps in practice what it has sown conceptually.[45] In a nutshell the Hegelian-Gnostic doctrine teaches that our world has fallen from its original unity into difference by a founding act of violence, whether that is the self-objectification of reason in matter as in Hegel or the primordial conflict of the human species with nature and the fall into the division of labor as in Marx. In either case, difference is experienced as threat rather than as gift. When we clearly understand this background of Gnostic mythology, we understand why Marxism failed — how Marxism, which promised to make everyone a comrade, instead *had* to make everyone cruel.

How precisely then is the image of *Homo faber* false? It is surely not false in lifting up humanity's creative capacities, nor the human vocation to make this earth a paradise. In Christian theological perspective, however, the doctrine of sin asserts that this human calling has been forfeited, that human powers are now falsely employed to exploit, to dominate, to destroy. That is to say with Augustine that it is not the evil body which causes the

---

45. See Milbank, "Ontological Violence or the Postmodern Problematic," in *Social Theory*, pp. 278-325.

good soul to sin (so Gnosticism), but the wicked soul which leads the good body astray. What is false in the image of *Homo faber* is its systematically rationalistic and activistic bias, which regards human "nature" (the passive physical as opposed to the active intellectual) as infinitely malleable. The root economic conflict between indifferent nature and the human species in Marxism-Hegelianism reappears in this way as an ominous and infinite dissatisfaction of mind with matter. Despite materialism, this essentially idealistic and dualistic prejudice allowed Marxist revolutionaries to think that humanity can be forcibly remolded according to a rational plan. Overlooked here is the fact that human nature is *essentially* embodied, thus not *infinitely* malleable; that human suffering in particular is part and parcel of biologically embodied existence, not merely a by-product of exploitation. When this natural limitation, and the natural law which corresponds to it protecting human bodies, are systematically overlooked, any fear of revolutionary *sin,* i.e., of using human powers to exploit, dominate, and destroy in the name of liberating transformation, is abolished in the conscience of the self-declared agents of the new humanity.

Hypothetically speaking, even in the communist paradise we would still need morality, though there it would be the morality of the angels. For even if we were angels, we would remain creatures, and that means that there would be differences among us and so also tensions between viewpoints and values as we learned to live together. Thus in Christian thinking even the angels can sin. By the mere fact that we are finite creatures, there are and always will be differences that must manifest when we work to live together. The point of this little thought experiment about angels is that here below in the material, embodied creation difference does not *necessitate* violence but is rather the *presupposition* of Beloved Community. Difference allows the possibility of sin, but *just because,* embodied as individuals with wills of their own, mortals are invited to create loving fellowship in imagining and realizing new forms of common life. Moral discourse, language about what is right in a fellowship of love and what is wrong, that is, what defeats a fellowship of love, will still be necessary so long as we remain differentiated creatures, though it be in paradise on a journey of infinite duration. Even then we will still have to ask who has what rights and duties, what are the facts, what are the pertinent values and how are they ranked. For Christians, even though they live under the leadership of the Holy Spirit, and are liberated from the accusation of the law, the moral content of the law as love binding us in community remains God's Word; indeed Beloved Community is the very goal of the gospel.[46] So, for example, we have developed in time and in light of the gospel's history with us a moral rule, that we may not in the name of Christ slaughter unbelievers or heretics who are also creatures beloved of God; if that happens it is heresy as well as crime. But Marxism fatefully refused on principle and in the name of an allegedly scientific knowledge, or better, Gnosis, of the highest good to entertain such moral reflection or to articulate for itself such moral rules.

Through this extended discussion I have shown that the Marxist objection against the alleged passivity of Luther's waiting faith on the God who comes itself succumbs to a similar fault as that alleged against Luther, but with by far graver consequence. By the minimalist maxim, "Do no harm," Luther's supposed passivity is justified, but Marxist activism eternally merits damnation. Revolutionary praxis has no criterion by which to discern a true *kairos* from its own will-to-power, while its pretension to holding the key to the riddle of history licenses the most fanatical violence in the fashion of self-fulfilling prophecy. Yet Luther cannot be justified as resource for political theology today merely by the maxim, "Do no harm." The law that judges Christian political theology is the double love commandment. The next task in meeting the objection to Luther as resource for political theology today then is to ask whether Lage was right in principle when he associated notions of earthly station and Christian vocation with an injurious social conservatism and the loss of radical discipleship. For if we are done with Marxism and other infantile fantasies, we are back on the earth as somatic selves seeking the right kinds of ecstasy, dealing then with the natural forms of human life in society,[47] structures of existence that are *not* infinitely malleable.

---

46. Robert Benne speaks of a contemporary "lack of ethical substance . . . [which has] shied away from the contemporary explications of the Decalogue that would give Old Testament content to the ethical life" in chap. 2, "Lutheran Ethics: Perennial Themes and Contemporary Challenges," in *The Promise of Lutheran Ethics*, ed. Karen L. Bloomquist and John R. Stumme (Minneapolis: Fortress, 1998), pp. 27-28. See the important study by Reinhold Hütter in the same volume, "The Twofold Center of Lutheran Ethics: Christian Freedom and God's Commandments" (pp. 31-54). The collapse of moral language into the theological category of "law" and the reduction of "law" to its purely accusative function are fundamental blunders of contemporary Lutheranism that cannot claim the Luther who wrote the catechisms as its source.

47. Bonhoeffer, *Ethics*, pp. 143ff., on restoring the category of the natural to Protestant theology as that in the fallen creation which is ordered nonetheless to Christ.

## Vocation in Battle-Stations of the New Creation

Luther's apocalyptic-Pauline and Augustinian theology, as we have so far in this book encountered it, tells of an overarching battle between God and the devil, the New Adam and the first Adam, *civitas dei* and *civitas terrena*. Without doubt, this entails the sober recognition that the state as a monopoly on the means of violence is part of the *civitas terrena* and as such never any part of the Beloved Community, but rather something at last to be left behind along with the sinful chaos it imperfectly holds at bay. Yet there is more to the body's redemption than this narrow arena of the state with its power politics. Indeed the claim of the state to represent the public, to occupy all of creation, not to mention also the community of redemption, is already totalitarian in tendency. As we saw in Chapter Six, a created form destined for redemption appears in marriage and family. We now want to explore other such arenas of social life that Luther identified as structural aspects of somatic existence, for they are as such the social objects of God's redeeming love and the places where cross-bearing disciples live out the high calling of the *imago Dei* in an as yet embattled world. Luther is often misunderstood by antinomian hawkers of cheap grace in his own camp to commend a Christian life without "sanctification" or the pursuit of "holiness." This misunderstanding is in fact the Lutheran "heresy," if there is one. In reality, Luther takes up the ideals of the monastic life or New Testament discipleship or Pauline imitation and applies them to social life, life in society. It is not that he has no teaching on Christian life, but that he has rigorously conceived of it as in self-giving service to the Beloved Community.

Robert Benne accordingly speaks of "the structures of life in which we are embedded," an (unintentional?) allusion to the Pauline *stoicheia tou kosmou*, which imprisoned humanity unto the coming of Christ. Divested of pretensions to ultimacy and now re-ordered by Christ to serve anew God's creative purposes, these structures of life have been variously termed by theology in Luther's tradition "'orders of creation' or 'mandates' (Dietrich Bonhoeffer) or 'natural orders' (Forell) or 'places of responsibility' (Benne). God works through these structures to provide moral contexts within which we can live."[48] Benne thus lays significant stress upon the *moral* nature of these structures (in contrast then to the Marxian refusal to speak morally in these areas). They are not to be conceived as

---

48. Benne in *The Promise of Lutheran Ethics*, p. 13.

fixed, static, ideal arrangements imposed upon life, but, with Bonhoeffer, as living social structures mandated by God's creative Word. The creative Word dynamically structures people into social forms intending Beloved Community and sustains this social life by moral discourse about the common good and each one's responsibility for it: "God gives these structures moral direction, using many means to sustain their moral character . . . the moral ordering of our common life."[49] Just this, however, can and does go wrong. Moral discourse can become a means of exclusion rather than inclusion, stilling conversation rather than opening it up, or it can be forgone altogether, as we saw in Marxism, in response to the moral hypocrisy of the privileged. Thus, as fundamentally moral phenomena, the very structures of existence are also "subject to the individual and corporate sins of humans, who can bend them away from God's intentions. They are battlefields upon which both God and Satan contend." The specific formations of life in community sustained by moral discourse can be frustrated or hijacked. Like a fundamental sociology, Benne's notion, "places of responsibility," seeks to identify the concrete dimensions of corporate existence and to put them to work by moral discourse for discovering the will of God on the way to the Beloved Community. "Discerning God's law in these structures is thus a great challenge for Christian ethics."[50] To say that the state, or the family, or the economy, or religion is a divinely mandated structure of life, then, is not to answer an ethical question, but to pose one.

In a classic study Gustav Wingren argued similarly. Are the stations in life sinful? Are they moral? Those are exactly the burning questions of life that must be discerned, to which task the doctrine of vocation arising from Christian baptism[51] directs us. All true stations in life are objectively oriented by God, in Luther's understanding, to service of others, though

49. Benne in *The Promise of Lutheran Ethics*, p. 13.

50. Benne in *The Promise of Lutheran Ethics*, p. 13.

51. "Baptism is the church's fundamental sacrament. . . . This takes place day by day through the putting to death of the old man and the rising of the new man out of sin. This is completely effected in death, when the body of sin withers, and God's new creation appears in the consummation. . . . God must help man to die daily . . . learn to suffer and die. . . . In one's vocation there is a cross . . . and on this cross the old human nature is to be crucified. . . . Christ died on the cross, and one who is baptized unto death with Christ must be put to death by the cross." Gustaf Wingren, *Luther on Vocation*, trans. Carl C. Rasmussen (Philadelphia: Muhlenberg Press, 1957), pp. 28-29. "Baptism is therefore completely fulfilled only in death . . ." (p. 31). No self-chosen crosses, "the cross comes to us uninvoked in our vocation" (p. 53), "not in deserted places apart from the company of people, but right in the social and political order" (57, WA 43, 214).

their sinful occupants abuse them for self-serving. In this theological intention of structuring life toward others in society, "it is the station itself which is the ethical agent."[52] This means that there is no "private" sphere on earth; that socialization goes all the way down; that what is called "private" is actually something seeking to be concealed, hidden — like Adam and Eve in the garden. But they are not hidden from the Creator. "It is only before God, i.e. in heaven, that the individual stands alone. In the earthly realm man always stands *in relatione,* always bound to another."[53] On earth God the Creator is active in the stations to relate creatures to one another in mutual care. "All is the ceaseless work of the God of creation, which goes forward through the labors of mankind . . . care for one's office is, in its very frame of reference on earth, participation in God's own care for human beings."[54]

Here we encounter again that difficulty which ceaselessly plagued Luther in communicating his new understanding of what makes good works truly good, namely, that they are not expiatory sacrifices of the private individual aimed at placating or influencing the Deity for her own benefit, but rather propitiatory sacrifices of the public person, in imitation of Christ himself, undertaking the burden of others here on the earth for their benefit. "Good works and vocation (love) exist for the earth and one's neighbor, not for eternity and God. God does not need our good works, but our neighbor does."[55] Indeed, since "the reign of Christ is in giving, and in grace and the gospel, to proffer gifts here is an attempt to depose Christ from his throne . . . at the same time, his neighbor on earth is neglected since his good works have clearly been done, not for the sake of his neighbor, but to parade before God. Faith is revoked in heaven, and love on earth. Neither God nor one's neighbor receives that which is properly his."[56] This new "demarcation between earth and heaven," Wingren argued, is the main point of the mature Luther texts, *De servo arbitrio* (discussed above in Chapter Five) and the 1535 Galatians commentary (discussed in Chapter Seven) and the true sense of the so-called *Zweireichenlehre.* True human agency is passively received by the new birth of Spirit-wrought baptism into Christ, and just so is activated in imitation of Christ on the earth out this heavenly source. The *cooperatio* of the new man with God "is entirely limited to the

---

52. Wingren, *Luther on Vocation,* p. 6.
53. Wingren, *Luther on Vocation,* p. 5.
54. Wingren, *Luther on Vocation,* p. 9.
55. Wingren, *Luther on Vocation,* p. 10.
56. Wingren, *Luther on Vocation,* p. 13.

sphere 'below,' 'under us,'"[57] where this activated faith is not "passivity: man can receive from God only in prayer, and prayer is struggle, just as faith is struggle."[58] The Christian vocation, the true "religious life," is to be sought and found not in retreating from society into utopian communes or private gardens, but in the "structures of life in which we are embedded" where agents of the new humanity are to live "by prayer and righteous action" (Bonhoeffer).

Oswald Bayer has labored to retrieve Luther's teaching about the three estates from the notoriety given the teaching by Paul Althaus and lesser lights during the Nazi period, pointing to the seminal exegesis of Genesis 2:16-17 from 1535: "After the church was instituted, the household was established as well. . . . So the temple comes before the house, just as it is also placed on a higher level. There was no state before there was sin, since it was not yet necessary. The state is the necessary means for dealing with the depraved condition of nature."[59] Bayer's exposition is profound. The establishment of the estate of the "church" is fundamental in the sense that "the human being who is addressed by God [is] furnished with the ability to respond freely in thankfulness." Although the religions (including Christianity!) are "corrupted by human ingratitude, because of sin,"[60] they nevertheless presuppose even in this state of corruption the underlying mandate of the Creator, "Let there be! Let us make humankind in our image. . . ." That the religions respond to this gift of life with acts of expiation rather than the sacrifice of praise and works of love is testimony both to the reality of the first estate and to its corruption. Under the second estate, household, Luther understands not only the partnership of male and female in marriage discussed in Chapter Six, but also the household economy: the relations between parents and children, employer and employed, farmer and field for the acquisition of sustenance. This estate too has been corrupted by sin, yet together with the church it is "not destroyed." They endure as surely as the creative command, "Let there be . . ." endures. But Luther "would not recognize the third estate,"[61] which is, as he colorfully put it, God's "punishing one jackass with another": "the state came into being because of the fall into sin, with its ability to force compliance to maintain just order." This relative delegitimizing of the state is important to Lu-

57. Wingren, *Luther on Vocation*, p. 17.
58. Wingren, *Luther on Vocation*, p. 18.
59. Cited in Bayer, *Luther's Theology*, p. 122, from LW 1:103-4.
60. Bayer, *Luther's Theology*, p. 123.
61. Bayer, *Luther's Theology*, p. 123.

ther; he will have no Hobbsean Leviathan with its totalizing claim to be a god on the earth. As the monopoly on violence the state's reality is rather temporary; its very existence is always testimony to the reality of sin against which it so imperfectly struggles.

Bayer makes a striking claim about this teaching on the three estates: it "carries much greater weight for [Luther] than the teaching about the two realms of God."[62] The significance of this observation is that it helps to undermine the predominant, dualistic, Cartesian-Kantian reading of the *Zweireichenlehre* which assigns most of life to a secular sphere under the jurisdiction of Universal Reason and religion in turn to a sphere of idiosyncratic inwardness and privacy. "In Neo-Protestantism of the Kantian variety, [Luther's] *pro me* has been and continues to be misused as a methodological principle, in order to eliminate anything that is objective concerning what faith believes, and to characterize faith as that which happens to each one individually."[63] This is not what Luther means by the personalizing appropriation of ecstatic faith in the Christ who is *pro me:* "That God is gracious to me is thus identical with the fact that he has bound himself for all time to the human being, Jesus of Nazareth, to this life, suffering and death."[64] The real God who is *pro me,* then, is the God who meets us in "the structures of life," "born of a woman, under the law," not one who calls us away from them. That is not the only connection between the estates and Jesus Christ. As we have already noted, the "structures of life" may be equated with the Pauline *stoicheia,* that is to say, as pedagogues, even tyrants constraining the power of sin from wanton destruction of the groaning creation unto the coming of the Redeemer, who both liberates the imprisoned and re-orders those wayward powers to serve anew God's creative purposes. The liberation then is not escape or removal from these areas of responsibility, but rather freedom for cross-bearing discipleship here in the Galilee of human existence. As Luther repudiated the convent and monastery as false, escapist attempts at radical discipleship, and regarded marriage as the true religious order, so also he thinks of radical discipleship not as a self-proclaimed refusal to live in the world, but as the vocation there to live as the people of God, concretely in the basic social areas

---

62. Bayer, *Luther's Theology,* p. 124. See also the important work of John Witte Jr., *Law and Protestantism: The Legal Teachings of the Lutheran Reformation,* with a foreword by Martin E. Marty (Cambridge: Cambridge University Press, 2002), and the author's review in *Sixteenth Century Journal* 35, no. 2 (2004): 534-36.

63. Bayer, *Luther's Theology,* p. 132.

64. Bayer, *Luther's Theology,* p. 133.

of marriage and family, economy and ecology, church in society, even in service of that monopoly on violence, the temporal state. (One can of course imagine a renewed monastic vocation along these lines.) But is such worldly discipleship really the imitation of Christ? Lage's study is helpful and convincing in reply to this question. Luther did "not subscribe to a literalist sola scriptura. . . . We have no way of knowing which characteristics or actions of the historical Jesus are contingent to particular circumstances and which transcend their time and place and have relevance for us. . . . [Anabaptists] represented a legalism grounded in Biblical literalism."[65] Literally to follow Jesus, one would have to return in time through some science-fiction machine and join Jesus on the dusty by-ways of Galilee. The only true possibility is to follow Jesus spiritually, that is, by the leading of the same Spirit which led him to fulfill the law of neighbor love by making the burden of the perishing sinner His own. On the other hand, conscience is an insufficient guide, "in that the conscience is a prisoner of sin as well, it cannot in and of itself witness to good, just and right activity. It is the Spirit-mediated presence of Christ which witnesses to good, just and right activity, thereby enabling the conscience to judge ourselves and our actions and to condemn the self when we place our own self-interest before the needs of another."[66] It is the presence of Christ *as the One narrated in the gospel,* as something followable, which example directs the believer, as in Philippians 2, to have the same mind as was in Christ Jesus: something revealed in the story which follows of His humiliation and obedience for humanity's sake. So the true imitation of Christ is an *imitatio mentis,* not an *imitatio operas.*[67] By the same token, Luther is *not* "claiming that the Holy Spirit directs our actions. . . . Luther rejected the unmediated autodidacticism of the Divine-inspiration pneumatology as advocated by the Enthusiasts. The Spirit sets the conscience free to make moral choices which may not be in the immediate best interests of the self; but the Spirit does not make our choices for us. To claim the direct guidance or teaching of the Holy Spirit is to be absolved of

---

65. Lage, *Christology and Ethics,* p. 139. "To codify and prescribe the imitation of Christ in terms of particulars and rigid norms is to turn Christology into ideology, at which point the Spirit is silenced and faith is dead. For, without the reality of the Spirit, the Word is only law; without faith, works have no meaning; and without the Christus sacramentum, Christ is merely a prophet . . . a law and a prescription for living rather than the joyful experience of inner freedom in God's presence" (p. 140).

66. Lage, *Christology and Ethics,* p. 141.

67. Lage, *Christology and Ethics,* p. 144.

responsibility for our actions (as incidentally is the consequence of a narrow legalism as well). However, to reject responsibility is to deny the continuing corruption of self-will and complicity of evil. . . ."[68] Imitation manifests the real agency of the new self in Christ; it is not a mere modality of Christ or the Spirit.

I will now illustrate these claims about true human agency in basic social forms by presenting three samples of theological agency: a public pastor, a public intellectual, and a public advocate for social justice — in Luther, Niebuhr, and King respectively. Meeting Marx's objection can certainly start with Luther and indeed take its point of departure in his essential affirmation of the unity of passive and active obedience, but it must also go beyond what was imaginable to him in the sixteenth century and on account of his apocalypticism. The case of Niebuhr is a fascinating retooling of certain essential insights of Luther, in discovering new paths of emancipating history in ways that Luther could never have imagined. It is in King, however, that our thesis is almost visibly incarnated: in passive receptivity before God in Christ, His servant becomes a mighty agent of the new humanity on the earth. In linking these three as examples of this teaching, incidentally, I am not claiming immanent historical causality. I am not saying that Luther's teachings influenced Niebuhr who influenced Martin Luther King Jr., even though in an indirect way that case might be made. I am rather saying that Luther's teaching about this, i.e., that passive before God in Christ we become on the earth real agents of the new humanity of the Beloved Community, is true, and that truth can be seen as such in tracing out these three examples.

## Luther's Admonition to Peace

"I shall never advise a heathen or a Turk, let alone a Christian to attack another or begin a war."[69] It is a little recognized fact — due undoubtedly to distortions created by the alliance of Throne and Altar, the dualistic

---

68. Lage, *Christology and Ethics,* p. 142. "For Luther, the Holy Spirit must not be understood as a supernatural or transcendent causality which endows the self with a new nature, faculty or attribute. The Spirit does not infuse . . . the Holy Spirit sets the conscience free to accuse and condemn self-will . . . the Spirit permits a moral life. But it does not automatically provide instruction, teaching or perception, nor does it direct the self to perform particular works." Lage, *Christology and Ethics,* p. 142.

69. "On War against the Turk" (1529) LW 46:161-205.

Two Kingdoms doctrine stemming from the nineteenth century, and the memory of Luther's "harsh" words in the Peasants' War — that the historical Martin Luther was a consistent opponent of war. He had virtually advocated a pacifist capitulation when he declared: "To fight against the Turk is the same as resisting God, who visits our sins upon us with this rod." Pope Leo X cited this statement of the young Luther in the Bull of Excommunication and Luther eventually had to revisit the matter in his significant treatise of 1529, *On War against the Turk*. There he executed an incisive theological critique of the holy war tradition of the Christian crusades against Islam, and in its place he tried to rehabilitate the just war tradition, reaching back once again to Augustine. Luther explains what motivated him: "they undertook to fight against the Turk in the name of Christ, and taught and incited men to do this, as though our people were an army of Christians against the Turks, who were enemies of Christ. This is absolutely contrary to Christ's doctrine and name." In place of this, Luther spoke of the Holy Roman Emperor, "not as the head of Christendom or defender of the gospel or the faith," but as "regular ruler, appointed by God, to defend his own" as a matter of moral duty and subject accordingly to criteria of the just war tradition. Today the latter is often impugned as little more than ineffective, if not often an actual pretext for war. Be that as it may, what is noteworthy is how vigorously and consistently (even against his own interest) Luther the public Christian intervened in the volatile politics of his day consistently to argue against resort to the sword.

In the treatise on *Temporal Authority*[70] (1523) Luther offered counsel to the prince who would be a Christian. First, he must be devoted to the welfare of his subjects. Second, he must be wary of flatterers. Third, he must deal justly with evildoers and as a result "must not follow the advice of those counselors and fire-eaters who would stir and incite him to start a war." The objection is raised: "Is a prince then not to go to war, and are his subjects not to follow him into battle?" Luther calls this a "far reaching question," but answers it briefly as follows. First, there should be no rebellion against higher authority; the "governing authority must not be resisted by force, but only by confession of the truth." It should be noted that Luther allows both for *resistance* with the Word and that this Luther who disallows violent resistance is an excommunicated heretic, at any moment liable to be handed over to that higher authority for the flames. Luther's re-

---

70. "Temporal Authority: To What Extent It Should Be Obeyed" (1523) LW 45:81-129.

fusal of violent rebellion then begins with his own case. Luther continues next to discuss war with antagonists who are one's equal. Here one "should first offer justice and peace," and only upon refusal "defend yourself against force by force." If it comes to such justified war of defense, Luther understands the vigorous prosecution of it to be "both Christian and an act of love." (He speaks somewhat recklessly here of using "every method of warfare.") Upon the defeat of the aggressor, "one should offer mercy and peace." But what if the prince is wrong and the war is unjust? If we know this, Luther says, we must not obey the prince, but rather obey God (Acts 5:29). If we do not know, we can in good faith obey the prince and leave the matter to God. Thus Luther endorses conscientious objection to an unjust war.

On the whole, it is evident that Luther follows the guidance of the just war tradition, with its bias against war and demand for stringent moral justification. Such a conclusion would also be borne out by examination of the later treatise, *Whether Soldiers Too Can Be Saved* (1526). Such general counsel soon became actual in the ferment leading up to the Peasants' War. In 1525 Luther published his *Admonition to Peace*[71] addressed to the peasants in Swabia and their temporal lords. This tract opens with a scathing denunciation of the latter: "We have no one on earth to blame for this disastrous rebellion [in the making] except you princes and lords. . . . You do not cease to rant and rave against the holy gospel. . . . In addition, as temporal rulers you do nothing but cheat and rob the people so that you may lead a life of luxury and extravagance." With the first point Luther contends for religious tolerance, since "no ruler can or ought to prevent anyone from teaching or believing what he pleases, whether it is the gospel or lies." With the second point, Luther comments on the "economic injustices": these "protests are also right and just, for rulers are not appointed to exploit their subjects for their own profit and advantage, but to be concerned about the welfare of their subjects." The modern thought, "if you want peace, work for justice," is already Luther's.

When he turns to address the peasants, he expresses solidarity with them *coram Deo:* "the princes and lords who forbid the preaching of the gospel and oppress the people unbearably deserve to have God put them down from their thrones." Yet the same principles of justice apply to the oppressed; with their oppressors they belong to a common moral order: "you, too, must be careful that you take up your cause justly and with a

---

71. "Admonition to Peace" (1525) LW 46:17-43.

good conscience . . . if you act unjustly and have a bad conscience you will be defeated." As "a Christian association," the peasants must beware, lest they take God's name in vain. They are to recall the word of Christ, "all who take the sword will perish by the sword." They must realize that the "fact that the rulers are wicked and unjust does not excuse disorder and rebellion." Luther appeals to reason and the "natural law of all the world, that no one may sit as judge in his own case or take his own revenge." He backs this with "divine law": "Vengeance is mine, says the Lord. I will repay." Luther warns prudentially that war unleashes a firestorm: "The wolf that eats the whole sheep will also eat its ear." If we take justice into our hands, there will be "nothing but murder and bloodshed." Luther concludes by turning to the "law of Christ": "Resist not evil." With this, he warns against the false prophet in their midst (the reference is to Thomas Müntzer) who teaches that the godless have no right to live. But the true prophet of the "law of Christ" preaches otherwise: "Suffering! Suffering! Cross! Cross! This and nothing else is the Christian law!" Christians are to suffer before recourse to war, let alone rebellion. This is then the identical counsel he gave about resistance to the Turk years earlier. It will be the same witness that he makes when the Emperor threatens the invasion of Germany to crush the Reformation in a few years.

When this admonition to peace failed to dissuade the peasants under the sway of Müntzer's zealotry, Luther published "harsh words"[72] exhorting the lords to put down the rebellion. This they were all too happy to do. As Luther warned, the defeat of the peasants was as predictable as it was massive and cruel. Luther's judgment in publishing the tract against the peasants is certainly questionable. The princes hardly needed his cheerleading. As discussed in the Appendix to this book, Luther's outburst is a manifestation of his apocalyptic demonology. "See what a mighty prince the devil is, how he has the world in his hands and can throw everything into confusion. . . ." In his medieval mind, what Luther actually sees is not the desperation of starving, humiliated peasants but the devil at work in Müntzer's preaching to them, to catch, deceive, blind, harden, and throw them into revolt. A "rebel [i.e., under the spell of Satan] is not worth rational arguments, for he does not accept them,"[73] but must rather be stopped

---

72. "Against the Robbing and Murdering Hordes of Peasants" (1525) LW 46:49-55.

73. His frame of mind is also shown in the statement from "Open Letter on the Harsh Book" (1525): "The devil intended to lay all Germany to utter waste because there was no other way by which he could suppress the gospel." LW 46:79.

with a fist. By the same token, lending evangelical counsel to the princes now to suppress the devil's work in stirring up a rebellion is Luther's duty as a public Christian, who must also be concerned to differentiate the gospel of peace that he preaches from Müntzer's false and disastrous agitation to storm heaven.

Embarrassed by his own "harsh words," however, Luther followed up in the aftermath of the revolt with *An Open Letter on the Harsh Book*.[74] It contains one of the starkest formulations of the so-called Two Kingdoms doctrine: "the kingdom of the world, which is nothing else than the servant of God's wrath upon the wicked and is a real precursor of hell and everlasting death, should not be merciful but strict, severe and wrathful in fulfilling its work and duty. Its tool is not a wreath of roses or a flower of love, but a naked sword. . . ." As the state *is* the *monopoly* on the means of violence, it *cannot* tolerate rebellion. "You must make a very, very great distinction between a rebel and a thief. . . ." Taking moral responsibility for supporting the suppression of the revolt, though not for the excesses of the princes, Luther makes the fundamental point of *Mitsein:* "If you want to live in a community, you must share the community's burdens, dangers, and injuries, even though not you, but your neighbor has caused them." This is said in reference to the excessive violence and disproportionate cruelty of the princes. Luther closes the *Open Letter* openly mocking the machismo of these "furious, raving, senseless tyrants": "one of these big shots summoned the poor wife of Thomas Müntzer, now a pregnant widow, fell on one knee before her, and said, 'Dear lady, let me \*\*\* you.' O a knightly noble deed, done to a poor, helpless, pregnant little woman! That is a brave hero for you!" Mockery was all that remained in the preacher's power.

It "is not fitting for me, a preacher, vested with the spiritual office, to wage war or to counsel war or to incite it." This last example comes from *Dr. Martin Luther's Warning to His Dear German People* following the Diet of Augsburg in 1531. Charles V was threatening to invade Germany and violently suppress the Reformation; Luther's prince and his allies now debated the right of resistance by lesser magistrates. Luther, who would have been first to the flames in the event of an imperial conquest, stayed with that principled witness against war that he so clumsily made in the time of the Peasants' War. Indeed, he reminds readers of what he has written and taught so emphatically: "not to resort to rebellion, but to suffer the mad-

---

74. "Open Letter on the Harsh Book" (1525) LW 46:63-85.

ness even of tyrants, and not to defend oneself. "This is what I teach," he confessed, perhaps thinking back to the Peasants' War, "but I cannot create the doers of this teaching." If war comes, he will let the lesser authorities' resistance against the Emperor pass as self-defense. As for himself, "they can do no more than deprive me of a sack of ailing flesh." So against his own interest Luther once again counseled against rebellion. Anticipating martyrdom, Luther next turns attention to what a subjugated people might do after he has gone up in flames. To my knowledge, for the first time in Christian history, Luther articulates civil disobedience as a Christian social duty. The "bloodhounds," he says, do not have the right to define obedience or rebellion for Christians who must obey God rather than men. It is not insurrection to disobey unjust laws, but only if one attacks "with a view to making [oneself] ruler and establishing the law, as Müntzer did." If the emperor calls to arms to suppress the Reformation, "no one should lend himself to it or obey the emperor." Indeed, whoever "does obey him can be certain that he is disobedient to God and will lose both body and soul eternally." Luther goes on to give reasons for his summons to civil disobedience before the court of public opinion. In the end he reiterates his consistent admonition to peace: I do not "want to be known before God or the world as having counseled or desired anyone to wage war or offer [violent] resistance. . . ."

Luther's public Christian witness against war was principled and consistent, even though some of his political judgments were badly bungled. He was not the master of events, but a participant in tumultuous times that he deciphered in part by means of a superstitious demonology which we today cannot and should not imitate. A proper theology of the state needs Luther's realism about the monopoly of violence which the state is, but not Luther's overconfidence in the good behavior of the princes and underconfidence in the poor and oppressed. Luther thought of himself as a pastor advising consciences and in this he was as innocent as a dove. But political theology needs also to be as cunning as a serpent. Beyond these measured evaluations of the mixed success of the historical Martin Luther on the most perplexing problem of the state and war, however, the broader point is that as a public Christian, Luther engaged with the powers on behalf of peace at the most dangerous juncture, when the sword was being drawn from the sheath. He was in fact a political witness for peace in a violence-prone world.

In the following two vignettes, we speed forward to near contemporaries in a vastly changed world, a world in which the estate of domestic economy (the pre-modern household of Luther's time) was sundered by the Industrial Revolution, and the "common order of charity" was corroded by colonialism, by the rationalizing of chattel slavery, and by new theories of racial degeneration. In this transformed world, Niebuhr discovered the social form of public economy and King the social form of public religion as arenas of responsibility where the new agency of the total Christ could set to work on behalf of the Beloved Community. Both agencies involve forms of non-violent coercion, illustrating and developing Luther's inchoate ideas.

### Niebuhr's Rediscovery of Economic Power

Vision not distorted by Luther's superstitious demonology, Niebuhr arguably put Luther's Augustinian insights to work in bearing witness against the false consciousness of the privileged, who persistently justify their "special interests in terms of general interest," a "very potent instrument for maintaining an unjust status quo." Niebuhr's analysis from the pathbreaking *Moral Man and Immoral Society* is worth quoting at length:

> Those who would eliminate the injustice are therefore always placed at the moral disadvantage of imperiling its peace . . . even if the efforts toward justice are made in the most pacific terms. They will claim that it is dangerous to disturb a precarious equilibrium and will feign to fear anarchy as the consequence of the effort. This passion for peace need not always be consciously dishonest. Since those who hold special privileges in society are naturally inclined to regard their privileges as their rights and to be unmindful of the effects of inequality upon the underprivileged, they will have a natural complacency toward injustice. Every effort to disturb the peace, which incorporates the injustice, will therefore seem to them to spring from unjustified malcontent. They will furthermore be only partly conscious of the violence and coercion by which their privileges are preserved and will therefore be particularly censorious of the use of force or the threat of violence by those who oppose them. The force they use is either the covert force of economic power or it is the police power of the state, seemingly sanctified by the supposedly impartial objectives of the government which wields it, but nevertheless amenable to their interests. They are thus able in perfect good faith to express abhorrence of the violence of a

strike by workers and to call upon the state in the same breath to use violence in putting down the strike.[75]

Underlying Niebuhr's analysis is the same Augustinian doctrine of the state as a precarious monopoly on the means of coercion — a band of brigands apart from justice. One can also discern Niebuhr's Luther-like disdain for the pretenses of reason, which sells itself to rationalize anything in a world in which nothing is sacred and everything has its price: the "human mind is so weak an instrument, and is so easily enslaved and prostituted by human passions, that one is never certain to what degree the fears of the privileged classes, of anarchy and revolution, are honest. . . ."[76] Yet Luther's admonition to peace in the revolutionary situation has lost its absolute force for Niebuhr for several reasons.

The end of superstition permits people of conscience to see the desperation of the oppressed rather than to fixate upon diabolic agitation. The modern view of history opens up the prospect of social change in the direction of greater justice. The state has lost its aura of sanctity. Its monopoly on the means of violence can be radically questioned in the name of justice. Niebuhr, in other words, lives in a world populated as much by Müntzers as by Luthers. So, for example, Niebuhr quotes the influential and powerful voice (at the time) of Trotsky: "As for us, we were never concerned with the Kantian priestly and vegetarian-Quaker prattle about the 'sacredness of human life.' We were revolutionaries in opposition and remain revolutionaries in power. To make the individual sacred we must destroy the social order which crucifies him and this problem can only be solved by blood and iron."[77] In such a world, Luther's absolute call for Christians to bear the cross and suffer injustice rather than unleash anarchy has been thwarted, in part, by Luther's own realistic doctrine of the state: "Once we have made the fateful concession of ethics to politics, and accepted coercion as a necessary instrument of social cohesion, we can make no absolute distinction between non-violent and violent types of coercion or between coercion used by governments and that which is used by revolutionaries."[78] Just as the oppressed can become the new oppressor,[79]

75. Reinhold Niebuhr, *Moral Man and Immoral Society: A Study in Ethics and Politics* (New York: Charles Scribner's Sons, 1960), pp. 129-30.

76. Niebuhr, *Moral Man*, p. 136 et passim.

77. Niebuhr, *Moral Man*, pp. 177-78.

78. Niebuhr, *Moral Man*, p. 179.

79. Niebuhr, *Moral Man*, pp. 192-93.

so also wars on terrorism can themselves become wars of terrorism. Demystifying both sides, Niebuhr concludes that the "real question is: what are the political possibilities of establishing justice through violence?"[80]

With this question, a Luther-like argument against Trotskyite fanaticism can appear, not with the historical Martin Luther's admonition to peace so much as an admonition to non-absolutist struggle for social justice. At a time when liberal Protestants from America regularly made the Moscow tour and proclaimed the coming of the Kingdom under Papa Stalin, Niebuhr in his most Marxian period presciently wrote: "Perhaps a society which gradually approximates the idea will not be so very inferior morally to one which makes one desperate grasp after the ideal, only to find that the realities of history and nature dissolve it."[81] Not only are the fates of millions put at risk when revolutionaries gamble everything on attaining the absolute, but that cruelty unique to Marxism "shuts the gates of mercy on mankind." "[S]ince coercion is an invariable instrument of their policy, absolutism transmutes this instrument into unbearable tyrannies and cruelties."[82] Arguing for the long, slow, "non-violent" struggle for justice, Niebuhr finds himself repeating Luther's analysis of civil disobedience: "The chief difference between violence and non-violence is not in the degree of destruction, though the difference is usually considerable, but in the aggressive character of the one and the negative character of the other. Non-violence is essentially non-co-operation . . . ," employing economic tools such as refusing taxation, boycotts and strikes.[83] Non-violence is resistance; it is coercive. It is not mere passivity. It confronts the oppressor; it protests injustice. It is not only "soul-force," as Gandhi said, but is also physically forceful, though its tool is not the fist, but rather the dollar.

Niebuhr has discovered, then, a mediating power between the brutal state's monopoly on violence and the sentimental appeal to love by the churches: the economy. Class analysis reveals the economic basis, of course, for the attitudes of the privileged and working classes that make up the bulk of Niebuhr's *Moral Man and Immoral Society*. Moral theorists and ethical idealists "persist in hoping that some force of reason and conscience can be created, powerful enough to negate or to transcend the economic interests which are basic to class divisions. The whole history of hu-

---

80. Niebuhr, *Moral Man*, p. 180.
81. Niebuhr, *Moral Man*, p. 199.
82. Niebuhr, *Moral Man*, p. 199.
83. Niebuhr, *Moral Man*, p. 240.

manity is witness to the futility of this hope."[84] Niebuhr also rejected, however, the "economic determinism" of Marx and Engels, because it reduced culture as superstructure to its material base, rather than seeing economy along with state and religion as independent variables, distinct forms of social power.[85] Niebuhr's appropriation is differentiated: "We have seen how inevitably special privilege is associated with power, and how the ownership of the means of production is the significant power in modern society." Niebuhr calls this Marxism's "greatest ethical contribution" even though it "may at times not see with sufficient clarity" that the state must check and balance concentrations of economic power, even as the churches must uphold in society that absolute standard of love against both. But the rediscovery of economic power puts a previously unrecognized lever of non-violent coercion into the hands of those who hoping against hope will struggle for justice without resort to absolutism.

Niebuhr tied this economic strategy to the plight of the "Negro" in America: "non-violence is a particularly strategic instrument for an oppressed group which is hopelessly in the minority and has no possibility of developing sufficient power to set against its oppressors. The emancipation of the Negro race in America probably waits upon the adequate development of this kind of social and political strategy. It is hopeless for the Negro to expect complete emancipation . . . merely by trusting in the moral sense of the white race. It is equally hopeless to attempt emancipation through violent revolution."[86] The commendation of non-violent struggles for justice instead of revolutionary fanaticism, however, raised a new issue about the spiritual resources for struggle, for that Pauline "hope against hope." Those who would undertake this struggle are sorely tempted to cynicism. "Since liberal Protestantism is, on the whole, the religion of the privileged classes of Western civilization, it is not surprising that its espousal of the ideal of love, in a civilization reeking with social injustice, should be cynically judged and convicted of hypocrisy by those in whom bitter social experiences destroy the sentimentalities and illusions of the comfortable."[87] In a book with precious little overt theology, the few notes that Niebuhr sounds strike home. "A sentimental generation has destroyed the apocalyptic note in the vision of the Christ. It thinks the king-

---

84. Niebuhr, *Moral Man*, p. 116.
85. Niebuhr, *Moral Man*, pp. 145-46.
86. Niebuhr, *Moral Man*, p. 252.
87. Niebuhr, *Moral Man*, p. 80.

dom of God is around the corner, while [Christ] regarded it as impossible of realization, except by God's grace." Can that apocalyptic Christ help sustain the struggle for justice? The cross "is a symbol of love triumphant in its own integrity, but not triumphant in the world and society." Can this symbol as such soar in the souls of those who struggle "beyond the possibilities of history"?[88] That is what is needed. For "the vision of a just society is an impossible one," Niebuhr announces in a Luther-like paradox, "which can be approximated only by those who do not regard it as impossible."[89] Niebuhr concluded his book on this apocalyptic note. The most effective agents of redemption will be "men who have substituted some new illusions for the abandoned ones . . . [in] a sublime madness of the soul. Nothing but such madness will do battle with malignant power and 'spiritual wickedness in high places.'"[90] Such an ecstatic self is and can be the agent of the new humanity.

John Milbank has sharply criticized the "poverty" of Niebuhr's approach, by which he means that Niebuhr's "realism" concedes far too much to a classical tragic-Stoic interpretation of existence. I have no deep quarrel with Milbank's quarrel with Niebuhr. In important ways Niebuhr never transcended the Kantian dualism of nature and spirit that he inherited from the nineteenth-century theology of the social gospel. In fact, he found his peculiar version of that dualism vital for resisting reduction of human history to natural mechanism, arguing that the peculiar freedom of humanity lies in its incalculable imaginative power to remake its environment, of which adventures human history is the story. On the other hand, he wanted to maintain the recalcitrant nature of nature, so to say, as a wall against fanatical attempts to remake human nature (recall the previous discussion of Marxism's eternal dissatisfaction with nature). These, in any case, were the motives behind his "realism." Milbank is certainly right to inveigh against a "realism" whose real sources are tragedy and Stoicism and to hold that "Christians see a different historical reality. We must realize this if we are not to confine Christianity to a realm of 'pure value,' or else to cordon off the narratives of the New Testament as a sacred enclave within an otherwise secular process."[91] The ministry of Dr. Martin Luther

88. Niebuhr, *Moral Man*, p. 82.

89. Niebuhr, *Moral Man*, p. 81.

90. Niebuhr, *Moral Man*, p. 277.

91. I thus read Niebuhr's realism differently than that which Milbank subjects to trenchant criticism in his essay on "the poverty of Niebuhrianism" in *Word Made Strange*, pp. 233-54. I am in any case in material agreement with Milbank's remarks on the cognitive

Some Objections regarding Justification, the Church, and Political Theology

King Jr., however, who found in Niebuhr's analysis a valuable resource, indicates that a more charitable interpretation of Niebuhr is possible. It was his discovery of the economic realm as a social power alongside church and state which opened up a "realistic" path to social justice. But even more important, King knew about Niebuhr's "sublime madness of the soul."

### The Reverend Dr. Martin Luther King Jr.'s Public Ministry of Redemptive Love

From his childhood in a middle-class parsonage, King was a man on a mission, not a detached thinker. From his earliest youth, he thought vaguely of his mission as leading descendants of African slaves to full participation in American life. He shared, as he famously proclaimed in 1963, the dream of America as a covenant for freedom, a national union as Lincoln had famously said, dedicated to the moral proposition inscribed in the *Declaration* that all are created equal. He thought of himself as one who would perform the role of a prophet from the script of Hebrew Scriptures,[92] speaking truth to power by recalling the nation to this founding covenant. He was baptized as teenager, in the customary way of evangelical Baptists. Although he earned a doctorate in Systematic Theology from Boston University, King was never interested in an academic career devoted to developing a system of thought for its own sake. He declined teaching offers upon completion of his course work at Boston and took a congregation in Montgomery, Alabama, where he finished writing his doctorate between the baptisms and weddings, parish visits and congregational meals of happy early years of peaceful pastoring.

Later in life, however, King often spoke of a specific event of divine calling. It took place in his own kitchen in the middle of the night during the tense times of the Montgomery Bus Boycott. The phone rang and an angry voice full of hate made a death threat against him and his family. He felt himself losing all courage and wanting out. And the "Lord Jesus," he

---

weight of interpretation of history in Christian theology (pp. 248-89), though the model I am working with here is less Augustine's than Luther's distinction of the old language of philosophy and the new language of theology; see Hinlicky, *The Substance of Faith: Luther on Doctrinal Theology* (Minneapolis: Fortress, 2008), pp. 138-44.

92. Richard Lischer, *The Preacher King: Martin Luther King, Jr. and the Word That Moved America* (New York and Oxford: Oxford University Press, 1995), pp. 217ff.

said, spoke to him in his despair: "Martin Luther, stand up for righteousness. Stand up for justice. Stand up for truth. And lo, I am with you, even until the end of the world."[93] From 1956 onward, King would refer back to this "kitchen experience" as his own Road to Damascus, the source and assurance of his calling to proclaim God's will for the redemption of America's soul from its original sin of racism. King constantly recalled this sense of divine commissioning to strengthen his resolve; he struggled all his life with fear of violent death, a sense of personal inadequacy, the embarrassment of contradictory desires in his own soul and indeed behaviors in his own body, particularly in relation to his marriage. The reluctant prophet was no "saint." Others close to him would speak of deep-seated feelings of guilt. "He wanders around in a daze," an old schoolmate once observed, "asking, 'Why has God seen fit to catapult me into such a situation?'"[94] Prophets learn in their human weakness, including moral weakness, to depend entirely on the God whose reign they proclaim. King's final address, "I See the Promised Land," has in this respect the ring of authenticity.[95]

His calling was to be a Baptist preacher, as Richard Lischer has stressed in his outstanding study, *The Preacher King.* What he learned at Crozier Seminary and Boston University amounted to the insight that the God of Moses and the biblical prophets is interested and involved in setting free the oppressed in this world, not pie in the sky in the sweet bye and bye. King frequently noted this doctrine in express disagreement with the Feuerbachian-Marxian doctrine that religion is the opiate of the people, previously discussed. One can make that kind of accusation against false religion, King would grant, but this is the very kind of religion that the prophets themselves attacked. King loved to recite a saying from the prophet Amos, the full citation reading as follows: "Thus says the LORD: I hate, I despise your festivals, and I take no delight in your solemn assemblies. Even though you offer me your burnt offerings and grain offerings, I will not accept them; and the offerings of well-being of your fatted animals I will not look upon. Take away from me the noise of your songs; I will not listen to the melody of your harps. But let justice roll down like waters, and righteousness like an ever-flowing stream" (Amos 5:21-24, NRS). In reliance on such biblical sources, delivered from dualistic construals, King activated these traditional biblical sources in

---

93. Marshall Frady, *Martin Luther King, Jr.* (New York: Penguin, 2002), p. 46.

94. Frady, *Martin Luther King, Jr.,* p. 44.

95. *Essential Writings, A Testament of Hope: The Essential Writings of Dr. Martin Luther King, Jr.,* ed. James Melvin Washington (San Francisco: Harper, 1986), pp. 279-86.

a creative social application of the Black Baptist's Christian gospel of redemption from America's original sin of racism.

King would have been first to insist that his movement of non-violent direct action for racial justice was not original with him, but derived. When the Black clergy of Montgomery drafted him as their spokesperson for the boycott movement in protest against Rosa Parks's arrest, King had this to say in his first appearance as a leader in the civil rights movement: "Now let us say that we are not here advocating violence, we have overcome that. I want it to be known throughout Montgomery and throughout this nation that we are — a *Christian* people. . . . If we are wrong, God Almighty is wrong! . . . If we are wrong, Jesus of Nazareth was merely a utopian dreamer and never came down to earth."[96] The *gospel* is the specific source of King's notion of non-violent direct action for racial justice: God who in the person of his own Son takes away the sin of the world by taking it upon himself, Jesus who goes to the cross forgiving his executioners. Reflecting on this, fellow Baptist preacher and Birmingham collaborator, Fred Shuttlesworth, said some years after King's death: "I think number one, Dr. King recognized himself as a messenger of God. A person who was speaking God's word, and interpreted God's will for people. That's what makes anybody powerful. King has said that this personal commitment is the source of any man's power . . . non-violence didn't just begin with King or Gandhi or others of us of whatever generation who spoke about non-violence. *Non-violence actually began in the mind of God and is included in the Word of God.* So when you preach the real Word of God in terms of the words of Christ Jesus as they are really meant, then you will do unto each other as you shall do unto yourself."[97] As King himself averred: "This business of passive resistance and nonviolence is the gospel of Jesus. I went to Gandhi through Jesus."[98]

King did find conceptual help at Boston University for the social diagnosis of racism as sin in a school of philosophy called Personalism, which is based on the contrast between the natural realm of necessity and the ethical realm of freedom. It holds that the evolutionary emergence from impersonal natural necessity of human personality into the ethical realm of freedom is the key to understanding of social reality. Along the

---

96. Frady, *Martin Luther King, Jr.*, p. 35.

97. Russel Moldovan, *Martin Luther King, Jr.: An Oral History of His Religious Witness and His Life* (San Francisco: International Scholars Publications, 1999), p. 128. Emphasis added.

98. Frady, *Martin Luther King, Jr.*, p. 39.

same lines, King was deeply influenced by Jewish theologian Martin Buber's distinction between I-It and I-Thou relations. In the realm of natural necessity, relations are between impersonal objects, Its. In the ethical realm of freedom, relations are between persons, Thous. King used both of these sources as aids in conceptualizing what racism is and why it is a sin. Racism subordinates an entire class of people in I-It relations, resulting in a deformation of both parties in a constructed social reality, that is, racism is a form of perception in which all are entangled. A false sense of inferiority is thus systematically instilled in the one, a false sense of superiority in the other. In both, human personality, which ought to flourish in I-Thou relations of Beloved Community, is instead violated and social reality is injuriously segregated. This violence against human personality is sin, because it refuses to receive and acknowledge the other as person, as gift from the supreme person, God. In more traditional language, King would say that the monogenist biblical narrative (e.g., Acts 17:26) tells that all of us come from Adam, that we are all the children of God, that racial differences become human pretexts for refusing to receive our own life with the lives of manifold others as the gift of Beloved Community.

Empowered by such thinking, Martin Luther King Jr. went on a mission to redeem the American soul from this sinful refusal of the Beloved Community in favor of racist segregation. Like Lincoln, he did not aspire merely to see individuals protected from the oppression of others, but simultaneously looked for a new birth of positive freedom, freedom for others, the Beloved Community characterized by malice toward none, charity toward all.[99] Redemption, therefore, converts the sinner through repentance and forgiveness. Redemption does not whitewash the sin, but confronts with truth in order that mercy can then restore fellowship. Redemption eschews both the literal violence of vengeful destruction of the sinner and at the same time intends in that sinner a spiritual death and resurrection. It is spiritually coercive. It is also publicly so. As the human self is social, it is of the essence of the matter for King that this happen openly. Redemption *publicly* draws the violence of the offender onto oneself and just so exposes it to public view. Thus that truth in its ugly brutality is seen by one and all, arousing the community to remedial action based upon this truer self-knowledge, and so working at length a redemptive change in self-understanding in the wrongdoer.

99. Paul R. Hinlicky, "Lincoln's Theology of the Republic According to the Second Inaugural Address," *The Cresset* 65, no. 6 (May 2002): 7-14.

King thus took evangelical ideas of redemption and translated them into his program of non-violent direct action. "We will wear you down by our capacity to suffer, and one day we will win our freedom . . . ," King would say repeatedly to Dixiecrat and Segregationist, "and so appeal to your heart and conscience that we will win a double victory."[100] In Birmingham, King put it this way: "God's love was poured out on the cross of Christ for unlikable people, people who don't move us, whose ways are not our ways. With this kind of love, we, that is, all in this room, will transform those who have persecuted us all these years and create a new Birmingham. But it won't happen without a sacrificial effort on our part."[101] The "I" who acts sacrificially in this way in the world is the same self who lives by this faithfulness of Christ poured out on the cross. King thus saw his social movement as the extension of his ministry as a Baptist preacher. He would not have objected to being described as a civil rights leader. But in his own self-understanding such a designation only touched the surface, not the depth; it described the fruit, not the root of his particular righteousness: a recipient of God's agape love who would return that agape love even to racist enemies and persecutors. This is the "I" who believes according to King's own self-understanding.

To explain the real source of King's life and work this way — to say that this exemplary agency under the conditions of modernity was rooted in faith formed by the gospel as handed on in the evangelical Black church and applied to its concrete experience of racist exclusion — leaves us with several problems. First, America is a nation, not a church. In his discovery in seminary that God is no dualist, King tended to connect nation and religion, state and church, law and gospel, justice and redemption so tightly, that he was baffled to the point of disillusionment when Americans acted like Americans, pursuing happiness as each sees fit, rather than like disciples of Jesus on the way to Beloved Community. Why would they not rather do the heavenly Father's will, no matter what the cost in bearing the cross? Moreover, in the final years of his life King confronted an alternative message of redemption proclaimed by the Black Muslim movement personified in Malcolm X, which he found deeply disturbing. This was not a message asking Black people to suffer even more for the redemption of white devils.

100. See, for example, King's last Christmas "Sermon on Peace," in *Essential Writings*, pp. 253-58, which I paraphrased to speak to the Trent Lott fiasco in the *Roanoke Times*, December 25, 2002, p. A11, "MLK Sermon Still Rings True."

101. Cited in Lischer, *The Preacher King*, p. 261.

It was a message of self-defense in bitter but clear-sighted recognition of intractable racial conflict. Black people are to redeem themselves with *power,* not redeem their white oppressors by sacrificial suffering. There *is* dissonance here. What is the relation between King's redemptive mission to free the soul of America from the sin of racism and Malcolm X's protective mission to defend the bodies and souls of oppressed Blacks from the ravages of racism? Many issues of political theology arise here. What is the relationship between coercive justice to protect the innocent from violence and merciful justice that aims at the redemption of the sinner? What is our natural diversity on the one hand and what is unnatural perversity on the other, and how are we to tell the difference? How do we relate law and gospel, force and persuasion, sword and spirit, justice and love, state and beloved community? At best, both terms in these dynamic polarities are and should be in their proper relation to one another taken as the works of the one God who creates, redeems, and fulfills one world through Jesus Christ. Thus Christian political theology can and should recognize what is truthful in Malcolm X's Islamic critique as a check against "realized eschatology," that is, against Christian illusions that the Kingdom has already come, that Christian people have already arrived, that the believer is already righteous with an achieved righteousness of her own rather than remaining still in the grip, albeit broken, of this world, that is, as a sinner in ways conscious and unconscious, whose righteousness remains Christ, whose progress is faith, whose Beloved Community is paradoxically present in hope, not yet in reality. Just so, the truth of the Christian claim that the grip of this world is a broken one, and that in faith a new subject has arisen from the old, is attested by the *martyr's* willingness to sacrifice life, precious life itself, as King acknowledged in the ecstatic sermon he delivered on the night before his assassination.

Thus while there is perhaps a little more overlap on these questions between King and (at least the later) Malcolm X than King was able to recognize in his lifetime, James Cone concluded that the two men represent truths that, though often opposed to one another, really ought to be kept together in a dialectic. Indeed, Cone asserted, we need Malcolm X as a reality check to keep King from being turned into a harmless American hero.[102] King was not in any event as starry-eyed as his Black nationalist detractors portrayed him. He had learned from Niebuhr about "moral

---

102. James H. Cone, *Martin and Malcolm and America: A Dream or a Nightmare* (Maryknoll, NY: Orbis, 1991), p. 316.

man and immoral society," i.e., about the paradox of caring slaveholders, sincere Klansmen, and born-again segregationists. As we have noted, in his personal experience King knew a signature doctrine of his namesake, that the Christian is *simul iustus et peccator*. King knew that agape love at its best has a paradoxical relation to recalcitrant human reality; that it achieves incarnation only in the ebb and flow of battle with an ongoing resistance; that law therefore must sometimes coerce what love cannot morally compel. In support of civil rights legislation King once declared: "The law cannot make you love me but it can sure stop you from lynching me!" The law can only do this because it is *not* agape by Word and Spirit forming a new subject for the Beloved Community but is temporal force justly, lawfully, and therefore inevitably punitively applied to protect others from what is against love. To the extent that we must be compelled in this way, naturally, we are not yet converted, not yet redeemed. The "I" who believes presides over a divided self, as depicted in Romans 7. Our righteousness in this life consists for the most part in the forgiveness of sins. Life together demands patience, just as patience is the eschatological virtue.

On the other hand, without Word and Spirit of the Beloved Community, law forgets that agape is the point of law. It becomes law for law's sake without any true and final goal to orient it, except to impose order on perceived chaos, or fanatically to remake human nature. All that then matters is order, or the revolution, backed by the threat of force. In such a world obsessed with security no matter what the moral cost, no one can ever afford painful truth; no one dares to be a sinner or to hope for mercy. Here there is and can be no safe zone of mercy. Everyone, for survival itself, maintains at all costs the Stoic appearance of innocence in a godless struggle for social recognition. People fight mercilessly in verbal if not physical violence, because they know they will receive no mercy if they lose. Against the prospect of a war of all against all that he saw in Malcolm X, King preferred to err on the side of agape, redemption, and mercy. Yet in this he was not blind to the *morally coercive*, if I may put it this way, the *spiritually confrontational* nature of non-violent direct action.

### Who Believes?

The examples of theological agency we have just surveyed in three arenas of social life provide a contemporary model of faith. Each shows that the passion of faith in its agencies of love and hope is not a matter of the repristination of some golden past but of the contemporaneousness of Jesus Christ. Even though the present "post-Christian" culture of the West in much resembles the society of the pre-Constantinian church, ours today is a peculiar and historically unprecedented situation in Europe and North America. We live culturally *after* the critique of pious humanity, *after* "the death of God," *after* the collapse of the Constantinian arrangement, *after* the institutional deformation of the modern churches into thousands of contending and competing sects marketing religion, *after* the decay within them of classic Christian doctrine, *after* the disasters of Hitler, Hiroshima, and Stalin — which lessons in secular salvation the secular intelligentsia still willfully refuses to learn.[103] Patriotic Romans despised early Christians as atheists because believing in the living and true God of the gospel meant disbelieving the idols, which were the civic gods of the Roman people. But today Western culture is becoming "atheistic" toward the God of the gospel, and new messages of human emancipation constitute a culturally viable, religiously plausible alternative to the gospel. The political passions of this age supplant the passion of faith for the age to come. How are we to proceed in this unprecedented situation?

While the broken churches of Euro-America surely need to repent of disunity, obeisance to secular power, and accommodation to the *Zeitgeist*, they need even more to renew their first love. What connects today's believers to those of the earlier church and of every time and place is "Jesus Christ, the same, yesterday, today and forever" (Heb. 13:8). Contemporary Western Christians cannot and should not retreat culturally to the catacombs, nor could they repristinate some golden past, even if they wanted to, without the aura of antiquarianism. *That* is a sure sign that the game is over. But it is not necessary to "go back," whether to the Bible, the early church, the Reformers, the civil rights movement, or anything else. The way forward with exemplary sisters and brothers from ages past lies in the Easter recognition that not only is Christ the same *object* of faith for us and for them as described by creedal faith, even more profoundly He is the original and proper *subject* of faith. Indeed, in this light we better understand how Jesus Christ is properly believed as also faith's *object*. Who is the subject of faith? Jesus Christ. He is the one who believed for us, and in whom, newborn, anyone believes who believes. *In Him* we *have the unity of the passive and active obedience, the One who suffered* our *loss of God out of love for* us all. The plural pronouns here are decisive. Our faith, such as it

---

103. Tinder, *Political Meaning*, p. 10.

is individually, is participation in His, and through Him therefore with all the others who are His. That is why in principle and sometimes in power, even the individual believer activates in love for the loveless and in hope against hope for this godless world. Whatever the individual lacks is made up in the whole, who is the total Christ, from Easter morn to the Parousia. Individual failings and maximal idiosyncrasy aside, all the saints have celebrated, together through space-time, the total Christ who is the agent of the new humanity, on the way to the Beloved Community.

Consider the alternative to this proposal. If Christ were merely the same *object* for us and for earlier believers, we could at best only speak of a community of intention (not even of action!) through the ages. Which Jesus is really He? How is He correctly to be "objectified" so that we can imitate Him? The Jewish Rabbi? The Kyrios of the Hellenistic congregation? The Logos? The Byzantine King of Kings? The Medieval Man of Sorrows? The Pietist's Bridegroom of the Soul? The Pacifist's Prince of Peace? Liberator of the Oppressed? Cynic Trickster of the Society of Recovering Fundamentalists, aka "The Jesus Seminar"? All things to all people? Nothing, then, in Himself? In fact we cannot easily see how Christ through the ages is one and the same object of faith. So long as we are thinking this way about faith as a literal imitation of Jesus' works as represented or objectified in such a more or less genuine way, we have no choice but to choose our own preferred sectarian image from the list above. Or, make up a new one. But, as the Letter to the Hebrews so wonderfully makes clear, Jesus *is* the subject who believed in God for us, and just so became the object of our unbelief when we nailed Him to the tree, but nevertheless lives in Easter glory as great High Priest on our behalf, the One true agent who loved the unworthy once and for all.[104] Because Jesus is this *subject* of faith, even as object, creedal faith in Him does not call us back to a classical past or previous representations, but forward together to His Father's victory of agapic love that reigns forever, that Beloved Community of the resurrection of the dead and the life everlasting. Jesus Christ crucified and risen is

---

104. Edward Schillebeeckx, *Christ: The Experience of Jesus as Lord,* trans. J. Bowden (New York: Crossroads, 1981), pp. 237-93. The ancient author's new interpretation of Jesus as high priest, Schillebeeckx concludes, is theologically liberating: "It leaves open the possibility that, inspired by what we have read in the New Testament about interpretative experiences of Jesus Christ, we should again be able to experience the same Jesus differently within a new and different horizon of experience" (p. 293). This can be the same Jesus when by Jesus we understand the public subject, in His *persona* as the messianic priest, who is in solidarity with human suffering (pp. 262ff.).

this present and active *subject* of faith because he has "descended into hell" — also this "hell" of post-Christian culture in Euro-America, also into all the other false or distorted "objectifications" and idolatrous associations of His more or less faithful people through the ages. He meets us in these "hells" as the living *subject* of faith or he meets us not at all. If He meets us there, what he brings is an "eschatological message," of "the kingdom of God . . . given us as a promise."[105] Understood this way, Marx's objection (not merely to Luther, but) to Jesus Christ is met and defeated: the path to the Beloved Community is the total Christ, which gives rise to real agencies in the world: in admonitions to peace by those afflicted with a sublime madness of a soul, since they hear and obey the voice of the Lord Jesus, *Stand up for justice!*

What finally about the *Zweireichenlehre?* Its lasting value lies merely in Luther's and Niebuhr's and King's *Augustinian* realism about the state as a monopoly on the means of violence,[106] which is how the state is and must be construed by the gospel of the resurrection of *the Crucified.* This regime as such is temporary. Yet so long as it exists, it is living testimony to the fact that the Kingdom has not yet fully come, that neither love nor community yet prevails. For punishment, like the sin that is punished, cannot enter the kingdom of God. In principle, then, the state does not belong to the Beloved Community, even if in God's economy it can and is made to serve it. But redemption is eternal. Faith in Jesus and with Jesus "looks to things which are invisible and unknowable . . . because they are not yet visible, not yet knowable. Faith directs itself to that which is to come — faith is the proper way to wait"[107] in the world in which human beings are not in final control and so must learn to live together in prospect of the reign, the City of God, the Beloved Community.

---

105. Wingren, *Vocation,* pp. 20-21.

106. A realism shared by Asad, *Formations,* pp. 6, 8, 22, in his trenchant critique of contemporary Western secularity.

107. Wingren, *Vocation,* p. 23, quoting M. A. H. Stomps, *Die Anthropologie Luthers* (Frankfurt: Klostermann, 1935).

# CHAPTER TEN

By Way of Conclusion:

# What Luther Meant by *theologia crucis*

## What Luther Meant

What *Luther* meant by the theology of the cross is that God heals us by afflicting us. The theologian of the cross "knows that it is sufficient if he suffers and is brought low by the cross in order to be annihilated all the more. It is this that Christ says in John 3[:7], 'You must be born anew.' To be born anew, one must consequently first die and then be raised up with the Son of Man. To die, I say, means to feel death at hand."[1] The death of the centered self and the birth of the ecstatic self by bodily union with Jesus Christ in faith — that is what Luther meant by the *theologia crucis*. A generation ago, John Douglas Hall wrote about what Luther's meaning would mean for theology in North America: it will require us to dispense "with the habit of regarding the gospel as a word that meets, answers, conquers and so annuls the negative. Instead, one would have to look upon the gospel of Jesus Christ as a vantage point from which to engage the negative: to engage it, not to overcome it. To live with and in it, not to displace it with a theoretically unassailable positive."[2] The negative is to be lived with and engaged because, taken from our hands and restored to God's, it becomes the "severe mercy" (Augustine) of "costly grace" (Luther) that brings us to the Beloved Community. There is no doubt, on the other hand, that this *theologia crucis*

---

1. "The Heidelberg Disputation" (1518) LW 31:55.
2. John Douglas Hall, *Lighten Our Darkness: Towards an Indigenous Theology of the Cross* (Philadelphia: Westminster, 1976), p. 209.

raises dangerous and sensitive questions of theodicy, which theology cannot refuse to consider. The world in which the cross of Jesus stood is a world in which the One he called Father permits the natural evils of flood and famine no less than the moral evil of created wills actually contravening His own. In such a world affliction belongs to life, and human beings can no more disown their pains than the bodies that feel them from birth day to death day. The gospel never delivers us from natural evil as such and does not easily or cheaply deliver us from moral evil. Indeed, even to understand this much as a theologian of the cross is to have owned one's affliction in faith as the birth pangs of God's new humanity. Such insight cannot be shared with the old Adam, who can only protest it. *Theologia crucis* is wisdom for those who boast in "in the cross of our Lord Jesus Christ, through which the world has been crucified to me and I to the world" (Gal. 6:14). It is the new "epistemology at the turn of the ages" (Martyn).

If that is so, it is "wicked sophistry," as Dietrich Bonhoeffer once wrote, "to justify the worldliness of the Church by the cross of Jesus[,]" that is, by a "'Reformation theology' which boldly claims the name of *theologia crucis* and pretends to prefer to Pharisaic ostentation a modest invisibility, which in practice means conformity to the world."[3] Thinking along the same lines, but endeavoring to reclaim the proper sense of Luther's *theologia crucis,* Jürgen Moltmann likewise wrote, "Radical reflection on the origin of Christian faith from the night of the cross makes this faith not only homeless in a religious world strange to it, but also homeless in the syncretistic world of bourgeois Christendom today. Consequently, the task for theology is no longer to present itself as the self-consciousness of Christendom in its world-historical appearance, but rather to re-orient itself radically to the originative events of faith in the cross, and thus to become theology of the cross."[4] Moltmann continued that as theology of the cross, faith "does not lead human beings into better harmony with themselves and their surroundings, but into contradiction with themselves and their surroundings. It does not domesticate and socialize, but makes 'homeless' and 'unbound' and through the discipleship of the homeless and unbound Christ it makes free."[5] If these authors point us in the right

---

3. Dietrich Bonhoeffer, *The Cost of Discipleship,* trans. R. Fuller (New York: Macmillan, 1979), pp. 132-33.

4. Jürgen Moltmann, *Der gekreuzigte Gott* (München: Chr. Kaiser, 1976), p. 39. My translation. I cite with approval the given passage, but it will be clear that I do not share in Moltmann's patripassionism.

5. Moltmann, *Der gekreuzigte Gott,* p. 42. My translation.

direction, central then to the project of a postmodern critical dogmatics "after Christendom" is the complex of anthropological ideas that I have designated by the terminology of the somatic, the centered, and the ecstatic self. Everything depends on this discourse being understood as theology not philosophy, thinking the canonical narrative of Trinitarian advent bearing the demand and promise of the Beloved Community in contest with the prevailing society of this world (even when it wears the mask of Christendom). The proclamation of the cross of Jesus ever marks this turn of the ages. In the proclamation of it, God afflicts in order to console, to heal, and at last to make all things new.

Nowhere is Luther's insight into this controversial contention of the gospel for human transformation[6] toward the Beloved Community more pointedly and yet as problematically articulated than in the 1518 statement of the *theologia crucis,* "The Heidelberg Disputation." "The law says, 'do this,' and it is never done. Grace says, 'believe in this,' and everything is already done."[7] Left on the level of anthropology, this is unintelligible. Such rhetoric only yields ambiguous paradoxes, vulnerable to misunderstanding, not to say also misuse. That occurs when it is not clear that the "this" which grace commands us to believe is the Christ who comes to live in us as the One who was, is, and will be for us; but apart from this new power and possibility of Christ with His earthly body, it is not clear why the doing of the law never accomplishes salvation, that is, inclusion in the Beloved Community. In fact the final thesis of the Heidelberg Disputation eloquently tells of this new power and hence possibility. "Thus Christ says: 'For I came not to call the righteous, but sinners' [Matt. 9:13]. This is the love of the cross, born of the cross, which turns in the direction where it does not find good which it may enjoy, but where it may confer good upon the bad and needy person. 'It is more blessed to give than to receive' [Acts 20:35], says the Apostle. Hence Psalm 41[:1] states, 'Blessed is he who considers the poor.'" Whether as successful doer or as failure by the same promethean measure, the centered self is and remains isolated, ultimately

---

6. Daphne Hampson, *Christian Contradictions: The Structures of Lutheran and Catholic Thought* (Cambridge: Cambridge University Press, 2001). Hampson wants "the transformation of the self rather than the breaking of the self," i.e., a "much more optimistic" view of "a self being able to be centered-in-relation" (p. 238). I regard a self-centered-in-relationship something of a contradiction in terms; instead we should speak of an eccentric or ecstatic or idiosyncratic self. Hampson's is an optimism without foundation in reality. See *Christian Contradictions,* pp. 239-40.

7. "The Heidelberg Disputation" (1518) LW 31:56.

from the body itself whose pain must be disowned; but salvation is communion, in the redeemed Body, bearing one another's burdens. This is the total Christ, agent of the new humanity and harbinger of the Beloved Community, the Israel of God.

Anthropological interpretation has been drawn to the early Luther and indeed predominated since the rediscovery of this early thought almost a century ago. In a classical study from the Luther Renaissance, one of Holl's students, Erich Vögelsang, analyzed the early Luther's use of the medieval tropological sense to impute the cry of the psalmist to the humanity of Christ. By this trope, Christ "unconditionally subjected Himself to the judgment of God, condemned Himself and acknowledged God's right in God's damning judgment; [this] was the fundamental claim of Luther's theology which was already irretrievably established for him prior to the engagement with the Psalms . . ."[8] — the exegesis simply working out this motif of *odium sui*. Building on such ideas, Walter von Loewenich in his classical study of the *theologia crucis* defended "the thesis that the theology of the cross is a principle of Luther's entire theology."[9] In this approach, the decisive thing is that the humanity of Christ in its human experience of *Anfechtung* is thought to form a bridge with our humanity in a continuum of understanding of the experience of God's judgment, the "crisis" of the Crisis theology of the 1920s.

Yet Loewenich had to deal with the difficulty that Luther in fact abandoned this rhetorically powerful differentiation of the theologies of the cross and of glory almost immediately after delivering the Heidelberg Disputation in 1518. He explained this interesting fact in a chapter on mysticism, in which he argued that Luther abandoned the rhetoric, but not the principle of the theology of the cross, because it was too easily confounded with mystical endeavor to crucify the flesh in order attain union of the intellectual soul with the divine: "the cross is not seen, in the first place, as God's way to man, but man's way to God."[10] Lage too sees that Luther has drawn the ideas of the theology of the cross from the mystical tradition of Tauler, Pseudo-Dionysius, and Meister Eckhart.[11] "In Tauler Luther found

8. Erich Vögelsang, *Die Anfänge von Luthers Christologie* (Berlin: Walter de Gruyter, 1929), p. 95. My translation.

9. Walter von Loewenich, *Luther's Theology of the Cross,* trans. H. Bouman (Minneapolis: Augsburg, 1976), p. 13.

10. Loewenich, *Luther's Theology of the Cross,* p. 164.

11. "The cosmological presupposition of this tradition was that the individual simultaneously lives in a world of multiplicity and flux, which is visible to the senses, and in a

*By Way of Conclusion:*

a Christological orientation distinct from that advocated by the medieval scholastic traditions. . . . While the imitation of Christ helps to create the precondition of *similitudo* necessary for conformity to occur, it is ultimately the living Christ who takes form in the Christian, conforming the Christian to himself . . . replacing the self's orientation with that of Christ."[12] It seems likely then that this early Luther of the Heidelberg Disputation is in motion, groping toward a view of the cross as God's way to the suffering creature, as *sacramentum* first and only as such then also *exemplum*.

Yet in the rhetoric of 1518 that is not yet quite clear, as David Yeago pointed out; he asked whether here "salvation [is] a matter of replicating a *pattern* displayed in Christ, or of communion with his *person,* sharing in what is his and in what he is? Both ways of thinking are present in Luther's thought from the beginning, and the motif of the 'happy exchange,' certainly presses towards an understanding of salvation as communion with Christ's person. . . ."[13] The overlap between pattern and person is understandable: this person *is* the Crucified but Risen One, whose narrative

---

world of unity, which is not visible to the senses. The invisible world is only available to the upper part of the soul with which it is in constant, although unconscious, contact. The consequence of this metaphysical dualism is that it is only possible to know God, who is the source of unity, meditatively without interference from the knowing subject. It was believed that a penetration into the being of God, resulting in a fusion of the knower and the known, was experientially possible. The entire purpose of the ascetic methodology was the destruction or loss of the self in the attempt to attain an 'essentialist' union with the Divine. The dissolution of individual form which characterizes the unio mystica is best illustrated by Bernard's example of the drop of water lost in the wind or Meister Eckhart's example of the drop of wine lost in the sea. . . . The unio mystica was possible because the imago Dei was said to reside in embryonic form in 'the soul's little spark.' A part of the self, namely the soul, thus shared a common ground of being with the Divine, commonly referred to as the Seelengrund. . . . Whereas the Dionysian mystical tradition emphasized the destruction or loss of the self in the ecstasy and bliss of absorption into Divinity, Tauler placed the emphasis on overcoming self-will in order to restore the true self to its prefallen nature." Dietmar Lage, *Martin Luther's Christology and Ethics: Texts and Studies in Religion,* vol. 45 (Lewiston, NY: Edwin Mellen Press, 1990), pp. 77-78.

12. Lage, *Luther's Christology,* p. 79. Further, ". . . resignation or Gelassenheit . . . ascent, therefore, plays only a minor or restricted preparatory role. Conformitas Christi entailed not only the ascent of the soul, but more significantly, the descent of God in Christ. Humanity's preparatory ascent meets God's gracious descent" (p. 80).

13. David Yeago, "The Catholic Luther," *First Things* 61 (March 1996): 37-41; originally a paper delivered at the conference, "The Catholicity of the Reformation," in Northfield, MN, on 27 February 1995; revised 24 October 1.

constitutes the saving transformation from the centered self to the ecstatic self for those who communicate to Him their sin and receive in exchange His righteousness.[14] Yet tension between the two motifs is unavoidable because the theology of the cross, when taken as a pattern to be imitated for reaching salvation, "*excludes* the sort of confident assurance of God's favor that Luther later came to teach." Indeed, "for the early theology of the cross, *uncertainty* of salvation plays an important part in weaning us from self-interested piety."[15] Ironically, if Yeago is right, the stance of Luther's earliest Reformation theology turns out to be closer to the position eventually taken by the Council of Trent on Justification (which anathematized the teaching of "faith alone without works" as leading to false security) than to his own mature theology!

## Some Feminist Concerns

It is clear in any case that what one means by *theologia crucis* and how it might comport with Luther's legacy for contemporary theology is not immediately obvious. As Christine Helmer has recently pointed out, there is or seems to be a "divide" between Luther and Feminist theology in just this respect, which several theologians have attempted to bridge[16] with perhaps varying levels of success. This "divide," however, may be a function of several variables: first, the various "Luthers" in play today still streaming from the mighty intellectual world of German Protestant scholarship (as the preceding paragraphs attest), and second, the various feminisms (liberal? radical? Marxist? womanist? Christian commonsense?) that purport to speak in the name of (historical? essential? all? sisters in Christ?) women's experience. The proposal of this book will in any case not accord

---

14. So Lage, *Luther's Christology:* "Faith in Christ, properly understood as itself the gift of the Holy Spirit, is the only form of relationship with Christ not infected by self-righteous claims. . . . Luther's Christ-mysticism stressed the pneumatic presence of the crucified and risen Christ in the Christian — 'the spiritual birth of the incarnate Word' — rather than merely a psychological presence or the speculative presence of the *synteresis* as conceived by the various medieval schools . . . a contemporaneousness in life and destiny rather than merely in knowing, willing or feeling. . . . Furthermore, Luther held that *conformitas Christi* is the locus of the 'wonderful' or 'happy exchange' of *iustitia* and *peccata* . . ." (p. 86).

15. Yeago, "The Catholic Luther."

16. Christine Helmer, "The American Luther," *Dialog: A Journal of Theology* 47, no. 2 (Summer 2008): 115. I am grateful to Helmer for bringing this article to my attention.

with *any* Jamesian appeal to a theology of religious experience, feminist or otherwise, just as it has also tried to avoid a repristinating Luther-theology. The approach this book has taken is to ask whether Luther can provide help for a creedal Christian theology in Euro-America today that looks to the social salvation of the Beloved Community, and from that perspective asks centrally about the moral burden of the individual and the atoning work of Christ. Nevertheless, two objections stemming from Feminist theology broadly speaking to what Luther meant by the theology of the cross are worthy of consideration by way of conclusion. They will point us on to the "proper distinction," so to say, of the theology of the cross and the theology of glory.

The first concern has to do with the traumatized, that is, with those who are said to have been so profoundly abused, especially by structures of male privilege, that there is no centered, egocentric self in need of Luther's kind of salvation — what Daphne Hampson criticized the "breaking" of an already broken self.[17] Such a battered self is thought to need healing first, and only then, if ever, justification (as breaking and remaking). This I take to be an important concern that merits an important qualification: a theology of the cross that eclipses the healing and liberating Christ of the gospel narrative cuts the ground from under its own feet. If some Hitler or Stalin were crucified, it would be cruelty upon cruelty to hail such an abuser's resurrection as our salvation or to think that we too are to be broken and refashioned to become a true person on their pattern. A theology of the cross only helps if the One who was crucified for us is Jesus, friend of women and children as well as sinners and tax-collectors, healer of the diseased, liberator of the possessed, stiller of the storm, feeder of the multitude, singularly moved in all these things by compassion for the sheep without a shepherd. This is in fact as much the good news about Jesus for Luther as the Pauline kerygma of the resurrection of this One crucified or the Johannine teaching of the Incarnation as the glory of God dwelling among us.

In a memorable sermon Luther described "the good report that Christ was a pious man and cheerfully helped everyone" from the Synoptic Gospels. But Luther took sides in his sermon with the Syro-Phoenician woman who dared to trust in this report about Christ. Thus she is a "true example of firm and perfect faith" in the good news about Jesus; she overcame "great and hard battles" to teach us "in a beautiful manner the true

---

17. See above, n. 4.

way and virtue of faith, namely, that it is a hearty trust in the grace and goodness of God as experienced and revealed through his Word."[18] Luther roots for this woman, because she will not take "No" for an answer to her plea of faith; she protests her "experience" of rebuff and rejection by "cling[ing] alone to God's bare Word, until she experienced the contrary."[19] She will not give in to feelings of unworthiness but in fact she finally sasses Christ with a "masterly stroke," catching him "in his own words"[20] when she turns the statement about the dogs eating crumbs that fall from the master's table to her own advantage.

Reading the story this way, Luther lifts up her *faith as the healing virtue* for all the marginalized and disregarded, new *courage* to believe in one's own value as valued also by the God who is coming to bring in that Beloved Community. The story is an important testimony to the fact that for Luther the experience of God's hiddenness is an experience of faith, in faith, for faith in Jesus — not an alternative to faith.[21] "Christ like a hunter exercises and chases faith in his followers that it may become strong and firm. . . ."[22] This divine sport[23] of God who hides in His revelation[24] provides a clue also to the harsh rhetoric of the *odium sui,* parsed by Luther's re-preaching of the Synoptic story about this foreign woman whom Christ compared to a dog: "she concedes it, and asks nothing more than that he let her be a dog, as he himself has judged her to be. Where will Christ now take refuge? He is caught. . . . Therefore Christ now completely opens his

---

18. "Second Sunday in Lent" on Matthew 15:21-28 in *Sermons of Martin Luther,* 7 vols., trans. John Nicholas Lenker (Grand Rapids: Baker, 1983), II:149.

19. *Sermons* II:150.

20. *Sermons* II:152.

21. "It is not the case that there are two Gods: a loving God and a wrathful God. Nor is it the case that the two expressions of God's wrath and love are in conflict with each other. If this were the case, the Ockhamist God of pure arbitrariness and capriciousness, the Deus exlex bound by no law, to which Luther had always objected, would be introduced. God's true nature is love, and wrath is alien to that nature. But wrath is the means which God has chosen to help a sinful humanity fight against its own sinfulness." Lage, *Luther's Christology,* p. 65. "Beyond the subjective perception of the paradoxical dyadic will of God, which both damns and justifies, lies a loving and transcendent God with a salvific will for humanity" (p. 66).

22. *Sermons* II:149.

23. "God's wrath is most terrible when the sinner is not punished but allowed to remain sinful." Lage, *Luther's Christology,* p. 66. For then the unafflicted sinner is left to its own destruction.

24. Steinmetz concludes his chapter on the Hidden God with a discussion of this sermon, *Luther in Context,* p. 30.

heart to her and yields to her will, so that she is now no dog, but even a child of Israel."[25] Lage has the nuance here precisely right. "The believer's relationship to Christ is a 'coincidence of opposites' such that it is only possible to say 'I am Christ' because Christ has first said to me, 'I am that sinner.'" [WA 40 I, 285] — it is a "communion of faith in which the Divine/human encounter is bridged by the activity of the Holy Spirit . . ." [Gal. 2:20][26] in the bold, feisty, divine faith of a woman who would not take "No" for an answer.

Even so, this *odium sui* rhetoric of Luther will not likely be our contemporary idiom. It is too vulnerable to misunderstanding and misapplication. Yet the truth of what Luther is saying here must inform any theology of salvation for the traumatized, whose healing begins with the courage to believe in one's own value as the good and redeemed creature of God against profoundly internalized experience of inferiority. This liberation to faith in God our heavenly Father through Jesus Christ in the power of their Spirit does not come by denying the trauma, but by owning it as one's incorrigible experience, even in all its terror. So it is. But it is not the final truth, the truth that comes to the traumatized in the figure of Christ, the Good Physician. This advent brings about the battle that actually must be now fought by the traumatized as new agents in Christ in this their own idiosyncrasy, namely, daily whether to yield to victimization or to stand up, walk, and be crippled no more. However faltering these latter steps, they signal the healing that begins now in faith and is fulfilled in that promised community of love, when every tear is wiped away.

There is another kind of feminist objection to Luther's theology of the cross, which Rosemary Ruether famously put when she asked: Whatever kind of good news can it be (for anyone, but especially for women) about a father killing a son? This second objection has been quite influential, but, as should be evident from the argument of this book, it is quite equally misplaced. It does not hit its target when and where theology is vigorously Trinitarian. Whatever subtle objection might be lodged against Anselm, or more profoundly against expiatory sacrifice, we have seen that

---

25. *Sermons* II:152. As for example when "we feel in our own conscience that God rebukes us as sinners and judges us unworthy of the kingdom of heaven, then we experience hell, and we think we are lost forever. Now whoever understands here the actions of this poor woman and catches God in his own judgment and says: Lord, it is true, I am a sinner and not worthy of thy grace; but still thou hast promised sinners forgiveness. . . . Behold, then must God according to his own judgment have mercy upon us" (p. 153).

26. Lage, *Luther's Christology*, p. 85.

the Son is not for him a hapless mortal at the mercy of an all-powerful and egocentric "Father": God as masculinist bully. On the contrary, the very reason that this Son can help in Anselm's scheme is that His suffering is supremely active, voluntary, and transformative, as Milbank rightly sees. The point is worthy of emphasis, because the feminist critique of theological sadism presupposes post-Cartesian notions of a private god with a narcissist's ego superintending a privatized religion. No doubt, this mutation of Christianity has been particularly injurious to the privatized women of modernity, and in this respect it is an emphatically worthy object of criticism. Such religiosity interiorizes oppression even as it sanctions interiority. As a serious critique of Luther, however, it is only as valid as Marx's original version of it, discussed above in Chapter Nine. As we saw there, what is at stake is retaining Luther's motif of punishment, the passive obedience of the divine Son of God (which was of course for Luther also a voluntary act of loving identification, as we saw), as well as Anselm's motif of the active obedience of the man Christ (but with rather greater weight on Him who was first the Healer of our diseases and so became at length the disease He healed), together with the patristic *Christus Victor* breaking the grip of the contra-divine powers. Indeed what is at stake is *integrating* these three New Testament teachings about atonement to reflect the cosmic rather than acosmic interpretation of Christianity, as labor of and for the Beloved Community in conflict with the *civitas terrena*.

## What's Wrong with Glory?

If that suffices to meet several feminist concerns, another way of posing the question about the validity for us today of Luther's theology of the cross is to ask just what is wrong with its antipode, the *theologia gloriae*. I have argued throughout this book that this notion is regularly confused with Kantian strictures on the limits of reason rather than Luther's strictures against Satanic curiosity prying into God's secrets. There is a horizon of mystery against which the *deus incarnatus/revelatus* appears, such that faith remains venture and risk, a condition that decisively qualifies the nature and task of theology itself. All sides are agreed on this much. But twentieth-century Protestant theology has witnessed two divergent interpretations stemming from just this common point of departure in the *theologia crucis*.

Karl Barth could write that "dogmatics is possible only as *theologia crucis,* in the act of obedience which is certain in faith, but which for this very reason is humble, always being thrown back to the beginning and having to make a fresh start."[27] Barth considered the relation between the "word of the cross" and the "Word of God" on the analogy of form to content: "The speech of God is and remains the mystery of God supremely in its secularity"[28] in that "its form is not a suitable but an unsuitable medium for God's self-presentation." So Barth interprets Luther's *sub contrario:* "It does not correspond to the matter but contradicts it. It does not unveil it but veils it."[29] Thus one must ever and afresh listen in humble obedience to hear what the Spirit intends, since there is no ready, self-evident analogy available for understanding. The *theologia crucis* "is an attack on the attempt to evade the necessity of believing by trying to get a direct or only relatively indirect knowledge of God apart from the secularity and resultant mystery of the incarnate Word. When Luther points to the crib of Bethlehem and the cross of Golgotha, he is not saying that direct knowledge of God is possible and actual here in this very secular phenomenon as such . . . what he is pointing to is the total secularity, i.e., the hiddenness of the Word, and therewith the sole reality of indirect knowledge. . . ."[30] Hence, we have the interpretation of the theology of the cross as patient, obedient, trusting *nachdenken,* as opposed then to the *theologia gloriae* as speculation aiming at a direct knowledge of God. For Barth, this latter will in fact end up only in idolatry, as humans construct a monster-god from their own perverse imaginations — a monster-god that will in turn devour them. This interpretation reflects, then, Barth's realized eschatology in the sense that howsoever indirect the knowledge of God under the contrary of the cross is, it *is* the one true God who so *truly presents Himself* here as an *object* to be known and trusted by human beings. Any thought of a *deus absconditus* apart from manger and cross consequently is and can be only speculation, the *theologia gloriae.* Barth indeed passionately inveighs against any other God than the Baby in the manger, insisting that the monsters of speculative theology have been defeated forever at the cross. Theology must leave those idols behind, treating them as the nothing which actually they are.

Oswald Bayer represents an interpretation of the *theologia gloriae*

27. Karl Barth, *Church Dogmatics* I/1, trans. G. Bromiley (Edinburgh: T. & T. Clark, 1975), p. 14.

28. Barth, *Church Dogmatics* I/1:165.

29. Barth, *Church Dogmatics* I/1:166.

30. Barth, *Church Dogmatics* I/1:173.

that may be fairly described as the precise opposite of Barth's, a protest against realized eschatology which insists that there is no theological way — especially not Barth's way by means of a master-principle of self-revelation — to bridge the gap that Luther actually described. This is the gap between the hidden God who does not deplore death but omnipotently works all things and the revealed God who (ineffectively?) weeps for the lost and the dying. For Bayer, the *deus absconditus* is no no-thing, but an uncanny and incomprehensible power, indeed God as incommunicable It, God as God truly appears apart from Christ and faith, as God can appear when faith turns away from the manger and the cross and just so becomes unfaith. Bayer seems in this to come very close to dualism, though he denies that his position entails it.[31] Rather he argues that there is a true theology of glory, but it is the one that essentially belongs to the eschaton, since this gap is one that only God can traverse; as such, the theology of glory becomes false when it ceases to be future eschatology, the final theology of God who makes all things new. Consequently, faith lives in the interim and here takes on the form of a "dispute with God, summoning [the revealed] God against [the hidden] God."[32] Faith remains faith just because it must *believe* the eschatological unity of the hidden and revealed God, that is to say, believing now in the act and light of that future glory when faith gives way to sight and so comes to see what now it can only trust to be true. For Bayer, then, no one who follows Luther can then be a "Barthian," but instead confesses: "In praise of God I believe and hope with all the church that God the Trinity is wholly Love. In the eschaton the difference which appears between Law and Gospel will be transcended in favor of the Gospel, the difference between the hidden and revealed God in favor of the revealed God, the difference between the two regiments in favor of the spiritual regiment, and the difference between what faith be-

31. As also does Ebeling, who is in the background here: ". . . in order that God may be truly God Luther maintains to the utmost degree the contradiction between God in Jesus Christ and the God of omnipotence and omniscience, between faith and experience. . . . Jesus, the crucified, allows us to God in God as omnipotence in impotence, and only in this way makes God really God for us at all. For faith and God belong together." Gerhard Ebeling, *Luther: An Introduction to His Thought* (Philadelphia: Fortress, 1972), pp. 240-41. I confess to finding this unintelligible, unless tacitly "Jesus, the Crucified" bridges this "contradiction" by virtue of being the Incarnate Son suffering the Father's abandonment for His loving solidarity with us, and returned to the Father by the Spirit of the resurrection, as explicated in Chapter Three. But Ebeling never says such things, as Luther does.

32. Oswald Bayer, *Martin Luther's Theology: A Contemporary Interpretation,* trans. Thomas H. Trapp (Grand Rapids: Eerdmans, 2007), p. 213.

lieves and what appears to reason in favor of faith."[33] The light of grace is not yet glory's. Faith sees in a glass darkly, but it does envision the victory of the God of love.

There is of course yet another solution, as old and as venerable as Plato: to cut the Gordian knot of Luther's *theologia crucis* by denying divine responsibility for the suffering creation and so speaking in principle of a suffering, or more precisely, a helpless God. Bonhoeffer famously wrote that only a suffering God can help, though for the Lutheran Bonhoeffer, this is surely a Christological statement about the Man-for-others who is also Luther's Man-who-created-the-world. In principle, a helpless god cannot help, except in the sense of modeling for us a poignant *affectus*. But the Christian gospel has wanted to speak of God who helps and is able to help. Eschewing Platonism, we thus find ourselves between Bayer and Barth: on the one side, a realized eschatology, which dissolves the *deus absconditus* as no more than the illusory vestige of natural theology in the name of the true, revealed (albeit indirect) theology of the cross, and on the other side, a future eschatology of God's coming glory, only visible at the eschaton, lest we confuse faith with sight.[34]

---

33. "Mit der Doxologie glaube und hoffe ich inmitten der ganzen Kirche, daß Gott der dreieine und ganz und gar Liebe ist. Im Eschaton wird die Differenz zwischen Gesetz und Evangelium zugunsten des Evangeliums, die Differenz zwischen dem verborgenen und offenbaren Gott zugunsten des offenbaren, die Differenz zwischen den beiden Regimenten zugunsten des geistlichen und die Differenz zwischen Glauben und Schauen zugunsten eines Glaubens, der schaut, aufgehoben sein." Personal correspondence, 1/28/09.

34. B. A. Gerrish rightly groups Luther interpreters along just these lines stemming back to Theodosius Harnack's dualistic reading of the God of wrath outside of Christ, and Ferdinand Kattenbusch's monistic reading of God who hides Himself in His revelation. B. A. Gerrish, *The Reformation Heritage* (Chicago: University of Chicago Press, 1982), p. 133. While the latter reading stemming from the *theologia crucis*, he claims, "has been fully appreciated and appropriated," the former "has been found something of an embarrassment" (p. 134). Tracing Luther's argument through *De servo arbitrio*, Gerrish concludes that taken rationally the dualistic argument amounts to the "collapse of Luther's doctrine of God at this point: the two wills fall apart in a bifurcation that he does not profess himself able to overcome" (p. 137). At this juncture, in a fashion quite similar to Bayer, Gerrish appeals against systematic coherence to the messy reality of religious experience to vindicate what Luther attempts here to say about faith having "the character of a turning from the hidden God. The luminous object of faith is set against a dark, threatening background. Awareness of the hidden God, therefore, qualifies faith in Christ" (p. 138). In short, "To reason, it may well seem like desperation to invoke a sacred mystery. But that is the way things are" (p. 141). It is not an accident, in my view, that Gerrish ends this essay invoking Pascal (p. 148). On the other hand, if the "faith" turning to the revealed God were the divine faith of the Spirit, then the movement to the revealed God would be God's own movement incorporating believers.

Bayer is surely right in orienting his interpretation to the conclusion of the more mature Luther in the *DSA* with its discussion of the three lights of nature, grace, and glory[35] rather than to the early, problematic Heidelberg Disputation. On the other hand, it cannot be right simply to exclude Barth's understanding of *nachdenken* as false *theologia gloriae,* when it is charitably interpreted in terms of its own intention, certainly in keeping with Luther's, to flee to the *deus revelatus* and to eschew speculation as the factory of idols. Two lines of thought suggest themselves as a way forward for theology in Luther's tradition that wants to respect both strictures: Barth's against speculation and Bayer's against gnosis.

First, we recall what was promised in Chapter One. There I noted how Luther cited John 1:13, when commenting on Galatians 1:4, "There is another reason why Paul refers to the will of the Father here, a reason cited in many passages in the Gospel of John also, where Christ, in asserting His commission, calls us back to the will of the Father, so that in His words and works we are to look, not at Him but at the Father. For Christ came into the world so that he might take hold of us and so that we, by gazing upon Christ, might be drawn and carried directly to the Father."[36] Johannine theology is also a kind of (deliteralized) apocalyptic theology, which Luther fittingly cites here, if apocalypse is the true and abiding import of the early Luther's *theologia crucis.* Indeed, we might speculate (historically, not theologically) that increasing appreciation for the Johannine theology of glory is the theological reason why Luther abandoned the terminology of the Heidelberg Disputation as misleading (i.e., John 1:18). When the importance of John is taken into consideration, then a third way of *inaugurated eschatology* leading beyond the impasse between Barth and Bayer commends itself. That entails something like an old-fashioned Patristic theology, which conceives of the Gospel of John as the bridge between the New Testament and the developed creedal theology of the early Catholic Church; this would have to be argued in tandem with a greater appreciation of Luther's affinity with the Fourth Gospel. Thus it is not only wrong to isolate Luther from the Synoptic Jesus; he is to be seen as equally indebted to the Johannine. How these apparent contraries (as it seems for us today) can be understood together is a major question for future consider-

---

35. Martin Luther, *The Bondage of the Will,* trans. J. I. Packer and O. R. Johnston (Westwood, NJ: Fleming Revell, 2000), pp. 317-18; cf. also Thomas Reinhuber, *Kämpfender Glaube: Studien zu Luthers Bekenntnis am Ende von* De servo arbitrio (Berlin and New York: Walter de Gruyter, 2000), pp. 102-43.

36. "Commentary on Galatians" (1535) LW 26:42.

ation. This much can be said now: Luther's biblical theology is not that of a harmonizer but of an integrator; conversely, his historical and critical exegesis is a function of the discipline I am calling critical dogmatics (not an alternative to dogmatics).

Second, and in precise accord with the foregoing, there is an important dispute in scholarship about how to interpret the motif of the "withdrawal of the Deity" in Luther's mature discussions of the spiritual suffering of Christ.[37] Lienhard puts it with his usual frankness: "In Luther's view Christ was not only 'humiliated' by God, but 'abandoned' by him. God failed him. God withdrew himself from him."[38] He is "*a patre derelictus.*"[39] The Latin has the merit of putting the question in a way that specifies *the hidden God is the very One whom Jesus knew as His Abba-Father: a patre derelictus.* In this way, the tension between the Father and the Son is not eclipsed, as in Barth's notion of divine self-revelation, especially if taken along modalist lines of the One self-positing Ego *("God reveals Himself as Lord")* that minimize the personal distinctions.[40] Nor, on the other hand, is the Trinitarian heresy entertained of imagining some all-powerful deity not bound by its word. Rather, something much sharper in profile comes into view. Faith's knowledge of the *deus revelatus* continually depends on the real mediation of the Spirit in time, who returns the Father to the Son and the Son to the Father in the resurrection of the Crucified One, so also in the proclamation of the gospel in Word and Sacrament, as also in the life of faith which is participation in the *pistos Iesou.* This formulation of the question contains several implications for the task of theology today. I will mention three in conclusion.

---

37. E.g., Commentary on Psalm 8, WA 45:205-50; trans. LW 12:95-136. One could also reference here the Sermons for Wednesday after St. Elizabeth on Nov. 21, 1537, on Jesus Christ True God and Man and on His Office and Kingdom which He Conducts in Christendom, and Thursday, Nov. 22, 1537, On the Humanity of Christ and Its Office, WA 45:265-324; no English translation.

38. Marc Lienhard, *Martin Luther: Witness to Jesus Christ, Stages and Themes of the Reformer's Christology,* trans. Edwin H. Robertson (Minneapolis: Augsburg, 1982), p. 64.

39. Lienhard, *Martin Luther,* p. 67.

40. See the critique of Barth's Trinitarianism in Hinlicky, *Paths Not Taken: Theology from Luther through Leibniz* (Grand Rapids: Eerdmans, 2009), pp. 128-38.

## Three Conclusions

First, *cognition as interpretation.* Many think of theology after Schleiermacher as a work of the human imagination, a work of construction, of self- or communal expression in metaphors, symbols, or models that articulate some otherwise ineffable *Grunderfahrung.* Another form of noncognitivism in modern theology is to make — perhaps in reaction against the former — so strong a distinction between first-order kerygma and second-order doctrine that the notion of doctrinal knowledge of God seems out of place. In a sympathetic critique of George Lindbeck, Reinhard Hütter makes the latter point that the *fides quae creditur* and the *fides qua creditur* can hardly be so artificially segregated, least of all in preaching. Liberal theology in analogy to philosophical aesthetics conceives of its task as historical-critical description of past cultural productions and new constructive production of symbolic artifacts (more or less modeled upon the discoveries of the historians). Lindbeck's postliberal cultural-linguistic model brackets propositional truth claims and adopts a stance of referential neutrality on doctrine, which is rather taken as *regula fidei.* This approach allows (rare) truth claims to be made in first-order discourse of kerygma, but not by doctrine per se, unless doctrine comes to function as kerygma.[41] In first-order kerygma, a claim to ontological correspondence may take place if and when a proposition is used in a way that corresponds with the truth it bears, but in second-order doctrine, there is only a claim to coherence with other beliefs we hold as true, as in a system of doctrinal rules. The latter to be sure finally depends on the former, where it will be as a total life form that there is or rather may be correspondence with God, which must in turn be eschatologically verified.[42]

Hütter argues that Lindbeck's strong distinction between the two orders breaks down. On his own account Lindbeck requires the descriptive critical-historical task to ascertain those first-order propositions that second-order doctrines are to regulate. Does that not entail normative judgments? For example, why shouldn't the majority position in the German Protestant church of the 1930s, "Jesus was an Aryan," be reckoned as doctrine on purely historical grounds, as Steigmann-Gall has recently

---

41. Reinhard Hütter, *Suffering Divine Things: Theology as Church Practice,* trans. D. Stott (Grand Rapids: Eerdmans, 2000), p. 45.

42. Hütter, *Suffering Divine Things,* pp. 52-53.

*By Way of Conclusion:*

done?[43] Why wouldn't any given consensus count as Christian doctrine, which second-order reflection then must simply receive? "How can normative explication be the task of a 'descriptive' discipline . . . ? does not an explication oriented toward a norm imply a notion of 'correct' and 'false' that precisely does not coincide with pure description, and is rather the implicate of some concrete judgment?"[44] For Hütter himself, following Luther's notion of the Christian life as a *vita passiva,* formed by a *verbum externum,* theology cannot avoid its pathos under God's activity as *Spiritus Creator.*[45] It must therefore discriminate true kerygma from false on the first-order level. Preaching itself must therefore also instruct and teach.[46] Confessional theology in the primitive sense of the word is theology that "same-says" (Greek: *homologizein*) the speech-act of God's proclaimed word, which in turn must be discerned. If revelation is understood as God's self-interpretation to the world in the life, death, resurrection, and exaltation of the man Christ Jesus, then theology is this kind of cognition, the church's interpretation of God's self-interpretation to continually new human experience. There is of course a strong distinction to be made between doctrine and theology, since the latter must be free to explore and to discern in every changing circumstance. But whenever theology knows anything, it knows it as doctrine, or not at all; and it

43. The question represents an extreme case but it is not idle. Richard Steigmann-Gall, adopting a radically empiricist method that eschews normative conceptions, asks just this question in his useful and provocative *The Holy Reich: Nazi Conceptions of Christianity 1919-1945* (Cambridge: Cambridge University Press, 2003).

44. Hütter, *Suffering Divine Things,* p. 59. Hütter goes on to "expose" Lindbeck as a catechist (p. 62) and a Lutheran (pp. 64, 65), which undermines the putative formality and neutrality of Lindbeck's model and the strictness of the first/second order distinction. In Lindbeck's defense: his book had a limited goal, heuristic form, and a tone of ecumenical reserve (p. 64).

45. Hütter, *Suffering Divine Things,* p. 62.

46. Gerhard Forde would strongly agree with Hütter about this "pathos" of theology. Indeed, he executed a scathing critique of the bathos of contemporary constructivism in theology. "'The suffering of God,' or the 'vulnerability of God,' and such platitudes become the stock-in-trade of preachers and theologians who want to stroke the psyche of today's religionists. . . . But in the theology of the cross it is soon apparent that we cannot ignore the fact that suffering comes about because we are at odds with God and are trying to rush headlong into some sort of cozy identification with him . . ." Gerhard O. Forde, *On Being a Theologian of the Cross: Reflections on Luther's Heidelberg Disputation, 1518* (Grand Rapids: Eerdmans, 1997), p. viii. Sentimentalism is the inevitable price. "Sooner or later a disastrous erosion of the [biblical] language sets in. It must constantly be adjusted to be made appealing. Gradually it sinks to the level of maudlin sentimentality" (p. 17).

knows it as doctrine, when, and only when, it is interpretation of God's self-interpretation in Jesus Christ by the Holy Spirit, hence as *sacra doctrina*.

Second, *the Monothelite controversy*. Luther's daring speech about the withdrawal of the deity *would be* problematic, if it reflected a non-Trinitarian notion of Christ the man being carried about by deity in an account at once modalistic and Nestorian.[47] On this view, the withdrawal of the deity to leave the mortal man all alone to fight is at least a coherent idea and admittedly an attractive one to contemporary existentialists, who find themselves in the same situation. But it does not comport with Luther's otherwise well-attested anti-Nestorian convictions in Christology or with the Trinitarian personalism that has been urged in this study. The better solution is to resort to Philippians 2. In this view, it is the eternal Son who goes freely out of love to the ignominy and disgrace of the cross, who suffers not a human's "withdrawal of deity" but abandonment as Son by His own Father, whom He nevertheless trusts and obeys. In that case, when we think of the spiritual sufferings of Christ, we are up against the Christological problem of the two wills in Christ, a problem that long antedates Luther. The problem becomes apparent with a simple comparison of the Synoptic and Johannine accounts of the agony in the Garden.

**Mark 14:32-36** And they went to a place which was called Gethsemane; and he said to his disciples, "Sit here, while I pray." And he took with him Peter and James and John, and began to be greatly distressed and troubled. **And he said to them, "My soul is very sorrowful, even to death; remain here, and watch." And going a little farther, he fell on the ground and prayed that, if it were possible, the hour might pass from him.** And he said, "Abba, Father, all things are possible to thee; **remove this cup from me**; yet not what I will, but what thou wilt."

47. So Luther in the *Disputatio de divinitate et humanitate Christi*: "46. But none have spoken more insipidly than the Modernists, as they are called, who of all men wish to seem to speak most subtly and properly. 47. These say that the human nature was sustained or supposited by the divine nature, or by a divine supposit. 48. This is said monstrously and nearly forces God as it were to carry or bear the humanity." Translated from the Latin text of WA 39/2, 92-121, by Christopher B. Brown for *Project Wittenberg*. The translation is in the public domain and may be found at: www.iclnet.org/pub/resources/text/wittenberg/wittenberg-home.html.

*By Way of Conclusion:*

**John 12:22-33** And Jesus answered them, "The hour has come for the Son of man to be glorified. Truly, truly, I say to you, unless a grain of wheat falls into the earth and dies, it remains alone; but if it dies, it bears much fruit. He who loves his life loses it, and he who hates his life in this world will keep it for eternal life. If any one serves me, he must follow me; and where I am, there shall my servant be also; if any one serves me, the Father will honor him. **"Now is my soul troubled. And what shall I say? 'Father, save me from this hour'? No, for this purpose I have come to this hour.** Father, glorify thy name."

The Johannine account does not strictly speaking contradict Mark's but, so to say, supervenes it. John's Jesus *does acknowledge that his soul is troubled, yet this natural human aversion to suffering and disgrace is assumed or integrated into the mission of the divine Son, who is the real agent at work in the persona,* Jesus Christ. Here again we have an indication that the next step forward on the path to Christian theology after Christendom is to retrace the steps of patristic theology by understanding the Gospel we call John as the bridge between the later doctrinal development and the Synoptic testimony to Jesus as also the Pauline proclamation of this One crucified and risen.

Through the efforts of Maximus the Confessor the ancient Eastern church solved this tension in its doctrine of two wills, but one theandric energy in Christ. Commenting on Matthew 26:39, Maximus wrote: "Thus he possesses a human will . . . only it was not opposed to God. But this will is not at all deliberative, but properly natural, eternally formed and moved by its essential Godhead to the fulfillment of the economy . . . and can properly be said to have truly become divine in virtue of the union, but not by nature. For nothing at all changes in nature by being deified."[48] While the Western church has largely ignored the latter three ecumenical councils claimed by Eastern Orthodoxy, it is intriguing to note, as we have seen in Chapter Two, how Luther's Christology comports with the theopaschite neo-Chalcedonianism of the Fifth Council. Likewise the problem of the "withdrawal of the deity" fairly cries out for Maximus, whose doctrine of the natural "gnomic" human will (as indicated in the citation above) comports well with Luther's teaching on the "bound" will, *voluntas,* the unfreedom of desire (recall Chapter Five) as well as with the Christological teaching on the anhypostatic human nature. Here too a thesis for future work arises: Luther's great concern to accentuate

48. "Opuscule 7," in Andrew Louth, *Maximus the Confessor* (London: Routledge, 1996), pp. 186-87.

376

the spiritual sufferings of Christ will be underwritten, not subverted, by a fuller turn to Trinitarianism than Luther was capable of historically. On the other hand, the modalist-suppositional Christology apparently reflected in undifferentiated discourse of the deity's withdrawal does threaten to reduce the sufferings of Christ to nothing other than the well-justified despair of one more misguided fanatic among history's countless who finally threw himself on the wheel of fate (recall the discussion of Schweitzer's Jesus in Chapter Two).

Third, *Gethsemane of the soul.* This I think provides for us today the true "existential" import of the *theologia crucis.* Much ink has been spilled over the years on Luther's *Anfechtungen.* But Luther ties his stories of such spiritual suffering in Job's afflictions or Paul's thorn in the flesh to the agony of Christ in Gethsemane. One worries, however, that contemporary appropriations of Luther's experience of *Anfechtung* are less informed by Gethsemane than by, say, Pascal's early modern dread at the vastness of the cosmos. "When I consider the brief span of my life absorbed into the eternity which comes before and after — as the remembrance of a guest that tarrieth but a day — the small space I occupy and which I see swallowed up in the infinite immensity of spaces of which I know nothing and which know nothing of me, I take fright and am amazed to see myself here rather than there: there is no reason for me to be here rather than there, now rather than then. Who put me here? By whose command and act were this time and place allotted to me?"[49] Or consider Kant's similar account of dread at the experience of the sublime in nature: "bold, overhanging and, as it were, threatening rocks, thunderclouds piling up in the sky and moving about accompanied by lightning and thunderclaps, volcanoes with all their destructive power, hurricanes with all the devastation they leave behind, the boundless ocean heaved up, the high waterfall of a mighty river, and so on. Compared to the might of any of these, our ability to resist becomes an insignificant trifle."[50] Is Luther's *Anfechtung* to be understood along these lines?

Certainly not, if we recall that these are always for Luther martyr-

---

49. Blaise Pascal, *Pensées,* trans. A. J. Krailsheimer (London: Penguin, 1995), #68, p. 19.

50. Immanuel Kant, *Critique of Judgment,* trans. W. S. Pluhar (Indianapolis: Hackett, 1987), p. 120. Kant immediately goes on to argue that he has found in human reason a "nonsensible standard that has this infinity itself under it as a unit; and since in contrast to this standard everything in nature is small, we found in our mind a superiority over nature itself in its immensity . . . [which] reveals in us at the same time an ability to judge ourselves independent of nature. . . . This keeps the humanity in our person from being degraded . . ." (pp. 120-21). How much of liberal Protestant theology is but commentary on this humanocentric illusion?

iological arguments. In the Sermon on Psalm 8, for example, Christ is proclaimed as the One who on "our account was deserted and raised, adorned and made Lord over heaven and earth." Therefore, when believers fall into the hands of the persecutors, they know that they have not fallen out of the hands of God. "All things are in his power. Adam's kingdom too belongs to Christ. . . . But that kingdom also will be under Christ. All both pious and impious must be under the king Christ. All things are in his hands." Even when believers fail, i.e., "when death and sin take hold of us, we know that he holds us who is pleased to help us and obtains access to the Father." The testing of the saints, Job or Paul, is parsed by the prayer of the Son in Gethsemane, and His ultimate surrender to the will of His Father describes the actual passage in which salvation consists. The Gethsemane of the Christian soul, as we saw in the contemporary example of Dr. Martin Luther King Jr., is about the corroboration in life of the Kingdom prayer: Thy kingdom come! Thy will be done! This is what the martyr learns by the Gethsemane of the soul, when the doctrine of Christ forms his or her life, redeeming the body by forming the new person who lives outside its own body now as member of Another's, re-centered by faith in the God who comes, by hope with the groaning of creation for the glorious liberty of the children of God, by love in the needs of the neighbor, the body which is the total Christ, on the way to the Beloved Community of God.

# The Problem of Demonization
# in Luther's Apocalyptic Theology

Consider the following Luther texts:

"It ought surprise no one that I call him a devil. For I am not thinking of Dr. Karlstadt or concerned about him. I am thinking of him by whom he is possessed and for whom he speaks, as St. Paul says, 'For we are not contending against flesh and blood — but against the spiritual hosts of wickedness in the heavenly places' [Eph. 6:12]."[1]

"He is Satan, and Satan is his name, i.e. an adversary. He must obstruct and cause misfortune; he cannot do otherwise. Moreover, he is the prince and god of this world, so that he has sufficient power to do so. . . . Choose, then, whether you prefer to wrestle with the devil or whether you prefer to belong to him."[2]

"So I shall once more set myself against the devil and his fanatics, not for their sake, but for the sake of the weak and simple. For I have no hope that the teachers of a heresy or fanaticism will be converted. . . . I would like to request them, in all kindness, not to become angry that I condemn their doctrine and ascribe it to the devil."[3]

"They are angry because I detect the devil speaking through them. My dear friend, can reason itself say that we have here only human error, and not the devil's mockery?"[4]

---

1. "Against the Heavenly Prophets" (1525) LW 40:149; cf. "This Is My Body" (1527) LW 37:23, 270.
2. "This Is My Body" (1527) LW 37:17.
3. "This Is My Body" (1527) LW 37:19-20, 21.
4. "Confession concerning Christ's Supper" (1528) LW 37:179.

Such texts — which could be multiplied beyond measure — evince the apocalyptic frame of reference of Luther's theology; again, from the same writings: "Once more there will arise a brawl over the Scriptures, and such dissention and so many factions that we may well say with St. Paul, 'The mystery of lawlessness is already at work' [1 Thess. 2:7], just as he also said that many more factions would arise after him. If the world lasts much longer. . . ."[5] In this apocalyptic frame of reference, erroneous teaching is not mere human error or logical blunder but touches on the certainty of saving faith, bestowed by the Spirit who is holy in battle with the unholy spirit. Luther makes this abundantly clear: "But what kind of spirit is it who directs his ingenuity only to rendering Scripture passages uncertain and doubtful . . . well, this is easy to see. Christ's Spirit it surely is not; he makes sure and certain all that he teaches, as St. Paul extols the *plerophoria*. . . ."[6] Or again, "What kind of spirit is it that tries to make this side uncertain and confused, and yet cannot make his own certain or secure — indeed, does not even want to and is not interested in making it certain? Surely it is no other spirit than the devil, who takes pleasure in jarring men's hearts everywhere, and permits them on no side to be certain and sure, but keeps them dangling and hovering whichever way his wind blows, like an aspen leaf. The Holy Spirit, however, is the sort of teacher who is sure and makes men sure . . . *plerophoria* in Christ, a full, certain, sure understanding, upon which a man can die and risk everything."[7] The certain doctrine of which faith is fully persuaded and for which it is willing to suffer and die is the work of the Holy Spirit in battle with the unholy spirit who works to render it doubtful.

Luther is aware that both he and his opponents take this rhetoric of demonization *ad hominem*. He admits: "it is not surprising that I feel irritation over this Satan who makes a fickle fool of my Lord and Savior Jesus Christ . . ."[8] and he acknowledges how "Oecolampadius complains bitterly against me that I blaspheme, and that my writing takes its start from the devil, as Zwingli also foolishly fusses; and some say that I have mentioned the devil seventy-seven times. This is a laudable, honorable thing to do, and highly necessary for them to write since they have no answers to the real questions. Why don't they also count how often I mentioned God and

5. "This Is My Body" (1527) LW 37:16.
6. "This Is My Body" (1527) LW 37:107.
7. "This Is My Body" (1527) LW 37:125-26.
8. "Confession concerning Christ's Supper" (1528) LW 37:261.

Christ, and how I fight for Christ against the devil?"[9] He insists, however, that the rhetoric of demonization is public not private, official not personal, touching upon doctrine not character. And there is at least some evidence that Luther kept to this distinction, for example, in taking the "demon-possessed"[10] Karlstadt with his family into his own household during one of that troubled man's periods of remorse[11] and then interceding for support of his widow and orphans after his death.[12]

The problem is, whether Luther's theology — touching upon the certainty of faith, the work of the Spirit, and the role of doctrine — is so easily understood apart from this demonology. The contemporary American biblical theologian, J. Louis Martyn, who before all others in our times, as we have seen in Chapters Two and Seven, has followed Ernst Käsemann in contending for an "apocalyptic" interpretation of Paul, notes this problem in receiving Luther's Paul interpretation today at the outset of his insightful commentary on Galatians. Even though we have to repudiate "Luther's pejorative and indefensible references to 'Jews, Turks, papists, and sectarians,'" and register "notable reservations related to Luther's portrait of Judaism," nevertheless Luther's captivation "by the message of God's free and powerful grace" produced an "interpretation that has happily influenced — to one degree or another — most readings of the letter since his time."[13] Yet the question is: Are these two aspects of Luther's legacy separable? Is the proclamation of the free and powerful grace of God *separable* from the reduction of all who do not believe it (or believe it rightly) to the status of hardened reprobates, minions of the devil, whose disbelief renders grace dubious? If not, is Paul's apocalyptic theology, however happily appropriated by Luther, guilty of "historicizing the eschatological"[14] in the very notion that in Christ the ages have turned, the new creation begun? Does not this affirmation of the presence

---

9. "Confession concerning Christ's Supper" (1528) LW 37:269.

10. Martin Brecht, *Martin Luther: Shaping and Defining the Reformation, 1521-1532,* trans. J. L. Schaaf (Minneapolis: Fortress, 1990), p. 162.

11. Brecht, *Martin Luther: Shaping,* pp. 170-71.

12. Martin Brecht, *Martin Luther: The Preservation of the Church, 1532-1546,* trans. J. L. Schaaf (Minneapolis: Fortress, 1993), p. 326.

13. J. Louis Martyn, *Galatians,* The Anchor Bible, vol. 33A (New York: Doubleday, 1997), p. 35. See particularly Comment #51, "The Apocalyptic Antinomies and the New Creation," pp. 570-74.

14. Rosemary Radford Ruether, *Faith and Fratricide: The Theological Roots of Anti-Semitism* (New York: Seabury, 1979), pp. 246ff.

of the new creation in our midst necessarily always mean: here and not there, for Paul, in the *ecclesia* and not yet the world? *Yes,* some such differentiation *is* required. The difficulty is not wiped away by attributing it to Luther's personal limitations. The "apocalyptic antinomies" (Martyn) of the greatly appreciated Galatians 3:27-28 are engendered by the in-breaking of new creation in the field of the *ecclesia.* This Pauline eschatology of the *imminent* new creation provided Luther the basis upon which he refused and sharply criticized the traditional, *immanent* dualisms, like spirit and flesh. Apocalypse as promise of inclusion in God's coming reign by the grace of Christ provides the reason why Luther can conceive of the doctrinal beliefs brought with the gospel as a new language of the Spirit. But the question remains whether this new language of the Spirit can be retrieved without hauling along with it the division of faith from unbelief, and with it the theological potential for invective, which Luther learned also from Paul (cf. Gal. 5:12; Phil. 3:2). As respected a Luther scholar as Heiko Oberman has argued that in general this is the correct way to read Luther's theological legacy today,[15] and Oberman was accordingly careful to distinguish Luther's contribution, as he wanted to appropriate it, from "the origins of anti-Semitism."[16] Yet there is little doubt that we are here treading on dangerous ground. The question is twofold: Is some rhetoric of the devil and with it some theological demonology indispensable in understanding and appropriating Luther's theology? If so, can this legacy be somehow reformed? Can you have a devil without demonization? This *is* a problem.

The pope is a god on earth over everything heavenly, earthly, spiritual, and secular, and all is his own. No one is permitted to say to him:

15. "Holding fast to the Gospel was indeed much, but it did not constitute a 'success.' For Luther reformation was the beginning not of modern times but of the Last Days. . . . The only progress he expected from the reformation was the Devil's rage, provoked by the rediscovery of the Gospel. . . . God himself would bring about reformation through consummation; it would be preceded by the Devil's counterreformation." Heiko Oberman, *Luther: Man between God and the Devil,* trans. E. Walliser-Schwarzbart (New Haven: Yale University Press, 1989), pp. 266-67.

16. Heiko Oberman, *The Roots of Anti-Semitism in the Age of Renaissance and Reformation,* trans. J. I. Porter (Philadelphia: Fortress, 1984), which demonstrates in the manner of *Sachkritik* the material, theological contradiction between Luther's venomous statements of 1543 and his own gospel: "Our heinous crime and weighty sin nailed Jesus to the cross, God's true Son. Therefore, we should not in bitterness scold you, poor Judas, or the Jewish host. The guilt is our own" (p. 124). Paul R. Hinlicky, "A Lutheran Contribution to the Theology of Judaism," *Journal of Ecumenical Studies* 31, nos. 1-2 (Winter-Spring 1994): 123-52.

"What are you doing?" That is the abomination and stench of which Christ speaks in Matt. 24 [:15]: "So when you see the desolating sacrilege spoken of by the prophet Daniel [Dan. 9:27; 12:11], standing in the holy place (let the reader understand)," etc. And St. Paul writes: "He will take his seat in the temple of God (that is, in Christendom), proclaiming himself to be God."[17]

. . . in this particular case insurrection is most certainly a suggestion of the devil. He sees the bright light of the truth exposing his idols, the pope and the papists, before all the world; and he simply cannot cope with it. Its brilliant rays have so dazzled his eyes and blinded him that he can do nothing more than lie, blaspheme, and suggest errant nonsense. He even forgets to assume the hypocritical appearance of respectability. . . . Now he is at work trying to stir up an insurrection through those who glory in the gospel, hoping thereby to revile our teaching as if it came from the devil and not from God. [18] . . . [A]nyone who perishes on the peasants' side is an eternal firebrand of hell, for he bears the sword against God's word and is disobedient to him, and is a member of the devil.[19]

What are we poor preachers to do meanwhile? In the first place, we will believe that our Lord Jesus Christ is truthful when he declares of the Jews who did not accept but crucified him, "You are a brood of vipers and children of the devil" [cf. Matt. 12:34]. . . . He knows that these Jews are a brood of vipers and children of the devil, that is, people who will accord us the same benefits as does their father, the devil — and by now we Christians should have learned from Scripture as well as experience just how much he wishes us well. . . . I have read and heard many stories about the Jews which agree with this judgment of Christ, namely, how they have poisoned wells, made assassinations, kidnapped children, as related before. I have heard that one Jew sent another Jew, and this by means of a Christian, a pot of blood, together with a barrel of wine, in which when drunk empty, a dead Jew was found. There are many other similar stories. For their kidnapping of children they have often been burned at the stake or banished (as we

---

17. "Why the Books of the Pope Were Burned" (1520) LW 31:393.
18. "A Sincere Admonition by Martin Luther to All Christians" (1522) LW 45:63.
19. "Against the Robbing and Murdering Hordes" (1525) LW 46:53.

already heard). I am well aware that they deny all of this. However, it all coincides with the judgment of Christ which declares that they are venomous, bitter, vindictive, tricky serpents, assassins, and children of the devil, who sting and work harm stealthily wherever they cannot do it openly. For this reason I should like to see them where there are no Christians. . . . That is what I had in mind when I said earlier, that, next to the devil, a Christian has no more bitter and galling foe than a Jew. There is no other to whom we accord as many benefactions and from whom we suffer as much as we do from these base children of the devil, this brood of vipers.[20]

Such invective was not some highly regrettable but inexplicable personal "tragedy," though it surely became the occasion of personal *sin*. Luther saw the devil in rabbinic exegesis, the same in Müntzer's agitation of the Peasants' Revolt, and the same again, actually originally, in his condemnation as a heretic by the pope. It was this demonology that in each case permitted him to abandon the theological task of interpretation or the martyr's stance of defenseless witness and instead lash out in these noxious jeremiads that would have such fateful histories ahead of them.[21] That these others too are responsible for their own sins is both true and beside the point; no one is asking theology in Luther's tradition to become uncritical, but rather to become more critical, truly critical, self-critical in the very process of executing any necessary critiques on others. The three samples of Luther's writing above are pieces of apocalyptic-political polemic aimed, in Oberman's words, "not to a crusade against the Turks, nor to hatred of Rome or the Jews, but to keeping the gospel afloat in the world's last ravaged hour."[22] What we must see is that all these evil judgments of Luther are cut from the same apocalyptic cloth, and we cannot execute the needed act of hermeneutical violence against this real, historical Luther unless we break the spell of confessionalism with its need for a "prophet," a "martyr," a "hero."[23]

What we need from Luther is a *theologian*, a teacher of the *common*

20. "On the Jews and Their Lies" (1543) LW 47:276.

21. Paul Hinlicky, *The Substance of Faith: Luther on Doctrinal Theology* (Minneapolis: Fortress, 2008), pp. 174-80.

22. Oberman, *The Roots of Anti-Semitism*, p. 122.

23. James M. Stayer, *Martin Luther: German Saviour. German Evangelical Theological Factions and the Interpretation of Luther, 1917-1933* (Kingston/Montreal: McGill-Queen's University Press, 2000).

faith, *doctor ecclesiae,* fallible like the rest of us, uncommonly gifted unlike the rest of us, but just *wrong* so far as he took himself, as also did some of his followers, as God's "end-time prophet."[24] One cannot properly extricate what is valuable in Luther — his Christologically modified apocalyptic — without more consistently than he abandoning that remnant of unmodified apocalyptic that despairs of the world God created and redeemed in Christ and is seeking for the reign by the Spirit through the gospel. Luther's sin here against peasant, pope, and Jew is the sin of despair of God, which as a result really does leave the world to the devil, as if Christ were not risen, but effectively still in the tomb.

---

24. Scott Hendrix, "'More Than a Prophet': Martin Luther in the Work of Heiko Oberman," in *The Work of Heiko Oberman: Papers from the Symposium on His Seventieth Birthday,* ed. Thomas A. Brady Jr. (Leiden, Boston, Köln: E. J. Brill, 2003), pp. 11-29.

# Works Cited

*A Commentary on "Ecumenism: The Vision of the ELCA."* Edited by William G. Rusch. Minneapolis: Augsburg, 1990.

Althaus, Paul. *The Divine Command: A New Perspective on Law and Gospel.* Philadelphia: Fortress, 1966.

————. *The Ethics of Martin Luther.* Philadelphia: Fortress, 1972.

Anselm of Canterbury. *Why God Became Man* and *The Virgin Conception and Original Sin.* Translation, introduction, and notes by Joseph M. Colleran. Albany, NY: Magi Books, 1969.

Arendt, Hannah. *Eichmann in Jerusalem: A Report on the Banality of Evil,* revised and enlarged edition. London: Penguin, 1994.

Asad, Talal. *Formations of the Secular: Christianity, Islam, Modernity.* Stanford, CA: Stanford University Press, 2003.

Augustine of Hippo. *City of God.* Introduced by Etienne Gilson. Edited by Vernon J. Bourke. New York: Doubleday, 1958.

Aulén, Gustaf. *Christus Victor.* London: Society for Promoting Christian Knowledge; New York and Toronto: Macmillan, 1931.

————. *The Faith of the Christian Church.* Translated by Eric H. Wahlstrom. Philadelphia: Muhlenberg, 1962.

Aune, Michael B. *To Move the Heart: Philip Melanchthon's Rhetorical View of Rite and Its Implications for Contemporary Ritual Theory.* San Francisco: Christian Universities Press, 1994.

Ayres, Lewis. *Nicea and Its Legacy: An Approach to Fourth-Century Trinitarian Theology.* Oxford and New York: Oxford University Press, 2006.

Azar, Thomas P. "The Estate of Marriage, 1522," *Lutheran Forum* 30, no. 2 (May 1996): 41-43.

Bainton, Roland H. *Here I Stand: A Life of Martin Luther.* New York: Mentor, 1955.

Barth, Karl. *Church Dogmatics* I/1. Translated by G. Bromiley. Edinburgh: T. & T. Clark, 1975.

―――. *Community, State and Church*. Garden City, NY: Doubleday, 1960.

Bauer, Walter. *Orthodoxy and Heresy in Early Christianity*. Edited by R. Kraft and G. Krodel. Mifflintown, PA: Sigler Press, 1996.

Bayer, Oswald. "Freedom? The Anthropological Concepts in Luther and Melanchthon Compared," *Harvard Theological Review* 91, no. 4 (1998): 373-78.

―――. *Martin Luther's Theology: A Contemporary Interpretation*. Translated by Thomas H. Trapp. Grand Rapids: Eerdmans, 2007.

―――. *Martin Luthers Theologie: Eine Vergegenwärtigung*, 2 Auflage. Tübingen: Mohr Siebeck, 2004.

―――. *Theology the Lutheran Way*. Edited and translated by Jeffery G. Silcock and Mark C. Mattes. Lutheran Quarterly Books. Grand Rapids: Eerdmans, 2007.

Benne, Robert. *The Paradoxical Vision: A Public Theology for the Twenty-first Century*. Minneapolis: Fortress, 1995.

Bergen, Doris L. *Twisted Cross: The German Christian Movement in the Third Reich*. Chapel Hill: University of North Carolina Press, 1996.

Berkouwer, G. C. *The Triumph of Grace in the Theology of Karl Barth*. Translated by Harry R. Boer. Grand Rapids: Eerdmans, 1956.

Berlin, Sir Isaiah. *Karl Marx: His Life and Environment*. New York: Time, 1963.

*Biblical Studies: Meeting Ground of Jews and Christians*. Edited by Lawrence Boadt, Helga Croner, and Leon Klenicki. New York: Paulist Press, 1980.

Bielfeldt, Dennis, Mickey Mattox, and Paul R. Hinlicky. *The Substance of Faith: Luther on Doctrinal Theology*. Minneapolis: Fortress, 2008.

Bluhm, Heinz. "Nietzsche's Final View of Luther and the Reformation," *Proceedings of the Modern Language Association* 71, no. 1 (1956): 75-83.

―――. "Nietzsche's View of Luther and the Reformation in *Morgenroethe* and *Die Froehliche Wissenschaft*," *Proceedings of the Modern Language Association* 63 (1953): 111-27.

Bonhoeffer, Dietrich. *Christ the Center*. Translated by Edwin H. Robertson. New York: Harper & Row, 1978.

―――. *Ethics*. Edited by E. Bethge. New York: Macmillan, 1978.

―――. *Letters and Papers from Prison*, new greatly enlarged edition. Edited by E. Bethge. New York: Macmillan Collier, 1972.

―――. *Sanctorum Communio*. Minneapolis: Fortress, 1998.

―――. *Sanctorum Communio: A Theological Study of the Sociology of the Church*. Edited by C. J. Green. Translated by R. Kraus and N. Lukens, Dietrich Bonhoeffer Works, vol. 1. Minneapolis: Fortress, 1998.

―――. *The Cost of Discipleship*. Translated by R. Fuller. New York: Macmillan, 1979.

Brecht, Martin. *Martin Luther: Shaping and Defining the Reformation, 1521-1532.* Translated by J. L. Schaaf. Minneapolis: Fortress, 1990.

————. *Martin Luther: His Road to Reformation 1483-1521.* Translated by J. L. Schaf. Minneapolis: Fortress, 1993.

————. *Martin Luther: The Preservation of the Church, 1532-1546.* Translated by J. L. Schaaf. Minneapolis: Fortress, 1993.

Brown, Christopher B., trans. *Disputation on the Humanity and Deity of Christ* by Martin Luther. Project Wittenberg. www.ielnet.org/pub/resources/text/wittenberg/wittenberg-home.html.

Brown, Peter. *Augustine of Hippo: A Biography.* Berkeley and Los Angeles: University of California Press, 1969.

————. *The Body and Society: Men, Women and Sexual Renunciation in Early Christianity.* New York: Columbia University Press, 1988.

Bullock, Alan. *Hitler and Stalin: Parallel Lives.* London: Fontana Press, 1991.

Burke, Edmund. *Reflections on the Revolution in France.* New York: Knopf.

Calvin, John. *Institutes of the Christian Religion,* 4 volumes. Edited by J. T. McNeil. Translated by F. W. Battles. Philadelphia: Westminster, 1975.

*Canons and Decrees of the Council of Trent.* Translated by Rev. H. J. Schroeder, O.P. St. Louis and London: Herder, 1960.

*Christian Dogmatics,* 2 volumes. Edited by Carl E. Braaten and Robert W. Jenson. Philadelphia: Fortress, 1984.

Cone, James H. *Martin and Malcolm and America: A Dream or a Nightmare.* Maryknoll, NY: Orbis, 1991.

*Confessing the One Faith: A Joint Commentary on the Augsburg Confession by Lutheran and Catholic Theologians.* Edited by George W. Forell and James F. McCue. Minneapolis: Augsburg, 1982.

*Creator est creatura: Luthers Christologie als Lehre von der Idiomenkommunikation.* Edited by Oswald Bayer and Benjamin Gleede. Berlin: Walter de Gruyter, 2007.

Crowe, Benjamin D. *Heidegger's Religious Origins: Destruction and Authenticity.* Bloomington and Indianapolis: Indiana University Press, 2006.

Cullmann, Oscar. *The Christology of the New Testament.* Translated by Shirley C. Guthrie and Charles A. M. Hall. London: SCM Press, 1963.

Dahl, Nils. *Jesus in the Memory of the Early Church.* Minneapolis: Augsburg, 1976.

————. *Jesus the Christ: The Historical Origins of Christological Doctrine.* Edited by Donald H. Juel. Minneapolis: Fortress, 1991.

Damasio, Antonio R. *Descartes' Error: Emotion, Reason and the Human Brain.* London: Papermac, 1996.

de Lubac, Henri, S.J. *Augustinianism and Modern Theology.* Translated by Lancelot Sheppard. New York: Crossroad, 2000.

Derrida, Jacques. *The Gift of Death.* Translated by David Wills. Chicago and London: University of Chicago Press, 1995.

Douglas, Ann. *The Feminization of American Culture.* New York: Anchor Press/ Doubleday, 1977.

Dunn, James D. G. "The New Perspective on Paul," *Bulletin of the John Rylands Library* 65 (1983): 95-122.

Ebeling, Gerhard. *Luther: An Introduction to His Thought.* Philadelphia: Fortress, 1972.

Eckhardt, Burnell F., Jr. *Anselm and Luther on the Atonement: Was It "Necessary"?* San Francisco: Mellen Research University Press, 1992.

Ehrman, Bart D. *Lost Christianities: The Battles for Scripture and the Faiths We Never Knew.* New York: Oxford University Press, 2003.

Elert, Werner. *Law and Gospel.* Philadelphia: Fortress, 1967.

Elshtain, Jean Bethke. *Public Man, Private Woman.* Princeton: Princeton University Press, 1981.

Elton, G. R. "Commemorating Luther," *Journal of Ecclesiastical History* 35, no. 4 (October 1984): 614-19.

Ericksen, Robert B. *Theologians Under Hitler: Gerhard Kittel, Paul Althaus and Emanuel Hirsch.* New Haven and London: Yale University Press, 1985.

*Evangelisches Kirchengesangbuch.* Evangelisch-Lutherische Kirche in Bayern.

Feuerbach, Ludwig. *The Essence of Christianity.* Translated by G. Eliot. New York: Harper Torchbooks, 1957.

Forde, Gerhard O. *On Being a Theologian of the Cross: Reflections on Luther's Heidelberg Disputation, 1518.* Grand Rapids: Eerdmans, 1997.

————. "Caught in the Act: Reflections on the Work of Christ," *Word and World* 3, no. 1 (1984): 28-30.

Frady, Marshall. *Martin Luther King, Jr.* New York: Penguin, 2002.

Franks, Robert S. *A History of the Doctrine of the Work of Christ in Its Ecclesiastical Development.* London: Hodder & Stoughton, 1918.

Frei, Hans W. *The Eclipse of Biblical Narrative: A Study in Eighteenth and Nineteenth Century Hermeneutics.* New Haven and London: Yale University Press, 1974.

Freke, Timothy, and Peter Gandy. *The Laughing Jesus: Religious Lies and Gnostic Wisdom.* New York: Three Rivers Press, 2005.

Gaebler, Ulrich. *Huldrych Zwingli: His Life and Work.* Translated by Ruth C. L. Gritsch. Philadelphia: Fortress, 1986.

*German Churches and the Holocaust.* Edited by Robert P. Ericksen and Susannah Heschel. Minneapolis: Fortress, 1999.

Gerrish, B. A. *Grace and Reason: A Study in the Theology of Luther.* Oxford: Clarendon Press, 1962.

————. *The Reformation Heritage.* Chicago: University of Chicago Press, 1982.

Girard, René. *Violence and the Sacred.* Translated by Patrick Gregory. Baltimore: Johns Hopkins University Press, 1979.

*Gregory of Nyssa.* Translated by Anthony Meredith, S.J. London and New York: Routledge, 1999.

Hagen, Kenneth. "From Testament to Covenant in the Early Sixteenth Century," *Sixteenth Century Journal* 3, no. 1 (April 1972): 1-24.

————. *Luther's Approach to Scripture as Seen in His "Commentaries" on Galatians 1519-1538.* Tübingen: J. C. B. Mohr (Paul Siebeck), 1993.

Haile, H. G. *Luther: An Experiment in Biography.* Garden City, NY: Doubleday, 1980.

Hall, Douglas John. *Lighten Our Darkness: Towards an Indigenous Theology of the Cross.* Philadelphia: Westminster, 1976.

Hampson, Daphne. *Christian Contradictions: The Structures of Lutheran and Catholic Thought.* Cambridge: Cambridge University Press, 2001.

Härle, Wilfried. "Rethinking Paul and Luther," *Lutheran Quarterly* 20, no. 3 (Autumn 2006): 303-17.

Harrisville, Roy A. "The Life and Work of Ernst Käsemann (1906-1998)," *Lutheran Quarterly* 21, no. 3 (2007): 294-319.

Hart, David Bentley. *The Beauty of the Infinite: The Aesthetics of Christian Truth.* Grand Rapids: Eerdmans, 2003.

Helmer, Christine. "The American Luther," *Dialog: A Journal of Theology* 47, no. 2 (Summer 2008): 114-24.

————. *The Trinity and Martin Luther: A Study on the Relationship between Genre, Language and the Trinity in Luther's Works (1523-1546).* Mainz: Verlag Philipp von Zabern, 1999.

Hendrix, Scott H. *Luther and the Papacy: Stages in a Reformation Conflict.* Philadelphia: Fortress, 1981.

————. *Recultivating the Vineyard: The Reformation Agendas of Christianization.* Louisville and London: Westminster/John Knox, 2004.

————. "'More Than a Prophet': Martin Luther in the Work of Heiko Oberman," in *The Work of Heiko Oberman: Papers from the Symposium on His Seventieth Birthday.* Edited by Thomas A. Brady Jr. Leiden, Boston, Köln: E. J. Brill, 2003, pp. 11-29.

————. "Luther on Marriage," *Lutheran Quarterly* 14, no. 3 (2000): 335-50.

————. "Masculinity and Patriarchy in Reformation Germany," *Journal of the History of Ideas* 56, no. 2 (April 1995).

Hengel, Martin. *Between Jesus and Paul: Studies in the Earliest History of Christianity.* Translated by John Bowden. Minneapolis: Fortress, 1983.

Heschel, Susannah. *The Aryan Jesus: Christian Theologians and the Bible in Nazi Germany.* Princeton: Princeton University Press, 2008.

Hinlicky, Paul R. "A Response to the Vatican's Response: I. The Persistence of Sin in the Life of the Redeemed," *Lutheran Forum* 32, no. 3 (Fall 1998): 5-7.

————. "A Response to the Vatican's Response: II. Is There a Lutheran Communion?" *Lutheran Forum* 32, no. 4 (Winter 1998): 9-11.

————. "Luther Against the Contempt of Women," *Lutheran Quarterly* 2, no. (Winter 1989): 515-30.

————. "A Lutheran Contribution to the Theology of Judaism," *Journal of Ecumenical Studies* 31, nos. 1-2 (Winter-Spring 1994): 123-52.

————. "A Lutheran Encyclical: Benedict's Deus Caritas Est," *August 2006 Journal of Lutheran Ethics (online),* volume 6, issue 8.

————. "Appreciation and Critique of the ELCA Draft Social Statement on Sexuality," *August 2008, Journal of Lutheran Ethics (online),* volume 8, issue 8.

————. "Lincoln's Theology of the Republic According to the Second Inaugural Address," *The Cresset* 65, no. 6 (May 2002): 7-14.

————. "Luther and Heidegger," *Lutheran Quarterly* 22, no. 1 (Spring 2008): 78-86.

————. "Luther and Liberalism," in *A Report from the Front Lines: Conversations on Public Theology. A Festschrift in Honor of Robert Benne.* Edited by Michael Shahan. Grand Rapids: Eerdmans, 2009, pp. 89-104.

————. "Process, Convergence, Declaration: Reflections on Doctrinal Dialogue," *The Cresset* 64, no. 6 (Pentecost 2001): 13-18.

————. "The Lutheran Dilemma," *Pro Ecclesia* 8, no. 4 (Fall 1999): 391-422.

————. *Paths Not Taken: Theology from Luther through Leibniz.* Grand Rapids: Eerdmans, 2009.

————. "Recognition not Blessing," *August 2005 Journal of Lutheran Ethics (online),* volume 5, issue 8.

————. John Witte Jr. *Law and Protestantism: The Legal Teachings of the Lutheran Reformation.* Foreword by Martin E. Marty. Cambridge: Cambridge University Press, 2002. Reviewed in *Sixteenth Century Journal* 35, no. 2 (2004): 534-36.

Hinlicky, Paul R., and Ellen I. Hinlicky. "Gnosticism: Old and New," *Dialog* 28, no. 1 (Winter 1989): 12-17.

Hobbes, Thomas. *Leviathan,* with selected variants from the Latin edition of 1668. Edited by E. Curley. Indianapolis: Hackett, 1994.

Holl, Karl. *The Reconstruction of Morality.* Translated by F. W. Meuser and W. R. Wietzke. Minneapolis: Augsburg, 1979.

Hoskyns, Sir Edwin, and Francis Noel Davey. *The Riddle of the New Testament.* London: Faber & Faber, 1941.

Hultgren, Arland J. *The Rise of Normative Christianity.* Minneapolis: Fortress, 1994.

Hunsinger, George. *Disruptive Grace: Studies in the Theology of Karl Barth.* Grand Rapids: Eerdmans, 2000.

Huntington, Samuel P. *The Clash of Civilizations and the Remaking of World Order.* London: Simon & Schuster, 2002.

Hütter, Reinhard. *Suffering Divine Things: Theology as Church Practice.* Translated by D. Stott. Grand Rapids: Eerdmans, 2000.

Works Cited

*In Search of Christian Unity: Basic Consensus/Basic Differences.* Edited by Joseph A. Burgess. Minneapolis: Fortress, 1991.

James, William. *The Varieties of Religious Experience: A Study in Human Nature.* Mineola, NY: Dover, 2002.

Jenson, Robert W. "An Ontology of Freedom in the DSA of Luther," *Modern Theology* 10, no. 3 (July 1994): 247-52.

————. *Systematic Theology,* 2 volumes. *The Triune God.* New York and Oxford: Oxford University Press, 1997.

————. *The Triune Identity: God according to the Gospel.* Philadelphia: Fortress, 1982.

————. *Unbaptized God: The Basic Flaw in Ecumenical Theology.* Minneapolis: Fortress, 1992.

Juel, Donald H. *Messianic Exegesis: Christological Interpretation of the Old Testament in Early Christianity.* Philadelphia: Fortress, 1988.

Jüngel, Eberhard. *The Doctrine of the Trinity: God's Being Is in Becoming.* Grand Rapids: Eerdmans, 1976.

Juntunen, Sammeli. "The Christological Background of Luther's Understanding of Justification," Lecture. Salem, VA: Roanoke College, 2002; later published under the same title in the *Seminary Ridge Review* 2 (Gettysburg, 2003): 6-36.

*Justification and the Future of the Ecumenical Movement.* Edited by William G. Rusch. Collegeville, MN: Liturgical Press, 2003.

*Justification: What's at Stake in the Current Debates.* Edited by Mark Husbands and Daniel Treier. Downers Grove and Leicester, UK: InterVarsity and Apollos, 2004.

Kant, Immanuel. *Critique of Judgment.* Translated by W. S. Pluhar. Indianapolis: Hackett, 1987.

————. *Religion and Rational Theology.* Translated by Allen W. Wood and George di Giovanni. Cambridge: Cambridge University Press, 2001.

Käsemann, Ernst. *Commentary on Romans.* Translated by Geoffrey W. Bromiley. Grand Rapids: Eerdmans, 1980.

————. *Perspectives on Paul.* Translated by Margaret Kohl. Philadelphia: Fortress, 1978.

Keck, Leander E. *A Future for the Historical Jesus: The Place of Jesus in Preaching and Theology.* Philadelphia: Fortress, 1981.

Kelly, J. N. D. *Early Christian Doctrines,* revised edition. New York: Harper, 1978.

Kidd, Colin. *The Forging of Races: Race and Scripture in the Protestant Atlantic World, 1600-2000.* Cambridge: Cambridge University Press, 2006.

King, Martin Luther, Jr. *Essential Writings, A Testament of Hope: The Essential Writings of Dr. Martin Luther King, Jr.* Edited by James Melvin Washington. San Francisco: Harper, 1986.

Koestler, Arthur. *The God That Failed.* New York: Harper, 1949.

Kolb, Robert. *Bound Choice, Election, and Wittenberg Theological Method: From Martin Luther to the Formula of Concord.* Lutheran Quarterly Books. Grand Rapids: Eerdmans, 2005.

Kuklick, Bruce. *Josiah Royce: An Intellectual Biography.* Indianapolis: Hackett, 1985.

Lage, Dietmar. *Martin Luther's Christology and Ethics: Texts and Studies in Religion,* vol. 45. Lewiston, NY: Edwin Mellen Press, 1990.

Lasch, Christopher. *Haven in a Heartless World: The Family Besieged.* New York: Basic Books, 1977.

————. *The Culture of Narcissism: American Life in an Age of Diminishing Expectations.* New York: W. W. Norton, 1978.

Lazareth, William H. *Christians in Society: Luther, the Bible and Social Ethics.* Minneapolis: Fortress, 2001.

————. *Luther on the Christian Home.* Philadelphia: Muhlenberg Press, 1960, with the republication of its final chapter and new preface in *Lutheran Quarterly* (1993): 235-68.

Lee, Philip J. *Against the Protestant Gnostics.* New York: Oxford University Press, 1987.

Lienhard, Marc. *Martin Luther: Witness to Jesus Christ, Stages and Themes of the Reformer's Christology.* Translated by Edwin H. Robertson. Minneapolis: Augsburg, 1982.

Lindbeck, George. *The Nature of Doctrine: Religion and Theology in a Postliberal Age.* Louisville: Westminster/John Knox, 1984.

Lindhardt, Jan. *Martin Luther: Knowledge and Mediation in the Renaissance.* Texts and Studies in Religion, vol. 29. Lewiston, NY: Edwin Mellen Press, 1986.

Lischer, Richard. *The Preacher King: Martin Luther King, Jr. and the Word That Moved America.* New York and Oxford: Oxford University Press, 1995.

Lochman, Jan Milic. *Christ and Prometheus? A Quest for Theological Identity.* Geneva: WCC Publications, 1988.

Locke, John. *Second Treatise of Government.* Edited by C. B. Macpherson. Indianapolis: Hackett, 1980.

Lohse, Bernard. *Martin Luther's Theology: Its Historical and Systematic Development.* Translated by Roy A. Harrisville. Minneapolis: Fortress, 1999.

Lotz, David. *Luther and Ritschl: A Fresh Perspective on Albrecht Ritschl's Theology in the Light of His Luther Study.* Nashville: Abingdon, 1974.

Louth, Andrew. *Maximus the Confessor.* London: Routledge, 1996.

Lukes, Steven. *Marxism and Morality.* Oxford: Oxford University Press, 1987.

Luther, Martin. *The Bondage of the Will.* Translated by J. I. Packer and O. R. Johnston. Westwood, NJ: Fleming Revell, 2000.

*Luther on Women: A Sourcebook.* Edited and translated by Susan C. Karant-Nunn and Merry E. Wiesner-Hanks. Cambridge: Cambridge University Press, 2003.

## Works Cited

*Luther: Lecture on Romans.* Translated by Wilhelm Pauck. Philadelphia: Westminster, 1961.

*Lutherans and Catholics in Dialogue I-III.* Edited by Paul C. Empie and T. Austin Murphy. Minneapolis: Augsburg, n.d.

*Lutherans and Catholics in Dialogue IV: Eucharist and Ministry.* USA National Committee of the Lutheran World Federation and the Bishops' Committee for Ecumenical and Interreligious Affairs, 1970.

*Lutherans and Catholics in Dialogue V: Papal Primacy and the Universal Church.* Edited by Paul C. Empie and T. Austin Murphy. Minneapolis: Augsburg, 1974.

*Lutherans and Catholics in Dialogue VIII: The One Mediator, the Saints, and Mary.* Edited by H. George Anderson, J. Francis Stafford, and Joseph A. Burgess. Minneapolis: Augsburg, 1992.

*Lutherforschung im 20. Jarhundert: Rückblick-Bilanz-Ausblick.* Edited by Rainer Vinke. Mainz: Philipp von Zabern, 2004.

*Luther's Ecumenical Significance: An Interconfessional Consultation.* Edited by Peter Manns and Harding Meyer in collaboration with Carter Lindberg and Harry McSorley. Philadelphia: Fortress, 1984.

MacIntyre, Alasdair. *Marxism and Christianity.* Notre Dame: University of Notre Dame Press, 1984.

———. *Three Rival Versions of Moral Enquiry: Encyclopaedia, Genealogy and Tradition.* Notre Dame: University of Notre Dame Press, 1990.

Mannermaa, Tuomo. *Der im Glauben Gegenwärtige Christus: Rechtfertigung und Vergottung. Zum ökumenischen Dialog.* Arbeiten zur Geschichte und Theologie des Luthertums, Neue Folge Band 8. Hannover: Lutherisches Verlagshaus, 1989.

Marcuse, Herbert. *Eros and Civilization: A Philosophical Inquiry into Freud.* Boston: Beacon Press, 1955.

Marshall, Bruce. *Christology in Conflict: The Identity of a Saviour in Rahner and Barth.* Oxford: Basil Blackwell, 1987.

———. *Trinity and Truth.* Cambridge: Cambridge University Press, 2000.

Martyn, J. Louis. "Epistemology at the Turn of the Ages: 2 Cor. 5:16," in *Christian History and Intepretation: Studies Presented to John Knox.* Edited by W. R. Father, C. F. D. Moule, and R. R. Niebuhr. Cambridge: Cambridge University Press, 1967.

———. *Galatians.* The Anchor Bible Vol. 33A. New York: Doubleday, 1997.

Marx, Karl. *On Religion.* Translated by Saul K. Padover. New York: McGraw-Hill, 1974.

———. *Writings of the Young Marx on Philosophy and Society.* Translated by Loyd D. Easton and Kurt H. Guddat. Garden City, NY: Anchor, 1967.

Mattes, Mark C. *The Role of Justification in Contemporary Theology.* Lutheran Quarterly Books. Grand Rapids: Eerdmans, 2004.

Mattox, Mickey L. *"Defender of the Most Holy Matriarchs": Martin Luther's Interpretation of the Women of Genesis in the* Enarrationes in Genesin. *1535-45.* Leiden and Boston: E. J. Brill, 2003.

———. "Martin Luther's Reception of Paul," in *The Reception of Paul in the Sixteenth Century.* Edited by Ward Holder. Leiden/Boston: E. J. Brill, forthcoming.

McLellan, David. *The Thought of Karl Marx: An Introduction.* New York: Harper Torchbooks, 1971.

McSorley, Harry J., C.S.P. *Luther: Right or Wrong? An Ecumenical-Theological Study of Luther's Major Work.* The Bondage of the Will. New York: Newman Press; Minneapolis: Augsburg, 1969.

———. "Use and Underuse of Luther in the Lutheran-Roman Catholic Dialogues in the United States," *Lutheran Theological Seminary Bulletin* 71 (Winter 1991): 3-12.

Melanchthon, Philip. *On Christian Doctrine: Loci Communes, 1555,* Translated by C. L. Manschreck. Grand Rapids: Baker Book House, 1982.

———. *Orations on Philosophy and Education.* Edited by Sachiko Kusukawa. Cambridge: Cambridge University Press, 1999.

Menand, Louis. *The Metaphysical Club: A Story of Ideas in America.* New York: Farrar, Straus & Giroux, 2001.

Meyer, Harding. "The Ecumenical Dialogues: Situations, Problems, Perspectives," *Pro Ecclesia* 3, no. 1 (Winter 1994): 24-35.

Milbank, John. "The Ethics of Self-Sacrifice," *First Things* 91 (March 1999): 33-38.

———. *The Word Made Strange: Theology, Language, Culture.* Cambridge, MA: Blackwell, 1997.

———. *Theology and Social Theory: Beyond Secular Reason.* Oxford: Blackwell, 1997.

Moldovan, Russel. *Martin Luther King, Jr. An Oral History of His Religious Witness and His Life.* San Francisco: International Scholars Publications, 1999.

Moltmann, Jürgen. *Der gekreuzigte Gott.* München: Chr. Kaiser, 1976.

Morse, Christopher. *Not Every Spirit: A Dogmatics of Christian Disbelief.* Harrisburg, PA: Trinity Press International, 1994.

Mouw, Richard J. "Violence and the Atonement," chap. 10 in *Must Christianity Be Violent? Reflections on History, Practice and Theology.* Edited by Kenneth R. Chase and Alan Jacobs. Grand Rapids: Brazos, 2003.

Neusner, Jacob, with William Scott Green. *Writing with Scripture: The Authority and the Uses of the Hebrew Bible in the Torah of Formative Judaism.* Minneapolis: Augsburg/Fortress, 1989.

Niebuhr, Reinhold. *Moral Man and Immoral Society: A Study in Ethics and Politics.* New York: Charles Scribner's Sons, 1960.

Niebuhr, H. Richard. *The Kingdom of God in America.* New York: Harper Torchbooks, 1959.

## Works Cited

Nietzsche, Friedrich. *Beyond Good and Evil: Prelude to a Philosophy of the Future.* Translated by Walter Kaufmann. New York: Vintage, 1966.

————. *The Will to Power.* Translated by W. Kaufmann and R. J. Hollingdale. New York: Vintage, 1967.

Novak, David. *Jewish-Christian Dialogue: A Jewish Justification.* New York and Oxford: Oxford University Press, 1989.

Nygren, Anders. *Agape and Eros.* Translated by Philip S. Watson. New York and Evanston: Harper & Row, 1969.

O'Regan, Cyril. *The Heterodox Hegel.* Albany: State University of New York Press, 1994.

Oakes, Edward T. *Pattern of Redemption: The Theology of Hans Urs von Balthasar.* New York: Continuum, 2002.

Oberman, Heiko. "Teufelsdreck: Eschatology and Scatology in the 'Old' Luther," *Sixteenth Century Journal* 19, no. 3 (1998): 435-50.

————. *The Dawn of the Reformation: Essays in Late Medieval and Early Reformation Thought.* Edinburgh: T. & T. Clark, 1986.

————. *The Harvest of Medieval Theology: Gabriel Biel and Late Medieval Nominalism.* Grand Rapids: Baker Academic, 2000.

————. *Luther: Man between God and the Devil.* Translated by E. Walliser-Schwarzbart. New Haven: Yale University Press, 1989.

————. *The Roots of Anti-Semitism in the Age of Renaissance and Reformation.* Translated by J. I. Porter. Philadelphia: Fortress, 1984.

Ozment, Steven. *When Fathers Ruled: Family Life in Reformation Europe.* Cambridge, MA: Harvard University Press, 1983.

Pannenberg, Wolfhart. *Jesus: God and Man.* Translated by Lewis L. Wilkins and Duane A. Priebe. Philadelphia: Westminster, 1975.

Pascal, Blaise. *Pensees.* Translated by A. J. Krailsheimer. London: Penguin, 1995.

*Pauline Theology, Vol. 1: Thessalonians, Philippians, Galatians, Philemon.* Edited by Jouette M. Bassler. Minneapolis: Fortress, 1991.

Peacocke, Arthur. *Theology for a Scientific Age,* enlarged edition. London: SCM Press, 1993.

Pelikan, Jaroslav. *Obedient Rebels: Catholic Substance and Protestant Principle in Luther's Reformation.* New York and Evanston: Harper & Row, 1964.

————. *The Christian Tradition: A History of the Development of Doctrine.* Chicago and London: University of Chicago Press, 1975.

————. *The Riddle of Roman Catholicism.* New York: Abingdon, 1959.

Percesepe, Gary. "Against Appropriation," in *Postmodern Philosophy and Christian Thought.* Edited by Merold Westphal. Bloomington: Indiana University Press, 1999, chap. 4, pp. 69-87.

Pesch, Otto Hermann, O.P. *The God Question in Thomas Aquinas and Martin Luther.* Translated by Gottfried G. Krodel. Philadelphia: Fortress, 1972.

Peters, Ted. *God — the World's Future: Systematic Theology for a New Era,* 2nd edition. Minneapolis: Fortress, 2000.

Pigden, Charles R. "Ought-Implies-Can: Erasmus, Luther and R. M. Hare," *Sophia* 29, no. 1 (1990): 2-30.

Prager, Dennis. "Judaism's Sexual Revolution: Why Judaism (and then Christianity) Rejected Homosexuality," *Crisis* 11, no. 8 (September 1993).

Raitt, Jill. *The Colloquy of Montbéliard: Religion and Politics in the Sixteenth Century.* New York and Oxford: Oxford University Press, 1993.

Ratzinger, Joseph Cardinal. *Principles of Catholic Theology: Building Stones for a Fundamental Theology.* Translated by Sister Mary Frances McCarthy, S.N.D. San Francisco: Ignatius, 1987.

Raunio, Antti. *Summe des Christlichen Lebens: Die 'Goldene Regel' als Gesetz der Liebe in der Theologie Martin Luthers von 1510 bis 1527.* Helsinki, 1993.

*Reinhold Niebuhr: His Religious, Social, and Political Thought.* Edited by Robert W. Bretall and Charles W. Kegley. New York: Macmillan, 1956.

Reinhuber, Thomas. *Kämpfender Glaube: Studien zu Luthers Bekenntnis am Ende von De servo arbitrio.* Berlin and New York: Walter de Gruyter, 2000.

Richardson, Alan. *Christian Apologetics.* New York: Harper & Brothers, 1947.

Ridley, Matt. *The Origins of Virtue.* London: Penguin, 1997.

Riley, Gregory J. *One Jesus, Many Christs: How Jesus Inspired Not One True Christianity But Many.* Minneapolis: Fortress, 2000.

Ritschl, Albrecht. *The Christian Doctrine of Justification and Reconciliation: The Positive Development of the Doctrine.* Translated by H. R. MacIntosh and A. B. Macaulay. Clifton, NJ: Reference Book Publishers, 1966.

Rorty, Richard. *Philosophy and the Mirror of Nature.* Princeton: Princeton University Press, 1979.

Royce, Josiah. *The Problem of Christianity.* Washington, DC: Catholic University of America Press, 2001.

Ruether, Rosemary Radford. *Faith and Fratricide: The Theological Roots of Anti-Semitism.* New York: Seabury, 1979.

Russell, William R. *The Schmalkald Articles: Luther's Theological Testament.* Minneapolis: Fortress, 1995.

Saarinen, Risto. "The Pauline Luther and the Law: Lutheran Theology Reengages the Study of Paul," *Pro Ecclesia* 15, no. 1 (Winter 2006): 64-86.

Safranski, Rüdiger. *Nietzsche: A Philosophical Biography.* Translated by Shelley Frisch. New York: W. W. Norton, 2002.

Sanders, E. P. *Paul and Palestinian Judaism: A Comparison of Patterns of Religions.* London and Philadelphia: SCM and Fortress, 1977.

Schell, Jonathan. *The Fate of the Earth.* New York: Knopf, 1982.

Schillebeeckx, Edward. *Christ: The Experience of Jesus as Lord.* Translated by J. Bowden. New York: Crossroads, 1981.

Schleiermacher, Friedrich. *The Christian Faith,* 2 volumes. Edited by H. R. Macintosh and J. S. Steward. New York: Harper & Row, 1963.

————. *The Life of Jesus.* Edited by J. C. Verheyden. Philadelphia: Fortress, 1975.

Schneider, Carolyn. "Luther's Preface to Bugenhagen's Edition of Athanasius," *Lutheran Quarterly* 7, no. 5 (2003): 226-30.

Schulze, Manfred. "Martin Luther and the Church Fathers," in *The Reception of the Church Fathers in the West.* Leiden and New York: E. J. Brill, 1997.

Schweitzer, Albert. *The Quest of the Historical Jesus,* with a new Introduction by James M. Robinson. New York: Macmillan, 1978.

*Sermons of Martin Luther,* 7 volumes. Translated by John Nicholas Lenker. Grand Rapids: Baker, 1983.

Siggins, Ian D. Kingston. *Martin Luther's Doctrine of Christ.* New Haven and London: Yale University Press, 1970.

Soloveichik, Meir Y. "The Virtue of Hate," *First Things* (February 2003).

*Sophocles: The Three Theban Plays.* Translated by Robert Fagles. London: Penguin, 1984.

Spinoza, Baruch. *Ethics, Treatise on the Emendation of the Intellect and Selected Letters.* Translated by S. Shirley. Indianapolis: Hackett, 1992.

Stayer, James M. *Martin Luther: German Saviour. German Evangelical Theological Factions and the Interpretation of Luther, 1917-1933.* Kingston/Montreal: McGill-Queen's University Press, 2000.

Steiger, Johan Anselm. "The *communicatio idiomatum* as the Axle and Motor of Luther's Theology," *Lutheran Quarterly* 14, no. 2 (2000): 125-58.

Steigmann-Gall, Richard. *The Holy Reich: Nazi Conceptions of Christianity 1919-1945.* Cambridge: Cambridge University Press, 2003.

Steinmetz, David C. *Luther in Context.* Grand Rapids: Baker Academic, 2002.

Stendahl, Krister. *Paul among Jews and Gentiles.* Philadelphia: Fortress, 1976.

Strohl, Jane. "Luther's New View of Marriage, Sexuality and the Family," International Congress for Luther Research in São Paulo, Brazil.

Strommen, Merton P. *The Church and Homosexuality: Searching for a Middle Ground,* 2nd edition. Minneapolis: Kirk, 2001.

Stuhlmacher, Peter. *Revisting Paul's Doctrine of Justification: A Challenge to the New Perspective.* Translated by Daniel P. Bailey, with an essay by Donald A. Hagner. Downers Grove, IL: InterVarsity Press Academic, 2001.

*Styri Prednasky* [Four Lectures]. Mikulas: Tranoscius, 1938.

Tavard, George. *Justification: An Ecumenical Study.* New York: Paulist Press, 1983.

*The Augsburg Confession: A Collection of Sources.* Edited by J. M Reu. Reprinted by Concordia Seminary Press (Winter 1966).

*The Book of Concord.* Edited by Robert Kolb and Timothy J. Wengert. Minneapolis: Fortress, 2000.

*The Christian Theology Reader.* Edited by Alister E. McGrath. Oxford: Blackwell, 1999.

*The Collected Dialogues of Plato.* Edited by Edith Hamilton and Huntington Cairns. Princeton: Princeton University Press, 1971.

*The Doctrinal Theology of the Evangelical Lutheran Church.* Edited by H. Schmid. Translated by C. Hay and H. Jacobs. Philadelphia: Lutheran Publication Society, 1899.

*The Documents of Vatican II.* Edited by Walter M. Abbott, S.J. New York: American Press, 1966.

*The Latin Works of Huldreich Zwingli,* 2 volumes. Translated by Samuel Macauley Jackson. Philadelphia: Heidelberg Press, 1922.

*The Philosophy of Kant: Immanuel Kant's Moral and Political Writings.* Edited by Carl J. Friedrich. New York: The Modern Library, 1949.

*The Promise of Lutheran Ethics.* Edited by K. Bloomquist and J. Stumme. Minneapolis: Fortress, 1998.

*The Role of the Augsburg Confession: Catholic and Lutheran Views.* Edited by Joseph A. Burgess. Philadelphia: Fortress, 1980.

Tillard, J.-M. R., O.P. *Church of Churches: The Ecclesiology of Communion.* Translated by R. C. DePeaux, O.P. Collegeville, MN: Liturgical Press, 1992.

Tillich, Paul. *Systematic Theology,* 3 volumes. Chicago: University of Chicago Press, 1967.

Tinder, Glenn. *The Political Meaning of Christianity.* Baton Rouge and London: Louisiana State University Press, 1989.

Torrance, T. F. *The Trinitarian Faith: The Evangelical Theology of the Ancient Catholic Church.* Edinburgh: T. & T. Clark, 1993.

Troeltsch, Ernst. *Religion in History.* Translated by James Luther Adams and Walter F. Bense. Minneapolis: Fortress, 1991.

———. *The Social Teachings of The Christian Churches,* volume 2. Translated by O. Wyon. New York: Harper Torchbooks, 1961.

Vainio, Olli-Pekka. *Justification and Participation in Christ: The Development of the Lutheran Doctrine of Justification from Luther to the Formula of Concord (1580).* Leiden and Boston: E. J. Brill, 2008.

Vignaux, Paul. "On Luther and Ockham," in *The Reformation in Medieval Perspective.* Edited by Steven E. Ozment. Chicago: Quadrangle Books, 1971, pp. 107-18.

Vögelsang, Erich. *Die Anfänge von Luthers Christologie.* Berlin: Walter de Gruyter, 1929.

von Balthasar, Hans Urs. *Theo-Drama: Theological Dramatic Theory, IV: The Action.* Translated by G. Harrison. San Francisco: Ignatius, 1994.

von Harnack, Adolph. *History of Dogma,* 7 volumes. Translated by N. Buchanan. New York: Dover, 1961.

von Loewenich, Walter. *Luther's Theology of the Cross.* Translated by H. Bouman. Minneapolis: Augsburg, 1976.

# Works Cited

Ware, Kallistos. *The Orthodox Way.* Crestwood, NY: St. Vladimir's Seminary Press, 1979.

Wengert, Timothy J. *Law and Gospel: Philip Melanchthon's Debate with John Agricola of Eisleben over Poenitentia.* Grand Rapids: Baker Books, 1997.

————. "Philip Melanchthon and Augustine of Hippo," *Lutheran Quarterly* 22, no. 3 (Autumn 2008): 249-67.

Werner, Martin. *The Formation of Christian Dogma: An Historical Study of Its Problem.* New York: Harper, 1957.

White, Graham. *Luther as Nominalist: A Study of the Logical Methods Used in Martin Luther's Disputations in the Light of Their Medieval Background.* Schriften der Luther-Agricola-Gesellschaft 30. Helsinki: Luther-Agricola Society, 1994.

Wicks, Jared, S.J. *Luther and His Spiritual Legacy.* Collegeville, MN: Michael Glazer, 1984.

Wilson, Sarah Hinlicky. "Blessed Are the Barren," *Christianity Today* 51, no. 12 (December 2007): 22-28.

————. "Luther and Cyril on Christology." Unpublished paper, Princeton Theological Seminary, 2006.

————. "Luther on the 'Atonement.'" Unpublished paper, Princeton Theological Seminary, 2007.

Wingren, Gustaf. *Luther on Vocation.* Translated by Carl C. Rasmussen. Philadelphia: Muhlenberg Press, 1957.

Witte, John, Jr. *Law and Protestantism: The Legal Teachings of the Lutheran Reformation,* with a Foreword by Martin E. Marty. Cambridge: Cambridge University Press, 2002.

————. *From Sacrament to Contract: Marriage, Religion and Law in the Western Tradition.* Louisville: Westminster/John Knox, 1997.

Wolf, Jacob. "Luther's Concept of Deus Absconditus." Unpublished lecture, University of Aarhus, 2003; cf. *Den skjulte Gud.* Copenhagen: ANIS, 2001.

Wood, Susan K. "Communion Ecclesiology: Source of Hope, Source of Controversy," *Pro Ecclesia* 2, no. 4 (Fall 1993): 424-32.

Wright, N. T. *Paul in Fresh Perspective.* Minneapolis: Fortress, 2005.

————. *The Climax of the Covenant: Christ and the Law in Pauline Theology.* Minneapolis: Fortress, 1991.

————. *What Saint Paul Really Said: Was Paul of Tarsus the Real Founder of Christianity?* Grand Rapids: Eerdmans, 1997.

Yeago, David. "The Catholic Luther," *First Things* 61 (March 1996): 37-41.

————. "The Bread of Life: Patristic Christology and Evangelical Soteriology in Martin Luther's Sermons on John 6," *St. Vladimir's Theological Quarterly* 39, no. 3 (2004).

# Index of Names and Selected Topics

Abbott, Walter M., S.J., 262

Agape, 55, 70, 103, 148, 162, 189-90, 199, 226-27, 250-51, 264, 286, 304, 333

Althaus, Paul, 110, 111, 186-87, 194, 203, 307, 309, 334

Anderson, H. George, 269

Anselm of Canterbury, xx, 58-59, 67, 69-70, 72-73, 75-76, 80, 81-91, 102, 117, 119-21, 129, 166, 366-67

Anti-Judaism, 107, 190, 225, 228-29, 232-34, 241

Anti-Semitism, 232, 381-82, 384

Apocalyptic Theology (or, Revealed Theology), xxi, 32, 37, 39, 42, 58, 114, 124, 126, 153-62, 186, 245, 371, 379-85

Arendt, Hannah, 134-35

Asad, Talal, 22, 145-47, 313, 357

Augustine of Hippo, 16-17, 37, 49, 72, 75, 88, 103-4, 112, 118-19, 131, 141-44, 147, 168, 171-72, 183-84, 187-88, 198, 203-4, 208, 217, 221-22, 224-25, 227, 230, 235-36, 241, 256, 259, 290, 298, 302, 305, 328, 338, 348, 358

Aulén, Gustaf, 60, 75-76, 80, 83

Aune, Michael B., xxi

Ayres, Lewis, 6, 50

Azar, Thomas P., 186

Bainton, Roland H., 186

Barth, Karl, xvi, xx, 35, 49, 55, 67, 92, 95, 105-13, 139, 143, 161, 173, 194, 225, 254, 367-72

Bassler, Jouette M., 229

Bauer, Walter, 29

Bayer, Oswald, xv, xvii, 5-6, 33, 39, 49, 52, 58-60, 67, 73-74, 81, 106, 109, 111-12, 122, 124-26, 128, 152-53, 161, 191, 195-97, 223, 230, 259, 290, 307, 316, 334-35, 368-71

Benne, Robert, 101, 213, 267, 302, 307, 330-32

Bergen, Doris L., 107

Berkouwer, G. C., 95

Berlin, Sir Isaiah, 316, 318

Bielfeldt, Dennis, xv, 57, 117, 223

Bloomquist, Karen, 189, 330

Bluhm, Heinz, 70

Boadt, Lawrence, 231

Bonhoeffer, Dietrich, 5, 43-44, 91, 113-14, 186, 189, 191-92, 194-97, 214, 237, 279, 307, 330-32, 334, 359, 370

Braaten, Carl E., 83

Brecht, Martin, 193, 197, 199, 203, 259, 292, 381

Bretall, Robert W., 314

Brown, Christopher, 46, 375

Brown, Peter, 119, 182-84, 198
Bullock, Alan, 310
Burgess, Joseph A., 269, 280-81, 298
Burke, Edmund, 197-98

Cairns, Huntington, 145
Calvin, John, 63, 87, 107, 150
Christ, Subject of Faith *(pistos Iesou)*,
  xx, 105-6, 108, 252-54, 355-57, 372;
  Object of Faith, 63, 297-98, 355-56,
  370
Communication of Properties
  *(communicatio idiomatum)*, xv, 51-65,
  67
Concupiscence, 187, 198, 200, 201-9, 214
Cone, James H., 353
Critical Dogmatics, xiii, xv, xvii-ix, 3, 5-
  17, 40-43, 46, 48, 86, 116, 225, 233, 235,
  257, 279, 286, 308, 360, 372
Croner, Helga, 231
Crowe, Benjamin D., 29
Cullmann, Oscar, 104

Dahl, Nils, 45
Damasio, Antonio R., 212
Darwinism, 21-24, 201, 212, 216, 350
Davey, Francis Noel, 45
de Lubac, Henri, S.J., 142, 204
Demonology, 6, 340-43, 379-85
Derrida, Jacques, xviii, 96-97, 134
Di Giovanni, George, 234
Douglas, Ann, 188, 209
Dunn, James D. G., xxii, 225-30, 234,
  241, 247

Ebeling, Gerhard, xix, 36-37, 43, 112,
  142, 149, 156, 170-71, 250-51, 369
Eckhardt, Burnell F., Jr., 72, 74-75, 80-
  81, 86, 119-22
Ehrman, Bart D., 41
Elert, Werner, 27, 110-11, 113, 125, 132
Elshtain, Jean Bethke, 322
Elton, G. R., xix
Empie, Paul C., 269
Epistemology, 7, 10, 19, 32-45, 170, 359
Ericksen, Robert B., 307

Eros, 188, 206-8, 275
Experiential Theology, 17-21

Feuerbach, Ludwig, 48, 302
Forde, Gerhard O., 36, 67-68, 80, 83-84,
  374
Forell, George W., 264, 331
Frady, Marshall, 349-50
Franks, Robert S., 78-79
Frei, Hans W., 9, 42
Freke, Timothy, 41
Freud, Sigmund, 188, 207
Friedrich, Carl J., 322

Gaebler, Ulrich, 163-65
Gandy, Peter, 41
Gerrish, B. A., 117, 141, 370
Girard, René, xx, 92-93, 98-103, 109,
  140, 190, 222
Gleede, Benjamin, xv, 39
God, Hidden and Revealed *(Deus
  absconditus et revelatus)*, xiv, 4, 6, 27,
  32-33, 101, 109, 127, 151, 161-63, 166,
  173-75, 365, 368-70, 372, 374
Good Works, 34, 108, 123, 148, 158, 162,
  189, 190, 199, 226-27, 250-51, 264, 286,
  304, 333
Green, William Scott, 254
Gregory of Nyssa, 12

Häerle, Wilfried, 38, 180-81, 191, 226
Hagen, Kenneth, 37, 45, 118, 131, 153,
  240, 260
Haile, H. G., 186
Hall, Douglas John, 358
Hamilton, Edith, 145
Hampson, Daphne, 360, 364
Harrisville, Roy A., 237, 240
Hart, David Bentley, 70
Hay, C., 82, 191, 307
Helmer, Christine, xx, 27-29, 58, 112,
  114, 122, 125-33, 363
Hendrix, Scott H., 70, 185-86, 193-94,
  201, 260, 291-92, 385
Hengel, Martin, 34
Heschel, Susannah, 107

Heterosexual Marriage, 184, 186-87, 196-98, 210, 217
Historical Jesus, xix, 37, 39, 41-46, 72, 222, 336
Hobbes, Thomas, 101, 212
Holl, Karl, 86-87, 361
Homosexual Union, 197, 199, 214-18
Hoskyns, Sir Edwin, 45
Hultgren, Arland J., 4
Hunsinger, George, xvi, 107
Huntington, Samuel P., 116
Husbands, Mark, 108
Hütter, Reinhard, 189, 204, 279, 330, 373, 374

Image of God *(imago Dei)*, 140, 159, 169, 179-91, 197, 199, 206, 212-13, 324, 331, 362

Jacobs, H., 82, 191, 307
James, William, xix, 17-26, 30, 32, 146, 200, 228, 235
Jenson, Robert W., xxii, 35, 53-54, 58, 76, 83, 160, 188, 194-97, 211, 280-81, 297-98
Joyful Exchange *(commercium admirabile, fröhliche Wechsel)*, xv, xxii, 33, 57, 80-81, 91, 94, 97, 102, 281, 288, 293, 299
Juel, Donald H., 45-46
Jüngel, Eberhard, 49
Juntunen, Sammeli, xxiii, 36, 186-87, 199-205, 211

Kant, Immanuel, xvii, 140-41, 233-34, 240, 322, 377
Kantianism, xxii, 7-8, 18-19, 34, 63, 83, 98, 114, 207, 224, 229, 306, 316, 335, 344, 347, 367
Karant-Nunn, Susan C., 185
Käsemann, Ernst, xxii, 112, 134, 139, 141, 145-47, 221-22, 224, 228-29, 236-42, 245, 247, 250-51, 255, 381
Keck, Leander E., 41-46, 48, 72
Kegley, Charles W., 314
Kelly, J. N. D., 29

Kidd, Colin, 17
King, Martin Luther, Jr., xxiii, 16-17, 308, 337, 343, 348-54, 357, 378
Klenicki, Leon, 231
Koestler, Arthur, 312
Kolb, Robert, 27, 38, 126, 141, 150, 153, 167, 173-74, 191, 282, 322
Kuklick, Bruce, 3, 8, 16, 20

Lage, Dietmar, 95, 274, 303-7, 330, 336-37, 361-66
Lasch, Christopher, 188
Law and Gospel (also, Gospel and Law), xi, xii, 105-17, 122, 127, 133, 189, 223, 271, 305, 352-53, 369
Lazareth, William H., 111, 186-87, 189, 200, 203, 208, 215
Lee, Philip J., 29
Leibniz, Gottfried, xv-xvi, 71, 74, 107, 140-41, 167, 176, 236, 372
Lenin, Vladimir, 310, 313, 320, 327
Lenker, John Nicholas, 365
Lienhard, Marc, 36, 54-55, 58-59, 68-69, 80, 372
Lindbeck, George, 5, 261, 299, 373-74
Lindberg, Carter, 277
Lindhardt, Jan, 143-46, 204
Lischer, Richard, 348-49, 352
Lochman, Jan Milič, 311
Locke, John, 212
Lohse, Bernard, xiii, 52, 77, 112, 259
Lotz, David, 69, 106-8, 127
Louth, Andrew, 376
Lukes, Steven, 311, 321, 325

MacIntyre, Alasdair, 148
Mannermaa, Tuomo, 106-7, 274
Manns, Peter, 276-77, 298
Marcuse, Herbert, 188, 197
Marshall, Bruce, 55, 64, 257, 349
Martyn, J. Louis, xxii, 32-33, 36, 134, 161, 181-82, 185, 227, 229, 242, 244-48, 251-54, 359, 381-82
Marx, Karl, xxii-xxiii, 301-3, 306-8, 311, 313-19, 320-21, 323-28, 337
Marxism, 308-30, 332, 345-47

# Index of Names and Selected Topics

Mattes, Mark C., 114, 153, 223
Mattox, Mickey, xi-xv, xxiii, 57, 178, 185, 189, 191, 194, 223, 231-32, 236
McCue, James F., 264
McGrath, Alister E., 81
McLellan, David, 316
McSorley, Harry 164, 175-78, 267, 269, 273, 277
Melanchthon, Philip, xvi, xxi, xxiii, 11, 55, 61-63, 70, 81-82, 85, 94, 107, 122, 144, 150, 152, 156, 188-89, 223, 249, 277-78, 282-83, 287
Menand, Louis, 21
Meredith, Anthony, S.J., 12
Metaphysics, 20, 26, 49, 51, 56, 59, 67, 121, 155
Meyer, Harding, 272, 277, 298
Milbank, John, 101-4, 146, 207, 314, 324-25, 328, 347, 367
Moldovan, Russel, 350
Moltmann, Jürgen, 92, 359
Morse, Christopher, 121, 184-85, 214-16, 286
Mouw, Richard J., 98-99
Murphy, T. Austin, 269

Neusner, Jacob, 254
Niebuhr, Reinhold, xxiii, 32, 72-73, 308, 314, 337, 343-48, 353, 357
Nietzsche, Friedrich, 24, 66, 70-74, 96-97, 99, 103, 114, 118, 157-58
Novak, David, 228
Nygren, Anders, 206-7

O'Regan, Cyril, 325
Oakes, Edward T., 94
Oberman, Heiko, xiii, 151, 186-87, 192, 198, 224, 282, 382-85
Original Sin, 78, 142, 166, 197, 349-50
Osusky, Samuel Stefan, 310
Ozment, Steven, 161, 193, 201

Pannenberg, Wolfhart, 34, 44, 92-93, 96, 167
Pascal, Blaise, 370, 377

Patience (vita passive), 93, 144, 303, 323, 374
Pauck, Wilhelm, 87
Peacocke, Arthur, 216-17
Pelikan, Jaroslav, xxii, 27, 29, 54, 58, 62, 264-66
Percesepe, Gary, xvii-xviii, 5
Perspectivalism, 170
Pesch, Otto Hermann, O.P., 4
Pigden, Charles R., 140
Plato, 71, 145, 148, 157, 370
Platonism, 56, 71, 98, 140, 143, 145, 148, 168, 370
Prager, Dennis, 198-99

Raitt, Jill, 150, 152
Ratzinger, Joseph Cardinal, xxii, 266, 268, 275-84, 293-94, 296, 298-99
Raunio, Antti, 77
Reinhuber, Thomas, 371
Reu, J. M., 282-87
Richardson, Alan, 316
Ridley, Matt, 212
Riley, Gregory J., 41
Ritschl, Albrecht, 63, 69, 71, 83, 106-7, 127
Rorty, Richard, 7
Royce, Josiah, xv, xvii, xix, 3-8, 10-21, 25-26, 30, 32, 146, 225, 235, 267
Ruether, Rosemary Radford, 366, 381
Rusch, William G., 294, 300
Russell, William R., 38

Saarinen, Risto, 77, 90, 226
Safranski, Ruediger, 118
Salvation History, 112, 124, 221, 227-29, 233-34, 236-42, 245
Sanders, E. P., xxii, 228-34, 239
Schell, Jonathan, 198
Schillebeeckx, Edward, 356
Schleiermacher, Friedrich, 39, 43, 62-63, 122, 229, 373
Schmid, H., 82, 191, 307
Schneider, Carolyn, 35
Schroeder, Rev. H. J., O.P., 151
Schulze, Manfred, 37, 53, 56

Schweitzer, Albert, 39, 40-45, 222, 229, 235, 377
Second Vatican Council, 262, 264, 268-75, 297
Siggins, Ian D. Kingston, 46
Sophocles, 101
Spinoza, Baruch, 9, 11, 42, 71, 99, 141, 165-67, 176-77
Stafford, J. Francis, 269
Stalin, Josef, 55, 100, 310, 313, 324, 327, 345, 355, 364
Stayer, James M., xix, 384
Steiger, Johan Anselm, 51, 58, 65
Steigmann-Gall, Richard, 107, 373-74
Steinmetz, David, 124, 152, 157, 188, 235, 255, 290, 365
Stendahl, Krister, xxii, 118, 222, 227-28, 233-41, 245, 247
Strauss, David Friedrich, 42, 48
Strohl, Jane, 186
Strommen, Merton P., 217
Stuhlmacher, Peter, 229
Stumme, John, 189, 330

Tavard, George, 287-88
Theology of the Cross *(theologia crucis)*, xxiii, 32, 34, 153, 275, 290, 358-62, 364, 367-68, 370, 374
Three Estates, xxi, xxiii, 186, 189, 191-97, 199, 200, 203-4, 211, 308, 334-35, 342
Tillard, J.-M. R., O.P., 294-95
Tillich, Paul, 207-8, 223, 314
Tinder, Glenn, 311, 355
Torrance, T. F., 64
Treier, Daniel, 108
Trinitarianism, 16, 50, 59, 372, 377
Troeltsch, Ernst, 60, 306
Two Kingdoms Doctrine *(Zweireichenlehre)*, xii, xxii, 104, 194, 275, 306, 308, 333, 335, 338, 341, 357

Vainio, Olli-Pekka, 223
Vignaux, Paul, 161
Vinke, Rainer, 262
Vocation *(vocatio)*, 145, 192, 307-8, 328, 330, 331-37, 357
Vögelsang, Erich, 361
von Balthasar, Hans Urs, 91-95, 167
von Harnack, Adolph, 26-30, 52, 57, 83-84, 127, 232, 240, 260-61, 265
von Harnack, Theodosius, 370
von Loewenich, Walter, 361

Ware, Kallistos, 295-96
Wengert, Timothy J., 27, 38, 126, 188-89, 191, 223, 282, 322
Werner, Martin, 29
White, Graham, 17, 117
Wicks, Jared, S.J., 263-64, 288
Wiesner-Hanks, Merry E., 185
Wilson, Sarah Hinlicky, xxiii, 52, 56, 75, 77, 217
Wingren, Gustaf, 145, 307, 332-34, 357
Witte, John, Jr., 191, 193-94, 213, 335
Wolf, Jacob, 161
Wood, Allen W., 234
Wood, Susan K., 297-98
Wrath of God, xx, 55, 59, 66-73, 77, 82, 84, 99, 103, 111, 113, 202, 210, 242, 248, 251-54
Wright, N. T., xxii, 34, 180-81, 221, 225, 229, 242-48, 253, 254

Yeago, David, 52, 125, 289-91, 300, 352-53

Zwingli, Huldreich, xxi, 46, 141, 152, 159-69, 174-77, 260-61, 380